Why Do You Need This New Edition?

Why should you buy this new edition of *Patterns of Exposition*? Here are five excellent reasons!

P9-EDV-644

❶ **Twenty-five new readings** from acclaimed writers of past and present whose works raise questions important to today's readers. The result is a fresh, balanced, and exciting collection of works from a wide range of differing viewpoints.

❷ **Works by an expanded selection of writers**—including former U.S. Vice President Al Gore, blogger Michael Jernigan, Pulitzer Prize–winning author Jhumpa Lahiri, journalist Amy Sutherland, novelist Amy Tan, and professor and theorist Stanley Fish—provide you with insights into a wide range of topical issues with flair and mastery. In addition to these contemporary voices are celebrated writers Henry David Thoreau, Mark Twain, George Orwell, Virginia Woolf, and Ernest Hemingway, whose classic works demonstrate that powerful exposition speaks to all eras.

❸ **An analysis of an** irreverent 1900s greeting-card image provides a vivid example of the analogy mode of exposition and gives you a springboard to an array of unexpected topics.

❹ **Issues and ideas sections are focused to help you identify** ways in which authors use the different rhetorical patterns to achieve a specific objective: In Chapter 5, for example, Bharati Mukherjee and William Ouchi use the comparison mode to evaluate tradition. In Chapter 7, Stanley Fish and Ernest Hemingway use process analysis to demystify everyday rituals.

❺ **A further expanded selection of persuasive argumentative** essays by contemporary and classic authors give you a broad range of viewpoints and subjects on a variety of ethical issues.

PEARSON

PATTERNS OF EXPOSITION

Patterns of Exposition

Twentieth Edition

Robert A. Schwegler
University of Rhode Island

PEARSON

Boston Columbus Indianapolis New York San Francisco Upper Saddle River
Amsterdam Cape Town Dubai London Madrid Milan Munich Paris Montreal Toronto
Delhi Mexico City São Paulo Sydney Hong Kong Seoul Singapore Taipei Tokyo

Senior Sponsoring Editor: Virginia Blanford
Senior Marketing Manager: Sandra McGuire
Senior Supplements Editor: Donna Campion
Production Manager: Denise Phillip
Project Coordination, Text Design, and Electronic Page Makeup: PreMediaGlobal
Cover Design Manager: John Callahan

Cover Images (Top to Bottom): Ellen Beijers/Shutterstock; Mushakesa/Shutterstock; Markovka/Shutterstock; Maaike Boot/Shutterstock
Senior Manufacturing Manager: Dennis J. Para
Printer and Binder: R.R. Donnelley/Crawfordsville
Cover Printer: R.R. Donnelley/Crawfordsville

Credits and acknowledgments borrowed from other sources and reproduced, with permission, in this textbook appear either on the page within text or on page 571.

Library of Congress Cataloging-in-Publication Data

Patterns of exposition / [edited by] Robert A. Schwegler. — 20th ed.
    p. cm.
  Includes index.
  ISBN-13: 978-0-205-22045-8
  ISBN-10: 0-205-22045-2
  1. College readers. 2. Exposition (Rhetoric) 3. English language—Rhetoric. I. Schwegler, Robert A.
  PE1417.P3954 2011
  808'.0427—dc23

                                                    2011031154

6 2019

ISBN-13: 978-0-205-22045-8
ISBN-10:   0-205-22045-2

Contents

Thematic Contents

Politics and Leaders

Personality and Behavior

Nature and the Environment

Morals, Crime, and Punishment

Growing Up, Getting Old

Differences

Families and Children

Society and Social Change

Media

Essay Pairs

Preface

Instructors familiar with *Patterns of Exposition* will notice that this new edition retains the discussions of rhetorical patterns, student essay examples, and comprehensive chapters on reading and writing that have been well received in previous editions. And it continues the tradition of providing many new and interesting readings. The discussions of patterns of exposition and argument and the essays illustrating these strategies demonstrate the ways in which rhetorical patterns enable writers and readers to explore, understand, and take a stand on questions of culture, identity, and value in the college community, the workplace, and in society at large.

NEW TO THIS EDITION

This edition features twenty-five inspiring new readings by acclaimed writers of past and present, such as Virginia Woolf, Langston Hughes, Robert Benchley, Amy Tan, Sandra Cisneros, and Al Gore. Their works raise timeless questions vital to today, showing readers that powerful use of the rhetorical patterns of exposition is not limited to the college classroom.

Of special note is a vivid new addition to the chapter on analogy, a visual text providing its readers with a wordless glimpse at post-Victorian attitudes about romantic love. This telling illustration, from a greeting card of the 1900s, speaks volumes about its times and raises questions about our own. Our visual-text selection also serves to spotlight an alternative avenue for understanding the use of analogy as a rhetorical mode, not only for students who are visual thinkers, but for all critical thinkers.

THE CORE OF THIS BOOK

Chapter 1, "Reading for Writing," introduces students to reading strategies especially useful for the essays in this text, for academic reading in general, and for turning reading into writing. The chapter pays particular attention to critical reading and reading for technique as well as reading for understanding. It introduces students to concrete reading strategies for use in composition courses, in other college courses, and beyond.

Chapter 2, "Ways of Writing," introduces students to the composing process and to a variety of useful techniques for discovering ideas and information, planning an essay, developing a thesis, drafting, and revising. The chapter also provides numerous student examples, including a student essay in draft and revised form. Our emphasis here and elsewhere in the text is on the practical: concrete writing strategies, specific suggestions, and concise illustrations.

Each chapter covering a pattern of exposition (or argument) begins with a discussion of the roles the particular pattern can play for writers and readers. The discussions provide a definition of the pattern; a paragraph example taken from the work of an accomplished, professional writer; a discussion of the various uses of the pattern ("Why Use . . . ?"); suggestions for designing essays that employ the pattern ("Choosing a Strategy"); and techniques for developing the content of an essay as well as individual paragraphs and sentences ("Developing. . . .").

The first few essay selections in each chapter illustrate some of the many roles a pattern can play in organizing thought and expression within an essay or the roles a pattern can play in working with other rhetorical patterns to create an organized, purposeful, effective exposition (or argument).

Each chapter concludes with a cluster of essays focusing on "Issues and Ideas" that speak to a common purpose, such as "Clarifying Values and Roles," "Dramatizing Ethical Dilemmas," or "Fathoming Consequences." The primary goal of these clusters is to help students develop an awareness of rhetorical strategies as a critical tool for understanding differing perspectives and to demonstrate the variety of purposes a strategy can serve. It is precisely the broad similarity in subject matter and strategy among the essays in a cluster that serves to highlight for students the important differences and the varied models for expression the selections provide.

The questions at the end of each selection highlight important issues of meaning, technique, and style that help develop students' abilities as readers and the range of options available to them as they write. "Read to Write" activities follow the questions. The first activity in each set, labeled "Collaborating," offers students a chance to work with their classmates to develop ideas, essay plans, brief essays, and, occasionally, a collaboratively written essay. The second activity, labeled "Considering Audience," directs students' attention to readers' expectations and audience constraints. Some of the activities ask them to consider the likely reactions of readers to the essay presented in the text; other activities call for speculation about readers' reactions to different writing strategies. The third activity, "Developing an Essay," helps students view the sample essay in the text as a broad model for their own work—a model that they are encouraged to alter and develop in a fashion appropriate to their own perspectives and purposes. These activities provide practice in linking reading to writing—one of the primary focuses of the book as a whole. The "Writing Suggestions" at the end of each chapter include collaborative activities and offer further avenues for students to follow from reading into writing.

In choosing new essays and retaining those from previous editions, we have looked first for selections that are well written and insightful and that reward careful (re)reading, and then for selections that can serve as useful models for thought, organization, and expression. We have also drawn on suggestions from the text's instructor-users and have reviewed the responses of students. We have seriously considered and fully appreciated all of them, and we have incorporated many suggestions into this new edition. We have responded, as well, to requests for added essays in some of the most heavily used chapters of the book.

The wealth of excellent and recent nonfiction writing reflecting the perspectives of many different cultural and social groups has made it possible for us to choose selections reflecting the intellectual ferment and challenge of our times. In drawing on this diversity, we have not tried to represent every identity in an unimaginative and rigid fashion but have instead tried to use it to create an exciting mixture of perspectives and backgrounds designed to encourage varied, engaged responses from students.

Because so many instructors find it useful, we continue to retain the table of contents listing pairs of essays. Each pair provides contrasts (or similarities) in theme, approach, and style that are worth studying. The essay pairs can form the focus of class discussion or writing assignments.

The "Further Readings: Combining Patterns" chapter provides contemporary and classic selections to provoke discussion. The pieces also suggest some intriguing combinations of patterns and goals for writing essays that can be pursued in the hands of skilled and daring writers. The essays in this section can be used on their own or with the other chapters of the book.

Throughout *Patterns of Exposition*, Twentieth Edition, we have tried to make possible the convenient use of all materials in whatever ways instructors think best for their own classes. With a few exceptions, only complete essays or freestanding units of larger works have been included. With their inevitable overlap of patterns, they are more complicated than excerpts illustrating single principles, but they are also more realistic examples of exposition and more useful for other classroom purposes. Versatility has been an important criterion in choosing materials.

Thirty-six of the selections best liked in previous editions have been kept. Twenty-five selections are new.

The arrangement of essays is but one of the many workable orders; instructors can easily develop another if they so desire. The thematic table of contents and the table of essay pairs also suggest a variety of arrangements.

We have tried to vary the study questions from the purely objective to those calling for some serious self-examination by students. (The Instructor's Manual supplements these materials.)

"A Guide to Terms," at the end of the book, briefly discusses matters from *Abstract* to *Unity* and refers whenever possible to the essays themselves for illustrations. Its location is designed to permit easy access, and there are cross-references to it in the study questions following each selection.

In all respects—size, content, arrangement, format—we have tried to keep *Patterns of Exposition* uncluttered and easy to use.

ACKNOWLEDGMENTS

We'd like to thank the users of this text and the reviewers: Connie S. Adair. Marshalltown Community College; Jacqueline A. Blackwell, Thomas Nelson Community College; Paul Friskney, Cincinnati Christian University; Vicki Houser, Northeast State Community College; Lillie Miller Jackson, Southwest Tennessee Community College; and Kaushalya Jagasia, Illinois Valley Community College. In addition, we'd like to give special thanks to Paula Bryant Bonilla for her assistance in preparing this revision.

Reading for Writing

Reading and writing work together. Good writers draw ideas and information from their reading. They use reading to help understand an audience's likely reactions. They read to discover techniques of expression. They use critical reading as a springboard for their own writing. You can read for all of these purposes— understanding, critical response, and discovery of technique—or for only a few, depending on your goals as a writer.

To develop your skills as a reader and writer of expository and argumentative texts, you need to pay attention to three ways of approaching a text: reading for understanding, critical reading, and reading for technique. No matter what your approach, however, you need to pay attention to the elements of the **reading process: previewing, reading,** and **reviewing**. These elements are important whether you are reading **expository writing** (including essays, magazine articles, reports, memos, newspaper reports, and nonfiction books) or **argumentative writing** (including editorials, opinion essays, reports and proposals, policy statements, investigative reporting, or professional articles).

If you plunge right into reading, moving quickly through an article, essay, or book and then put it aside, you are missing important opportunities. Effective readers treat reading as a process consisting of **previewing, reading,** and **reviewing**. They develop techniques for each of these stages of the reading process.

PREVIEW YOUR READING

Previewing means "reading before you start reading." Newspapers provide headlines to tell you what to expect in an article. Books and articles have titles. Authors and editors often provide brief summaries at the beginning of a chapter or in a table of contents. Magazine editors often take key statements from an article and reprint them in large type within boxes where readers can see them as they flip through the pages. Paying attention to these features is important because the knowledge and expectation you bring to a text can affect how well you understand it.

Look for Help from the Editor or Writer

Writers and editors often provide you with considerable help for previewing. Titles are a good place to start. Many will tell you much about a work's contents and organization, as does the title of Don Aslett's book, *How Do I Clean the Moosehead? And 99 More Tough Questions About Housecleaning.*

A table of contents provides detailed information about the coverage and purpose of a work and perhaps even a summary of individual sections of the work.

If an article or book does not have a table of contents, skim the text looking for headings and subheadings that reveal the writer's plan and the topics being discussed.

If an editor highlights important passages in an essay or article, pay attention to them. Here are three passages from a magazine article entitled "What Makes Sammy Walk?" that the editor chose to reprint in large type in the middle of a page.

> Less than 70 percent of U.S. men are now full-time year-round workers.
>
> "You don't have a social life," Dave's daughter says, "and you don't do anything."
>
> "I just put in a proposal to cut my hours to thirty-two a week and take a 20 percent pay cut," says a woman. "It's been accepted. I'm so happy."

Look for Help from the Context

The kind of magazine, scholarly journal, or newspaper in which an essay appears can tell you important things about its outlook. Some publications have a reputation for publishing articles with a particular social, cultural, or political point of view. Look for any statements of the periodical's editorial outlook. Pay attention to the magazine's title and to the titles of the other articles it contains.

For books, look at the back cover or dust jacket. They may provide a brief summary of the contents or the writer's outlook. They may also offer quotations from reviewers that highlight a book's main points.

READ FOR UNDERSTANDING, CRITICAL RESPONSE, AND TECHNIQUE

The reading strategies you employ should vary according to your goals for reading: to understand, to respond critically, or to understand writing techniques. These goals can overlap, of course, but whenever you try to do too many things as you read, your effectiveness at each task suffers. For this reason, you may often need to read a selection more than once, concentrating on a different goal each time.

Understanding

When you read for understanding, you focus on ideas and information by asking questions as you read. You try to identify the main idea (**thesis**) and the line of reasoning that supports it. You explore meanings and values. Questions can help guide your reading.

What Is This Selection About?

Some essays focus on one topic throughout. Other essays, just as effective, discuss several related topics, such as the effect of television on attitudes towards violence and its consequences for family life. Brent Staples's essay, "Just Walk On By," (pp. 56–60) presents a variety of examples and brief incidents, but they all illustrate how people reacted to the author's presence as a black man.

As a reader, you need to be able to identify the topic or related topics around which an essay is constructed. Avoid the temptation to pay attention only to ideas and information that interest you. You risk misunderstanding the real focus of the essay if you give selective attention to the elements that interest you.

- **Look for cues.** Writers frequently use a title, headings in the text, or direct statements as cues identifying an essay's topic or focus.

> **Title:** "Women, Men, and the Media"
> **Heading:** "Stereotypical Portrayals of Men and Women"
> **Direct Statements:** "But in what ways are our behaviors, especially those of children, shaped by the inaccurate and oversimplified portraits of men and women that populate the mass media?"

- **Make a list of topics.** Review what you have read and make a list of the topics or important ideas discussed in the essay. If the elements in your list fit clearly within a broader topic, state it; or if they do not, try stating their relationship in a way that identifies the essay's focus.

  > local restaurants replaced by fast food
  > small shops replaced by malls
  > family farms turn into agribusinesses
  > hardware stores replaced by home building centers
  > small towns replaced by sprawling suburbs

  > **Overall Topic:** change from small, individualized social organizations to large, more impersonal ones

- **Look for repetition.** Identify words, ideas, or subjects that appear repeatedly in the text. Such repetitions provide evidence of an essay's focus and may even be intentional signals provided by the writer. In his essay "Just Walk On By," (pp. 56–60) for example, Brent Staples uses words like "softy," "embarrassed," and "frightening" to refer to himself, his feelings, and his reaction to the incidents he describes. He uses a contrasting set of words like "fearsomeness," "dangerous," and "terror" to describe people's (mistaken) reactions to him and to other young black men like him.

What Does This Selection Mean?
Expository writing offers conclusions and insights. Argumentative writing offers opinions or proposes a course of action. Much of the value of these kinds of writing lies in the insights, ideas, and opinions conveyed: What the writing means.

Sometimes direct statements announce the meaning(s) of an essay. Often, however, conclusions are presented less directly or even implied, requiring you to provide an answer to the question, "What does it mean?" Good writing generally offers more than one insight or conclusion, typically a main point and several related points. Identifying the main point is an important step for any reader trying to understand an essay.

- **Highlight direct statements.** While you read or when you have finished reading an essay, try highlighting or otherwise making note of conclusions, generalizations, or opinions stated directly to readers. These can include statements (or restatements) of an essay's main idea or *thesis* like the following.

"Taboos, big or small, are always about having to respect somebody's (often irrational) boundary—or else."

—Michael Ventura
"Don't Even Think About It!"

For many essays, a list of such statements would provide a rough but revealing outline of the writer's exploration of a subject or of the chain of argument supporting a thesis. Here is the list Shauna Benoit compiled from her reading of Cullen Murphy's essay, "Hello, Darkness" (pp. 268–272). Note how the list clarifies the way the writer has arranged the essay.

"The average American a hundred years ago was able to sleep 20 percent longer than the average American today."
"Other evidence seems to indicate that the rate of sleep loss is in fact accelerating."
"We are laboring under a large and increasingly burdensome 'sleep deficit'. . . ."
"Many commentators would blame it on what might be called the AWOL factor—that is, the American Way of Life. We are by nature a busy and ambitious people whom tectonic social forces . . . have turned into a race of laboratory rats on a treadmill going nowhere ever faster."
"Yet electricity's ubiquitous and seemingly most innocuous use—to power the common light bulb—could not help exacting a price in sleep."
"Whatever it is that we wish or are made to do—pursue leisure, earn a living—there are simply far more usable hours now in which to do it."

• **Look for repetition and emphasis.** Look for words, phrases, details, and ideas that the writer repeats throughout a text. They are cues to ideas or issues that receive special emphasis within the text—even if not all the repetition was consciously intended by the writer. Repetitions can help you interpret the meanings and values around which an essay has been constructed and can also act as evidence for your conclusions about the essay.

- **Pause and summarize.** As you read an essay you will likely pause at a number of "resting places," between sections or paragraphs, for example. When you pause, take a moment to summarize what the essay has already said and to predict what it will say next. Then read ahead to test the accuracy of your predictions as well as your understanding of the essay.

What Is This Selection's Purpose?

Expository and argumentative writing each have general purposes: expository—to explain and explore; and argumentative—to convince and persuade. To understand an individual essay, you need to recognize its more specific purpose(s), however.

By taking purpose into account as you read, you can more easily grasp an essay's meaning and evaluate its likely effect on readers. Sometimes, writers state their purpose directly; at other times, you will need to pay attention to repeated phrases and ideas in a text to understand its purpose. Remember, too, that essays often have secondary purposes as well as primary ones.

How Is The Main Idea Developed or Supported?

Once you have identified the main idea (thesis) and related ideas in an essay, you can pay attention to the distinction between them and the examples, information, and discussions that develop or support them. To do so, try keeping two questions in mind as you read: How is the main idea developed or supported? How adequate is the development/support?

Writers often make your job easier by using familiar words or phrases to signal supporting details, discussions, or examples. Here are a few of the most familiar.

for example	supports	in the case of
for instance	explains	sheds light on
contributes to	because	illustrates
justifies	as a consequence	explains

Critical Response

Critical reading questions and challenges a text. It treats the text as a starting point, not the final word on a subject or issue. It helps you develop your own ideas and conclusions and evaluate the ideas and information in a text. Critical reading also suggests directions for your own writing. Above all, critical reading calls for activity on your part.

- **Keeping a reading journal.** A **reading journal** is a notebook, folder, or computer file in which you keep your responses to reading: notes, questions, ideas, criticisms, and the like. Turning the fleeting ideas, questions, and responses that occur to you as you read into sentences in a journal helps you remember them and makes them available for later use, perhaps in an essay of your own.

  You can organize entries in a reading journal according to the particular selection, allotting a few pages to each article, chapter, or book, for example. Or you can organize the journal by categories, such as "Responses (and Objections) to Readings About New Roles for Men and Women" or "Quotations and Information for Use in My 'Dangers of Dieting' Paper."

  A reading journal can be particularly valuable when you plan to integrate sources into your writing. Are you looking for conclusions or perspectives that differ from yours? Summarize or quote any that you encounter and explore them in writing along with your own point of view so you can discover ways to incorporate both in an essay of your own and jot down relevant information about your source.

- **Create marginal notes. Marginal notes** are the scribbles, jottings, abbreviations, and other annotations you make in the margins of a book or magazine. Typically, you make such annotations when something you read prompts a strong response that you can record in brief form. You may wish to use marginal notes to record agreements or disagreements with what the writer says, to highlight passages or techniques you admire, or to note important ideas and information.

  Your marginal notes are most likely to be of use to you when they indicate ways to turn the text or your response to it into material for your own writing, as with the following.

> No! Putting attractive people in an ad is not necessarily a way of using sex to sell.
> People can be attractive without being sexy, for example.
> And the people belong in the ad because they show how the product works. (They wear safety goggles, for example.)
> Would it be better to have ugly people? Or just plain-looking people? I bet audiences would be critical of that approach, too.

To make your marginal annotations as useful as possible, try to give some variety to your responses. Consider making comments in categories like these.

Interpretations of what the author is trying to say
Questions you wish the author had answered
Objections to the author's conclusions
Counterarguments the writer fails to mention
Notes on passages you find confusing
Evaluations of the writer's conclusions or techniques of expression

Technique

Reading for technique helps you identify and understand writing strategies you can adapt for your own work. Patterns of organization, ways to explore ideas, strategies for presenting supporting details, and ways to use words and sentences—reading for technique brings all of these to your attention.

The questions on "Expository (or Argumentative) Techniques" and "Diction and Vocabulary" following each selection in this book focus on technique. They help you develop your ability to analyze the techniques writers employ. They also suggest ways various techniques help writers achieve a range of purposes.

- **Pay attention to expository (and argumentative) patterns.** Writers use expository and argumentative patterns in varied ways: alone or in combination, for whole essays or sections of essays. The introductions to Chapters 3–13 in this book discuss patterns and their uses. The following questions can also help you identify patterns and the roles they play.
- **Turn to "A Guide to Terms."** "A Guide to Terms" at the end of this book (pp. 551–569) contains entries for important writing techniques, from subjects such as essay introductions and closings to creating emphasis and using the correct choice of words ("Diction") or sentence structure ("Syntax"). Before reading a selection in this book or elsewhere, turn to the Guide, choose an entry that interests you, and then read with attention to the technique described in the entry.

REVIEW

Take some time to review what you have read. Think of directions for your own writing that are suggested by your reading. Evaluate a text in whole or part, and consider any unanswered question you might wish to address.

One good place to start your review is with the kinds of questions that follow the essays in this text: Meanings and Values, Expository (or Argumentative) Techniques, and Diction or Vocabulary.

When you focus on meanings and values, you look back at the different topics covered in a text and the writer's conclusions about them.

When you focus on expository or argumentative techniques, you pay attention to overall patterns of organization and development, to opening and closing strategies, to paragraph and sentence techniques, to the use of detail and kinds of support and to patterns in words and groups of words.

- **Identify opportunities for writing.** By responding to your reading with questions like the following, you can identify opportunities for your own writing.

    1. What topics or issues does the writer address satisfactorily and completely? What questions are left unanswered, problems left unsolved, or issues left unresolved?
    2. Does the writer present a balanced perspective in offering conclusions or are important explanations and points of view left unconsidered?
    3. Does the writer reason fairly and provide adequate support for conclusions? Or is the writing clearly biased, omitting evidence or misrepresenting facts and distorting others' positions?
    4. Are there other kinds of information and experiences or different ideas and approaches that might lead to conclusions differing from those offered by the writer?

- **Evaluate a source's reliability and usefulness.** Evaluating the trustworthiness of a source and identifying its strengths and limitations are important parts of a review. Ask questions like these.

    1. What conclusions or generalizations does the source offer? Are they supported adequately or do they go beyond the facts presented in the text? Are they consistent with my knowledge of the topic?
    2. What is the reputation of the author, the publisher, or the publication in which the text appeared? Is the reputation one of thoroughness and balance or of bias and carelessness? How does this piece of writing compare with others on the topic?
    3. Are there any obvious errors? Which parts of the discussion are detailed and well documented?

4. Does the text acknowledge and document its own sources? Does it appear to treat others' opinions fairly, presenting them in clear summaries or through quotations?

• **Evaluate electronic sources with special care.** Electronic sources such as Web pages and discussion groups pose some special problems—and opportunities. These sites can be rich and provocative sources of ideas and details. At the same time, electronic sites are often produced by individuals or organizations whose trustworthiness or bias are difficult to determine—unlike those for sources in scholarly journals, well-known magazines, or books from reputable publishers. Use questions like these to evaluate electronic sources.

1. Who is responsible for the site? Are there any obvious signs of bias or distortion, such as highly selective information or exaggerated language and points of view? In what ways does the site serve the interests of the person or organization that produced it, and how might this affect its reliability?
2. Are sources for information indicated clearly, or are details, examples, and ideas presented without attribution or documentation? Is information presented clearly and carefully? Are ideas and opinions explained thoroughly? Are alternate points of view acknowledged and discussed?

2

Ways of Writing

Confident writers know the importance of each of the stages of the composing process: discovering, drafting, revising, editing, and proofreading. They also know there is no single formula for all writing tasks, so they develop a variety of techniques. Making choices among strategies means paying attention to the needs of readers and the demands of a writing task.

The stages of the writing process may look regular and orderly: Discovering, Planning, Drafting, Revising, Editing, and Proofreading. The lines between these activities often blur, however. Writers often discover worthwhile new ideas as they draft and revise or amend an essay's plan based on readers' responses.

DISCOVERING

Most writing begins with an assignment or invitation: an essay for a college course, a report at work, or a call for submissions to a local newspaper, for example. Good writing can also be self-sponsored, growing from a writer's experiences and feelings and taking initial shape in the writer's journal or personal writing. Some of the best writers are those able to blend an understanding of task and audience with the impulse toward personal expression.

Look for the Assignment's Focus and Purpose—Nouns

When your writing begins with an assignment, make sure you have the exact wording—along with any explanatory comments from the person making the assignment.

Sometimes an assignment will announce a topic clearly. Often, however, assignments use nouns and noun phrases to introduce the various elements of the topic. Consider underlining any direct statements and associated nouns and noun phrases in your assignment. Then, draw on them as you write out the topic focus of the assignment. Student Rachel Baez underlined terms in the following assignment, then summarized it for herself.

> Many of the <u>studies</u> we have read about <u>violent behavior among teens</u> point to the influence of <u>violent scenes on television and in movies</u>. In the <u>interviews</u> we read, however, teenagers themselves point to <u>different causes</u>: social pressures, the personalities of individuals, drug and alcohol use, or a "desire for excitement and adventure." Analyze the differences among these explanations, tell which you find most convincing, and support your conclusions.

What do I see as the focus of this assignment? Two sets of explanations, one set in the studies and one set in the interviews.

Look for Purposes and Patterns in an Assignment—Verbs

The verbs and verb phrases in an assignment set goals (purposes) for your writing and may even suggest patterns for organizing and developing an essay. Verbs like *inform, explain, analyze, discuss,* and *show* suggest that your purpose will be *expository*: helping readers understand ideas, events, and information and offering carefully reasoned and supported conclusions about a subject. Words like *argue, persuade,* and *evaluate* suggest that your purpose will be argumentative: presenting reasoned arguments and supporting evidence designed to convince readers to share your opinion on an issue.

Underline such words in your assignment and write a purpose statement for your task, including information about the topic. When she went back to her assignment, here are the action words Rachel Baez underlined and the purpose statement she prepared.

> Many of the studies we have read about violent behavior among teens point to the influence of violent scenes on television and in movies. In the interviews we read, however, teenagers themselves point to different causes: social pressures, the personalities of individuals, drug and alcohol use, or a "desire for excitement and adventure." <u>Analyze</u> the differences among these explanations, <u>tell</u> which you find most convincing, and <u>support</u> your conclusions.

What are my purposes for this assignment? To give specific information about the differences, to offer my conclusion about the causes, and to give reasons and information that will help readers understand why my conclusions are reasonable.

Verbs and other words in the assignment may suggest (or require) patterns of exposition (or argument) for you to employ in all or part of an essay, alone or in combination with other patterns. Look for words like the following (or their synonyms) and consult the appropriate chapters in this book for ideas on using these patterns:

> *illustrate* or provide *examples* (Chapter 3)
> *classify* or *classification* (Chapter 4)
> *compare* and *contrast* (Chapter 5)
> create an *analogy* (Chapter 6)
> analyze or explain a *process* or *process analysis* (Chapter 7)
> analyze *cause* and *effect* (Chapter 8)
> *define* or provide a *definition* (Chapter 9)
> *describe* or create a *description* (Chapter 10)
> *narrate* or use *narration* (Chapter 11)
> reason *inductively* and *deductively* or use *induction* and *deduction* (Chapter 12)
> *argue* or present an *argument* (Chapter 13)

Use these words, combined with information about your topic and purpose, to create a *design statement* for your writing, as did Rachel Baez.

I plan to begin with a section contrasting the sets of explanations for violent behavior among teens and indicating the specific differences. Then I will state clearly those I find convincing: media influence, social pressures, and the personalities of individuals. Finally, I will present examples and reasons why I think these are probably the most important causes for violent behavior.

Keep a Writing Journal

A *writing journal* (or *academic journal*) is a place (often a notebook or a computer file) in which you jot down ideas and discoveries, try out different perspectives on a topic, prepare rough drafts of paragraphs or essays, and note responses to readings or observations. Journals are not diaries: journals are starting places for public writing while diaries are places to record and keep your private observations.

This passage from Scott Giglio's journal, made in response to an article in his local newspaper, illustrates some of the ways journals can provide an imaginative start for the essay-writing process while at the same time be hard for anyone but the author to read.

> Article in PrJo 6/10/09 "Hispanics losing ground in employ-ment" hadn't thought about this. Why? Article claims—uh, where is it—Census Bureau claims Hispanic families income down 5.1% more than others (can get rest of stats from article if impt. cut it out of pa-per) Ok Ok why happening and why important is this something to argue about or can I use it as part of paper on how people just seem to be same but lead diff. lives??

Ask Questions to Focus and Develop a Topic

Focusing questions help you identify goals or main ideas for your writing and may suggest general ways to divide a topic into parts and organize an essay around key points. They may even point to-ward a thesis around which you can build an essay (see pp. 16–18).

Here are some focusing questions that ask you to consider both your perspective on a topic and your readers' likely responses.

- What parts of this subject or ways of looking at it interest me the most? Is the subject as a whole interesting or does some part of it or specific way of looking at it seem more intriguing?
- What aspect of the subject is most likely to interest readers?
- What would I most like to learn about this subject? Would read-ers like to learn the same thing?
- What feelings about the subject do I want to share with readers? What knowledge, opinions, or insights do I want to share?
- How is my perspective different from the ones readers will likely bring with them?
- What are two (three? four?) fresh, unusual, unsettling, or con-troversial insights I have to share? Why may some readers have trouble understanding or accepting them?

PLANNING

Planning before you draft does not mean deciding ahead of time the exact order in which you will present each detail or idea. It does not mean determining at the start the precise conclusions you will offer and support in each paragraph. Why not?

For most writers, writing is itself a form of discovery. Putting sentences and paragraphs together brings ideas and information into often unanticipated relationships that create fresh perspectives worth sharing.

Nonetheless, if you begin writing without any plan, you are probably dooming yourself to false starts and long periods of inactivity when you try to decide what to say next—or whether to scrap the whole draft and start over.

Sometimes your exploration of a topic suggests a clear pattern and direction for your writing. Sometimes your **discovering** activities (pp. 11–14) suggest a point or **thesis** as a focus. And still other times, you have gathered so many ideas, opinions, and details that you need to move ahead before you are overwhelmed. All these are good times to begin planning.

Cluster and Diagram

Both clustering and diagramming (creating tree diagrams) lead to conceptual maps that group ideas to help you see relationships and develop focal points for your writing.

In **clustering**, you develop ideas related to a central topic and link the ideas with lines to display how they are associated. Clustering encourages the interconnection of ideas. You may begin by developing a single idea into several seemingly unconnected nodes, but on further reflection recognize some connections you hadn't yet considered.

Begin by writing a concept, idea, or topic in the center of a page, and circle it. Then randomly jot down associations with the central idea, circling them and connecting them with lines to the center, like the spokes of a wheel. As you continue to generate ideas around the central focus, think about the interconnections among subsidiary ideas, and draw lines to show those.

You can also create clusters in cycles, each subsidiary idea becoming the central focus on a new page. You'll soon find that some clusters begin petering out once you've exhausted your fund of knowledge. Stand back and assess what you have. Is there enough to go on, without further consideration? If so, you may be ready to start some harder, more critical consideration of your paper's direction. If not, perhaps further strategies will open up additional ideas.

Tree diagrams resemble clusters, but their branches tend to be a little more linear, with few interconnections. Tree diagrams rely on the notion of subordination: each larger branch can lead to smaller and smaller branches. For this reason, tree diagramming can provide a useful way to visualize the components of your paper. You can even revise a tree diagram into a sort of preliminary outline (see p. 18) to use when deciding what to place in each paragraph of your paper.

Develop a Thesis

Perhaps the most important and useful planning technique involves focusing on what you want to say and do. In a finished essay, a **thesis statement** creates focus by announcing your main idea(s) to readers and helping organize supporting ideas, evidence, and discussions. An effective thesis statement is specific and limited; it announces and highlights the main idea without getting bogged down in details.

> **Specific:** A good community exercise program makes provisions for four kinds of exercisers: people dedicated to fitness, people wanting to become fit, people struggling with health problems, and children building a base for a healthy lifestyle.
>
> **Vague:** A community exercise program is good when it has room for people who want to exercise for all sorts of different reasons.

> **Limited:** Extensive use of fossil fuels and widespread changes in agriculture have had significant effects on our climate in the last seventy-five years.
>
> **Too Broad:** The last several centuries have seen massive changes in industrial production, in the use of fossil fuels, in transportation, in the development of cities, in agriculture, and in many other areas that have had an impact on our climate.

> **Direct:** Despite all their protests to the contrary, people tend to value appearance, likelihood of success, and similarity of background in choosing a mate.
>
> **Bogged:** People may say they look for spiritual qualities rather than looks in choosing a mate, yet research points out that they are more likely to be influenced by some traditional factors, and these are likely to include how a person looks, whether or not a person is likely to succeed financially or

in social terms, and the extent to which the people's families, experiences, and social class are similar.

Effective thesis statements seldom start out specific, limited, and direct. They begin as **tentative thesis statements** that provide a focus for planning. As you draft and revise, they become clearer and more sharply focused, eventually taking final form in a finished essay.

Here are some techniques for developing a tentative thesis statement as part of your planning.

- *List Your Conclusions and Evidence*
  Create a list of possible conclusions and evidence you wish to offer in an essay. Then sum them up in a **generalization**, which highlights the main idea linking them all.

  Support: Fashions in children's toys change quickly—sometimes several times a year.

  Support: Toy manufacturers must make product decisions a year before the toys appear in stores, so they need to predict trends a year ahead.

  Support: Bringing a new toy to market can cost millions of dollars.

  Support: Most new toys are not successes; many make very little money.

  Support: There are many well-managed and imaginative companies competing for business in the toy market.

  Generalization (Tentative Thesis): Manufacturing children's toys is a risky business.

- *Create a Tentative Purpose Statement*
  Try writing yourself a note stating your potential topic along with your conclusions and possible goals for writing. To remain flexible and open to new ideas, you might begin your statement with a phrase like "I'd like to. . . ." or "I'm planning to. . . ."

  I'm planning to explain the reasons why many college students lose their motivation to work hard at their studies.

  —Bippin Kumar

  I'd like to tell what it felt like to be forced to leave my homeland, Haiti, so that my readers can understand why to leave something you love is to die a little.

  —Fredza Léger

Create a Rough Purpose/Thesis Outline

When you have in mind the various ideas and details you wish to present in an essay, create a **purpose/thesis outline** arranging the ideas and details in groups by clustering the details and summing up your conclusions and purpose for each section of an essay.

Here is Bippin Kumar's purpose outline for a paper exploring the reasons why college students may lose the motivation necessary to succeed at their studies.

1. Get readers' attention by mentioning the *bad habits* most of us have and that we may be able to correct on our own. (minor causes of the problem)

   lack of sleep

   disorganization

   distractions (television, video games, etc.)

2. Show how we are often responsible because of the choices we make and explain that we need to make wiser choices. (more serious causes)

   sports and other extracurricular activities

   friends and socializing

   Greek life

   letting ourselves get frustrated and angry over daily hassles (bookstores, commuting)

3. Conclude with problems that we can't avoid and that may require special planning or counseling to overcome. (more serious causes)

   work

   financial stresses

   family demands or problems

   lack of necessary skills

DRAFTING

Drafting involves a good deal more than setting pen to paper or fingers to keyboard and letting the words flow according to your plan. It means paying attention to the way each section of an essay relates to the other sections and to the central theme. It means making sure you begin and end the essay in ways that are clear, helpful, and interesting to readers. And it means making sure each section and each paragraph present sufficient, detailed information so that readers can understand your subject and have reasons to agree with your explanations and conclusions.

Drafting does not mean getting everything right the first time. Such a goal is likely to prove both exhausting and impossible to achieve. A much better goal is to draft with the most important features of an essay in mind and to work quickly enough so that you have sufficient time to revise later and then pay attention to details.

Keep Your Plan in Mind

As you draft, therefore, make sure that you introduce readers to your topic, indicate its importance, generate interest in it, and suggest the direction your essay will take. The essays in this collection can provide you with models of successful strategies for the beginnings of essays, and the *Introductions* entry in the Guide to Terms (at the back of the text, pp. 551–569) offers a detailed list of opening strategies. The Guide also provides advice about another important feature that should be a focus during drafting—your essay's conclusion.

Keep in mind the various sections you have planned for your essay, or keep at hand a copy of any planning strategies you have used, especially those that identify the planned parts of your essay, their general content, and their purposes.

Keep Your Focus (Thesis) in Mind

Most likely, you will also alter, revise, or change the main point (theme or thesis) of your essay as you write, and such changes often make for a better essay. By the time your essay is complete, moreover, you will also have to decide whether to announce your main point directly to readers in a concise **thesis statement** (see below), to present it less directly in a series of statements in the body of the essay, or to imply it through the details and arrangement of the paper. No matter which strategy you choose, you should have a relatively clear idea of your thesis before you begin drafting. Try stating your thesis to yourself in a tentative form. You can do this in several ways:

- Start with a phrase like "I want my readers to understand. . . ." or "The point of the whole essay is. . . ."
- Make up a title that embodies your main idea.

- Send an imaginary note to your readers: "By the time you are finished with this essay, I hope you will see (or agree with me) that...."

If you want to share your knowledge of bicycling as a sport, for instance, you might try one or more of these thesis-building strategies, as in the following examples.

1. The point of the whole essay is that people can choose what kind of bicycle riders they want to be—recreational, competitive, or cross-country.
2. What Kind of Bicycle Rider Do You Want to Be?
3. By the time you finish this essay, I hope you will be able to choose the kind of bicycle riding—recreational, competitive, or cross-country—that is best for you.

A **tentative thesis statement** can guide your drafting by reminding you of your essay's main point. You can create a tentative thesis statement by summing up in a sentence or two your main point, the conclusion you plan to draw from the information and ideas you will present, or the proposition for which you plan to argue. You may eventually use a revised form of the tentative thesis statement in your completed essay as a way of announcing clearly to readers the main idea behind your writing.

For example, when Ken Chin was preparing a paper on different meanings of the phrase *recent immigrant* he used the following tentative thesis statement: "For some people, *recent immigrant* means a threat to their jobs or more strain on the resources of schools and social service agencies. For others, it means fresh ideas and a broadening of our culture and outlook." In his final paper he used this thesis statement: "For some, *recent immigrant* means *cheap labor* or *higher taxes;* for others, it means *fresh ideas* and *a richer, more diverse culture.*"

Pay Attention to Sections

As you write, include statements that alert readers to the various sections, along with transitions marking the movement from one section to the next or from paragraph to paragraph (see "Guide to Terms": *Transition*).

Make sure, too, that in making shifts in time, place, ideas, and content you do not confuse readers, but instead give them adequate indication of the shifts. Remember to provide readers with concrete, specific details and evidence that will give them the information they need about your topic, or the support necessary to make your explanations or arguments convincing.

Pay attention to the arrangement of your essay, especially to the patterns of exposition or argument you are employing. In any essay that classifies, for example, don't provide a detailed treatment of one category in the classification but skimpy treatment of the others—unless you have a special reason for doing so. Let your readers know, directly or indirectly, whatever pattern(s) you are employing. This will make them aware of your essay's design and will help to guide their attention to the key points you cover.

Make every effort to stick to your main idea (perhaps using your tentative thesis statement as a guide), and check to see that the parts of the essay are clearly related to and support the main idea. If you have trouble developing a section because you need more information, or because you can't express ideas as clearly as you want, make a note of the things that need to be done and then move on.

REVISING

When you shift your focus to revising, you pay special attention to the success with which your draft essay embodies your intentions and meets your readers' likely expectations. You examine the draft to see if it does a good job presenting insights, reasoning, and details. You look at the draft from a reader's perspective to see if the discussions are clear and informative, the reasoning is logical, and the examples and supporting details are related to the central theme.

Read for Revision

Revision starts with rereading—looking over your draft with a dual perspective: as an author and as a member of your potential audience. As you read for revision, keep track of the places that need more work and make note of the directions your rewriting might take, perhaps in the margins of your text. Most writers find it hard to read for revision directly from a computer screen, and they print a hard copy of their drafts on which to make notes.

Whether you are working with a handwritten text, an on-screen copy, or a printout from a word processor, you may find reading for revision most effective if you do it with a pencil or pen in hand to record your reactions and plans for revision.

Reading for revision can be even more effective when another writer does it for you (and you return the favor). Remember, collaborative readings of this sort are best done in a cooperative, rather than harshly critical, atmosphere. Your job and that of your reader(s) is to identify strengths as well as weaknesses and to suggest (if possible) ways to turn weaknesses into strong points. (For more about collaborative revising and editing, see pp. 27–28.)

Whether you are reading your own work or someone else's, you may find symbols (see box) useful shortcuts for making marginal comments to guide revision.

Reader Response Symbols

?	Could you explain this a bit more? I can't really understand this.
Add?	I would like to know more about this. I think you could use more detail here.
Leave out?	This information or this passage may not be necessary. You have already said this.
Missing?	Did you leave something out? I think there is a gap in the information, explanation, or argument here.
Confusing?	I have trouble following this explanation/argument. The information here is presented in a confusing manner.
Reorganize?	I think this section (or paper) would be more effective if you presented it in a different order.
Interesting, Good, Effective, etc.	Your writing really works here. I like it.

You may be tempted to revise as you read, and for sentences or paragraphs that need a quick fix, this approach is often adequate. In most cases, however, your revisions need to go beyond tinkering with words and sentences if they are to lead to real improvement. You will need to pay attention to the overall focus, to the need for additional paragraphs presenting detailed evidence, and to the arrangement of the steps in an explanation or argument. To see the need for such large-scale changes, you need to read the draft paying attention to the essay as a whole, something you cannot do if you stop frequently to rework the parts. In addition, it makes little sense to correct the flaws in a sentence if you realize later on that the entire paragraph ought to be dropped.

Read with Questions

One good way to read for revision is to prepare questions that will focus your attention as you read—questions appropriate for your topic, your purposes, your pattern(s) of exposition or argument, and your intended readers. Following are some possible questions to help you evaluate your draft.

Revision Checklist

General

Does my essay have a clear topic and focus?
Does it stick to the topic and focus throughout?
How have I signaled the topic and focus to readers?
Is the essay divided into parts? What are they?
Are the parts clearly identified for readers?

Thesis and theme

Does the essay have a thesis statement? Is it clearly stated?
Is the thesis statement in the best possible location?
Should the thesis statement be more (or less) specific?
Are all the different parts of the essay clearly related to the thesis statement or the central theme?
In what ways have I reminded readers of the thesis or theme in the course of the essay? Do I need to remind them more often or in other ways?

Introductions and conclusions

Does my introduction make the topic clear? Does it interest readers in what I will have to say?
Does my introduction give readers some indication of the arrangement of the essay and its purpose(s)?
Does the conclusion help tie together the main points of the essay or remind readers of the significance of the information and ideas I have presented?
Does my conclusion have a clear purpose or have I ended the essay without any clear strategy?

Information and ideas

Have I presented enough information and enough details so that readers will feel they have learned something worthwhile about the topic?

At what specific places would the essay be improved if I added more information?

What information can be cut because it is repetitive, uninteresting, or unrelated to the topic or theme of the essay?

Is my information fresh and worth sharing? Do I need to do more thinking or research so that the content of my essay is worth sharing?

Do the examples and details I present support my conclusions in a convincing way? Do I need to explain them more fully?

Would more research or thinking enable me to offer better support? What kinds of support would readers find helpful?

Have I learned something new or worthwhile about my topic and communicated it to readers?

Sentences and paragraphs

Have I divided the essay into paragraphs that help readers identify shifts in topic, stages in an explanation, steps in a line of reasoning, key ideas, or important segments of information?

Does each paragraph make its topic or purpose clear to readers?

Which short paragraphs need greater development through the addition of details or explanations?

Which long paragraphs could be trimmed or divided?

Do the sentences reflect what I want to say? Which sentences could be clearer?

Are the sentences varied in length? Do they provide appropriate emphasis to key ideas?

Can I word the explanations or arguments more clearly?

Can I use more vivid and concrete language?

Would the paper benefit from more complicated or imaginative language? From simpler, more direct wording?

Readers' perspective

In what ways are my readers likely to view this topic or argument? Have I taken their perspectives into account?

What do I want my readers to learn from this essay? What opinion do I want them to share? What do I want them to do?

Have I considered what my readers are likely to know or believe and how this will shape their response to my purpose(s) for writing?

Sample Student Essay

Here is the draft of an essay Sarah Lake produced in response to an assignment asking her to write about a community of some sort, taking the perspective of an outsider trying to understand how the community works and what kinds of relationships people in the community form. The marginal comments on the paper are notes she has addressed to the classmates (peer readers) who will be responding to her paper with revision suggestions.

Welcome to the Gym!

As I stepped up to the door to the field house I saw myself in the reflection from the door. I had chosen mesh shorts, a white v-neck T-shirt, and tattered old sneakers in hope to "fit in" with the crowd. Luckily, I still possess the Ram sticker on the back of my I.D. I was all set. I was in. A cheery eyed student asked for my I.D., and pointed me towards the training room. So far, so good, I thought. My only hopes were that the gym was going to be a great place.

I've tried to make this interesting. Is it?

This is the community I studied. Is my purpose clear?

The smell was rather distinct; one part sweat, one part machine oil, and one part cleaner, or maybe it was the chlorine coming from the pool. Surprisingly, it was a rather welcoming smell. The kind of smell that says "Come on in, have fun, work out, sweat, be hot and sticky and smelly, it's O.K." I liked what it had to say, so I continued on, farther into the training room. As I stepped inside to the training room, heavy breathing and strenuous shouts of "One!, Two!, Three!" could be heard. The shouting seemed common, and went unnoticed by regulars. Weightlifters, mostly men, would grunt, scream, moan, and sometimes yell in agony as they tried to lift weights two, three times the weight they could handle. Their heads turned a tomato red and looked as if they were about to explode. Their veins,

I added a lot of detail. Does it work?

like thick rope, popped through the skin on their necks, arms, and legs. Due to the fact that I'm not a weight-lifter or a man, I surely don't understand the meaning behind this behavior. It looked rather painful, and it wasn't very flattering to them, but it was entertaining.

I squirmed my way through the machines, and people, and found myself a spot on one of the stair masters. I curiously stared at the screen in front of me. Blinking letters zoomed across the screen reading enter your weight and then press enter. Enter my weight? That's a lot to ask of a girl. I thought about it, and even considered lying to the machine, but reality set in, I realized it was just a machine. Why lie to a machine? I punched in my weight, and continued to answer the questions the screen produced.

As I started my workout, I began to gaze around and inspect everyone's interaction with each other. "Rules of the Gym" were listed on the wall and were followed by everyone. Everyone respected everyone and everything. On the other hand rules for socializing weren't posted, but underlying rules seemed to be understood. Socializing while working out or better yet, while in motion was not encouraged. Talking only took place while one was motionless or waiting for a machine. It seemed as if it took so much concentration to work out that no one could even talk while doing so. I, on the other hand, couldn't wait to talk when I got finished. I felt like I had gone through withdrawal. I needed some sort of outlet to make the time go by and my workout faster so I turned from people behavior watching to people's attire watching.

Gym attire was rather diverse. Some wore the typical workout uniform, which consisted of tight spandex. It included tops, tops over tops, bottoms, bottoms over bottoms, etc., etc. Others wore outfits very similar to my own which was very comforting. My favorite outfit (I'm being sarcastic) was on a young woman, about 21, who turned more heads in twenty minutes than most

I think my punctuation and grammar got a bit out of control at times in this draft. Help!

supermodels do in their careers. It consisted of, from top to bottom: a bright pink scrunchie (one of those cloth elastics), a black headband, a bright pink jog bra, black lycra spandex, covered by a workout g-string, also bright pink in color. As I worked my eyes down to her legs and then to her feet I noticed she had boxing sneakers on. Smashing, was the only word to describe her ensemble.

Is this too much detail?

Peer Response

Before you revise (or in between successive drafts), getting a look at your work through another's eyes can help you spot strengths and weaknesses and identify steps you can take to improve your essay. To do this, ask a person or a group of people to read and comment on the strengths and weaknesses of your draft essay. Ask them, too, to suggest ways the writing might be improved. Their comments are most likely to be useful if you ask them to respond to specific questions (like those in the list on pp. 23–25) and to make concrete suggestions for improvement.

Here are some comments students Tonya Williams and Dave Cisneros made on Sarah Lake's essay.

Does this essay have a clear and interesting thesis statement or generalization?

TONYA: I don't see any thesis statement. The assignment asked us to make a generalization about the community. What is yours?

DAVE: In the planning materials you shared with us, you talked about the reasons people were exercising. Could you add a generalization about the motivations of people in this community?

Does this essay provide detailed examples that support or explain the essay's thesis statement or generalization?

TONYA: I like some of the pictures of gym life that you provide, but I don't see how they fit with any kind of generalization. The last example probably talks too much about clothes.

DAVE: I suggest cutting the last paragraph. It doesn't fit with the rest of the paper.

Are the sentences clear and effective? How might they be improved?

TONYA: A lot of the sentences begin with "I," so the paper seems to focus on you rather than the community you are exploring.

DAVE: I like the way you write. I think your sentences are easy to read in general. At times, though, the paper seems a bit informal. I'm not sure whether the writing is too informal in style or whether you are focusing more on your personal feelings than on the kinds of observations and conclusions you are trying to explain.

Are there any places the grammar and spelling might be improved?

TONYA: I think you have some grammar problems, especially fragments and run-ons. I put a question mark next to these on the paper.

DAVE: I noticed a few spelling problems and other small errors. I tried to mark them, but I may have missed a few.

EDITING, PROOFREADING, AND FINAL REVISION

After you have carefully rewritten your essay at least one time and perhaps several, you can focus on editing and on the final revision. In creating your finished paper, pay special attention to matters such as the style and clarity of sentences and paragraphs as well as correctness in grammar and usage. Before you hand in your final draft, carefully correct any typographical errors along with any mistakes in spelling or expression that remain.

   Here is the final version of Sarah Lake's paper, including some revisions that she made during a last reading and some editing before she typed the final copy. In revising, Sarah took into account the comments of her classmates and those her instructor wrote on a copy of her draft. In addition, she went back to her planning document for ideas she left out of the draft, and she developed these ideas at some length in the revised version of the paper. The comments in the margin of the paper below have been added to highlight features of the essay.

Welcome to the Gym:

A Community of Worriers

As I stepped up to the door of the field house, I saw
my reflection in the glass, and I started worrying. I had
chosen mesh shorts, a white V-necked T-shirt, and

tattered old sneakers in hopes of fitting in with the community I planned to observe: people exercising for fitness inside the gym. I was worrying about how well I would fit in. After my visit, I realized I fit in quite well. Not only had I dressed appropriately, but I was also worried, and worrying about appearance seemed to be one trait everybody at the gym shared. <u>It seems to be the attribute that defines this community and ties its members together.</u>

Moves from personal experience to the conclusion that will be explored in the essay

Thesis statement

Paragraph presents observations

As I stepped inside the training room I heard heavy breathing and strenuous shouts of "One! Two! Three!" Weightlifters, mostly men, were grunting, screaming, moaning, and yelling in agony as they tried to lift weights two, three times more than they could handle. Their heads turned tomato red, and they looked as if they were about to explode. I'm neither a man nor a weightlifter, and I had no idea why they were trying to overexert themselves, or so it seemed to me.

When I spoke with several of the weightlifters, they admitted that for many people who spend time lifting weights, appearance is a primary concern. They claimed that many male weightlifters begin exercising because they feel inferior about their physical appearance or because they want to get that "He-man" or "Caveman" look that they consider an ideal for men. Though the men I talked to said that they, personally, weren't that anxious about the way they looked, they also admitted that they felt that potential dates pay more attention to a man who has "bulked up." I asked why they felt it was important to have a muscular and masculine appearance in today's society, especially when a lot of people (women especially) talk about the need for men to be "sensitive." I was surprised by the answers because they seemed to reveal worry and insecurity—which was surprising coming from a group of very well-muscled college men. The weightlifters said they thought sensitivity was a good thing, and they claimed to work toward it in their relationships. They also said that sensitivity grows

Evidence supports overall thesis

Observations likely to surprise and intrigue reader

out of self-confidence, and that for men self-confidence often comes through physical fitness and athletic ability.

Though the weightlifters seemed sincere, as a woman I felt rather awed by their appearance and kept waiting for one of them to knock one of the female exercisers over the head and drag her back to his cave. This thought made me shift my attention to the women, most of whom were working on machines like Stair Masters, stationary bicycles, or Nautilus. To enter into the women's part of this community, I squirmed my way through the machines and people, and I found a spot on one of the Stair Masters. I stared curiously at the screen in front of me. Blinking letters zoomed across the screen asking me to enter my weight. "Enter my weight," I thought. "That's a lot to ask of a girl." I even thought about lying, but then I got embarrassed about lying to a machine. Later, when I shared this worry with some of the women at the gym, I realized they shared my apprehension and a lot of my other worries.

Like the men, the women shared many concerns about their appearance, especially about their attractiveness and about the relationship of appearance to self-confidence. They spoke of how the *Baywatch* girls are the ideals of appearance for women in our society, and of how they felt a need to compete with the "Barbies" of this world, even though such an appearance is unrealistic for the average woman. They also talked about having a kind of balance scale in their heads. As their weight increases, they feel less attractive, and as their weight decreases, they feel more attractive. They pointed out how magazines, TV programs, and movies seem to equate thinness with attractiveness and link attractiveness to self-confidence. Though they admitted that working women with responsibilities as wives and mothers might not have time or energy to work out in a gym, they worried about how their self-confidence might suffer if they didn't have the opportunity to exercise to control their weight.

Transition to second set of observations

Personal experience supports thesis

Observations act as evidence for thesis

Summarizes interviews

After my time on the Stair Master came to an end and I had finished talking to the members of the gym community, I left, feeling as though I fit in. I was a worrier and I had dressed like many of the women. On my way out, however, I passed a woman dressed in a daring pink and black outfit who began turning heads as soon as she walked in the door. I started worrying again, and I knew the people in the gym were now worrying even more about their looks.

Conclusion echoes main point

3

Illustrating Ideas
by Use of *Example*

The use of examples to illustrate an idea under discussion is the most common, and frequently the most efficient, pattern of exposition. It is a method we use almost instinctively; for instance, instead of talking in generalities about the qualities of a good city manager, we cite Angela Lopes as an example. We may go further and illustrate her virtues as a manager by a specific account of her handling a crucial situation during the last power shortage or hurricane. In this way, we put our abstract ideas into concrete form—making them clearer and more convincing. As readers, we look for examples as well, often responding to general statements with a silently voiced question, "For instance?" and expecting the writer to provide us with appropriate specifics.

Examples can be short or long: a brief illustration within a sentence or a fully developed instance filling a paragraph or more. They can appear singly, or they can work together in clusters, as in the following paragraph where brief examples serve to make a generalization vivid and convincing.

> *There were many superstitions regarding food.* Dropping a fork meant that company would be coming. If we were to take a second helping of potatoes while we still had some left on our plate, someone always predicted that a person more hungry than we were would drop in during the day. Every housewife believed that food from a tin can had to be removed immediately after opening, or it would become deadly poison within a few seconds. My mother always ran across the room to dump the contents immediately.
>
> —Lewis Hill, "Black Cats and Horse Hairs"

Generality

> Example 1
> Example 2
> Example 3
> Example 4

Whether making an explanation clear, a generality more convincing, or an argument more persuasive, examples work in the same way. They make the general more specific, the abstract more concrete, and in so doing they illustrate a sound principle of writing.

WHY USE EXAMPLES?

Examples clarify by showing readers what a general statement means in terms of individual events, people, or ideas. By pointing out students who use lucky pens to take a test, lawyers who wear special ties or shoes to a big day in court, and engineers who begin a new project with a special breakfast, a writer can aid understanding of the statement, "Even educated people often make superstition part of their everyday lives."

On the other hand, lack of clear illustrations may leave readers with only a hazy conception of the points the writer has tried to make. Even worse, readers may try to supply examples from their own knowledge or experience, leading them to an impression different from that intended by the author. Since writers are the ones trying to communicate, clarity is primarily their responsibility.

Not only do good examples put into clear form what otherwise might remain vague and abstract, but they also serve to make generalizations and conclusions convincing. Not every generality requires supporting examples, of course. An audience with even a passing familiarity with films probably does not need extended examples to understand and accept the statement, "Action films are characterized by physical violence, explosions, chase scenes, and broadly drawn characters." Conclusions about unfamiliar or complicated subjects, technical discussions, and perspectives that may be difficult for readers to share initially usually call for examples. College instructors, for instance, will usually look for examples to render an interpretation convincing; business and public audiences will search reports and memorandums for examples that make the writer's judgments plausible.

With something specific for readers to visualize, a statement becomes more convincing—but convincing within certain limitations.

If you use the Volvo as an example of Swedish manufacturing, the reader is probably aware that this car may not be entirely typical. For ordinary purposes of explanation, the Volvo example could make its point convincingly enough. In supporting an argument, however, you need either to choose an example that is clearly typical or to present several examples to show that you have represented the situation fairly.

CHOOSING A STRATEGY

As a writer, you need to recognize not only places where individual examples can aid your writing but also occasions when your ideas might be most effectively presented through the use of examples as the primary strategy for an essay. If you have a fresh, unusual, or surprising conclusion to offer readers, consider using examples in a **thesis-and-support strategy**. Announce your thesis (perspective, interpretation) to readers, then offer evidence of its reasonableness in the form of varied, carefully developed examples, as illustrated in the following plan for an essay.

Tentative Thesis	Modern technology offers many creative outlets for writers, musicians, and artists.
Supporting Point	Cable television provides opportunities for creative work through the large number of television programs on its schedule.
	Example: It provides work for scriptwriters of all kinds: dramatic, documentary, news, sports, and comedy.
	Example: It creates opportunities for actors, cinematographers, and directors.
	Example: It produces programs calling for original music, art, and graphics.
Supporting Point	Software development calls for creative artists as well as software engineers.
	Example: Games require scriptwriters, artistic designers, graphic artists, and composers (for music to accompany the action).
	Example: Office programs require graphic design; home and landscape design programs

involve artistic and graphic design; educational software calls for writers and designers (sometimes even music).

Supporting Point   The World Wide Web provides the means to create and distribute works of art without significant financial resources.

Example: Composers and performers can create musical works without hiring performers or renting a studio and distribute their work on the Web.

Example: Desktop publishing allows writers to create printed copies of their novels, essays, and other writing without the expense or difficulty of working with publishers and printers.

Example: Design programs and drawing/painting programs let visual artists create without having to maintain a studio or buy expensive materials, and the Web gives them a way to advertise and distribute their work.

If an extended, especially detailed example covers all aspects of your topic that need explaining or provides a particularly appropriate instance of your main idea, consider using a **representative example strategy**. A representative example needs to be interesting in itself because it will serve as the main focus of the writing, preceded or followed (or both) by the main idea it illustrates.

In this chapter, Andy Rooney's "In and of Ourselves We Trust" (pp. 45–46) provides a particularly successful instance of a representative example (stopping at a red light when no one is around) followed by the writer's conclusion that "the whole structure of our society depends on mutual trust, not distrust."

CHOOSING EXAMPLES

Successful writers select and use examples cautiously, keeping in mind their readers and their own specific purposes for communicating. To be effective, an example must be pertinent to the chief qualities of the generality it illustrates. In writing about horror films, for instance, you might offer this interpretation: "The films generally have contemporary settings, yet most reinforce traditional, even old-fashioned, roles for both men and women." To be pertinent, examples would need to address the various elements of this thesis, including the contrast between the contemporary setting and the old-fashioned values, the roles of both men and women, and exceptions to the conclusion (the interpretation applies to "most" horror films, but not all).

Examples should be representative as well, presenting in a fair manner the range of situations, people, or ideas to which a generality applies. In discussing a new approach to education, you should be ready to consider it in terms of urban and rural as well as suburban communities. Your interpretation of a play, film, novel, or recording should take into account the work as a whole, not simply those parts corresponding most directly to your thesis. If you wish readers to adopt your perspective, you should choose examples that represent any important differences among their outlooks, often the product of differences in background, gender, ethnicity, or education.

It is possible to provide too many examples and make them too long, but for most writers, the opposite is usually the problem. We frequently underestimate the number of examples needed because we pay attention only to those that come to mind most readily. Almost any part of a subject can provide potential examples, however. With your generality or thesis in mind, look for representative events, situations, quotations, or people; typical attitudes, opinions, or ideas; and characteristic physical and emotional details. Make a conscious effort to draw examples from a variety of sources.

- *Your Experiences:* Draw on your involvement with the topic. For an essay on work, draw on jobs you have held. For an essay on sports, think of your experiences (pleasant and unpleasant) as an athlete or spectator. For a report on health care, begin with your own broken bones, doctor's appointments, sessions in the dentist's chair, and trips to the hospital either as patient or visitor.
- *Your Reading:* Add to your knowledge of a topic by searching a library catalog or using an Internet search engine. Choose articles and reports that expand your understanding and suggest the ways others may respond to your conclusions. Draw examples (including statistics) from your reading, being careful to acknowledge your sources using whatever documentation strategies your audience considers appropriate (such as the Modern Language Association or American Psychological Association styles).
- *Other People:* Think about other people whose experiences are consistent with your conclusions: the neighbor whose job history

reflects a changing view of loyalty to an employer or your cousin whose reliance on the Internet for shopping illustrates changing patterns of consumption.

- *One from a Group:* When your thesis or generalization applies to a wide variety of people, situations, organizations, or experiences, you may be tempted to provide numerous examples as a way of representing the group as a whole but instead end up with a cluster of indistinct, ineffective illustrations. Instead, consider focusing on one or two examples and presenting them in extended detail that explains and supports your conclusions. To illustrate the features of science fiction movies, for example, turn to one or two films likely to be familiar to your readers.

There is no set length for effective examples. They can be as short as a few words or as long as several paragraphs in length, depending on the purpose they serve. For a thesis-and-support essay, however, a paragraph of four to six sentences provides a good measure.

Each paragraph supporting your main idea should provide several brief examples (as in the sample paragraph on p. 33) or several sentences presenting the example and discussing it in detail. Writers often overestimate how much their readers know about a subject and offer examples lacking in important ideas and information, as in the following student example from a paper for a course on public health policy.

> Nonprescription drugs are still drugs and can be dangerous if misused. Many people make themselves ill by doubling or tripling the dosage of nonprescription drugs in order to get a greater effect.

When her instructor and fellow students pointed out the lack of information in this paragraph, the writer realized that she could have included examples of the toxic effects of high dosages of aspirin and other painkillers, of allergic reactions to excessive intake of vitamin and mineral supplements, and of physical damage that can result from overuse of digestive remedies—examples her readers would have found informative and useful.

Remember, a good example must be either instantly obvious to readers or fully developed so that they learn exactly what it illustrates, and how. Sometimes, however, illustration may be provided best by something other than a real-life example—a fictional anecdote, an analogy, or perhaps a parable that demonstrates the general idea. Here even greater care is needed to be sure these examples are both precise and clear.

Student Essay

If you looked back over the events in your life, how would you interpret them? Would you be able to state the perspective or idea that ties them together? The generality that runs through them? How would you select and present examples to illustrate the generality and help readers understand and share your perspective?

Adrian Boykin's experiences as a stutterer and his struggles to deal with the impediment shaped many of the events in his life, and he is able to share an understanding of his experiences and his perspective through carefully selected examples in the essay that follows.

Overcoming an Impediment: A Rite of Passage

Adrian Boykin

"Sp, sp, sp, sp spit it out already, Adrian!" These were among the insults I received from classmates throughout elementary and junior high school. Inheriting the stuttering, dominantly linked phenotype from my father's side of my family has affected my speech, and in turn my relationships, since I first began to speak.

Starting when I was only eight years old and in the third grade, I took speech lessons at school in an attempt to overcome a speech impediment. The trait dates back to my great-grandfather. In the last four generations, many Boykin men have expressed a stutter, while others, such as my younger brother, have not. Throughout childhood I often encountered a block in my speech at the first word of each sentence when beginning to speak. From third grade through my freshman year in high school, I participated in monthly, one-on-one speech classes. Through my working diligently with a speech specialist, I have, for the most part, been able to overcome this genetic defect successfully and speak without impediment.

As a stutterer, it is difficult to explain to a nonstutterer why we sometimes just can't get the words out. Speaking in a casual one-on-one situation has never been a problem for me. Only in stressful situations where a large group of people were gathered, or in a

Margin notes:

Dramatic opening

Thesis statement

Short examples of how his family has been affected

Background explanation of stuttering

setting where everyone is attempting to speak, did my speech impediment become evident. At these times I would compare the first word of my sentence to ice cream that has been in the freezer for a month on the coldest setting. No matter how hard you try to get a full scoop out of the container, only small tastes of the ice cream will come out. Unfortunately, for the stutterer, that small, unfulfilling taste of ice cream is the first syllable of the stutterer's first word. Repeatedly.

Uses an analogy to explain—see Chapter 6

The problems I encountered with speech never rivaled what my dad experienced growing up. Unable to answer the telephone, speak in class, or even speak without incessant stuttering at the dinner table, my father attended a summer camp in Michigan for three months each summer, four summers in a row, with the hopes of correcting his impediment. Today, though he still often stutters momentarily at the beginning of his sentences, he is a successful custom furniture designer and businessman. About ten years ago, still having difficulty speaking in front of groups, Dad completed the Toastmasters speaking course. Because his speech impediment hindered his social development for so many years and in so many ways, he was determined to never let my impediment hold me back socially.

Examples of how his father's life was affected

Because children are often cruel, I was picked on many times by my peers in elementary and junior high school for stuttering. Friends often made fun of me by imitating the stutter I had at the beginning of my sentences. Furthermore, I grew up watching television shows such as *In Living Color* and movies such as *Harlem Nights* and *Billy Madison*, which depict people with speech impediments as being stupid outcasts or class clowns. Looking back at these television shows and movies, I sometimes ask myself why dehumanization of stutterers is tolerated by the public. Racist stabs at minorities are viewed as disgusting and intolerable by the masses, but attacks and mockery aimed at stutterers are seen as hilarious.

Short examples of how stuttering made him feel in elementary school and junior high school

Fortunately, my speech impediment was never something that hindered me from experiencing all the things that other students with normal speech experienced. Because my father knew firsthand what it was like to have a speech impediment, he made sure that I was given therapy to correct my stutter. My father first sent me to a speech therapist affiliated with my elementary school in Denver. Only eight years old, I saw speech therapy as a fun way to get out of class and meet another boy, Michael, who also had a "block in his throat." Attending therapy with another child helped me get away from the feeling that I was alone in my speech problem. During speech class, though, I really never concentrated on Michael. What I remember is my therapist, Mrs. Rainart. "Wow," I always thought, "she is the nicest lady, and pretty too!" This was better than playing with G.I. Joes! By fifth grade, the main reason I liked going to therapy was because I liked seeing her.

Fifth grade was a time of physical change and of change in how I looked at the girls. Mrs. Rainart's milky white teeth and spiral, burgundy-colored hair made speech therapy more than tolerable for me. You know how elementary school children all have a crush on a teacher at one time or another? I guess that teacher was Mrs. Rainart for me.

My mother got a job in Boulder with Celestial Seasonings Tea Company when I was eleven. As a result we moved to a house in a suburb called Broomfield, wherein my father promptly found me another speech therapist in Boulder. The change in scenery made me nervous. Entering Birch Elementary School, I had to make all new friends. Fortunately, everyone at Birch was really nice. My confidence was soaring, and I was convinced that I no longer needed to go to some stupid speech class.

Then came my worst-ever stuttering experience. For my seventh-grade birthday, my parents let me have a party for both my boy friends and my girl friends.

Extended example

Elementary school— relationships with another stutterer and with therapist

Extended example

Begins to develop new kinds of relationships— successfully

Extended example

The night started well, with my friends and I boogying down to the latest Michael Jackson album. I was wearing my nicest polyester shirt to go with my loafers and tight Wranglers. My parents interrupted our disco party for cake, ice cream, and presents.

With the speech impediment seemingly gone, I started socializing with the group while I was opening my gifts. My girl friend, Emily, gave me the coolest Michael Jordan poster. I began to tell Emily how much I appreciated her gift, when out of nowhere, a heavy encompassing piece of cake got stuck in my throat, and I could only stutter to Emily. I ran to the sink to get water when I realized it wasn't the cake that wasn't letting me speak, but that frickin' stutter. Trying to regain my composure, I went back into the family room and said to Emily, "Th, th, th, th." Once more, I tried to thank Emily, "Th, th, th, th."

Junior high school stuttering undermines relationships

Embarrassed, I could not speak, but only heard the laughter of ten wild seventh graders reverberating throughout the room. My good friend Shawn, always quick-witted, decided to slash open my wound a little further and promptly pour a tablespoon of salt on it. He said clearly and loudly, "Dang, Adrian speaks about as well as a cat barks."

More than anything, my stuttering as a child pushed me to aspire to excel socially. Throughout high school, I struggled to become a class leader whom others admired as someone who would express the concerns and wants of the school and group.

High school stuttering pushes him to excel

At the end of my junior year, my speech impediment was rarely noticeable. Furthermore, I wanted to prove to myself that I could speak in the most pressure-packed situations without a problem. Thus, I decided to run for senior class vice president. I gave my election speech in front of my senior class of about 300 and Broomfield High School's faculty. Approaching the podium, I was nervous, but confident in my speech. Usually having difficulties with my first word, I concentrated on my

Extended example

Meets and overcomes challenges

Develops new relationships and self-confidence

therapy tactics. "Keep it slow in the first word," I reminded myself. "Breathe deeply and imagine being in a one-on-one conversation." The sweat flowing in large beads down my back, I delivered a strong, stutter-free, three-minute speech. The crowd could not concentrate on my impediment because there was none. My classmates were forced to concentrate on the content of my speech. The next day I was given word of my election as class vice president.

During my senior year I realized that I was no longer getting any comments about my speech. I also started using my techniques learned from seven years of speech therapy without thinking about them. I had not been in a dusty brown, eight-by-twelve cubicle for three years. Even better, there was no reason for me to ever foresee going back. My father and I sat down and discussed our impediment from time to time, but his assistance was all I would need.

No longer needs speech therapy

By the time I graduated from high school, I had overcome the biggest fear of my speech impediment. Speaking in front of large groups was no longer a time where my speech impediment would reveal itself. As the senior class vice president, I was responsible for giving the closing address at graduation, probably the most high-pressure speech of all. For three weeks I rehearsed my graduation speech.

Extended example

On his own— biggest challenge

The biggest speech of my life was delivered in front of 2,000 friends, classmates, faculty, and family. The football stadium stands were packed like a Mexican piñata for a Cinco de Mayo celebration. Over 2,000 were in attendance, all to hear my closing address. Walking into the stadium, I looked at the happy but tightly squeezed crowd and realized that this was going to be a special moment in my eighteen-year-old life. More than the high school graduation that the class was celebrating, I was celebrating my ability to speak in front of crowds.

For the following two hours I tried listening intently to all of the other speeches. I found myself getting very nervous, but my stutter did not once come to my mind as being a problem. I was only nervous because I was soon going to be on the biggest stage I had ever been on before. Principal Martin gave a short address after we received our diplomas. He then said, "Ladies and gentlemen, the closing address will be given by Class Vice President Adrian Boykin."

I looked to the crowd, started slowly, and let my voice flow continuously and smoothly, similar to an eagle soaring through the sky. As I concluded, I looked into the dots of faces in the crowd and my eyes met my father's.

Throwing my graduation cap into the still, windless sky, I celebrated a rite of passage.

Builds to climax emphasizing his victory over the impediment and the barriers it creates

ANDY ROONEY

ANDREW A. ROONEY was born in 1919 in Albany, New York. Drafted into the army while still a student at Colgate University, he served in the European theater of operations as a *Stars and Stripes* reporter. After the war Rooney began what has been a prolific and illustrious career as a writer-producer for various television networks—chiefly for CBS—and has won numerous awards, including the Writers Guild Award for Best Script of the Year and three National Academy Emmy awards. The author of a number of magazine articles in publications like *Esquire, Harper's,* and *Playboy,* Rooney is nonetheless probably most familiar for his regular appearances as a commentator on the television program *60 Minutes.* Rooney also writes a syndicated column, which appears in more than 250 newspapers, and has lectured on documentary writing at various universities. His books include *My War* (1995), *Sincerely, Andy Rooney* (1999), *Common Nonsense* (2002), *Years of Minutes* (2003), *Out of My Mind* (2006), and *60 Years of Wisdom and Wit* (2009). He lives in Rowayton, Connecticut.

In and of Ourselves We Trust

"In and of Ourselves We Trust" was one of Rooney's syndicated columns. Rooney's piece uses one simple example to illustrate a generality. He draws from it a far-reaching set of conclusions: that we have a "contract" with each other to stop for red lights—and further, that our whole system of trust depends on everyone doing the right thing.

L ast night I was driving from Harrisburg to Lewisburg, Pa., a distance of about 80 miles. It was late, I was late, and if anyone asked me how fast I was driving, I'd have to plead the Fifth Amendment to avoid self-incrimination. 1

At one point along an open highway, I came to a crossroads with a traffic light. I was alone on the road by now, but as I approached the light, it turned red, and I braked to a halt. I looked left, right, and behind me. Nothing. Not a car, no suggestion of headlights, but there I sat, waiting for the light to change, the only human being, for at least a mile in any direction. 2

I started wondering why I refused to run the light. I was not afraid of being arrested, because there was obviously no cop anywhere around and there certainly would have been no danger in going through it. 3

Much later that night, after I'd met with a group in Lewisburg   4
and had climbed into bed near midnight, the question of why I'd
stopped for that light came back to me. I think I stopped because it's
part of a contract we all have with each other. It's not only the law,
but it's an agreement we have, and we trust each other to honor it:
We don't go through red lights. Like most of us, I'm more apt to be
restrained from doing something bad by the social convention that
disapproves of it than by any law against it.

It's amazing that we ever trust each other to do the right thing,   5
isn't it? And we do, too. Trust is our first inclination. We have to
make a deliberate decision to mistrust someone or to be suspicious
or skeptical.

It's a darn good thing, too, because the whole structure of our   6
society depends on mutual trust, not distrust. This whole thing we
have going for us would fall apart if we didn't trust each other most
of the time. In Italy they have an awful time getting any money for
the government because many people just plain don't pay their income tax. Here, the Internal Revenue Service makes some gestures
toward enforcing the law, but mostly they just have to trust that
we'll pay what we owe. There has often been talk of a tax revolt
in this country, most recently among unemployed auto workers in
Michigan, and our government pretty much admits that if there
were a widespread tax revolt here, they wouldn't be able to do any
thing about it.

We do what we say we'll do. We show up when we say we'll   7
show up.

I was so proud of myself for stopping for that red light. And   8
inasmuch as no one would ever have known what a good person I
was on the road from Harrisburg to Lewisburg, I had to tell
someone.

Meanings and Values

1.   Explain the concept of a "contract we all have with each other"
(Par. 4). How is the "agreement" achieved (Par. 4)?

2.   Why do you suppose exceeding the speed limit (Par. 1) would not
also be included in the "contract"? Or is there some other reason for
Rooney's apparent inconsistency?

3.   Explain the significance of the title of this selection.

Expository Techniques

1. How does the example of the red light "work" for readers? How does an analysis of this example help us better understand each other?

2. What other uses of example do you find in the selection?

3. What, if anything, do the brief examples in Paragraph 6 add to this piece? (See "Guide to Terms": *Evaluation*.)

Diction and Vocabulary

1. Does it seem to you that the diction and vocabulary levels of this selection are appropriate for the purpose intended? Why or why not? (Guide: *Diction*.)

2. Could this be classified as a formal essay? Why or why not? (Guide: *Essay*.)

3. Rooney uses the word "trust" six times in Paragraphs 4–6. How effective is the repetition of such a word? Why might Rooney have chosen this strategy?

Read to Write

1. **Collaborating:** Working in groups of three, list several examples that could help convey a main idea similar to the generality Rooney advances in his essay. Then, together, write a brief essay using these examples and employing a casual tone of voice similar to Rooney's.

2. **Considering Audience:** Andy Rooney often appears on television as an oral commentator on events and social behavior. The style of this essay is more similar in some ways to spoken language than written language. How effective is this style for the essay's audience? Why is it or isn't it effective? Rewrite Rooney's essay in a more formal style and analyze the effectiveness of your new version.

3. **Developing an Essay:** Choose an experience that revealed to you something about your personal characteristics, the traits of family or friends, or the "character" of a larger cultural or social group to which you belong. Using Rooney's essay as a model, use this experience as an example to illustrate a generality about your subject, and draw also on briefer examples in the course of your essay.

(NOTE: Suggestions for topics requiring development by EXAMPLE are on pp. 69–70 at the end of this chapter.)

WIL HAYGOOD

After graduating from college, Wıʟ Hᴀʏɢᴏᴏᴅ began his career as a writer with the *Charlestown Gazette* and the *Pittsburgh Post-Gazette.* He then spent seventeen years with the *Boston Globe* as a staff writer and currently writes for the Style section of the *Washington Post.* His nonfiction books are *Two on the River* (1987), *King of Cats: The Life and Times of Adam Clayton Powell, Jr.* (1993), *The Haygoods of Columbus: A Love Story* (1997), *In Black and White: The Life of Sammy Davis, Jr.* (2003), and *Sweet Thunder: The Life and Times of Sugar Ray Robinson* (2011).

Underground Dads

Parents generally play key roles in shaping our identities, but what happens to someone who has not one parent or two, but a number of people who fill the role? Using as examples the men who acted as "underground fathers" for him, Haygood explains how unconventional parenting of the kind he experienced as a boy can be loving, supportive, and successful. This essay first appeared in the *New York Times Magazine.*

For years, while growing up, I shamelessly told my playmates   1
that I didn't have a father. In my neighborhood, where men went to work with lunch pails, my friends thought there was a gaping hole in my household. My father never came to the park with me to toss a softball, never came to see me in any of my school plays. I'd explain to friends, with the simplicity of explaining to someone that there are, in some woods, no deer, that I just had no father. My friends looked at me and squinted. My mother and father had divorced shortly after my birth. As the years rolled by, however, I did not have the chance to turn into the pitiful little black boy who had been abandoned by his father. There was a reason: other men showed up. They were warm, honest (at least as far as my eyes could see) and big-hearted. They were the good black men in the shadows, the men who taught me right from wrong, who taught me how to behave, who told me, by their very actions, that they expected me to do good things in life.

There are heartbreaking statistics tossed about regarding   2
single-parent black households these days, about children growing up fatherless. Those statistics must be considered. But how do you count the other men, the ones who show up—with perfect timing,

with a kind of soft-stepping loveliness—to give a hand, to take a boy to watch airplanes lift off, to show a young boy the beauty of planting tomatoes in the ground and to tell a child that all of life is not misery?

In my life, there was Jerry, who hauled junk. He had a lean   3
body and a sweet smile. He walked like a cowboy, all bowlegged, swinging his shoulders. It was almost a strut. The sound of his pickup truck rumbling down our alley in Columbus, Ohio, could raise me from sleep.

When he wasn't hauling junk, Jerry fixed things. More than   4
once, he fixed my red bicycle. The gears were always slipping; the chain could turn into a tangled mess. Hearing pain in my voice, Jerry would instruct me to leave my bike on our front porch. In our neighborhood, in the 60s, no one would steal your bike from your porch. Jerry promised me he'd pick it up, and he always did. He never lied to me, and he cautioned me not to tell lies. He was, off and on, my mother's boyfriend. At raucous family gatherings, he'd pull me aside and explain to me the importance of honesty, of doing what one promised to do.

And there was Jimmy, my grandfather, who all his life paid his   5
bills the day they arrived: that was a mighty lesson in itself—it taught me a work ethic. He held two jobs, and there were times when he allowed me to accompany him on his night job, when he cleaned a Greek restaurant on the north side of Columbus. Often he'd mop the place twice, as if trying to win some award. He frightened me too. It was not because he was mean. It was because he had exacting standards, and there were times when I didn't measure up to those standards. He didn't like shortcutters. His instructions, on anything, were to be carried out to the letter. He believed in independence, doing as much for yourself as you possibly could. It should not have surprised me when, one morning while having stomach pains, he chose not to wait for a taxi and instead walked the mile to the local hospital, where he died a week later of stomach cancer.

My uncles provided plenty of good background music when I   6
was coming of age. Uncle Henry took me fishing. He'd phone the night before. "Be ready. Seven o'clock." I'd trail him through woods—as a son does a father—until we found our fishing hole. We'd sit for hours. He taught me patience and an appreciation of the outdoors, of nature. He talked, incessantly, of family—his family, my family, the family of friends. The man had a reverence for family. I knew to listen.

I think these underground fathers simply appear, decade to de-   7
cade, flowing through the generations. Hardly everywhere, and
hardly, to be sure, in enough places, but there. As mystical, sometimes, as fate when fate is sweet.

Sometimes I think that all these men who have swept in and   8
out of my life still couldn't replace a good, warm father. But inasmuch as I've never known a good, warm father, the men who entered my life, who taught me right from wrong, who did things they
were not asked to do, have become unforgettable. I know of the cold
statistics out there. And yet, the mountain of father-son literature
does not haunt me. I've known good black men.

MEANINGS AND VALUES

1.   What are some of the important things that fathers are supposed to
teach their sons? Why in Paragraph 1 does Haygood compare a boy
without a father to woods without deer?

2.   Twice in the essay Haygood mentions "good black men." Why do
you think he makes race an issue with this reference?

3.   In the beginning of Paragraph 2, Haygood speaks of "heartbreaking
statistics tossed about regarding single-parent households. . . ." He
says that these figures must be considered, yet he goes on to talk
about households such as his, where "good black men" have helped
raise children. Why does he mention such statistics if he does not
plan to focus on them in the essay?

EXPOSITORY TECHNIQUES

1.   What examples does the author present of fatherly acts he experienced while growing up?

2.   Would the examples of fatherly acts be sufficient to convince most
readers that the writer should not be pitied for the lack of a father in
his home? (See "Guide to Terms": *Evaluation*.)

3.   Why does Haygood list several men who had an effect on his life and
attitudes? Would his essay have been more effective if he had built it
around one representative example of an influential man?

DICTION AND VOCABULARY

1.   Why does the writer use the words "gaping hole" to describe his
friends' image of his household? Is this a figure of speech? (Guide:
Figures of Speech.)

2. How does the word "shamelessly" (Par. 1) help define the image of himself the writer presents to readers? What other words and phrases does he employ to shape his audience's responses to himself?

READ TO WRITE

1. **Collaborating:** Prepare a list of men (not including your biological or adoptive father) who have had a profound impact on your life. Note also their relationship to you. Share your list with two other students in your class. Compare the roles that these men have had in shaping you into an adult. Write a two-page essay analyzing the similarities and differences between the adult males in your life and those in the lives of your classmates.

2. **Considering Audience:** Haygood's essay may strike chords in readers who have been raised without a father at home. However, even readers who have had fathers in their daily lives are likely to respond strongly to this essay. Why would both groups of readers understand the points Haygood makes? What similarities exist between children raised with fathers as a daily presence and those without? What are important differences, if any? Consider the varied ways in which readers might react to this essay based on their upbringing. Prepare a short essay explaining the different reactions readers might have to Haygood's essay.

3. **Developing an Essay:** Haygood mentions his mother briefly in Paragraph 1 of his essay; however, he does not discuss her effect on his life or the expectations he held for her. Make a list of the traditional "teaching" responsibilities of mothers and of fathers. Using these responsibilities as examples, prepare an essay supporting or refuting the notion that one person can take on the roles of both parents.

(NOTE: Suggestions for topics requiring development by EXAMPLE are on pp. 69–70 at the end of this chapter.)

MARY KARR

Mary Karr's highly praised memoir of her Texas childhood and unusual family, *The Liar's Club,* was first published in 1995. It won a
PEN Prize and is frequently cited as among the best of the many
moving and insightful accounts of growing up that have appeared
in recent years. Her memoir of teenage years, *Cherry* (2000), has
also been widely praised. Karr, who teaches literature at Syracuse
University, has also published several volumes of poetry, including
Abacus (1987), *The Devil's Tour* (1993), and *Sinners Welcome*
(2006). Karr's most recent book is *Lit: A Memoir* (2009).

Dysfunctional Nation

To make the point that her dysfunctional family was far from
unique, Karr draws examples from the many stories of other families she heard on a tour to promote her memoir. She suggests, in
addition, that growing up in such a setting may not prevent a person from achieving a healthy identity and sense of self as an adult.

When I set out on a book tour to promote the memoir about my   1
less-than-perfect Texas clan, I did so with soul-sucking dread.
Surely we'd be held up as grotesques, my beloveds and I. Instead, I
shoved into bookstores where sometimes hundreds of people stood
claiming to identify with my story, which fact stunned me.

For one thing, my artist mother had been married seven times,   2
twice to my Texas oil-worker daddy, who was Nos. 5 and 7. Both of
my parents drank hard enough to hit some jackpots. Both were well
armed. (The tile man who came to redo my mother's kitchen last
spring pried more than one .22 slug from the wall.)

Yet in towns across this country I sat at various bookstore ta-   3
bles till near closing and heard people posit that reading about my
tribe brought not slack-jawed horror, but recognition. Maybe these
peoples' family lives differed from mine in terms of surface
pyrotechnics—houses set afire and fortunes squandered. But
the feelings didn't. After eight weeks of travel, I ginned up this
working definition for a dysfunctional family: any family with
more than one person in it.

Even the most perfect-looking clan seemed to suffer a rough   4
patch. "I'm from one of these Donna Reed households you always
wanted to belong to," said the elegant woman in Chicago. But her

doctor daddy got saddled with a wicked malpractice suit, a few more martinis than usual got poured from his silver shaker every night. Rumor was he took up with his nurse.

What happened? "We worked it out. It passed." But not before 5
his Cadillac plowed over her bicycle one drunken night and her mother threatened divorce. Like me, she'd lain awake listening to her parents storm around in the masks of monsters and felt the metaphorical foundations of her house tremble, hopeless to prop it all up.

Not all folks reported such rough times as mere blips on the 6
family time line. In fact, I met dozens of people from way more chaotic households than mine. One guy's drug-dealer parents allegedly dragged him across several borders with bags of heroin taped under his Doctor Denton sleeper. Another woman had, at age 5, watched her alcoholic mother stick her head in a noose and step off a kitchen stool while the girl fought to shield her toddler brother's eyes. Surely many don't survive such childhoods intact (or they don't go to book signings because they're too busy being serial killers). But the myth that such a childhood condemns you to a life curled up in the back ward of a mental institution dissolved for me. On the surface, people seemed to have got over their troubled upbringings.

The female therapist in a Portland bookstore talked specifically 7
about the power of narrative in her life. She'd been raised by a chronic schizophrenic. On a given day, her school clothes were selected by God himself talking to her mother through scalp implants. The girl got good at worming her way into the homes of neighbors and any halfway decent teacher. In college, she fought depression with counseling she continued for nearly 10 years.

At 50, happily married, she wore a Burberry raincoat and toted 8
a briefcase of fine leather. She showed no visible signs of trauma. The real miracle? She was in fairly close touch with her mother, whose psychosis had diminished with new medications.

In part, this woman claimed to have survived through stories. 9
Traditional therapy, of course, starts with retelling family dramas. Talk about it, in the old wisdom, and the hurt eventually recedes. From narratives about her childhood, a self eventually emerged. Her tendency otherwise would have been to lop herself off from her own past, to make a false self for navigating the world. But false selves rarely withstand the real blows life delivers, hence, her need for stories, her own and other peoples'.

In our longing for some assurance that we're behaving O.K. in- 10
side fairly isolated families, personal experience has assumed some new power. Just as the novel form once took up experiences

of urban, industrialized society that weren't being handled in epic poems or epistles, so memoir—with its single, intensely personal voice—wrestles subjects in a way readers of late find compelling. The good ones I've read confirm my experience in a flawed family. They reassure the same way belonging to a community reassures.

My bookstore chats did the same. On the road, I came to believe   11 that our families are working, albeit in new forms. People go on birthing babies and burying dead and loving those with whom they've shared deeply wretched patches of history. We do this partly by telling stories, in voices that seek neither to deny family struggles nor to make demons of our beloveds.

MEANINGS AND VALUES

1. What conclusion about families does Karr offer in Paragraph 3? What examples does she provide to illustrate and support this generality?

2. Does Karr believe our identities and well being are primarily determined by our family backgrounds? If so, where in the essay does she make this point? If not, what else does she believe shapes who we are?

EXPOSITORY TECHNIQUES

1. Explain how the statement, "On the surface, people seemed to have got over their troubled upbringings" (Par. 6), serves both to separate the two halves of the essay and to link them (see "Guide to Terms": *Transition*). In what ways does the second half of the essay answer questions suggested by the statement?

2. In what specific ways does the example in the second half of the essay (Pars. 7–9) and the way it is presented differ from the examples in the first half? How much space does the writer devote to presenting the later example and how much to commenting on and interpreting it?

3. What strategy does the writer employ to conclude the essay? (Guide: *Closings.*)

DICTION AND VOCABULARY

1. Karr uses a number of vivid phrases in the course of the essay: "soul-sucking dread" (Par. 1); "drank hard enough to hit some jackpots" (2); "in the masks of monsters" and "the metaphorical foundations of

her house" (5). Tell what each of these phrases means and what it contributes to the essay's effectiveness.

2. If you do not know the meaning of any of the following words, look them up in a dictionary: *memoir, grotesques* (Par. 1); *pyrotechnics, squandered, ginned, dysfunctional* (3); *trauma, psychosis* (8); *epistles* (10); *albeit* (11).

READ TO WRITE

1. **Collaborating:** Karr's essay touches on a variety of subjects, including storytelling, alcoholism, and family relationships. Make a list of all the subjects she mentions, and then choose two that you find most interesting. Then for each subject, make a list of topics or issues you might wish to explore in an essay of your own. Share your list with a group of classmates, asking them to identify topics they find most intriguing. Do the same for their lists, and, as a group, decide which topics are the most compelling and why.

2. **Considering Audience:** Other than the ones Karr discusses, what situations, relationships, or social forces make it hard for people to establish healthy identities? How many of these is the average person likely to encounter in his or her life? How many are they likely to know about from other people's experiences? How do people learn about such matters if not from their own experiences? Prepare a short essay discussing why readers in general would be likely to be comfortable or uncomfortable with an essay that presents examples of each type of negative situation, relationship, or social force. Include an explanation of why different groups of readers might react in different ways.

3. **Developing an Essay:** Karr begins her essay by describing a situation that surprised her by turning out to be the opposite of what she expected. Use this strategy to begin an essay of your own, and then go on to explore what you learned through the experience (just as Karr does).

(NOTE: Suggestions for topics requiring development by EXAMPLE are on pp. 69–70 at the end of this chapter.)

Issues and Ideas

Characterizing Behavior

- Brent Staples, *Just Walk on By*
- Jonah Lehrer, *The Uses of Reason*

BRENT STAPLES

BRENT STAPLES was born in 1951 in Chester, Pennsylvania. He received his B.A. in 1973 from Widener University and his Ph.D. (in psychology) in 1982 from the University of Chicago. He is a member of the *New York Times* editorial board, writing on matters of culture and society. He was formerly a reporter for the *Chicago Sun Times* and an editor of the *New York Times Book Review*. Staples is the author of *Parallel Time* (1994), a memoir.

Just Walk on By

The power of examples to enable a reader to see through someone else's eyes is evident in this selection. Though many of the examples in the essay draw on a reader's sympathy, their main purpose appears to be explanatory; hence, the author accompanies them with detailed discussions. The result is a piece that is both enlightening and moving.

My first victim was a woman—white, well dressed, probably in her early twenties. I came upon her late one evening on a deserted street in Hyde Park, a relatively affluent neighborhood in an otherwise mean, impoverished section of Chicago. As I swung onto the avenue behind her, there seemed to be a discreet, uninflammatory distance between us. Not so. She cast back a worried glance. To her, the youngish black man—a broad six feet two inches with a beard and billowing hair, both hands shoved into the pockets of a bulky military jacket—seemed menacingly close. After a few more quick glimpses, she picked up her pace and was soon running in earnest. Within seconds she disappeared into a cross street. 1

That was more than a decade ago. I was 22 years old, a graduate student newly arrived at the University of Chicago. It was in the 2 echo of that terrified woman's footfalls that I first began to know the unwieldy inheritance I'd come into—the ability to alter public space in ugly ways. It was clear that she thought herself the quarry of a mugger, a rapist, or worse. Suffering a bout of insomnia, however, I was stalking sleep, not defenseless wayfarers. As a softy who is scarcely able to take a knife to a raw chicken—let alone hold it to a person's throat—I was surprised, embarrassed, and dismayed all at once. Her flight made me feel like an accomplice in tyranny. It also made it clear that I was indistinguishable from the muggers who occasionally seeped into the area from the surrounding ghetto. That first encounter, and those that followed, signified that a vast, unnerving gulf lay between nighttime pedestrians—particularly women—and me. And I soon gathered that being perceived as dangerous is a hazard in itself. I only needed to turn a corner into a dicey situation, or crowd some frightened, armed person in a foyer somewhere, or make an errant move after being pulled over by a policeman. Where fear and weapons meet—and they often do in urban America—there is always the possibility of death.

In the first year, my first away from my hometown, I was to become thoroughly familiar with the language of fear. At dark, shadowy intersections in Chicago, I could cross in front of a car stopped at a traffic light and elicit the *thunk, thunk, thunk, thunk* of the driver—black, white, male, or female—hammering down the door locks. On less traveled streets after dark, I grew accustomed to but never comfortable with people who crossed to the other side of the street rather than pass me. Then there were the standard unpleasantries with police, doormen, bouncers, cab drivers, and others whose business it is to screen out troublesome individuals *before* there is any nastiness.

I moved to New York nearly two years ago and I have remained an avid night walker. In central Manhattan, the near-constant crowd cover minimized tense one-on-one street encounters. Elsewhere—visiting friends in SoHo, where sidewalks are narrow and tightly spaced buildings shut out the sky—things can get very taut indeed.

Black men have a firm place in New York mugging literature. Norman Podhoretz in his famed (or infamous) 1963 essay, "My Negro Problem—And Ours," recalls growing up in terror of black males; they "were tougher than we were, more ruthless," he writes—and as an adult on the Upper West Side of Manhattan, he continues, he cannot constrain his nervousness when he meets black men on certain streets. Similarly, a decade later, the essayist and novelist Edward Hoagland extols a New York where once

"Negro bitterness bore down mainly on other Negroes." Where some see mere panhandlers, Hoagland sees "a mugger who is clearly screwing up his nerve to do more than just *ask* for money." But Hoagland has "the New Yorker's quick-hunch posture for broken-field maneuvering," and the bad guy swerves away.

I often witness that "hunch posture," from women after dark   6
on the warrenlike streets of Brooklyn where I live. They seem to set their faces on neutral and, with their purse straps strung across their chests bandolier style, they forge ahead as though bracing themselves against being tackled. I understand, of course, that the danger they perceive is not a hallucination. Women are particularly vulnerable to street violence, and young black males are drastically overrepresented among the perpetrators of that violence. Yet these truths are no solace against the kind of alienation that comes of being ever the suspect, against being set apart, a fearsome entity with whom pedestrians avoid making eye contact.

It is not altogether clear to me how I reached the ripe old age of   7
22 without being conscious of the lethality nighttime pedestrians attributed to me. Perhaps it was because in Chester, Pennsylvania, the small, angry industrial town where I came of age in the 1960s, I was scarcely noticeable against a backdrop of gang warfare, street knifing, and murders. I grew up one of the good boys, had perhaps a half-dozen fist fights. In retrospect, my shyness of combat has clear sources.

Many things go into the making of a young thug. One of those   8
things is the consummation of the male romance with the power to intimidate. An infant discovers that random flailings send the baby bottle flying out of the crib and crashing to the floor. Delighted, the joyful babe repeats those motions again and again, seeking to duplicate the feat. Just so, I recall the points at which some of my boyhood friends were finally seduced by the perception of themselves as tough guys. When a mark cowered and surrendered his money without resistance, myth and reality merged—and paid off. It is, after all, only manly to embrace the power to frighten and intimidate. We, as men, are not supposed to give an inch of our lane on the highway; we are to seize the fighter's edge in work and in play and even in love; we are to be valiant in the face of hostile forces.

Unfortunately, poor and powerless young men seem to take   9
all this nonsense literally. As a boy, I saw countless tough guys locked away; I have since buried several. They were babies,

really—a teenage cousin, a brother of 22, a childhood friend in his mid-twenties—all gone down in episodes of bravado played out in the streets. I came to doubt the virtues of intimidation early on. I chose, perhaps even unconsciously, to remain a shadow—timid, but a survivor.

The fearsomeness mistakenly attributed to me in public places often has a perilous flavor. The most frightening of these confusions occurred in the late 1970s and early 1980s when I worked as a journalist in Chicago. One day, rushing into the office of a magazine I was writing for, with a deadline story in hand, I was mistaken for a burglar. The office manager called security and, with an ad hoc posse, pursued me through the labyrinthine halls, nearly to my editor's door. I had no way of proving who I was. I could only move briskly toward the company of someone who knew me.   10

Another time I was on assignment for a local paper and killing time before an interview. I entered a jewelry store on the city's affluent Near North Side. The proprietor excused herself and returned with an enormous red Doberman pinscher straining at the end of a leash. She stood, the dog extended toward me, silent to my questions, her eyes bulging nearly out of her head. I took a cursory look around, nodded, and bade her good night. Relatively speaking, however, I never fared as badly as another black male journalist. He went to nearby Waukegan, Illinois, a couple of summers ago to work on a story about a murderer who was born there. Mistaking the reporter for the killer, police hauled him from his car at gunpoint and but for his press credentials would probably have tried to book him. Such episodes are not uncommon. Black men trade tales like this all the time.   11

In "My Negro Problem—And Ours," Podhoretz writes that the hatred he feels for blacks makes itself known to him through a variety of avenues—one being his discomfort with that "special brand of paranoid touchiness" to which he says blacks are prone. No doubt he is speaking here of black men. In time, I learned to smother the rage I felt at so often being taken for a criminal. Not to do so would surely have led to madness—via that special "paranoid touchiness" that so annoyed Podhoretz at the time he wrote the essay.   12

I began to take precautions to make myself less threatening. I move about with care, particularly late in the evening. I give a wide berth to nervous people on subway platforms during the wee hours, particularly when I have exchanged business clothes for jeans. If I happen to be entering a building behind some people who   13 appear skittish, I may walk by, letting them clear the lobby before I return, so as not to seem to be following them. I have been calm and extremely congenial on those rare occasions when I've been pulled over by the police.

And on late-evening constitutionals along streets less traveled   14
by, I employ what has proved to be an excellent tension-reducing measure: I whistle melodies from Beethoven and Vivaldi and the more popular classical composers. Even steely New Yorkers hunching toward nighttime destinations seem to relax, and occasionally they even join in the tune. Virtually everybody seems to sense that a mugger wouldn't be warbling bright, sunny selections from Vivaldi's *Four Seasons*. It is my equivalent of the cowbell that hikers wear when they know they are in bear country.

MEANINGS AND VALUES

1. Identify the contradictions the author presents through the example in the first two paragraphs.

2. Can any of the contradictions in the opening paragraphs be considered ironic? Please explain. (See "Guide to Terms": *Irony*.)

EXPOSITORY TECHNIQUES

1. Identify each of the major (two sentences or more) examples in this essay.

2. Select three major examples and discuss what important purposes they play in the essay.

3. This essay was first published in 1986. Are the examples still relevant and accurate? If not, how would you suggest changing them?

DICTION AND VOCABULARY

1. What words does Staples use in Paragraph 9 to highlight the contrast between the ideas expressed in this paragraph and those presented in Paragraph 8? (Guide: *Diction*.)

2. If you do not know the meaning of some of the following words, look them up in a dictionary: *affluent, impoverished, discreet* (Par. 1); *quarry, wayfarers, indistinguishable* (2); *taut* (4); *infamous* (5); *bandolier* (6); *lethality, retrospect* (7); *consummation* (8); *bravado* (9); *perilous* (10); *constitutionals* (14).

READ TO WRITE

1. **Collaborating:** Young African American males are not the only group from whom specific kinds of behavior are expected—or whose behavior often contradicts expectations, as in Staples's case. Working with a group of classmates, identify two other social groups from whom certain kinds of behavior (positive or negative) are often expected. Choose one of the social groups, and drawing from your general knowledge or experiences, write collaboratively two paragraph-length examples of actions or events that demonstrate behaviors contrary to the expected behaviors you listed.

2. **Considering Audience:** This essay was first published in 1986. How are readers' attitudes likely to have changed since then? In what ways are they likely to have remained the same? Prepare a paragraph-length introduction to this essay in which you explain how readers' reactions are likely to have changed or not changed since it first appeared.

3. **Developing an Essay:** Using Staples's approach of developing a generalization through examples, develop an essay in which you explain how people have consistently misjudged or misunderstood you (or someone you know).

(NOTE: Suggestions for essays requiring development by EXAMPLE are on pp. 69–70 at the end of this chapter.)

JONAH LEHRER

As an undergraduate, JONAH LEHRER attended Columbia University. From there he went to Oxford University as a Rhodes Scholar. Currently, he blogs at *The Frontal Cortex*. He has worked in the lab of Nobel Prize–winning neuroscientist Eric Kandel—and in the kitchens of Le Cirque 2000 and Le Bernardin. His writing has appeared in *The New Yorker, Nature, Seed, Wired*, the *Washington Post*, the *Boston Globe, NPR*, and *NOVAScienceNow*. Lehrer's two books are *Proust Was a Neuroscientist* (2007) and *How We Decide* (2009). In *How We Decide*, Lehrer explains how our best decisions make use of both emotion and reason.

The Uses of Reason

"The Uses of Reason" tells a dramatic story about firefighters that has been told before (most notably in Norman Maclean's *Young Men and Fire*) for a variety of purposes. Lehrer uses it as an example to explain an important generalization about the role of reason in decisions made in highly emotional situations. The story loses none of its power when used as an example; indeed, it adds to the forcefulness of the generalization Lehrer draws from it.

The summer of 1949 had been long and dry in Montana; the grassy highlands were like tinder. On the afternoon of August 5—the hottest day ever recorded in the area—a stray bolt of lightning set the ground on fire. A parachute brigade of firefighters, known as smokejumpers, was dispatched to put out the blaze. Wag Dodge, a veteran with nine years of smokejumping experience, was in charge. When the jumpers took off from Missoula in a C-47, a military transport plane left over from World War II, they were told that the fire was small, just a few burning acres in the Mann Gulch river valley. As the plane approached the fire, the jumpers could see the smoke in the distance. The hot wind blew it straight across the sky.

Mann Gulch is a place of geological contradiction. It is where the Rocky Mountains meet the Great Plains, pine trees give way to prairie grass, and the steep cliffs drop onto the steppes of the Midwest. The gulch is just over three miles long, but it marks the border between these two different terrains.

The fire began on the Rockies' side, on the western edge of the gulch. By the time the firefighters arrived at the gulch, the blaze had grown out of control. The surrounding hills had all been burned; the landscape was littered with the skeletons of pine trees. Dodge moved his men over to the grassy side of the gulch and told them to head downhill, toward the placid Missouri River. Dodge didn't trust this blaze. He wanted to be near water; he knew this fire could crown.

Crowns occur when flames get so high they reach into the top   4 branches of trees. Once that happens, the fire has too much fuel. Hot embers begin to swirl in the air, spreading the fire across the prairie. The smokejumpers used to joke that the only way to control a crown fire was to pray like hell for rain. Norman Maclean, in his seminal history *Young Men and Fire*, described what it was like to be close to such a fire:

> It sounds like a train coming too fast around a curve and may get so high-keyed that the crew cannot understand what their foreman is trying to do to save them. Sometimes, when the timber thins out, it sounds as if the train were clicking across a bridge, sometimes it hits an open clearing and becomes hushed as if going through a tunnel, but when the burning cones swirl through the air and fall on the other side of the clearing, the new fire sounds as if it were the train coming out of the tunnel, belching black unburned smoke. The unburned smoke boils up until it reaches oxygen, then bursts into gigantic flames on top of its cloud of smoke in the sky. The new [novice] firefighter, seeing black smoke rise from the ground and then at the top of the sky turn into flames, thinks that natural law has been reversed.

Dodge looked at the dry grass and the dry pine needles. He felt   5 the hot wind and the hot sun. The conditions were making him nervous. To make matters worse, the men had no map of the terrain. They were also without a radio, since the parachute on the radio pack had failed to open and the transmitter had been smashed on the rocks. The small crew of smokejumpers was all alone with this fire; there was nothing between them and it but a river and a thick tangle of ponderosa pine and Douglas fir trees. And so the jumpers set down their packs and watched the blaze from across the canyon. When the wind parted the smoke, as it did occasionally, they could see inside the fire as the flames leaped from tree to tree.

It was now five o'clock—a dangerous time to fight wilderness   6 fires because the twilight wind can shift without warning. The breeze had been blowing the flames up the canyon, away from the river. But then, suddenly, the wind reversed. Dodge saw the ash swirl in the air. He saw the top of the flames flicker and wave. And then he saw the fire leap across the gulch and spark the grass on his side.

That's when the updraft began. Fierce winds began to howl   7
through the canyon, blowing straight toward the men. Dodge could
only watch as the fire became an inferno. He was suddenly staring
at a wall of flame two hundred feet tall and three hundred feet deep
on the edge of the prairie. In a matter of seconds, the flames began
to devour the grass on the slope. The fire ran toward the smokejumpers at thirty miles per hour, incinerating everything in its path.
At the fire's center, the temperature was more than two thousand
degrees, hot enough to melt rock.

Dodge screamed at his men to retreat. It was already too late to   8
run to the river, since the fire was blocking their path. Each man
dropped his fifty pounds of gear and started running up the bru-
tally steep canyon walls, trying to get to the top of the ridge and escape the blowup. Because heat rises, a fire that starts burning on flat
prairie accelerates when it hits a slope. On a 50 percent grade, a fire
will move nine times faster than it does on level land. The slopes at
Mann Gulch are 76 percent.

When the fire first crossed the gulch, Dodge and his crew had a   9
two-hundred-yard head start. After a few minutes of running,
Dodge could feel the fierce heat on his back. He glanced over his
shoulder and saw that the fire was now fewer than fifty yards away
and gaining. The air began to lose its oxygen. The fire was sucking
the wind dry. That's when Dodge realized the blaze couldn't be outrun. The hill was too steep, and the flames were too fast.

So Dodge stopped running. He stood perfectly still as the fire   10
accelerated toward him. Then he started yelling at his men to do the
same. He knew they were racing toward their own immolation and
that in fewer than thirty seconds the fire would run them over, like a
freight train without brakes. But nobody stopped. Perhaps the men
couldn't hear Dodge over the deafening roar of flames. Or perhaps
they couldn't bear the idea of stopping. When confronted with a
menacing fire, the most basic instinct is to run away. Dodge was telling the men to stand still.

But Dodge wasn't committing suicide. In a fit of desperate cre-   11
ativity, he came up with an escape plan. He quickly lit a match and
ignited the ground in front of him. He watched as those flames
raced away from him, up the canyon walls. Then Dodge stepped
into the ashes of this smaller fire, so that he was surrounded by a
thin buffer of burned land. He lay down on the still smoldering embers. He wet his handkerchief with some water from his canteen
and clutched the cloth to his mouth. He closed his eyes tight and
tried to inhale the thin ether of oxygen remaining near the ground.

Then he waited for the fire to pass around him. After several terrifying minutes, Dodge emerged from the ashes virtually unscathed.

Thirteen smokejumpers were killed by the Mann Gulch fire. Only two men in the crew besides Dodge managed to survive, and that was because they found a shallow crevice in the rocky hillside. As Dodge had predicted, the flames were almost impossible to outrun. White crosses still mark the spots where the men died; all of the crosses are below the ridge.   12

Dodge's escape fire is now a standard firefighting technique. It has saved the lives of countless firefighters trapped by swift blazes. At the time, however, Dodge's plan seemed like sheer madness. His men could think only about fleeing the flames, and yet their leader was starting a new fire. Robert Sallee, a first-year smokejumper who survived the blaze, later said he'd thought that "Dodge had gone nuts, just plain old nuts."   13

But Dodge was perfectly sane. In the heat of the moment he managed to make a very smart decision. The question, for those of us looking back on it, is how? What allowed him to resist the urge to flee? Why didn't he follow the rest of his crew up the gulch? Part of the answer is experience. Most of the smokejumpers were teenagers working summer jobs. They had fought only a few fires, and none of them had ever seen a fire like that. Dodge, on the other hand, was a grizzled veteran of the forest service; he knew what prairie flames were capable of. Once the fire crossed the gulch, Dodge realized that it was only a matter of time before the men were caught by the hungry flames. The slopes were too steep and the wind was too fierce and the grass was too dry; the blaze would beat them to the top. Besides, even if the men managed to reach the top of the mountain, they were still trapped. The ridge was covered with high, dry grass that hadn't been trimmed by cattle. It would burn in an instant.   14

For Dodge, it must have been a moment of unspeakable horror: to know that there was nowhere to go; to realize that his men were running to their deaths and that the wall of flame would consume them all. But Dodge's fear wasn't what saved him. In fact, the overwhelming terror of the situation was part of the problem. After the fire started burning uphill, all of the smokejumpers became fixated on getting to the ridge, even though the ridge was too far away for them to reach. Walter Rumsey, a first-year smokejumper, later recounted what was going through his mind when he saw Dodge stop running and get out his matchbook. "I remember thinking that that was a very good idea," Rumsey said, "but I don't remember what   15

I thought it was good for . . . I kept thinking the ridge—if I can make it. On the ridge I will be safe." William Hellman, the second in command, looked at Dodge's escape fire and reportedly said, "To hell with that, I'm getting out of here." Hellman did reach the ridge, the only smokejumper who managed to do so, but he died the next day from third-degree burns that covered his entire body. The rest of the men acted the same way. When Dodge was asked during the investigation why none of the smokejumpers followed his orders to stop running, he just shook his head. "They didn't seem to pay any attention," he said. "That is the part I didn't understand. They seemed to have something on their minds—all headed in one direction . . . They just wanted to get to the top."

Dodge's men were in the grip of panic. The problem with panic   16 is that it narrows one's thoughts. It reduces awareness to the most essential facts, the most basic instincts. This means that when a person is being chased by a fire, all he or she can think about is running from the fire.

This is known as perceptual narrowing. In one study, people   17 were put one at a time in a pressure chamber and told that the pressure would slowly be increased until it simulated that of a sixty-foot dive. While inside the pressure chamber, the subject was asked to perform two simple visual tasks. One task was to respond to blinking lights in the center of the subject's visual field, and the other involved responding to blinking lights in his peripheral vision. As expected, each of the subjects inside the pressure chamber exhibited all the usual signs of panic—a racing pulse, elevated blood pressure, and a surge of adrenaline. These symptoms affected performance in a very telling way. Although the people in the pressure chamber performed just as well as control subjects did on the central visual task, those in the pressure chamber were twice as likely to miss the stimuli in their peripheral vision. Their view of the world literally shrank.

The tragedy of Mann Gulch holds an important lesson about   18 the mind. Dodge survived the fire because he was able to beat back his emotions. Once he realized that his fear had exhausted its usefulness—it told him to run, but there was nowhere to go—Dodge was able to resist its primal urges. Instead, he turned to his conscious mind, which is uniquely capable of deliberate and creative thought. While automatic emotions focus on the most immediate variables, the rational brain is able to expand the list of possibilities. As the neuroscientist Joseph LeDoux says, "The advantage of the emotional brain is that by allowing evolution to do the thinking for you at first, you basically buy the time that you need to think about the situation and do the most reasonable thing." And so Dodge stopped running. If he was going to survive the fire, he needed to think.

MEANINGS AND VALUES

1. According to this essay, what are the uses of reason? List them, and be ready to explain each.
2. What is the generality explained in this essay?
3. In what ways was fear "part of the problem" (Par. 15)?

EXPOSITORY TECHNIQUES

1a. Where in the essay does the writer indicate that the events are an extended example used to illustrate a generalization?

b. How does the writer signal this expository purpose? Does he do so successfully? (See "Guide to Terms": *Evaluation*.)

2. What technique does the writer use at the beginning of Paragraph 10 to create a strong contrast with the preceding paragraphs?

3. Explain how the contrast between Paragraphs 7–9 and 10 reflects the overall theme (generality) presented in the essay. (Guide: *Unity*.)

DICTION AND VOCABULARY

1. What words does the writer use in Paragraphs 7–9 to emphasize the intensity of the events and the corresponding strong emotions they provoke in the firefighters? (Guide: *Diction*.)

2. If you do not know the meaning of some of the following words, look them up in a dictionary: *tinder* (Par. 1); *updraft* (7); *immolation* (10); *unscathed* (11); *grizzled* (14); *perceptual, peripheral* (17).

READ TO WRITE

1. **Collaborating:** Working in a group, pool your experiences to create a list of emotional situations in which the ability to think carefully and rationally would be a benefit. Next, create a list of strategies people can use to help them think rationally when emotions threaten to overcome them.

2. **Considering Audience:** Readers are likely to have many different ideas about the importance or unimportance of emotions in decision

making and behavior. Beginning with the insights offered by "The Uses of Reason," make two lists: one about the positive roles emotions can play and one about the negative roles emotions can play.

3. **Developing an Essay:** Use the lists you developed in #2 as a basis for an essay on the roles of emotion—one that takes into account readers' likely perspectives on the topic. Develop and explain your own generalization through examples, but acknowledge that other people may have different outlooks.

(NOTE: Suggestions for topics requiring development by EXAMPLE follow.)

Writing Suggestions for Chapter 3

EXAMPLE

Use one of the following statements or another suggested by them as your central theme. Develop it into a unified composition, using examples from history, current events, or personal experience to illustrate your ideas. Be sure to have your reader-audience clearly in mind, as well as your specific purpose for the communication.

1. Successful businesses keep employees at their highest level of competence.

2. In an age of working mothers, fathers spend considerable time and effort helping raise the children.

3. Family life can create considerable stress.

4. Laws holding parents responsible for their children's crimes would (or would not) result in serious injustices.

5. Letting people decide for themselves which laws to obey and which to ignore would result in anarchy.

6. Many people find horror movies entertaining.

7. Service professions are often personally rewarding.

8. Religion in the United States is not dying.

9. Democracy is not always the best form of government.

10. A successful career is worth the sacrifices it requires.

11. "An ounce of prevention is worth a pound of cure."

12. The general quality of television commercials may be improving (or deteriorating).

13. An expensive car can be a poor investment.

14. "Some books are to be tasted; others swallowed; and some few to be chewed *and* digested." (Francis Bacon, English scientist-author, 1561–1626)

15. Most people are superstitious in one way or another.

16. Relationships within the family are much more important than relationships outside the family.

COLLABORATIVE EXERCISE

Working in a group, begin with the statement "Many people find horror movies entertaining," and ask each person to identify two examples to illustrate and support the generality advanced in the statement. (This task will probably require each group member to do some research.) After the examples have been collected, group members should present them, and the group as a whole should vote for those that best illustrate the generality. Each group member should then create a short essay using the examples to explain and support the statement. (Statements 7, 10, 12, and 13 also lend themselves well to this activity.)

4
Analyzing a Subject by *Classification*

People naturally like to sort and classify things. A young child, moving into a new dresser of her own, will put her scarves together, socks and underwear in separate stacks, and hair clips in a pretty holder for the dresser top. Another young child may classify animals as those with legs, those with wings, and those with neither. As they get older, they may find schoolteachers have ways of classifying *them*, not only into reading or math groups, but periodically on the basis of "A," "B," or "C" papers. On errands to the grocery store, they discover macaroni in the same department as spaghetti, pork chops somewhere near the ham, and apples just down from the miniature carrots (themselves part of larger groups like "carrots" and "root vegetables"). In reading the local newspaper, they observe that its staff has done some classifying for them, putting most of the comics together and seldom mixing sports stories with news of social affairs and marriage announcements (classifications based in turn on traditional categories of behavior). Eventually, they find courses neatly classified in college catalogs, and they know enough not to look for biology courses under "Social Science" or "Arts and Letters."

Classification also helps writers and readers sort through and understand detailed information or ideas. It groups people, ideas, objects, experiences, or concepts according to shared qualities and helps point out patterns of relationships among them. For example, if you were writing an article to help people understand their personal characteristics, you might draw on the ancient Indian concept of "ayurveda," as does the author of the following paragraph.

The three ayurvedic types (or doshas) are vata, pitta, and kapha. Vatas (space and air) are creative, thin people with light bones and dark hair and eyes who are light sleepers, dislike routine, and tend toward fear and anxiety when they're under stress. Pittas (fire and water) are medium built, light-eyed, oily-skinned people who enjoy routine, make good leaders and initiators, are opinionated, and tend toward anger and frustration when they're under stress. Kaphas (water and earth) are amply built, thick-skinned and thick-haired people who are good at running projects, love leisure, sleep soundly, and tend to avoid difficult situations.

—Lynette Lamb, "Living the Ayurvedic Way"

WHY USE CLASSIFICATION?

A classification creates groups on the basis of shared characteristics. It is a useful strategy when you are dealing with facts, events, or ideas whose differences are worth detailed examination. Many subjects that you may need to write and think about will remain a hodgepodge of facts and opinions unless you can find some system of analyzing the material, dividing the subject into categories, and classifying individual elements into those categories. The two patterns, **division** and **classification**, or *dividing* and *grouping*, move in different directions, at least to begin with. But when put in use for analysis and understanding, the two processes become inevitable companions that lead to a system of classification you can employ in your writing.

Expository writing both explains and informs, and classification is a pattern that enables writers to bring clarity to discussions of complicated subjects. Exercise programs, undergraduate majors, investment strategies, personal computers, ways to prepare for tests, even used cars—all these come in various types that are worth understanding. So, too, do other possible subjects for writing: behavior patterns; literary or anthropological theories; careers in engineering, business, or communications; management techniques; or environmental policies.

When readers encounter a classification, however, they expect more than a simple identification of categories. They look for an explanation of the qualities that distinguish each category and an explanation of the overall arrangement of the categories. In short, they expect the writer to provide a conclusion—a thesis—about the categories themselves, perhaps an explanation of why the subject falls into a particular set of categories or what implications the pattern of sorting has. A conclusion helps readers decide what to do with the information being presented; it helps them choose among alternatives, understand the specific uses of each set of policies or products; or grasp the implications of different psychological perspectives and social groupings.

CHOOSING A STRATEGY

If you choose to employ classification as a strategy for sharing information and ideas, your readers will expect you to take them into account from the beginning. They will want to know what information you are going to present and why it is important to them. They will expect you to make clear the purpose for your classification and the main idea or thesis tying it together.

From the start, therefore, you need to focus clearly on a **principle of classification**, that is, the quality that members of each group share and what distinguishes them from the members of other groups. The simplest classifications form two groups, those with a particular quality and those without it: vegetarians and meat-eaters, closed-end mutual funds and open-ended funds, introverts and extroverts, environmentally sensitive policies and environmentally destructive policies. But such simple classifications often break down, usually because the differences among groups are matters of degree or level (varying levels of environmental sensitivity; different degrees of strictness in adhering to a vegetarian diet) and not absolute.

In creating a classification, then, choose a strategy that reflects your purpose for writing while allowing you to maintain clear and logical distinctions among the categories. If your purpose is to help people understand dietary options available to them—vegan, ovo-lacto-vegetarian, avoidance of all meat except fish, and meat eating, for example—then your categories should be built around the kinds of food that people choose to include or avoid in their diet. In addition, the principle of classification should be consistent throughout the categories and complete with respect to the subject being investigated.

It would not be logical to divide movies into categories such as action films, science fiction films, romantic films, political films, serious films, and entertaining films because the principles of classification are not consistent and the categories therefore overlap: romantic films can be serious, entertaining, or both, for example. Likewise, it would not make sense to limit discussion of religious practices in North America to those of Christians, Jews, and Muslims because to do so would exclude, for example, the many people who identify themselves as Buddhists and Hindus. A more limited system might be appropriate, however, when discussing the religious backgrounds of residents in a particular region (southwest Louisiana, rural Mexico) or from a particular cultural or ethnic group (Hungarians, Native Americans in Alaska or northern Canada). Although your classification system need not be exhaustive, it should at the same time not omit significant numbers of whatever behaviors, people, or ideas you are planning to discuss.

In many cases, the pattern of classification you choose will also serve to organize your writing, as the following tentative plan for an essay illustrates.

Tentative Thesis

> People who love sports but have only limited athletic talent need not give up their dreams of a career in professional sports because being a player is only one of many career paths.

Category

> Name: administrators. Definition: people involved in management of sports teams. Members: managers, coaches, public relations specialists, personnel managers.

Category

> Name: medical staff. Definition: people concerned with physical and mental health of athletes. Members: trainers, team doctors, sports psychologists.

Category

> Name: facilities staff. Definition: people who create and maintain sports facilities. Members: sports architects and designers, engineers, groundskeepers, facilities managers.

Category

> Name: equipment specialists. Definition: people who design, manufacture, and sell sports equipment. Members: designers, testers, advertisers, manufacturing engineers, sales representatives.

A plan like this could logically include players' agents and legal representatives, people who work in financing sports, and people who arrange travel for sports teams. But although this would be a logical classification, it would be far too detailed for most readers. You should therefore limit the number of categories you present in an essay to avoid overwhelming and confusing your readers, but make sure you do not leave out any categories that are essential to the subject.

Any plan like this seems almost absurdly obvious, of course—*after* the planning is done. It appears less obvious, however, to inexperienced writers who are dealing with a jumble of information they must explain to someone else. This is when writers should be aware of the patterns at their disposal, and one of the most useful of these, alone or combined with others, is classification.

DEVELOPING CATEGORIES

At the center of any essay employing classification are the paragraphs that present, explain, and illustrate categories. There is no single strategy for presenting categories, and the way you approach the task should vary according to your subject and purpose for writing. Nonetheless, many writers find the following techniques useful for alerting readers to the structure of an essay, structuring the presentation of categories, and making sure they present each category with enough explanatory detail.

- *Use Transitions:* You can make effective use of transitional terms to signal the beginning of a new category.

type	sort	trait	segment
category	kind	species	characteristic
class	aspect	element	component
part	subcategory	subset	group

- *Name the Categories:* To help identify categories and also help readers remember them, try giving each a name when you explain it. The names can be purely descriptive ("supporters/opponents/compromisers of the policy") or they can be somewhat imaginative ("lookers/browsers/testers/buyers").
- *Provide Detailed Examples:* To help readers visualize and understand each category, consider providing at least one extended example or a cluster of shorter ones. By making the examples detailed and specific, you help explain the categories while making them more memorable.
- *Explain:* Remind readers of the principle of classification, of the qualities that characterize a category, and of the ways it differs

from other categories. Let them know, too, how the categories are related: Do they represent differing or contradictory approaches to a problem? Are they different products with similar functions? Will readers be faced with sharply differing options or a gradual range of choices?

Here is how one student, Hung Bui, put these techniques to work in a paragraph.

> Cigarettes play an even larger role in the lives of the next group, habitual smokers. They cannot quit as readily as the casual smoker can because of one key factor: habit. When the phone rings, they quickly grab an ashtray and cigarettes and chat. When having a cup of coffee in the morning, they simply must have a cigarette because "the coffee won't taste as good without it." And always, without fail, a good meal is followed by a good cigarette. Habitual smokers also smoke on a regular basis—a pack or two a day, never more, never less. They become irritated when they discover they are down to their last cigarette and rush to buy another pack. They also play games by buying only packs instead of cartons, rationalizing that because cigarettes aren't always on hand, they can't be smoking too much. They are constantly trying to cut down and tell everyone so, but never actually do, because in reality, smoking is an essential part of their lives.

Student Essay

Whenever you are learning, you do so in stages, from beginner, to novice, to (perhaps) expert. Heather Farnum applied these stages to a task she knew well (playing the piano) and came up with a system of classification that readers can apply to musicians in general and extend to other learners as well.

Piano Recitals

by Heather Farnum

Last night while I was sitting at the piano and relaxing by playing some old recital pieces, memories of playing in piano recitals as a child and high school student came flooding back to me. I remember looking at each pianist intently, watching how she or he presented a piece, and imagining myself sitting at the piano and playing in a similar way. I watched how each presented a selection—whether or not the person gave

Begins with anecdote introducing the topic and creating interest

feeling to the music and was comfortable with playing it. Most of all, I watched how the pianist interpreted a piece, for there are several quite different ways to interpret the same selection for an audience.

Novice pianists, intermediate pianists, and top-class pianists all approach the job of interpretation in different and characteristic ways. You can help me explain these differences if you will imagine a stage in a brightly lit church hall or school auditorium. Stretched across the stage is a grand piano, set up so the audience of parents, friends, and fellow students can see the recitalist.

Thesis statement

The first person to walk tentatively across the stage to polite applause is a novice pianist. Like all novices, this one either rushes through the piece or plays much too slowly. He bobs his head up and down trying to maintain the tempo, messes up notes, and plays too loudly or too softly, but seldom in between.

Category 1 example

The best example of a novice pianist I can recall is Stephany Cody, a girl of about 7. For her first recital, Stephany played "Twinkle, Twinkle, Little Star" as loudly as she could, bobbing her head throughout the familiar piece. Every time she reached the "twinkle, twinkle, little star" she speeded up because she knew that part best. However, when she reached "up above the sky so gray," she slowed way down as she struggled through the less familiar notes.

Another example (detailed)

Next across the stage is an intermediate pianist. Sitting down, she strives for a professional look in form and stature. Unlike the novice pianist, she has control over dynamics, yet she is more tense because she is more aware of the things she needs to do and the things that can go wrong.

Category 2 example

John Cody (Stephany's ten-year-old brother) comes to my mind as an image of the intermediate pianist. For one of his recitals, John played a piece called "Festival of Arragon." He sat down at the piano with a serious disposition, like a professional. When he began playing, however, his form fell apart. His shoulders sagged and he held his head at an awkward angle because he was

Another example (detailed)

paying more attention to the correct tempo and the correct shade of loudness or softness than to the image he was presenting of himself and the music.

Last across the stage is an advanced pianist. She (or he) sits in a relaxed yet formal manner at the piano. When she plays, the dynamics and shades of sound are balanced and put the piece on display rather than the pianist. The tempo is even and steady, and the audience senses a performer in control with a strong stage presence.

My piano teacher, Ann Fitch, remains in my mind as an image of the advanced pianist. Whenever she sits at the piano, she is calm and relaxed; her disposition alone makes the audience feel relaxed and at ease—ready for the piece to begin. She plays with tempos and rhythms that are steady and gradual. Most of all, however, she makes the audience members feel they are living the music.

An advanced pianist like Ann goes even further with her performance. She plays with a mood and a stage presence that enable listeners to share the pianist's emotions. A top-flight pianist can convey feelings of love, romance, anger, sadness, depression, and excitement and arrange them in ways that guide listeners to the heart of the music without overwhelming them. Finally, if advanced pianists have a secret, it is that they keep four questions always in mind:

1. What is the tempo I want to follow for this piece?
2. What mood do I wish to present?
3. What emotions do I want to convey?
4. How can I play so that the audience can live the piece of music at the same time I do?

*Category 3
example*

*Another
example
(detailed)*

*Example
continues*

*In place of a
conventional
conclusion—a
list of things
all pianists
should keep in
mind*

WILLIAM ZINSSER

WILLIAM ZINSSER, who lives in New York City, is a nonfiction writer and teacher of writing who began his career as a journalist at the *New York Herald Tribune* in 1946. During the 1970s, he taught a popular writer's workshop at Yale University. Zinsser tells writers to simplify their language in order to empower their writing. He has authored numerous books, including the classic guide *On Writing Well* (1976). Other titles by Zinsser include *Writing to Learn* (1993), *Writing Places* (2010), and *Going on Faith* (2011). He currently posts a weekly blog on writing, the arts, and popular culture to the website The American Scholar, titled *Zinsser on Friday*.

College Pressures

William Zinsser's experiences as a seasoned college professor allow him to empathize with the perennial challenges confronting each new generation of college student. This reading first appeared in *Country Journal* magazine in 1979.

Dear Carlos: I desperately need a dean's excuse for my chem midterm which will begin in about 1 hour. All I can say is that I totally blew it this week. I've fallen incredibly, inconceivably behind.

Carlos: Help! I'm anxious to hear from you. I'll be in my room and won't leave it until I hear from you. Tomorrow is the last day for . . .

Carlos: I left town because I started bugging out again. I stayed up all night to finish a take-home make-up exam & am typing it to hand in on the 10th. It was due on the 5th. P.S. I'm going to the dentist. Pain is pretty bad.

Carlos: Probably by Friday I'll be able to get back to my studies. Right now I'm going to take a long walk. This whole thing has taken a lot out of me.

Carlos: I'm really up the proverbial creek. The problem is I really *bombed* the history final. Since I need that course for my major I . . .

Carlos: Here follows a tale of woe. I went home this weekend, had to help my Mom, & caught a fever so didn't have much time to study. My professor . . .

Carlos: Aargh! Trouble. Nothing original but everything's piling up at once. To be brief, my job interview . . .

Hey Carlos, good news! I've got mononucleosis.

Who are these wretched supplicants, scribbling notes so laden   1
with anxiety, seeking such miracles of postponement and balm?
They are men and women who belong to Branford College, one of
the twelve residential colleges at Yale University, and the messages
are just a few of the hundreds that they left for their dean, Carlos
Hortas—often slipped under his door at 4 A.M.—last year.

But students like the ones who wrote those notes can also be   2
found on campuses from coast to coast—especially in New England
and at many other private colleges across the country that have high
academic standards and highly motivated students. Nobody could
doubt that the notes are real. In their urgency and their gallows humor they are authentic voices of a generation that is panicky to
succeed.

My own connection with the message writers is that I am mas-   3
ter of Branford College. I live in its Gothic quadrangle and know the
students well. (We have 485 of them.) I am privy to their hopes and
fears—and also to their stereo music and their piercing cries in the
dead of the night ("Does anybody *ca-a-are?*"). If they went to Carlos
to ask how to get through tomorrow, they come to me to ask how to
get through the rest of their lives.

Mainly I try to remind them that the road ahead is a long one   4
and that it will have more unexpected turns than they think. There
will be plenty of time to change jobs, change careers, change whole
attitudes and approaches. They don't want to hear such liberating
news. They want a map—right now—that they can follow unswerv-
ingly to career security, financial security, Social Security and, presumably, a prepaid grave.

What I wish for all students is some release from the clammy   5
grip of the future. I wish them a chance to savor each segment of
their education as an experience in itself and not as a grim preparation for the next step. I wish them the right to experiment, to trip
and fall, to learn that defeat is as instructive as victory and is not the
end of the world.

My wish, of course, is naïve. One of the few rights that America   6
does not proclaim is the right to fail. Achievement is the national
god, venerated in our media—the million-dollar athlete, the wealthy
executive—and glorified in our praise of possessions. In the presence
of such a potent state religion, the young are growing up old.

I see four kinds of pressure working on college students today: 7
economic pressure, parental pressure, peer pressure, and self-
induced pressure. It is easy to look around for villains—to blame the
colleges for charging too much money, the professors for assigning

too much work, the parents for pushing their children too far, the students for driving themselves too hard. But there are no villains; only victims.

"In the late 1960s," one dean told me, "the typical question that 8 I got from students was 'Why is there so much suffering in the world?' or 'How can I make a contribution?' Today it's 'Do you think it would look better for getting into law school if I did a double major in history and political science, or just majored in one of them?'" Many other deans confirmed this pattern. One said: "They're trying to find an edge—the intangible something that will look better on paper if two students are about equal."

Note the emphasis on looking better. The transcript has become 9 a sacred document, the passport to security. How one appears on paper is more important than how one appears in person. *A* is for Admirable and *B* is for Borderline, even though, in Yale's official system of grading, *A* means "excellent" and *B* means "very good." Today, looking very good is no longer good enough, especially for students who hope to go on to law school or medical school. They know that entrance into the better schools will be an entrance into the better law firms and better medical practices where they will make a lot of money. They also know that the odds are harsh. Yale Law School, for instance, matriculates 170 students from an applicant pool of 3,700; Harvard enrolls 550 from a pool of 7,000.

It's all very well for those of us who write letters of recommen- 10 dation for our students to stress the qualities of humanity that will make them good lawyers or doctors. And it's nice to think that admission officers are really reading our letters and looking for the extra dimension of commitment or concern. Still, it would be hard for a student not to visualize these officers shuffling so many transcripts studded with *A*s that they regard a *B* as positively shameful.

The pressure is almost as heavy on students who just want to 11 graduate and get a job. Long gone are the days of the "gentleman's *C*," when students journeyed through college with a certain relaxation, sampling a wide variety of courses—music, art, philosophy, classics, anthropology, poetry, religion—that would send them out as liberally educated men and women. If I were an employer I would rather employ graduates who have this range and curiosity than those who narrowly pursued safe subjects and high grades. I know countless students whose inquiring minds exhilarate me. I like to hear the play of their ideas. I don't know if they are getting *A*s or *C*s, and I don't care. I also like them as people. The country needs them, and they will find satisfying jobs. I tell them to relax. They can't.

Nor can I blame them. They live in a brutal economy. Tuition,   12
room, and board at most private colleges now comes to at least $7,000
[in 1979], not counting books and fees. This might seem to suggest
that the colleges are getting rich. But they are equally battered by in-
flation. Tuition covers only 60 percent of what it costs to educate a
student, and ordinarily the remainder comes from what colleges receive in endowments, grants, and gifts. Now the remainder keeps
being swallowed by the cruel costs—higher every year—of just
opening the doors. Heating oil is up. Insurance is up. Postage is up.
Health-premium costs are up. Everything is up. Deficits are up. We
are witnessing in America the creation of a brotherhood of paupers—
colleges, parents, and students, joined by the common bond of debt.

Today it is not unusual for a student, even if he works part time   13
at college and full time during the summer, to accrue $5,000 in loans
after four years—loans that he must start to repay within one year
after graduation. Exhorted at commencement to go forth into the
world, he is already behind as he goes forth. How could he not feel
under pressure throughout college to prepare for this day of reckoning? I have used "he," incidentally, only for brevity. Women at Yale
are under no less pressure to justify their expensive education to
themselves, their parents, and society. In fact, they are probably under more pressure. For although they leave college superbly
equipped to bring fresh leadership to traditionally male jobs, society
hasn't yet caught up with this fact.

Along with economic pressure goes parental pressure. Inevita-   14
bly, the two are deeply intertwined:

I see many students taking pre-medical courses with joyless   15
tenacity. They go off to their labs as if they were going to the dentist.
It saddens me because I know them in other corners of their life as
cheerful people.

"Do you want to go to medical school?" I ask them.   16

"I guess so," they say, without conviction, or "Not really."   17

"Then why are you going?"   18

"Well, my parents want me to be a doctor. They're paying all
this money and . . . "   19

Poor students, poor parents. They are caught in one of the old-   20
est webs of love and duty and guilt. The parents mean well; they are
trying to steer their sons and daughters toward a secure future. But
the sons and daughters want to major in history or classics or philosophy—subjects with no "practical" value. Where's the payoff on
the humanities? It's not easy to persuade such loving parents that

the humanities do indeed pay off. The intellectual faculties developed by studying subjects like history and classics—an ability to synthesize and relate, to weigh cause and effect, to see events in perspective—are just the faculties that make creative leaders in business or almost any general field. Still, many fathers would rather put their money on courses that point toward a specific profession—courses that are pre-law, pre-medical, pre-business, or, as I sometimes heard it put, "pre-rich."

But the pressure on students is severe. They are truly torn. One part of them feels obligated to fulfill their parents' expectations; after all, their parents are older and presumably wiser. Another part tells them that the expectations that are right for their parents are not right for them.

I know a student who wants to be an artist. She is very obviously an artist and will be a good one—she has already had several modest local exhibits. Meanwhile she is growing as a well-rounded person and taking humanistic subjects that will enrich the inner resources out of which her art will grow. But her father is strongly opposed. He thinks that an artist is a "dumb" thing to be. The student vacillates and tries to please everybody. She keeps up with her art somewhat furtively and takes some of the "dumb" courses her father wants her to take—at least they are dumb courses for her. She is a free spirit on a campus of tense students——no small achievement in itself—and she deserves to follow her muse.

Peer pressure and self-induced pressure are also intertwined, and they begin almost at the beginning of freshman year.

"I had a freshman student I'll call Linda," one dean told me, "who came in and said she was under terrible pressure because her roommate, Barbara, was much brighter and studied all the time. I couldn't tell her that Barbara had come in two hours earlier to say the same thing about Linda."

The story is almost funny—except that it's not. It's symptomatic of all the pressures put together. When every student thinks every other student is working harder and doing better, the only solution is to study harder still. I see students going off to the library every night after dinner and coming back when it closes at midnight. I wish they would sometimes forget about their peers and go to a movie. I hear the clacking of typewriters in the hours before dawn. I see the tension in their eyes when exams are approaching and papers are due. *Will I get everything done?*

Probably they won't. They will get sick. They will get "blocked." They will sleep. They will oversleep. They will bug out. *Hey, Carlos, help!*

Part of the problem is that they do more than they are expected   27
to do. A professor will assign five-page papers. Several students will
start writing ten-page papers to impress him. Then more students
will write ten-page papers, and a few will raise the ante to fifteen.
Pity the poor student who is still just doing the assignment.

"Once you have twenty or thirty percent of the student popula-   28
tion deliberately overexerting," one dean points out, "it's bad for
everybody. When a teacher gets more and more effort from his class,
the student who is doing normal work can be perceived as not doing well. The tactic works, psychologically."

Why can't the professor just cut back and not accept longer pa-   29
pers? He can, and he probably will. But by then the term will be half
over and the damage done. Grade fever is highly contagious and
not easily reversed. Besides, the professor's main concern is with his
course. He knows his students only in relation to the course and
doesn't know that they are also overexerting in their other courses.
Nor is it really his business. He didn't sign up for dealing with the
student as a whole person and with all the emotional baggage
the student brought along from home. That's what deans, masters,
chaplains, and psychiatrists are for.

To some extent this is nothing new: a certain number of profes-   30
sors have always been self-contained islands of scholarship and
shyness, more comfortable with books than with people. But the
new pauperism has widened the gap still further, for professors
who actually like to spend time with students don't have as much
time to spend. They are also overexerting. If they are young, they
are busy trying to publish in order not to perish, hanging by their
fingernails onto a shrinking profession. If they are old and tenured,
they are buried under the duties of administering departments—as
departmental chairmen or members of committees—that have been
thinned out by the budgetary axe.

Ultimately it will be the students' own business to break the   31
circles in which they are trapped. They are too young to be prisoners of their parents' dreams and their classmates' fears. They must
be jolted into believing in themselves as unique men and women
who have the power to shape their own future.

"Violence is being done to the undergraduate experience," says   32
Carlos Hortas. "College should be open-ended: at the end it should
open many, many roads. Instead, students are choosing their goal in
advance, and their choices narrow as they go along. It's almost as if
they think that the country has been codified in the type of jobs that

exist—that they've got to fit into certain slots. Therefore, fit into the best-paying slot.

"They ought to take chances. Not taking chances will lead to a   33
life of colorless mediocrity. They'll be comfortable. But something in the spirit will be missing."

I have painted too drab a portrait of today's students, making   34
them seem a solemn lot. That is only half of their story; if they were so dreary I wouldn't so thoroughly enjoy their company. The other half is that they are easy to like. They are quick to laugh and to offer friendship. They are not introverts. They are unusually kind and are more considerate of one another than any student generation I have known.

Nor are they so obsessed with their studies that they avoid   35
sports and extracurricular activities. On the contrary, they juggle their crowded hours to play on a variety of teams, perform with musical and dramatic groups, and write for campus publications. But this in turn is one more cause of anxiety. There are too many choices. Academically, they have 1,300 courses to select from; outside class they have to decide how much spare time they can spare and how to spend it.

This means that they engage in fewer extracurricular pursuits   36
than their predecessors did. If they want to row on the crew and play in the symphony they will eliminate one; in the '60s they would have done both. They also tend to choose activities that are self-limiting. Drama, for instance, is flourishing in all twelve of Yale's residential colleges as it never has before. Students hurl themselves into these productions—as actors, directors, carpenters, and technicians—with a dedication to create the best possible play, knowing that the day will come when the run will end and they can get back to their studies.

They also can't afford to be the willing slave of organizations   37
like the *Yale Daily News*. . . . At the one-hundredth anniversary banquet of that paper—whose past chairmen include such once and future kings as Potter Stewart, Kingman Brewster, and William F. Buckley, Jr.—much was made of the fact that the editorial staff used to be small and totally committed and that "newsies" routinely worked fifty hours a week. In effect they belonged to a club; Newsies is how they defined themselves at Yale. Today's student will write one or two articles a week, when he can, and he defines himself as a student. I've never heard the word Newsie except at the banquet.

If I have described the modern undergraduate primarily as a   38
driven creature who is largely ignoring the blithe spirit inside who
keeps trying to come out and play, it's because that's where the
crunch is, not only at Yale but throughout American education. It's
why I think we should all be worried about the values that are nurturing a generation so fearful of risk and so goal-obsessed at such an
early age.

I tell students that there is no one "right" way to get ahead—   39
that each of them is a different person, starting from a different point
and bound for a different destination. I tell them that change is a
tonic and that all the slots are not codified nor the frontiers closed.
One of my ways of telling them is to invite men and women who
have achieved success outside the academic world to come and talk
informally with my students during the year. They are heads of
companies or ad agencies, editors of magazines, politicians, public
officials, television magnates, labor leaders, business executives,
Broadway producers, artists, writers, economists, photographers,
scientists, historians—a mixed bag of achievers.

I ask them to say a few words about how they got started. The   40
students assume that they started in their present profession and
knew all along that it was what they wanted to do. Luckily for me,
most of them got into their field by a circuitous route, to their surprise, after many detours. The students are startled. They can hardly
conceive of a career that was not pre-planned. They can hardly imagine allowing the hand of God or chance to nudge them down some
unforeseen trail.

Meanings and Values

1. State the four categories of college pressure developed by the author
   in this essay.

2. What is the significance of the phrase "change is a tonic" (Par. 39)?
   Why do you suppose the writer talks about change in an essay about
   college pressures?

3. Explain what the writer means when he says, "I think we should
   all be worried about the values that are nurturing a generation so
   fearful of risk and so goal-obsessed at such an early age" (Par. 38).
   How do you think being goal-obsessed differs from being
   goal-oriented?

EXPOSITORY TECHNIQUES

1. "Along with economic pressure goes parental pressure" (Par. 14) serves Zinsser as a transitional sentence to signal that he is about to begin discussion of a new category. Point to another, similar transition sentence later in the essay.

2. The author begins his essay by quoting a selection of notes left for Dean Carlos Hortas by Branford College students. Do you suppose that this cluster of short examples is intended to help the reader understand the abstract concept about to be classified? Is the strategy successful?

3. Although the writer presents detailed examples to explain each category of college pressure, he doesn't repeat the names of the categories. Does this make it hard to follow the author's presentation of each category? Why or why not?

DICTION AND VOCABULARY

1. What purpose do you think the informal interjection *"Hey, Carlos, help!"* serves (Par. 26)?

2. The writer repeats the word *intertwined* when he names each pair of categories (Par. 14 and Par. 23). Why do you think he emphasizes this word?

3. If you do not know the meaning of some of the following words, look them up in a dictionary: *supplicants* (Par. 1), *synthesize* (20), *vacillates, furtively* (22), *codified* (32), *tonic* (39), *circuitous* (40).

READ TO WRITE

1. **Collaborating:** Working in a group, choose one of Zinsser's four categories of college pressure (economic, parental, peer, or self-induced) and further divide it into subcategories. Brainstorm examples for each subcategory. Choose one of these examples and use it to write an anecdote to serve as an introduction to a classification essay on college pressures today.

2. **Considering Audience:** The negative term *helicopter parent* applies to a parent who pays exceedingly close attention to a child's experiences and problems, particularly in educational settings. Imagine that you are a helicopter parent reading Zinsser's essay. Write a letter to the magazine in which it first appeared, *Country Journal*, responding to the issue of college pressures from your point of view.

3. **Developing an Essay:** Using Zinsser's essay as inspiration, prepare your own essay describing the range of pressures facing high school students to get into a prestigious college. Or prepare an essay that discusses the range of pressures some high school students feel to fit in socially while in high school.

(NOTE: Suggestions for topics requiring development by CLASSIFICATION are on pp. 125–126 at the end of this section.)

AMY TAN

Novelist AMY TAN was born in Oakland, California, to Chinese immigrant parents. She earned a B.A. in English and an M.A. in linguistics from San Jose State University. Her books explore the Chinese American experience and mother-daughter relationships. Among other works, Tan is the author of several novels, including *The Joy Luck Club* (1989), *The Kitchen God's Wife* (1991), *The Bonesetter's Daughter* (2001), and *Saving Fish from Drowning* (2005).

Mother Tongue

In this essay, originally published in 1990 in *The Threepenny Review,* Amy Tan looks at the many different "Englishes" she and her mother have spoken, separately and together, as well as the unspoken language between the generations.

I am not a scholar of English or literature. I cannot give you much   1
more than personal opinions on the English language and its variations in this country or others.

I am a writer. And by that definition, I am someone who has al-   2
ways loved language. I am fascinated by language in daily life. I spend a great deal of my time thinking about the power of language—the way it can evoke an emotion, a visual image, a complex idea, or a simple truth. Language is the tool of my trade. And I use them all—all the Englishes I grew up with.

Recently, I was made keenly aware of the different Englishes   3
I do use. I was giving a talk to a large group of people, the same talk I had already given to half a dozen other groups. The nature of the talk was about my writing, my life, and my book, *The Joy Luck Club.* The talk was going along well enough, until I remembered one major difference that made the whole talk sound wrong. My mother was in the room. And it was perhaps the first time she had heard me give a lengthy speech, using the kind of English I have never used with her. I was saying things like, "The intersection of memory upon imagination" and "There is an aspect of my fiction that relates to thus-and-thus"—a speech filled with carefully wrought grammatical phrases, burdened, it suddenly seemed to me, with nominalized forms, past perfect tenses, conditional phrases, all the forms of standard English that I had learned in school and through books, the forms of English I did not use at home with my mother.

Just last week, I was walking down the street with my mother, 4
and I again found myself conscious of the English I was using, and
the English I do use with her. We were talking about the price of
new and used furniture and I heard myself saying this: "Not waste
money that way." My husband was with us as well, and he didn't
notice any switch in my English. And then I realized why. It's because over the twenty years we've been together I've often used that
same kind of English with him, and sometimes he even uses it with
me. It has become our language of intimacy, a different sort of English that relates to family talk, the language I grew up with.

So you'll have some idea of what this family talk I heard sounds 5
like, I'll quote what my mother said during a recent conversation
which I video-taped and then transcribed. During this conversation
my mother was talking about a political gangster in Shanghai who
had the same last name as her family's, Du, and how the gangster in
his early years wanted to be adopted by her family, which was rich
by comparison. Later, the gangster became more powerful, far richer
than my mother's family, and one day showed up at my mother's
wedding to pay his respects. Here's what she said in part:

"Du Yusong having business like fruit stand. Like off the street 6
kind. He is Du like Du Zong—but not Tsung-ming Island people.
The local people call putong, the river east side, he belong to that
side local people. The man want to ask Du Zong father take him in
like become own family. Du Zong father wasn't looking down on
him, but didn't take seriously, until that man big like become a
mafia. Now important person very hard to inviting him. Chinese
way, come only to show respect, don't stay for dinner. Respect for
making big celebration, he shows up. Mean gives lots of respect.
Chinese custom. Chinese social life that way. If too important won't
have to stay too long. He come to my wedding. I didn't see. I heard
it. I gone to boy's side, they have YMCA dinner. Chinese age I was
nineteen."

You should know that my mother's expressive command of 7
English belies how much she actually understands. She reads the
Forbes report, listens to *Wall Street Week,* converses daily with her
stockbroker, reads all of Shirley MacLaine's books with ease—all
kinds of things I can't begin to understand. Yet some of my friends
tell me they understand 50 percent of what my mother says. Some
say they understand 80 to 90 percent. Some say they understand
none of it, as if she were speaking pure Chinese. But to me, my
mother's English is perfectly clear, perfectly natural. It's my mother's
tongue. Her language, as I hear it, is vivid, direct, full of observation

and imagery. This was the language that helped shape the way I saw things, expressed things, made sense of the world.

Lately, I've been giving more thought to the kind of English my   8
mother speaks. Like others, I have described it to people as "broken" or "fractured" English. But I wince when I say that. It has always bothered me that I can think of no way to describe it other than "broken," as if it were damaged and needed to be fixed, as if it lacked a certain wholeness and soundness, I've heard other terms used, "limited English," for example. But they seem just as bad, as if everything is limited, including people's perceptions of the limited English speaker.

I know this for a fact, because when I was growing up, my   9
mother's "limited" English limited *my* perception of her. I was ashamed of her English. I believed that her English reflected the quality of what she had to say. That is, because she expressed them imperfectly her thoughts were imperfect. And I had plenty of empirical evidence to support me: the fact that people in department stores, at banks, and at restaurants did not take her seriously, did not give her good service, pretended not to understand her, or even acted as if they did not hear her.

My mother has long realized the limitations of her English as   10
well. When I was fifteen, she used to have me call people on the phone to pretend I was she. In this guise, I was forced to ask for information or even complain and yell at people who had been rude to her. One time it was a call to her stockbroker in New York. She had cashed out her small portfolio and it just so happened we were going to go to New York the next week, our very first trip outside California. I had to get on the phone and say in an adolescent voice that was not very convincing, "This is Mrs. Tan."

And my mother was standing in the back whispering loudly,   11
"Why he don't send me check, already two weeks late. So mad he lie to me, losing me money."

And then I said in perfect English, "Yes, I'm getting rather concerned. You had agreed to send the check two weeks ago, but it hasn't arrived."   12

Then she began to talk more loudly. "What he want, I come to   13
New York tell him front of his boss, you cheating me?" And I was trying to calm her down, make her be quiet, while telling the stockbroker, "I can't tolerate any more excuses. If I don't receive the check immediately I am going to have to speak to your manager when I'm in New York next week." And sure enough, the following week there we were in front of this astonished stockbroker, and I was sitting there red-faced and quiet, and my mother, the

real Mrs. Tan, was shouting at his boss in her impeccable, broken English.

We used a similar routine just five days ago, for a situation that 14 was far less humorous. My mother had gone to the hospital for an appointment, to find out about a benign brain tumor a CAT scan had revealed a month ago. She said she had spoken very good English, her best English, no mistakes. Still, she said, the hospital did not apologize when they said they had lost the CAT scan and she had come for nothing. She said they did not seem to have any sympathy when she told them she was anxious to know the exact diagnosis, since her husband and son had both died of brain tumors. She said they would not give her any more information until the next time and she would have to make another appointment for that. So she said she would not leave until the doctor called her daughter. She wouldn't budge. And when the doctor finally called her daughter, me, who spoke in perfect English—lo and behold—we had assurances the CAT scan would be found, promises that a conference call on Monday would be held, and apologies for any suffering my mother had gone through for a most regrettable mistake.

I think my mother's English almost had an effect on limiting my 15 possibilities in life as well. Sociologists and linguists probably will tell you that a person's developing language skills are more influenced by peers. But I do think that the language spoken in the family, especially in immigrant families which are more insular, plays a large role in shaping the language of the child. And I believe that it affected my results on achievement tests, IQ tests, and the SAT. While my English skills were never judged as poor, compared to math, English could not be considered my strong suit. In grade school I did moderately well, getting perhaps B's, sometimes B-pluses, in English and scoring perhaps in the sixtieth or seventieth percentile on achievement tests, But those scores were not good enough to override the opinion that my true abilities lay in math and science, because in those areas I achieved A's and scored in the ninetieth percentile or higher.

This was understandable. Math is precise; there is only one 16 correct answer. Whereas, for me at least, the answers on English tests were always a judgment call, a matter of opinion and personal experience. Those tests were constructed around items like fill-in-the-blank sentence completion, such as "Even though Tom was_____, Mary thought he was_____." And the correct answer always seemed to be the most bland combinations of thoughts, for example, "Even though Tom was shy, Mary thought he was charming," with the grammatical structure "even though" limiting the correct answer to some sort of semantic opposites, so you wouldn't get answers like, "Even though Tom was foolish, Mary thought he was ridiculous." Well, according to my mother, there were very few limitations as to what Torn could have been and what Mary might have thought of him. So I never did well on tests like that.

The same was true with word analogies, pairs of words in which 17 you were supposed to find some sort of logical, semantic relationship—for example, "*Sunset* is to *nightfall* as _____ is to _____." And here you would be presented with a list of four possible pairs, one of which showed the same kind of relationship: *red* is to *stoplight, bus* is to *arrival, chills* is to *fever, yawn* is to *boring.* Well, I could never think that way. I knew what the tests were asking, but I could not block out of my mind the images already created by the first pair, "*sunset* is to *nightfall*"—and I would see a burst of colors against a darkening sky, the moon rising, the lowering of a curtain of stars. And all the other pairs of words—red, bus, stoplight, boring— just threw up a mass of confusing images, making it impossible for me to sort out something as logical as saying: "A sunset precedes nightfall" is the same as "a chill precedes a fever." The only way I would have gotten that answer right would have been to imagine an associative situation, for example, my being disobedient and staying out past sunset, catching a chill at night, which turns into feverish pneumonia as punishment, which indeed did happen to me.

I have been thinking about all this lately, about my mother's 18 English, about achievement tests. Because lately I've been asked, as a writer, why there are not more Asian Americans represented in American literature. Why are there few Asian Americans enrolled in creative writing programs? Why do so many Chinese students go into engineering? Well, these are broad sociological questions I can't begin to answer. But I have noticed in surveys—in fact, just last week—that Asian students, as a whole, always do significantly better on math achievement tests than in English. And this makes me think that there are other Asian-American students whose English spoken in the home might also be described as "broken" or "limited." And perhaps they also have teachers who are steering them away from writing and into math and science, which is what happened to me.

Fortunately, I happen to be rebellious in nature and enjoy the 19 challenge of disproving assumptions made about me. I became an English major my first year in college, after being enrolled as pre-med. I started writing nonfiction as a freelancer the week after I was told by my former boss that writing was my worst skill and I should hone my talents toward account management.

But it wasn't until 1985 that I finally began to write fiction. And 20
at first I wrote using what I thought to be wittily crafted sentences,
sentences that would finally prove I had mastery over the English
language. Here's an example from the first draft of a story that later
made its way into *The Joy Luck Club,* but without this line: "That was
my mental quandary in its nascent state." A terrible line, which I can
barely pronounce.

Fortunately, for reasons I won't get into today, I later decided 21
I should envision a reader for the stories I would write. And the
reader I decided upon was my mother because these were stories
about mothers. So with this reader in mind—and in fact she did
read my early drafts—I began to write stories using all the Englishes
I grew up with: the English I spoke to my mother, which for lack of a
better term might be described as "simple"; the English she used
with me, which for lack of a better term might be described as
"broken"; my translation of her Chinese, which could certainly be
described as "watered down" and what I imagined to be her translation of her Chinese if she could speak in perfect English, her internal language, and for that I sought to preserve the essence, but
neither an English nor a Chinese structure. I wanted to capture what
language ability tests can never reveal: her intent, her passion, her
imagery, the rhythms of her speech and the nature of her thoughts.

Apart from what any critic had to say about my writing, I knew 22
I had succeeded where it counted when my mother finished reading
my book and gave me her verdict: "So easy to read."

Meanings and Values

1. At what point in the essay does the writer name the different types of
   Englishes she grew up with? List these categories. What category
   does Tan's mother's speech in Paragraph 6 belong to?

2. How is the phrase "mother tongue" significant?

3. Explain what you think the author means by "internal language" (Par. 21).

Expository Techniques

1. In your view, does the author treat all the categories of English discussed in this essay equally? How so?

2. In Paragraph 4, the writer uses an example to illustrate the use of
   "simple" English, similar to the kind she speaks with her mother.

In this case, however, she is speaking to her husband. What point is Tan making about her use of "simple" English in this example?

DICTION AND VOCABULARY

1. Tan emphasizes the impact of her mother's English-speaking style on her own life by offering some examples of her mother's conversation patterns (Par. 6). Did Tan provide enough quotes to illustrate her mother's English-speaking style, or should she have provided more examples? Explain your opinion.

2. In Paragraph 3, the writer quotes herself giving a formal speech, saying that she has never used this type of English-speaking style with her mother. Which style would you prefer to listen to, Tan's style in her formal speech or Tan's mother's conversation style quoted in Paragraph 6? Explain.

READ TO WRITE

1. **Collaborating:** Survey group members about the various "Englishes" they use and under what circumstances. Discuss why they prefer to use certain styles of speech at some times rather than at others. Together, write a report that identifies each kind of language style used by group members, when it is used, and why.

2. **Considering Audience:** Children of recent immigrants, or those for whom English was not the first language spoken in the home, can relate well to Tan's essay. However, the essay also appeals to people who were not exposed to languages other than English as children. Why is this so? Point to specific examples in Tan's essay to explain your response.

3. **Developing an Essay:** An *idiolect* is a language or speech pattern used by a person at a certain time in his or her life. Drawing strategies from Tan's essay, prepare an essay that classifies, defines, and illustrates your own idiolect or that of a person you know.

(NOTE: Suggestions for topics requiring development by CLASSIFICATION are on pp. 125–126 at the end of this chapter.)

MICHAEL VENTURA

MICHAEL VENTURA worked as an editor for the *Austin Sun* and the *L.A. Weekly* (which he cofounded). He has been a columnist for the *Austin Chronicle* and the *Los Angeles Village View.* His books include *The Mollyhawk Poems* (1977); *Night Time, Losing Time* (1989); and *The Zoo Where You're Fed to God* (1994). His most recent book is a novel, *The Death of Frank Sinatra* (2000).

Don't Even Think About It!

In this essay, Michael Ventura explains how taboos, which many readers might associate with primitive societies or superstitions, help shape the things we do in our daily lives. By showing how many different kinds of taboos we routinely observe (more categories than readers usually encounter in an essay), Ventura demonstrates their prevalence and importance. The concrete examples that Ventura provides help keep the numerous categories from seeming overwhelming and abstract. The illustrations also help readers recognize taboos in their own behavior.

Taboos come in all sizes. Big taboos: when I was a kid in the Italian neighborhoods of Brooklyn, to insult someone's mother meant a brutal fight—the kind of fight no one interferes with until one of the combatants goes down and stays down. Little taboos: until the sixties, it was an insult to use someone's first name without asking or being offered permission. Personal taboos: Cyrano de Bergerac would not tolerate the mention of his enormous nose. Taboos peculiar to one city: in Brooklyn (again), when the Dodgers were still at Ebbets Field, if you rooted for the Yankees you kept it to yourself unless you wanted a brawl. Taboos, big or small, are always about having to respect somebody's (often irrational) boundary—or else.

There are taboos shared within one family: my father did not feel free to speak to us of his grandmother's suicide until his father died. Taboos within intellectual elites: try putting a serious metaphysical or spiritual slant on a "think-piece" (as we call them in the trade) written for the *New York Times,* the *Washington Post,* or most

1

2

big name magazines—it won't be printed. Taboos in the corporate and legal worlds: if you're male, you had best wear suits of somber colors, or you're not likely to be taken seriously; if you're female, you have to strike a very uneasy balance between the attractive and the prim, and even then you might not be taken seriously. Cultural taboos: in the Jim Crow days in the South, a black man who spoke with familiarity to a white woman might be beaten, driven out of town, or (as was not uncommon) lynched.

Unclassifiable taboos: in Afghanistan, as I write this, it is a sin— punishable by beatings and imprisonment—to fly a kite. Sexual taboos: there are few communities on this planet where two men can walk down a street holding hands without being harassed or even arrested; in Afghanistan (a great place for taboos these days) the Taliban would stone them to death. Gender taboos: how many American corporations (or institutions of any kind) promote women to power? National taboos: until the seventies, a divorced person could not run for major public office in America (it wasn't until 1981 that our first and only divorced president, Ronald Reagan, took office); today, no professed atheist would dare try for the presidency. And most readers of this article probably approve, as I do, of this comparatively recent taboo: even the most rabid bigot must avoid saying "nigger," "spic," or "kike" during, say, a job interview—and the most macho sexist must avoid words like "broad."

Notice that nearly all of our taboos, big and small, public and intimate, involve silence—keeping one's silence, or paying a price for not keeping it. Yet keeping silent has its own price: for then silence begins to fill the heart, until silence becomes the heart—a heart swelling with restraint until it bursts in frustration, anger, even madness.

The taboos hardest on the soul are those which fester in our intimacies—taboos known only to the people involved, taboos that can make us feel alone even with those to whom we're closest. One of the deep pains of marriage—one that also plagues brothers and sisters, parents and children, even close friends—is that as we grow more intimate, certain silences often become more necessary. We discover taboo areas, both in ourselves and in the other, that cannot be transgressed without paying an awful price. If we speak of them, we may endanger the relationship; but if we do not speak, if we do not violate the taboo, the relationship may become static and tense, until the silence takes on a life of its own. Such silences are corrosive. They eat at the innards of intimacy until, often, the silence itself causes the very rupture or break-up that we've tried to avoid by keeping silent.

The Cannibal in Us All

You may measure how many taboos constrict you, how many ta-   6
boos you've surrendered to—at home, at parties, at work, with your
lover or your family—by how much of yourself you must suppress.
You may measure your life, in these realms, by what you cannot say,
do, admit—cannot and must not, and for no better reason than that
your actions or words would disrupt your established order. By this
measure, most of us are living within as complex and strictured a
system of taboos as the aborigines who gave us the word in the first
place. You can see how fitting it is that the word "taboo" comes from
a part of the world where cannibalism is said to be practiced to this
day: the islands off eastern Australia—Polynesia, New Zealand,
Melanesia. Until 1777, when Captain James Cook published an account of his first world voyage, Europe and colonial America had
many taboos but no word that precisely meant taboo. Cook introduced this useful word to the West. Its instant popularity, quick assimilation into most European languages, and constant usage since,
are testimony to how much of our lives the word describes. Before
the word came to us, we'd ostracized, coerced, exiled, tormented,
and murdered each other for myriad infractions (as we still do), but
we never had a satisfying, precise word for our reasons.

We needed cannibals to give us a word to describe our behav-   7
ior, so how "civilized" are we, really? We do things differently from
those cannibals, on the surface, but is the nature of what we do all
that different? We don't cook each other for ceremonial dinners, at
least not physically (though therapists can testify that our ceremonial seasons, like Christmas and Thanksgiving, draw lots of
business—something's cooking). But we stockpile weapons that can
cook the entire world, and we organize our national priorities
around their "necessity," and it's a national political taboo to seriously cut spending for those planet-cookers. If that's "progress," it's
lost on me. In China it's taboo to be a Christian, in Israel it's taboo to
be a Moslem, in Syria it's taboo to be a Jew, in much of the United
States it's still taboo to be an atheist, while in American academia
it's taboo to be deeply religious. Our headlines are full of this stuff.
So it's hardly surprising that a cannibal's word still describes much
of our behavior.

I'm not denying the necessity of every society to set limits and   8
invent taboos (some rational, some not) simply in order to get on
with the day—and to try to contain the constant, crazy, never-to-be-
escaped longings that blossom in our sleep and distract or compel

us while awake. Such longings are why even a comparatively tiny desert tribe like the ancient Hebrews needed commandments and laws against coveting each other's wives, stealing, killing, committing incest. That tribe hadn't seen violent, sexy movies, hadn't listened to rock 'n' roll, hadn't been bombarded with ads featuring half-naked models, and hadn't watched too much TV. They didn't need to. Like us, they had their hearts, desires, and dreams to instruct them how to be very, very naughty. The taboo underlying all others is that we must not live by the dictates of our irrational hearts—as though we haven't forgiven each other, or ourselves, for having hearts.

If there's a taboo against something, it's usually because a con-   9
siderable number of people desire to do it. The very taboos that we employ to protect us from each other and ourselves, are a map of our secret natures. When you know a culture's taboos (or an individual's, or a family's) you know its secrets—you know what it really wants.

Favorite Taboos

It's hard to keep a human being from his or her desire, taboo or not.   10
We've always been very clever, very resourceful, when it comes to sneaking around our taboos. The Aztecs killed virgins and called it religion. The Europeans enslaved blacks and called it economics. Americans tease each other sexually and call it fashion.

If we can't kill and screw and steal and betray to our heart's   11
desire, and, in general, violate every taboo in sight—well, we can at least watch other people do it. Or read about it. Or listen to it. As we have done, since ancient times, through every form of religion and entertainment. The appeal of taboos and our inability to escape our longing for transgression (whether or not we ourselves transgress) are why so many people who call themselves honest and law-abiding spend so much time with movies, operas, soaps, garish trials, novels, songs, Biblical tales, tribal myths, folk stories, and Shakespeare—virtually all of which, both the great and the trivial, are about those who dare to violate taboos. It's a little unsettling when you think about it: the very stuff we say we most object to is the fundamental material of what we call culture.

That's one reason that fundamentalists of all religions are so   12
hostile to the arts. But fundamentalists partake of taboos in the sneakiest fashion of all. Senator Jesse Helms led the fight against the National Endowment for the Arts because he couldn't get the

(vastly overrated) homosexual art of Robert Mapplethorpe or the most extreme performance artists out of his mind—he didn't and doesn't want to. He, like all fundamentalists, will vigorously oppose such art and all it stands for until he dies, because his very opposition gives him permission to concentrate on taboo acts. The Taliban of Afghanistan will ride around in jeeps toting guns, searching out any woman who dares show an inch of facial skin or wear white socks (Taliban boys consider white socks provocative), and when they find such a woman they'll jail and beat her—because their so-called righteousness gives them permission to obsess on their taboos. Pat Robertson and his ilk will fuss and rage about any moral "deviation," any taboo violation they can find, because that's the only way they can give themselves permission to entertain the taboos. They get to not have their taboo cake, yet eat it too.

We are all guilty of this to some extent. Why else have outlaws   13
from Antigone to Robin Hood to Jesse James to John Gotti become folk heroes? Oedipus killed his father and slept with his mother, and we've been performing that play for 2500 years because he is the ultimate violator of our deepest taboos. Aristotle said we watch such plays for "catharsis," to purge our desires and fears in a moment of revelation. Baloney. Ideas like "catharsis" are an intellectual game, to glossy-up our sins. What's closer to the truth is that we need Oedipus to stand in for us. We can't have changed much in 2500 years, if we still keep him alive in our hearts to enact our darkest taboos for us. Clearly, the very survival of Oedipus as an instantly recognizable name tells us that we still want to kill our fathers and screw our mothers (or vice versa).

A Country of Broken Taboos

Taboos are a special paradox for Americans. However much we   14
may long for tradition and order, our longings are subverted by the inescapable fact that our country was founded upon a break with tradition and a challenge to order—which is to say, the United States was founded upon the violation of taboos. Specifically, this country was founded upon the violation of Europe's most suffocating taboo: its feudal suppression (still enforced in 1776, when America declared its independence) of the voices of the common people. We were the first nation on earth to write into law that any human being has the right to say anything, and that even the government is (theoretically) not allowed to silence you.

At the time, Europe was a continent of state-enforced religions,   15
where royalty's word was law and all other words could be crushed

by law. (Again: taboo was a matter of enforced silence.) We were the first nation to postulate verbal freedom for everyone. All our other freedoms depend upon verbal freedom; no matter how badly and how often we've failed that ideal, it still remains our ideal.

Once we broke Europe's verbal taboos, it was only a matter of   16
time before other traditional taboos fell too. As the writer Albert Murray has put it, Americans could not afford piety in their new homeland: "You can't be over respectful of established forms; you're trying to get through the wilderness of Kentucky." Thus, from the moment the Pilgrims landed, our famous puritanism faced an inherent contradiction. How could we domesticate the wilderness of this continent; how could peasants and rejects and "commoners" form a strong and viable nation; how could we develop all the new social forms and technologies necessary to blend all the disparate peoples who came here—without violating those same Puritan taboos which are so ingrained, to this day, in our national character?

It can't be over-emphasized that America's fundamental stance   17
against both the taboos of Europe and the taboos of our own Puritans, was our insistence upon freedom of speech. America led the attack against silence. And it is through that freedom, the freedom to break the silence, that we've destroyed so many other taboos. Especially during the last 40 years, we've broken the silence that surrounded ancient taboos of enormous significance. Incest, child abuse, wife-battering, homosexuality, and some (by no means all) forms of racial and gender oppression, are not merely spoken of, and spoken against, they're shouted about from the rooftops. Many breathe easier because of this inevitable result of free speech. In certain sections of our large cities, for the first time in modern history, gay people can live openly and without fear. The feminist movement has made previously forbidden or hidden behaviors both speakable and doable. The National Organization of Women can rail against the Promise Keepers all they want (and they have some good reasons), but when you get a million working-class guys crying and hugging in public, the stoic mask of the American male has definitely cracked. And I'm old enough to remember when it was shocking for women to speak about wanting a career. Now virtually all affluent young women are expected to want a career.

Fifty years ago, not one important world or national leader   18
was black. Now there are more people of color in positions of influence than ever. Bad marriages can be dissolved without social stigma. Children born out of wedlock are not damned as "bastards" for something that wasn't their fault. And those of us who've

experienced incest and abuse have finally found a voice, and through our voices we've achieved a certain amount of liberation from shame and pain.

These boons are rooted in our decidedly un-Puritan freedom of speech. But we left those Puritans behind a long time ago—for the breaking of silence is the fundamental political basis of our nation, and no taboo is safe when people have the right to speak. 19

Keeper of Your Silence

In the process, though, we've lost the sanctity of silence. We've lost the sense of dark but sacred power inherent in sex, in nature, even in crime. Perhaps that is the price of our new freedoms. 20

It's also true that by breaking the silence we've thrown ourselves into a state of society's structure. Without them, that structure has undeniably weakened. We are faced with shoring up the weakened parts, inventing new ways of being together that have pattern and order—for we cannot live without some pattern and order—but aren't so restrictive. Without sexual taboos, for instance, what are the social boundaries between men and women? When are they breached? What is offensive? Nobody's sure. Everybody's making mistakes. This is so excruciating that many are nostalgic for some of the old taboos. But once a taboo is broken, then for good or ill it's very hard, perhaps impossible, to reinstate it. 21

But there is another, subtler confusion: yes, enormous taboos have fallen, but many taboos, equally important, remain. And, both as individuals and as a society, we're strained enough, confused enough, by the results of doing away with so many taboos in so short a time, that maybe we're not terribly eager for our remaining taboos to fall. We may sincerely desire that, but maybe we're tired, fed up, scared. Many people would rather our taboos remain intact for a couple of generations while we get our act together again, and perhaps they have a point. But the price of taboos remains what it's always been: silence and constriction. 22

What do we see, when we pass each other on the street, but many faces molded by the price paid for keeping the silences of the taboos that remain—spirits confined within their own, and their society's, silences? Even this brief essay on our public and intimate strictures is enough to demonstrate that we are still a primitive race, bounded by fear and prejudice, with taboos looming in every direction—no matter how much we like to brag and/or bitch that modern life is liberating us from all the old boundaries. 23

The word taboo still says much more about us than most prefer to admit.

What is the keeper of your silence? The answer to that question 24 is your own guide to your personal taboos. How must you confine yourself in order to get through your day at the job, or to be acceptable in your social circle? The answer to that is your map of your society's taboos. What makes you most afraid to speak? What desire, what word, what possibility, freezes and fevers you at the same time, making any sincere communication out of the question? What makes you vanish into your secret? That's your taboo, baby. You're still in the room, maybe even still smiling, still talking, but not really—what's really happened is that you've vanished down some hole in yourself, and you'll stay there until you're sure the threat to your taboo is gone and it's safe to come out again. If, that is, you've ever come out in the first place. Some never have.

What utterance, what hint, what insinuation, can quiet a room 25 of family or friends? What makes people change the subject? What makes those at a dinner party dismiss a remark as though it wasn't said, or dismiss a person as though he or she wasn't really there? We've all seen conversations suddenly go dead, and just as suddenly divert around a particular person or subject, leaving them behind in the dead space, because something has been said or implied that skirts a silently shared taboo. If that happens to you often, don't kid yourself that you're living in a "free" society. Because you're only as free as your freedom from taboos—not on some grand abstract level, but in your day-to-day life.

It is probably inherent in the human condition that there are no 26 "last" taboos. Or perhaps it just feels that way because we have such a long way to go. But at least we can know where to look; right in front of our eyes, in the recesses of our speechlessness, in the depths of our silences. And there is nothing for it but to confront the keepers of our silence. Either that, or to submit to being lost, as most of us silently are, without admitting it to each other or to ourselves— lost in a maze of taboos.

MEANINGS AND VALUES

1. Ventura says, "Taboos, big or small, are always about having to respect somebody's (often irrational) boundary—or else" (Par. 1). Do you agree with this definition of the word "taboo"? Why, or

why not? Why do you think that we must honor other people's boundaries? What does "or else" mean?

2. Explain the connection that Ventura makes in Paragraph 5 between silence and taboos. How does silence impact us personally and in relationships?

3. Why does much of our popular culture violate many societal taboos? How do the media encourage this?

EXPOSITORY TECHNIQUES

1. Ventura places taboos into many categories. Some are broad (e.g., "big taboos" and "little taboos") while others are very specific (e.g., "corporate taboos" and "language taboos"). Does he deliberately give equal standing to specific taboos? If so, why?

2. Beginning in Paragraph 14, Ventura explains how enforced silence led to a whole series of taboos. What are some of the subcategories of taboos that disappeared with the American practice of free speech, and what connection does Ventura make between these subcategories and Americans' willingness to talk?

DICTION AND VOCABULARY

1. Ventura uses the expression "social stigma" in Paragraph 18 in conjunction with dissolved marriages. He uses the words "shame" and "pain" connected to incest and abuse. Why does he use such words when he is comparing American society before its willingness to speak openly with contemporary, more open American society? (See "Guide to Terms": *Diction.*)

2. Why does Ventura provide us with the etymology (history) of the word "taboo" and an explanation of its assimilation into languages (Par. 6)?

3. If you do not know the meaning of some of the following words, look them up in a dictionary: *assimilation, ostracized, coerced* (Par. 6); *garish* (11); *catharsis* (13); *piety, disparate* (16); *stoic* (17).

READ TO WRITE

1. **Collaborating:** Ventura makes clear his opinion that taboos, though a reflection of human nature, are dangerous to society because they cause us to be silent about many horrible things that may be happening in our lives. Can you think of cases in which silence and taboos might be positive? In a small group, create a list of such instances, and as a team prepare a short essay classifying and explaining these taboos.

2. **Considering Audience:** Society's taboos about premarital and extramarital sex are less strong now than they were in the first half of the

twentieth century. Other taboos have changed as well. Consider an audience reading this essay in the 1960s. What parts of the discussion and examples might have worked well for most readers at the time? What taboos were probably no longer as forceful for these readers as they might have been for readers earlier in the century? Prepare an essay examining how one or more taboos changed during the course of the century.

3.   **Developing an Essay:** Look over one or more editions of a local newspaper. Identify and list some issues or behaviors that the articles treat as taboos. Separate the items in the list into categories. Adding further examples from your experience and knowledge, develop the list into an essay on the way newspapers and similar media such as magazines reinforce or undermine taboos. You might also examine the various kinds of news programs on television (both "hard" and "soft" news) and write about the way they treat taboos.

(NOTE: Suggestions for topics requiring development by CLASSIFICATION are on pp. 125–126 at the end of this chapter.)

Issues and Ideas

Sorting Out How We Communicate

- Deborah Tannen, *But What Do You Mean?*
- Stephanie Ericsson, *The Ways We Lie*

DEBORAH TANNEN

Linguist DEBORAH TANNEN holds an M.A. in English literature from Wayne State University and an M.A. and a Ph.D. in linguistics from the University of California, Berkeley. She is a specialist in discourse analysis, the study of naturally occurring language, and interpersonal communication, dialogue between participants who have a shared history. Tannen's best-known book is *You Just Don't Understand* (1990). She has also authored *You're Wearing That?* (2006) and *You Were Always Mom's Favorite!* (2010), among many other popular general-audience books on how people use language.

But What Do You Mean?

The modern workplace emphasizes being a team player. Do gender differences in the way men and women exchange information hinder employees' efforts to collaborate on the job? Tannen categorizes workplace communication gaps in this reading selected from *Talking from 9 to 5* (1994).

Conversation is a ritual. We say things that seem obviously the thing to say without thinking of the literal meaning of our words, any more than we expect the question "How are you?" to call forth a detailed account of aches and pains.

Unfortunately, women and men often have different ideas about what's appropriate, different ways of speaking. Many of the conversational rituals common among women are designed to take the other person's feelings into account, while many of the conversational rituals common among men are designed to maintain the one-up position, or at least avoid appearing one-down. As a result, when men and women interact—especially at work—it's often women who are at the disadvantage. Because women are not trying to avoid the one-down position, that is unfortunately where they may end up.

Here, the biggest areas of miscommunication.   3

1. Apologies

Women are often told they apologize too much. The reason they're   4
told to stop doing it is that, to many men, apologizing seems synonymous with putting oneself down. But there are many times
when "I'm sorry" isn't self-deprecating, or even an apology; it's an
automatic way of keeping both speakers on an equal footing. For
example, a well-known columnist once interviewed me and gave
me her phone number in case I needed to call her back. I misplaced
the number and had to go through the newspaper's main switch-
board. When our conversation was winding down and we'd both
made ending-type remarks, I added, "Oh, I almost forgot—I lost
your direct number, can I get it again?" "Oh, I'm sorry," she came
back instantly, even though she had done nothing wrong and *I* was
the one who'd lost the number. But I understood she wasn't really
apologizing; she was just automatically reassuring me she had no
intention of denying me her number.

Even when "I'm sorry" is an apology, women often assume it   5
will be the first step in a two-step ritual: I say "I'm sorry" and take
half the blame, then you take the other half. At work, it might go
something like this:

> **A:** When you typed this letter, you missed this phrase I inserted.
> **B:** Oh, I'm sorry, I'll fix it.
> **A:** Well, I wrote it so small it was easy to miss.

When both parties share blame, it's a mutual face-saving   6
device. But if one person, usually the woman, utters frequent apologies and the other doesn't, she ends up looking as if she's taking the
blame for mishaps that aren't her fault. When she's only partially to
blame, she looks entirely in the wrong.

I recently sat in on a meeting at an insurance company where   7
the sole woman, Helen, said "I'm sorry" or "I apologize" repeatedly.
At one point she said, "I'm thinking out loud. I apologize." Yet the
meeting was intended to be an informal brainstorming session, and
everyone was thinking out loud.

The reason Helen's apologies stood out was that she was the   8
only person in the room making so many. And the reason I was

concerned was that Helen felt the annual bonus she had received was unfair. When I interviewed her colleagues, they said that Helen was one of the best and most productive workers—yet she got one of the smallest bonuses. Although the problem might have been outright sexism, I suspect her speech style, which differs from that of her male colleagues, masks her competence.

Unfortunately, not apologizing can have its price too. Since so many women use ritual apologies, those who don't may be seen as hard-edged. What's important is to be aware of how often you say you're sorry (and why), and to monitor your speech based on the reaction you get.

2. Criticism

A woman who cowrote a report with a male colleague was hurt when she read a rough draft to him and he leapt into a critical response— "Oh, that's too dry! You have to make it snappier!" She herself would have been more likely to say, "That's a really good start. Of course, you'll want to make it a little snappier when you revise."

Whether criticism is given straight or softened is often a matter of convention. In general, women use more softeners. I noticed this difference when talking to an editor about an essay I'd written. While going over changes she wanted to make, she said, "There's one more thing. I know you may not agree with me. The reason I noticed the problem is that your other points are so lucid and elegant." She went on hedging for several more sentences until I put her out of her misery: "Do you want to cut that part?" I asked—and of course she did. But I appreciated her tentativeness. In contrast, another editor (a man) I once called summarily rejected my idea for an article by barking, "Call me when you have something new to say."

Those who are used to ways of talking that soften the impact of criticism may find it hard to deal with the right-between-the-eyes style. It has its own logic, however, and neither style is intrinsically better. People who prefer criticism given straight are operating on an assumption that feelings aren't involved: "Here's the dope, I know you're good; you can take it."

3. Thank-Yous

A woman manager I know starts meetings by thanking everyone for coming, even though it's clearly their job to do so. Her "thank-you" is simply a ritual.

A novelist received a fax from an assistant in her publisher's of-   14
fice; it contained suggested catalog copy for her book. She immediately faxed him her suggested changes and said, "Thanks for
running this by me," even though her contract gave her the right to
approve all copy. When she thanked the assistant, she fully expected
him to reciprocate: "Thanks for giving me such a quick response."
Instead, he said, "You're welcome." Suddenly, rather than an equal
exchange of pleasantries, she found herself positioned as the recipi-
ent of a favor. This made her feel like responding, "Thanks for
nothing!"

Many women use "thanks" as an automatic conversation   15
starter and closer; there's nothing literally to say thank you for. Like
many rituals typical of women's conversation, it depends on the
goodwill of the other to restore the balance. When the other speaker
doesn't reciprocate, a woman may feel like someone on a seesaw
whose partner abandoned his end. Instead of balancing in the air,
she has plopped to the ground, wondering how she got there.

4. Fighting

Many men expect the discussion of ideas to be a ritual fight—   16
explored through verbal opposition. They state their ideas in the
strongest possible terms, thinking that if there are weaknesses someone will point them out, and by trying to argue against those objections, they will see how well their ideas hold up.

Those who expect their own ideas to be challenged will respond   17
to another's ideas by trying to poke holes and find weak links—as a
way of *helping*. The logic is that when you are challenged you will
rise to the occasion: Adrenaline makes your mind sharper, you get
ideas and insights you would not have thought of without the spur
of battle.

But many women take this approach as a personal attack.   18
Worse, they find it impossible to do their best work in such a contentious environment. If you're not used to ritual fighting, you begin to hear criticism of your ideas as soon as they are formed. Rather
than making you think more clearly, it makes you doubt what you
know. When you state your ideas, you hedge in order to fend off
potential attacks. Ironically, this is more likely to *invite* attack because it makes you look weak.

Although you may never enjoy verbal sparring, some women   19
find it helpful to learn how to do it. An engineer who was the only
woman among four men in a small company found that as soon as

she learned to argue she was accepted and taken seriously. A doctor attending a hospital staff meeting made a similar discovery. She was becoming more and more angry with a male colleague who'd loudly disagreed with a point she'd made. Her better judgment told her to hold her tongue, to avoid making an enemy of this powerful senior colleague. But finally she couldn't hold it in any longer, and she rose to her feet and delivered an impassioned attack on his position. She sat down in a panic, certain she had permanently damaged her relationship with him. To her amazement, he came up to her afterward and said, "That was a great rebuttal. I'm really impressed. Let's go out for a beer after work and hash out our approaches to this problem."

5. Praise

A manager I'll call Lester had been on his new job six months when   20 he heard that the women reporting to him were deeply dissatisfied. When he talked to them about it, their feelings erupted; two said they were on the verge of quitting because he didn't appreciate their work, and they didn't want to wait to be fired. Lester was dumbfounded: He believed they were doing a fine job. Surely, he thought, he had said nothing to give them the impression he didn't like their work. And indeed he hadn't. That was the problem. He had said *nothing*—and the women assumed he was following the adage "If you can't say something nice, don't say anything." He thought he was showing confidence in them by leaving them alone.

Men and women have different habits in regard to giving   21 praise. For example, Deirdre and her colleague William both gave presentations at a conference. Afterward, Deirdre told William, "That was a great talk!" He thanked her. Then she asked, "What did you think of mine?" and he gave her a lengthy and detailed critique. She found it uncomfortable to listen to his comments. But she assured herself that he meant well, and that his honesty was a signal that she, too, should be honest when he asked for a critique of his performance. As a matter of fact, she had noticed quite a few ways in which he could have improved his presentation. But she never got a chance to tell him because he never asked—and she felt put down. The worst part was that it seemed she had only herself to blame, since she *had* asked what he thought of her talk.

But had she really asked for his critique? The truth is, when she   22 asked for his opinion, she was expecting a compliment, which she felt was more or less required following anyone's talk. When he

responded with criticism, she figured, "Oh, he's playing 'Let's critique each other'"—not a game she'd initiated, but one which she
was willing to play. Had she realized he was going to criticize her
and not ask her to reciprocate, she would never have asked in the
first place.

It would be easy to assume that Deirdre was insecure, whether   23
she was fishing for a compliment or soliciting a critique. But she
was simply talking automatically, performing one of the many conversational rituals that allow us to get through the day. William may
have sincerely misunderstood Deirdre's intention—or may have
been unable to pass up a chance to one-up her when given the
opportunity.

6. Complaints

"Troubles talk" can be a way to establish rapport with a colleague.   24
You complain about a problem (which shows that you are just folks)
and the other person responds with a similar problem (which puts
you on equal footing). But while such commiserating is common
among women, men are likely to hear it as a request to *solve* the
problem.

One woman told me she would frequently initiate what she   25
thought would be pleasant complaint-airing sessions at work. She'd
talk about situations that bothered her just to talk about them,
maybe to understand them better. But her male office mate would
quickly tell her how she could improve the situation. This left her
feeling condescended to and frustrated. She was delighted to see
this very impasse in a section in my book *You Just Don't Understand*,
and showed it to him. "Oh," he said, "I see the problem. How can
we solve it?" Then they both laughed, because it had happened
again: He short-circuited the detailed discussion she'd hoped for
and cut to the chase of finding a solution.

Sometimes the consequences of complaining are more serious: 26
A man might take a woman's lighthearted griping literally, and she
can get a reputation as a chronic malcontent. Furthermore, she may
be seen as not up to solving the problems that arise on the job.

7. Jokes

I heard a man call in to a talk show and say, "I've worked for two   27
women and neither one had a sense of humor. You know, when you
work with men, there's a lot of joking and teasing." The show's host

and the guest (both women) took his comment at face value and assumed the women this man worked for were humorless. The guest said, "Isn't it sad that women don't feel comfortable enough with authority to see the humor?" The host said, "Maybe when more women are in authority roles, they'll be more comfortable with power." But although the women this man worked for *may* have taken themselves too seriously, it's just as likely that they each had a terrific sense of humor, but maybe the humor wasn't the type he was used to. They may have been like the woman who wrote to me: "When I'm with men, my wit or cleverness seems inappropriate (or lost!) so I don't bother. When I'm with my women friends, however, there's no hold on puns or cracks and my humor is fully appreciated."

The types of humor women and men tend to prefer differ. Research has shown that the most common form of humor among men is razzing, teasing, and mock-hostile attacks, while among women it's self-mocking. Women often mistake men's teasing as genuinely hostile. Men often mistake women's mock self-deprecation as truly putting themselves down. 28

Women have told me they were taken more seriously when they learned to joke the way the guys did. For example, a teacher who went to a national conference with seven other teachers (mostly women) and a group of administrators (mostly men) was annoyed that the administrators always found reasons to leave boring seminars, while the teachers felt they had to stay and take notes. One evening, when the group met at a bar in the hotel, the principal asked her how one such seminar had turned out. She retorted, "As soon as you left, it got much better." He laughed out loud at her response. The playful insult appealed to the men—but there was a trade-off. The women seemed to back off from her after this. (Perhaps they were put off by her using joking to align herself with the bosses.) 29

There is no "right" way to talk. When problems arise, the culprit may be style differences—and *all* styles will at times fail with others who don't share or understand them, just as English won't do you much good if you try to speak to someone who knows only French. If you want to get your message across, it's not a question of being "right": it's a question of using language that's shared—or at least understood. 30

MEANINGS AND VALUES

1. What is "troubles talk," and in what ways do men and women respond differently to it, according to Tannen?

2. Explain how understanding style differences in workplace conversation can be beneficial to both male and female employees, according to the writer.

3. State what the author considers to be the different purposes of each gender for engaging in conversational rituals. Do you find this to be true about your own gender?

EXPOSITORY TECHNIQUES

1. What clear-cut technique does the writer use to signal each category of miscommunication between men and women to readers?

2. Is the author's use of short clusters of examples to illustrate each category effective, in your opinion? How so?

3. Locate a paragraph in the essay where Tannen discusses the consequences of one of the categories of miscommunication she has illustrated, and restate the consequences she defines. Do you agree with her?

DICTION AND VOCABULARY

1. Consider the simile the author uses in Paragraph 15. Is it effective? (See "Guide to Terms": *Figurative Language.*)

2. What is the author's tone? (Guide: *Style/Tone.*) Is her diction formal or informal? (Guide: *Diction.*) Give examples to support your answers.

3. If you do not know the meaning of some of the following words, look them up in a dictionary: *self-deprecating* (Par. 4), *face-saving* (6), *reciprocate* (14), *contentious* (18), *rebuttal* (19), *commiserating* (24), *razzing* (28).

READ TO WRITE

1. **Collaborating:** In a group of other writers, brainstorm a list of other characteristics, aside from communication style, in which you perceive men and women to differ. Choose three characteristics from the list and prepare a group report on how the genders seem to differ to you, using examples.

2. **Considering Audience:** A likely audience for Tannen's essay categorizing gender differences in workplace communication styles is employees and managers. Using Tannen's essay for inspiration, prepare

a classification essay about differences in playground communication styles between boys and girls. Address an audience of parents or teachers.

3.   **Developing an Essay:** Drawing strategies from Tannen's essay and from the brainstorming list in question 1, prepare your own essay classifying gender differences in a different area of social activity, for example, behavior at social gatherings, game-playing styles, exercise or study habits, grooming, or some other. Remember to explain the significance of these differences in addition to categorizing and describing them.

(NOTE: Suggestions for topics requiring development by CLASSIFICATION are on pp. 125–126 at the end of this chapter.)

STEPHANIE ERICSSON

STEPHANIE ERICSSON is a screenwriter and advertising copywriter originally from San Francisco. She began her writing career in the 1970s as a story editor for films and as a screenwriter for the television sitcom *Mork and Mindy*. Her husband's death during her pregnancy with their first child prompted her to transform the journals she kept after he died into the book *Companion through the Darkness: Inner Dialogues on Grief* (1993).

The Ways We Lie

In the fourth century, St. Augustine of Hippo wrote *On Lying*, in which he divided lies into eight categories, including "lies that harm no one and help someone" and "lies for the pleasure of lying." Although today we call some lies white, the question of lying is never truly black and white, as Ericsson explores in this essay, originally published in *The Utne Reader* in 1992.

The bank called today and I told them my deposit was in the mail, 1
even though I hadn't written a check yet. It'd been a rough day. The baby I'm pregnant with decided to do aerobics on my lungs for two hours, our three-year-old daughter painted the living room couch with lipstick, the IRS put me on hold for an hour, and I was late to a business meeting because I was tired.

I told my client that traffic had been bad. When my partner 2
came home, his haggard face told me his day hadn't gone any better than mine, so when he asked, "How was your day?" I said, "Oh, fine," knowing that one more straw might break his back. A friend called and wanted to take me to lunch. I said I was busy. Four lies in the course of a day, none of which I felt the least bit guilty about.

We lie. We all do. We exaggerate, we minimize, we avoid con- 3
frontation, we spare people's feelings, we conveniently forget, we keep secrets, we justify lying to the big-guy institutions. Like most people, I indulge in small falsehoods and still think of myself as an honest person. Sure I lie, but it doesn't hurt anything. Or does it?

I once tried going a whole week without telling a lie, and it was 4
paralyzing. I discovered that telling the truth all the time is nearly impossible. It means living with some serious consequences: The bank charges me $60 in overdraft fees, my partner keels over when I tell him about my travails, my client fires me for telling her I didn't feel like being on time, and my friend takes it personally when I say I'm not hungry. There must be some merit to lying.

But if I justify lying, what makes me any different from slick   5
politicians or the corporate robbers who raided the S&L industry?[1]
Saying it's okay to lie one way and not another is hedging. I cannot
seem to escape the voice deep inside me that tells me: When someone lies, someone loses.

What far-reaching consequences will I, or others, pay as a result   6
of my lie? Will someone's trust be destroyed? Will someone else pay
my penance because I ducked out? We must consider the *meaning of
our actions.* Deception, lies, capital crimes, and misdemeanors all
carry meanings. *Webster's* definition of *lie* is specific:

> 1: a false statement or action especially made with the intent to deceive;
> 2: anything that gives or is meant to give a false impression.

A definition like this implies that there are many, many ways to   7
tell a lie. Here are just a few.

The White Lie

*A man who won't lie to a woman has very little consideration for her
feelings.*

—Bergen Evans

The white lie assumes that the truth will cause more damage   8
than a simple, harmless untruth. Telling a friend he looks great
when he looks like hell can be based on a decision that the friend
needs a compliment more than a frank opinion. But, in effect, it is
the liar deciding what is best for the lied to. Ultimately, it is a vote of
no confidence. It is an act of subtle arrogance for anyone to decide
what is best for someone else.

Yet not all circumstances are quite so cut-and-dried. Take, for   9
instance, the sergeant in Vietnam who knew one of his men was
killed in action but listed him as missing so that the man's family
would receive indefinite compensation instead of the lump-sum pittance the military gives widows and children. His intent was honorable. Yet for twenty years this family kept their hopes alive, unable
to move on to a new life.

---

[1]Reference to the savings and loan scandal of the 1980s, in which corrupt owners of
bank-like institutions defrauded the federal government of vast amounts of money
(editors' note).

Façades

Et tu, Brute?
—Caesar

We all put up façades to one degree or another. When I put on a   10
suit to go to see a client, I feel as though I am putting on another
face, obeying the expectation that serious businesspeople wear suits
rather than sweatpants. But I'm a writer. Normally, I get up, get the
kid off to school, and sit at my computer in my pajamas until four in
the afternoon. When I answer the phone, the caller thinks I'm wearing a suit (though the UPS man knows better).

But façades can be destructive because they are used to seduce   11
others into an illusion. For instance, I recently realized that a former
friend was a liar. He presented himself with all the right looks and
the right words and offered lots of new consciousness theories, fab-
ulous books to read, and fascinating insights. Then I did some business with him, and the time came for him to pay me. He turned out
to be all talk and no walk. I heard a plethora of reasonable excuses,
including in-depth descriptions of the big break around the corner.
In six months of work, I saw less than a hundred bucks. When I confronted him, he raised both eyebrows and tried to convince me that
I'd heard him wrong, that he'd made no commitment to me. A simple investigation into his past revealed a crowded graveyard of dis-
enchanted former friends.

Ignoring the Plain Facts

Well, you must understand that Father Porter is only human. . . .
—A Massachusetts priest

In the '60s, the Catholic Church in Massachusetts began hearing   12
complaints that Father James Porter was sexually molesting children. Rather than relieving him of his duties, the ecclesiastical authorities simply moved him from one parish to another between
1960 and 1967, actually providing him with a fresh supply of unsus-
pecting families and innocent children to abuse. After treatment in
1967 for pedophilia, he went back to work, this time in Minnesota.
The new diocese was aware of Father Porter's obsession with children, but they needed priests and recklessly believed treatment had
cured him. More children were abused until he was relieved of his

duties a year later. By his own admission, Porter may have abused as many as a hundred children.

Ignoring the facts may not in and of itself be a form of lying, but   13
consider the context of this situation. If a lie is *a false action done with the intent to deceive*, then the Catholic Church's conscious covering for Porter created irreparable consequences. The church became a co-perpetrator with Porter.

Deflecting

When you have no basis for an argument, abuse the plaintiff.

—Cicero

I've discovered that I can keep anyone from seeing the true me by   14
being selectively blatant. I set a precedent of being up-front about intimate issues, but I never bring up the things I truly want to hide; I just let people assume I'm revealing everything. It's an effective way of hiding.

Any good liar knows that the way to perpetuate an untruth is   15
to deflect attention from it. When Clarence Thomas[2] exploded with accusations that the Senate hearings were a "high-tech lynching," he simply switched the focus from a highly charged subject to a radioactive subject. Rather than defending himself, he took the offensive and accused the country of racism. It was a brilliant maneuver. Racism is now politically incorrect in official circles—unlike sexual harassment, which still rewards those who can get away with it.

Some of the most skillful deflectors are passive-aggressive[3] peo-   16
ple who, when accused of inappropriate behavior, refuse to respond to the accusations. This you-don't-exist stance infuriates the accuser, who, understandably, screams something obscene out of frustration. The trap is sprung and the act of deflection successful, because now the passive-aggressive person can indignantly say, "Who can talk to someone as unreasonable as you?" The real issue is forgotten and the sins of the original victim become the focus. Feeling guilty of namecalling, the victim is fully tamed and crawls into a hole, ashamed. I have watched this fighting technique work thousands of times in disputes between men and women, and what I've learned is that the real culprit is not necessarily the one who swears the loudest.

---

[2]Nominated to the Supreme Court in 1993, Clarence Thomas, an African American jurist, was accused by former colleague Anita Hill of sexual harassment. Much of Thomas's confirmation hearing, televised nationwide, focused on this issue (editors' note).

[3]A psychological pattern in which hostility is expressed through an infuriating detachment and nonresponsiveness (editors' note).

Omission

The cruelest lies are often told in silence.
—R. L. Stevenson

Omission involves telling most of the truth minus one or two   17
key facts whose absence changes the story completely. You break a
pair of glasses that are guaranteed under normal use and get a new
pair, without mentioning that the first pair broke during a rowdy
game of basketball. Who hasn't tried something like that? But what
about omission of information that could make a difference in how
a person lives his or her life?

For instance, one day I found out that rabbinical legends tell of   18
another woman in the Garden of Eden before Eve. I was stunned.
The omission of the Sumerian goddess Lilith from Genesis—as well
as her demonization by ancient misogynists as an embodiment of
female evil—felt like spiritual robbery. I felt like I'd just found out
my mother was really my stepmother. To take seriously the tradition
that Adam was created out of the same mud as his equal counter-
part, Lilith, redefines all of Judeo-Christian history.

Some renegade Catholic feminists introduced me to a view of   19
Lilith that had been suppressed during many centuries when this
strong goddess was seen only as a spirit of evil. Lilith was a proud
goddess who defied Adam's need to control her, attempted negotiations, and when this failed, said adios and left the Garden of Eden.

This omission of Lilith from the Bible was a patriarchal strategy   20
to keep women weak. Omitting the strong-woman archetype of Lilith from Western religions and starring the story with Eve the Rib
has helped keep Christian and Jewish women believing they were
the lesser sex for thousands of years.

Stereotypes and Clichés

Where opinion does not exist, the status quo becomes stereotyped and
all originality is discouraged.
—Bertrand Russell

Stereotype and cliché serve a purpose as a form of shorthand.   21
Our need for vast amounts of information in nanoseconds has made
the stereotype vital to modern communication. Unfortunately, it often shuts down original thinking, giving those hungry for
the truth a candy bar of misinformation instead of a balanced meal.

The stereotype explains a situation with just enough truth to seem unquestionable.

All the "isms"—racism, sexism, ageism, et al.—are founded on   22
and fueled by the stereotype and the cliché, which are lies of exaggeration, omission, and ignorance. They are always dangerous. They take a single tree and make it a landscape. They destroy curiosity. They close minds and separate people. The single mother on welfare is assumed to be cheating. Any black male could tell you how much of his identity is obliterated daily by stereotypes. Fat people, ugly people, beautiful people, old people, large-breasted women, short men, the mentally ill, and the homeless all could tell you how much more they are like us than we want to think. I once admitted to a group of people that I had a mouth like a truck driver. Much to my surprise, a man stood up and said, "I'm a truck driver, and I never cuss." Needless to say, I was humbled.

Groupthink

*Who is more foolish, the child afraid of the dark,
or the man afraid of the light?*

—Maurice Freehill

Irving Janis, in *Victims of Group Think,* defines this sort of lie as a   23
psychological phenomenon within decision-making groups in which loyalty to the group has become more important than any other value, with the result that dissent and the appraisal of alternatives are suppressed. If you've ever worked on a committee or in a corporation, you've encountered groupthink. It requires a combination of other forms of lying—ignoring facts, selective memory, omission, and denial, to name a few.

The textbook example of groupthink came on December 7,   24
1941. From as early as the fall of 1941, the warnings came in, one after another, that Japan was preparing for a massive military operation. The Navy command in Hawaii assumed Pearl Harbor was invulnerable—the Japanese weren't stupid enough to attack the United States' most important base. On the other hand, racist stereotypes said the Japanese weren't smart enough to invent a torpedo effective in less than 60 feet of water (the fleet was docked in 30 feet); after all, U.S. technology hadn't been able to do it.

On Friday, December 5, normal weekend leave was granted to   25
all the commanders at Pearl Harbor, even though the Japanese

consulate in Hawaii was busy burning papers. Within the tight, good-ole-boy cohesiveness of the U.S. command in Hawaii, the myth of invulnerability stayed well entrenched. No one in the group considered the alternatives. The rest is history.

Out-and-Out Lies

The only form of lying that is beyond reproach is lying for its own sake.

—Oscar Wilde

Of all the ways to lie, I like this one the best, probably because   26
I get tired of trying to figure out the real meanings behind things. At least I can trust the bald-faced lie. I once asked my five-year-old nephew, "Who broke the fence?" (I had seen him do it.) He answered, "The murderers." Who could argue?

At least when this sort of lie is told it can be easily confronted.   27
As the person who is lied to, I know where I stand. The bald-faced lie doesn't toy with my perceptions—it argues with them. It doesn't try to refashion reality, it tries to refute it. *Read my lips . . .* No sleight of hand.[4] No guessing. If this were the only form of lying, there would be no such things as floating anxiety[5] or the adult, children-of-alcoholics movement.

Dismissal

Pay no attention to that man behind the curtain! I am the Great Oz!

—The Wizard of Oz

Dismissal is perhaps the slipperiest of all lies. Dismissing feel-   28
ings, perceptions, or even the raw facts of a situation ranks as a kind of lie that can do as much damage to a person as any other kind of lie.

The roots of many mental disorders can be traced back to the   29
dismissal of reality. Imagine that a person is told from the time she is a tot that her perceptions are inaccurate. *"Mommy, I'm scared."*

---

[4]A phrase used by presidential candidate George H. W. Bush during the 1988 campaign (and often parodied thereafter): "Read my lips.... No new taxes" (editors' note).

[5]A psychological condition in which a person feels generalized anxiety for no specific reason (editor's note).

"No you're not, darling." "*I don't like that man next door, he makes me feel icky.*" "Johnny, that's a terrible thing to say, of course you like him. You go over there right now and be nice to him."

I've often mused over the idea that madness is actually a sane   30
reaction to an insane world. Psychologist R. D. Laing supports this hypothesis in *Sanity, Madness and the Family*, an account of his investigations into the families of schizophrenics. The common thread that ran through all of the families he studied was a deliberate, staunch dismissal of the patient's perceptions from a very early age. Each of the patients started out with an accurate grasp of reality, which, through meticulous and methodical dismissal, was demolished until the only reality the patient could trust was catatonia.

Dismissal runs the gamut. Mild dismissal can be quite handy   31
for forgiving the foibles of others in our day-to-day lives. Toddlers who have just learned to manipulate their parents' attention sometimes are dismissed out of necessity. Absolute attention from the parents would require so much energy that no one would get to eat dinner. But we must be careful and attentive about how far we take our "necessary" dismissals. Dismissal is a dangerous tool, because it's nothing less than a lie.

Delusion

We lie loudest when we lie to ourselves.

—Eric Hoffer

I could write the book on this one. Delusion, a cousin of dis-   32
missal, is the tendency to see excuses as facts. It's a powerful lying tool because it filters out information that contradicts what we want to believe. Alcoholics who believe that the problems in their lives are legitimate reasons for drinking rather than results of the drinking offer the classic example of deluded thinking. Delusion uses the mind's ability to see things in myriad ways to support what it wants to be the truth.

But delusion is also a survival mechanism we all use. If we were   33
to fully contemplate the consequences of our stockpiles of nuclear weapons or global warming, we could hardly function on a day-to-day level. We don't want to incorporate that much reality into our lives because to do so would be paralyzing.

Delusion acts as an adhesive to keep the status quo intact. It   34
shamelessly employs dismissal, omission, and amnesia, among
other sorts of lies. Its most cunning defense is that it cannot
see itself.

•   •   •

The liar's punishment . . . is that he cannot believe anyone else.
—George Bernard Shaw

These are only a few of the ways we lie. Or are lied to. As I said   35
earlier, it's not easy to entirely eliminate lies from our lives. No matter how pious we may try to be, we will still embellish, hedge, and
omit to lubricate the daily machinery of living. But there is a world
of difference between telling functional lies and living a lie. Martin
Buber[6] once said, "The lie is the spirit committing treason against
itself." Our acceptance of lies becomes a cultural cancer that eventually shrouds and reorders reality until moral garbage becomes as invisible to us as water is to a fish.

How much do we tolerate before we become sick and tired of   36
being sick and tired? When will we stand up and declare our *right* to
trust? When do we stop accepting that the real truth is in the fine
print? Whose lips do we read this year when we vote for president?
When will we stop being so reticent about making judgments?
When do we stop turning over our personal power and responsibility to liars?

Maybe if I don't tell the bank the check's in the mail I'll be less   37
tolerant of the lies told me every day. A country song I once heard
said it all for me: "You've got to stand for something or you'll fall for
anything."

MEANINGS AND VALUES

1.   Explain the concept of a white lie. According to the author, in what
way is a white lie "an act of subtle arrogance"?

2.   Why do you suppose Ericsson classifies deflecting as a form of lying?

3.   Explain the concept of groupthink.

---

[6]A German Jewish scholar and philosopher (1878–1965) (editors' note).

EXPOSITORY TECHNIQUES

1. What do you think is the author's purpose for introducing each category of lie with a quotation? Is this strategy effective?

2. In Paragraph 17, the writer uses the device of a rhetorical question (see "Guide to Terms": *Rhetorical Questions*) to directly address the reader: "Who hasn't tried something like that?" In your opinion, is this question successful as a technique to emphasize her point about the insignificance of some lies of omission? Explain your response.

3. Ericsson writes her essay in the first person, and her tone is informal. Does this undermine the effectiveness of her classification or strengthen it? How so?

DICTION AND VOCABULARY

1. Why do you suppose the writer chose to begin a classification essay on lying with a personal anecdote? Was this a successful choice?

2. If you do not know the meaning of some of the following words, look them up in a dictionary: *hedging* (Par. 5), *pittance* (9), *façades* (10), *blatant* (14), *bald-faced* (26), *foibles* (31).

3. Consider the metaphors (Guide: *Figures of Speech*) the writer uses near the end of her essay (Par. 35). To what two things does she compare our acceptance of lies? Do you think that these metaphors succeed in conveying her opinion effectively?

READ TO WRITE

1. **Collaborating:** In a group of writers, choose one of the ten types of lying Ericsson describes in her essay. Together, craft a written statement, in a sentence or two, that defines that particular type of lying and restates Ericsson's opinion about it. Share stories in your group about when each of you might have told, or been told, this type of lie. Choose one of your group members' stories and, as a group, write an extended example suitable for use in an essay on this type of lying. Introduce or conclude your group anecdote with the statement you wrote about this category.

2. **Considering Audience:** After reading this essay, most readers are probably persuaded to agree with its author that the acceptance of lies can be a slippery slope that leads to worse social ills. Whether or not you agree with Ericsson's conclusion, choose one of the types of lying she categorizes and write an essay defending it, taking the point of view of a reader who supports lying as a necessity of human life.

3. **Developing an Essay:** Drawing ideas and strategies from Ericsson's essay and from the group exercise in question 1, write an essay on groupthink, classifying this category into further subdivisions

explaining different types of groupthink that you have heard or read about. Include in your essay a definition of groupthink, vivid examples illustrating each of your subcategories of groupthink, and an opinion statement about the consequences of groupthink. Or reproduce Ericsson's own experiment and try to go for a week (or just a day) without lying. Classify your results into categories and write an informal essay using clusters of examples and/or extended examples about the results of your attempt.

(NOTE: Suggestions for topics requiring development by CLASSIFICATION follow.)

Writing Suggestions for Chapter 4

CLASSIFICATION

Use classification (into at least three categories) as your basic method of analyzing one of the following subjects from an interesting point of view. (Your instructor may have good reason to place limitations on your choice of subject.) Narrow the topic as necessary to enable you to do a thorough job.

1. College students
2. College teachers
3. Athletes
4. Coaches
5. Salespeople
6. Hunters (or fishers)
7. Parents
8. Drug users
9. Police officers
10. Summer (or part-time) jobs
11. Sailing vessels
12. TV show hosts
13. Friends
14. Careers
15. Horses (or other animals)
16. Television programs
17. Motivations for study
18. Methods of studying for exams
19. Lies
20. Selling techniques
21. Tastes in clothes
22. Contemporary music or films
23. Love
24. Ways to spend money
25. Attitudes toward life
26. Fast foods (or junk foods)
27. Smokers
28. Investments
29. Actors
30. Books or magazines

COLLABORATIVE EXERCISES

1. Working in a group, prepare a classification essay on college life using numbers 1–4 in the preceding exercise as the major sections for your classification. Assign group members to divide each of the four sections into two or three subcategories and to prepare a section of an essay explaining these subcategories. Then prepare a collaboratively written essay linking

each section with clear transitions and unifying the whole with a central idea on which all members of the group agree. (See "Guide to Terms": *Unity.*)

2. As a group, create three or more categories from the subject "careers" (see number 14). Have each member of the group research one of the types of careers and then create a collaboratively written essay with an appropriate introduction, conclusion, thesis, and transitions.

5

Explaining by Means of Comparison and Contrast

One of the first expository methods we used as children was **comparison,** noticing similarities of objects, qualities, and actions, or **contrast,** noticing their differences. We compared the color of the new puppies with that of their mother, contrasted a parent's height with our own. Then the process became more complicated. Now we employ it frequently in college essay examinations or term papers when we compare or contrast forms of government, reproductive systems of animals, or ethical philosophies of humans. In the business or professional world, we prepare important reports based on comparison and contrast—between kinds of equipment for purchase, the personnel policies of different departments, or precedents in legal matters. Nearly all people use the process of comparison (meaning both *comparing* and *contrasting*) many times a day—in choosing a head of lettuce, in deciding what to wear to school, in selecting a house, or a friend, or a religion.

In expository writing, brief comparisons—a sentence or two— may serve to alert readers to similarities or highlight differences. Longer comparisons need to do more; they need to explore the subject and convey the writer's perspective. For a longer comparison or contrast that explains or explores ideas, you need an ordered plan to avoid having a mere list of characteristics or a frustrating jumble of similarities and differences. You also need to give attention to all the important points of similarity (or difference). The following paragraph accomplishes all these things.

We really are terribly confused about our relationship with nature. On the one hand, we like to live in houses that are tidy and clean,

127

and if nature should be rude enough to enter—in the form of a bat in the attic, or a mouse in the kitchen, or a cockroach crawling along the skirting boards—we stalk it with the blood-lust of a tabby cat; we resort to chemical warfare. In fact, we judge people harshly if their house is full of dust and dirt. And yet, on the other hand, we just as obsessively bring nature indoors. We touch a switch and light floods the room. We turn a dial and suddenly it feels like summer or winter. We live in a perpetual breeze or bake of our devising. We buy posters and calendars with photographs of nature. We hang paintings of landscapes on our walls. We scent everything that touches our lives. We fill our houses with flowers and pets. We try hard to remove ourselves from all the dramas and sensations of nature, and yet without them we feel lost and disconnected. So, subconsciously, we bring them right back indoors again. Then we obsessively visit nature—we go swimming, jogging, or cross-country skiing, we take strolls in a park. Confusing, isn't it?

—Diane Ackerman, *Deep Play*

WHY USE COMPARISON?

Highlighting similarities and differences is the most obvious use for comparison, but merely a starting point for effective writing. Whenever you employ the pattern, therefore, make sure you give it a worthwhile purpose. You can contrast llamas with pot-bellied pigs, for example, but your efforts will likely seem silly or trivial unless tied to some larger goal such as their relative suitability as pets.

The question of purpose is especially important in a formal, full-scale analysis by comparison and contrast where the pattern lends shape to an entire essay. Sometimes the purpose may be merely to reveal *surprising or frequently overlooked likenesses and differences,* with the goal of adding to readers' knowledge, satisfying their curiosity, or developing their self-awareness. For example, an essay on generational differences over responsibility for housework might explain that younger people are more likely to share the work of cooking and cleaning, but that all generations seem to be maintaining traditional gender differences in the responsibility of home maintenance. Mark Twain, in the selection "Two Ways of Seeing a River" (pp. 142–143), contrasts his view of the Mississippi as a young man with his perspective as an experienced river pilot. In doing so, he helps readers understand how radically experience and changes in attitude can affect our perceptions of the external world—even making the same stretch of scenery appear a different place.

The aim may be to show *the superiority* of one thing over another. Or it may be to *explain* and *evaluate*, as in a discussion of alternatives or of differing points of view on an issue. For instance, you might examine competing proposals for an antismoking campaign, one designed by teenagers and the other by advertising professionals, evaluating the strengths and limitations of each.

The purpose could be to explain the *unfamiliar* (wedding customs in Ethiopia) by comparing it to the *familiar* (wedding customs in Kansas). Or it could be to support and explore a thesis, as is the case with several of the essays in this chapter. Bill McKibben ("Old MacDonald Had a Farmer's Market" pp. 152–156), for example, uses comparison to advance the thesis that our modern insistence on self-reliance may be at odds with the earlier idea that we are meant to rely on one another.

CHOOSING A STRATEGY

To take a comparison beyond the obvious and develop knowledge and insight worth sharing with readers, you need to begin by identifying **points of comparison** (or **points of contrast**), both major and minor. Some important points of comparison will be apparent to you (and your readers) from the outset, and therefore should be part of your analysis. Others will be less apparent, though not necessarily less important. Including them will enable you to provide a fresh or more thorough perspective, adding to your reader's understanding. Consider using the following questions to identify and explore points of comparison, adapted, of course, to the particular demands of your subjects.

What are the similar (or different) **physical aspects** (shape, color, size, texture, movement) of the subjects you are analyzing?

> **Parts and Processes** (elements and their relationships, methods of operation, instructions)?
> **Benefits** (individual, social, political, environmental)?
> **Problems** (dangers, difficulties, limitations)?
> **Costs** (financial, emotional, political)?
> **Uses** (personal, social, environmental; to provide benefits, to create relationships, to accomplish a particular goal)?

As you develop responses to questions like these, keep in mind that you are trying to develop fresh insights both for yourself and your readers. Consider using questions like these to help you develop such a perspective.

What similarities (or differences) are readers likely to consider. . . .

Intriguing or surprising?

Useful or worth learning about?

Quite different from what they expected before they began reading?

Significant enough to make them more likely to consider different opinions on an issue or approaches to a problem?

Important enough to guide their choice among alternative policies, products, or conclusions?

The points of comparison you choose, along with your tentative thesis, your purpose for writing, and the complexity of your materials, will usually suggest an arrangement for your writing. The number of subjects making up any comparison (two or more) and the likelihood that you will be exploring multiple points of comparison along with their supporting details mean that you should plan the organization of an essay carefully and remember to make this arrangement clear to readers.

One of the two basic methods of comparison is to present all the information on the two (or more) subjects, one at a time, and to summarize by combining their most important similarities and differences. Here is a subject-by-subject plan for an essay.

Subject-by-Subject Pattern

Introduction

Subjects: Bella Costa Medical Center (curing illness) and Foothills Regional Health Complex (creating wellness)

Tentative Thesis: Today's health care dilemmas have gone beyond choices among insurance plans to choices between two very different kinds of medical treatment: one focused on curing illness (represented by Bella Costa M.C.), the other focused on creating wellness (represented by Foothills R.H.C.).

Subject 1: Bella Costa Medical Center

Feature 1: Traditional medicine—curing illness

Feature 2: Large hospital, newest equipment

Feature 3: Large staff of physicians

Feature 4: Emphasis on drugs, surgery, physical therapy

Subject 2: Foothills Regional Health Complex
    Feature 1: Preventive medicine—creating wellness
    Feature 2: Small hospital, limited facilities, local clinics
    Feature 3: Some physicians, other staff including nutrition-
        ists, exercise specialists, and alternative therapists
    Feature 4: Emphasis on diet, exercise, alternative therapies
        (acupuncture, holistic medicine), healthy lifestyle
Conclusion (summary): Summarize reasons for choosing either
    one and suggest that personal preferences may play an
    important role.

This method may be desirable if there are few points to compare, or if the individual points are less important than the overall
picture they present.

However, if there are several points of comparison to be considered, or if the points are of individual importance, alternation of the
material would be a better arrangement.

Point-by-Point Pattern

Subjects: *The Mummy* (1932) starring Boris Karloff
    The Mummy (1999) starring Brendan Fraser
Tentative Thesis: The original version of *The Mummy* (1932)
    takes itself and the horror movie form seriously and pro-
    vides an often scary portrait of evil. The remake (1999)
    takes itself only half-seriously and gently pokes fun at the
    conventions of the horror movie, so it is only occasionally
    scary and conveys no sense of evil.

Feature 1: Acting
    Original version of *The Mummy*: Boris Karloff, serious acting
        style, dramatic scenes and speeches
    Remake of *The Mummy*: Brendan Fraser, comic or ironic acting
        style, action scenes and physical comedy

Feature 2: Script
    Original version of *The Mummy*: Provides motivation for char-
        acters, emphasizes force of evil desires
    Remake of *The Mummy*: Little motivation for characters, high-
        lights stereotypes and conventions of horror movies

Feature 3: Special Effects
>   Original version of *The Mummy*: Support story line, emphasize
>   unnatural desires and presence of evil
>   Remake of *The Mummy*: Call attention to themselves, empha-
>   size unreal and exaggerated elements of horror stories

Conclusion (summary):
>   Original and remake show changing attitudes toward horror
>   movie as portrait of evil

Often the subject matter or the purpose itself will suggest a more casual treatment, or some combination or variation of the two basic methods. We might present the complete information on the first subject, then summarize it point by point within the complete information on the second. And although expository comparisons and contrasts are frequently handled together, it is sometimes best to present all similarities first, then all differences—or vice versa, depending on the emphasis desired. In any basic use of comparison, the important thing is to have a plan that suits the purpose and material, thoughtfully worked out in advance.

DEVELOPING COMPARISONS

In writing an essay using comparison as a primary pattern of exposition, keep these two important tasks in mind: 1) take care that your comparisons are logical and arranged in a manner that will be clear to your readers and 2) provide detailed explanations of the similarities and differences in order to support your conclusions.

Above all, your comparison needs to be *logical*. A logical comparison or contrast can be made only between subjects of the same general type. (Analogy, a special form of comparison used for another purpose, is discussed in the next chapter.) For example, contrasting modern medicine (prescription drugs, surgery) and traditional medicine (herbal remedies, acupuncture) could be useful or meaningful, but little would be gained by contrasting surgery and carpentry.

Transition words and phrases are a big help with both logic and the arrangement of an essay, reminding you of an essay's plan as you write and signaling the arrangement to readers. Some transition words identify the elements of a subject, some indicate logical relationships or highlight the place of a paragraph in

the overall organization, and some identify conclusions and supporting detail.

> Elements of a Subject: trait, characteristic, element, part, seg-
>   ment, unit, feature
> Logical Relationships and Arrangement: in comparison, in
>   contrast, on the other side, on the other hand, likewise,
>   moreover, similarly, in the same (or different) manner, in
>   addition, then, further, yet, but, however, nonetheless, first,
>   second, third, although, still
> Conclusions and Supporting Detail: in conclusion, to sum up,
>   finally, for example, for instance

Paragraphs are especially important in writing that compares
or contrasts. Typically, they are devoted to one of the major steps in
the exposition, often to one of the main points of comparison. In focusing on points of similarity or dissimilarity, be thorough. Provide
facts, concrete details, and examples. Consider those that support
your conclusions or recommendations as well as those that provide
contrary evidence. Remember, too, that effective comparisons serve
a purpose, so include details that support your overall thesis and
further the purpose for which you are writing.

Student Essay

In the following essay, Amy Bell uses comparison as a pattern of
thinking: a way to raise questions about and explore her topic. She
inquires into the "truthfulness" of two pieces of writing that claim
to be portrayals of events that really happened, and in so doing she
raises questions about what really constitutes "truth" in writing.
Amy uses comparison effectively in her own writing both as a way
of representing her thinking and as a way of helping readers understand the many detailed similarities and differences she analyzes.

Perception of Truth

by Amy Bell

"The following motion picture is based on a true
story." How many times have you seen this on the movie
screen and thought, "Yeah, right, 'true' story my foot"?
We all know that the movie producers/directors take
huge liberties with the facts and portray events differently from the way they actually occurred. The same is

true in non-fiction writing. Each author chooses what information to give to the reader and what information to withhold. In doing this the "truth" is blurred and the author's personal bias emerges. Truman Capote and Norman Mailer are both hailed as authors who succeeded in writing "true-story" novels. In describing Norman Mailer's *The Executioner's Song*, critics have said he is "our greatest chronicler" and "the best journalist in the country" (Mailer cover). Critics have described Truman Capote's *In Cold Blood* as a "superbly written 'true account'" and "the best documentary of an American crime" (Capote cover). All of these book reviews imply that Mailer and Capote gave only the truth in their books. However, this is not possible. Mailer's and Capote's personal opinions also must be in these novels. So which novel is more truthful? This question cannot be answered. How can we ever know what information these authors changed or what information they left out completely? However, it is possible to show which novel creates a greater impression of truth. Truman Capote's novel, *In Cold Blood*, seems more truthful than Mailer's *The Executioner's Song*. The impression of truth in these novels was partly created by the way in which each author portrayed the murderer in his story.

Norman Mailer and Truman Capote both had unlimited access to the facts about the murderers, Gary Gilmore and Perry Smith [respectively]. In researching Gilmore, Mailer collected interview manuscripts, court records, and documents. He also conducted nearly 300 interviews, which added up to a manuscript of 15,000 pages (Mailer 1020). Capote also collected numerous official records and conducted interviews (Capote acknowledgments page). Capote and Mailer used carefully selected bits of truth from this multitude of information to portray their murderers differently.

One obvious way in which Mailer and Capote described the murderers was to directly quote them.

Margin annotations:

Focuses on general topic/issue to be explored

Focuses on specific topic of essay

Purpose of essay—to be accomplished by comparing and contrasting

Thesis statement

General plan for essay—compare the works

Background—both Mailer and Capote

Feature 1: Quotations

Norman Mailer put a numerous amount of quotations from Gilmore in his novel. Nearly forty letters written by Gilmore to his girlfriend Nicole were printed in the book. Mailer also included a great deal of interviews between Gilmore and his two lawyers. A lot of "truth" is divulged because so much personal information about Gilmore is given. However, for the reader this truth becomes blurred because of Gilmore's contradicting feelings and intense emotions. For instance, in one letter Gilmore writes to Nicole he says, "I saw a simple, quiet Truth, a profound, deep, and personal Truth of beauty and love" (qtd. in Mailer 345). It would seem that through these words the reader might see who the "true" Gary is. However, in the next letter the reader is bombarded with ". . . these chickens——t pricks. Give a motherf——er a little authority and they think they have to start taking privileges away from people . . . bunch of slack-jawed . . . gurgling . . . punks" (Mailer 348). Gilmore's variety of raving emotions weaves in and out of the letters in the book, leaving the reader wary of believing anything Gilmore says. Norman Mailer gives us too much information from an unreliable Gilmore, and in doing so there seems to be less truth.

    Capote also quotes his murderer, Perry Smith; however, he uses fewer, carefully selected quotations. Capote only uses enough quotations to give an ample description of Smith. This creates less confusion for the reader about Smith. Smith could have been just as confusing to understand as Gilmore was; after all, Smith did kill four people without knowing why he did it. For example, Capote includes a few carefully selected quotations to describe Smith's childhood. Smith is describing the brutality of the nuns in an orphanage he lived in as a child: "She woke me up. She had a flashlight, and she hit me with it. Hit me and hit me. And when the flashlight broke, she went on hitting me in the dark" (qtd. in Capote 93). This well-chosen quotation gives the reader an understanding of Smith's childhood and gives a

Discussion of Mailer

Supporting details

Interpretation of details

Feature 1: Quotations

Discussion of Capote

Supporting details

glimpse into the mind of Smith. Capote tells the reader who Smith is, instead of the reader having to figure out who Smith is by sorting through hundreds of Smith's thoughts. Capote gives us what he thinks the truth about Smith is, and he does it in such a way that the reader is compelled to believe it.

Interpretation of details

One way to make a story more believable and truthful is to give equal weight to everyone's side of the story. Mailer thoroughly gives Gilmore's side of the story; however, the stories of the victims are hardly mentioned. In chapters twelve and fifteen of part four, Mailer gives a basic description of the lives of the Bushnells and the Jensens. He only devotes about twenty pages out of 1,000 pages to these people. Also, Mailer's description of these people is not an intimate one. He gives an overview of their lives in a distant, journalistic style. Mailer writes, "It was at Utah State that Colleen was introduced to her future husband, Max Jensen" (Mailer 212). This is simply a description, and the voices and feelings of Max and Colleen are not seen.

Feature 2: Equal weight in presentation

Discussion of Mailer

Conclusion followed by supporting details

Capote, on the other hand, gives an equal amount of time to everyone's side of the story. In the first chapter, "Last to See Them Alive," Capote describes the Clutter family while also describing Dick [Smith's accomplice] and Perry [Smith]. Capote shows each member of the Clutter family, their relationships with each other and with the community. Capote includes a lot of dialogue between members of the family, so that the reader can see the murder victims as real people. The following is a conversation between Nancy Clutter and her brother, Kenyon. [Nancy speaks first.]

Feature 2: Equal weight in presentation

Discussion of Capote

Conclusion followed by supporting details

"I keep smelling cigarette smoke."

"On your breath?" inquired Kenyon.

"No funny one. Yours." (Capote 19)

In this interplay between brother and sister the reader can relate to the Clutters as human beings and not just as murder victims. Capote gives an in-depth, intimate description of every person's side of the story.

Interpretation of details

For the reader this creates a perception that Capote was less biased, and therefore the story seems truthful.

Using basic logic, it would seem that Mailer probably wrote down more "truth" in a 1,000-page book than Capote wrote in a meager 350-page book. However, the amount of truth and the perception of truth are two very different things. Truman Capote's *In Cold Blood* gives a greater perception of truth than Norman Mailer's *The Executioner's Song*. Then again, this statement is merely my opinion. As the author of this essay, I selected only the "appropriate" bits of information from these two novels to give my reader(s) my perception of what "truth" is.

Summary conclusion: Capote seems more truthful

Works Cited

Capote, Truman. *In Cold Blood*. New York: Modern Library, 1965. Print.

Mailer, Norman. *The Executioner's Song*. New York: Warner, 1979. Print.

RACHEL CARSON

RACHEL CARSON (1907–1964), a marine biologist and naturalist, earned a master's degree in zoology from Johns Hopkins University in 1932. A few years later, the *Atlantic Monthly* published an essay of Carson's that brought the ocean to vibrant life for the nonscientist. She embarked on an writing career that resulted in *The Sea Around Us* (1951), winner of the 1952 National Book Award. Carson's later work focused on conservationism and helped inspire today's environmental movement.

A Fable for Tomorrow

In the 1940s, Carson began investigating the misuse of pesticides. Her inquiries led to the publication of *Silent Spring* in 1962. The controversial book initially provoked threats of litigation from chemical companies but ultimately has been recognized on many lists of the best nonfiction, including its selection by *Discover Magazine* as one of the 25 greatest science books of all time. This selection is drawn from the book's first chapter.

There was once a town in the heart of America where all life   1
seemed to live in harmony with its surroundings. The town lay in the midst of a checkerboard of prosperous farms, with fields of grain and hillsides of orchards where, in spring, white clouds of bloom drifted above the green fields. In autumn, oak and maple and birch set up a blaze of color that flamed and flickered across a backdrop of pines. Then foxes barked in the hills and deer silently crossed the fields, half hidden in the mists of the fall mornings.

Along the roads, laurel, viburnum and alder, great ferns and   2
wildflowers delighted the traveler's eye through much of the year. Even in winter the roadsides were places of beauty, where countless birds came to feed on the berries and on the seed beads of the dried weeds rising above the snow. The countryside was, in fact, famous for the abundance and variety of its bird life, and when the flood of migrants was pouring through in spring and fall people traveled from great distances to observe them. Others came to fish the streams, which flowed clear and cold out of the hills and contained shady pools where trout lay. So it had been from the days many years ago when the first settlers raised their houses, sank their wells, and built their barns.

Then a strange blight crept over the area and everything began to   3
change. Some evil spell had settled on the community: mysterious
maladies swept the flocks of chickens; the cattle and sheep sickened
and died. Everywhere was a shadow of death. The farmer spoke of
much illness among their families. In the town the doctors had become more and more puzzled by new kinds of sickness appearing
among their patients. There had been several sudden and unex-
plained deaths, not only among adults but even among children, who
would be stricken suddenly while at play and die within a few hours.

There was a strange stillness. The birds, for example—where   4
had they gone? Many people spoke of them, puzzled and disturbed.
The feeding stations in the backyards were deserted. The few birds
seen anywhere were moribund; they trembled violently and could
not fly. It was a spring without voices. On the mornings that had
once throbbed with the dawn chorus of robins, catbirds, doves, jays,
wrens, and scores of other bird voices there was now no sound; only
silence lay over the fields and woods and marsh.

On the farms the hens brooded, but no chicks hatched. The   5
farmers complained that they were unable to raise any pigs—the lit-
ters were small and the young survived only a few days. The apple
trees were coming into bloom but no bees droned among the blossoms, so there was no pollination and there would be no fruit.

The roadsides, once so attractive, were now lined with browned   6
and withered vegetation as though swept by fire. These, too, were
silent, deserted by all living things. Even the streams were now lifeless. Anglers no longer visited them, for all the fish had died.

In the gutters under the eaves and between the shingles of the   7
roofs, a white granular powder still showed a few patches; some
weeks before it had fallen like snow upon the roofs and the lawns,
the fields and streams.

No witchcraft, no enemy action had silenced the rebirth of new   8
life in this stricken world. The people had done it themselves.

This town does not actually exist, but it might easily have a   9
thousand counterparts in America or elsewhere in the world. I know
of no community that has experienced all the misfortunes I describe.
Yet every one of these disasters has actually happened somewhere,
and many real communities have already suffered a substantial
number of them. A grim specter has crept upon us almost unnoticed, and this imagined tragedy may easily become a stark reality
we all shall know.

MEANINGS AND VALUES

1. Explain the significance of this essay's title.

2. What is the effect of the "strange blight" that the writer introduces in Paragraph 3?

3. What is the significance of the "white granular powder" that the author describes in Paragraph 7?

EXPOSITORY TECHNIQUES

1. Does the writer use a subject-by-subject or a point-by-point pattern of comparison in this essay? Do you think her choice is a good one?

2. Does Carson give equal time to each subject she compares? Does she nevertheless succeed in showing the superiority of the town before the blight over the town after the blight?

3. Explain the writer's purpose in comparing the before and after versions of this imaginary town. Does she achieve that purpose, in your opinion?

DICTION AND VOCABULARY

1. What do you consider to be the overall tone of this essay? (See "Guide to Terms": *Style/Tone.*) Is it effective?

2. In her so-called fable, Carson's word choices (see Guide: *Diction*) are often similar to those found in a fable, fairy-tale, or child's bedtime story. Point to some examples of this style of diction.

READ TO WRITE

1. **Collaborate:** In her essay, Carson presents two descriptions of the same town: first before a change, then after that change. In a group of writers, brainstorm together other people, places, or things that group members have seen or read about that have undergone a distinct change, for better or for worse. List some of these subjects together with some sensory details—sights, sounds, textures, and so on—that you might use to describe them, both before the change and after.

2. **Considering Audience:** When Carson's *Silent Spring,* the book from which this selection is drawn, was first published, pesticide manufacturers tried to discredit her as an alarmist who was overreacting to a harmless product. Write a journal entry from the point of view of the chief executive officer of a company that makes a product that is considered harmful to the environment or to people's health, imitating Carson's subject-by-subject comparison, with the goal of showing the positive effects of your product.

3. **Developing an Essay:** Using the subject-by-subject comparison method, write an essay about an attitude that you held about something that subsequently changed after some event occurred. For example, write about how your attitude changed about a teacher, a parent, a sport, a romantic partner, a style of music, a choice of major, a city, or some other. Use vivid descriptive language and detailed examples to make the before and after comparison clear and state in a conclusion how the change in attitude affected you positively or negatively.

(NOTE: Suggestions for topics requiring development by COMPARISON are on pp. 170–171 at the end of this chapter.)

MARK TWAIN

MARK TWAIN was the pen name of Samuel Clemens (1835–1910). He was born in Missouri and became the first author of importance to emerge from "beyond the Mississippi." Although best known for bringing humor, realism, and Western local color to American fiction, Mark Twain wanted to be remembered as a philosopher and social critic. Still widely read, in most languages and in all parts of the world, are his numerous short stories (his "tall tales," in particular), autobiographical accounts, and novels, especially *Adventures of Huckleberry Finn* (1884). Ernest Hemingway called the last "the best book we've had," an appraisal with which many critics agree.

Two Ways of Seeing a River

"Two Ways of Seeing a River" (editor's title) is from Mark Twain's "Old Times on the Mississippi," which was later expanded and published in book form as *Life on the Mississippi* (1883). It is autobiographical. The prose of this selection is vivid, as is all of Mark Twain's writing, but considerably more reflective in tone than most.

Now when I had mastered the language of this water and had come to know every trifling feature that bordered the great river as familiarly as I knew the letters of the alphabet, I had made a valuable acquisition. But I had lost something, too. I had lost something which could never be restored to me while I lived. All the grace, the beauty, the poetry, had gone out of the majestic river! I still kept in mind a certain wonderful sunset which I witnessed when steamboating was new to me. A broad expanse of the river was turned to blood; in the middle distance the red hue brightened into gold, through which a solitary log came floating, black and conspicuous; in one place a long, slanting mark lay sparkling upon the water; in another the surface was broken by boiling, tumbling rings that were as many-tinted as an opal; where the ruddy flush was faintest was a smooth spot that was covered with graceful circles and radiating lines, ever so delicately traced; the shore on our left was densely wooded, and the somber shadow that fell from this forest was broken in one place by a long, ruffled trail that shone like silver; and high above the forest wall a clean-stemmed dead

1

tree waved a single leafy bough that glowed like a flame in the un-obstructed splendor that was flowing from the sun. There were graceful curves, reflected images, woody heights, soft distances, and over the whole scene, far and near, the dissolving lights drifted steadily, enriching it every passing moment with new marvels of coloring.

I stood like one bewitched. I drank it in, in a speechless rapture. 2 The world was new to me and I had never seen anything like this at home. But as I have said, a day came when I began to cease from noting the glories and the charms which the moon and the sun and the twilight wrought upon the river's face; another day came when I ceased altogether to note them. Then, if that sunset scene had been repeated, I should have looked upon it without rapture and should have commented upon it inwardly after this fashion: "This sun means that we are going to have wind tomorrow; that floating log means that the river is rising, small thanks to it; that slanting mark on the water refers to a bluff reef which is going to kill somebody's steamboat one of these nights, if it keeps on stretching out like that; those tumbling 'boils' show a dissolving bar and a changing chan-nel there; the lines and circles in the slick water over yonder are a warning that that troublesome place is shoaling up dangerously; that silver streak in the shadow of the forest is the 'break' from a new snag and he has located himself in the very best place he could have found to fish for steamboats; that tall dead tree, with a single living branch, is not going to last long, and then how is a body ever going to get through this blind place at night without the friendly old landmark?"

No, the romance and beauty were all gone from the river. All 3 the value any feature of it had for me now was the amount of use-fulness it could furnish toward compassing the safe piloting of a steamboat. Since those days, I have pitied doctors from my heart. What does the lovely flush in a beauty's cheek mean to a doctor but a "break" that ripples above some deadly disease? Are not all her visible charms sown thick with what are to him the signs and symbols of hidden decay? Does he ever see her beauty at all, or doesn't he simply view her professionally and comment upon her unwholesome condition all to himself? And doesn't he sometimes wonder whether he has gained most or lost most by learning his trade?

MEANINGS AND VALUES

1. What is the point of view in Paragraph 1? (See "Guide to Terms": *Point of View.*) Where, and how, does it change in Paragraph 2? Why is the shift important to the author's contrast?

2. Show how the noticeable change of tone between Paragraphs 1 and 2 is related to the change in point of view. (Guide: *Style/Tone.*) Specifically, what changes in style accompany the shift in tone and attitude? How effectively do they all relate to the central theme itself? (Remember that such effects seldom just "happen"; the writer *makes* them happen.)

3. Is the first paragraph primarily objective or subjective? (Guide: *Objective/Subjective.*) How about the latter part of Paragraph 2? Are your answers related to point of view? If so, how?

4. Do you think the last sentence refers only to doctors? Why, or why not?

EXPOSITORY TECHNIQUES

1. Where do you find a second comparison or contrast? Which is it? Is the comparison/contrast made within itself, with something external, or both? Explain.

2. Is the second comparison/contrast closely enough related to the major contrast to justify its use? Why, or why not?

3. In developing the numerous points of the major contrast, would an alternating, point-to-point system have been better? Why, or why not? Show how the author uses organization within the groups to assist in the overall contrast.

4. What is the most noteworthy feature of syntax in Paragraphs 1 and 2? (Guide: *Syntax.*) How effectively does it perform the function intended?

5. What is gained by the apparently deliberate decision to use rhetorical questions only toward the end? (Guide: *Rhetorical Questions.*)

DICTION AND VOCABULARY

1. In what ways do the word choices in Paragraph 1 differ from those in Paragraph 2? (Guide: *Diction.*)

2. Compare the quality of metaphors in the quotation of Paragraph 2 with the quality of those preceding it. (Guide: *Figures of Speech.*) Is the difference justified? Why or why not?

READ TO WRITE

1. **Collaborate:** We spend much of our lives preparing for work, working, and thinking about work. As Twain's essay points out, moreover, work shapes the way we perceive things and respond to them. Work can therefore be an excellent source of writing topics that are

interesting to both writers and readers. Working in a group, add five more questions about work to the following list, and then use it to help generate possible topics for an essay: How do specific kinds of work shape perceptions and values? Are people's outlooks likely to vary according to the kinds of jobs they hold (or want to hold)? How do my work habits, preferences, or experiences set me apart from others (or bring me closer)?

2. **Considering Audience:** Would readers of Twain's era, used to traveling by steamboat, horse-drawn carriage, steam-powered trains, and horseback, respond differently than readers of today to this essay? Write a brief essay of your own (one to three paragraphs) explaining why readers might or might not respond differently. In doing so, consider the ways in which modern means of transportation affect our perceptions and values.

3. **Developing an Essay:** Twain's essay not only describes two scenes but also explains what changes in outlook and experience make them seem different. Prepare an essay of your own with a similar purpose. Choose a scene or event that you have observed more than once and from differing perspectives. Explain to readers the ways in which the scene appeared different and what it was about your perceptions that accounted for the difference.

(NOTE: Suggestions for topics requiring development by COMPARISON are on pp. 170–171 at the end of this chapter.)

BRUCE CATTON

> Bruce Catton (1899–1978) was a Civil War specialist whose early
> career included reporting for various newspapers. In 1954 he re-
> ceived both the Pulitzer Prize for historical work and the National
> Book Award. He served as director of information for the United
> States Department of Commerce and wrote many books, includ-
> ing *Mr. Lincoln's Army* (1951), *Glory Road* (1952), *A Stillness at
> Appomattox* (1953), *This Hallowed Ground* (1956), *America Goes to
> War* (1958), *The Coming Fury* (1961), *Terrible Swift Sword* (1963),
> *Never Call Retreat* (1966), *Waiting for the Morning Train: An Ameri-
> can Boyhood* (1972), and *Gettysburg: The Final Fury* (1974). For five
> years, Catton edited *American Heritage.*

Grant and Lee: A Study in Contrasts

"Grant and Lee: A Study in Contrasts" was written as a chapter of
The American Story, a collection of essays by noted historians.
In this study, as in most of his other writing, Catton does more
than recount the facts of history: he shows the significance within
them. It is a carefully constructed essay, using contrast and comparison as the entire framework for his explanation.

When Ulysses S. Grant and Robert E. Lee met in the parlor of   1
a modest house at Appomattox Court House, Virginia, on
April 9, 1865, to work out the terms for the surrender of Lee's Army
of Northern Virginia, a great chapter in American life came to a
close, and a great new chapter began.

These men were bringing the Civil War to its virtual finish.   2
To be sure, other armies had yet to surrender, and for a few days the
fugitive Confederate government would struggle desperately and
vainly, trying to find some way to go on living now that its chief
support was gone. But in effect it was all over when Grant and Lee
signed the papers. And the little room where they wrote out the
terms was the scene of one of the most poignant, dramatic contrasts
in American history.

They were two strong men these oddly different generals, and   3
they represented the strengths of two conflicting currents that,
through them, had come into final collision.

Back of Robert E. Lee was the notion that the old aristocratic   4
concept might somehow survive and be dominant in American life.

Lee was tidewater Virginia, and in his background were family,   5
culture, and tradition . . . the age of chivalry transplanted to a New

World which was making its own legends and its own myths. He embodied a way of life that had come down through the age of knighthood and the English country squire. America was a land that was beginning all over again, dedicated to nothing much more complicated than the rather hazy belief that all men had equal rights and should have an equal chance in the world. In such a land Lee stood for the feeling that it was somehow of advantage to human society to have a pronounced inequality in the social structure. There should be a leisure class, backed by ownership of land; in turn, society itself should be keyed to the land as the chief source of wealth and influence. It would bring forth (according to this ideal) a class of men with a strong sense of obligation to the community; men who lived not to gain advantage for themselves, but to meet the solemn obligations which had been laid on them by the very fact that they were privileged. From them the country would get its leadership; to them it could look for the higher values—of thought, of conduct, of personal deportment—to give it strength and virtue.

Lee embodied the noblest element of this aristocratic ideal.   6
Through him, the landed nobility justified itself. For four years, the Southern states had fought a desperate war to uphold the ideals for which Lee stood. In the end, it almost seemed as if the Confederacy fought for Lee; as if he himself was the Confederacy . . . the best thing that the way of life for which the Confederacy stood could ever have to offer. He had passed into legend before Appomattox. Thousands of tired, underfed, poorly clothed Confederate soldiers, long since past the simple enthusiasm of the early days of the struggle, somehow considered Lee the symbol of everything for which they had been willing to die. But they could not quite put this feeling into words. If the Lost Cause, sanctified by so much heroism and so many deaths, had a living justification, its justification was General Lee.

Grant, the son of a tanner on the Western frontier, was every-   7
thing Lee was not. He had come up the hard way and embodied nothing in particular except the eternal toughness and sinewy fiber of the men who grew up beyond the mountains. He was one of a body of men who owed reverence and obeisance to no one, who were self-reliant to a fault, who cared hardly anything for the past but who had a sharp eye for the future.

These frontier men were the precise opposites of the tidewater   8
aristocrats. Back of them, in the great surge that had taken people over the Alleghenies and into the opening Western country, there was a deep, implicit dissatisfaction with a past that had settled into grooves. They stood for democracy, not from any reasoned

conclusion about the proper ordering of human society, but simply because they had grown up in the middle of democracy and knew how it worked. Their society might have privileges, but they would be privileges each man had won for himself. Forms and patterns meant nothing. No man was born to anything, except perhaps to a chance to show how far he could rise. Life was competition.

Yet along with this feeling had come a deep sense of belonging to a national community. The Westerner who developed a farm, opened a shop, or set up in business as a trader could hope to prosper only as his own community prospered—and his community ran from the Atlantic to the Pacific and from Canada down to Mexico. If the land was settled, with towns and highways and accessible markets, he could better himself. He saw his fate in terms of the nation's own destiny. As its horizons expanded, so did his. He had, in other words, an acute dollars-and-cents stake in the continued growth and development of his country. 9

And that, perhaps, is where the contrast between Grant and Lee becomes most striking. The Virginia aristocrat, inevitably, saw himself in relation to his own region. He lived in a static society which could endure almost anything except change. Instinctively, his first loyalty would go to the locality in which that society existed. He would fight to the limit of endurance to defend it, because in defending it he was defending everything that gave his own life its deepest meaning. 10

The Westerner, on the other hand, would fight with an equal tenacity for the broader concept of society. He fought so because everything he lived by was tied to growth, expansion, and a constantly widening horizon. What he lived by would survive or fall with the nation itself. He could not possibly stand by unmoved in the face of an attempt to destroy the Union. He would combat it with everything he had, because he could only see it as an effort to cut the ground out from under his feet. 11

So Grant and Lee were in complete contrast, representing two diametrically opposed elements in American life. Grant was the modern man emerging; beyond him, ready to come on the stage, was the great age of steel and machinery, of crowded cities and a restless burgeoning vitality. Lee might have ridden down from the old age of chivalry, lance in hand, silken banner fluttering over his head. Each man was the perfect champion of his cause, drawing both his strengths and his weaknesses from the people he led. 12

Yet it was not all contrast, after all. Different as they were—in background, in personality, in underlying aspiration—these two 13 great soldiers had much in common. Under everything else, they were marvelous fighters. Furthermore, their fighting qualities were really very much alike.

Each man had, to begin with, the great virtue of utter tenacity   14
and fidelity. Grant fought his way down the Mississippi Valley in spite of acute personal discouragement and profound military handicaps. Lee hung on in the trenches at Petersburg after hope itself had died. In each man there was an indomitable quality . . . the born fighter's refusal to give up as long as he can still remain on his feet and lift his two fists.

Daring and resourcefulness they had, too: the ability to think   15
faster and move faster than the enemy. These were the qualities which gave Lee the dazzling campaigns of Second Manassas and Chancellorsville and won Vicksburg for Grant.

Lastly, and perhaps greatest of all, there was the ability, at the   16
end, to turn quickly from war to peace once the fighting was over. Out of the way these two men behaved at Appomattox came the possibility of a peace of reconciliation. It was a possibility not wholly realized, in the years to come, but which did, in the end, help the two sections to become one nation again . . . after a war whose bitterness might have seemed to make such a reunion wholly impossible. No part of either man's life became him more than the part he played in their brief meeting in the McLean house at Appomattox. Their behavior there put all succeeding generations of Americans in their debt. Two great Americans, Grant and Lee— very different, yet under everything very much alike. Their encounter at Appomattox was one of the great moments of American history.

MEANINGS AND VALUES

1. Clarify the assertions that through Lee "the landed nobility justified itself" and that "if the Lost Cause . . . had a living justification," it was General Lee (Par. 6). Why are these assertions pertinent to the central theme?

2. Does it seem reasonable that "thousands of tired, underfed, poorly clothed Confederate soldiers" (Par. 6) had been willing to fight for the aristocratic system in which they would never have had even a chance to be aristocrats? Why or why not? Can you think of more likely reasons why they were willing to fight?

3.   What countries of the world have recently been so torn by internal war and bitterness that reunion has seemed, or still seems, impossible? Do you see any basic differences between the trouble in those countries and that in America at the time of the Civil War?

4.   The author calls Lee a symbol (Par. 6). Was Grant also a symbol? If so, of what? (See "Guide to Terms": *Symbol*.) How would you classify this kind of symbolism?

EXPOSITORY TECHNIQUES

1.   Make an informal list of paragraph numbers from 3 to 16, and note by each number whether the paragraph is devoted primarily to Lee, to Grant, or to direct comparison or contrast of the two. This chart will show you Catton's basic pattern of development. (Notice, for instance, how the broad information of Paragraphs 4–6 and 7–9 seems almost to "funnel" down through the narrower summaries in Paragraphs 10 and 11 into Paragraph 12, where the converging elements meet and the contrast is made specific.)

2.   What new technique of development is started in Paragraph 13?

3.   What is gained, or lost, by using one sentence for Paragraph 3? For Paragraph 4?

4.   How many paragraphs does the introduction comprise? How successfully does it fulfill the three basic requirements of a good introduction? (Guide: *Introductions*.)

5.   Show how Catton has constructed the beginning of each paragraph so that there is a smooth transition from the one preceding it. (Guide: *Transition*.)

6.   What seems to be the author's attitude toward Grant and Lee? Show how his tone reflects this attitude. (Guide: *Style/Tone*.)

DICTION AND VOCABULARY

1.   Why would a use of colloquialisms have been inconsistent with the tone of this writing?

2.   List or mark all metaphors in Paragraphs 1, 3, 5, 7–11, and 16. (Guide: *Figures of Speech*.) Comment on their general effectiveness.

3.   If you are not already familiar with the following words, study their meanings as given in the dictionary and as used in this essay: *virtual, poignant* (Par. 2); *concept* (4); *sinewy, obeisance* (7); *implicit* (8); *tenacity* (11); *diametrically, burgeoning* (12); *aspiration* (13); *fidelity, profound, indomitable* (14); *succeeding* (16).

READ TO WRITE

1. **Collaborating:** Catton focuses on a dramatic moment in history and explains its long-range significance. Drawing on his approach, list some dramatic moments in history. In a group, compare your lists. Does your definition of "dramatic moment" match those of other group members? Decide as a group on one moment you all agree is dramatic and, in a short essay, explain its long-range significance.

2. **Considering Audience:** Ask yourself how much you knew about the topic of "Grant and Lee" before you began reading the essay, then go through the text and highlight sections that present information that was new to you. To what extent do you think that your initial knowledge of the topic was similar to that of most readers? Why? Study the ways Catton introduces information that most readers are likely to be unfamiliar with, and identify techniques you could use to present new information in your own writing.

3. **Developing an Essay:** One special achievement of Catton's "Grant and Lee: A Study in Contrasts" is its portrait of the two generals as embodiments of contrasting societies and cultures. Consider using this strategy in an essay offering a contrast between ideas, values, or cultures by means of a contrast between people who embody the differences. The strategy can be applied to a wide variety of subjects, not simply to public or political ones. You might use it to talk about different parenting strategies, for example, or about various religious beliefs or value systems.

(NOTE: Suggestions for topics requiring development by COMPARISON are on pp. 170–171 at the end of this chapter.)

BILL McKIBBEN

Bill McKibben grew up in Lexington, Massachusetts, and attended Harvard University, where he was editor of the Harvard Crimson newspaper. After college he became a staff writer for the New Yorker magazine. When he left the magazine, he moved to the Adirondack Mountains in New York to work as a writer. He has published numerous books beginning with The End of Nature (1989) and The Age of Missing Information (1992) and including Deep Economy: The Wealth of Communities and the Durable Future (2007), The Bill McKibben Reader (2008), Eaarth: Making a Life on a Tough New Planet (2010), and The Global Warming Reader (2011). He has written articles for many magazines, including The Atlantic, Harper's, Rolling Stone, and Outside.

Old MacDonald Had a Farmer's Market

To most Americans, Henry David Thoreau represents an ideal of self-sufficiency, simplicity, and independence for living on his own on the shores of rural Walden Pond, as recorded in his book, Walden (1854). McKibben contrasts this view of Thoreau with the reality of Thoreau's life in a nineteenth-century community. He also takes a further step, comparing the earlier ideas of community and individuality with our modern views, explaining why our modern concepts may be hiding an important truth: "we're built to rely on each other."

Generations of college freshmen, asked to read *Walden*, have sputtered with indignation when they learned that Henry David went back to Concord for dinner with his family every week or two. He's *cheating*; his grand experiment is a fraud. This outrage is a useful tactic; it prevents them from having to grapple with the most important (and perhaps the most difficult) book in the American canon, one that asks impossibly searching questions about the emptiness of a consumer economy, the vacuity of an information-soaked era. But it also points to something else: Thoreau, our apostle of solitary, individual self-reliance, out in his cabin with his hoe and his beans, the most determinedly asocial man of his time—nonetheless was immersed in his community to a degree few people today can comprehend.

Consider the sheer number of people who happened to drop by the cabin of an obscure eccentric. "I had three chairs in my house; one for solitude, two for friendship, three for society," he writes.

Often more visitors came than could sit—sometimes twenty or thirty at a time. "Half-witted men from the almshouse," busybodies who "pried into my cupboard and bed when I was out," a French-Canadian woodchopper, a runaway slave "whom I helped to forward toward the north star," doctors, lawyers, the old and infirm and the timid, the self-styled reformers. It's not that Thoreau was necessarily a cheerful host—there were visitors "who did not know when their visit had terminated, though I went about my business again, answering them from greater and greater remoteness." Instead, it was simply a visiting age—as most of human history has been a visiting age, and every human culture a visiting culture.

Until ours. I doubt if many people reading these words have 3 had a spontaneous visit from a neighbor in the past week—less than a fifth of Americans report visiting regularly with friends and neighbors, and the percentage is declining steadily. The number of close friends that an American claims has dropped steadily for the last fifty years too; three-quarters of us don't know our *next-door neighbors*. Even the people who share our houses are becoming strangers: *The Wall Street Journal* reported recently that "major builders and top architects are walling off space. They're touting one-person 'internet alcoves,' locked-door 'away rooms,' and his-and-her offices on opposite ends of the house." The new floor plans, says the director of research for the National Association of Home Builders, are "good for the dysfunctional family." Or, as another executive put it, these are the perfect homes for "families that don't want anything to do with one another." Compared to these guys, Thoreau with his three-chair cabin was practically Martha Stewart.

Every culture has its pathologies, and ours is self-reliance. 4 From some mix of our frontier past, our *Little House on the Prairie* heritage, our Thoreauvian desire for solitude, and our amazing wealth we've derived a level of independence never seen before on this round earth. We've built an economy where we need no one else; with a credit card, you can harvest the world's bounty from the privacy of your room. And we've built a culture much the same—the dream houses those architects build, needless to say, come with a plasma screen in every room. As long as we can go on earning good money in our own tiny niche, we don't need a helping hand from a soul—save, of course, from the invisible hand that cups us all in its benign grip.

There are a couple of problems with this fine scenario, of course. 5 One is: we're miserable. Reported levels of happiness and life-satisfaction are locked in long-term one-way declines, almost certainly *because* of this lack of connection. Does this sound subjective and airy? Find one of the tens of millions of Americans who don't belong to *anything* and convince them to join a church, a softball league, a bird-watching group. In the next year their mortality—the risk that they will die in the next year—falls by half.

The other trouble is that our self-reliance is actually a reliance 6
on cheap fossil fuel and the economy it's built. Take that away—either because we start to run out of oil, or because global warming forces us to stop using it in current quantities—and our vaunted independence will start to lurch like a Hummer with four flat tires. Just think for a moment about that world and then decide if you want to live on an acre all your own in the outermost ring of suburbs.

The idea of self-reliance is so deep in our psyches, however, that 7
even when we attempt to escape from the unhappy and unsustainable cul-de-sac of our society, we're likely to turn toward yet more "independence." The "back-to-the-land" movement, for instance, often added the words "by myself." Think about how proudly a certain kind of person talks about his "off-the-grid" life—he makes his own energy and grows his own food, he can deal with whatever the world throws at him. One such person may be left-wing in politics (à la Scott and Helen Nearing); another may be conservative. But they are united in their lack of need for the larger world. Not even to school their kids—they'll take care of that as well.

Such folks are admirable, of course—they have a wide variety 8
of skills now missing in most Americans; they're able to amuse themselves; they work hard. But as an ideal, especially an economic ideal, that radical self-reliance strikes me as being almost as empty as the consumer society from which it dissents. Consider, for instance, the idea of growing all your own food. It's clearly better than relying on food from thousands of miles away—from our current industrialized food economy, which figures "it's always summer somewhere" and so orders take-out from that distant field every night of the year. Compared with that, an enormous garden and a root cellar full of all you'll need for the winter is virtue incarnate. But if you believe in many of the (entirely plausible) horror stories about what's to come—peak oil, climate change—then the world ends with you standing shotgun in hand above your vegetable patch, protecting your carrots from the poaching urban horde.

Contrast that with another vision, one taking shape in at least a 9
few places around the country: a matrix of small farmers growing food for their local areas. Farmers' markets are the fastest-growing

part of our food economy, with sales showing double-digit growth annually. Partly that's because people want good food (all kinds of people: immigrants and ethnic Americans tend to be the most avid farmers' market shoppers). And partly it's because they want more *company*. One team of sociologists reported recently that shoppers at farmers' markets engaged in ten times more conversations per visit than customers in supermarkets. I spent the past winter eating only from my valley; a little of the food I grew myself, but the idea of my experiment was to see what remained of the agricultural infrastructure that had once supported this place. And the payoff was not only a delicious six months, but also a deep network of new friends, a much stronger sense of the cultural geography of my place.

Or consider energy. Since the 1970s, a particular breed of noble   10 ex-hippie has been building "off-the-grid" homes, often relying on solar panels. This has been important work—they've figured out many of the techniques and technologies that we desperately need to get free of our climate change predicament. But the most exciting new gadget is a home-scale inverter, one that allows you to send the power your rooftop generates down the line instead of down into the basement. Where the isolated system has a stack of batteries, the grid-tied solar panel uses the whole region's electric system as its battery: my electric meter spins merrily backward all afternoon because while the sun shines I'm a utility; then at night I draw from somewhere else. It's a two-way flow, in the same way that the internet allows ideas to bounce in many directions.

You can do the same kind of calculation with almost any com-   11 modity. Music doesn't need to come from Nashville or Hollywood on a small disc, for instance. But you don't have to produce it all yourself either. More fun to join with the neighbors, to make music together or to listen to the local stars. A hundred years ago, Iowa had 1,300 opera houses. Radio doesn't need to come from the ClearChannel headquarters in some Texas office park; new low-power FM lets valleys make their own. Even currency can become a joint local project—all it takes is the trust that underwrites any system of money. In hundreds of communities, people are trying to build that trust locally, with money that only works within the region.

Thinking this way won't be easy. We're used to independence   12 as the prime virtue—so used to it that three quarters of American Christians believe the phrase "God helps those who help themselves" comes from the Bible, instead of Ben Franklin. "Love your neighbor as yourself" is harder advice, but sweeter and more sage.

We don't need to live on communes (though more and more old people are finding themselves enrolling in "retirement communities" that are gray-haired, upscale versions). But we will, I think, need to figure out how to stop relying on both oil and ourselves, and instead learn the lesson that the other primates and the other human cultures never forgot: we're built to rely on each other.

———————————

Meanings and Values

1.   State what the writer considers as our culture's pathology.

2.   a. Explain why you think most readers would be likely at first to agree or disagree with the writer's opinions about the pathology.

   b. What reasons does the writer offer readers for agreeing with his point of view?

3.   What are the ecological effects of self-reliance, according to this essay?

Expository Techniques

1.   Specify the examples this essay offers of our culture's pathology. Include examples the writer offers of the negative effects of this pathology.

2.   What words does the writer use in the opening sentences of Paragraphs 3, 6, 9, and 10 to emphasize comparisons or contrasts? (See "Guide to Terms": *Diction*.)

3.   Which paragraphs does McKibben devote primarily to discussing the past and which to the present?

Diction and Vocabulary

1.   Identify the transition words or repeated words and phrases the writer uses in Paragraphs 2, 3, and 5–10 to identify the different topics he is explaining and to indicate the stages of his explanation. (Guide: *Diction*.)

2.   Identify the following figures of speech and discuss their use: *allusion* (Par. 3); *simile* (6); and *allusion* (7) (Guide: *Figures of Speech*).

3.   If you do not know the meaning of some of the following words, look them up in a dictionary: *indignation, vacuity, asocial* (Par. 1); *eccentric, almshouse* (2); *spontaneous, alcoves* (3); *bounty, niche, benign* (4); *scenario* (5); *psyches, cul-de-sac* (7); *incarnate, poaching* (8); *matrix, infrastructure* (9); *predicament* (10); *sage* (12).

READ TO WRITE

1. **Collaborating:** Working in a group, survey each individual to see how often each week they drop by to visit someone unannounced. Then see how often their families do the same. Write together a brief report summarizing the visiting habits of your group.

2. **Considering Audience:** Some readers are likely to have a negative opinion of McKibben's view of "self-reliance." Others may agree with his outlook. Write two paragraphs, each one summarizing the different reactions readers may have and explaining the probable reasons behind these reactions.

3. **Developing an Essay:** McKibben looks at two different and often contrasting values: self-reliance and community. Choose another pair: nationalism and internationalism, for example; humility and reasonable pride; self-interest and charity; hard work and leisure; or any others you consider important. Create an essay comparing and contrasting these values, paying special attention to their positive and negative outcomes for our society.

(NOTE: Suggestions for topics requiring development by COMPARISON are on pp. 170–171 at the end of this chapter.)

Issues and Ideas

Evaluating Traditions

- Bharati Mukherjee, *Two Ways to Belong in America*
- William Ouchi, *Japanese and American Workers*

BHARATI MUKHERJEE

A native of Calcutta (now Kolkata), India, BHARATI MUKHERJEE has also lived in Europe, Canada, and the United States. She earned a B.A. from the University of Calcutta in 1959 and received an M.F.A. from the University of Iowa Writer's Workshop and a Ph.D. from that university's department of comparative literature. She and her husband, Clark Blaise, co-authored the memoir *Days and Nights in Calcutta* (1977). Mukherjee is the author of many other books, including *The Middleman and Other Stories* (1988), *Desirable Daughters* (2002), and *The Tree Bride* (2004). She is currently a professor of English at the University of California, Berkeley.

Two Ways to Belong in America

Bharati Mukherjee's fiction often contains female characters who are torn between two cultures. This essay, originally published in the *New York Times* on September 22, 1996, responds to legislation proposed at that time to deny government benefits to immigrants who lived in the United States legally but did not apply for citizenship. The essay addresses the issue by examining two kinds of immigrants, Mukherjee herself and her sister, Mira.

This is a tale of two sisters from Calcutta, Mira and Bharati, who have lived in the United States for some 35 years, but who find themselves on different sides in the current debate over the status of immigrants. I am an American citizen and she is not. I am moved that thousands of long-term residents are finally taking the oath of citizenship. She is not.

Mira arrived in Detroit in 1960 to study child psychology and preschool education. I followed her a year later to study creative writing at the University of Iowa. When we left India, we were almost

1

2

identical in appearance and attitude. We dressed alike, in saris; we expressed identical views on politics, social issues, love, and marriage in the same Calcutta convent-school accent. We would endure our two years in America, secure our degrees, then return to India to marry the grooms of our father's choosing.

Instead, Mira married an Indian student in 1962 who was getting his business administration degree at Wayne State University. They soon acquired the labor certifications necessary for the green card of hassle-free residence and employment.

3

Mira still lives in Detroit, works in the Southfield, Mich., school system, and has become nationally recognized for her contributions in the fields of pre-school education and parent-teacher relationships. After 36 years as a legal immigrant in this country, she clings passionately to her Indian citizenship and hopes to go home to India when she retires.

4

In Iowa City in 1963, I married a fellow student, an American of Canadian parentage. Because of the accident of his North Dakota birth, I bypassed labor-certification requirements and the race-related "quota" system that favored the applicant's country of origin over his or her merit. I was prepared for (and even welcomed) the emotional strain that came with marrying outside my ethnic community. In 33 years of marriage, we have lived in every part of North America. By choosing a husband who was not my father's selection, I was opting for fluidity, self-invention, blue jeans and T-shirts, and renouncing 3,000 years (at least) of caste-observant, "pure culture" marriage in the Mukherjee family. My books have often been read as unapologetic (and in some quarters overenthusiastic) texts for cultural and psychological "mongrelization." It's a word I celebrate.

5

Mira and I have stayed sisterly close by phone. In our regular Sunday morning conversations, we are unguardedly affectionate. I am her only blood relative on this continent. We expect to see each other through the looming crises of aging and ill health without being asked. Long before Vice President Gore's "Citizenship U.S.A." drive, we'd had our polite arguments over the ethics of retaining an overseas citizenship while expecting permanent protection and economic benefits that come with living and working in America.

6

Like well-raised sisters, we never said what was really on our minds, but we probably pitied one another. She, for the lack of structure in my life, the erasure of Indianness, the absence of an unvarying daily core. I, for the narrowness of her perspective, her

7

uninvolvement with the mythic depths or the superficial pop culture of this society. But, now, with the scapegoatings of "aliens" (documented or illegal) on the increase, and the targeting of long-term legal immigrants like Mira for new scrutiny and new self-consciousness, she and I find ourselves unable to maintain the same polite discretion. We were always unacknowledged adversaries, and we are now, more than ever, sisters.

"I feel used," Mira raged on the phone the other night. "I feel   8
manipulated and discarded. This is such an unfair way to treat a person who was invited to stay and work here because of her talent. My employer went to the I.N.S. and petitioned for the labor certification. For over 30 years, I've invested my creativity and professional skills into the improvement of *this* country's pre-school system. I've obeyed all the rules, I've paid my taxes, I love my work, I love my students, I love the friends I've made. How dare America now change its rules in midstream? If America wants to make new rules curtailing benefits of legal immigrants, they should apply only to immigrants who arrive after those rules are already in place."

To my ears, it sounded like the description of a long-enduring,   9
comfortable yet loveless marriage, without risk or recklessness. Have we the right to demand, and to expect, that we be loved? (That, to me, is the subtext of the arguments by immigration advocates.) My sister is an expatriate, professionally generous and creative, socially courteous and gracious, and that's as far as her Americanization can go. She is here to maintain an identity, not to transform it.

I asked her if she would follow the example of others who have   10
decided to become citizens because of the anti-immigration bills in Congress. And here, she surprised me. "If America wants to play the manipulative game, I'll play it, too," she snapped. "I'll become a U.S. citizen for now, then change back to India when I'm ready to go home. I feel some kind of irrational attachment to India that I don't to America. Until all this hysteria against legal immigrants, I was totally happy. Having my green card meant I could visit any place in the world I wanted to and then come back to a job that's satisfying and that I do very well."

In one family, from two sisters alike as peas in a pod, there   11
could not be a wider divergence of immigrant experience. America spoke to me—I married it—I embraced the demotion from expatriate aristocrat to immigrant nobody, surrendering those thousands of years of "pure culture," the saris, the delightfully accented English. She retained them all. Which of us is the freak?

Mira's voice, I realize, is the voice not just of the immigrant 12
South Asian community but of an immigrant community of the millions who have stayed rooted in one job, one city, one house, one
ancestral culture, one cuisine, for the entirety of their productive
years. She speaks for greater numbers than I possibly can. Only
the fluency of her English and the anger, rather than fear, born of
confidence from her education, differentiate her from the seam-
stresses, the domestics, the technicians, the shop owners, the millions of hard-working but effectively silenced documented
immigrants as well as their less fortunate "illegal" brothers and
sisters.

Nearly 20 years ago, when I was living in my husband's ances- 13
tral homeland of Canada, I was always well-employed but never allowed to feel part of the local Quebec or larger Canadian society.
Then, through a Green Paper that invited a national referendum on
the unwanted side effects of "nontraditional" immigration, the
Government officially turned against its immigrant communities,
particularly those from South Asia.

I felt then the same sense of betrayal that Mira feels now. I will 14
never forget the pain of that sudden turning, and the casual racist
outbursts the Green Paper elicited. That sense of betrayal had its
desired effect and drove me, and thousands like me, from the
country.

Mira and I differ, however, in the ways in which we hope to 15
interact with the country that we have chosen to live in. She is hap-
pier to live in America as expatriate Indian than as an immigrant
American. I need to feel like a part of the community I have
adopted (as I tried to feel in Canada as well). I need to put roots
down, to vote and make the difference that I can. The price that the
immigrant willingly pays, and that the exile avoids, is the trauma
of self-transformation.

MEANINGS AND VALUES

1. Restate the ways in which, when they left India, the two sisters were
    "almost identical in appearance and attitude" (Par. 2).

2. Explain how the sisters' U.S. citizenship statuses differ.

3. In your opinion, what is the significance of the essay's concluding
    sentence?

EXPOSITORY TECHNIQUES

1. Locate the transitional sentence in Paragraph 15 that signals a contrast between the writer and her sister.

2. This essay is an example of a point-by-point comparison. What are the points? Do you think the strategy succeeds?

3. Does the writer favor the experience of one sister over that of the other? Explain.

DICTION AND VOCABULARY

1. In Paragraph 11, the writer uses the cliché "alike as peas in a pod" (see "Guide to Terms": *Clichés*). What other phrase could she have used that would have been fresher and more effective?

2. In the last sentence of her essay, Mukherjee makes a distinction between an immigrant and an exile. With which term would the writer rather be identified, and why?

3. If you do not already know the meaning of some of the following words or phrases, look them up in a dictionary: *saris* (Par. 2); *green card* (3); *renouncing* (5); *curtailing* (8); *referendum* (13).

READ TO WRITE

1. **Collaborating:** In a group, discuss the question of which sister has made the right choice and why. Or discuss other similar experiences of first-generation immigrants that you know or have read about. Prepare a report that compares and contrasts your group's responses.

2. **Considering Audience:** Mukherjee writes for an educated, U.S. audience of readers of the *New York Times* who was familiar with the legislation she is describing. Do you think her essay as it stands would resonate well with an audience unfamiliar with the issue at stake? How would she modify her essay for such an audience?

3. **Developing an Essay:** In the last sentence of her essay, the writer refers to "the trauma of self-transformation." Write a point-by-point comparison or contrast essay in which you show how you experienced a self-transformation—traumatic or otherwise—as a result of a physical relocation from one city or country to another. (Alternatively, the relocation could be a move from high school to college or from one workplace to another.)

(NOTE: Suggestions for topics requiring development by COMPARISON are on pp. 170–171 at the end of this chapter.)

WILLIAM OUCHI

Professor and author WILLIAM OUCHI, born and raised in Honolulu, Hawaii, earned an M.B.A. from Stanford University and a Ph.D. in business administration from the University of Chicago. He currently teaches at the Anderson School of Business Management, University of California, Los Angeles. A recognized expert on management styles, Ouchi has also extensively studied the issues of school effectiveness and school district administration. His recent books on that subject are *Making Schools Work* (2003) and *The Secret of TSL* (2009).

Japanese and American Workers

Large companies in Japan often stress consensus as a way of arriving at decisions, and managers serve as consensus-builders rather than as authoritarians. This harmonious management style has long fascinated U.S. business experts. In his best-selling book in which this selection appears, *Theory Z* (1981), Ouchi considers company management styles in Japan and in the United States.

Perhaps the most difficult aspect of the Japanese for Westerners to comprehend is the strong orientation to collective values, particularly a collective sense of responsibility. Let me illustrate with an anecdote about a visit to a new factory in Japan owned and operated by an American electronics company. The American company, a particularly creative firm, frequently attracts attention within the business community for its novel approaches to planning, organizational design, and management systems. As a consequence of this corporate style, the parent company determined to make a thorough study of Japanese workers and to design a plant that would combine the best of East and West. In their study they discovered that Japanese firms almost never make use of individual work incentives, such as piecework or even individual performance appraisal tied to salary increases. They concluded that rewarding individual achievement and individual ability is always a good thing.

In the final assembly area of their new plant long lines of young Japanese women wired together electronic products on a piece-rate system: The more you wired, the more you got paid. About two months after opening, the head foreladies approached the plant manager. "Honorable plant manager," they said humbly as they bowed, "we are embarrassed to be so forward, but we must speak to you because all of the girls have threatened to quit work this Friday." (To have this happen, of course, would be a great disaster for all concerned.) "Why," they wanted to know, "can't our plant have the same compensation system as other Japanese companies? When you hire a new girl, her starting wage should be fixed by her age. An eighteen-year-old should be paid more than a sixteen-year-old. Every year on her birthday, she should receive an automatic increase in pay. The idea that any one of us can be more productive than another must be wrong, because none of us in final assembly could make a thing unless all of the other people in the plant had done their jobs right first. To single one person out as being more productive is wrong and is also personally humiliating to us." The company changed its compensation system to the Japanese model.

Another American company in Japan had installed a suggestion system much as we have in the United States. Individual workers were encouraged to place suggestions to improve productivity into special boxes. For an accepted idea the individual received a bonus amounting to some fraction of the productivity savings realized from his or her suggestion. After a period of six months, not a single suggestion had been submitted. The American managers were puzzled. They had heard many stories of the inventiveness, the commitment and the loyalty of Japanese workers, yet not one suggestion to improve productivity had appeared. 3

The managers approached some of the workers and asked why the suggestion system had not been used. The answer: "No one can come up with a work improvement idea alone. We work together, and any ideas that one of us may have are actually developed by watching others and talking to others. If one of us was singled out for being responsible for such an idea, it would embarrass all of us." The company changed to a group suggestion system, in which workers collectively submitted suggestions. Bonuses were paid to groups which would save bonus money until the end of the year for a party at a restaurant or, if there was enough money, for family vacations together. The suggestions and productivity improvements rained down on the plant. 4

One can interpret these examples in two quite different ways. Perhaps the Japanese commitment to collective values is an anachronism that does not fit with modern industrialism but brings economic success despite that collectivism. Collectivism seems to be inimical to the kind of maverick creativity exemplified in Benjamin Franklin, Thomas Edison, and John D. Rockefeller. Collectivism does not seem to provide the individual incentive to excel which has made a great 5 success of American enterprise. Entirely apart from its economic effects, collectivism implies a loss of individuality, a loss of the freedom to be different, to hold fundamentally different values from others.

The second interpretation of the examples is that the Japanese 6 collectivism is economically efficient. It causes people to work well together and to encourage one another to better efforts. Industrial life requires interdependence of one person on another. But a less obvious but far-reaching implication of the Japanese collectivism for economic performance has to do with accountability.

In the Japanese mind, collectivism is neither a corporate or indi- 7 vidual goal to strive for nor a slogan to pursue. Rather, the nature of things operates so that nothing of consequence occurs as a result of individual effort. Everything important in life happens as a result of teamwork or collective effort. Therefore, to attempt to assign individual credit or blame to results is unfounded. A Japanese professor of accounting, a brilliant scholar trained at Carnegie-Mellon University who teaches now in Tokyo, remarked that the status of accounting systems in Japanese industry is primitive compared to those in the United States. Profit centers, transfer prices, and computerized information systems are barely known even in the largest Japanese companies, whereas they are commonplace in even small United States organizations. Though not at all surprised at the difference in accounting systems, I was not at all sure that the Japanese were primitive. In fact, I thought their system a good deal more efficient than ours.

Most American companies have basically two accounting sys- 8 tems. One system summarizes the overall financial state to inform stockholders, bankers, and other outsiders. That system is not of interest here. The other system, called the managerial or cost accounting system, exists for an entirely different reason. It measures in detail all of the particulars of transactions between departments, divisions, and key individuals in the organization, for the purpose of untangling the interdependencies between people. When, for example, two departments share one truck for deliveries, the cost accounting system charges each department for part of the cost of maintaining the truck and driver, so that at the end of the year, the performance of each department can be individually assessed, and the better department's manager can receive a larger raise. Of course, all of this information processing costs money, and furthermore may lead to arguments between the departments over whether the costs charged to each are fair.

In a Japanese company a short-run assessment of individual per- 9 formance is not wanted, so the company can save the considerable expense of collecting and processing all of that information. Companies still keep track of which department uses a truck how often and for what purposes, but like-minded people can interpret some simple numbers for themselves and adjust their behavior accordingly. Those insisting upon clear and precise measurement for the purpose of advancing individual interests must have an elaborate information system. Industrial life, however, is essentially integrated and interdependent. No one builds an automobile alone, no one carries through a banking transaction alone. In a sense the Japanese value of collectivism fits naturally into an industrial setting, whereas the Western individualism provides constant conflicts. The image that comes to mind is of Chaplin's silent film *Modern Times* in which the apparently insignificant hero played by Chaplin successfully fights against the unfeeling machinery of industry. Modern industrial life can be aggravating, even hostile, or natural: All depends on the fit between our culture and our technology.

The *shinkansen* or "bullet train" speeds across the rural areas of   10 Japan giving a quick view of cluster after cluster of farmhouses surrounded by rice paddies. This particular pattern did not develop purely by chance, but as a consequence of the technology peculiar to the growing of rice, the staple of the Japanese diet. The growing of rice requires construction and maintenance of an irrigation system, something that takes many hands to build. More importantly, the planting and the harvesting of rice can only be done efficiently with the cooperation of twenty or more people. The "bottom line" is that a single family working alone cannot produce enough rice to survive, but a dozen families working together can produce a surplus. Thus the Japanese have had to develop the capacity to work together in harmony, no matter what the forces of disagreement or social disintegration, in order to survive.

Japan is a nation built entirely on the tips of giant, suboceanic   11 volcanoes. Little of the land is flat and suitable for agriculture. Terraced hillsides make use of every available square foot of arable land. Small homes built very close together further conserve the land. Japan also suffers from natural disasters such as earthquakes and hurricanes. Traditionally homes are made of light construction materials, so a house falling down during a disaster will not crush its occupants and also could be quickly and inexpensively rebuilt. During the feudal period until the Meiji restoration of 1868, each feudal lord sought to restrain his subjects from moving from one village to the next for fear that a neighboring lord might amass enough peasants with which to produce a large agricultural surplus, hire an army, and pose a threat. Apparently bridges were not commonly built across rivers and streams until the late nineteenth century, since bridges increased mobility between villages.

Taken all together, this characteristic style of living paints the picture of a nation of people who are homogeneous with respect to race, history, language, religion, and culture. For centuries and generations these people have lived in the same village next door to the same neighbors. Living in close proximity and in dwellings which gave very little privacy, the Japanese survived through their capacity to work together in harmony. In this situation, it was inevitable at the one most central social value which emerged, the one value without which the society could not continue, was that an individual does not matter.

To the Western soul this is a chilling picture of society. Subordinating individual tastes to the harmony of the group and knowing that individual needs can never take precedence over the interest of all is repellent to the Western citizen. But a frequent theme of Western philosophers and sociologists is that individual freedom exists only when people willingly subordinate their self-interests to the social interest. A society composed entirely of self interested individuals is a society in which each person is at war with the other, a society which has no freedom. This issue, constantly at the heart of understanding society, comes up in every century, and in every society, whether the writer be Plato, Hobbes, or B. F. Skinner. The question of understanding which contemporary institutions lie at the heart of the conflict between automatism and totalitarianism remains. In some ages, the kinship group, the central social institution, mediated between these opposing forces in preserve the balance in which freedom was realized; in other times the church or the government was most critical. Perhaps our present age puts the work organization as the central institution.

In order to complete the comparison of Japanese and American living situations, consider a flight over the United States. Looking out of the window high over the state of Kansas, we see a pattern of a single farmhouse surrounded by fields, followed by another single homestead surrounded by fields. In the early 1800s in the state of Kansas there were no automobiles. Your nearest neighbor was perhaps two miles distant; the winters were long, and the snow was deep. Inevitably, the central social values were self-reliance and independence. Those were the realities of that place and age that children had to learn to value.

The key to the industrial revolution was discovering that non-human forms of energy substituted for human forms could increase

12

13

14

15

the wealth of a nation beyond anyone's wildest dreams. But there was a catch. To realize this great wealth, non-human energy needed huge complexes called factories with hundreds, even thousands of workers collected into one factory. Moreover, several factories in one central place made the generation of energy more efficient. Almost overnight, the Western world was transformed from a rural and agricultural country to an urban and industrial state. Our technological advance seems to no longer fit our social structure: In a sense, the Japanese can better cope with modern industrialism. While Americans still busily protect our rather extreme form of individualism, the Japanese hold their individualism in check and emphasize cooperation.

MEANINGS AND VALUES

1. Restate in your own words the anecdote in Paragraphs 1 and 2 that serves to illustrate the Japanese worker's "strong orientation to collective values." Do you consider this anecdote effective in clarifying the author's point? How so?

2. Explain why the Japanese workers were not using the suggestion system. What change did the company make that resulted in a surge in suggestions and productivity improvements? Why did this work?

3. According to the author, how does it follow that the Japanese tradition of favoring the group over the individual results in a society that is better suited for modern industrialism?

EXPOSITORY TECHNIQUES

1. Locate the transitional sentence in this essay that serves to reinforce the comparison mode while at the same time introduces an example.

2. In Paragraph 9, the writer compares the Western individualist's hostile attitude toward modern industrial life to a role played by actor Charlie Chaplin in the silent film *Modern Times*. Do you consider this comparison effective? Do you think it works even for readers unfamiliar with this film? Explain.

3. In his essay, the author sometimes gives his own opinion of the two philosophies he is contrasting, for example: "In fact, I thought their system a good deal more efficient than ours" (Par. 7). Overall, which philosophy toward work (the Japanese collectivist approach or the American individualist approach) would you say that the author prefers, and why does he seem to prefer it?

DICTION AND VOCABULARY

1. In Paragraph 13, Ouchi refers to the concept of subordinating one's self-interest in a positive way. What effect do you think this has on the reader?

2. If you do not know the meaning of some of the following words, look them up in a dictionary: *collectivism, inimical* (Par. 5); *homogeneous* (12); *automatism, totalitarianism* (13).

READ TO WRITE

1. **Collaborating:** In a group of writers, survey group members, asking each whether they think they work better as an individual or in a group (collectively) and why. Write together a group report on the results, analyzing and explaining the differences between attitudes toward work in your group.

2. **Considering Audience:** Suppose the writer were to deliver this reading as a speech to a group who strongly believe in expressing individualism at all costs. Would the speech go over well? How might the author modify it for this audience?

3. **Developing an Essay:** In the author's final sentence, he states that "the Japanese hold their individualism in check and emphasize cooperation." Write an essay exploring the topic of cooperation in some area that interests you (workplace, home life, a friendship, or some other) in order to explain it to readers. Decide which elements that make up the topic you are going to emphasize. Contrast or compare each element using one or more of the following comparative strategies: positive and negative; honest and dishonest; traditional and innovative; effective and ineffective.

(NOTE: Suggestions for topics requiring development by COMPARISON follow.)

Writing Suggestions for Chapter 5

COMPARISON AND CONTRAST

1. Base your central theme on one of the following, and develop your composition primarily by use of comparison and/or contrast. Use examples liberally for clarity and concreteness, chosen always with your purpose and reader-audience in mind.

   1. Two kinds of families
   2. Two Internet search engines
   3. The innate qualities needed for success in two different careers
   4. Dog people versus cat people
   5. Two musicians
   6. Two radio personalities
   7. Two methods of parental handling of teenage problems
   8. Two family attitudes toward the practice of religion
   9. Two "moods" of the same town at different times
   10. The personalities (or atmospheres) of two cities or towns of similar size
   11. Two politicians with different leadership styles
   12. Careers versus jobs
   13. Two different attitudes toward the same thing or activity: one "practical," the other romantic or aesthetic
   14. The beliefs and practices of two religions or denominations concerning one aspect of religion
   15. Two courses on the same subject: one in high school and one in college
   16. The differing styles of two players of some sport or game
   17. The hazards of frontier life and those of life today
   18. Two companies with very different styles or business philosophies
   19. Two recent movies or music videos
   20. Two magazines focusing on similar subjects but directed at different audiences
   21. The "rewards" of two different kinds of jobs

2. Comparison can be a way of exploring a topic in order to explain it to others. To make this work in your own writing, start by choosing a topic that interests you. Then compare or

contrast the elements that make it up by using one or more of these comparative strategies: past and present; good and bad; useful and frivolous; kind and unkind; traditional and innovative; honest and dishonest; honorable and dishonorable; self-serving and dedicated to others; public and private; business and government; old and young; before and after; or momentary and long-lasting.

3. When we make choices among events or other forms of entertainment and learning, we often compare them to decide which to attend or recommend to friends. Choose two of the following, and prepare an essay explaining the differences between them to guide reader's choices.

    films   television shows   music DVDs or songs   books

    comics   graphic novels   theater performances   anime

    parks   musical groups   sporting events   outdoor experiences

4. Things that we often regard as different are often very much alike in important ways. Think about things, people, events, values, or experiences that most people consider very different, and create an essay explaining the important ways in which they are the same. Or do the opposite: Demonstrate how subjects, feelings, or ideas that many people think are the same are actually very different.

COLLABORATIVE EXERCISES

1. Choose a partner, and using topic number 19 from writing suggestion 1, write an essay comparing and contrasting two movies or music videos. Each member of the team should be responsible for researching one of the movies or videos.

2. Working with a partner, choose a topic on which you have differing perspectives and prepare an essay, each writing a section of the essay reflecting his or her own perspective. Combine the sections into a draft, then revise each other's section so that the essay reads as a smooth, consistent, and logical whole.

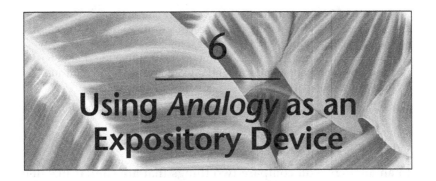

6

Using *Analogy* as an Expository Device

Analogy is a special form of comparison you can use to explain something abstract or difficult to understand. You can show its similarity to something concrete or something easier to understand. A much less commonly used technique than comparison (and contrast), analogy is, nonetheless, a highly efficient means of explaining difficult concepts or giving added force to explanations.

When you use comparison as an explanatory strategy, you need to make sure both subjects belong to the same general class of things, and you assume that readers will be more or less equally interested in both subjects. This is not the case with analogy. In analogy, you and your readers are really concerned only with one of the subjects; the second serves just to help explain the first. The two subjects, which may have little in common, also do not belong to the same class of things. The few elements they do share, however, are what give analogy the power to explain—and even to speculate about how things *might* be.

Certainly, for example, the universe is nothing like raisin bread—or so any reasonable person would think. But an analogy between the two can help explain a very difficult concept, as the following paragraph illustrates.

> If distant galaxies are really receding from the earth, and if more distant galaxies are receding faster than nearby ones, a remarkable picture of the universe emerges. Imagine that the galaxies were raisins scattered through a rising lump of bread dough. As the dough expanded, the raisins would be carried farther and farther apart from each other. If you were standing on one of the raisins, how would

things look? You wouldn't feel any motion yourself, of course, just as you don't feel the effects of the earth's motion around the sun, but you would notice that your nearest neighbor was moving away from you. This motion would be due to the fact that the dough between you and your nearest neighbor would be expanding, pushing the two of you apart.

—James Trefil, *The Dark Side of the Universe*

WHY USE ANALOGY?

In an analogy, you compare two things that are similar in some specifics but otherwise unlike. You can use this strategy to explain a complex, abstract, or unusual subject in familiar and easy-to-understand terms. Or you can use it to speculate about possible interpretations and consequences. For example, to explain how an electromagnetic field transmits radio signals from a station's transmitter to the radio in a listener's home or car, the physicist Richard Feynman asked his readers to imagine two corks floating in a pool of water. If we jiggle one cork, he pointed out, the waves in the water transmit the influence of our action and the second cork begins to jiggle, too. Like the water, an electromagnetic field transmits energy from sender to receiver in the form of waves— electromagnetic waves—conveying radio signals, a television picture, a radar image, or even plain light.

Analogy is not limited to scientific subjects, however. You can use it to explain and support your conclusions about other kinds of topics as well. For instance, a music critic, trying to explain her conclusion that jazz has influenced and will continue to influence modern music of all kinds, compares the jazz tradition to a tune that plays in the back of your mind all day, affecting your mood, the rhythm of your walk, and your tone of voice. Jazz, she explains, is a presence in the minds of composers and performers that shapes their choice of harmonies and rhythms, influences the tone of their compositions and the choice of instruments, and makes "hipness" (a mixture of sophistication, intensity, and emotional distancing) an attitude to which many of them aspire.

CHOOSING A STRATEGY

For a writer, the choice between using a brief analogy or an extended analogy is a significant one. A brief analogy, a sentence or two in length, can serve as an illustration or explanation of a difficult point or concept. To explain the need for a wide selection of college courses and the need for balance in a course of study, you might draw an analogy to a cafeteria, which serves desserts as well as meat, vegetables, and potatoes, allowing for various combinations adding up to balanced, full-course meals. If you wanted to extend this analogy to explain issues of curriculum and course choice in depth, however, you might run into problems with logic and with the adequacy of the particular analogy as an explanatory tool. Which courses, for example, should be classified as "desserts," and would all teachers and students agree on the classification? Does the concept of a well-balanced meal offer an adequate framework for understanding the specific kinds of balance appropriate for course choices?

An extended analogy, if carefully chosen for its logic and the points of comparison it offers, can serve as a framework for detailed explanation. In addition, it can offer a way to gain a fresh perspective on a problem, a controversy, or a puzzling phenomenon. For example, we often unconsciously draw on what we learn about relationships through family life in order to develop relationships within social organizations. Thus although businesses and other organizations are certainly different from families in many ways, there are still enough similarities to make an analogy worthwhile. Such an analogy asks readers to adopt a creative, "as if" perspective: let us examine the conflicts within an organization *as if* they were arguments among various members of a family to see whether the conflicts might be resolved in ways similar to those that work successfully in families. An analogy like this can be extended logically and consistently to explore a relatively broad topic, and it provides reasons for considering seriously the conclusions or interpretations the writer offers.

Analogies can take many different forms, and this flexibility is one of their appeals for both writers and readers. When you use an extended analogy to structure an essay, however, consider adopting a point-by-point arrangement to avoid confusing readers with too many comparisons at once. This is the approach taken in the following plan for an essay.

> Tentative thesis: We can better understand corporations by viewing them as if they were large, extended families.
> Point 1: Employee ranks are similar to family roles (CEOs, board members = grandparents; VPs = parents; and so on).

Point 2: Different parts of the company are similar to different parts of an extended family (main office = nuclear family; branch offices = families of uncles, aunts, cousins, and so forth).

Point 3: Conflicts over resources within a company are similar to rivalry among cousins or struggles over a will.

Point 4: Struggles over advancement within a company is similar to sibling rivalry.

Point 5: Training programs aim to help employees work together for the good of the company while family therapy tries to help maintain healthy relationships that preserve the family.

Point 6, 7, 8. . . . (if necessary)

DEVELOPING ANALOGIES

Simply stating an analogy and the specific grounds of similarity is seldom enough to make it an effective strategy, especially in the case of an extended analogy. The analogy needs to be clear to readers and developed in enough detail so that it provides convincing explanations and support for the writer's conclusions.

For an analogy to be effective, readers need to be familiar enough with the easier subject so that it really helps explain the more difficult one. Or the easier subject must be one that readers can understand with minimal discussion. An explanation of the human circulatory system, including the heart and arteries, in terms of a pump forcing water through the pipes of a plumbing system would be easily apprehended by readers. The analogy could be carried further to liken the effect of cholesterol deposits on the inner walls of the arteries to that of mineral deposits that accumulate inside water pipes and eventually close them entirely.

It is not enough for you as a writer simply to state an analogy, leaving for readers the job of understanding its significance. You need to explain both the analogy itself and its implications so that readers view it in the same way you do. To say that the world is like an overcrowded lifeboat will mean little in itself. You need also to explain that the lifeboat is in danger of sinking unless the number of passengers is reduced or the craft gains extra flotation power. And then you need to point out the implications: the world is overpopulated, and we must either limit population growth or increase our ability to sustain and feed people—without destroying the environment and, in effect, sinking the boat in which we are traveling.

Student Essay

People often use sports analogies to explain relationships and events in their lives. Kevin Nomura heard such analogies when he was growing up, especially comparisons between life and baseball. His essay draws on baseball for an extended analogy, but he uses it for a surprising purpose: to show how the analogy *fails* to explain much about life. Nonetheless, his essay makes effective use of analogy as a pattern and develops each element of the comparison in interesting, effective, and humorous detail.

Life Isn't Like Baseball

by Kevin Nomura

My father loves baseball. So does my mom. My sister was a star softball player in high school, and she is the regular shortstop on her college team. When my father tried to sign me up for Little League, however, I let him know that I would rather be playing soccer or tennis. It was about this time that he ⟩ **Introduces the analogy**

started trying to convince me that "life is like baseball." I wasn't convinced the first time he told me and I'm still not. Let me explain why. ⟩ **Thesis statement**

Striking Out. People who think life is like baseball often talk about "striking out," "staying ahead on the count," or "taking a big swing." When you are up to bat in baseball, you get a lot of chances—not just three strikes but also four balls and any number of fouled-off pitches. I have made some serious mistakes at work, at school, and in my love life, but while I have been lucky enough to get an occasional second chance, I have never gotten any more. When I have failed at something, I have never failed as completely, as obviously, and as publicly as a baseball player does striking out. I suppose that getting booed off the stage is like striking out, but when I sang off-tune in my high school's production of *Bye, Bye Birdie*, no one yelled at me or called me back to the dugout (woops, dressing room). Instead my parents told me they were proud of me no matter what,

First element of the analogy

Why the comparison is illogical

An inaccurate example

and the director told me ways to get through my part
of the song fast.

Hitting a Home Run. People seldom strike out in
real life, and they do not hit home runs either. When
baseball fans talk about "hitting a home run" at work
or in some other activity, they mean accomplishing
something dramatic whose success and importance
no one can deny. Who has a job that is big enough or
important enough to allow for a home run? Can the
manager of a McDonald's hit a home run? Can a clerk
in a department store or a steelworker do it? Who has
a job that allows for dramatic and significant achievement? Can a teacher create brilliant students overnight
or an artist become famous for one drawing rather
than a lifetime of careful, patient effort? I don't think
so, or only so seldom that such an achievement is unrealistic for us mortals.

Like a Spitball. People who believe that life is like
baseball often ignore those parts of the game that don't
fit very well with everyday experience or that are not
very pleasant. Is life like a spitball? Are successful people
the ones who load things up with petroleum jelly or
scuff them with emery boards, then lie when confronted
with evidence—and boast about their deception afterwards? And if some do, should we pretend their actions
are good sport and hold them up as examples for the
kids? Should we praise people for "stealing" and put
the biggest thieves in the record books? Should we
treat every botched move—every balk—as a serious error and a public humiliation? Would you like it if a slight
slip on your part automatically allowed your competitors
to advance a base and maybe even bring home the winning run?

I realize that I probably haven't convinced any real
baseball fans to stop seeing life in terms of their game.
I also realize that people will go on talking about "taking a good cut" or "winding up too long before the
pitch." My younger brother says he agrees with me, but
then he thinks life is a slap shot.

Margin notes:

Second element of the analogy

Questions pointing out why the analogy is faulty

Third element of the analogy

Questions and examples that highlight the usefulness of the analogy

Conclusion—maintains humorous tone of the essay

ALICE WALKER

ALICE WALKER was born in Georgia in 1944, the youngest in a family of eight. Her parents were sharecroppers, and she attended rural schools as a child, going on eventually to attend Spelman College and Sarah Lawrence College, from which she graduated. She worked as an editor of *Ms.* magazine and taught at several colleges. At present she teaches at the University of California, Berkeley and lives in northern California. Her work as a poet, novelist, and essayist has been highly acclaimed, and one of her novels, *The Color Purple* (1982), received both a Pulitzer Prize and the American Book Award for fiction. Some of her other works are *Her Blue Body Everything We Know: Earthling Poems 1989–1990* (1991) (poems); *In Love and Trouble* (1973) (short stories); *Meridian* (1976), *The Temple of My Familiar* (1989), *Possessing the Secret of Joy* (1992), and *By the Light of My Father's Smile* (1998) (novels); *In Search of Our Mothers' Gardens* (1983), *Living by the Word* (1988), and *The Same River Twice: Honoring the Difficult* (1996) (essays); *The Way Forward Is with a Broken Heart* (2000) (stories); *We Are the Ones We Have Been Waiting For* (2006) (nonfiction); *Devil's My Enemy* (2008) (fiction); and *Overcoming Speechlessness* (2010) (nonfiction).

Am I Blue?

In this essay from *Living by the Word,* Alice Walker demonstrates that, despite obvious differences, humans and animals are essentially alike—at least in important matters, such as the capacity to love and to communicate.

"Ain't these tears in these eyes tellin' you?" 1

For about three years my companion and I rented a small house 2 in the country that stood on the edge of a large meadow that appeared to run from the end of our deck straight into the mountains. The mountains, however, were quite far away, and between us and them there was, in fact, a town. It was one of the many pleasant aspects of the house that you never really were aware of this.

It was a house of many windows, low, wide, nearly floor to ceil- 3 ing in the living room, which faced the meadow, and it was from one of these that I first saw our closest neighbor, a large white horse, cropping grass, flipping its mane, and ambling about—not over the entire meadow, which stretched well out of sight of the house, but over the five or so fenced-in acres that were next to the twenty-odd that we had rented. I soon learned that the horse, whose name was Blue, belonged to a man who lived in another town, but was boarded by our neighbors next door. Occasionally, one of the children, usually a stocky teenager, but sometimes a much younger girl or boy, could be seen riding Blue. They would appear in the meadow, climb up on his back, ride furiously for ten or fifteen minutes, then get off, slap Blue on the flanks, and not be seen again for a month or more.

There were many apple trees in our yard, and one by the fence   4
that Blue could almost reach. We were soon in the habit of feeding him apples, which he relished, especially because by the middle of summer the meadow grasses—so green and succulent since January—had dried out from lack of rain, and Blue stumbled about munching the dried stalks half-heartedly. Sometimes he would stand very still just by the apple tree, and when one of us came out he would whinny, snort loudly, or stamp the ground. This meant, of course: I want an apple.

It was quite wonderful to pick a few apples, or collect those that   5
had fallen to the ground overnight, and patiently hold them, one by one, up to his large, toothy mouth. I remained as thrilled as a child by his flexible dark lips, huge, cubelike teeth that crunched the apples, core and all, with such finality, and his high, broad-breasted *enormity;* beside which, I felt small indeed. When I was a child, I used to ride horses, and was especially friendly with one named Nan until the day I was riding and my brother deliberately spooked her and I was thrown, head first, against the trunk of a tree. When I came to, I was in bed and my mother was bending worriedly over me; we silently agreed that perhaps horseback riding was not the safest sport for me. Since then I have walked, and prefer walking to horseback riding— but I had forgotten the depth of feeling one could see in horses' eyes.

I was therefore unprepared for the expression in Blue's. Blue   6
was lonely. Blue was horribly lonely and bored. I was not shocked that this should be the case; five acres to tramp by yourself, endlessly, even in the most beautiful of meadows—and his was— cannot provide many interesting events, and once rainy season turned to dry that was about it. No, I was shocked that I had forgotten that human animals and nonhuman animals can communicate quite well; if we are brought up around animals as children we take this for granted. By the time we are adults we no longer remember. However, the animals have not changed. They are in fact *completed* creations (at least they seem to be, so much more than we) who are not likely to change; it is their nature to express themselves. What

else are they going to express? And they do. And, generally speaking, they are ignored.

After giving Blue the apples, I would wander back to the house, aware that he was observing me. Were more apples not forthcoming then? Was that to be his sole entertainment for the day? My partner's small son had decided he wanted to learn how to piece a quilt; we worked in silence on our respective squares as I thought. . . .

Well, about slavery: about white children, who were raised by black people, who knew their first all-accepting love from black women, and then, when they were twelve or so, were told they must "forget" the deep levels of communication between themselves and "mammy" that they knew. Later they would be able to relate quite calmly, "My old mammy was sold to another good family." "My old mammy was _____." Fill in the blank. Many more years later a white woman would say: "I can't understand these Negroes, these blacks. What do they want? They're so different from us."

And about the Indians, considered to be "like animals" by the "settlers" (a very benign euphemism for what they actually were), who did not understand their description as a compliment.

And about the thousands of American men who marry Japanese, Korean, Filipina, and other non-English-speaking women and of how happy they report they are, "*blissfully*," until their brides learn to speak English, at which point the marriages tend to fall apart. What then did the men see, when they looked into the eyes of the women they married, before they could speak English? Apparently only their own reflections.

I thought of society's impatience with the young. "Why are they playing the music so loud?" Perhaps the children have listened to much of the music of oppressed people their parents danced to before they were born, with its passionate but soft cries for acceptance and love, and they have wondered why their parents failed to hear.

I do not know how long Blue had inhabited his five beautiful, boring acres before we moved into our house; a year after we had arrived—and had also traveled to other valleys, other cities, other worlds—he was still there.

But then, in our second year at the house, something happened in Blue's life. One morning, looking out the window at the fog that lay like a ribbon over the meadow, I saw another horse, a brown one, at the other end of Blue's field. Blue appeared to be afraid of it, and for several days made no attempt to go near. We went away for a week. When we returned, Blue had decided to make friends and the two horses ambled or galloped along together, and Blue did not come nearly as often to the fence underneath the apple tree.

When he did, bringing his new friend with him, there was a different look in his eyes. A look of independence, of self-possession, of inalienable *horse*ness. His friend eventually became pregnant. For months and months there was, it seemed to me, a mutual feeling between me and the horses of justice, of peace. I fed apples to them both. The look in Blue's eyes was one of unabashed "this is *it*ness." 14

It did not, however, last forever. One day, after a visit to the city, I went out to give Blue some apples. He stood waiting, or so I thought, though not beneath the tree. When I shook the tree and jumped back from the shower of apples, he made no move. I carried some over to him. He managed to half-crunch one. The rest he let fall to the ground. I dreaded looking into his eyes—because I had of course noticed that Brown, his partner, had gone—but I did look. If I had been born into slavery, and my partner had been sold or killed, my eyes would have looked like that. The children next door explained that Blue's partner had been "put with him" (the same expression that old people used, I had noticed, when speaking of an ancestor during slavery who had been impregnated by her owner) so that they could mate and she conceive. Since that was accomplished, she had been taken back by her owner, who lived somewhere else. 15

Will she be back? I asked. 16

They didn't know. 17

Blue was like a crazed person. Blue *was*, to me, a crazed person. He galloped furiously, as if he were being ridden, around and around his five beautiful acres. He whinnied until he couldn't. He tore at the ground with his hooves. He butted himself against his single shade tree. He looked always and always toward the road down which his partner had gone. And then, occasionally, when he came up for apples, or I took apples to him, he looked at me. It was a look so piercing, so full of grief, a look so *human*, I almost laughed (I felt too sad to cry) to think there are people who do not know that animals suffer. People like me who have forgotten, and daily forget, all that animals try to tell us. "Everything you do to us will happen to you; we are your teachers, as you are ours. We are one lesson" is essentially it, I think. There are those who never once have even considered animals' rights: those who have been taught that animals actually want to be used and abused by us, as small children "love" to be 18 frightened, or women "love" to be mutilated and raped. . . . They are the great-grandchildren of those who honestly thought, because someone taught them this: "Women can't think," And "niggers can't faint." But most disturbing of all, in Blue's large brown eyes was a new look, more painful than the look of despair: the look of disgust with human beings, with life; the look of hatred. And it was odd what the look of hatred did. It gave him, for the first time, the look of a beast. And what that meant was that he had put up a barrier within to protect himself from further violence; all the apples in the world wouldn't change that fact.

And so Blue remained, a beautiful part of our landscape, very   19 peaceful to look at from the window, white against the grass. Once a friend came to visit and said, looking out on the soothing view: "And it *would* have to be a white horse; the very image of freedom." And I thought, yes, the animals are forced to become for us merely "images" of what they once so beautifully expressed. And we are used to drinking milk from containers showing "contented" cows, whose real lives we want to hear nothing about, eating eggs and drumsticks from "happy" hens, and munching hamburgers advertised by bulls of integrity who seem to command their fate.

As we talked of freedom and justice one day for all, we sat   20 down to steaks. I am eating misery, I thought, as I took the first bite. And spit it out.

Meanings and Values

1. In which paragraphs does Walker describe what she believes to be Blue's thoughts and feelings?

2. According to Walker, in what ways is Blue similar to a human? In what ways is he different? To what other groups does the author compare Blue and his relationships with humans in Paragraphs 8–11?

3. What thematic purposes are served by the following phrases:

    a. "human animals and nonhuman animals" (Par. 6)

    b. "who did not understand their description as a compliment" (Par. 9)

    c. "Am I Blue?" (title)

    d. "If I had been born into slavery, and my partner had been sold or killed, my eyes would have looked like that." (Par. 15)

    e. "It gave him, for the first time, the look of a beast." (Par. 18)

EXPOSITORY TECHNIQUES

1. Why do you think Walker chose to wait until near the end of the essay (Par. 18) for a detailed discussion of its theme? (See "Guide to Terms": *Unity*.) To what extent does the placement of this discussion give the essay an expository rather than an argumentative purpose? (Guide: *Argument*.)

2. Discuss how the "'images'" presented in Paragraph 19 can be regarded as ironic symbols. (Guide: *Symbol; Irony*.)

3. Describe the way Walker alters the tempo of the sentences and builds to a climax in the concluding paragraph of the essay. (Guide: *Closings*.)

4. Some readers might consider the ending effective. Others might consider it overly dramatic or distasteful. Explain which reaction you consider most appropriate. (Guide: *Evaluation*.)

DICTION AND VOCABULARY

1. Describe the ways in which Walker uses syntax and figurative language (simile) for thematic purposes in this passage: "Blue was like a crazed person. Blue *was*, to me, a crazed person" (Par. 18). (Guide: *Syntax; Figures of Speech*.)

2. In speaking of the "'settlers,'" Walker says that this term is "a very benign euphemism for what they actually were" (Par. 9). What does she mean by this comment? What other terms might be applied to them (from Walker's point of view)? Why might she have chosen not to use such terms?

3. The title of this essay is taken from a song of the same name. In terms of the content of the essay, to what ideas or themes does it refer? Can it be considered a paradox? (Guide: *Paradox*.) The quotation from the song that opens the essay points to some of the ideas discussed in the essay. What are they?

READ TO WRITE

1. **Collaborating:** Working in groups of four, discuss different animals that you have known. What have you learned from these animals? Can you apply what you have learned to your human relationships? To your understanding of human nature? How would you contrast the behavior of animals in specific situations with typical human behavior in such situations? As a group, plan an essay that draws an analogy between likely animal and human behavior in a set of situations you have chosen.

2. **Considering Audience:** Walker repeatedly refers to expressions and feelings seemingly conveyed through Blue's eyes. How might readers who have their own pets react to Walker's descriptions of the animal's eyes? How might readers without pets react? Will readers who

have pets understand Walker's comparison of animal owners and slave owners better than non-pet owners? Will most pet owners be offended by such a comparison? Who, if anyone, might be offended by the conclusions Walker draws about Blue's and other animals' feelings and intelligence? In two to three paragraphs, offer your answers to some or all of these questions as a way of describing readers' likely reactions to Walker's essay.

3. **Developing an Essay:** Walker's analogy essay moves from obvious differences to surprising similarities, getting there through careful observation of horses and humans. Apply this pattern to an analogy of your own choosing, using it to express hidden similarities you have already noticed or to reveal similarities as you write.

(Note: Suggestions for topics requiring development by analogy are on pp. 208–209 at the end of this chapter.)

ROBERT BENCHLEY

> Humorist, newspaper columnist, and film actor ROBERT BENCHLEY
> (1889–1945) was notable for finding the remarkable in the ordi-
> nary. He received his diploma from Harvard University after com-
> pleting a paper on a fisheries dispute—written from the point of
> view of a cod. He wrote for *Vanity Fair* and *The New Yorker* and
> won an Academy Award for his short film, *How to Sleep.* His defini-
> tion of humor: anything that makes people laugh. Benchley was a
> member of the Algonquin Round Table, a group of New York City
> writers and actors who met regularly between 1919 and 1929 at
> the Algonquin Hotel.

Advice to Writers

> Is learning to ice skate like learning to write? If so, how should
> writing be taught? Benchley explains it all in this critique of two
> how-to manuals. The review was included in *Love Conquers All,* an
> anthology of Benchley's magazine essays from 1921 to 1922.

Two books have emerged from the hundreds that are being pub-   1
lished on the art of writing. One of them is *The Lure of the Pen,* by
Flora Klickmann, and the other is *Learning to Write,* a collection of
[Robert Louis] Stevenson's meditations on the subject, issued by
Scribner's. At first glance one might say that the betting would be at
least eight to one on Stevenson. But for real, solid, sensible advice in
the matter of writing and selling stories in the modern market, Miss
Klickmann romps in an easy winner.

It must be admitted that John William Rogers Jr., who collected   2
the Stevenson material, warns the reader in his introduction that the
book is not intended to serve as "a macadamized, mile-posted road
to the secret of writing," but simply as a help to those who want to
write and who are interested to know how Stevenson did it. So we
mustn't compare it too closely with Miss Klickmann's book, which
is quite frankly a mile-posted road, with little sub-headings along
the side of the page such as we used to have in Fiske's Elementary
American History. But Miss Klickmann will save the editors of the
country a great deal more trouble than Stevenson's advice ever will.
She is the editor of an English magazine herself, and has suffered.

Where Miss Klickmann enumerates the pitfalls which the can-   3
didate must avoid and points out qualities which every good piece
of writing should have, Stevenson writes a delightful essay on

"The Profession of Letters" or "A Gossip on Romance." These essays are very inspiring. They are too inspiring. They make the reader feel that he can go out and write like Stevenson. And then a lot of two-cent stamps are wasted and a lot more editors are cross when they get home at night.

On the other hand, the result of Miss Klickmann's book is to make the reader who feels a writing spell coming on stop and give pause. He finds enumerated among the horrors of manuscript-reading several items which he was on the point of injecting into his own manuscript with considerable pride. He may decide that the old job in the shipping-room isn't so bad after all, with its little envelope coming in regularly every week. As a former member of the local manuscript-readers' union, I will give one of three rousing cheers for any good work that Miss Klickmann may do in this field. One writer kept very busy at work in the shipping-room every day is a victory for literature. I used to have a job in a shipping-room myself, so I know.

4

If, for instance, the subject under discussion were that of learning to skate, Miss Klickmann might advise as follows:

5

Don't try to skate if your ankles are weak.

6

Get skates that fit you. A skate which can't be put on when you get to the pond, or one which drags behind your foot by the strap, is worse than no skate at all.

7

If you are sure that you are ready, get on your feet and skate.

8

On the same subject, Scribner's might bring to light something that Stevenson had written to a young friend about to take his first lesson in skating, reading as follows:

9

To know the secret of skating is, indeed, I have always thought, the beginning of winter-long pleasance. It comes as sweet deliverance from the tedium of indoor isolation and brings exhilaration, now with a swift glide to the right, now with a deft swerve to the left, now with a deep breath of healthy air, now with a long exhalation of ozone, which the lungs, like greedy misers, have cast aside after draining it of its treasure. But it is not health that we love nor exhilaration that we seek, though we may think so; our design and our sufficient reward is to verify our own existence, say what you will.

10

And so, my dear young friend, I would say to you: Open up your heart; sing as you skate; sing inharmoniously if you will, but sing! A man may skate with all the skill in the world; he may glide forward with incredible deftness and curve backward with divine grace, and yet if he be not master of his emotions as well as of his feet, I would say—and here Fate steps in—that he has failed.

11

There is, of course, plenty of good advice in the Stevenson book.   12
But it is much better as pure reading matter than as advice to the
young idea or even the middle-aged idea. It may have been all right
for Stevenson to "play the sedulous ape" and consciously imitate
the style of Hazlitt, Lamb, Montaigne and the rest, but if the rest of
us were to try it there would result a terrible plague of insufferably
artificial and affected authors, all playing the sedulous ape and all
looking the part.

On the whole, the Stevenson book makes good reading and   13
Miss Klickmann gives good advice.

Meanings and Values

1. Which book on writing, Stevenson's or Klickmann's, does the
    reviewer say misleads people into thinking that excellent writing is
    easy to achieve? Give reasons for your answer.

2. In the reading selection's last sentence, Benchley states his opinion
    that Klickmann's book gives good advice. In your own words, what
    might that advice be?

3. Benchley imagines Miss Klickmann advising, "Don't try to skate
    if your ankles are weak." Restate this analogy as if you were advising
    a beginning writer.

Expository Techniques

1. What is the main analogy in this reading? Is Benchley's analogy
    effective, in your opinion?

2. Locate another analogy offered by the writer earlier in the reading
    selection. What is being compared? How is that comparison related
    to the main analogy?

3. What other mode does the writer employ in this selection besides
    analogy?

Diction and Vocabulary

1. Benchley's tone is light and humorous (see Guide: *Style/Tone*). At
    what points in his review, if any, does he signal that he is serious
    about the topic of books that offer writing advice? Give examples.

2. Robert Louis Stevenson, one of the authors Benchley reviews in
    this reading, suggested in an essay titled "The Sedulous Ape" that
    writers should imitate the writing styles of authors they respect.

(Benchley refers to Stevenson's essay in this reading selection.) In Par. 10, beginning with "To know the secret of skating . . .," Benchley exaggeratedly mimics Stevenson's writing style. What is his purpose in doing so?

3.   If you do not know the meaning of some of the following words, consult a dictionary: *macadamized* (Par. 2); *deft* (10); *sedulous, affected* (12).

READ TO WRITE

1.   **Collaborating:** In a group of writers, brainstorm ways to fill in the blanks in this sentence: *Teaching someone to_____ well is like _____.* Choose one of your completed sentences by group consensus, then list examples of how that sentence is true.

2.   **Considering Audience:** Suppose that you want to use an analogy to help clarify the idea of giving good advice to writers. Your audience is a group of college students. What analogy would you employ for this audience?

3.   **Developing an Essay:** Prepare a comparison essay that develops an extended analogy. For your topic, use the completed sentence your group came up with in question 1. Alternatively, think of another topic that is complex or abstract—such as a mechanical process, an outlook on life, or an emotional reaction—and plan to compare it to something simpler. Structure your essay as a point-by-point pattern, with each point as one aspect of the extended analogy. Explain each element of your extended analogy thoroughly, and make clear to the reader why your analogy is a meaningful one.

(NOTE: Suggestions for topics requiring development by ANALOGY are on pp. 208–209 at the end of this chapter.)

VIRGINIA WOOLF

British novelist, essayist, and publisher VIRGINIA WOOLF (1882–1941) was born in London. In the early 1900s, she was a member of the Bloomsbury Group, a circle of writers and artists. Joining forces with her husband Leonard Woolf, she founded the Hogarth Press in 1917, publishing works by important artists and writers, including modernist poet T. S. Eliot. Woolf is known for her groundbreaking writing style, characterized by lyric, stream-of-consciousness prose and intense explorations of the psychology and emotions of her upper-middle-class characters. Her novels include *The Voyage Out* (1915), *Jacob's Room* (1922), and *Mrs. Dalloway* (1925). The celebrated extended essay *A Room of One's Own* (1929) champions women's right to write.

The Death of the Moth

This selection, combining description and narration in an extended analogy, appeared in a posthumous collection of Woolf's writings, *The Death of the Moth and Other Essays* (1942).

Moths that fly by day are not properly to be called moths; they do not excite that pleasant sense of dark autumn nights and ivy-blossom which the commonest yellow-underwing asleep in the shadow of the curtain never fails to rouse in us. They are hybrid creatures, neither gay like butterflies nor sombre like their own species. Nevertheless the present specimen, with his narrow hay-coloured wings, fringed with a tassel of the same colour, seemed to be content with life. It was a pleasant morning, mid-September, mild, benignant, yet with a keener breath than that of the summer months. The plough was already scoring the field opposite the window, and where the share had been, the earth was pressed flat and gleamed with moisture. Such vigour came rolling in from the fields and the down beyond that it was difficult to keep the eyes strictly turned upon the book. The rooks too were keeping one of their annual festivities; soaring round the tree tops until it looked as if a vast net with thousands of black knots in it had been cast up into the air; which, after a few moments, sank slowly down upon the trees until every twig seemed to have a knot at the end of it. Then, suddenly, the net would be thrown into the air again in a wider circle this time, with the utmost

1

clamour and vociferation, as though to be thrown into the air and settle slowly down upon the tree tops were a tremendously exciting experience.

The same energy which inspired the rooks, the ploughmen, the horses, and even, it seemed, the lean bare-backed downs, sent the moth fluttering from side to side of his square of the window-pane. One could not help watching him. One was, indeed, conscious of a queer feeling of pity for him. The possibilities of pleasure seemed that morning so enormous and so various that to have only a moth's part in life, and a day moth's at that, appeared a hard fate, and his zest in enjoying his meagre opportunities to the full, pathetic. He flew vigorously to one corner of his compartment, and, after waiting there a second, flew across to the other. What remained for him but to fly to a third corner and then to a fourth? That was all he could do, in spite of the size of the downs, the width of the sky, the far-off smoke of houses, and the romantic voice, now and then, of a steamer out at sea. What he could do he did. Watching him, it seemed as if a fibre, very thin but pure, of the enormous energy of the world had been thrust into his frail and diminutive body. As often as he crossed the pane, I could fancy that a thread of vital light became visible. He was little or nothing but life.

Yet, because he was so small, and so simple a form of the energy that was rolling in at the open window and driving its way through so many narrow and intricate corridors in my own brain and in those of other human beings, there was something marvellous as well as pathetic about him. It was as if someone had taken a tiny bead of pure life and decking it as lightly as possible with down and feathers, had set it dancing and zigzagging to show us the true nature of life. Thus displayed one could not get over the strangeness of it. One is apt to forget all about life, seeing it humped and bossed and garnished and cumbered so that it has to move with the greatest circumspection and dignity. Again, the thought of all that life might have been had he been born in any other shape caused one to view his simple activities with a kind of pity.

After a time, tired by his dancing apparently, he settled on the window ledge in the sun, and, the queer spectacle being at an end, I forgot about him. Then, looking up, my eye was caught by him. He was trying to resume his dancing, but seemed either so stiff or so awkward that he could only flutter to the bottom of the window-pane; and when he tried to fly across it he failed. Being intent on other matters I watched these futile attempts for a time without thinking, unconsciously waiting for him to resume his flight, as one waits for a machine, that has stopped momentarily, to start again without considering the reason of its failure. After perhaps a seventh attempt he slipped from the wooden ledge and fell, fluttering his wings, on to his back on the window sill. The helplessness of his attitude roused me. It flashed upon me that he was in difficulties; he could no longer raise himself; his legs struggled vainly. But, as I stretched out a pencil, meaning to help him to right himself, it came over me that the failure and awkwardness were the approach of death. I laid the pencil down again.

The legs agitated themselves once more. I looked as if for the   5
enemy against which he struggled. I looked out of doors. What had happened there? Presumably it was midday, and work in the fields had stopped. Stillness and quiet had replaced the previous animation. The birds had taken themselves off to feed in the brooks. The horses stood still. Yet the power was there all the same, massed outside, indifferent, impersonal, not attending to anything in particular. Somehow it was opposed to the little hay-coloured moth. It was useless to try to do anything. One could only watch the extraordinary efforts made by those tiny legs against an oncoming doom which could, had it chosen, have submerged an entire city, not merely a city, but masses of human beings; nothing, I knew, had any chance against death. Nevertheless after a pause of exhaustion the legs fluttered again. It was superb, this last protest, and so frantic that he succeeded at last in righting himself. One's sympathies, of course, were all on the side of life. Also, when there was nobody to care or to know, this gigantic effort on the part of an insignificant little moth, against a power of such magnitude, to retain what no one else valued or desired to keep, moved one strangely. Again, somehow, one saw life, a pure bead. I lifted the pencil again, useless though I knew it to be. But even as I did so, the unmistakable tokens of death showed themselves. The body relaxed, and instantly grew stiff. The struggle was over. The insignificant little creature now knew death. As I looked at the dead moth, this minute wayside triumph of so great a force over so mean an antagonist filled me with wonder. Just as life had been strange a few minutes before, so death was now as strange. The moth having righted himself now lay most decently and uncomplainingly composed. O yes, he seemed to say, death is stronger than I am.

Meanings and Values

1. Explain why you think the writer chose to compare the life force to a struggling moth rather than to something far grander, like an exploding volcano, a flaming torch, or a soaring eagle.

2. In what way is the short sentence "What he could do he did" meaningful?

3. What is the significance of the moth's struggle against death? Why is the writer fascinated by it?

Expository Techniques

1. Find the place in the essay where the author introduces her analogy. Should she have introduced it sooner?

2. The writer embeds the elements of her analogy—a comparison of the life force to a moth—within the structure of a narrative, telling the brief story of a moth's life and death. Reread the essay, underlining separate elements of the analogy as you read.

3. Characterizing an insect as having the qualities and emotions of a person, as Woolf does in this essay, is a form of personification (see "Guide to Terms": *Figures of Speech*). Find several examples of personification in the essay. Does the writer's use of personification add to or subtract from the effectiveness of the essay, in your opinion? How so?

Diction and Vocabulary

1. Woolf chooses to refer to the moth by the pronoun "he" instead of "it." She also occasionally uses the pronoun "one" instead of "I." Why do you think she chooses to do so?

2. The elevated tone of this essay would be considered far too grand for the topic if Woolf were merely describing an actual moth. However, for an essay on life and death itself, this tone seems appropriate. Point to examples of ordinary, everyday events in this essay that are described using elevated diction.

3. If you do not know the meaning of some of the following words, consult a dictionary: *vociferation* (Par. 1); *zest* (2); *bossed, circumspection* (3); *vainly* (4).

Read to Write

1. **Collaborating:** Discuss in your writer's group whether Woolf's extended analogy essay succeeds or fails in conveying the frailty and tenacity of life. List group members' opinions pro and con. Write a brief report together that compares and contrasts your opinions about the essay.

2. **Considering Audience:** Would a sixth-grader without the maturity to appreciate the abstract concepts of life and death be able to follow the thread of Woolf's narrative? What aspects of the reading selection might get in the way of such an understanding of this simple story about a moth?

3. **Developing an Essay:** Woolf's essay is the product of close observation. Carefully observe a brief scene in which you are not a participant, for example, a couple ordering food, children playing, a worker taking a break. The scene you observe should have a natural beginning, middle, and end. Write detailed notes about what you observe and your feelings and thoughts about it. Then use these notes as a basis for an extended analogy essay in which you compare what you have observed to something important in your life, using the Woolf essay as inspiration.

(NOTE: Suggestions for topics requiring development by ANALOGY are on pp. 208–209 at the end of this chapter.)

Issues and Ideas

Perceiving Likeness in Differences

- Henry David Thoreau, *The Battle*
- Anne Morrow Lindbergh, *Oyster Bed*
- Visual Text, *"To My Valentine"*

HENRY DAVID THOREAU

HENRY DAVID THOREAU (1817–1862), the renowned writer, philosopher, naturalist, abolitionist, and free thinker, was born in Concord, Massachusetts. He was an early follower of the Transcendentalist movement and its emphasis on personal intuition over religious doctrine. His famous writings include the essay *Civil Disobedience* (1849) and the classic spiritual memoir *Walden* (1854). In *Walden*, Thoreau explained his rationale for conducting his experiment in simple living in the forest around Walden Pond: "I went to the woods because I wished to live deliberately, to front only the essential facts of life, and see if I could not learn what it had to teach, and not, when I came to die, discover that I had not lived."

The Battle

In his later years, Thoreau became fascinated with nature, keeping detailed notes on his observations. This keen eye for the natural world, as well as his penchant for drawing larger inferences from what he saw, is evident in this extended analogy from *Walden, or Life in the Woods* (1854).

You only need sit still long enough in some attractive spot in the woods that all its inhabitants may exhibit themselves to you by turns.   1

I was witness to events of a less peaceful character. One day when I went out to my wood-pile, or rather my pile of stumps, I observed two large ants, the one red, the other much larger, nearly half an inch long, and black, fiercely contending with one another. Having once got hold they never let go, but struggled and wrestled   2 and rolled on the chips incessantly. Looking farther, I was surprised to find that the chips were covered with such combatants, that it was not a *duellum*, but a *bellum*, a war between two races of ants, the red always pitted against the black, and frequently two red ones to one black. The legions of these Myrmidons covered all the hills and vales in my wood-yard, and the ground was already strewn with the dead and dying, both red and black. It was the only battle which I have ever witnessed, the only battle-field I ever trod while the battle was raging; internecine war; the red republicans on the one hand, and the black imperialists on the other. On every side they were engaged in deadly combat, yet without any noise that I could hear, and human soldiers never fought so resolutely. I watched a couple that were fast locked in each other's embraces, in a little sunny valley amid the chips, now at noonday prepared to fight till the sun went down, or life went out. The smaller red champion had fastened himself like a vice to his adversary's front, and through all the tumblings on that field never for an instant ceased to gnaw at one of his feelers near the root, having already caused the other to go by the board; while the stronger black one dashed him from side to side, and, as I saw on looking nearer, had already divested him of several of his members. They fought with more pertinacity than bulldogs. Neither manifested the least disposition to retreat. It was evident that their battle-cry was "Conquer or die." In the meanwhile there came along a single red ant on the hillside of this valley, evidently full of excitement, who either had dispatched his foe, or had not yet taken part in the battle; probably the latter, for he had lost none of his limbs; whose mother had charged him to return with his shield or upon it. Or perchance he was some Achilles, who had nourished his wrath apart, and had now come to avenge or rescue his Patroclus. He saw this unequal combat from afar—for the blacks were nearly twice the size of the red—he drew near with rapid pace till he stood on his guard within half an inch of the combatants; then, watching his opportunity, he sprang upon the black warrior, and commenced his operations near the root of his right foreleg, leaving the foe to select among his own members; and so there were three united for life, as if a new kind of attraction had been invented which put all other locks and cements to shame. I should not have wondered by this time to find that they had their respective musical bands stationed on some eminent chip, and playing their national airs the while, to excite the slow and cheer the dying combatants. I was myself excited somewhat even as if they had been men. The more you think of it, the less the difference. And certainly there is not the fight recorded in Concord history, at least, if in the history of America, that will bear a moment's comparison with this, whether for the numbers engaged in it, or for the patriotism and heroism displayed. For numbers and for carnage it was an Austerlitz or Dresden. Concord Fight! Two killed on the patriots' side, and Luther Blanchard wounded! Why here every ant was a Buttrick—"Fire! for God's sake fire!"—and thousands shared the fate of Davis and Hosmer. There was not one hireling there. I have no doubt that it was a principle they fought for, as much as our ancestors, and not to avoid a three-penny tax on their tea; and the results of this battle will be as important and memorable to those whom it concerns as those of the battle of Bunker Hill, at least.

I took up the chip on which the three I have particularly described were struggling, carried it into my house, and placed it under a tumbler on my window-sill, in order to see the issue. Holding a microscope to the first-mentioned red ant, I saw that, though he was assiduously gnawing at the near foreleg of his enemy, having severed his remaining feeler, his own breast was all torn away, exposing what vitals he had there to the jaws of the black warrior, whose breastplate was apparently too thick for him to pierce; and the dark carbuncles of the sufferer's eyes shone with ferocity such as war only could excite. They struggled half an hour longer under the tumbler, and when I looked again the black soldier had severed the heads of his foes from their bodies, and the still living heads were hanging on either side of him like ghastly trophies at his saddle-bow, still apparently as firmly fastened as ever, and he was endeavoring with feeble struggles, being without feelers and with only the remnant of a leg, and I know not how many other wounds, to divest himself of them, which at length, after half an hour more, he accomplished. I raised the glass, and he went off over the window-sill in that crippled state. Whether he finally survived that combat, and spent the remainder of his days in some Hôtel des Invalides, I do not know; but I thought that his industry would not be worth much thereafter. I never learned which party was victorious, nor the cause of the war; but I felt for the rest of that day as if I had had my feelings excited and harrowed by witnessing the struggle, the ferocity and carnage, of a human battle before my door.

Kirby and Spence tell us that the battles of ants have long been celebrated and the date of them recorded, though they say that Huber is the only modern author who appears to have witnessed them. "Aeneas Sylvius," say they, "after giving a very circumstantial account of one contested with great obstinacy by a great and small species on the trunk of a pear tree," adds that "this action was fought in the pontificate of Eugenius the Fourth, in the presence of

Nicholas Pistoriensis, an eminent lawyer, who related the whole history of the battle with the greatest fidelity." A similar engagement between great and small ants is recorded by Olaus Magnus, in which the small ones, being victorious, are said to have buried the bodies of their own soldiers, but left those of their giant enemies a prey to the birds. This event happened previous to the expulsion of the tyrant Christiern the Second from Sweden. The battle which I witnessed took place in the Presidency of Polk, five years before the passage of Webster's Fugitive-Slave Bill.

MEANINGS AND VALUES

1. What do you think the writer is trying to communicate in this extended analogy? Is he successful, in your opinion? How so?

2. What are some of the points of comparison the author makes between human and ant behavior in wartime?

3. Explain the significance of Thoreau's observation, "I never learned which party was victorious, nor the cause of the war."

EXPOSITORY TECHNIQUES

1. The first time the writer explicitly states that he is developing an analogy between men at war and ants fighting over a wood pile is his comment, "The more you think of it, the less the difference." Point to details earlier in the essay in which the analogy is made without being directly stated.

2. Does the author directly explain what he thinks his analogy means and why we should find it significant? If not, is the comparison meaningful nonetheless? What clues can you find that hint at the author's true opinion of the "ferocity and carnage" he describes?

3. As in the essay *The Death of the Moth*, this reading selection employs personification (see "Guide to Terms": *Figures of Speech*), or attributing human feelings to nonhuman creatures or things. Select one of the many instances of personification in this essay and explain its significance.

DICTION AND VOCABULARY

1. Is Thoreau's admiration for the ants sincere or ironic (see Guide: *Irony*)? Explain your answer.

2. In addition to analogy, this reading selection uses narrative as an expository form, telling a story to make a point. The story of the battle

takes place within a particular time frame. Reread the selection and underline phrases that signal time order.

3. If you do not know the meaning of some of the following words, consult a dictionary: *Myrmidons, internecine* (Par. 2); *carbuncles, harrowed, carnage* (3).

READ TO WRITE

1. **Collaborating:** In this reading, Thoreau compares the sublime to the ridiculous, drawing an analogy between something considered serious (humanity's warlike nature) with something ordinary (a common species of insect). With the other writers in your group, brainstorm other pairings of the sublime and the ridiculous. List the pairs. As a group, write a paragraph that develops an analogy using one of the pairs.

2. **Considering Audience:** What prior knowledge about history does Thoreau expect from his audience, and how can you tell? Does Thoreau also assume that the reader has prior knowledge about his own political and philosophical views? Explain. How well would this reading selection go over as a speech given to anti-war activists? How about as a speech given to pro-war activists? Why?

3. **Developing an Essay:** Prepare an essay in which you contrast or compare the use of extended analogy in Virginia Woolf's *The Death of the Moth* and Henry David Thoreau's *The Battle*. Illustrate your comparison with examples, using either the point-by-point or subject-by-subject pattern. Remember to make clear the purpose of your comparison.

(NOTE: Suggestions for topics requiring development by ANALOGY are on pp. 208–209 at the end of this chapter.)

ANNE MORROW LINDBERGH

> Noted aviator and author ANNE MORROW LINDBERGH (1906–2001) earned a B.A. from Smith College in 1928. Wife of fellow aviator Charles Lindbergh, she was inducted into the National Aviation Hall of Fame and the National Women's Hall of Fame. Her many books include *North to the Orient* (1935), *The Wave of the Future* (1940), and the last installment in a series of published diaries and letters, *War Within and Without* (1980).

Oyster Bed

> Marriage has been compared to many things, including a journey (John Steinbeck), a funeral (Eddie Cantor), and communism (Bill Maher), but Anne Morrow Lindbergh is probably the only close observer ever to draw attention to the similarities between marriage and a bed of oysters. This extended analogy is drawn from her inspirational meditation on marriage, solitude, and women's lives, *Gift from the Sea* (1955).

But surely we *do* demand duration and continuity of relationships, at least of marriage. That is what marriage is, isn't it—continuity of a relationship? Of course, but not necessarily continuity in one single form or stage, not necessarily continuity in the double-sunrise stage. There are other shells to help me, to put in the row on my desk. Here is one I picked up yesterday. Not rare, there are many of them on the beach and yet each one is individual. You never find two alike. Each is fitted and formed by its own life and struggle to survive. It is an oyster, with small shells clinging to its humped back. Sprawling and uneven, it has the irregularity of something growing. It looks rather like the house of a big family, pushing out one addition after another to hold its teeming life—here a sleeping porch for the children, and there a veranda for the play-pen; here a garage for the extra car and there a shed for the bicycles. It amuses me because it seems so much like my life at the moment, like most women's lives in the middle years of marriage. It is untidy, spread out in all directions, heavily encrusted with accumulations and, in its living state—this one is empty and cast up by the sea—firmly imbedded on its rock.   1

Yes, I believe the oyster shell is a good one to express the middle years of marriage. It suggests the struggle of life itself. The oyster has fought to have that place on the rock to which it has fitted itself   2 perfectly and to which it clings tenaciously. So most couples in the growing years of marriage struggle to achieve a place in the world. It is a physical and material battle first of all, for a home, for children, for a place in their particular society. In the midst of such a life there is not much time to sit facing one another over a breakfast table. In these years one recognizes the truth of Saint-Exupéry's line: "Love does not consist in gazing at each other (one perfect sunrise gazing at another!) but in looking outward together in the same direction." For, in fact, man and woman are not only *looking* outward in the same direction; they are *working* outward. (Observe the steady encroachment of the oyster bed over the rock.) Here one forms ties, roots, a firm base. (Try and pry an oyster from its ledge!) Here one makes oneself part of the community of men, of human society.

Here the bonds of marriage are formed. For marriage, which is   3
always spoken of as a bond, becomes actually, in this stage, many bonds, many strands, of different texture and strength, making up a web that is taut and firm. The web is fashioned of love. Yes, but many kinds of love: romantic love first, then a slow-growing devotion and, playing through these, a constantly rippling companionship. It is made of loyalties, and interdependencies, and shared experiences. It is woven of memories of meetings and conflicts, of triumphs and disappointments. It is a web of communication, a common language, and the acceptance of lack of language too; a knowledge of likes and dislikes, of habits and reactions, both physical and mental. It is a web of instincts and intuitions, and known and unknown exchanges. The web of marriage is made by propinquity, in the day-to-day living side by side, looking outward and working outward in the same direction. It is woven in space and in time of the substance of life itself.

But the bond—the bond of romantic love is something else. It   4
has so little to do with propinquity or habit or space or time or life itself. It leaps across all of them, like a rainbow—or a glance. It is the bond of romantic love which fastens the double-sunrise shell, only one bond, one hinge. And if that fragile link is snapped in the storm, what will hold the halves to each other? In the oyster stage of marriage, romantic love is only one of the many bonds that make up the intricate and enduring web that two people have built together.

I am very fond of the oyster shell. It is humble and awkward and   5
ugly. It is slate-colored and unsymmetrical. Its form is not primarily beautiful but functional. I make fun of its knobbiness. Sometimes I resent its burdens and excrescences. But its tireless adaptability and tenacity draw my astonished admiration and sometimes even my tears.

And it is comfortable in its familiarity, its homeliness, like old garden gloves which have moulded themselves perfectly to the shape of the hand. I do not like to put it down. I will not want to leave it.

But is it the permanent symbol of marriage? Should it—any more than the double-sunrise shell—last forever? The tide of life recedes. The house, with its bulging sleeping porches and sheds, begins little by little to empty. The children go away to school and then to marriage and lives of their own. Most people by middle age have attained, or ceased to struggle to attain, their place in the world. That terrific tenacity to life, to place, to people, to material surroundings and accumulations—is it as necessary as it was when one was struggling for one's security or the security of one's children? Many of the physical struggles have ceased, due either to success or to failure. Does the shell need to be so welded to its rock? Married couples are apt to find themselves in middle age, high and dry in an outmoded shell, in a fortress which has outlived its function. What is one to do—die of atrophy in an outstripped form? Or move on to another form, other experiences?   6

Perhaps, someone will suggest, this is the moment to go back to the simple self-enclosed world of the sunrise shell? Alone at last again over the muffins and the marmalade! No, one cannot go back to that tightly closed world. One has grown too big, too many-sided, for that rigidly symmetrical shell. I am not sure that one has not grown too big for any shell at all.   7

Perhaps middle age is, or should be, a period of shedding shells; the shell of ambition, the shell of material accumulations and possessions, the shell of the ego. Perhaps one can shed at this stage in life as one sheds in beach-living; one's pride, one's false ambitions, one's mask, one's armor. Was that armor not put on to protect one from the competitive world? If one ceases to compete, does one need it? Perhaps one can at last in middle age, if not earlier, be completely oneself. And what a liberation that would be!   8

It is true that the adventures of youth are less open to us. Most of us cannot, at this point, start a new career or raise a new family. Many of the physical, material and worldly ambitions are less attainable than they were twenty years ago. But is this not often a relief? "I no longer worry about being the belle of Newport," a beautiful woman, who had become a talented artist, once said to me. And I always liked that Virginia Woolf hero who meets middle age admitting: "Things have dropped from me. I have outlived certain desires . . . I am not so gifted as at one time seemed likely. Certain things lie beyond my scope. I shall never understand the harder problems of philosophy. Rome is the limit of my   9 travelling . . . I shall never see savages in Tahiti spearing fish by the light of a blazing cresset, or a lion spring in the jungle, or a naked man eating raw flesh . . ." (Thank God! you can hear him adding under his breath.)

The primitive, physical, functional pattern of the morning of   10
life, the active years before forty or fifty, is outlived: But there is still the afternoon opening up, which one can spend not in the feverish pace of the morning but in having time at last for those intellectual, cultural and spiritual activities that were pushed aside in the heat of the race. We Americans, with our terrific emphasis on youth, action and material success, certainly tend to belittle the afternoon of life and even to pretend it never comes. We push the clock back and try to prolong the morning, overreaching and overstraining ourselves in the unnatural effort. We do not succeed, of course. We cannot compete with our sons and daughters. And what a struggle it is to race with these overactive and under-wise adults! In our breathless attempts we often miss the flowering that waits for afternoon.

For is it not possible that middle age can be looked upon as a   11
period of second flowering, second growth, even a kind of second adolescence? It is true that society in general does not help one accept this interpretation of the second half of life. And therefore this period of expanding is often tragically misunderstood. Many people never climb above the plateau of forty-to-fifty. The signs that presage growth, so similar, it seems to me, to those in early adolescence: discontent, restlessness, doubt, despair, longing, are interpreted falsely as signs of decay. In youth one does not as often misinterpret the signs, one accepts them, quite rightly, as growing pains. One takes them seriously, listens to them, follows where they lead. One is afraid. Naturally. Who is not afraid of pure space—that breathtaking empty space of an open door? But despite fear, one goes through to the room beyond.

But in middle age, because of the false assumption that it is a   12
period of decline, one interprets these life-signs, paradoxically, as signs of approaching death. Instead of facing them, one runs away, one escapes—into depressions, nervous breakdowns, drink, love affairs or frantic, thoughtless, fruitless overwork. Anything, rather than face them. Anything, rather than stand still and learn from them. One tries to cure the signs of growth, to exorcise them, as if they were devils, when really they might be angels of annunciation.

Angels of annunciation of what? Of a new stage in living when,   13
having shed many of the physical struggles, the worldly ambitions, the material encumbrances of active life, one might be free to fulfill the neglected side of one's self. One might be free for growth of mind, heart and talent; free at last for spiritual growth; free of the

clamping sunrise shell. Beautiful as it was, it was still a closed world one had to outgrow. And the time may come when—comfortable and adaptable as it is—one may outgrow even the oyster shell.

MEANINGS AND VALUES

1. Explain why you think the author says she likes the oyster shell even though it is unattractive. In expressing her fondness for the ugly shell, what do you think the writer is saying about her feelings about marriage?

2. In what way is the observation "one may outgrow even the oyster shell" significant?

3. What is the purpose, in your opinion, of the writer's development of an analogy between a mature marriage and an oyster shell? What leads you to that opinion?

EXPOSITORY TECHNIQUES

1. In this reading, Lindbergh compares something abstract—the complexities of the middle years of marriage—to something concrete—an ordinary shell (see "Guide to Terms": *Concrete/Abstract*). The analogy is an unexpected one: Does it work, in your opinion? Explain your answer.

2. In addition to the main analogy, the author uses a secondary analogy, that of the double-sunrise shell as compared to romantic love. In your own words, restate what the author seems to be saying about romantic love through her double-sunrise shell analogy.

3. Locate the sentence where the writer directly states her analogy to the reader.

DICTION AND VOCABULARY

1. In addition to the extended analogy of marriage to the oyster shell, the writer uses simile and metaphor in this reading selection (Guide: *Figures of Speech*). Point to one example of each.

2. Lindbergh makes repeated use of the device of the rhetorical question (Guide: *Rhetorical Questions*) in this selection. Reread the selection and underline incidences of rhetorical questions. Why do you think she chooses to use them?

3. If you do not know the meaning of some of the following words, consult a dictionary: *tenaciously* (Par. 2); *propinquity* (3); *atrophy* (6); *presage* (11); *annunciation* (12); *encumbrances* (13).

READ TO WRITE

1. **Collaborating:** Bring to your writer's group an object from nature, such as a rock, pinecone, leaf, or the like. Consider the object brought by each group member in turn. Discuss the analogies suggested by each natural object. Choose one object and, as a group, write about the analogy you came up with in the manner of the Lindbergh reading selection.

2. **Considering Audience:** In your opinion, does the reader of this essay need to be involved in the middle years of a marriage in order to appreciate what the writer is saying? Explain your answer.

3. **Developing an Essay:** Through extended analogy, compare another aspect of relationships, such as a second marriage, dating one person exclusively, or remaining single, with a concrete object (not necessarily from nature). Alternatively, develop the analogy from question 1 into an essay using extended analogy, simile, and metaphor, using the Lindbergh reading selection as inspiration.

(NOTE: Suggestions for topics requiring development by ANALOGY are on pp. 208–209 at the end of this chapter.)

VISUAL TEXT

"To My Valentine"

1900s Greeting Card, UK

MEANINGS AND VALUES

1. What is taking place in this visual analogy? Why do you think the greeting card designer chose this image for a valentine? What is the intended message of this image?

2. What is love being compared to in this image? Do you think the comparison is effective?

3. Cupid is the Roman god of erotic love and is often pictured as a naked, winged boy carrying arrows that inspired love or passion in the victims he targeted. Moreover, Cupid was sometimes portrayed wearing armor. Does this greeting card offer a traditional representation of Cupid? If not, what is different?

READ TO WRITE

1. **Collaborating:** Working in a group of writers, brainstorm other analogies to love. Song lyrics might provide inspiration. (For example, "love is a rose," or "love is the ring of a telephone.") Represent your group's visual analogy by creating together a valentine to share with the rest of the class. Write together a brief explanation of how you came to choose this image and why.

2. **Considering Audience:** Consider the historical context of the visual text "To My Valentine," created in Britain between 1900 and 1909. In the British colony of South Africa, the British had just defeated the Dutch guerilla rebels in the brutal Boer War (1899 to 1902), and Britain was widely criticized for brutality throughout Europe. The serious and repressed Victorian era had come to a close with the death of Queen Victoria in 1901, and the new century represented a time of optimism for Britain. Women had not yet received the right to vote, and the country had yet to experience the horrors of World War I. How might that explain the tone (Guide: *Style/Tone*) of this visual text?

3. **Developing an Essay:** In the United States, *courtship* (the act of seeking the affection of another) has changed. For example, whereas in 1900 an unmarried couple might go on a sedate walk accompanied by a chaperone, today an unmarried couple might go to a hotel casino accompanied by an overnight bag containing skimpy lingerie. Search the Web for visual images of courtship in the first decade of the twentieth century and those of today. Then choose one image to analyze as a visual text from each time frame (one from 1900 to 1909 and one from the present). What does each image reveal about the prevailing attitude toward courtship? Use a subject-by-subject pattern for your essay.

(NOTE: Suggestions for topics requiring development by ANALOGY follow.)

Writing Suggestions for Chapter 6

ANALOGY

In any normal situation, the analogy is chosen to help explain a theme-idea that already exists—such as those in the first group below. But for imagination and fresh insight, you may wish to work from the other direction, to develop a theme that fits a preselected analogy-symbol.

1a. State a central theme about one of the following general topics or a suitable one of your own, and develop it into a composition by use of an analogy of your own choosing.

  a. A well-organized school system

  b. Starting a new business or other enterprise

  c. The long-range value of programs for underprivileged children

  d. Learning a new skill

  e. The need for cooperation in solving environmental problems

  f. Dealing with stress

 b. Select an analogy-symbol from the list below and fashion a theme that it can illustrate. Develop your composition as instructed.

  a. A freeway at commuting time

  b. Building a bridge across a river

  c. A merry-go-round

  d. A wedding or a divorce

  e. A car wash

  f. The tending of a garden

  g. An animal predator stalking prey

  h. A baseball game

  i. A juggling act

  j. An airport

2. Some topics are hard for most readers to understand without analogies to more familiar subjects. Think about some knowledge you have gained through study in the natural sciences

(chemistry, biology, physics, or physical anthropology, for example) or in the social sciences (sociology, psychology, or economics, for instance). Prepare an essay that uses one or more analogies to explain a subject from your studies for readers who have little experience with it. You do not need to structure the entire essay around a single analogy; you can use several different ones in the course of the essay.

3. To understand our everyday lives, we often think about them in terms of an analogy: my job is like a march through the desert; our relationship is like a hurricane; working with this organization is like walking around in the dark; being part of this political campaign has been like taking a roller coaster ride. Most often, we state such analogies (or just think about them). Choose one that you often use or think of one to describe your experiences. Develop it into an essay that helps readers either understand their own lives or learn something about experiences they have not had.

4. At the library, find a book that explains a complicated topic to the average reader, such as one that explains recent developments in astronomy, genetics or human DNA, or ecology. Look for a section that makes use of analogies, and prepare a paper discussing the ways the writer uses analogies to explain and explore. (You may wish to choose a Web site that make similar use of analogies.)

COLLABORATIVE EXERCISES

1. Working with a partner, choose a topic from a–f in Exercise 1a on page 208, and decide on an appropriate analogy. One member of the pair should outline the points that need to be made about the theme. The other member should outline comparative (analogous) details. Combine the two outlines, and write a well-developed essay from the combined plan.

2. In groups of three or more, come up with an appropriate analogy for the theme of "adapting to college life in the freshman year." Members should brainstorm to determine the best point of analogy. Once you determine that as a group, each member should provide one point of expansion that fits the analogy, and group members should then write essays of their own drawing on material developed by the group and adding their own ideas and examples.

7

Explaining Through
Process Analysis

Process analysis focuses on *how* something happens. As an expository pattern, it appears most frequently in *instructions* that tell us how to do something, or in *explanations* that explain how something is or was done. Instructions can range from the simple and everyday to the complex and challenging: from the directions for using a new appliance or piece of electronic equipment to a detailed plan showing how to make the United Nations more effective. Effective instructions do more than simply list the steps to be taken. They generally provide detailed justification for individual steps or for the plan as a whole, and they take into account readers' background knowledge and abilities.

Explanations, on the other hand, might explain the stages of a wide variety of operations or actions, of mental or evolutionary process—how stress affects judgment and health, how volcanoes cause earthquakes and mudslides, or how digital telephones work. Effective explanations take into account the things readers want or need to know about, but they can also appeal to curiosity and imagination. You can speculate how space exploration might work or how societies might be better organized.

The following process analysis by L. Rust Hills shows how process analysis can be used in imaginative ways to talk about everyday matters. It takes the form of a set of directions, and though it is short, it is a whole essay in miniature. The second example by Ira Flatow is an explanation that helps readers understand some of the reasons hurricanes can be so dangerous.

This is admittedly not a problem qualitatively on the order of what to do about the proliferation of nuclear weaponry, but quantitatively it disturbs a great deal of Mankind—all those millions, in fact, who've ever used a bar of soap—except, of course, me. I've solved the problem of what to do about those troublesome, wasteful, messy little soap ends, and I'm ready now to deliver my solution to a grateful world.

The solution depends on a fact not commonly known, which I discovered in the shower. Archimedes made his great discovery about displacement ("Eureka!" and all that) in the bathtub, but I made mine in the shower. It is not commonly known that if, when you soap yourself, you hold *the same side* of the bar of soap cupped in the palm of your hand, that side will, after a few days, become curved and rounded, while the side of the bar you're soaping yourself *with* will become flat. (In between showers or baths, leave the bar curved side down so it won't stick to whatever it's resting on.) When the bar diminishes sufficiently, the flat side can be pressed onto a new bar of soap and will adhere sufficiently overnight to become, with the next day's use, a just slightly oversized new bar, ready to be treated in the same way as the one that came before it, in perpetuity, one bar after another, down through the length of your days on earth, with never a nasty soap end to trouble you ever again. Eureka, and now on to those nuclear weapons. Man is at his best, I feel, when in his problem-solving mode.

—L. Rust Hills, "What to Do About Soap Ends"

It's not the wind, though, that's the most dangerous part of a hurricane. It's the water, especially when something called the "storm surge" occurs. As the low-pressure eye of the hurricane sits over the ocean, the sea level literally rises into a dome of water. For every inch drop in barometric pressure, the ocean rises a foot higher. Now, out at sea, that means nothing. The rise is not even noticeable. But when that mound of water starts moving toward land, the situation becomes crucial. As the water approaches a shallow beach, the dome of water rises. It may rise ten to fifteen feet in an hour and span fifty miles. Like a marine bulldozer, the surge may rise up twenty feet high, crash onto land, and wash everything away. Then with six- to eight-foot waves riding atop this mound of water, the storm surge destroys buildings, trees, cars, and anything else in its path. It's this storm surge that accounts for 90 percent of the deaths during a hurricane.

—Ira Flatow, "Storm Surge"

WHY USE PROCESS ANALYSIS?

In almost every part of our lives, we rely on **instructions.** They help us cook a meal, repair a car, get to a vacation spot, perform an experiment, and calculate income tax. Essays offering instruction appear in newspapers, magazines, and books on topics from fashion, fitness, and sports to technology, pets, and personal relationships.

We turn to **explanations** not when we want to do things but when we want to understand how things work. Explanations can focus on mechanical or technical subjects (how computer operating systems work), on social matters (how societies create groups of insiders and outsiders), on psychological topics (how stress builds up), or on natural subjects (how cancer cells take over from normal cells).

Process analysis can have imaginative uses as well, helping us speculate about building floating cities, changing our diets for better health, or considering steps that might close the ozone hole over the South Pole. Writers sometimes explain a process in order to amuse or criticize—analyzing with a critical eye some aspects of behavior (as do Fish and Frazier in this chapter) or looking at some surprising natural phenomenon. And process analysis often appears in combination with other expository patterns. You might use it to help readers understand the steps by which a cause (such as meditating) leads to an effect (reduced physical and mental stress), for example. Or you might explain differences in the processes of forming social relationships as part of an essay contrasting the behaviors of men and women.

Expository writing built around process analysis generally responds to a need for information and understanding. The need may be immediate (how to prepare for an upcoming sales meeting or an exam). It may be practical or helpful (understanding the ways our bodies respond to stress; strategies for incorporating a healthy diet and exercise into a busy schedule). Or it may be a matter of curiosity or a desire for understanding (discovering how puppeteers in Indonesia create hours-long shows that appeal to both children and adults; investigating the ways our brains process information).

CHOOSING A STRATEGY

Having encountered instructions and explanations many times before, your readers will probably expect you to employ some basic strategies. For example, they will expect the opening of a set of instructions to announce its purpose, establish the need for a step-by-step explanation of the process, and indicate any materials needed to accomplish it. The way you choose to accomplish these things should vary from situation to situation and topic to topic, however. If you are addressing a need your readers can readily recognize, such as finding effective ways to take a test, make a speech, or apply for a student loan, you might begin with a brief example of how important such knowledge is. Or you might even state the need directly: "Would you like to know how to give a speech without getting so flustered that you forget half of what you planned to say?" or "Wouldn't you like to know how to get a student loan without all the hassle and paperwork most people encounter?"

In many instances, however, you will have to convince readers that they ought to be interested in the instructions you are offering. This is the situation Heather Kaye faced when she decided to tell readers how to play the game "Bones." In response, she created an opening paragraph reminding her readers how often they get bored and telling them of the simple equipment they will need to pass the time with an amusing game.

> When boredom strikes, what can you do if you are tired of computer games, don't like chess, and don't have the money or time to go to a movie? Just collect a pad of paper, a pen, six dice, and a friend, and you are ready to play a game called "Bones." Bones provides fun and excitement, and you don't have to be Einstein to learn how to play. It is a game of chance and luck, laughter and friendship.

For an explanation, however, you may need to appeal to readers' curiosity or their desire for understanding (practical or otherwise). Emphasizing the mystery, adventure, or even oddity of a process will engage most readers' curiosity: What bodily processes allow pearl divers to stay underwater for several minutes when most of us can hold our breath for only ten or twenty seconds? How do bats produce a kind of "radar" that enables them to fly in the dark and catch minute insects? When you appeal to readers' desire for understanding, you will be most likely to succeed when you suggest a practical dimension for the knowledge. For instance, some readers interested in the natural world may be interested in the complex stages of the honey-making process. Yet to attract the majority of readers you may need to suggest that such knowledge can help them understand honey's virtues as a sweetener or choose among different kinds of honey as they shop.

Most process analyses are organized into simple, chronological units, either the *steps* involved in accomplishing the task or the *stages* of operation. In planning a set of instructions, begin by breaking it down into steps, approaching the activity as if you were doing it for the first time so that you do not leave out any necessary elements that have become so routine you might easily overlook them. Then create an organization that will help readers keep track of the many steps, perhaps dividing the task into several units, each containing smaller steps. Consider building your plan around a framework like the following.

> Introduction: Need for the information, materials, statement of purpose
> Step 1: Explanations, details
> > Substeps 1, 2, 3. . . . (if any)
> Step 2: Explanations, details
> > Substeps 1, 2, 3. . . .
> Step 3: Explanations, details
> > Substeps 1, 2, 3. . . .
> Summary (if necessary)

In planning an explanation, identify the various stages or components, including any that overlap, and create an organization that presents them in an easy-to-follow, logical order. If the process is complex, divide it into major components and subdivide each in turn, just as the following rough plan does.

> Introduction (tentative thesis identifying need for the information): Because most people do not understand the amount of energy, natural resources, and human effort needed to create paper, they use it wastefully; understanding the process and the resources it requires is an important first step for all of us concerned with preserving our environment.
> Stage 1: Bringing together natural resources
> > a. Wood—logging
> > b. Water—drawing from rivers or lakes
> > c. Fuel for heat and power (oil, gas, or electric)
> Stage 2: Turning logs into pulp
> > a. Grinding up logs (uses water and power) *or*
> > b. Breaking wood into pulp using chemicals
> Stage 3: Turning pulp into paper
> > a. Paper machine
> > > 1. Feeding pulp into machine
> > > 2. Using heated screen to congeal pulp into a mushy sheet of paper

   b. Dryer
      1. Using heat to further congeal pulp
      2. Using rollers to stretch and thin the sheet (consumes
         energy)
Stage 4: Turning paper into paper products (energy and labor
   intensive)
   a. Creating giant rolls of paper
   b. Cutting and folding rolls of paper into tissues, newsprint,
      pads, paper towels, and other everyday products

Maintaining the exact order of a process is sometimes of greatest importance, as in a recipe. But occasionally the organization of an analysis may present problems. You may need to interrupt the step-by-step format to give descriptions, definitions, and other explanatory asides. Some processes may even defy a strict chronological treatment because several things occur simultaneously. In explaining the operating process of a gasoline engine, for example, you would be unable to convey at once everything that happens at the same time. Instead, you would need to present the material in *general* stages, each with subdivisions, so your readers could see each stage by itself yet also become aware of interacting relationships.

DEVELOPING A PROCESS ANALYSIS

In developing the paragraphs and sentences that make up an explanation of a process, you also need to pay attention to your readers' expectations. When you are presenting instructions, your readers will expect you to tell them of any necessary materials and will look for frequent summaries to allow them to check if they have followed the steps correctly. They will benefit from warnings of special difficulties they may encounter or any dangers the procedure entails. In addition, they will appreciate words of encouragement ("The procedure may seem strange, but it *will* work") or reminders of the goal of the process ("No pain, no gain: the only way to a flat tummy is through the hard work of repeating these exercises").

Effective explanations and instructions alike often have a visual element. Drawings can show how the parts of a mechanism fit together or help readers recognize the differences among the elements of a natural process, such as the growth of an insect or the eruption of a volcano. Pictures can help readers identify ingredients or components and show them what a finished product will look like.

To guide readers through the steps or stages of a process, to remind them of changes that will occur, or to highlight the sequence of events, consider using words that point out relationships among the various elements.

> Words identifying different stages—*step, event, element, component, phase, state, feature, occurrence*
> Words emphasizing relationships in time—*after, next, while, first, second, third, fourth, concurrently, the next week, later, preceding, following*
> Words indicating changes—*becomes, varies, transforms, causes, completes, alters, revises, uncovers, synthesizes, cures, builds*

Make sure you include enough details to allow readers to visualize the steps or stages of the process, but not so many that the details become confusing. Present major steps (or stages) in considerable detail, minor ones in less. If you choose to write in the second person (*you*), as in a set of directions ("You should then blend the ingredients"), make sure you use this point of view consistently and do not shift to the first person (*I* or *we*) or the third person (*he, she, it,* or *they*) without good reason. If you choose the first person or third person for your perspective, make sure likewise that your presentation is consistent.

Student Essay

Losing weight is not easy for most people, nor is the process a simple one, as Karin Gaffney explains in the essay that follows. As a result, she provided detailed explanations along with her dieting instructions so that readers can understand not only *how* to diet but also *why* they should follow certain steps and avoid others.

Losing Weight
by Karin Gaffney

Across the board, regardless of age, gender, race, or background, most people spend time trying to lose weight (Williamson et al.). Some people want to lose only five or ten pounds while others worry about getting rid of seventy-five pounds or more. As a result, weight loss is both a universal concern and a highly individualized matter.

Losing weight must mean a lot to Americans. After all, they spend over three billion dollars on weight-loss programs each year ("Rating" 353). If you think you need to diet, think again. Many people think they are overweight because they compare themselves to impossibly thin models or imagine themselves in the slimmest of new fashions. So if you think you need to diet, consult a doctor and other reliable sources of health information. Then go to a good weight-loss program—if you really need one.

Why should you be careful about going on a diet? A study in 1988 by the Centers for Disease Control concluded that any change of weight either up or down led to a higher rate of heart disease in the people studied ("Losing" 350). This does not necessarily mean that you should forget about dieting, however, because weight loss can also help you avoid other health problems ("Losing" 348, 350).

To lose weight, some people turn to commercial diets and hospital programs, yet the majority rely on self-help. For those people who are trying to lose weight on their own, I can offer some general advice along with a simple weight-loss program. The simple advice is no different from what most of us have already heard, but it probably still needs to be repeated: 1) cut down on high-fat foods, 2) eat moderate portions of healthy foods, and 3) get regular exercise. Above all, consult your doctor not only to determine whether you should diet but to make sure your dietary and exercise programs are appropriate for you (and not for the models and athletes who appear on exercise tapes or talk about their health and muscle-power diets in magazines).

A person who is overweight probably has a diet heavy in fat (Beitz 281). A calorie of fat in food becomes part of body fat much more easily than does a calorie of carbohydrate, which is easily burned as energy (Delaney 46). In other words, the body often keeps the fat it takes in, but the carbohydrates it uses up. Moreover, a gram of fat has about 2.25 times as many calories as one gram of carbohydrate or protein does (Beitz 281).

The first step in a healthy weight-loss plan is to reduce the fat in your diet. If you eliminate high-fat foods such as ice creams, cheese, hamburgers, and butter from your diet, your body will respond immediately to the change. Low-fat substitutes, such as low-fat milk, can also have a positive effect, as can steps like cutting the fat off meat or taking the skin off poultry ("Losing" 352).

The second step is to eat more foods that are low in fat but high in fiber and carbohydrates. Here are several choices:

1. Potatoes (baked, not fried, and without butter or sour cream)
2. Beans (pinto, kidney, lentil, and so on)
3. Whole grains (cereals, pastas, breads)
4. Fresh fruits
5. Skim milk (and skim milk products)

When you eat foods like these, your blood sugar levels stabilize and you get "filled up," yet you take in only about one-half the number of calories that fatty alternatives provide (Delaney 44–45).

The third step is to snack wisely. Limit your snacks, of course, and choose from foods like the following: string cheese, corn-on-the-cob (without butter), vegetables, angel food cake, pita bread, soft pretzels, fruits, bagels, nonfat yogurt, juice, animal crackers, or fig bars ("30 Low Fat" 3). Food companies have also been adding fat-free items to grocery shelves in recent years, so when you shop, look for low-fat frozen desserts, low-fat cookies, and the like.

The fourth step is to exercise regularly. Exercise can burn up to 200–300 calories per day (Delaney 46). You may also be surprised to learn that exercise can decrease your weight even if you do not radically change your eating habits. Regular exercise increases basal metabolism, the energy needed just to stay alive. One-half of the calories in a person's diet, for example, can go to basal metabolism. Exercise can increase the basal metabolism rate so that a person can lose more calories by just living and breathing. The amount of muscle a person has also affects basal metabolism. A person with more muscle has a higher basal metabolism and burns up more of the calories in food through this means ("Losing" 357).

Your exercise routine does not have to be strenuous or exhausting like that of an Olympic trainee. Moderate exercise, such as one half-hour to an hour of good-paced walking, is beneficial. If you need an incentive to start your exercise program, remember that a person who goes from a nonexerciser to a moderate exerciser will notice the results more than someone going from moderate to advanced. There are other side benefits to exercise as well. For example, people who exercise regularly develop adult diabetes 40 percent less frequently than nonexercisers do ("Losing" 351).

The fifth step is to set reasonable goals for weight loss. Concentrate on losing a pound or two at a time, and try to maintain this small weight loss before continuing ("Losing" 350). This approach will help make you confident of your ability to lose weight and help you avoid the yo-yo effect of losing a lot of weight, then gaining it right back.

The final step is to keep several key points in mind.

1. Make eating right and exercising (not dieting) the focus of your attention and effort.
2. Concentrate on maintaining your healthy lifestyle so that you can make your weight loss permanent and benefit over the long term from good eating and exercise habits.
3. Remember that you are an individual and that the advice offered here may or may not apply to you. Always consult a doctor who knows you and your medical history.

Works Cited

Beitz, Donald C. "Nutrition." *McGraw-Hill Yearbook of Science and Technology.* New York: McGraw, 1993. Print.

Delaney, Lisa. "The 'No-Hunger' Weight-Loss Plan."
Prevention Sept. 1993: 43–46. Print.

"Losing Weight: What Works, What Doesn't." *Consumer Reports* June 1993: 347–52. Print.

"Rating the Diets." *Consumer Reports* June 1993: 353–57. Print.

"30 Low Fat Foods to Grab." *Thinline* Sept./Oct. 1993: 3. Print.

Williamson, David F., Mary K. Serdula, Robert F. Auclay, Alan Levy, and Tim Byers. "Weight Loss Attempts in Adults: Goals, Duration, and Rate of Weight Loss." *American Journal of Public Health* Sept. 1992: 82–89. Print.

AMY SUTHERLAND

> Journalist AMY SUTHERLAND grew up in suburban Cincinnati, Ohio, earned an M.A. from the Medill School of Journalism at Northwestern University, and worked as a reporter for several daily newspapers. Inspired by a visit to the 2000 Pillsbury Bake-Off in San Francisco, she wrote her first book, *Cookoff* (2003). Her research of exotic animal training led to her second book, *Kicked, Bitten, and Scratched* (2007).

What Shamu Taught Me About a Happy Marriage

> Should relationships come with owner's manuals? In this witty excerpt from her 2009 book *What Shamu Taught Me About Life, Love, and Marriage*, Sutherland draws upon techniques learned from animals and their trainers to fine tune her husband's behavior.

As I wash dishes at the kitchen sink, my husband paces behind me, irritated. "Have you seen my keys?" he snarls, then huffs out a loud sigh and stomps from the room with our dog, Dixie, at his heels, anxious over her favorite human's upset.   1

In the past I would have been right behind Dixie. I would have turned off the faucet and joined the hunt while trying to soothe my husband with bromides like, "Don't worry, they'll turn up." But that only made him angrier, and a simple case of missing keys soon would become a full-blown angst-ridden drama starring the two of us and our poor nervous dog.   2

Now, I focus on the wet dish in my hands. I don't turn around. I don't say a word. I'm using a technique I learned from a dolphin trainer.   3

I love my husband. He's well read, adventurous and does a hysterical rendition of a northern Vermont accent that still cracks me up after 12 years of marriage.   4

But he also tends to be forgetful, and is often tardy and mercurial. He hovers around me in the kitchen asking if I read this or that piece in *The New Yorker* when I'm trying to concentrate on the simmering pans. He leaves wadded tissues in his wake. He suffers from serious bouts of spousal deafness but never fails to hear me when I mutter to myself on the other side of the house, "What did you say?" he'll shout.   5

These minor annoyances are not the stuff of separation and divorce, but in sum they began to dull my love for Scott.   6

I wanted—needed—to nudge him a little closer to perfect, to make him into a mate who might annoy me a little less, who wouldn't keep me waiting at restaurants, a mate who would be easier to love.

So, like many wives before me, I ignored a library of advice   7
books and set about improving him. By nagging, of course, which only made his behavior worse: he'd drive faster instead of slower; shave less frequently, not more; and leave his reeking bike garb on the bedroom floor longer than ever.

We went to a counselor to smooth the edges off our marriage.   8
She didn't understand what we were doing there and complimented us repeatedly on how well we communicated. I gave up, I guessed she was right—our union was better than most—and resigned myself to stretches of slow-boil resentment and occasional sarcasm.

Then something magical happened. For a book I was writing   9
about a school for exotic animal trainers, I started commuting from Maine to California, where I spent my days watching students do the seemingly impossible: teaching hyenas to pirouette on command, cougars to offer their paws for a nail clipping, and baboons to skateboard.

I listened, rapt, as professional trainers explained how they   10
taught dolphins to flip and elephants to paint. Eventually it hit me that the same techniques might work on that stubborn but lovable species, the American husband.

The central lesson I learned from exotic animal trainers is that I   11
should reward behavior I like and ignore behavior I don't. After all, you don't get a sea lion to balance a ball on the end of its nose by nagging. The same goes for the American husband.

Back in Maine, I began thanking Scott if he threw one dirty shirt   12
into the hamper. If he threw in two, I'd kiss him. Meanwhile, I would step over any soiled clothes on the floor without one sharp word, though I did sometimes kick them under the bed. But as he basked in my appreciation, the piles became smaller.

I was using what trainers call "approximations," rewarding   13
the small steps toward learning a whole new behavior. You can't expect a baboon to learn to flip on command in one session, just as you can't expect an American husband to begin regularly picking up his dirty socks by praising him once for picking up a single sock. With the baboon you first reward a hop, then a bigger hop, then an even bigger hop. With Scott the husband, I began to praise every small act every time: if he drove just a mile an hour slower, tossed one pair of shorts into the hamper, or was on time for anything.

I also began to analyze my husband the way a trainer considers   14
an exotic animal. Enlightened trainers learn all they can about
a species, from anatomy to social structure, to understand how it
thinks, what it likes and dislikes, what comes easily to it and what
doesn't. For example, an elephant is a herd animal, so it responds to
hierarchy. It cannot jump, but can stand on its head. It is a
vegetarian.

The exotic animal known as Scott is a loner, but an alpha male.   15
So hierarchy matters, but being in a group doesn't so much. He has
the balance of a gymnast, but moves slowly, especially when getting
dressed. Skiing comes naturally, but being on time does not. He's an
omnivore, and what a trainer would call food-driven.

Once I started thinking this way, I couldn't stop. At the school   16
in California, I'd be scribbling notes on how to walk an emu or have
a wolf accept you as a pack member, but I'd be thinking, "I can't
wait to try this on Scott."

On a field trip with the students, I listened to a professional   17
trainer describe how he had taught African crested cranes to stop
landing on his head and shoulders. He did this by training the
leggy birds to land on mats on the ground. This, he explained, is
what is called an "incompatible behavior," a simple but brilliant
concept.

Rather than teach the cranes to stop landing on him, the trainer   18
taught the birds something else, a behavior that would make the undesirable behavior impossible. The birds couldn't alight on the mats
and his head simultaneously.

At home, I came up with incompatible behaviors for Scott to   19
keep him from crowding me while I cooked. To lure him away from
the stove, I piled up parsley for him to chop or cheese for him to
grate at the other end of the kitchen island. Or I'd set out a bowl of
chips and salsa across the room. Soon I'd done it: no more Scott hov-
ering around me while I cooked.

I followed the students to SeaWorld San Diego, where a dol-   20
phin trainer introduced me to least reinforcing syndrome (L.R.S.).
When a dolphin does something wrong, the trainer doesn't respond
in any way. He stands still for a few beats, careful not to look at the
dolphin, and then returns to work. The idea is that any response,
positive or negative, fuels a behavior. If a behavior provokes no response, it typically dies away.

In the margins of my notes I wrote, "Try on Scott!"   21

It was only a matter of time before he was again tearing around   22
the house searching for his keys, at which point I said nothing and

kept at what I was doing. It took a lot of discipline to maintain my calm, but results were immediate and stunning. His temper fell far shy of its usual pitch and then waned like a fast-moving storm. I felt as if I should throw him a mackerel.

Now he's at it again; I hear him banging a closet door shut, rus- 23 tling through papers on a chest in the front hall and thumping up-stairs. At the sink, I hold steady. Then, sure enough, all goes quiet. A moment later, he walks into the kitchen, keys in hand, and says calmly, "Found them."

Without turning, I call out, "Great, see you later." 24

Off he goes with our much-calmed pup. 25

After two years of exotic animal training, my marriage is far 26 smoother, my husband much easier to love. I used to take his faults personally; his dirty clothes on the floor were an affront, a symbol of how he didn't care enough about me. But thinking of my husband as an exotic species gave me the distance I needed to consider our differences more objectively.

I adopted the trainers' motto: "It's never the animal's fault." 27 When my training attempts failed, I didn't blame Scott. Rather, I brainstormed new strategies, thought up more incompatible behav-iors and used smaller approximations. I dissected my own behavior, considered how my actions might inadvertently fuel his. I also ac-cepted that some behaviors were too entrenched, too instinctive to train away. You can't stop a badger from digging, and you can't stop my husband from losing his wallet and keys.

Professionals talk of animals that understand training so well 28 they eventually use it back on the trainer. My animal did the same. When the training techniques worked so beautifully, I couldn't re-sist telling my husband what I was up to. He wasn't offended, just amused. As I explained the techniques and terminology, he soaked it up. Far more than I realized.

Last fall, firmly in middle age, I learned that I needed braces. 29 They were not only humiliating, but also excruciating. For weeks my gums, teeth, jaw and sinuses throbbed. I complained frequently and loudly. Scott assured me that I would become used to all the metal in my mouth. I did not.

One morning, as I launched into yet another tirade about how 30 uncomfortable I was, Scott just looked at me blankly. He didn't say a word or acknowledge my rant in any way, not even with a nod.

I quickly ran out of steam and started to walk away. Then I real- 31 ized what was happening, and I turned and asked, "Are you giving me an L.R.S.?" Silence. "You are, aren't you?"

He finally smiled, but his L.R.S. had already done the trick.   32
He'd begun to train me, the American wife.

Meanings and Values

1. What techniques from animal training does the writer apply in the process of trying to change her husband's behavior?

2. What is the result when Scott turns the tables on the writer and uses the least reinforcing syndrome (L.R.S.) himself?

3. What do you think the writer's purpose is for writing this process analysis?

Expository Techniques

1. In her explanation of the behavioral techniques she uses, does the author provide step-by-step instructions? List them.

2. How does the writer convince her readers that they ought to be interested in the process she is sharing?

3. In her examples, does the writer include enough details for you to understand various stages of training the American husband? Explain your answer.

Diction and Vocabulary

1. Why do you think the writer chooses to refer to Scott and herself as "the American husband" (Par. 10) and "the American wife" (32)?

2. The writer uses some technical terms, such as *incompatible behavior*, that are unfamiliar to most readers. Is she effective in getting their meanings across? How so?

3. If you do not know the meaning of some of the following words, consult a dictionary: *bromides, angst-ridden* (Par. 2); *approximations* (13); *hierarchy* (14); *incompatible* (17); *inadvertently* (27); *tirade* (30).

Read to Write

1. **Collaborating:** In addition to process analysis, Sutherland uses comparison—she compares changing the behavior of her husband to changing the behavior of an exotic animal. Working with a group of writers, make a list of pairs of processes (for example, writing a computer program and writing a novel, or going on a job interview and going on a first date). Then choose one pair of

processes and summarize the similarities between them in a paragraph.

2. **Considering Audience:** Do you think that both men and women would have the same response to this reading selection? Explain your answer.

3. **Developing an Essay:** Choose a social challenge (for example, overcoming shyness or stage fright, asking a new romantic interest out on a first date, behaving appropriately in a classroom or work situation, or some other) and write an explanation of a process for meeting that challenge.

(NOTE: Suggestions for topics requiring development by PROCESS ANALYSIS are on pp. 249–250 at the end of this chapter.)

BENJAMIN FRANKLIN

BENJAMIN FRANKLIN, one of the most remarkable of the Founding Fathers of the United States, was born in Boston in 1706, the tenth son of the seventeen children of a candle and soap maker. From this modest beginning, Franklin rose to become a drafter and signer of the Declaration of Independence, the U.S. representative in France during the American Revolution, and a delegate to the Constitutional Convention. In addition to his notable roles as states-man and diplomat, Franklin was a printer, publisher, and author whose writings include the best-selling *Poor Richard's Almanack*. Franklin, writing under the pseudonym of Richard Saunders, embellished this annual publication with his famously pithy, fre-quently cynical sayings, such as: "He that falls in love with himself will have no rivals"; "Three may keep a secret, if two of them are dead"; and "If you'd have it done, Go: if not, Send." In addition to his success as a man of letters, Benjamin Franklin made significant contributions to science, especially his pioneering experiments with electricity, which led to the discovery of the crucial scientific principle that we know today as the law of conservation of charge. Benjamin Franklin died in 1790 in Philadelphia.

The Art of Procuring Pleasant Dreams

In this instructive, eccentric, and engaging essay, originally written in the form of a letter in 1786, Benjamin Franklin displays his fond-ness for scientific theorizing while offering step-by-step advice on how to fall asleep, stay asleep, and dream well. (Similarly enter-taining scientific correspondence by Benjamin Franklin includes letters on topics as diverse as choosing eyeglasses, the cause of colds, and the behavior of oil and water.) More than two centuries after Franklin first penned this process analysis, its suggestions are still pertinent, and his prose still has the power to charm us while teaching us a thing or two about living the good life with a clear conscience.

As a great part of our life is spent in sleep, during which we have sometimes pleasant and sometimes painful dreams, it becomes of some consequence to obtain the one kind and avoid the other; for whether real or imaginary, pain is pain and pleasure is pleasure. If we can sleep without dreaming, it is well that painful dreams are avoided.   1

If, while we sleep, we can have any pleasant dreams, it is, as the French say, *autant de gagné*, so much added to the pleasure of life.   2

To this end it is, in the first place, necessary to be careful in pre-serving health by due exercise and great temperance; for in sickness   3 the imagination is disturbed, and disagreeable, sometimes terrible, ideas are apt to present themselves. Exercise should precede meals, not immediately follow them; the first promotes, the latter, unless moderate, obstructs digestion.

If, after exercise, we feed sparingly, the digestion will be easy　4 and good, the body lightsome, the temper cheerful, and all the animal functions performed agreeably. Sleep, when it follows, will be natural and undisturbed, while indolence, with full feeding, occasions nightmares and horrors inexpressible; we fall from precipices, are assaulted by wild beasts, murderers, and demons, and experience every variety of distress.

Observe, however, that the quantities of food and exercise are　5 relative things: those who move much may, and indeed ought to, eat more; those who use little exercise should eat little.

In general, mankind, since the improvement of cookery, eat about　6 twice as much as nature requires. Suppers are not bad if we have not dined; but restless nights follow hearty suppers after full dinners.

Indeed, as there is a difference in constitutions, some rest well　7 after these meals; it costs them only a frightful dream and an apoplexy, after which they sleep till doomsday. Nothing is more common in the newspapers than instances of people who, after eating a hearty supper, are found dead abed in the morning.

Another means of preserving health to be attended to is the having a constant supply of fresh air in your bedchamber. It has been a　8 great mistake, the sleeping in rooms exactly closed and the beds surrounded by curtains. No outward air that may come in to you is so unwholesome as the unchanged air, often breathed, of a close chamber.

As boiling water does not grow hotter by long boiling if the　9 particles that receive greater heat can escape, so living bodies do not putrefy if the particles, so fast as they become putrid, can be thrown off. Nature expels them by the pores of the skin and lungs, and in a free, open air they are carried off; but in a close room we receive them again and again, though they become more and more corrupt.

A number of persons crowded into a small room thus spoil the　10 air in a few minutes, and even render it mortal as the Black Hole at Calcutta. A single person is said to spoil only a gallon of air per minute, and therefore requires a longer time to spoil a chamberful; but it is done, however, in proportion, and many putrid disorders hence have their origin.

It is recorded of Methuselah, who, being the longest liver, may　11 be supposed to have best preserved his health, that he slept always in the open air; for when he had lived five hundred years an angel said to him: "Arise, Methuselah, and build thee an house, for thou shalt live yet five hundred years longer."

But Methuselah answered and said: "If I am to live but five   12
hundred years longer, it is not worth while to build me an house; I will sleep in the air, as I have been used to do."

Physicians, after having for ages contended that the sick should   13
not be indulged with fresh air, have at length discovered that it may do them good. It is therefore to be hoped that they may in time discover likewise that it is not hurtful to those who are in health, and that we may then be cured of the *aerophobia* that at present distresses weak minds, and makes them choose to be stifled and poisoned rather than leave open the window of a bedchamber or put down the glass of a coach.

Confined air, when saturated with perspirable matter, will not   14
receive more, and that matter must remain in our bodies and occasion diseases; but it gives us some previous notice of its being about to be hurtful by producing certain uneasiness, slight indeed at first, such as with regard to the lungs is a trifling sensation and to the pores of the skin a kind of restlessness which is difficult to describe, and few that feel it know the cause of it.

But we may recollect that sometimes, on waking in the night,   15
we have, if warmly covered, found it difficult to get asleep again. We turn often, without finding repose in any position. This fidgetiness (to use a vulgar expression for want of a better) is occasioned wholly by uneasiness in the skin, owing to the retention of the perspirable matter, the bedclothes having received their quantity, and being saturated, refusing to take any more.

To become sensible of this by an experiment, let a person keep   16
his position in the bed, throw off the bedclothes, and suffer fresh air to approach the part uncovered of his body; he will then feel that part suddenly refreshed, for the air will immediately relieve the skin by receiving, licking up, and carrying off the load of perspirable matter that incommoded it. For every portion of cool air that approaches the warm skin, in receiving its part of that vapor, receives therewith a degree of heat that rarefies and renders it lighter, when it will be pushed away with its burden by cooler and therefore heavier fresh air, which for a moment supplies its place, and then, being likewise changed and warmed, gives way to a succeeding quantity.

This is the order of nature, to prevent animals being infected by   17
their own perspiration. He will now be sensible of the difference between the part exposed to the air and that which, remaining sunk in

the bed, denies the air access; for this part now manifests its uneasiness more distinctly by the comparison, and the seat of the uneasiness is more plainly perceived than when the whole surface of the body was affected by it.

Here, then, is one great and general cause of unpleasing dreams. For when the body is uneasy the mind will be disturbed by it, and disagreeable ideas of various kinds will in sleep be the natural consequences. The remedies, preventive and curative, follow. **18**

1. By eating moderately (as before advised for health's sake) less perspirable matter is produced in a given time; hence the bedclothes receive it longer before they are saturated, and we may therefore sleep longer before we are made uneasy by their refusing to receive any more.
2. By using thinner and more porous bedclothes, which will suffer the perspirable matter more easily to pass through them, we are less incommoded, such being longer tolerable.
3. When you are awakened by this uneasiness and find you cannot easily sleep again, get out of bed, beat up and turn your pillow, shake the bedclothes well, with at least twenty shakes, then throw the bed open and leave it to cool; in the meanwhile, continuing undressed, walk about your chamber till your skin has had time to discharge its load, which it will do sooner as the air may be drier and colder. When you begin to feel the cold air unpleasant, then return to your bed, and you will soon fall asleep, and your sleep will be sweet and pleasant. All the scenes presented to your fancy will be, too, of a pleasing kind. I am often as agreeably entertained with them as by the scenery of an opera.

If you happen to be too indolent to get out of bed, you may, instead of it, lift up your bedclothes with one arm and leg, so as to draw in a good deal of fresh air, and by letting them fall force it out again. This, repeated twenty times, will so clear them of the perspirable matter they have imbibed as to permit your sleeping well for some time afterward. But this latter method is not equal to the former. **19**

Those who do not love trouble and can afford to have two beds will find great luxury in rising, when they wake in a hot bed, and going into the cool one. Such shifting of beds would also be of great service to persons ill of a fever, as it refreshes and frequently procures sleep. **20**

A very large bed that will admit a removal so distant from the   21
first situation as to be cool and sweet may in a degree answer the
same end.

One or two observations more will conclude this little piece.   22
Care must be taken, when you lie down, to dispose your pillow so
as to suit your manner of placing your head and to be perfectly easy;
then place your limbs so as not to bear inconveniently hard upon
one another, as, for instance, the joints of your ankles; for though a
bad position may at first give but little pain and be hardly noticed,
yet a continuance will render it less tolerable, and the uneasiness
may come on while you are asleep and disturb your imagination.

These are the rules of the art. But though they will generally   23
prove effectual in producing the end intended, there is a case in
which the most punctual observance of them will be totally fruitless.
I need not mention the case to you, my dear friend; but my account
of the art would be imperfect without it. The case is when the person who desires to have pleasant dreams has not taken care to preserve, what is necessary above all things, A GOOD CONSCIENCE.

MEANINGS AND VALUES

1. What act do people perform before going to bed that the author says
   can lead to "a frightful dream and an apoplexy, after which they
   sleep till doomsday"? What more serious consequence does Franklin
   say this act could have?

2. In addition to eating moderately (temperance) and exercise, what is
   another means of achieving a good night's sleep, according to
   Franklin? Do you agree? Why or why not?

3. In the course of discussing the best type of bed linens to use for a
   good night's rest, the author suggests that those who can afford to do
   so might consider having two beds. What is the alternative Franklin
   offers as a substitute for this rather impractical solution?

4. In the concluding paragraph of the reading, Franklin says that a person who wishes to have pleasant dreams should maintain one thing
   above all. What is it? Do you agree with him? Why or why not?

EXPOSITORY TECHNIQUES

1. Locate the three "remedies," listed as three numbered steps, that
   Benjamin Franklin suggests for curing "unpleasing dreams." Rewrite

all three in your own words. Which of the three steps does the author seem to believe is the most important? Explain how you can tell.

2. The author presents a brief dialogue between the biblical patriarch Methuselah and an angel. Is this a useful technique for underscoring the author's point about the benefits of fresh air? Why or why not?

3. In Paragraph 16, the author describes an experiment, using scientific terms such as "matter" and "vapor," that the reader can try in order to understand the "uneasiness in the skin" that creates a restless slumber. Even though this experiment uses outmoded terminology, do you find it convincing? Is the process that is being analyzed explained clearly enough for the reader to replicate it? Explain.

4. What comparison does Franklin draw in Paragraph 18?

DICTION AND VOCABULARY

1. What is the "vulgar expression" used by Franklin in Paragraph 15? What does *vulgar* probably mean in this context? Why do you think the author is somewhat apologetic about using this expression?

2. What is the "Black Hole at Calcutta," mentioned in Paragraph 10? Do you think that the author's use of this exaggeration is justified in making his point, or do you think that it weakens his point? Explain.

3. What is the tone of this essay? Explain.

READ TO WRITE

1. **Collaborating:** In your writer's group, discuss experiences you or people you know have had with insomnia. What were their remedies? Were they effective? Write a list as a group, then choose the most effective remedy for insomnia and write a one-paragraph process analysis to share with the class.

2. **Considering Audience:** The audience of this letter is someone who is a peer of Benjamin Franklin's, a person whom he can reasonably expect to be equally well read and to share many of his own experiences or concerns. Consider an audience of today that might be interested in Franklin's views on how to sleep well, for example, busy parents, fellow college students, children who are afraid of the dark, or exhausted coworkers. Write a letter of advice about how to have a good night's sleep addressed to one of these updated audiences or to another contemporary audience of your choice.

3. **Developing an Essay:** Using Benjamin Franklin's "The Art of Procuring Pleasant Dreams" as inspiration, prepare a how-to, process analysis essay with a title beginning with "The Art of Procuring . . ."

(Or use a synonym for *procuring*, such as *attaining, landing,* or *getting*.) Write to an audience of college students similar to yourself. Incorporate at least three numbered steps, as does Franklin, and, if your instructor requires it, also make a point using both a comparison (such as Franklin's comparison using the Black Hole of Calcutta) and made-up or actual dialogue (such as Franklin's dialogue between the angel and Methuselah).

(NOTE: Suggestions for topics requiring development by PROCESS ANALYSIS are on pp. 249–250 at the end of this chapter.)

IAN FRAZIER

IAN FRAZIER was born in Cleveland, Ohio, in 1951. He graduated from Harvard University in 1973 and soon after joined the staff of *The New Yorker*, where he wrote for the "Talk of the Town" section and published a variety of feature stories and humorous articles. He is known both for his success as a humorist and for employing a matter-of-fact, first-person narrative style when discussing topics that range from personal hobbies to history and life in the American West. Some of his other notable works include *Dating Your Mom* (1986), *Nobody Better, Better than Nobody* (1987), *Great Plains* (1989), *Family* (1994), *Coyote vs. Acme* (1996), *On the Rez* (2000), *The Fish's Eye* (2002), *Lamentations of the Father* (2008), and *Travels in Siberia* (2010).

How to Operate the Shower Curtain

One technique of humorous writing is to take a simple activity and explain it in such extensive, often irrelevant detail, that the explanation becomes ridiculous and funny. This technique pokes fun at the kinds of silly or pompous instructions and similar forms of writing we often encounter as well as the kinds of foolish situations we often find ourselves in. Sometimes writing of this sort includes parody, taking the form of serious writing but with exaggerated or outlandish content. That is the case with this essay from *The New Yorker*. It takes the form of a set of instructions but overstates them and includes loosely related details that poke fun at contemporary habits and customs while pointing out that we sometimes rely on written instructions when simple common sense might provide better guidance.

Dear Guest: The shower curtain in this bathroom has been purchased with care at a reputable "big box" store in order to provide maximum convenience in showering. After you have read these instructions, you will find with a little practice that our shower curtain is as easy to use as the one you have at home. 1

You'll note that the shower curtain consists of several parts. The top hem, closest to the ceiling, contains a series of regularly spaced holes designed for the insertion of shower-curtain rings. As this part receives much of the everyday strain of usage, it must be handled correctly. Grasp the shower curtain by its leading edge and gently pull until it is flush with the wall. Step into the tub, if you have not already done so. Then take the other edge of shower curtain and cautiously pull it in opposite direction until it, too, adjoins the wall. A little moisture between shower curtain and wall tiles will help curtain to stick. 2

Keep in mind that normal bathing will cause you unavoidably   3
to bump against shower curtain, which may cling to you for a moment owing to the natural adhesiveness of water. Some guests find
the sensation of wet plastic on their naked flesh upsetting, and over-
react to it. Instead, pinch the shower curtain between your thumb
and forefinger near where it is adhering to you and simply move
away from it until it is disengaged. Then, with the ends of your fingers, push it back to where it is supposed to be.

If shower curtain reattaches itself to you, repeat process above.   4
Under certain atmospheric conditions, a convection effect creates air
currents outside shower curtain which will press it against you on
all sides no matter what you do. If this happens, stand directly under showerhead until bathroom microclimate stabilizes.

Many guests are surprised to learn that all water pipes in our   5
system run off a single riser. This means that the opening of any hot
or cold tap, or the flushing of a toilet, interrupts flow to shower. If you
find water becoming extremely hot (or cold), exit tub promptly while
using a sweeping motion with one arm to push shower curtain aside.

REMEMBER TO KEEP SHOWER CURTAIN *INSIDE* TUB AT ALL TIMES!   6
Failure to do this may result in baseboard rot, wallpaper mildew,
destruction of living-room ceiling below, and possible dripping onto
catered refreshments at social event in your honor that you are
about to attend. So be careful!

This shower curtain comes equipped with small magnets in the   7
shape of disks which have been sewn into the bottom hem at intervals.
These serve no purpose whatsoever and may be ignored. Please do not
tamper with them. The vertical lines, or pleats, which you may have
wondered about, are there for a simple reason: user safety. If you
have to move from the tub fast, as outlined above, the easy accordion-
type folding motion of the pleats makes that possible. The gray substance in some of the inner pleat folds is a kind of insignificant mildew,
less toxic than what is found on some foreign cheeses.

When detaching shower curtain from clinging to you or when ex-   8
iting tub during a change in water temperature, bear in mind that
there are seventeen mostly empty plastic bottles of shampoo on tub
edge next to wall. These bottles have accumulated in this area over
time. Many have been set upside down in order to concentrate the last
amounts of fluid in their cap mechanisms, and are balanced lightly.
Inadvertent contact with a thigh or knee can cause all the bottles to be
knocked over and to tumble into the tub or behind it. If this should
somehow happen, we ask that you kindly pick the bottles up and put
them back in the same order in which you found them. Thank you.

While picking up the bottles, a guest occasionally will lose his   9
or her balance temporarily, and, in even rarer cases, fall. If you find
this occurring, remember that panic is the enemy here. Let your
body go limp, while reminding yourself that the shower curtain is
not designed to bear your weight. Grabbing onto it will only complicate the situation.

If, in a "worst case" scenario, you do take hold of the shower   10
curtain, and the curtain rings tear through the holes in the upper
hem as you were warned they might, remain motionless and relaxed in the position in which you come to rest. If subsequently you
hear a knock on the bathroom door, respond to any questions by
saying either "Fine" or "No, I'm fine." When the questioner goes
away, stand up, turn off shower, and lay shower curtain flat on floor
and up against tub so you can see the extent of the damage. With a
sharp object—a nail file, a pen, or your teeth—make new holes in
top hem next to the ones that tore through.

Now lift shower curtain with both hands and reattach it to   11
shower-curtain rings by unclipping, inserting, and reclipping them. If
during this process the shower curtain slides down and again goes
onto you, reach behind you to shelf under medicine cabinet, take nail
file or curved fingernail scissors, and perform short, brisk slashing
jabs on shower curtain to cut it back. It can always be repaired later
with safety pins or adhesive tape from your toiletries kit.

At this point, you may prefer to get the shower curtain out of   12
your way entirely by gathering it up with both arms and ripping it
down with a sharp yank. Now place it in the waste receptacle next
to the john. In order that anyone who might be overhearing you will
know that you are still all right, sing "Fat Bottomed Girls," by
Queen, as loudly as necessary. While waiting for tub to fill, wedge
shower curtain into waste receptacle more firmly by treading it un-
derfoot with a regular high-knee action as if marching in place.

We are happy to have you as our guest. There are many   13
choices you could have made, but you are here, and we appreciate
that. Operating the shower curtain is kind of tricky. Nobody is denying that. If you do not wish to deal with it, or if you would
rather skip the whole subject for reasons you do not care to reveal,
we accept your decision. You did not ask to be born. There is no
need ever to touch the shower curtain again. If you would like to
receive assistance, pound on the door, weep inconsolably, and
someone will be along.

Meanings and Values

1. At what point in this essay did you first become aware that it is not to be taken seriously, that it is, in fact, a parody? What specifically made you doubt the seriousness of the selection?

2. Choose two passages from the essay that can be considered examples of irony, and explain what makes them ironic. (See "Guide to Terms": *Irony*.)

3. This essay pokes fun at more than one subject. Review Paragraphs 3–6 carefully and identify as many targets of the humor as you can (including the "speaker" or persona in the essay, who seems to take simple things far too seriously). (Guide: *Persona*.)

Expository Techniques

1. One important technique in this essay is the creation of a persona, the person in the essay appears to be addressing the reader ("Dear Guest:" Par. 1) but who is in fact separate from the actual writer of the essay. Make a list of the apparent character traits and values of this persona. Indicate those which the essay appears to make fun of or criticize. (Guide: *Persona*.)

2. To what extent do the techniques in this essay move beyond simple humor into satire? Be ready to explain your answer by referring to specific sections of the text. For a definition of satire, see Guide: *Satire*.

3. Exaggeration is a frequent technique in humor and satire. Identify the exaggerations in Paragraphs 8–10 and tell for what purpose the writer seems to be using them. (Guide: *Purpose*.)

Diction and Vocabulary

1. The vocabulary in this selection often seems to be more formal and technical than the subject requires. Identify any such terms in Paragraph 2. (Guide: *Diction*.) Explain how the writer uses these terms to poke fun at the speaker (persona), readers who take the piece seriously, or both. (Guide: *Persona*.)

2. The last sentence in Paragraph 6 uses several words and phrases to poke fun at people who take cleanliness to extremes and at people who may fail to see a contrast between their cultural sophistication and their other values. What are these passages? State their meaning in your own words.

3. If you do not know the meaning of some of the following words, look them up in a dictionary: *reputable* (Par. 1); *hem* (2); *adhering* (3); *atmospheric, microclimate* (4); *riser* (5); *inconsolably* (13).

READ TO WRITE

1. **Collaborating:** Many of the experiences described in this essay are likely to have happened to readers, though few readers are likely to have experienced them all. Working with a group, identify those things that have happened to one or more members. Then decide if the essay can be considered somewhat realistic despite its exaggerations and humor.

2. **Considering Audience:** This essay takes experiences that most of us have encountered and looks at them humorously. Make a list of similar common experiences and explain why they are worth treating with humor or satire.

3. **Developing an Essay:** Following Frazier's example, create an essay using process analysis and a speaker, or persona, whose explanations are worth criticizing, or at least not worth taking seriously.

(NOTE: Suggestions for topics requiring development by PROCESS ANALYSIS are on pp. 249–250 at the end of this chapter.)

Issues and Ideas

Demystifying Everyday Rituals

- Stanley Fish, *Getting Coffee Is Hard to Do*
- Ernest Hemingway, *Camping Out*

STANLEY FISH

> STANLEY FISH is a university professor, literary theorist, and legal scholar. He earned a Ph.D. from Yale in 1962, served as chair of the English department at Duke, and has taught at several universities. Fish is the author of many books, including *Is There a Text in This Class?* (1980), *The Fugitive in Flight* (2010), and *How to Write a Sentence* (2011). He is a frequent contributor to the *Wall Street Journal* editorial page, and his blog on education, law, and society appears in the *New York Times*.

Getting Coffee Is Hard to Do

In the United States, we live in a coffee culture: many of our daily rituals and interactions revolve around this stimulating social lubricant. In the following selection, originally published in the *New York Times* on August 5, 2007, Fish examines the process of ordering a caffeinated beverage.

A coordination problem (a term of art in economics and management) occurs when you have a task to perform, the task has multiple and shifting components, the time for completion is limited, and your performance is affected by the order and sequence of the actions you take. The trick is to manage it so that the components don't bump into each other in ways that produce confusion, frustration, and inefficiency. 1

You will face a coordination problem if you are a general deploying troops, tanks, helicopters, food, tents, and medical supplies, or if you are the CEO of a large company juggling the demands of design, personnel, inventory, and production. 2

And these days, you will face a coordination problem if you want to get a cup of coffee. 3

It used to be that when you wanted a cup of coffee you went 4
into a nondescript place fitted out largely in linoleum, Formica, and
neon, sat down at a counter, and, in response to a brisk "What'll
you have, dear?" said, "Coffee and a cheese Danish." Twenty seconds later, tops, they arrived, just as you were settling into the
sports page.

Now it's all wood or concrete floors, lots of earth tones, soft, 5
high-style lighting, open barrels of coffee beans, Folk-rock and indie
music, photographs of urban landscapes, and copies of *The Onion*.
As you walk in, everything is saying, "This is very sophisticated,
and you'd better be up to it."

It turns out to be hard. First you have to get in line, and you 6
may have one or two people in front of you who are ordering a drink
with more parts than an internal combustion engine, something
about "double shot," "skinny," "breve," "grande," "au lait" and a lot
of other words that never pass my lips. If you are patient and stay in
line (no bathroom breaks), you get to put in your order, but then you
have to find a place to stand while you wait for it. There is no such
place. So you shift your body, first here and then there, trying not to
get in the way of those you can't help get in the way of.

Finally, the coffee arrives. 7

But then your real problems begin when you turn, holding your 8
prize, and make your way to where the accessories—things you put
in, on, and around your coffee—are to be found. There is a stagger-
ing array of them, and the order of their placement seems random in
relation to the order of your needs. There is no "right" place to start,
so you lunge after one thing and then after another with awkward
reaches.

Unfortunately, two or three other people are doing the same 9
thing, and each is doing it in a different sequence. So there is an endless round of "excuse me," "no, excuse me," as if you were in an old
Steve Martin routine.

But no amount of politeness and care is enough. After all, there 10
are so many items to reach for—lids, cup jackets, straws, napkins,
stirrers, milk, half and half, water, sugar, Splenda, the wastepaper
basket, spoons. You and your companions may strive for a ballet of
courtesy, but what you end up performing is more like bumper cars.
It's just a question of what will happen first—getting what you want
or spilling the coffee you are trying to balance in one hand on the
guy reaching over you.

I won't even talk about the problem of finding a seat. 11

And two things add to your pain and trouble. First, it costs a lot, $3   12
and up. And worst of all, what you're paying for is the privilege of doing the work that should be done by those who take your money. The
coffee shop experience is just one instance of the growing practice of
shifting the burden of labor to the consumer—gas stations, grocery and
drug stores, bagel shops (why should I put on my own cream cheese?),
airline check-ins, parking lots. It's insert this, swipe that, choose credit
or debit, enter your PIN, push the red button, error, start again. At least
when you go on a "vacation" that involves working on a ranch, the
work is something you've chosen. But none of us has chosen to take
over the jobs of those we pay to serve us.

Well, it's Sunday morning, and you're probably reading this   13
with a cup of coffee. I hope it was easy to get.

MEANINGS AND VALUES

1.   What is a coordination problem, according to the author? In what
     way does getting a cup of coffee in the way the author describes turn
     out to be a coordination problem?

2.   In Paragraph 12, Fish mentions some instances of "the growing prac-
     tice of shifting the burden of labor to the consumer." List some other
     examples of your own. Do you agree with the author that this practice
     is unpleasant, or do you think it makes life easier for consumers?

3.   What is the significance of the one-sentence paragraph, "I won't
     even talk about the problem of finding a seat"? (Par. 11).

EXPOSITORY TECHNIQUES

1.   The writer presents a scenario—getting a cup of coffee—and uses the
     step-by-step method to explain the process. List the steps the author
     describes.

2.   Many people already know what it is like to get a cup of coffee in the
     type of coffeehouse venue that Fish describes. What is his purpose in
     writing a process analysis of it? Explain your answer.

DICTION AND VOCABULARY

1.   In what ways does this reading selection represent irony of situation,
     in which there is a contradiction between what is expected to happen
     and what does happen? (See "Guide to Terms": *Irony*). Point to ex-
     amples in the reading.

2.   In Paragraph 6, the writer uses humorous exaggeration: ". . . you may have one or two people in front of you who are ordering a drink with more parts than an internal combustion engine . . ." Point to other examples of exaggeration. Why do you think the author uses this technique in a process analysis?

READ TO WRITE

1.   **Collaborating:** With a group of writers, reread Stanley Fish's definition of the term *coordination problem* in Paragraph 1, as well as his examples of it in Paragraph 2. Brainstorm other examples of coordination problems that you are personally familiar with or have read about. List them in order of least problematic to most problematic. As a group, write a summary of your findings.

2.   **Considering Audience:** Suppose that you work at a coffeehouse similar to the one the writer describes. This piece has just come out in the Sunday *New York Times,* and you have just finished reading it. Write a letter to the editor of the newspaper responding to it from the point of view of an overworked coffeehouse employee.

3.   **Developing an Essay:** Consider the instances of shifting the burden of labor to the consumer listed by the author in Paragraph 12. Choose one of these or some other as the topic for a step-by-step process analysis essay. When preparing your essay, decide whether your attitude about the process is positive or negative, and why. Be sure to convey that attitude in your essay, as well as why your process analysis should be important to the reader.

(NOTE: Suggestions for topics requiring development by PROCESS ANALYSIS are on pp. 249–250 at the end of this chapter.)

ERNEST HEMINGWAY

Ernest Hemingway (1889–1961) was an author and journalist whose fiction influenced other writers because of its understated style. His first novel, *The Sun Also Rises* (1926), was greeted as gripping, lean, hard, and athletic. Born in Oak Park, Illinois, to a physician father and musician mother, he served as an ambulance driver in World War I, wrote fiction in Paris in the 1920s, and was a war-news correspondent in the 1930s during the Spanish Civil War. In the 1940s, he lived in Cuba and went on safari in Africa. Hemingway received the Nobel Prize in Literature in 1954. His other major works include *A Farewell to Arms* (1929), *For Whom the Bell Tolls* (1940), and *The Old Man and the Sea* (1951).

Camping Out

Ernest Hemingway was proud of his reputation as an outdoorsman and athlete, and he cultivated a virile persona. In this selection, originally published in *The Toronto Daily Star* on June 26, 1920, he offers some succinct advice on how to camp like a man.

Thousands of people will go into the bush this summer to cut the high cost of living. A man who gets his two weeks' salary while he is on vacation should be able to put those two weeks in fishing and camping and be able to save one week's salary clear. He ought to be able to sleep comfortably every night, to eat well every day and to return to the city rested and in good condition.   1

But if he goes into the woods with a frying pan, an ignorance of black flies and mosquitoes, and a great and abiding lack of knowledge about cookery, the chances are that his return will be very different. He will come back with enough mosquito bites to make the back of his neck look like a relief map of the Caucasus. His digestion will be wrecked after a valiant battle to assimilate half-cooked or charred grub. And he won't have had a decent night's sleep while he has been gone.   2

He will solemnly raise his right hand and inform you that he has joined the grand army of never-agains. The call of the wild may be all right, but it's a dog's life. He's heard the call of the tame with both ears. Waiter, bring him an order of milk toast.   3

In the first place he overlooked the insects. Black flies, no-see-ums, deer flies, gnats and mosquitoes were instituted by the devil to force people to live in cities where he could get at them better. If it   4 weren't for them everybody would live in the bush and he would be out of work. It was a rather successful invention.

But there are lots of dopes that will counteract the pests. The   5
simplest perhaps is oil of citronella. Two bits' worth of this pur-chased at any pharmacist's will be enough to last for two weeks in the worst fly and mosquito-ridden country.

Rub a little on the back of your neck, your forehead and your   6
wrists before you start fishing, and the blacks and skeeters will shun you. The odor of citronella is not offensive to people. It smells like gun oil. But the bugs do hate it.

Oil of pennyroyal and eucalyptol are also much hated by   7
mosquitoes, and with citronella they form the basis for many pro-prietary preparations. But it is cheaper and better to buy the straight citronella. Put a little on the mosquito netting that covers the front of your pup tent or canoe tent at night, and you won't be bothered.

To be really rested and get any benefit out of a vacation a man   8
must get a good night's sleep every night. The first requisite for this is to have plenty of cover. It is twice as cold as you expect it will be in the bush four nights out of five, and a good plan is to take just double the bedding that you think you will need. An old quilt that you can wrap up in is as warm as two blankets.

Nearly all outdoor writers rhapsodize over the browse bed. It is   9
all right for the man who knows how to make one and has plenty of time. But in a succession of one-night camps on a canoe trip all you need is level ground for your tent floor and you will sleep all right if you have plenty of covers under you. Take twice as much cover as you think that you will need, and then put two-thirds of it under you. You will sleep warm and get your rest.

When it is clear weather you don't need to pitch your tent if   10
you are only stopping for the night. Drive four stakes at the head of your made-up bed and drape your mosquito bar over that, then you can sleep like a log and laugh at the mosquitoes.

Outside of insects and bum sleeping the rock that wrecks most   11
camping trips is cooking. The average tyro's idea of cooking is to fry everything and fry it good and plenty. Now, a frying pan is a most necessary thing to any trip, but you also need the old stew kettle and the folding reflector baker.

A pan of fried trout can't be bettered and they don't cost any   12
more than ever. But there is a good and bad way of frying them.

The beginner puts his trout and his bacon in and over a brightly   13
burning fire; the bacon curls up and dries into a dry tasteless cinder

and the trout is burned outside while it is still raw inside. He eats them and it is all right if he is only out for the day and going home to a good meal at night. But if he is going to face more trout and bacon the next morning and other equally well-cooked dishes for the remainder of two weeks he is on the pathway to nervous dyspepsia.

The proper way is to cook over coals. Have several cans of Crisco or Cotosuet or one of the vegetable shortenings along that are as good as lard and excellent for all kinds of shortening. Put the bacon in and when it is about half cooked lay the trout in the hot grease, dipping them in corn meal first. Then put the bacon on top of the trout and it will baste them as it slowly cooks. 14

The coffee can be boiling at the same time and in a smaller skillet pancakes being made that are satisfying the other campers while they are waiting for the trout. 15

With the prepared pancake flours you take a cupful of pancake flour and add a cup of water. Mix the water and flour and as soon as the lumps are out it is ready for cooking. Have the skillet hot and keep it well greased. Drop the batter in and as soon as it is done on one side loosen it in the skillet and flip it over. Apple butter, syrup or cinnamon and sugar go well with the cakes. 16

While the crowd have taken the edge from their appetites with flapjacks the trout have been cooked and they and the bacon are ready to serve. The trout are crisp outside and firm and pink inside and the bacon is well done—but not too done. If there is anything better than that combination the writer has yet to taste it in a lifetime devoted largely and studiously to eating. 17

The stew kettle will cook your dried apricots when they have resumed their predried plumpness after a night of soaking, it will serve to concoct a mulligan in, and it will cook macaroni. When you are not using it, it should be boiling water for the dishes. 18

In the baker, mere man comes into his own, for he can make a pie that to his bush appetite will have it all over the product that mother used to make, like a tent. Men have always believed that there was something mysterious and difficult about making a pie. Here is a great secret. There is nothing to it. We've been kidded for years. Any man of average office intelligence can make at least as good a pie as his wife. 19

All there is to a pie is a cup and a half of flour, one-half teaspoonful of salt, one-half cup of lard and cold water. That will make pie crust that will bring tears of joy into your camping partner's eyes. 20

Mix the salt with the flour, work the lard into the flour, make it up   21
into a good workmanlike dough with cold water. Spread some flour on
the back of a box or something flat, and pat the dough around a while.
Then roll it out with whatever kind of round bottle you prefer. Put a little more lard on the surface of the sheet of dough and then slosh a little
flour on and roll it up and then roll it out again with the bottle.

Cut out a piece of the rolled out dough big enough to line a pie   22
tin. I like the kind with holes in the bottom. Then put in your dried
apples that have soaked all night and been sweetened, or your apricots, or your blueberries, and then take another sheet of the dough
and drape it gracefully over the top, soldering it down at the edges
with your fingers. Cut a couple of slits in the top dough sheet and
prick it a few times with a fork in an artistic manner.

Put it in the baker with a good slow fire for forty-five minutes   23
and then take it out and if your pals are Frenchmen they will kiss
you. The penalty for knowing how to cook is that the others will
make you do all the cooking.

It is all right to talk about roughing it in the woods. But the real   24
woodsman is the man who can be really comfortable in the bush.

MEANINGS AND VALUES

1. What does the writer say are the advantages of camping out his way?

2. What is the significance of the sentence, "Waiter, bring him an order
   of milk toast" (Par. 3)?

3. What is the difference, according to the writer, between merely
   "roughing it" and being "really comfortable" on a camping trip?

EXPOSITORY TECHNIQUES

1. What process is the author describing when he uses the step-by-step
   method of process analysis?

2. In your opinion, why does the writer think his process analysis is
   worth sharing? What is he trying to communicate, in your opinion,
   aside from the practical steps of camping comfortably and
   efficiently?

3. Hemingway describes in detail the process of making a pie. Do you
   think the steps are thorough enough that you could make a good pie
   yourself if you had the right equipment and followed them to the
   letter?

DICTION AND VOCABULARY

1. Hemingway frequently refers to the camping experience as "the bush," a phrase suggesting an uncivilized wilderness. Why do you think he chooses to use this term?

2. The writer seems sincerely interested in conveying helpful pointers about camping out, yet he uses a humorous tone throughout. Does this humorous tone help your understanding of the process he is analyzing, or does it get in the way? Explain.

3. If you do not know the meaning of some of the following words, consult a dictionary: *grub* (Par. 2); *proprietary* (7); *rhapsodize* (9); *tyro* (11); *dyspepsia* (13); *soldering* (22).

READ TO WRITE

1. **Collaborating:** In a group of writers, interview members about their experiences with camping. What was the process like? What do people in your group know now that they wish they had known then? As a group, write an anecdote based on one of the group members' stories that could be used as an introduction to an essay like the selection you have just read.

2. **Considering Audience:** Who is Hemingway's intended audience in this essay? How can you tell? What does he want this audience to learn from his process analysis? Do you think he reaches his intended audience successfully? How so?

3. **Developing an Essay:** Think of processes that in the past (or even today) have been considered typically masculine or typically feminine. Examples: changing a tire, painting a house, sewing, putting on makeup, mowing the lawn. Write an encouraging step-by-step process analysis that urges the nontraditional gender to try this activity.

(NOTE: Suggestions for topics requiring development by PROCESS ANALYSIS follow.)

Writing Suggestions for Chapter 7

ANALOGY

From one of the following topics, develop a central theme into an informational process analysis, showing:

1. How you selected a college
2. How you selected your future career or major field of study
3. How your family selected a home
4. How an unusual sport is played
5. How religious faith is achieved
6. How gasoline is made
7. How the air (or water) in _____ becomes polluted
8. How lightning kills
9. How foreign policy is made
10. How political campaigns are financed
11. How _____ was rebuilt
12. How fruit blossoms are pollinated
13. How a computer chip is designed or made

EVERYDAY USES

1. Choose a useful everyday activity that you can do well but that others often do poorly (or are unable to accomplish), and create an essay that uses process analysis to share your skills with readers.
2. Choose an activity at which you excel but others don't. Share your pleasure at this skill through an essay that uses process analysis to explain your ability and suggests ways that others might develop a similar skill.

COLLABORATIVE EXERCISES

1. As a group, write an informative paper on the process of completing a collaborative project. Consider how you plan team meetings, team tasks, team evaluations, and so on.

2. For topics 2a–g that follow, have each member of a group write the directional process for a different audience-reader. Predefine each person's audience profile using an audience profile sheet.

   a. How to overcome shyness

   b. How to overcome stage fright

   c. How to make the best use of study time

   d. How to write a college composition

   e. How to sell an ugly house

   f. How to prepare livestock or any other entry for a fair

   g. How to start a club (or some other kind of recurring activity)

8

Analyzing *Cause-and-Effect* Relationships

W riting built around cause-effect analysis addresses questions like "Why did that happen?" and "What is likely to happen next?" It can grow from simple curiosity about the *why* of events or from a practical desire to avoid unpleasant or unforeseen consequences. Above all, cause-effect analysis focuses on relationships, the links between one phenomenon and another. When you employ the pattern in expository writing, you need to do more than identify possible causes or consequences. You need to establish a reasonable relationship among them by showing how both logic and the available evidence point to the relationship. After all, two things that often occur together, such as storms and tornadoes, are not *necessarily* related. Since many storms occur without the accompaniment of tornadoes, a cause-effect analysis would focus first on identifying those kinds of storms frequently associated with the appearance of tornadoes, then isolate specific causal features that can be demonstrably linked to funnel clouds and destructive winds.

A search for cause and effect can be rigorously scientific ("Researchers debate possible links between caffeine consumption and heart disease") or it can be personal ("Why do I always end up arguing with my parents over things we all know are unimportant?"). It can take the form of causal analysis, trying to identify all the links in a causal chain: remote causes, necessary conditions, and direct causes to immediate effects and more distant consequences. Or it can identify the many conditions and forces that work together in no particular pattern to shape a person's life, create a particular situation, or help bring about events.

Most expository uses of the pattern do not require scientific rigor, however. For social or cultural events, like the growth of a political movement or the rise of a new form of art, we can seldom hope to pinpoint exact causes and effects. Instead, we can identify the roots of contemporary phenomena and develop an awareness of the kinds of changes that may be going on today. This is the kind of explanation provided by the following paragraph, which looks at the early development of a popular kind of music.

> Rap started in the discos, not the midtown glitter palaces like Studio 54 or New York, New York, but at Mel Quinn's on 42nd Street and Club 371 in the Bronx, where a young Harlemite who called himself D.J. Hollywood spun on the weekends. It wasn't unusual for black club jocks to talk to their audiences in the jive style of the old personality deejays. Two of the top black club spinners of the day, Pete (D.J.) Jones and Maboya, did so. Hollywood, just an adolescent when he started, created a more complicated, faster style, with more rhymes than his older mentors and call-and-response passages to encourage reaction from the dancers. At local bars, discos, and many illegal after-hours spots frequented by street people, Hollywood developed a huge word-of-mouth reputation. Tapes of his parties began appearing around the city on the then new and incredibly loud Japanese portable cassette players flooding into America. In Harlem, Kurtis Blow, Eddie Cheeba, and D.J. Lovebug Star-ski; in the Bronx, Junebug Star-ski, Grandmaster Flash, and Melle Mel; in Brooklyn, two kids from the projects called Whodini; and in Queens, Russell and Joey, the two youngest sons from the middle-class Simmons household— all shared a fascination with Hollywood's use of the rhythmic breaks in his club mixes and his verbal dexterity. These kids would all grow up to play a role in the local clubs and, later, a few would appear on the national scene to spread Hollywood's style. Back in the 1970s, while disco reigned in the media, the Black Main Streets of New York were listening to D.J. Hollywood, and learning.
>
> —Nelson George, *The Death of Rhythm and Blues*

WHY USE CAUSE-EFFECT ANALYSIS?

Some causes and effects are not very complicated; at least their explanation requires only a simple statement. New parking facilities are not built because a college (or town) lacks the money in its budget. But frequently a much more thorough analysis is required. New parking facilities are not built partly because of expense and partly because they simply seem to encourage more traffic and rapidly become jammed. The college (or town) delays the project until it can study *why* parking facilities quickly become overloaded. In writing, cause-effect as an expository pattern helps address these kinds of complicated relationships.

Writers often respond to puzzling or intriguing phenomena with causal explanations. In its simplest form, the strategy consists of a description of a puzzling phenomenon (the persistence of alcoholism in families, for example) followed by an explanation or an examination of possible causes. The simplicity of this pattern gives it considerable power and flexibility. Writers speculating about social patterns and individual behavior often use the strategy or vary it to consider possible consequences. In dealing with effects, the strategy consists of discussion of a new or previously unnoticed phenomenon whose consequences are unfamiliar followed by consideration of its likely effects, or it begins with discussion of desired effects followed by examination of actions or arrangements most likely to produce these consequences.

Causal explanations appear frequently in academic and research writing. Scholars often look for a particularly puzzling element in a subject or for a point over which there has been much disagreement and then build an essay in an attempt to explain the phenomena: "Perhaps the most interesting feature of early jazz is. . . ."; "Over the last decade researchers have argued about the role of aggressive behavior in corporate organizations. . . ."

CHOOSING A STRATEGY

To explain fully the causes of a phenomenon, writers must seek not only *immediate* causes (the ones encountered first) but also *ultimate* causes (the basic, underlying factors that help to explain the more apparent ones). Business or professional people, as well as students, often have a pressing need for this type of analysis. How else could they fully understand or report on a failing sales campaign, diminishing church membership, a local increase in traffic accidents, or a decline in crime and the use of drugs? The immediate cause of a disastrous warehouse fire could be faulty electrical wiring, but this might be attributed in turn to the company's unwise economic measures, which might be traced even further to undue pressures on the management to show large profits. The written analysis might logically stop at any point of course, with the actual strategy a writer employs depending on the purpose of the writing and the audience for which it is intended.

Similarly, both the immediate and ultimate *effects* of an action or situation may, or may not, need to be fully explored. If a 5 percent pay raise is granted, what will be the immediate effect on the cost of production, leading to what ultimate effects on prices and, in some cases, on the economy of a business, a town, or perhaps the entire region?

Whatever the extent of the reasoning your writing task demands, you need to make certain strategic choices. Will you focus on causes, effects, or both? Will you focus on a single clear chain of causes and effects or provide a more general discussion, highlighting many contributing factors? How will you use the opening of your writing to convince readers of the importance of understanding the causes or effects of a phenomenon or situation and interest them in reading about the topic?

Because causes and effects often form intricate, potentially confusing relationships, you should develop a straightforward plan for your writing—an organization that will help readers understand the order you have discovered within the complexity. This is particularly important when a phenomenon has multiple causes, as in the following example.

> Introduction: Example of a diverse audience at a horror movie responding with both fear and pleasure to the film
>> Tentative thesis: People choose to watch horror films for many different reasons, each depending on the individual's taste and psychological makeup.
>
> Cause 1: The "thrill" of being shocked and scared
>> Support: Some people are psychologically disposed to get pleasure from danger, especially when it is imaginary.
>>
>> Support: Certain people's brain chemistry may mean that they (like people who engage in extreme sports) get a feeling of well-being after feeling that they have placed themselves in danger.
>
> Cause 2: The twists and turns of the plot
>> Support: Many people enjoy the kinds of complicated, surprising plots they find in horror movies (similar in some ways to the kinds of plots people enjoy in adventure stories).
>
> Cause 3: The pleasure of "escape"
>> Support: The dangers faced by characters in the films allow viewers to escape for a short time from their somewhat less serious but more real everyday problems.

Cause 4: Fashion
> Support: Horror movies are popular. Going to them with friends and talking about them afterwards is a pleasant social experience.

Summary

Your writing will need to do more than identify causes and effects. It will need to provide readers with evidence that you have correctly identified the relationships. As a result, much writing that employs this pattern relies on detailed research. Printed sources, television documentaries, and interviews can provide you with useful information. You should keep such research focused, however, so you don't stray too far into areas that are interesting but not really related to the causes or consequences you will be discussing.

DEVELOPING CAUSE-EFFECT ANALYSIS

Discussions of causes and effects can easily become complex and confusing, so consider using the following strategies for alerting readers to the relationships among causes and effects. A concise statement near the beginning of an essay can point out relationships you plan to examine. Statements in the body of an essay can remind readers of the points you are making and the supporting details and reasoning you are providing. Likewise, terms that identify causes and effects or that indicate their relationships can help guide readers' attention:

result	effect	accomplishment	development
outcome	antecedent	source	first
cause	instrument	as a result	second
means	thus	motive	third
consequence	reason	agent	next

When you analyze causes and effects, your readers must always have confidence in the thoroughness and logic of your reasoning. Here are some ways to avoid the most common faults in causal reasoning:

1. Never mistake the fact that something happens with or after another occurrence as evidence of a causal relationship—for example, that a black cat crossing the road caused the flat tire a few minutes later, or that a course in English composition caused a student's nervous breakdown that same semester.

2. Consider all possible relevant factors before attributing causes. Perhaps studying English did result in a nervous breakdown, but the cause may also have been ill health, trouble at home, the stress of working while attending college, or the anguish of a love affair. (The composition course, by providing an "emotional" outlet, may even have helped postpone the breakdown!)

3. Support the analysis by more than mere assertions: offer evidence. It would not often be enough to *tell* why Shakespeare's wise Othello believed the villainous Iago—the dramatist's lines should be used as evidence, possibly supported by the opinions of at least one literary scholar. If you are explaining that capital punishment deters crime, do not expect the reader to take your word for it—give before-and-after statistics or the testimony of reliable authorities.

4. Be careful not to omit any links in the chain of causes or effects unless you are certain that the readers for whom the writing is intended will automatically make the right connections themselves—and this is frequently a dangerous assumption. To unwisely omit one or more of the links might leave the reader with only a vague, or even erroneous, impression of the causal connection, possibly invalidating all that follows and thus making the entire writing ineffective.

5. Be honest and objective. Writers (or thinkers) who bring their old prejudices to the task of casual analysis, or who fail to see the probability of *multiple* causes or effects, are almost certain to distort their analyses or to make them so superficial, so thin, as to be almost worthless.

Student Essay

As an expository pattern, cause-effect can explore personal matters as well as those of broader public interest. Aware of her difficulties in coming to terms with her mother's death, Sarah Egri used the pattern to explore one possible reason for her feelings.

How a Public Document Affected My Life
by Sarah Egri

Public documents are a part of everyday life. The presence of these documents can affect a person's life in many different ways. However, the *absence* of such documents may also affect a person's life, such as my

Gives topic an interesting twist: an absence

own. I believe the absence of my mother's death certificate has affected my life.

When I was around 12 years old, my mother became very ill with cancer. She was diagnosed with lymphoma, which is cancer within the lymph nodes. She sought several types of medical treatment, but nothing seemed to help her. During this time, the doctor told my family that my mom did not have much longer to live. The doctor also told my mom this, but she did not believe him, nor did she want to. At this point, I did not know what was happening. Since I was so young, I did not understand. I listened to my mom and believed her because I did not want her to die. She and I were quite close. I was able to talk to her about anything and everything. There was still so much I had to learn from her, still so many more memories to be made.

When I was 14 years old my mother passed away. I will never forget that night, for it seemed like a dream; it seemed as though it were not really happening. I awoke to a phone call at one-thirty in the morning saying that my mom had passed away. No more would I be able to talk with her, or learn from her, or make precious memories. She was gone, yet it felt like it was not real. I could not grasp the concept that she would no longer be a part of my life. The years passed by and I only got *used* to my mom not being there; I never faced the fact that she had died. The day that my mother died, I never saw her death certificate. Perhaps if I had seen it, her death would have seemed more realistic.

Now as I think back, I *never* saw my mother's death certificate. A death certificate is a document that is signed by a doctor, giving information about the time, place, and cause of a person's death. This document finalizes everything. It may be that since I never saw this document, I never came to the realization that she had passed. Since I did not believe she *would* die, I cannot bring myself to believe that she *did* die. If I had seen the death certificate, I would have come to terms with her death.

rather than a presence is the cause

Thesis statement

Background to help readers understand the cause and the effects

One of the effects

The cause

Examines and explains the cause

Generalizes about the effects

How can such a *small* document make such a *big* difference in my life? All a death certificate is, is a small piece of paper with a person's name on it. I think it might have made a difference because it's an *official* notification of my mom's death. It's a *real*, physical thing; it is more real than just *thinking* someone has died.

My mother's death certificate has affected my life, even though I never did see it. The absence of this document affects my life, because if I had seen it, I would have come to the realization that she is really gone. If I had seen that document, her death would have been finalized in my mind and I would not just be *used to* her not being around; I would *know* that she has passed and is no longer with us. The death certificate finalizes a person's death, and if I had seen my mom's it would have finalized her death for me. Since I did not see this document, I have not brought my mom's death to a close. Perhaps the *absence* of some documents, such as my mother's death certificate, can affect a person's life more than the presence of other documents.

Explains the force and importance of public documents

Explores effects

Ends with a contrast between absence and presence

MICHAEL JERNIGAN

Blogger MICHAEL JERNIGAN retired from the Marine Corps in 2005 after being blinded by a roadside bomb explosion in Fallujah, Iraq. He has been a contributor to *Home Fires,* a *New York Times* blog written by U.S. military veterans. Topics he has addressed from this vantage point include war movies, relationship challenges, and returning to school. He described himself in a 2009 posting: "I am a husband. I am a stepfather. I am a student. I am a Marine. I am a combat veteran. I am a man who was violently attacked and left blind and tormented. I want to be normal. But I know there is no real normal."

Living the Dream

In this selection, Michael Jernigan discussed the effects of post-traumatic stress disorder (P.T.S.D.) on his life after Iraq. It originally appeared in the *New York Times* as a *Home Fires* blog post on October 11, 2009.

Greetings again from the Sunshine State.   1

As I mentioned in my first post I would like to bring some   2
awareness to an issue facing many of us returning war veterans. Post-traumatic stress disorder (P.T.S.D.) is a monster that war veterans have been facing since the beginning of armed conflict. In a nutshell, it is the stress brought on by a traumatic event. I understand that it is more complicated than that but I would like to keep it as simple as possible for our purposes here.

I am living with P.T.S.D., and I am thriving in some respects   3
and having problems in others. In this and future posts I plan to use myself and my experiences as examples.

Post-traumatic stress can manifest itself in many different ways.   4
It is usually brought on by a trigger mechanism, or what some might call a catalyst. It can be something very minor that can be easily controlled or it can be so large that it has life altering circumstances.

So what do I mean when I say I am both thriving and having   5
problems at the same time? Well, I can tell you that in school I am thriving. I have been back for a couple of years now and continue to pull a 3-plus grade point average every semester. It is in other parts of my life that I am struggling.

My relationship with my wife has been strained because of the   6
way I react to certain things; my relationship with my stepson has

suffered as well. I have quick reactions full of emotion that are not checked before they come out. In many cases they are very aggressive and quite counterproductive. I am impatient in numerous situations and become frustrated easily. To top it all off I often have to overcome bouts of anxiety, especially when I am outside my house. I do well in social situations but I find them physically taxing. I have been receiving help with all of these problems and I am improving at a good rate. My wife and I have worked hard to help me overcome a lot of these symptoms.

One of the most common problems facing our war veterans 7
when we return home is drug and alcohol abuse. We turn to these to escape from emotions. I drank heavily when I returned home. I would drink to the point that I would pass out at night. I would do this because I could not sleep. I could not sleep because there were a healthy wave of emotions that I refused to face. What made sleep hard was the P.T.S.D. in conjunction with a traumatic brain injury. When I would finally sleep I had to deal with some strange and horrific dreams.

I would have dreams that most people would be scared by. 8
I was scared, too, especially when I would have the same dream more than once. One of the strangest dreams took place in Iraq. We would be returning from a foot patrol at night. It was as if I were looking through a set of night vision goggles. There were two gates that we would have to come through at our forward operating base (F.O.B.). I can remember gaining access through the first gate but then not being able to enter the inner part of the base until daybreak. Since we could not get back to our hooches we would decide to sleep under the gun line (155-millimeter howitzers), something that would not be done for safety purposes. Just when I would be drifting off to sleep the gun line would open up. It was at that point that I would awake for real. I was never able to go back to sleep after that.

There were dreams that were both strange and violent. In one of 9
them, I was in the spare bedroom of a condominium that I had rented before I enlisted. When I lived there the only thing in this room was my gun cabinet with all of my rifles and shotguns in it. During my dream I was in this room waist deep in stuffed animals. Someone would enter the room (I could never identify the person) and attack me. We would be fighting in this room. At a certain point in the fight I would gain the advantage. I would bend over this individual and bite his throat out. It was always bloody. Just then I would wake up.

One of the hardest dreams to deal with came back many times. 10
It was one of the scariest in my mind. It look place in Iraq as well.

I can remember being on patrol in Mahmudiya. That is the town that I was wounded in. I was always on patrol with a group of Marines. At some point in the dream I would become separated from my patrol. Iraq can be a scary place to find yourself alone in. It got worse. I cannot remember how, but I would lose my rifle (a good Marine does not lose his weapon). I would see a small kid scampering off with my rifle and follow him. I was terrified of returning back to base without my rifle. The kid would enter a building and I knew that I would have to follow him into the building. Keep in mind that I am defenseless. When I would enter the building I always encountered hand to hand combat with a few different individuals at one time. I would always defeat those attacking me. I can remember that I also would find a number of weapons that had once belonged to Marines—pistols, rifles and shotguns. To my dismay I would never find my rifle.

I would see the kid again and chase him one more time. I al-   11
ways wound up chasing him into another building and encountering more and more hand to hand combat situations. I would always find more weapons but never mine. I always picked up the weapons that I would find and bring them with me before I gave pursuit to that kid again. This cycle would never end. I would thrash around in my bed until I would wake up hot and sweating. I could never get back to sleep and was quite disturbed by this dream.

While I was in Washington D.C. I started to make significant   12
progress on many different fronts. I found a counselor there named Carey Smith, a disabled veteran from the Vietnam War. He has been through what I have. He began to teach me how to interpret my dreams in a positive way. I know that this can be hard to do. When he first told me I was very hesitant. As he explained it to me I started to understand what he was talking about.

We came to the conclusion that the dreams were my mind's   13
way of reconciling problems I had. They usually dealt with some guilt I had over one thing or another. In many of these situations, I would have no way of making things better, so my brain would do it for me in my sleep. Once I grasped this concept the dreams became much easier to deal with. I would then wake up in the middle of the night and be able to tell myself that there was nothing wrong and return to sleep. It is great. Currently, I am not dealing with any harsh dreams. I use the term "harsh" because I no longer see these dreams as bad but as healthy and productive.

One of the things that I am learning as I am living with P.T.S.D.   14
is that these feelings can be dealt with positively, that these different

symptoms do not have to control my life. I am doing my best to live my life and be happy. There is no magic pill that will make things better. By facing the difficult emotions and learning how to positively react to them my life becomes easier. The emotions are still there—they will probably never go away. But when I face them sober and head on I can live my good dreams and not be controlled by the difficult ones.

Semper Fidelis,
Mike Jernigan

MEANINGS AND VALUES

1. What is the definition of post-traumatic stress disorder, according to the writer?

2. What do you think that the writer is referring to when he titles this blog post "Living the Dream"? Do you think the title has a double meaning? How so?

3. What is the significance of the phrase "semper fidelis," and why do you think Jernigan chose to close his blog post with this phrase?

EXPOSITORY TECHNIQUES

1. List several effects that post-traumatic stress disorder has had on Jernigan's life.

2. What is the ultimate cause of the writer's terrible dreams? What do you think was the ultimate cause of his post-traumatic stress disorder?

3. Cause-and-effect analyses can explore the *immediate* effects of a situation, the *ultimate* effects, or both. In Paragraphs 13 and 14, what does the author seem to be saying about the ultimate effect of his nightmares?

DICTION AND VOCABULARY

1. Although the writer's dreams are frightening, he describes them in a calm and matter-of-fact tone (see "Guide to Terms": *Style/Tone*). Is this choice effective, in your opinion, or would you have preferred him to use a more dramatic and emotional tone? Explain your answer.

2. If you do not know the meaning of some of the following words, consult a dictionary: *thriving* (Par. 3); *counterproductive, bouts* (6); *howitzers* (8); *dismay* (10).

READ TO WRITE

1. **Collaborating:** In a group of writers, survey members about traumatic events they may have experienced. Did these events have lingering effects on their everyday lives? What were those effects? Write, as a group, a brief summary of your findings. Alternatively, discuss positive events group members have experienced and their effects.

2. **Considering Audience:** What type of audience do you think reads the *Home Fires* blog in which Jernigan's entry was posted? Can Jernigan's posting appeal to other types of audiences? Who would they be, and why would they be responsive?

3. **Developing an Essay:** In this reading selection, the author explores how a negative event can have a positive outcome, depending upon a person's interpretation of it. Brainstorm a similar negative event in your own life and write about its immediate negative and ultimate positive effects. Alternatively, research post-traumatic stress disorder. Choosing one aspect of the topic, formulate a thesis statement, then plan a clear cause-and-effect analysis that discusses both immediate and ultimate effects.

(NOTE: Suggestions for topics requiring development by CAUSE AND EFFECT are on pp. 279–280 at the end of this chapter.)

NORMAN COUSINS

> NORMAN COUSINS (1915–1990), a writer and humanitarian, served as
> editor in chief of the magazine *Saturday Review* between 1942 and
> 1977. His best-selling book *Anatomy of an Illness* (1979) looks at
> how a patient's attitude can affect recovery. Other works include:
> *The Republic of Reason* (1988), *The Healing Heart* (1983), and *The
> Celebration of Life* (1991). A social critic, he was a proponent of cen-
> tralized world government. The year of his death, Cousins received
> the Albert Schweitzer Prize for Humanitarianism.

Who Killed Benny Paret?

> The welterweight boxer Benny "Kid" Paret (born Bernardo Paret in
> 1937 in Santa Clara, Cuba) died on April 3, 1962, of injuries resulting
> from a boxing match ten days earlier, when he went into a coma after
> being struck multiple times by his opponent. The televised incident
> sparked public debate about whether boxing should be banned as a
> sport. Norman Cousins's take on the controversial fight appears in
> *Present Tense: An American Editor's Odyssey* (1967).

Sometime about 1935 or 1936 I had an interview with Mike   1
Jacobs, the prize-fight promoter. I was a fledgling reporter at that
time; my beat was education but during the vacation season I found
myself on varied assignments, all the way from ship news to sports
reporting. In this way I found myself sitting opposite the most powerful figure in the boxing world.

There was nothing spectacular in Mr. Jacobs' manner or ap-   2
pearance; but when he spoke about prize fights, he was no longer a
bland little man but a colossus who sounded the way Napoleon
must have sounded when he reviewed a battle. You knew you were
listening to Number One. His saying something made it true.

We discussed what to him was the only important element in   3
successful promoting—how to please the crowd. So far as he was
concerned, there was no mystery to it. You put killers in the ring and
the people filled your arena. You hire boxing artists—men who are
adroit at feinting, parrying, weaving, jabbing, and dancing, but
who don't pack dynamite in their fists—and you wind up counting
your empty seats. So you searched for the killers and sluggers and
maulers—fellows who could hit with the force of a baseball bat.

I asked Mr. Jacobs if he was speaking literally when he said   4
people came out to see the killer.

"They don't come out to see a tea party," he said evenly. "They   5
come out to see the knockout. They come out to see a man hurt.
If they think anything else, they're kidding themselves."

Recently, a young man by the name of Benny Paret was killed   6
in the ring. The killing was seen by millions; it was on television. In
the twelfth round, he was hit hard in the head several times, went
down, was counted out, and never came out of the coma.

The Paret fight produced a flurry of investigations. Governor   7
Rockefeller was shocked by what happened and appointed a committee to assess the responsibility. The New York State Boxing Commission
decided to find out what was wrong. The District Attorney's office expressed its concern. One question that was solemnly studied in all three
probes concerned the action of the referee. Did he act in time to stop the
fight? Another question had to do with the role of the examining doctors who certified the physical fitness of the fighters before the bout. Still
another question involved Mr. Paret's manager; did he rush his boy into
the fight without adequate time to recuperate from the previous one?

In short, the investigators looked into every possible cause except   8
the real one. Benny Paret was killed because the human fist delivers
enough impact, when directed against the head, to produce a massive
hemorrhage in the brain. The human brain is the most delicate and
complex mechanism in all creation. It has a lacework of millions of
highly fragile nerve connections. Nature attempts to protect this exqui-
sitely intricate machinery by encasing it in a hard shell. Fortunately, the
shell is thick enough to withstand a great deal of pounding.
Nature, however, can protect a man against everything except man
himself. Not every blow to the head will kill a man—but there is always the risk of concussion and damage to the brain. A prize fighter
may be able to survive even repeated brain concussions and go on
fighting, but the damage to his brain may be permanent.

In any event, it is futile to investigate the referee's role and seek to   9
determine whether he should have intervened to stop the fight earlier.
That is not where the primary responsibility lies. The primary responsibility lies with the people who pay to see a man hurt. The referee
who stops a fight too soon from the crowd's viewpoint can expect to
be booed. The crowd wants the knockout; it wants to see a man
stretched out on the canvas. This is the supreme moment in boxing. It
is nonsense to talk about prize fighting as a test of boxing skills. No
crowd was ever brought to its feet screaming and cheering at the sight
of two men beautifully dodging and weaving out of each other's jabs.
The time the crowd comes alive is when a man is hit hard over the
heart or the head, when his mouthpiece flies out, when the blood

squirts out of his nose or eyes, when he wobbles under the attack and his pursuer continues to smash at him with pole-axe impact.

Don't blame it on the referee. Don't even blame it on the fight managers. Put the blame where it belongs—on the prevailing mores that regard prize fighting as a perfectly proper enterprise and vehicle of entertainment. No one doubts that many people enjoy prize-fighting and will miss it if it should be thrown out. And that is precisely the point.

MEANINGS AND VALUES

1. Restate what the three major areas were that investigators focused on in their search for the cause of Paret's death. Does Cousins think these possible causes have validity? Explain your answer.

2. In the writer's opinion, who or what is the true cause of Paret's death?

EXPOSITORY TECHNIQUES

1. In your view, does the author make his case convincingly? Why or why not?

2. What is the writer's purpose in his introduction when he tells the story of an interview with prize-fight promoter Mike Jacobs that took place roughly thirty years earlier? How does the story connect with the writer's concluding paragraphs?

DICTION AND VOCABULARY

1. In Paragraph 6, the author uses the phrase "the killing" when referring to the fight that put Benny Paret into a coma. Why do you think he chooses to use the term "killing" rather than some other term?

2. If you do not know the meaning of some of the following words, consult a dictionary: *fledgling* (Par. 1); *colossus* (2); *hemorrhage, concussion* (8); *futile* (9).

READ TO WRITE

1. **Collaborating:** Brainstorm in your writer's group other controversial and potentially dangerous sports besides boxing: for example, football, skiing, racecar driving, hang gliding. Together, make a chart listing the effects of these sports in one column and the causes of these effects in an opposite column.

2. **Considering Audience:** How would boxing fans react to Cousins's essay? Among the possible causes of Paret's death mentioned in the essay, which ones would boxing fans consider the most convincing? Why?

3. **Developing an Essay:** Research the topic of progressive brain damage in football players. Identify cause-and-effect relationships for this topic and write a focused cause-effect analysis. Be sure to provide readers with enough evidence to support your findings. Alternatively, research any sport that interests you, identify cause-and-effect relationships, positive or negative, and write a focused cause-effect analysis.

(NOTE: Suggestions for topics requiring development by CAUSE AND EFFECT are on pp. 279–280 at the end of this chapter.)

Issues and Ideas

Fathoming Consequences

- Cullen Murphy, *Hello, Darkness*
- Verlyn Klinkenborg, *Our Vanishing Night*

CULLEN MURPHY

CULLEN MURPHY grew up in Greenwich, Connecticut, and attended school in both Greenwich and Dublin, Ireland. He received a B.A. from Amherst College in 1974 and soon after began working in the production department of *Change* magazine. In 1977 he was named editor of the *Wilson Quarterly*. He was managing editor of *The Atlantic* from 1985 to 2002 and editor of that magazine from 2002 to 2006. He currently serves as editor at large for *Vanity Fair.* In his parallel career, he has written the comic strip *Prince Valiant* since the middle 1970s (a comic strip that his father draws). Murphy is an essayist and nonfiction writer as well. His essays on many different topics have appeared in the *Atlantic Monthly* and other magazines, including *Harper's.* His first book, *Rubbish!* (with William Rathje), appeared in 1992; a collection of his essays, *Just Curious,* was published in 1995; and *The World According to Eve* appeared in 1998. His most recent book is *Are We Rome?* (2007).

Hello, Darkness

"Hello, Darkness" was first published in the *Atlantic Monthly* in 1996. With touches of humor, Murphy looks at a subject that troubles many people: lack of sleep. His explanations of a phenomenon that most of us view as a matter of personal behavior may at first seem surprising; nonetheless, they point convincingly to technology and social change as the culprits who have stolen sleep.

A mericans today have plenty of reasons to be thankful that they   1
were not Americans a hundred years ago, but they also have more than a few reasons to wish they had been. On the one hand, a hundred years ago there was no Voting Rights Act, no penicillin, and no zipper, and the first daily comic strip was still more than a decade away. On the other hand there was no income tax, no nuclear bomb, and no

Maury Povich. Also on the plus side, the average American a hundred years ago was able to sleep 20 percent longer than the average American today.

That last figure, supported by various historical studies over 2 the years, comes from a report released by the Better Sleep Council. Americans in the late 1800s are believed to have slept an average of about nine and a half hours a night. The average today is about seven and a half hours. A survey by the Better Sleep Council reveals that on a typical weeknight almost 60 percent of Americans get *less* than seven hours of sleep. Other evidence seems to indicate that the rate of sleep loss is in fact accelerating.

Some may argue that the Better Sleep Council's news should be 3 discounted, on the grounds that the council has an interest in the story—it is supported (comfortably?) by the mattress industry.

I would counter that the data simply confirm what anecdotal 4 evidence already suggests is true. Independent experts at universities and hospitals speak as one on the subject, observing that as a nation we are laboring under a large and increasingly burdensome "sleep deficit," defined as the difference between how much sleep we need and how much we get.

Would that we could pass this particular deficit on to our chil- 5 dren! But the only way we can pay it back, the experts say, is by getting more sleep ourselves. Apparently, we're trying. A recent article in *The Wall Street Journal* took note of the growing phenomenon of employees napping at work, but I suspect that this barely covers the interest payments, which go right to Japan. (As you may have noticed, the Japanese are asleep most of the time that we're awake.)

Why, by degrees, are we banishing sleep? In a handful of in- 6 stances, arguably, the cause has been government over-regulation. I am thinking of the recent case of Sari Zayed, of Davis, California. Ms. Zayed, after being overheard by a neighbor, was awakened at 1:30 A.M. by a municipal "noise-abatement officer" who gave her a $50 citation for snoring too loudly. The amount of money that Ms. Zayed subsequently received in damages from the city of Davis would allow her to pay for nightly snoring citations from now to the end of the year.

America's sleep deficit, though, is surely a systemic phenome- 7 non. Many commentators would blame it on what might be called the AWOL factor—that is, the American Way of Life. We are by nature a busy and ambitious people whom tectonic social forces—declining average wage, high rate of divorce, two-paycheck families, instant telecommunications, jet travel across time zones, growing popularity of soccer for everyone older than four—have turned into a race of laboratory rats on a treadmill going nowhere ever faster. And there is obviously something to this explanation. It is noteworthy that television shows like *Seinfeld* and *Cheers,* on which nobody seems to have any real responsibilities (circumstances that accord more fully with most viewers' fantasies than with their actual lives), have come to constitute a distinct broadcast genre known as "time porn."

It is hard not to credit the importance of the AWOL factor, but I   8
wonder if the driving force behind the sleep deficit is in fact more pervasive, and indeed global in nature: the triumph of light. I am by no means a romantic or a Luddite when it comes to electricity (anyone who is should read Robert Caro's *The Years of Lyndon Johnson* for its haunting description of life in west Texas in the days before rural electrification), and I also don't subscribe to the fashionable opinion that electronic labor-saving devices (personal computers possibly excepted) end up consuming more labor than they save. Yet electricity's ubiquitous and seemingly most innocuous use—to power the common light bulb—could not help exacting a price in sleep. Electricity made it possible for the first time in history for masses of humanity to vanquish darkness.

I had never given much thought to the role of darkness in ordinary human affairs until I read a monograph prepared by John   9
Staudenmaier, a historian of technology and a Jesuit priest, for a recent conference at MIT. (The essay appears in a book called *Progress: Fact or Illusion,* edited by Leo Marx and Bruce Mazlish.) Staudenmaier makes the point—obvious when brought up, though we've mostly lost sight of it—that from the time of the hominid Lucy, in Hadar, Ethiopia, to the time of Thomas Edison, in West Orange, New Jersey, the onset of darkness sharply curtailed most kinds of activity for most of our ancestors. He writes,

> Living with electric lights makes it difficult to retrieve the experience of a non-electrified society. For all but the very wealthy, who could afford exorbitant arrays of expensive artificial lights, nightfall brought the works of daytime to a definitive end. Activities that need good light—where sharp tools are wielded or sharply defined boundaries maintained; purposeful activities designed to achieve specific goals; in short, that which we call work—all this subsided in the dim light of evening. Absent the press of work, people typically took themselves safely to home and were left with time in the evening for less urgent and more sensual matters: storytelling, sex, prayer, sleep, dreaming.

Staudenmaier's comments on electric light occupy only a few   10
passages. His larger subject is Western intellectual history, and

how metaphors of "enlightenment" came to be associated with or-
derliness, objectivity, and progress, even as metaphors of darkness
came to signify the chaotic, the nonrational, the terrifying. He argues that we have lost, to our detriment, the medieval view that
some aspects of life and understanding are not necessarily helped
by clarity or harmed by ambiguity. Observing that Enlightenment
ideals have "taken a fair beating" in the course of this century,
Staudenmaier wonders if it is time to rediscover the metaphysical
dark, that place "where visions are born and human purpose
renewed."

    I'll leave that thought where it is. But the implication of elec-   11
tricity in the sleep deficit seems hard to argue with. Whatever it
is that we wish or are made to do—pursue leisure, earn a living—
there are simply far more usable hours now in which to do it.
Darkness was once an ocean into which our capacity to venture
was greatly limited; now we are wresting vast areas of permanent lightness from the darkness, much the way the Dutch have
wrested polders of dry land from the sea. So vast are these areas
that in composite satellite photographs of the world at night the
contours of civilization are clearly illuminated—the boundaries
of continents, the metastases of cities. Even Wrigley Field, once a
reliable pool of nocturnal darkness, would now show up seventeen nights during the baseball season. In the United States at
midnight more than five million people are at work at full-time
jobs. Supermarkets, gas stations, copy shops—many of these
never close. I know of a dentist in Ohio who decided to open an
all-night clinic, and has had the last laugh on friends who believed that he would never get patients. The supply-side theory
may not have worked in economics, but it has certainly worked
with regard to light: the more we get, the more we find ways to
put it to use. And, of course, the more we get, the more we distance ourselves from the basic diurnal rhythm in which our evolution occurred.

    Thomas Edison, famous for subsisting on catnaps, would have   12
wanted it this way. In contrast, Calvin Coolidge, a younger man
with an older temperament, slept at least ten and often as much as
eleven hours a day. Two world views collide here, and somewhere
between them is a balance waiting to be struck. Where and how?
The only useful contribution I can make is to recall life in Ireland in
the mid-1960s. One of the elements that made it so congenial was a
shared expertise among engineers at the Electricity Supply Board
which resulted in regular but unpredictably occurring blackouts.

The relentless march of time would suddenly be punctuated by a limbo of uncertain duration. Lights were extinguished. Clocks stopped. Television screens went black. Drivers became hesitant and generous at traffic signals. Society and all its components took a blessed time out.

There was also something in Ireland called "holy hour," a   13 period in the afternoon when all the pubs would close. Perhaps what Americans need is a holy hour in the form of a blackout—a brief caesura in our way of life that might come every day at perhaps nine-thirty or ten at night. Not the least of the holy hour's benefits, I might add, would be an appealing new time slot for Maury Povich.

MEANINGS AND VALUES

1. The writer mentions "anecdotal evidence" of a "'sleep deficit'" (Par. 4) but does not present it directly. Why do you think he chose not to offer it in detail? Is the essay weakened—or perhaps strengthened—by this omission? Explain. (See "Guide to Terms": *Evaluation*.)

2. Are we to take the example in Paragraph 6 seriously? If not, what is its role in the essay? Is it an indication that we should not take other examples in the essay seriously? Why or why not?

3. Explain why the author might be justified in referring to certain television shows as "time porn." Do you think most readers will agree or disagree with his conclusion? Why?

4. According to this essay, what was lost when electricity made it possible to "vanquish darkness" (Par. 8)?

EXPOSITORY TECHNIQUES

1. Where does Murphy first announce the phenomenon he wishes to explain? Should this announcement be considered a thesis? Why or why not? (Guide: *Thesis*.)

2. What is the role of the rhetorical question that opens Paragraph 6? (Guide: *Rhetorical Questions*.)

3. Which causes of the sleep deficit does the author consider most important, and how does he signal their importance to readers? Which of the strategies for creating emphasis does he use with frequency in this essay? (Guide: *Emphasis*.)

4. Where in the essay does the author begin discussing the effects of electricity?

5. What is the role of the extended discussion of Staudenmaier's work in Paragraphs 9 and 10? To what extent do these paragraphs contradict or complement Murphy's tone and approach in the rest of the essay? (Guide: *Style/Tone.*)

6. What strategy does the writer use to conclude the essay? (Guide: *Closings.*) How effective is the conclusion?

DICTION AND VOCABULARY

1. To what does the title allude? (Guide: *Figures of Speech.*) How is the allusion related to the rest of the essay? Discuss how repetition of the word "darkness," beginning with the title, serves to create unity and coherence in the essay. (Guide: *Unity; Coherence.*) Is the title effective even for readers who do not recognize the allusion? Why or why not?

2. What choices of words and phrases does the writer make in Paragraph 8 to indicate the importance of electricity as one of the causes of the sleep deficit and the disappearance of "darkness" in our daily lives? (Guide: *Diction.*) Do you think the diction in this paragraph is appropriate to its purposes, or is it excessive? Explain. (Guide: *Evaluation.*)

3. If you do not know the meaning of some of the following terms, look them up in a dictionary: *anecdotal* (Par. 4); *systemic, tectonic* (7); *Luddite, innocuous, vanquish* (8); *hominid, curtailed* (9); *metastases, diurnal* (11); *subsisting, limbo, duration* (12); *caesura* (13).

READ TO WRITE

1. **Collaborating:** In a group, think of other modern inventions (airplanes, television, the Internet, credit cards) and the ways they have changed our society and shaped our lives. The inventions can be seemingly insignificant (cup holders in automobiles, telephone calling cards, zippers, or Velcro) and still be topics worth exploring because of their consequences, both good and bad. Then plan an essay exploring the consequences of one or more of the inventions.

2. **Considering Audience:** This essay is partly humorous, partly serious. Prepare an essay analyzing the role of each element and discussing how readers are likely to respond to the combination.

3. **Developing an Essay:** This essay makes effective use of the concept of a "deficit," that is, the difference between what we have and what we ought to have. Use a similar strategy to begin an essay of your own by introducing some other kind of "deficit" whose causes and consequences are worth exploring.

(NOTE: Suggestions for topics requiring development by CAUSE AND EFFECT are on pp. 279–280 at the end of this chapter.)

VERLYN KLINKENBORG

VERLYN KLINKENBORG was born in 1952 in Meeker, Colorado, attended Pomona College, and received a Ph.D. from Princeton University. During the 1980s and the early 1990s, he taught literature and creative writing at Fordham University, St. Olaf College, Bennington College, and Harvard University. Since 1997, Klinkenborg has held a position on the editorial board for *The New York Times*, and has published a number of notable opinion pieces, many of which center on the topic of rural farm life. His books include *Making Hay* (1986), *The Rural Life* (2002), *The Last Fine Time* (2004), and *Timothy, or, Notes of an Abject Reptile* (2006). In 2007, he received a Guggenheim Fellowship, which is being used to fund his forthcoming book about the English farmer and journalist, William Cobbett.

Our Vanishing Night

"Our Vanishing Night" appeared in *National Geographic* in 2008. In this article, Klinkenborg addresses the relatively recent concern regarding "light pollution" and describes the impact that our careless use of artificial light has had on the natural rhythms and biological processes of many species. He then goes on to relate this scientific data to a number of similar effects on human life in order to illustrate the fact that the dangers of this phenomenon are not limited to nonhuman species. His explanation of an issue with which many of us are probably not familiar delivers the unsettling message that progress and technological innovation have caused us to divorce ourselves from "our evolutionary and cultural patrimony."

If humans were truly at home under the light of the moon and   1
stars, we would go in darkness happily, the midnight world as visible to us as it is to the vast number of nocturnal species on this planet. Instead, we are diurnal creatures, with eyes adapted to living in the sun's light. This is a basic evolutionary fact, even though most of us don't think of ourselves as diurnal beings any more than we think of ourselves as primates or mammals or Earthlings. Yet it's the only way to explain what we've done to the night: We've engineered it to receive us by filling it with light.

This kind of engineering is no different than damming a river.   2
Its benefits come with consequences—called light pollution—whose effects scientists are only now beginning to study. Light pollution is largely the result of bad lighting design, which allows artificial light

to shine outward and upward into the sky, where it's not wanted, instead of focusing it downward, where it is. Ill-designed lighting washes out the darkness of night and radically alters the light levels—and light rhythms—to which many forms of life, including ourselves, have adapted. Wherever human light spills into the natural world, some aspect of life—migration, reproduction, feeding—is affected.

For most of human history, the phrase "light pollution" would   3
have made no sense. Imagine walking toward London on a moonlit night around 1800, when it was Earth's most populous city. Nearly a million people lived there, making do, as they always had, with candles and rushlights and torches and lanterns. Only a few houses were lit by gas, and there would be no public gaslights in the streets or squares for another seven years. From a few miles away, you would have been as likely to *smell* London as to see its dim collective glow.

Now most of humanity lives under intersecting domes of   4
reflected, refracted light, of scattering rays from overlit cities and suburbs, from light-flooded highways and factories. Nearly all of nighttime Europe is a nebula of light, as is most of the United States and all of Japan. In the south Atlantic the glow from a single fishing fleet—squid fishermen luring their prey with metal halide lamps—can be seen from space, burning brighter, in fact, than Buenos Aires or Rio de Janeiro.

In most cities the sky looks as though it has been emptied of   5
stars, leaving behind a vacant haze that mirrors our fear of the dark and resembles the urban glow of dystopian science fiction. We've grown so used to this pervasive orange haze that the original glory of an unlit night—dark enough for the planet Venus to throw shadows on Earth—is wholly beyond our experience, beyond memory almost. And yet above the city's pale ceiling lies the rest of the universe, utterly undiminished by the light we waste—a bright shoal of stars and planets and galaxies, shining in seemingly infinite darkness.

We've lit up the night as if it were an unoccupied country, when   6
nothing could be further from the truth. Among mammals alone, the number of nocturnal species is astonishing. Light is a powerful biological force, and on many species it acts as a magnet, a process being studied by researchers such as Travis Longcore and Catherine Rich, co-founders of the Los Angeles-based Urban Wildlands Group. The effect is so powerful that scientists speak of songbirds and seabirds being "captured" by searchlights on land or by the light from

gas flares on marine oil platforms, circling and circling in the thousands until they drop. Migrating at night, birds are apt to collide with brightly lit tall buildings; immature birds on their first journey suffer disproportionately.

Insects, of course, cluster around streetlights, and feeding at   7
those insect clusters is now ingrained in the lives of many bat species. In some Swiss valleys the European lesser horseshoe bat began to vanish after streetlights were installed, perhaps because those valleys were suddenly filled with light-feeding pipistrelle bats. Other nocturnal mammals—including desert rodents, fruit bats, opossums, and badgers—forage more cautiously under the permanent full moon of light pollution because they've become easier targets for predators.

Some birds—blackbirds and nightingales, among others—sing   8
at unnatural hours in the presence of artificial light. Scientists have determined that long artificial days—and artificially short nights—induce early breeding in a wide range of birds. And because a longer day allows for longer feeding, it can also affect migration schedules. One population of Bewick's swans wintering in England put on fat more rapidly than usual, priming them to begin their Siberian migration early. The problem, of course, is that migration, like most other aspects of bird behavior, is a precisely timed biological behavior. Leaving early may mean arriving too soon for nesting conditions to be right.

Nesting sea turtles, which show a natural predisposition for   9
dark beaches, find fewer and fewer of them to nest on. Their hatchlings, which gravitate toward the brighter, more reflective sea horizon, find themselves confused by artificial lighting behind the beach. In Florida alone, hatchling losses number in the hundreds of thousands every year. Frogs and toads living near brightly lit highways suffer nocturnal light levels that are as much as a million times brighter than normal, throwing nearly every aspect of their behavior out of joint, including their nighttime breeding choruses.

Of all the pollutions we face, light pollution is perhaps the most   10
easily remedied. Simple changes in lighting design and installation yield immediate changes in the amount of light spilled into the atmosphere and, often, immediate energy savings.

It was once thought that light pollution only affected astron-   11
omers, who need to see the night sky in all its glorious clarity. And, in fact, some of the earliest civic efforts to control light pollution—in Flagstaff, Arizona, half a century ago—were made to protect the view from Lowell Observatory, which sits high above

that city. Flagstaff has tightened its regulations since then, and in 2001 it was declared the first International Dark Sky City. By now the effort to control light pollution has spread around the globe. More and more cities and even entire countries, such as the Czech Republic, have committed themselves to reducing unwanted glare.

Unlike astronomers, most of us may not need an undiminished view of the night sky for our work, but like most other creatures we do need darkness. Darkness is as essential to our biological welfare, to our internal clockwork, as light itself. The regular oscillation of waking and sleep in our lives—one of our circadian rhythms—is nothing less than a biological expression of the regular oscillation of light on Earth. So fundamental are these rhythms to our being that altering them is like altering gravity. 12

For the past century or so, we've been performing an open-ended experiment on ourselves, extending the day, shortening the night, and short-circuiting the human body's sensitive response to light. The consequences of our bright new world are more readily perceptible in less adaptable creatures living in the peripheral glow of our prosperity. But for humans, too, light pollution may take a biological toll. At least one new study has suggested a direct correlation between higher rates of breast cancer in women and the nighttime brightness of their neighborhoods. 13

In the end, humans are no less trapped by light pollution than the frogs in a pond near a brightly lit highway. Living in a glare of our own making, we have cut ourselves off from our evolutionary and cultural patrimony—the light of the stars and the rhythms of day and night. In a very real sense, light pollution causes us to lose sight of our true place in the universe, to forget the scale of our being, which is best measured against the dimensions of a deep night with the Milky Way—the edge of our galaxy—arching overhead. 14

MEANINGS AND VALUES

1.   How does this essay define "light pollution" (Par. 2)?

2.   Where does the writer first outline the consequences of human-generated light spreading into the natural world, and what does he name as the general kinds of effects?

3.   What are the negative consequences of excessive light that the writer discusses in detail in this essay?

EXPOSITORY TECHNIQUES

1. a. What pronoun does the writer use throughout the essay to refer to himself: *I*, *we*, or *he*? What pronoun does he use to refer to readers: *you*, *they*, or *we*?

   b. In what ways are these choices related to the overall theme? (See "Guide to Terms": *Unity.*)

2. Is the discussion in this essay neatly divided between causes and effects? If so, where is the dividing line? If not, which sections are primarily devoted to causes and which to effects?

DICTION AND VOCABULARY

1. The word *light* often has positive connotations. In this essay, what other words does the writer associate with *light* to give it negative connotations and what negative synonyms does he use for *light*? Hint: Look at Paragraphs 2, 4, 5, 6, 9, and 11. (Guide: *Connotation/ Denotation.*)

2. If you do not know the meaning of some of the following words, look them up in a dictionary: *diurnal* (Par. 1); *refracted, nebula, halide* (4); *dystopian, pervasive* (5); *priming* (8); *predisposition, gravitate* (9); *circadian, oscillation* (12); *peripheral* (13); *patrimony* (14).

READ TO WRITE

1. **Collaborating:** In a group, brainstorm a list of modern advancements (airplanes or televisions, for example) whose consequences have been negative (rapid spread of diseases or changes in social patterns, for instance) as well as positive. Choose three advances and list negative consequences for each. Then use one of the subjects and its effects and plan an essay using this content.

2. **Considering Audience:** As displayed in this essay, environmental thinking encourages us to consider the harmful as well as helpful effects of our actions. Prepare an essay suggesting to readers the need to consider the full range of consequences for actions they generally consider positive. You need not limit yourself to environmental issues; even personal behaviors like honesty and hard work can have a variety of outcomes.

3. **Developing an Essay:** This essay uses the term *pollution* to turn a positive term, *light*, into a negative one, *light pollution*. Use a similar strategy to develop an essay of your own. Try terms like *music, sports,* or *food* to look at the downside of these subjects.

(NOTE: Suggestions for topics requiring development by CAUSE AND EFFECT follow.)

Writing Suggestions for Chapter 8

CAUSE AND EFFECT

Analyze the immediate and ultimate causes and/or effects of one of the following subjects or another suggested by them. (Be careful that your analysis does not develop into a mere listing of superficial reasons.)

1. The ethnic makeup of a neighborhood
2. Some *minor* discovery or invention
3. The popularity of some modern singer or other celebrity
4. The popularity of some fad of clothing or hairstyle
5. The widespread fascination for antique cars (or guns, furniture, dishes, motorcycles, old bottles, etc.)
6. The decision of some close acquaintance to enter the religious life
7. Some unreasonable fear or anxiety that afflicts you or someone you know well
8. The popularity of computer games
9. The mainstreaming of handicapped children
10. The appeal of a recent movie or current television series
11. The willingness of some people to sacrifice personal relationships for professional success
12. The disintegration of a marriage or family
13. A trend in the national economy
14. The concern with diet and physical fitness
15. Attention to gender roles
16. Willingness to take risks, even extreme ones

COLLABORATIVE EXERCISES

1. As a group, research the causes of a war or other armed conflict. Decide collectively which causes were most central, and together write an essay showing how the combination of such causes led to the conflict. Look at immediate (direct) causes as well as indirect causes.

2. Split into teams of four. Divide each team into two halves, one that will analyze the causes and one that will analyze the effects of number 12 (p. 279). Create a thesis based on your analyses that would work as a claim for an essay on the topic.

3. Perform the same task for the above question for the topic of "the high percentage of women in the workforce."

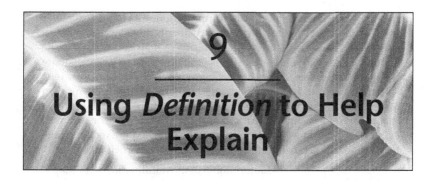

9

Using *Definition* to Help Explain

Few barriers to communication are as great as those created by key terms or concepts that have various meanings or shades of meaning. For this reason, expository writing often provides definitions of words and ideas whose precise meaning is important to the writer's purpose. Sometimes **definitions** merely clarify meanings of concrete or noncontroversial terms. This simple process is similar to that often used in dictionaries:

1. providing a synonym, for example

   cinema: a motion picture

   or

2. placing the word in a class and then showing how it differs from others of the same class, for example

   Term   Class   Details

   metheglin: an alcoholic liquor made of fermented honey

Often, however, definitions specify the meanings of abstract, unusual, or newly minted terms. Definitions of this sort are particularly useful when the experiences or knowledge of readers does little to help them with the meaning of a term or idea that is nonetheless a key element of an overall explanation.

Sometimes a term or concept (or perhaps a process, a natural phenomenon, a group of people, or a relationship) is itself the subject of an explanation, leading to an *extended definition*, as in the following example.

This is *orienteering,* a mixture of marathon, hike, and scavenger hunt, a cross-country race in which participants must locate a series of markers set in unfamiliar terrain by means of map and compass. The course, which may range from an acre of city park to twenty square miles of wilderness, is dotted with anywhere from four to fifteen "controls," red-and-white flags whose general locations are marked on the map by small circles. At each control there is a paper punch that produces a distinctive pattern on a card the racer carries. In most events the order in which the card must be punched is fixed; the route taken to reach each control, however, is up to the participant.

—Linton Robinson, "Marathoning with Maps"

Extended definitions may take a paragraph or two or may be the primary pattern for all or most of an essay, depending on the complexity of the subject being defined, the amount of controversy or confusion it has generated, the likely interest of readers in the discussion, and the writer's purpose.

WHY USE DEFINITION?

When your subject requires you to write about terms, ideas, or phenomena likely to be unfamiliar to your audience, or when the concepts and words you are using have conflicting or controversial meanings, then you probably need to prepare an extended definition for your readers. For years, discussions of how much people work each week excluded housework and other time spent on activities important to home and family. The definition of *work* included only labor outside the home for a specific wage. Women were rightly angered by this definition, which excluded the hours many of them labored creating homes and maintaining families. If you were to write today about how much work people do in an average week, you would need to provide an extended definition of work including such activities. Few people would argue your definition, but they would expect you to be aware of the different (and conflicting) meanings of the term and to make your choice among them clear. If some readers are likely to disagree with your choice, however, you will need to present reasons for it. You might even need to stipulate (or dictate) the meaning of the term as you use it in the essay so that your audience will not misread your essay by substituting their preferred meaning for your own.

When your writing focuses on a fashion, artistic trend, social phenomenon, political movement, or set of ideas or behaviors whose impact is widespread enough to interest most readers but new enough to require definition, you might consider creating an essay that presents an *informative definition*, one that explores and explains the various aspects of your subject. In contrast, when your readers already have some ideas about your subject, but you think these ideas (or perspectives) need to be changed, you could create a *redefinition* essay. A redefinition begins with the ideas readers hold and tries to substitute new and different ones. For example, people often try to make pets of wild animals because they consider the creatures cute, cuddly, or amusing. You might attempt to redefine the favorable images people hold of animals like koala bears, monkeys, boa constrictors, ocelots, or raccoons to show that these and similar creatures are likely to make troublesome, unpleasant, or even dangerous pets.

CHOOSING A STRATEGY

Extended definitions, unlike the simple dictionary type, follow no set pattern. Often when extended definitions are part of an essay, readers are not specifically aware of the process of definition. This lack of specific awareness arises because the definitions are frequently part of the overall subject, are written in the same tone as the rest of the exposition, and are closely tied to the writer's thesis and purpose.

When an extended definition is the primary pattern for an essay, however, the essay itself may follow one of several broad strategies. An informative definition often begins by explaining the reason for the subject's current importance as well as the need to define it. It may then move to a brief, sometimes formal definition; continue with a discussion of the historical background and present instances; and conclude with a review of the subject's features. The following informal plan for an essay includes these strategies in an order appropriate to the subject.

Introduction
 Tentative thesis: If you look carefully at your calendar for the month of December, you are likely to come across the holiday Kwanzaa, which may be unfamiliar to you but which is celebrated each year by an increasing number of your friends, coworkers, and neighbors.
 Current importance: Examples
Definition
 Brief formal definition
 Historical background

Features: Seven principles, various activities, clothing,
participants, meaning of celebration, food, stories,
and materials and resources
Present instances: Current and growing popularity
Conclusion: Summary and sources for further information

A redefinition essay grows from the assumption that readers
already have some ideas about the subject but these ideas should
be modified or discarded altogether. Redefinitions often begin in
the same manner as informative definitions—by creating interest
in the topic. Then they generally proceed to mention the ways the
subject is normally interpreted, following each with an alternate interpretation, or redefinition. Or they review various aspects of the
subject and suggest fresh ways of looking at each.

DEVELOPING DEFINITIONS

A definition helps writers and readers agree on the meaning of
a term, concept, or phenomenon by providing answers to some
important questions. As you develop a definition, try keeping in
mind the questions you will need to address in order to help readers understand your subject. These sample questions can provide
a start.

For subjects that can be observed, measured, and known:	**For concepts, values, or terms whose meaning depends on the ways people use them:**
What are its features?	How do people use it?
What is its history?	What has its meaning been historically, and how has the meaning changed?
What does it do?	
What doesn't it do?	
	How is this set of values or concepts different from others? Similar?

Definitions use many familiar techniques of expository writing, including examples, comparisons, and classifications. There
are, however, some techniques peculiar to definition. You can give
the *background* of a word, answering the question "What is the

history of the term or concept?" (that is, its *etymology*) and providing valuable hints to its meanings. For example, *catholic* originally, in ancient times, meant pertaining to the universal Christian church. Its present meaning—of or concerning the Roman Catholic Church—retains some of the original force because the Roman Catholic Church views itself as the direct descendant of the ancient, undivided Christian church.

You can also enumerate the *characteristics* of the term or subject, sometimes isolating an essential one for special treatment. In defining a social group, such as triathletes, for example, you might list the physical qualities they share (endurance, strength, versatility, and exceptional fitness), their mental qualities (high endurance for pain, desire to exceed normal levels of achievement, and pleasure in physical exertion), and their social preferences (tolerance for solitary training routines, desire to excel, and preference for individual achievement rather than group membership). In so doing, you would be explaining the common elements that define the group and distinguish it from other groups.

You might define by *negation,* sometimes called "exclusion" or "differentiation," by showing what is *not* the meaning of the term, concept, or phenomenon. (This is an important technique for a redefinition essay.) To do this, you answer the question, "What is it *not?*": "*Intelligence* is neither a puzzle-solving activity that enables people to do well on a standardized example like the SAT or ACT, nor the ability to remember columns of facts and figures that may have no real use." If you employ this technique, however, remember that readers will expect you also to provide a positive definition, indicating what the definition *is* as well as what it *is not.*

But perhaps the most dependable techniques for defining are basic expository patterns. You can illustrate the meaning of a term or define a phenomenon by drawing *examples* from your own experience, from newspaper or online reports, from books and magazines, or from interviews and surveys. For instance, you might help explain the range of behaviors included in the term *deviant behavior* by offering examples not only of thieves, drug dealers, and pornographers, but also of people who live alone in the wilderness for spiritual enlightenment or who participate in dangerous sports. You might even include yourself in the category by telling how you climbed the side of a glacier or parachuted from a bridge into a river gorge. Or you might define by *classifying,* sorting kinds of deviant behavior into those that are socially acceptable, even honorable (the search for spiritual enlightenment); those that are harmful only to the individual (dangerous sports); and those that harm other people (thievery and other activities generally considered criminal).

Comparisons are useful, too, both those that identify *synonyms* (*naïve* means innocent, unsophisticated, natural, unaffected, and artless) or that distinguish among concepts with similar, though not identical, meanings, such as *consensus* (general agreement among a group of people on their attitude toward an issue or problem) and *dissensus* (general agreement among a group of people on the ways their attitudes toward an issue or problem differ). Comparisons respond to the question, "What is the subject like or unlike?" So, too, do *similes* and *metaphors*, two techniques that are especially useful in defining concepts and attitudes that are difficult to grasp directly ("an *epiphany* is a moment of sudden clarity and insight, like the moment your eyes become accustomed to the dark and you can suddenly see your surroundings," "a *transition* in writing is a bridge between ideas").

A narrative or an account of a process can also help you define. An explanation of *courage*, for example, might include the story of a 10-year-old saving a friend from drowning in an icy pond. A discussion of *open-heart surgery* might include a description of the process.

Few extended definitions would use all these methods, but the extent to which you use them should depend on three factors: (1) the term or concept itself, since some are more elusive and subject to misunderstanding than others; (2) the function the term serves in your writing, since it is foolish to develop several pages defining a term that serves only a casual or unimportant purpose; and (3) your prospective audience, since the extent of your readers' knowledge and their likely responses to your definition of a disputed or controversial concept or phenomenon should lead you to choose the most convincing or persuasive strategies for the particular audience.

Finally, remember that reference works can be valuable sources for definition. The *Oxford English Dictionary*, for example, traces the meanings of a word during various historical periods; the *Dictionary of Slang and Unconventional English* or the *Encyclopedia of Pop, Rock, and Soul* can provide you with surprising and useful information. A reference librarian or an Internet search engine can provide you with many more sources.

Student Essay

In the following essay, Lori L'Heureux uses a variety of definition techniques to define and redefine *stars*.

Stars
by Lori L'Heureux

How many of us as children longed to be famous when we grew up? Many of us admired a certain celebrity and wanted to be just like him or her when we got older. We wanted to be a star.

Importance of term

Word/concept to be defined

The word "star," used to describe a celebrity, first came into use around 1830. Before this, there was no special term to label performers who, on their own, could draw large numbers of spectators to a performance or an athletic contest. The lack of a term for such a celebrity probably reflected a greater emphasis on the performance or athletic event than on the individual performer or athlete. But as the role of talented individuals became more important, a word for it was needed. Many words, old or newly fashioned, might have served, but the noun borrowed from gazing at the night sky somehow captured the emerging role (Braudy 9).

Background and history

Stars, indeed, have an enormous impact on our lives. They are recognized throughout society, observed closely onstage and off, thought about, talked about, emulated, even dreamed about. Stardom is a vital force in our culture.

Effects and importance

Because so many people perceive the work stars do as a form of upgraded play, they understand only imperfectly the work life of celebrity entertainers. According to Jib Fowles, many stars resent the stereotypes that have been created for them over the last century. Many people, thinking that the majority of stars spend the hours of the day at leisure, imagine them living a lavish lifestyle characterized by money and glamour. Stars are thought to be greedy and to associate only with people whose social status

Define by negation

matches their own. Stars are frequently imagined as leading relaxed lives: this one reclining in a chaise lounge, reading a script; that one stretched out on a massage table, getting worked on by a team's trainer; several others poolside and prone. But in reality, the life of most stars is quite the opposite (Fowles 59).

I conducted a survey of my own to see if most people hold these misconceptions of celebrities' lives. I asked 15 people to tell me what type of lives they felt celebrities lead. Twelve people said that stars were rich and had easy careers. Only three said celebrities led hard lives in the public eye and had difficult jobs. Two people added that they were never tempted to become stars (L'Heureux).

What readers believe

But what exactly is a star? Is there a downside to being constantly in the public eye? Is being a star really a lot of work? What is the cost of being famous?

Rhetorical questions provide structure

It must be understood that being a star is a social role that an individual adopts. Every day of our lives, we, too, take on social roles; we accept the obligations and behaviors of being an employee, a parent, a spouse, and so forth. Celebrity performers are similar; they wake up in the morning and step into the star role.

A star's talent delights audiences of all ages. A star acts or sings or cracks jokes or even just poses, and does these things with such style that we are fascinated and refreshed. We pay attention to stars because their performances are so successful at entertaining us. Because the audience for television shows, films, and recordings has become so large and so appreciative, the acclamation a star receives has become greater and more ferocious in recent decades. Through ticket sales, high ratings, and fan mail, an audience makes known its jubilant or waning response to a star's performance. When the response is good, the flow of good tidings certifies a star in public regard and elevates him or her to a special glory. At some

Examples

moments for certain stars and their captivated fans, the reaction can be manic, as when the Beatles first toured the U.S. in 1964.

Becoming a star is sometimes a difficult task. Trying to become known in the industry, to be liked by directors, and to get parts, hopefuls embark on endless rounds of auditions. Most will spend more time at auditions than they ever will before the camera. Athletes struggling to become star players generally spend many years in the minor leagues (or the equivalent) waiting for a call to "the show."

Redefining star

Examples

Meanwhile, between roles, struggling actors have to sustain themselves. Usually this means menial jobs of one sort or another. For example, Marilyn Monroe labored in a wartime defense plant where she packed parachutes. For aspiring athletes, a job in the off-season is generally a necessity.

Example

Fame may require much in the way of disappointment, strain, and heartache. Since so many people are striving to become stars, and since so few will make it, the typical aspirant's work life is a ceaseless round of rejection and exclusion. He or she may attempt to maintain motivation with visions of ultimate stardom, but the daily experience of trudging from audition to audition can prove devastating. Celebrity George C. Scott commented about acting, "I think it is a psychologically damaging profession, just too much rejection to cope with every day of your life."

Redefining

Example and quote

Aspirants may initially set themselves on the path to stardom because, in their rosy view, fame promises freedom beyond compare. But in fact the job of the celebrity performer is subject to suffocating impositions and strangling constraints. Asked what it means to become a star, Cary Grant replied, "Does it mean happiness? Yeah, for a couple of days. And then what happens? You find out that your life is not your own anymore, and that you're on show every time you step out on the street."

Example and quote

According to Yoti Lane, such a reaction is altogether typical, for "one of the most characteristic symptoms of having actually become a celebrity is a certain disillusionment, which sets in—after the first thrill of seeing one's name in headlines—upon discovering the obligations and inconveniences of being known by everyone everywhere" (130).

Underestimated by the public, a star's work is one of the most strenuous occupations that a person can have. Fred Astaire commented, "People will come up to me and say, 'Boy, it must have been fun making those old MGM musicals.' Fun? I suppose you could have considered them that—if you like beating your brains and feet out." Knocking oneself out to deliver first-rate performances to the public, time after time, is the fate of those ensconced in the star role. The occupation calls for extraordinary effort and ceaseless toil.

Redefinition continues

For most stars, the preparation for performing begins with a general readiness. Professional athletes work out for countless hours to maintain their physical condition. Singers exercise their voices daily, practicing their delivery and keeping their vocal cords in shape. Actors take classes to strengthen their performance or spend time carefully observing others.

Process

From a base of readiness, the star prepares for the performance. The rock band practices its songs for a concert, the comedian works on new material, and the actor concentrates on a new character to become familiar with it. Actors must go over their lines again and again, working to get them right. Before going on, the star has to be costumed and made up, a process that can be very time-consuming.

The hard work for a star truly begins when he or she must concentrate on the task at hand. What a performer must do is create wonderfully and completely, on cue. The star has been engaged to deliver, within the framework of the performance, the right act at the right moment. The audience expects the comedian to have the perfect punchline, the center fielder to catch the ball in the sun, and the actress to cry when required.

Being a star can also be dangerous. Actor Sylvester Stallone calculates that in making some of his action films he has broken his nose three times, his hand twice, and has suffered a concussion and a ruptured stomach. Also a danger to stars is their public. Fan letters pour in by the thousands each day, and the letter writers often want to enter into some sort of transaction with their idols. This can be dangerous when fans strive to encounter a star in person, pushing and shoving for contact, or when outraged fans try to injure a star.

For the privilege of staring at a star, fans will follow an entertainer into parties, restaurants, and even bathrooms. Sometimes stars have to live with the unremitting presence of fans camped at their front doors. The romance and obsession that are in a fan's mind can lead them to stalk an idol. Brooke Shields was the object of the affections of one Mark Bailey, who attempted to break into her New Jersey home; the judge put him on five years' probation. While David Letterman was on the West Coast, a mentally ill woman who claimed to be his wife installed herself in his East Coast home (Fowles 310).

The media can also invade the privacy of a star. Interviews may seem endless and prove to be very draining. The press tends to emphasize personal questions that make the subject of an interview understandably uncomfortable. Magazines such as *The National Enquirer* strive to create rumors about different stars, often relying on questionable sources and rumors that later prove to be unfounded. A personal problem that any of us could easily encounter and that most of us would like to face in privacy frequently ends up on the front pages of newspapers, creating stress and embarrassment for the celebrity and threatening his or her career.

Even if their lives do not fit within stereotypes, stars are not people who lead normal lives. Celebrities are

Effects of stardom

Summary

widely admired and often receive considerable money for their work, yet they must face situations that the general public does not fully understand. Stars face danger; give up their privacy; and work long, hard hours. Referring to celebrities as "stars" is quite appropriate because their lives are as far from ours as the stars are distant from the ground we stand on.

Works Cited

Braudy, Leo. *Frenzy of Renown: Fame and Its History.* New York: Oxford UP, 1986. Print.

Fowles, Jib. *Starstruck.* Chicago: Smithsonian, 1992. Print.

Lane, Yoti. *The Psychology of the Actor.* Westport: Greenwood, 1959. Print.

L'Heureux, Lori. Survey. U of Rhode Island, Kingston, 7–10 Nov. 1995. TS.

JOHN BERENDT

JOHN BERENDT was born in Syracuse, New York, in 1939. He was a
student at Harvard and received his B.A. in 1961. A journalist,
essayist, and writer of nonfiction, he has also worked as an editor
and columnist at *Esquire,* an editor at *Holiday* and *New York* magazines, and as an associate producer of the *David Frost Show* and the
Dick Cavett Show. His essays and articles have appeared in numerous magazines, including *Forbes, Publisher's Weekly, Esquire, Architectural Digest,* and the *New Yorker.* His best-selling book, *Midnight
in the Garden of Good and Evil* (1994) is a nonfiction account of unusual characters and scandalous goings-on in Savannah, Georgia.
He is also the author of *The City of Falling Angels* (2005).

The Hoax

In this essay, first published in *Esquire,* Berendt takes a relatively
straightforward approach to definition, yet through skillful writing and wit, he manages to offer a fresh and insightful understanding of a familiar term and the behavior it designates.

When the humorist Robert Benchley was an undergraduate at   1
Harvard eighty years ago, he and a couple of friends showed
up one morning at the door of an elegant Beacon Hill mansion,
dressed as furniture repairmen. They told the housekeeper they had
come to pick up the sofa. Five minutes later they carried the sofa out
the door, put it on a truck, and drove it three blocks away to another
house, where, posing as deliverymen, they plunked it down in the
parlor. That evening, as Benchley well knew, the couple living in
house A were due to attend a party in house B. Whatever the
outcome—and I'll get to that shortly—it was guaranteed to be a defining example of how proper Bostonians handle social crises. The
wit inherent in Benchley's practical joke elevated it from the level of
prank to the more respectable realm of hoax.

To qualify as a hoax, a prank must have magic in it—the word   2
is derived from *hocus-pocus,* after all. Daring and irony are useful
ingredients, too. A good example of a hoax is the ruse perpetrated
by David Hampton, the young black man whose pretense of being
Sidney Poitier's son inspired John Guare's *Six Degrees of Separation.*
Hampton managed to insinuate himself into two of New York's
most sophisticated households—one headed by the president of the
public-television station *WNET,* the other by the dean of the

Columbia School of Journalism. Hampton's hoax touched a number of sensitive themes: snobbery, class, race, and sex, all of which playwright Guare deftly exploited.

Hampton is a member of an elite band of famous impostors   3
that includes a half-mad woman who for fifty years claimed to be Anastasia, the lost daughter of the assassinated czar Nicholas II; and a man named Harry Gerguson, who became a Hollywood restaurateur and darling of society in the 1930s and 1940s as the ersatz Russian prince Mike Romanoff.

Forgeries have been among the better hoaxes. Fake Vermeers   4
painted by an obscure Dutch artist, Hans van Meegeren, were so convincing that they fooled art dealers, collectors, and museums. The hoax came to light when van Meegeren was arrested as a Nazi collaborator after the war. To prove he was not a Nazi, he admitted he had sold a fake Vermeer to Hermann Göring for $256,000. Then he owned up to having created other "Vermeers," and to prove he could do it, he painted *Jesus in the Temple* in the style of Vermeer while under guard in jail.

In a bizarre twist, a story much like van Meegeren's became the   5
subject of the book *Fake!*, by Clifford Irving, who in 1972 attempted to pull off a spectacular hoax of his own: a wholly fraudulent "authorized" biography of Howard Hughes. Irving claimed to have conducted secret interviews with the reclusive Hughes, and McGraw-Hill gave him a big advance. Shortly before publication, Hughes surfaced by telephone and denied that he had ever spoken with Irving. Irving had already spent $100,000 of the advance; he was convicted of fraud and sent to jail.

As it happens, we are used to hoaxes where I come from. I grew up   6
just a few miles down the road from Cardiff, New York—a town made famous by the Cardiff Giant. As we learned in school, a farmer named Newell complained, back in 1889, that his well was running dry, and while he and his neighbors were digging a new one, they came upon what appeared to be the fossilized remains of a man twelve feet tall. Before the day was out, Newell had erected a tent and posted a sign charging a dollar for a glimpse of the "giant"—three dollars for a longer look. Throngs descended on Cardiff. It wasn't long before scientists determined that the giant had been carved from a block of gypsum. The hoax came undone fairly quickly after that, but even so—as often happens with hoaxes—the giant became an even bigger attraction *because* it was a hoax. P. T. Barnum offered Newell a fortune for the giant, but Newell refused, and it was then that he got his comeuppance. Barnum simply made a replica and put it on display as the genuine Cardiff Giant. Newell's gig was ruined.

The consequences of hoaxes are what give them spice. Orson 7
Welles's lifelike 1938 radio broadcast of H. G. Wells's *War of the Worlds*
panicked millions of Americans, who were convinced that martians had
landed in New Jersey. The forged diary of Adolf Hitler embarrassed historian Hugh Trevor-Roper, who had vouched for its authenticity, and
Newsweek and the *Sunday Times* of London, both of which published excerpts in 1983 shortly before forensic tests proved that there were nylon
fibers in the paper it was written on, which wouldn't have been possible
had it originated before 1950. The five-hundred-thousand-year-old remains of Piltdown man, found in 1912, had anthropologists confused
about human evolution until 1953, when fluoride tests exposed the
bones as an elaborate modern hoax. And as for Robert Benchley's game
on Beacon Hill, no one said a word about the sofa all evening, although
there it sat in plain sight. One week later, however, couple A sent an
anonymous package to couple B. It contained the sofa's slipcovers.

MEANINGS AND VALUES

1. State Berendt's definition of a hoax in your own words, and indicate
   the difference between a hoax and a practical joke or prank. Look up
   hoax in a dictionary, and tell how Berendt's definition differs, if at all,
   from the one you encounter there.

2. Restate the meaning of this sentence, "The consequences of hoaxes
   are what give them spice" (Par. 7), and discuss whether the examples
   that follow it provide satisfactory support for the writer's conclusion. (See "Guide to Terms": *Evaluation.*)

3. Other than defining the term *hoax*, what purposes do you think the
   writer had in mind for this essay? (Guide: *Purpose.*)

EXPOSITORY TECHNIQUES

1. Discuss how the way Berendt presents the examples in Paragraphs 2,
   3, and 6 makes them seem imaginative (and somewhat harmless)
   escapades rather than criminal frauds or deceptions.

2. Determine what definition strategies Berendt uses in this essay.
   Which seem most effective, and why? (Guide: *Evaluation.*)

3. Evaluate the strategy Berendt uses to open and close the essay. What
   makes it successful or unsuccessful?

DICTION AND VOCABULARY

1. To what extent does Berendt's presentation of the hoaxes described in Paragraphs 2, 3, and 6 as escapades rather than crimes depend on the terms he uses to present them? (See Expository Techniques, Question 1.) (Guide: *Diction.*)

2. If you do not know the meaning of some of the following terms, look them up in a dictionary: *perpetrated* (Par. 2); *ersatz* (3); *reclusive* (5); *gypsum, gig* (6); *vouched, forensic* (7).

READ TO WRITE

1. **Collaborating:** Pranks, jokes, humorous events, adventures, and absurd occurrences make enjoyable examples in essays, and they often reveal a good deal about human beings and their relationships. Working in a group, make a list of possible examples of this sort. Then freewrite individually about the examples as a way of discovering a possible topic and thesis for an essay of your own.

2. **Considering Audience:** Make a list of words that most readers are likely to believe imply some sort of trickery and deception. Then prepare an essay in which you *redefine* one of the words and attempt to alter readers' views of its meaning.

3. **Developing an Essay:** Using Berendt's essay as a general pattern, create a definition of your own about a very different subject—such as the greatest loss, the most difficult task, or the biggest disappointment.

(NOTE: Suggestions for topics requiring development by DEFINITION are on pp. 326–327 at the end of this chapter.)

JHUMPA LAHIRI

Author JHUMPA LAHIRI was born in London to Bengali Indian parents. The family moved to the United States when she was three. She received a B.A. in English literature from Barnard College in 1989 and earned multiple graduate degrees from Boston University. The short stories in her first book, *Interpreter of Maladies* (1999), deal with the dilemmas of first and second generation Indian immigrants. The collection was awarded the Pulitzer Prize for Fiction in 2000. Her other works include the novel *The Namesake* (2003) and another short story collection, *Unaccustomed Earth* (2008).

My Two Lives

The complex, at times conflicted, sense of identity among many second-generation South Asian immigrants to the United States is a frequent topic of Lahiri's fiction. In this selection, which originally appeared in *Newsweek*, March 6, 2006, she considers her own self-image in relation to the term "Indian-American."

I have lived in the United States for almost 37 years and anticipate growing old in this country. Therefore, with the exception of my first two years in London, "Indian-American" has been a constant way to describe me. Less constant is my relationship to the term. When I was growing up in Rhode Island in the 1970s I felt neither Indian nor American. Like many immigrant offspring I felt intense pressure to be two things, loyal to the old world and fluent in the new, approved of on either side of the hyphen. Looking back, I see that this was generally the case. But my perception as a young girl was that I fell short at both ends, shuttling between two dimensions that had nothing to do with one another.

At home I followed the customs of my parents, speaking Bengali and eating rice and dal with my fingers. These ordinary facts seemed part of a secret, utterly alien way of life, and I took pains to hide them from my American friends. For my parents, home was not our house in Rhode Island but Calcutta, where they were raised. I was aware that the things they lived for—the Nazrul songs they listened to on the reel-to-reel, the family they missed, the clothes my mother wore that were not available in any store in any mall—were at once as precious and as worthless as an outmoded currency.

I also entered a world my parents had little knowledge or con-   3
trol of; school, books, music, television, things that seeped in and
became a fundamental aspect of who I am. I spoke English without
an accent, comprehending the language in a way my parents still do
not. And yet there was evidence that I was not entirely American. In
addition to my distinguishing name and looks, I did not attend Sunday school, did not know how to ice-skate, and disappeared to India
for months at a time. Many of these friends proudly called themselves Irish-American or Italian-American. But they were several
generations removed from the frequently humiliating process of
immigration, so that the ethnic roots they claimed had descended
underground whereas mine were still tangled and green. According
to my parents I was not American, nor would I ever be no matter
how hard I tried. I felt doomed by their pronouncement, misunderstood and gradually defiant. In spite of the first lessons of arithme-
tic, one plus one did not equal two but zero, my conflicting selves
always canceling each other out.

When I first started writing I was not conscious that my subject   4
was the Indian-American experience. What drew me to my craft was
the desire to force the two worlds I occupied to mingle on the page
as I was not brave enough, or mature enough, to allow in life. My
first book was published in 1999, and around then, on the cusp of a
new century, the term "Indian-American" has become part of this
country's vocabulary. I've heard it so often that these days, if asked
about my background, I use the term myself, pleasantly surprised
that I do not have to explain further. What a difference from my
early life, when there was no such way to describe me, when the
most I could do was to clumsily and ineffectually explain.

As I approach middle age, one plus one equals two, both in my   5
work and in my daily existence. The traditions on either side of the
hyphen dwell in me like siblings, still occasionally sparring, one out-
shining the other depending on the day. But like siblings they are in-
timately familiar with one another, forgiving and intertwined. When
my husband and I were married five years ago in Calcutta we invited friends who had never been to India, and they came full of
enthusiasm for a place I avoided talking about in my childhood,
fearful of what people might say. Around non-Indian friends, I no
longer feel compelled to hide the fact that I speak another language.
I speak Bengali to my children, even though I lack the proficiency to
teach them to read or write the language. As a child I sought perfection and so denied myself the claim to any identity. As an adult I
accept that a bicultural upbringing is a rich but imperfect thing.

While I am American by virtue of the fact that I was raised in   6
this country, I am Indian thanks to the efforts of two individuals.
I feel Indian not because of the time I've spent in India or because
of my genetic composition but rather because of my parents' steadfast presence in my life. They live three hours from my home;
I speak to them daily and see them about once a month. Everything will change once they die. They will take certain things with
them—conversations in another tongue, and perceptions about the
difficulties of being foreign. Without them, the back-and-forth life
my family leads, both literally and figuratively, will at last approach stillness. An anchor will drop, and a line of connection will
be severed.

I have always believed that I lack the authority my parents   7
bring to being Indian. But as long as they live they protect me from
feeling like an impostor. Their passing will mark not only the loss of
the people who created me but the loss of a singular way of life, a
singular struggle. The immigrant's journey, no matter how ultimately rewarding, is founded on departure and deprivation, but it
secures for the subsequent generation a sense of arrival and advantage. I can see a day coming when my American side, lacking the
counterpoint India has until now maintained, begins to gain ascendancy and weight. It is in fiction that I will continue to interpret the
term "Indian-American," calculating that shifting equation, whatever answers it may yield.

MEANINGS AND VALUES

1. The writer defines herself as "Indian-American," but she states that her
    relationship to the term has changed as she has gotten older (Par. 1).
    How so?

2. What is the significance of the phrase "approved of on either side of
    the hyphen" (Par. 1)?

EXPOSITORY TECHNIQUES

1. Is this reading selection an informative definition essay or a redefini-
    tion essay? Explain your answer.

2. What is the writer's purpose in writing an extended definition of
    herself in relation to the term Indian-American? Is she successful?
    How so?

DICTION AND VOCABULARY

1. Identify the simile Lahiri uses in Paragraph 5, and the metaphor she uses in Par. 6 (see Guide: *Figurative Language*). What larger meanings do they convey?

2. If you do not know the meaning of some of the following words, consult a dictionary: *shuttling* (Par. 1); *dal* (2); *cusp* (4); *steadfast* (6); *counterpoint, ascendancy* (7).

READ TO WRITE

1. **Collaborating:** Working in a group, create a list of terms that individual group members use to describe themselves, for example: brainiac, geek, Chinese American, athlete, conservative, underachiever, troublemaker, sports fan. Survey group members about how they interpret this self-definition, using Lahiri's discussion of her own self-definition as a model. Write a brief report as a group summarizing the results of your survey.

2. **Considering Audience:** Do you think that the author wrote this essay primarily to Indian American readers? Do you think that other readers who do not define themselves as Indian Americans would relate well to the essay? Explain your answers.

3. **Developing an Essay:** How do you define yourself? Use a term to define some aspect of your personality, either a common one like those in question 1, or create a new term to define yourself. Using Lahiri's essay as a model, develop an extended definition of this side of you. Be sure to communicate to the reader why he or she should be interested in your self-definition.

(NOTE: Suggestions for topics requiring development by DEFINITION are on pp. 326–327 at the end of this chapter.)

ANNE FADIMAN

ANNE FADIMAN was born in New York City in 1953 and attended Harvard University, where she served as the undergraduate columnist for *Harvard Magazine*. She later wrote for both *Life* and *Civilizations*, and she has received two National Magazine Awards for Reporting and Essays. She also received the National Book Critics Circle Award for her 1997 book, *The Spirit Catches You and You Fall Down*. Her other works include two collections of essays entitled *Ex-Libris: Confessions of a Common Reader* (1998) and *At Large and At Small: Familiar Essays* (2007). Fadiman currently serves as the Francis Chair in nonfiction writing at Yale University.

Coffee

Caffeine is perceived by many as a necessary crutch that is used to get us through early mornings, interminable hours at the office, and many of the other stressful situations that arise on a daily basis. In this essay, Anne Fadiman traces the transformation of coffee from the stigmatized ambrosia of the overworked to a kind of miracle drug that raised English society out of its drunken haze, inspired the feverishly brilliant writings of Balzac, fostered a public discourse that led to some of the great intellectual advances of the seventeenth and eighteenth centuries, and personally enabled her to survive one of the greatest emotional challenges of her life.

When I was a sophomore in college, I drank coffee nearly every 1 evening with my friends Peter and Alex. Even though the coffee was canned; even though the milk was stolen from the dining hall and refrigerated on the windowsill of my friends' dormitory room, where it was diluted by snow and adulterated by soot; even though Alex's scuzzy one-burner hot plate looked as if it might electrocute us at any moment; and even though we washed our *batterie de cuisine* in the bathroom sink and let it air-dry on a pile of paper towels next to the toilet—even though Dunster F-13 was, in short, not exactly Escoffier's kitchen, we considered our nightly coffee ritual the very acme and pitch of elegance. And I think that in many ways we were right.

Alex came from Cambridge, but Peter was alluringly interna- 2 tional. He had a Serbian father, an American mother, and a French coffeemaker. At my home in Los Angeles, the coffee-making process had taken about three seconds: you plunked a spoonful of Taster's Choice freeze-dried crystals in a cup, added hot water, and stirred.

With Peter's *cafetière à piston*, you could easily squander a couple of hours on the business of assembling, heating, brewing, pouring, drinking, disassembling, and cleaning (not to mention talking), all the while telling yourself that you weren't really procrastinating, because as soon as you were fully caffeinated you would be able to study like a fiend. The *cafetière* had seven parts: a cylindrical glass beaker; a four-footed metal frame; a chrome lid impaled through its center by a plunger rod topped with a spherical black knob; and three metal filtration discs that screwed onto the tip of the plunger in a sequence for whose mastery our high SAT scores had somehow failed to equip us. After all the pieces were in place, you dolloped some ground coffee into the beaker, poured in boiling water, and waited precisely four minutes. (In the title sequence of *The Ipcress File*, special agent Harry Palmer unaccountably fails to carry out this crucial step. As an eagle-eyed critic for *The Guardian* once observed, Palmer grinds his beans and pops them into his *cafetière*, but *fails to let the grounds steep before he depresses the plunger.* How could any self-respecting spy face his daily docket of murder and mayhem fueled by such an anemic brew?) Only then did you apply the heel of your hand to the plunger knob and ram the grounds to the bottom of the beaker, though the potable portion always retained a subtle trace of Turkish sludge. What a satisfying operation! The plunger fit *exactly* into its glass tunnel, presenting a sensuous resistance when you urged it downward; if you pressed too fast, hot water and grounds would gush out the top. The whole process involved a good deal of screwing and unscrewing and trying not to make too much of a mess. Truth to tell, it was a lot like sex (another mystery into which I was initiated that year, though not by Peter or Alex), and as soon as you'd done it once, you wanted to do it again and again and again.

Disdaining the dining hall's white polystyrene cups, most of which had gone a little gray around the rim, each of us had procured our own china mug. Mine had a picture of a polka-dotted pig on it, an allusion to the frequency with which it was refilled. I stirred its contents with a silver demitasse spoon whose bowl was engraved with the name of my hometown. "Firenze" or "Cap d'Antibes" would have been preferable to "Los Angeles," but I did like the feel of the calligraphy against my tongue. Although the whole point of coffee-drinking was to be grown up—no Pepsi-Cola for bohemian intellectuals like *us!*—the amount of milk and sugar with which we undermined our sophisticated brew suggested that we needed to regress as much as we yearned to evolve. The end product resembled melted coffee ice cream.

3

It was the last time in my life that coffee slowed the hours rather 4
than speeding them up. Those long, lazy nights—snow falling outside on Cowperthwaite Street, the three of us huddled inside in a
warm, bright room, talking of literature and politics until the rest of
Dunster House was asleep—were an essential part of my college
curriculum. After all, wasn't education a matter of infusing one's
life with flavorful essences, pressing out the impurities, and leaving
only a little sludge at the bottom?

It is said that around the seventh century, somewhere near the 5
Red Sea—whether it was Ethiopia or Yemen is a subject of debate—
a herd of goats ate the magenta berries of a local shrub and began to
act strangely. In a classic 1935 study called *Coffee: The Epic of a Com-
modity*, the German journalist Heinrich Eduard Jacob described their
behavior thus:

> All night, for five nights in succession—nay, for seven or eight—they
> clambered over rocks, cutting capers, chasing one another, bleating
> fantastically. They turned their bearded heads hither and thither; with
> reddened eyes they gambolled convulsively when they caught sight of
> the goatherds, and then they darted off swift as arrows speeding from
> the bow.

Having observed the frisky goats, the imam of a nearby 6
monastery—a sort of medieval Carlos Castaneda—roasted the
berries in a chafing dish, crushed them in a mortar, mixed them
with boiling water, and drank the brew. When he lay down, he
couldn't sleep. His heartbeat quickened, his limbs felt light, his
mood became cheerful and alert. "He was not merely thinking,"
wrote Jacob. "His thoughts had become concretely visible. He
watched them from the right side and from the left, from above
and from below. They raced like a team of horses." The imam
found that he could juggle a dozen ideas in the time it normally
took to consider a single one. His visual acuity increased; in the
glow of his oil lamp, the parchment on his table looked unusually lustrous and the robe that hung on a nearby peg seemed to
swell with life. He felt strengthened, as Jacob put it, "by heavenly
food brought to him by the angels of Paradise."

Whoa! Little did the hopped-up imam know that while he and 7
the goats were happily tripping, 1,3,7-trimethylxanthine (otherwise
known as caffeine) was coursing through their veins, stimulating
brain activity by blocking the uptake of adenosine, a neurotransmit-
ter that, if left to its own devices, makes people (and goats) sleepy and
depressed. Just enough of the stuff and you feel you've been fed by
the angels of Paradise; too much, and Mr. Coffee Nerves (a diabolical

cartoon character with a twirly mustache who graced Postum ads in the 1930s) gets you in his grip.

Caffeine was first isolated in 1819, when the elderly Johann   8
Wolfgang von Goethe, who had swallowed oceans of coffee in his younger days and regretted his intemperance, handed a box of Arabian mocha coffee beans to a chemist named Friedlieb Ferdinand Runge and enjoined him to analyze their contents. Runge extracted an alkaloid that, as Jacob put it, "presents itself in the form of shining, white, needle-shaped crystals, reminding us of swansdown and still more of snow." Caffeine is so toxic that laboratory technicians who handle it in its purified state wear masks and gloves. In *The World of Caffeine,* by Bennett Alan Weinberg and Bonnie K. Bealer, there is a photograph of the label from a jar of pharmaceutical-grade crystals. It reads in part:

> Warning! May be harmful if inhaled or swallowed. Has caused mutagenic and reproductive effects laboratory animals. Inhalation causes rapid heart rate, excitement, dizziness, pain, collapse, hypotension, fever, shortness of breath. May cause headache, insomnia, nausea, vomiting, stomach pain, collapse and convulsions.

Anyone who doubts that caffeine is a drug should read some of   9
the prose composed under its influence. Many of the books on coffee that currently crowd my desk share a certain . . . *velocity,* as if their authors, all terrifically buzzed at 3:00 A.M., couldn't get their words out fast enough and had to resort to italics, hyperbole, and sentences so long that by the time you get to the end you can't remember the beginning. (But that's only if you're uncaffeinated when you read them; if you've knocked back a couple of *cafés noirs* yourself, keeping pace is no sweat.) Heinrich Eduard Jacob boasts that his narrative was "given soul by a coffee-driven euphoria." Gregory Dicum and Nina Luttinger claim that while they were writing *The Coffee Book: Anatomy of an Industry from Crop to the Last Drop,* they

> sucked down 83 double Americanos, 12 double espressos, 4 perfect ristrettos, 812 regular cups (from 241 French press-loads, plus 87 cups of drip coffee), 47 Turkish coffees, a half-dozen regrettable cups of flavored coffee, 10 pounds of organic coffee, 7 pounds of fair trade coffee, a quarter pound of chicory and a handful of hemp seeds as occasional adjuncts, 1 can of ground supermarket coffee (drunk mostly iced), 6 canned or bottled coffee drinks, 2 pints of coffee beer, a handful of mochas, 1 pint of coffee concentrate, a couple of cappuccinos, 1 espresso soda, and, just to see, a lone double tall low-fat soy orange decaf latte.

Their book contains only 196 pages and doesn't look as if it took   10
very long to write; that decaf latte aside, the authors' caffeine quota

per day must have been prodigious. (But note their exactitude: coffee makes you peppy, but it doesn't make you sloppy.)

The contemporary master of the genre is Stewart Lee Allen,   11
known as "the Hunter S. Thompson of coffee journalism," whose gonzo masterwork, *The Devil's Cup*, entailed the consumption of "2,920 liters of percolated, drip, espresso, latte, cappuccino, macchiato, con panna, instant and americana." (It isn't very long, either. By the time Allen finished, his blood must have been largely composed of 1,3,7-trimethylxanthine.) Following the historical routes by which coffee spread around the globe, Allen gets wired in Harrar, Sana, Istanbul, Vienna, Munich, Paris, Rio de Janeiro, and various points across the United States, attempting to finance his travels and his coffee habit with complicated transactions involving forged passports and smuggled art. He ends up on Route 66, in search of the worst cup of coffee in America, in a Honda Accord driveaway filled with every form of caffeine he can think of: Stimu-Chew, Water Joe, Krank, hi-caf candy, and a vial of caffeine crystals (scored from an Internet site that features images of twitching eyeballs) whose resemblance to cocaine occasions some exciting psychopharmacological plot twists when a state trooper pulls him over in Athens, Tennessee.

But in the realm of twitching eyeballs, even Stewart Lee Allen   12
can't hold a candle to Honoré de Balzac, the model for every espresso-swilling writer who has followed in his jittery footsteps. What hashish was to Baudelaire, opium to Coleridge, cocaine to Robert Louis Stevenson, nitrous oxide to Robert Southey, mescaline to Aldous Huxley, and Benzedrine to Jack Kerouac, caffeine was to Balzac. The habit started early. Like a preppie with an expensive connection, he ran up alarming debts with a concierge who, for a price, was willing to sneak contraband coffee beans into Balzac's boarding school. As an adult, grinding out novels eighteen hours a day while listening for the rap of creditors at the door, Balzac observed the addict's classic regimen, boosting his doses as his tolerance mounted. First he drank one cup a day, then a few cups, then many cups, then forty cups. Finally, by using less and less water, he increased the concentration of each fix until he was eating dry coffee grounds: "a horrible, rather brutal method," he wrote, "that I recommend only to men of excessive vigor, men with thick black hair and skin covered with liver spots, men with big square hands and legs shaped like bowling pins." Although the recipe was hell on the stomach, it dispatched caffeine to the brain with exquisite efficiency.

From that moment on, everything becomes agitated. Ideas quick-
march into motion like battalions of a grand army to its legendary
fighting ground, and the battle rages. Memories charge in, bright flags
on high; the cavalry of metaphor deploys with a magnificent gallop;
the artillery of logic rushes up with clattering wagons and cartridges;
on imagination's orders, sharpshooters sight and fire; forms and
shapes and characters rear up; the paper is spread with ink.

Could that passage have been written on decaf? 13

Balzac's coffeepot is displayed at 47 rue Raynouard in Paris, 14
where he lived for much of his miserable last decade, writing *La
Cousine Bette* and *Le Cousin Pons*, losing his health, and escaping bill
collectors through a secret door. My friend Adam (who likes his
espresso strong but with sugar) visited the house a few years ago.
"The coffeepot is red and white china," he wrote me, "and bears Balzac's monogram. It's an elegant, neat little thing, almost nautical in
appearance. I can imagine it reigning serenely over the otherwise-
general squalor of his later life, a small pharos of caffeine amid the
gloom."

When I was fifteen, I went to Paris myself. I didn't realize it at 15
the time, but that summer I stood at a fateful crossroads. One way
led to coffee, the other to liquor.

I was a student on a high school French program in an era when 16
the construction of *in loco parentis* was considerably looser than it is
now. I began each day with a *café au lait* at a local patisserie and
ended it with a *crème de menthe frappé* at a bar. One afternoon, after
we had left Paris and were traveling through southern France, the
director of the program invited me to lunch at a three-star restaurant in Vienne, where we shared *pâté de foie gras en brioche, mousse de
truite Périgueux, turbot á la crème aux herbes, pintadeau aux herbes, gra-
tin dauphinois, fromages, gâteau aux marrons, petits fours*, and a Brut
Crémant '62. I'd never drunk half a bottle of wine before. Afterward,
en route to Avignon in Monsieur Cosnard's Mercedes, I was asked
to help navigate, a task that appeared inexplicably difficult until I
realized I was holding the map upside down.

The conclusion was clear: *Why would anyone want to feel like this?* 17
Although I never became a teetotaler, I knew—especially when I
woke up the next morning with a hangover—that I would cast my
lot with caffeine, not with alcohol. Why would I wish my senses to
be dulled when they could be sharpened? Why would I wish to forget when I could remember? Why would I wish to mumble when I
could scintillate? Of course, since even in those days I was a loqua-
cious workaholic who liked to stay up late, you might think I'd pick

a drug that would nudge me closer to the center of the bell curve instead of pushing me farther out on the edge—but of course I didn't. Who does? Don't we all just keep doing the things that make us even more like ourselves?

As I lay in bed with a godawful headache, sunlight streamed   18
through the open window, and so did the smell of good French coffee from the hotel kitchen downstairs.

Heinrich Eduard Jacob called coffee the "anti-Bacchus." By the   19
middle of the seventeenth century, when it had filtered westward from the Middle East and begun to captivate Europe, its potential consumers were in dire need of sobering up. "The eyes, the blood-vessels, the senses of the men of those days were soused in beer," observed Jacob. "It choked their livers, their voices, and their hearts." The average Englishman drank three liters of beer a day—nearly two six-packs—and spent a lot of time bumping into lamp-posts and falling into gutters. Coffee was hailed as a salubrious alternative. As an anonymous poet put it in 1674, "When foggy Ale, leavying up mighty trains/Of muddy vapours, had besieg'd our Brains,/Then Heaven in Pity . . ./First sent amongst us this All-healing Berry."

Between 1645 and 1750, as coffeehouses sprang up in Paris,   20
Vienna, Leipzig, Amsterdam, Rome, and Venice, the All-healing Berry defogged innumerable Continental brains. But until tea gained the upper hand around 1730, the English were the undisputed kings of coffee. By the most conservative estimates, London had five hundred coffeehouses at the turn of the eighteenth century. (If New York City were similarly equipped today, it would have nearly eight thousand.) These weren't merely places to drink the muddy liquid that one critic likened to "syrup of soot or essence of old shoes." In the days when public libraries were nonexistent and journalism was in its embryonic stages, they were a vital center of news, gossip, and education—"penny universities" whose main business, in the words of a 1657 newspaper ad, was "PUBLICK INTERCOURSE."

London had a coffeehouse for everyone (as long as you were   21
male). If you were a gambler, you went to White's. If you were a physician, you went to Garraway's or Child's. If you were a businessman, you went to Lloyd's, which later evolved into the great insurance house. If you were a scientist, you went to the Grecian, where Isaac Newton, Edmund Halley, and Hans Sloane once staged a public dissection of a dolphin that had been caught in the Thames. If you were a journalist, you went to Button's, where Joseph Addison had set up a "Reader's Letter-box" shaped like a lion's head; you

could post submissions to *The Guardian* in its mouth. And if you were a man of letters, you—along with Pope, Pepys, and Dryden—went to Will's, where you could join a debate on whether Milton should have written *Paradise Lost* in rhymed couplets instead of blank verse. These coffeehouses changed the course of English social history by demonstrating how pleasant it was to hang out in a place where (according to a 1674 set of Rules and Orders of the Coffee House) "Gentry, Tradesmen, all are welcome hither, / and may without affront sit down together." And they changed the course of English literature by turning monologuists into conversationalists. A 1705 watercolor that now hangs in the British Museum depicts a typical establishment, a high-ceilinged room dominated by a huge black coffee cauldron that simmers over a blazing fire. The periwigged patrons are sipping coffee, smoking pipes, reading news-sheets, and scribbling in notebooks, but most of all—you can tell from their gesticulations—they are talking.

Looking back, I see that my evenings in Dunster House were a   22
penny university in miniature. It therefore saddens me to report that these days my coffee-drinking is usually a solitary affair, a Balzacian response to deadlines (though in smaller doses) rather than an opportunity for PUBLICK INTERCOURSE. Time is scarcer than it used to be; I make my coffee with a disposable paper filter stuffed into a little plastic cone, not in a *cafetière a piston*. My customary intake is only a cup or two a day—still with milk and sugar—though I ratchet up my consumption when I'm writing. In the spirit of participatory journalism, every word of this essay has been written under the influence of 1,3,7-trimethylxanthine, in quantities sufficient to justify the use, after a respite of thirty years, of the mug with the polka-dotted pig.

My coffee is in every way a weaker brew than it once was, but   23
I could never give it up entirely. This is not just a matter of habit, sentiment, or taste; it is more akin to the reasons that, long ago, the Galla people of Ethiopia ate ground coffee mixed with animal fat before they went off to fight, or that the night before every battle of the Civil War, you would have seen hundreds of campfires flickering in the darkness, each surmounted by a pot of thick, black, courage-inducing coffee.

I remember a morning five years ago when I took a dawn flight to   24
Fort Myers, Florida. My father had just been hospitalized with what looked like—and in fact turned out to be—terminal cancer, and the task of dealing with doctors, nurses, and hospice workers had fallen to me. I'd been up all night, and I stumbled off the plane so bleary I could

hardly walk. There, shimmering like a mirage at the end of the jetway, in the midst of what on my last visit had been a wasteland of Pizza Huts and Burger Kings, stood a newly opened Starbucks.

I know, I know. Heartless corporate giant. Monster of coast-to-coast uniformity. Killer of mom-and-pop cafés. But that's not what I thought at that moment. I thought: I'm going to order a grande latte with whole milk. I'm going to pour in two packets of Sugar in the Raw, and stir really well so there are no undissolved crystals at the bottom. I'm going to sit down and drink it slowly. Then I'm going to drive to the hospital.   25

As I walked toward the counter, I said to myself: *I can do this.*   26

Meanings and Values

1. Paragraphs 1–4 focus on the writer's college experiences. What other sections does the essay have, and what subject areas do they cover as a way of defining *coffee*, its meanings, and its roles for people?

2. Why are Paragraphs 1–4 filled with sophisticated, unfamiliar terms along with extensive attention to trivial details?

3. What does the history of coffee and its uses in Paragraphs 5–14 add to the definition of coffee?

Expository Techniques

1. The writer opens each of these sections with references to time: 15–18, 19–21, and 22–26. What are these references? How do they serve to tie the parts of the essay together? What other sections open in similar ways? (See "Guide to Terms": *Transition.*)

2. Which definition strategies does the writer use in this essay, and where? (See "Developing Definitions," pp. 284–286.)

3. At times in the essay, the writer indicates more or less directly the effects of coffee and its meaning for coffee drinkers. Identify these statements.

4. Does the essay seem to indicate that it is possible to provide a concise definition of coffee? If so, state it in your own words. If not, explain where in the essay the writer comes closest to defining the meaning of coffee.

DICTION AND VOCABULARY

1. In the last sentence of Paragraph 4, Fadiman offers an extended comparison (an analogy). State it in your own words, and explain why you find it accurate and effective, or not. (See the introduction to Chapter 6 for a discussion of Analogy; see also Guide: *Analogy*.)

2. a. The opening four paragraphs of the essay contain many allusions. Identify as many as you can. (Guide: *Figures of Speech*.)

   b. Do you think readers are expected to understand these allusions? If not, why did the writer put them in the text?

3. This essay contains words likely to be unfamiliar to many readers. Some are used to indicate the writer's state of mind at the time of events. Others add an exotic or faraway feel to the essay. If you do not know the meaning of them, look them up in a dictionary.

READ TO WRITE

1. **Collaborating:** Coffee isn't the only substance or activity that people make an important part of their lives. Working in a group, brainstorm other such substances or activities as possible topics for papers, and choose one to list details that might be used in an essay that provides a definition of the topic.

2. **Considering Audience:** Are Anne Fadiman's college experiences or her love of coffee typical of college students today? In a paragraph or two, indicate how you would revise the essay so that it more clearly reflects the interests, attitudes, and values of the majority of contemporary college students.

3. **Developing an Essay:** Using Fadiman's approach, define something you love by its good effects in various times and places so that others can understand why you consider it so important.

(NOTE: Suggestions for essays requiring development by DEFINITION are on pp. 326–327 at the end of this chapter.)

Issues and Ideas

Clarifying Values and Roles

- Stephen L. Carter, *The Insufficiency of Honesty*
- Mary Pipher, *Beliefs About Families*

STEPHEN L. CARTER

STEPHEN L. CARTER is professor of law at Yale Law School and the author of several controversial but highly respected and tightly reasoned books that explore issues in contemporary ethics, politics, and social relationships. After graduating from Yale Law School, he had a variety of professional experiences, including clerking for U.S. Supreme Court Justice Thurgood Marshall and working in a prestigious law firm. Carter's books are *Reflections of an Affirmative Action Baby* (1992), *The Culture of Disbelief: How American Law and Politics Trivialize Religious Devotion* (1994), *The Confirmation Mess: Cleaning Up the Federal Appointments Mess* (1995), *Integrity* (1997), and *Civility* (1999) (nonfiction); and *The Emperor of Ocean Park* (2002) (a novel). His most recent works are *Jericho's Fall* (2009) and *The Violence of Peace: America's Wars in the Age of Obama* (2011).

The Insufficiency of Honesty

Integrity is not simply a term or idea. It refers to a way of acting and of discerning the qualities of our actions. Integrity may be something we all claim to admire and wish to have ourselves, but as Stephen L. Carter points out in this essay first published in the *Atlantic Monthly*, it can be very difficult to achieve.

A couple of years ago I began a university commencement address by telling the audience that I was going to talk about integrity. The crowd broke into applause. Applause! Just because they had heard the word "integrity": that's how starved for it they were. They had no idea how I was using the word, or what I was going to say about integrity, or, indeed, whether I was for it or against it. But they knew they liked the idea of talking about it.

Very well, let us consider this word "integrity." Integrity is like   2
the weather: everybody talks about it but nobody knows what to do
about it. Integrity is that stuff that we always want more of. Some
say that we need to return to the good old days when we had a lot
more of it. Others say that we as a nation have never really had
enough of it. Hardly anybody stops to explain exactly what we
mean by it, or how we know it is a good thing, or why everybody
needs to have the same amount of it. Indeed, the only trouble with
integrity is that everybody who uses the word seems to mean something slightly different.

For instance, when I refer to integrity, do I mean simply "hon-   3
esty"? The answer is no; although honesty is a virtue of importance,
it is a different virtue from integrity. Let us, for simplicity, think of
honesty as not lying; and let us further accept Sissela Bok's definition of a lie: "any intentionally deceptive message which is *stated*."
Plainly, one cannot have integrity without being honest (although,
as we shall see, the matter gets complicated), but one can certainly
be honest and yet have little integrity.

When I refer to integrity, I have something very specific in   4
mind. Integrity, as I will use the term, requires three steps: discerning what is right and what is wrong; acting on what you have dis-
cerned, even at personal cost; and saying openly that you are acting
on your understanding of right and wrong. The first criterion captures the idea that integrity requires a degree of moral reflective-
ness. The second brings in the ideal of a person of integrity as
steadfast, a quality that includes keeping one's commitments. The
third reminds us that a person of integrity can be trusted.

The first point to understand about the difference between hon-   5
esty and integrity is that a person may be entirely honest without
ever engaging in the hard work of discernment that integrity requires: she may tell us quite truthfully what she believes without
ever taking the time to figure out whether what she believes is good
and right and true. The problem may be as simple as someone's
foolishly saying something that hurts a friend's feelings; a few moments of thought would have revealed the likelihood of the hurt
and the lack of necessity for the comment. Or the problem may be
more complex, as when a man who was raised from birth in a society that preaches racism states his belief in one race's inferiority as a
fact, without ever really considering that perhaps this deeply held
view is wrong. Certainly the racist is being honest—he is telling us
what he actually thinks—but his honesty does not add up to
integrity.

Telling Everything You Know

A wonderful epigram sometimes attributed to the filmmaker Sam   6
Goldwyn goes like this: "The most important thing in acting is honesty; once you learn to fake that, you're in." The point is that honesty
can be something one *seems* to have. Without integrity, what passes
for honesty often is nothing of the kind; it is fake honesty—or it is
honest but irrelevant and perhaps even immoral.

Consider an example. A man who has been married for fifty   7
years confesses to his wife on his deathbed that he was unfaithful
thirty-five years earlier. The dishonesty was killing his spirit, he
says. Now he has cleared his conscience and is able to die in peace.

The husband has been honest—sort of. He has certainly unbur-   8
dened himself. And he has probably made his wife (soon to be his
widow) quite miserable in the process, because even if she forgives
him, she will not be able to remember him with quite the vivid image of love and loyalty that she had hoped for. Arranging his own
emotional affairs to ease his transition to death, he has shifted to his
wife the burden of confusion and pain, perhaps for the rest of her
life. Moreover, he has attempted his honesty at the one time in his life
when it carries no risk; acting in accordance with what you think is
right and risking no loss in the process is a rather thin and unadmi-
rable form of honesty.

Besides, even though the husband has been honest in a sense,   9
he has now twice been unfaithful to his wife: once thirty-five years
ago, when he had his affair, and again when, nearing death, he decided that his own peace of mind was more important than hers. In
trying to be honest he has violated his marriage vow by acting toward his wife not with love but with naked and perhaps even cruel
self-interest.

As my mother used to say, you don't have to tell people every-   10
thing you know. Lying and nondisclosure, as the law often recognizes, are not the same thing. Sometimes it is actually illegal to tell
what you know, as, for example, in the disclosure of certain financial information by market insiders. Or it may be unethical, as when
a lawyer reveals a confidence entrusted to her by a client. It may be
simple bad manners, as in the case of a gratuitous comment to a colleague on his or her attire. And it may be subject to religious punishment, as when a Roman Catholic priest breaks the seal of the
confessional—an offense that carries automatic excommunication.

In all the cases just mentioned, the problem with telling every-   11
thing you know is that somebody else is harmed. Harm may not be

the intention, but it is certainly the effect. Honesty is most laudable when we risk harm to ourselves; it becomes a good deal less so if we instead risk harm to others when there is no gain to anyone other than ourselves. Integrity may counsel keeping our secrets in order to spare the feelings of others. Sometimes, as in the example of the wayward husband, the reason we want to tell what we know is precisely to shift our pain onto somebody else—a course of action dictated less by integrity than by self-interest. Fortunately, integrity and self-interest often coincide, as when a politician of integrity is rewarded with our votes. But often they do not, and it is at those moments that our integrity is truly tested.

Error

Another reason that honesty alone is no substitute for integrity is   12
that if forthrightness is not preceded by discernment, it may result in the expression of an incorrect moral judgment. In other words, I may be honest about what I believe, but if I have never tested my beliefs, I may be wrong. And here I mean "wrong" in a particular sense: the proposition in question is wrong if I would change my mind about it after hard moral reflection.

Consider this example. Having been taught all his life that   13
women are not as smart as men, a manager gives the women on his staff less-challenging assignments than he gives the men. He does this, he believes, for their own benefit: he does not want them to fail, and he believes that they will if he gives them tougher assignments. Moreover, when one of the women on his staff does poor work, he does not berate her as harshly as he would a man, because he expects nothing more. And he claims to be acting with integrity because he is acting according to his own deepest beliefs.

The manager fails the most basic test of integrity. The question   14
is not whether his actions are consistent with what he most deeply believes but whether he has done the hard work of discerning whether what he most deeply believes is right. The manager has not taken this harder step.

Moreover, even within the universe that the manager has con-   15
structed for himself, he is not acting with integrity. Although he is obviously wrong to think that the women on his staff are not as good as the men, even were he right, that would not justify applying different standards to their work. By so doing he betrays both his obligation to the institution that employs him and his duty as a manager to evaluate his employees.

The problem that the manager faces is an enormous one in our   16
practical politics, where having the dialogue that makes democracy
work can seem impossible because of our tendency to cling to our
views even when we have not examined them. As Jean Bethke
Elshtain has said, borrowing from John Courtney Murray, our politics are so fractured and contentious that we often cannot even reach
disagreement. Our refusal to look closely at our own most cherished
principles is surely a large part of the reason. Socrates thought the
unexamined life not worth living. But the unhappy truth is that few
of us actually have the time for constant reflection on our views—on
public or private morality. Examine them we must, however, or we
will never know whether we might be wrong.

None of this should be taken to mean that integrity as I have de-   17
scribed it presupposes a single correct truth. If, for example, your
integrity-guided search tells you that affirmative action is wrong, and
my integrity-guided search tells me that affirmative action is right, we
need not conclude that one of us lacks integrity. As it happens, I believe—both as a Christian and as a secular citizen who struggles toward moral understanding—that we *can* find true and sound answers
to our moral questions. But I do not pretend to have found very many
of them, nor is an exposition of them my purpose here.

It is the case not that there aren't any right answers but that,   18
given human fallibility, we need to be careful in assuming that we
have found them. However, today's political talk about how it is
wrong for the government to impose one person's morality on
somebody else is just mindless chatter. *Every* law imposes one person's morality on somebody else, because law has only two functions: to tell people to do what they would rather not or to forbid
them to do what they would.

And if the surveys can be believed, there is far more moral agree-   19
ment in America than we sometimes allow ourselves to think. One of
the reasons that character education for young people makes so much
sense to so many people is precisely that there seems to be a core set
of moral understandings—we might call them the American Core—
that most of us accept. Some of the virtues in this American Core
are, one hopes, relatively noncontroversial. About 500 American communities have signed on to Michael Josephson's program to emphasize the "six pillars" of good character: trustworthiness, respect,
responsibility, caring, fairness, and citizenship. These virtues might
lead to a similarly noncontroversial set of political values: having an
honest regard for ourselves and others, protecting freedom of thought
and religious belief, and refusing to steal or murder.

Honesty and Competing Responsibilities

A further problem with too great an exaltation of honesty is that it   20
may allow us to escape responsibilities that morality bids us bear. If
honesty is substituted for integrity, one might think that if I say I am
not planning to fulfill a duty, I need not fulfill it. But it would be a
peculiar morality indeed that granted us the right to avoid our
moral responsibilities simply by stating our intention to ignore
them. Integrity does not permit such an easy escape.

Consider an example. Before engaging in sex with a woman, her   21
lover tells her that if she gets pregnant, it is her problem, not his. She
says that she understands. In due course she does wind up pregnant.
If we believe, as I hope we do, that the man would ordinarily have a
moral responsibility toward both the child he will have helped to
bring into the world and the child's mother, then his honest statement of what he intends does not spare him that responsibility.

This vision of responsibility assumes that not all moral obliga-   22
tions stem from consent or from a stated intention. The linking of
obligations to promises is a rather modern and perhaps uniquely
Western way of looking at life, and perhaps a luxury that only the
well-to-do can afford. As Fred and Shulamit Korn (a philosopher and
an anthropologist) have pointed out, "If one looks at ethnographic
accounts of other societies, one finds that, while obligations everywhere play a crucial role in social life, promising is not preeminent
among the sources of obligation and is not even mentioned by most
anthropologists." The Korns have made a study of Tonga, where
promises are virtually unknown but the social order is remarkably
stable. If life without any promises seems extreme, we Americans
sometimes go too far the other way, parsing not only our contracts
but even our marriage vows in order to discover the absolute mini-
mum obligation that we have to others as a result of our promises.

That some societies in the world have worked out evidently   23
functional structures of obligation without the need for promise or
consent does not tell us what *we* should do. But it serves as a reminder of the basic proposition that our existence in civil society creates a set of mutual responsibilities that philosophers used to capture
in the fiction of the social contract. Nowadays, here in America, people seem to spend their time thinking of even cleverer ways to avoid
their obligations, instead of doing what integrity commands and ful-
filling them. And all too often honesty is their excuse.

———————————————

MEANINGS AND VALUES

1. Most readers are likely to consider honesty a good trait. Why, there-fore, do you think Carter created a definition that points out its shortcomings? What do you think was his overall purpose in writing the essay? Do you believe the essay has more than one purpose? If so, what are they? (See "Guide to Terms": *Purpose.*)

2. List the reasons the author gives for considering honesty insufficient. State in your own words why the author believes that the men in Paragraphs 7–9 and 21 have honesty but lack integrity.

3. Does this essay have a thesis statement? If so, where is it? Does it ade-quately sum up the main idea of the entire essay? Why, or why not? If the essay does not have a thesis statement, is it nonetheless organized around a main idea or theme? What is it? (Guide: *Thesis.*) Explain why you consider the essay unified or not unified. (Guide: *Unity.*)

EXPOSITORY TECHNIQUES

1. If one of the main purposes of this essay is to define *integrity*, why does the writer spend so much time discussing the meaning of *hon-esty?* In formulating your answer, take into account various defini-tion strategies and the likely responses of readers to concepts like honesty.

2. What is the main definition strategy Carter employs in this essay? How is the organization of the essay related to this strategy? Be spe-cific in answering this question. What other definition patterns does the writer employ, and where in the essay does he use them?

3. Which paragraphs in the essay are devoted wholly, or mostly, to qualification? (Guide: *Qualification.*) What role(s) do they play in helping develop the definitions? Why would the essay be weaker without them?

4. Where in the essay does the writer use transitions at the beginnings of paragraphs to highlight the essay's organization and indicate the definition strategy he is employing? (Guide: *Transition.*)

DICTION AND VOCABULARY

1. Throughout the essay, Carter uses contrasting words and concepts to explain the difference between honesty and integrity. Sometimes the contrasts involve the denotation of words and sometimes the conno-tations. (Guide: *Connotation/Denotation.*) Discuss the contrasts as they appear in Paragraphs 6, 8, and 9, and explain the use Carter makes of them. (Guide: *Diction.*) Explain the extent to which Carter reinforces the contrasts through sentence structure. (Guide: *Syntax.*)

2. In the course of the essay, Carter repeats a small number of words quite frequently, often varying their form. What are the words? How

are they related to the essay's thesis (or theme)? How do they contribute to the essay's coherence? (Guide: *Coherence*.)

3.   If you do not know the meanings of some of the following terms, look them up in a dictionary: *discerning, criterion, steadfast* (Par. 4); *epigram* (6); *gratuitous, excommunication* (10); *laudable, counsel* (11); *forthrightness* (12); *contentious* (16); *presupposes* (17); *fallibility, impose* (18); *parsing* (22).

READ AND WRITE

1.   **Collaborating:** Working in a group, create a list of terms naming qualities that most people would agree are virtues (like *honesty* and *integrity*). Choose two and write three brief examples for each word that help define it. Choose examples that indicate what the term means and also some that indicate what it does not or should not mean. Include examples focusing on women as well as men.

2.   **Considering Audience:** Rewrite Carter's essay by substituting examples from women's experiences, or use the essay as a model for a discussion of moral concepts as they apply to both men and women.

3.   **Developing an Essay:** Carter's title, "The Insufficiency of Honesty," suggests both a focus for the essay and an interesting approach to explaining why a particular quality is inadequate. Borrow this approach for an essay. Explain why your subject is inadequate, insufficient, or incomplete.

(NOTE: Suggestions for topics requiring development by DEFINITION are on pp. 326–327 at the end of this chapter.)

MARY PIPHER

Clinical psychologist and author MARY PIPHER is best known for her influential bestseller, *Reviving Ophelia* (1994), a study of the spike in suicides, eating disorders, and other psychological disturbances in young girls. She earned a B.A. in anthropology from the University of California, Berkeley, in 1969 and a Ph.D. in clinical psychology from the University of Nebraska–Lincoln in 1977. Her most recent work is the memoir *Seeking Peace* (2009).

Beliefs About Families

What is a family? In this selection from her book *The Shelter of Each Other* (1996), Pipher spotlights nontraditional families and considers whether or not they support the needs of today's individual.

When I speak of families, I usually mean biological families. There is a power in blood ties that cannot be denied. But in our fragmented, chaotic culture, many people don't have biological families nearby. For many people, friends become family. Family is a collection of people who pool resources and help each other over the long haul. Families love one another even when that requires sacrifice. Family means that if you disagree, you still stay together.   1

Families are the people for whom it matters if you have a cold, are feuding with your mate or training a new puppy. Family members use magnets to fasten the newspaper clippings about your bowling team on the refrigerator door. They save your drawings and homemade pottery. They like to hear stories about when you were young. They'll help you can tomatoes or change the oil in your car. They're the people who will come visit you in the hospital, will talk to you when you call with "a dark night of the soul" and will loan you money to pay the rent if you lose your job. Whether or not they are biologically related to each other, the people who do these things are family.   2

If you are very lucky, family is the group you were born into. But some are not that lucky. When Janet was in college, her parents were killed in a car wreck. In her early twenties she married, but three years later she lost her husband to leukemia. She has one sister, who calls mainly when she's suicidal or needs money. Janet is a congresswoman in a western state, a hard worker and an idealist. Her family consists of the men, women, and children she's grown to   3 depend on in the twenty-five years she's lived in her community. Except for her beloved dog, nobody lives with her. But she brings the cinnamon rolls to one family's Thanksgiving dinner and has a Mexican fiesta for families at her house on New Year's Eve. She attends Bar Mitzvahs, weddings, school concerts, and soccer matches. She told me with great pride, "When I sprained my ankle skiing last year, three families brought me meals."

I think of Morgan, a jazz musician who long ago left his small   4
town and rigid, judgmental family. He had many memories of his father whipping him with a belt or making him sleep in the cold. Once he said to me, "I was eighteen years old before anyone ever told me I had something to offer." Indeed he does. He plays the violin beautifully. He teaches improvisation and jazz violin and organizes jazz events for his town. His family is the family of musicians and music lovers that he has built around him over the years.

If you are very unlucky, you come from a nuclear family that   5
didn't care for you. Curtis, who as a boy was regularly beaten by his father, lied about his age so that he could join the Navy at sixteen. Years later he wrote his parents and asked if he could return home for Christmas. They didn't answer his letter. When I saw him in therapy, I encouraged him to look for a new family, among his cousins and friends from the Navy. Sometimes cutoffs, tragic as they are, are unavoidable.

I think of Anita, who never knew her father and whose mother   6
abandoned her when she was seven. Anita was raised by an aunt and uncle, whom she loved very much. As an adult she tracked down her mother and tried to establish a relationship, but her mother wasn't interested. At least Anita was able to find other family members to love her. She had a family in her aunt and uncle.

Family need not be traditional or biological. But what family   7
offers is not easily replicated. Let me share a Sioux word, *tiospaye*, which means the people with whom one lives. The *tiospaye* is probably closer to a kibbutz than to any other Western institution. The *tiospaye* gives children multiple parents, aunts, uncles and grandparents. It offers children a corrective factor for problems in their nuclear families. If parents are difficult, there are other adults around to soften and diffuse the situation. Until the 1930s, when the *tiospaye* began to fall apart with sale of land, migration and alcoholism, there was not much mental illness among the Sioux. When all adults were responsible for all children, people grew up healthy.

What *tiospaye* offers and what biological family offers is a place   8
that all members can belong to regardless of merit. Everyone is

included regardless of health, likability or prestige. What's most valuable about such institutions is that people are in by virtue of being born into the group. People are in even if they've committed a crime, been a difficult person, become physically or mentally disabled or are unemployed and broke. That ascribed status was what Robert Frost valued when he wrote that home "was something you somehow hadn't to deserve."

Many people do not have access to either a supportive biological family or a *tiospaye*. They make do with a "formed family." Others simply prefer a community of friends to their biological families. The problem with formed families is they often have less staying power. They might not take you in, give you money if you lose a job or visit you in a rest home if you are paralyzed in a car crash. My father had a stroke and lost most of his sight and speech. Family members were the people who invited him to visit and helped him through the long tough years after his stroke. Of course, there are formed families who do this. With the AIDS crisis, many gays have supported their friends through terrible times. Often immigrants will help each other in this new country. And there are families who don't stick together in crisis. But generally blood is thicker than water. Families come through when they must.

Another problem with formed families is that not everyone has the skills to be included in that kind of family. Friendship isn't a product that can be obtained for cash. People need friends today more than ever, but friends are harder to make in a world where people are busy, moving, and isolated. Some people don't have the skills. They are shy, abrasive, or dull. Crack babies have a hard time making friends, as do people with Alzheimer's. Formed families can leave many people out.

From my point of view the issue isn't biology. Rather the issues are commitment and inclusiveness. I don't think for most of us it has to be either/or. A person can have both a strong network of friends and a strong family. It is important to define family broadly so that all kinds of families, such as single-parent families, multi-generational families, foster families and the families of gays are included. But I agree with David Blankenberg's conclusion in his book *Rebuilding the Nest:* "Even with all the problems of nuclear families, I will support it as an institution until something better comes along."

Americans hold two parallel versions of the family—the idealized version and the dysfunctional version. The idealized version portrays families as wellsprings of love and happiness, loyal, wholesome, and true. This is the version we see in *Leave It to Beaver* or

Father Knows Best. The dysfunctional version depicts families as disturbed and disturbing, and suggests that salvation lies in extricating oneself from all the ties that bind. Both versions have had their eras. In the 1950s the idealized version was at its zenith. Extolling family was in response to the Depression and war, which separated families. People who had been wrenched away from home missed their families and thought of them with great longing. They idealized how close and warm they had been.

In the 1990s the dysfunctional version of family seems the most   13
influential. This belief system goes along with the culture of narcissism, which sells people the idea that families get in the way of individual fulfillment. Currently, many Americans are deeply mistrustful of their own and other people's families. Pop psychology presents families as pathology-producing. Talk shows make families look like hotbeds of sin and sickness. Day after day people testify about the diverse forms of emotional abuse that they suffered in their families. Movies and television often portray families as useless impediments.

In our culture, after a certain age, children no longer have per-   14
mission to love their parents. We define adulthood as breaking away, disagreeing and making up new rules. Just when teenagers most need their parents, they are encouraged to distance themselves from them. A friend told me of walking with her son in a shopping mall. They passed some of his friends, and she noticed that suddenly he was ten feet behind, trying hard not to be seen with her. She said, "I felt like I was drooling and wearing purple plaid polyester." Later her son told her that he enjoyed being with her, but that his friends all hated their parents and he would be teased if anyone knew he loved her. He said, "I'm confused about this. Am I supposed to hate you?"

This socialized antipathy toward families is unusual. Most cul-   15
tures revere and respect family. In Vietnam, for example, the tender word for lover is "sibling." In the Kuma tribe of Papua New Guinea, family members are valued above all others. Siblings are seen as alter egos, essential parts of the self. The Kuma believe that mates can be replaced, but not family members. Many Native American tribes regard family members as connected to the self. To be without family is to be dead.

From the Greeks, to Descartes, to Freud and Ayn Rand, West-   16
erners have valued the independent ego. But Americans are the most extreme. Our founders were rebels who couldn't tolerate oppression. When they formed a new government they emphasized rights and freedoms.

American values concerning independence may have worked 17
better when we lived in small communities surrounded by endless
space. But we have run out of space and our outlaws live among us.
At one time the outlaw mentality was mitigated by a strong sense of
community. Now the values of community have been superseded
by other values.

We have pushed the concept of individual rights to the limits. 18
Our laws let adults sell children harmful products. But laws are not
our main problem. People have always been governed more by
community values than by laws. Ethics, rather than laws, determine
most of our behavior. Unwritten rules of civility—for taking turns,
not cutting in lines, holding doors open for others and lowering our
voices in theaters—organize civic life. Unfortunately, those rules of
civility seem to be crumbling in America. We are becoming a nation
of people who get angry when anyone gets in our way.

Rudeness is everywhere in our culture. Howard Stern, G. Gor- 19
don Liddy, and Newt Gingrich are rude. It's not surprising our children copy them. Phil Donahue and Jay Leno interrupt, and children
learn to interrupt. A young man I know was recently injured on a
volleyball court. The player who hurt him didn't apologize or offer
to help him get to an emergency room. An official told him to get off
the floor because he was messing it up with his blood and holding
up the game. I recently saw an old man hesitate at a busy intersection. Behind him drivers swore and honked. He looked scared and
confused as he turned into traffic and almost wrecked his car. At a
festival a man stood in front of the stage, refusing to sit down when
people yelled out that they couldn't see. Finally another man wrestled him to the ground. All around were the omnipresent calls of
"Fuck You." Over coffee a local politician told me she would no longer attend town meetings. She said, "People get out of control and
insult me and each other. There's no dialogue, it's all insults and
accusations."

We have a crisis in meaning in our culture. The crisis comes from 20
our isolation from each other, from the values we learn in a culture of
consumption and from the fuzzy, self-help message that the only
commitment is to the self and the only important question is—Am I
happy? We learn that we are number one and that our own immediate needs are the most important ones. The crisis comes from the message that products satisfy and that happiness can be purchased.

We live in a money-driven culture. But the bottom line is not 21
the only one, or even the best line for us to hold. A culture organized
around profits instead of people is not user friendly to families. We

all suffer from existential flu as we search for meaning in a culture that values money, not meaning. Everyone I know wants to do good work. But right now we have an enormous gap between doing what's meaningful and doing what is reimbursed.

MEANINGS AND VALUES

1. The author asserts that the definition of the word *family* has changed. List some examples she gives of new types of family groupings in society today.

2. Pipher classifies types of families into categories such as biological family, *tiospaye,* and formed family. Restate her definition of one of these three types of families.

3. In what ways does Pipher's discussion of "the outlaw mentality" (Par. 17), rudeness (19), and the "crisis in meaning in our culture" (20) relate to her definition of family?

EXPOSITORY TECHNIQUES

1. Is the writer's discussion of family an informative definition or a redefinition? Explain.

2. What mode does the author use to develop her definition of family in Paragraphs 12 and 13? Is her use of this mode effective? Explain.

3. In Paragraph 7, the writer clarifies the meaning of the Sioux word *tiospaye* because the term is important to the writer's purpose. Re-read Pipher's definition of *tiospaye* and then restate it in your own words. Do you think the definition is important in clarifying the overall point of the essay? Or could it have been left out? Explain.

DICTION AND VOCABULARY

1. The author often uses the first person in this essay: "When I speak of families..." (Par. 1); "I think of Morgan..." (4). Do you find this approach distracting or helpful? Why?

2. If you do not know the meaning of some of the following words, consult a dictionary: *nuclear family* (Par. 5); *kibbutz* (7); *abrasive* (10); *idealized, dysfunctional, extricating* (12); *narcissism* (13); *antipathy* (15); *omnipresent* (19).

READ TO WRITE

1. **Collaborating:** In a group of writers, brainstorm examples in popular culture (music, movies, TV, etc.) of ideal families, dysfunctional

families, and formed families. For example, drawing from classic or more recent TV, *The Brady Bunch* could be an example of an ideal family, *The Simpsons* or *Married with Children* can be examples of dysfunctional families, and *Friends* or *The Big Bang Theory* can be examples of formed families. Writing together, report how each example illustrates that particular definition of family (for example, in *The Brady Bunch*, Mrs. Brady rarely loses her temper).

2. **Considering Audience:** Although Pipher is a clinical psychologist, she has written extensively for general audiences. How well do you think she reaches a general audience in this essay? Explain your answer.

3. **Developing an Essay:** Using Pipher's essay as a jumping-off point, develop a definition essay explaining a formed family, an idealized family, or a dysfunctional family that you belong to or are familiar with. Alternatively, prepare a definition essay explaining the nature of friendship, marriage, mentorship, or some other social relationship that interests you. Or, write an essay giving your own definition with examples of the outlaw mentality described in Pipher's essay.

(NOTE: Suggestions for topics requiring development by DEFINITION follow.)

Writing Suggestions for Chapter 9

DEFINITION

Develop a composition for a specified purpose and audience, using whatever methods and expository patterns will help convey a clear understanding of your meaning of one of the following terms:

1. Country music
2. Conscience
3. Religion
4. Bigotry
5. Success
6. Empathy
7. Family
8. Hypocrisy
9. Humor
10. Sophistication
11. Naïveté
12. Cowardice
13. Wisdom
14. Integrity
15. Morality
16. Greed
17. Social poise
18. Intellectual (the person)
19. Pornography
20. Courage
21. Patriotism
22. Equality (or equal opportunity)
23. Loyalty
24. Stylishness (in clothing or behavior)
25. Fame
26. Obesity

27. Cheating
28. Hero
29. Feminine
30. Masculine

COLLABORATIVE EXERCISE

Working in a group, choose a term from the list below. Have each member of your group define the term for a reader/audience of a particular age group. As a group, compare your choices of definition strategies based on each intended audience.

a. Success
b. Family
c. Cowardice
d. Loyalty
e. Hero
f. Integrity

10

Explaining with the Help of *Description*

You can make your expository writing more vivid, and hence more understandable, with the support of **description,** sometimes even using the pattern as the basic plan for an exposition. In writing, you can use sensory details—sight, sound, touch, taste, and smell—to re-create *places:* a portrait of the steamy closeness of the Brazilian jungle; the gray stone, narrow streets, tall houses, and church spires of an Eastern European city. You can create portraits of *people, qualities, emotions,* or *moods:* a beloved aunt whose cheerfulness was part of a long fight against pain and illness, the physical and spatial on-court "intelligence" of a star basketball player, the despair of a child crying for her puppy just killed by a car, or the contrasting moods of a city where excited theatergoers pass a drunk slumped against a building.

Descriptive writing depends on detail, and your first and most important job as a writer employing description is to select the details to be included. There are usually many from which to choose, and it is easy to become so involved in a subject—especially one that is visually or emotionally intriguing—that you lose sight of the expository purpose of your writing. As you draft and revise, therefore, you need to keep in mind the kind of picture you want to paint with words, one that accomplishes *your* purpose for *your* intended audience. Such a word picture need not be entirely visual, for the dimensions of sound, smell, and even touch can create a vivid and effective image in your readers' minds.

When used as a pattern for much or all of an expository essay, description does more than set a mood, add a vivid touch to an explanation, or provide an occasional supporting detail. It becomes the primary strategy for explaining a subject or supporting a thesis, as in the following example.

> It's not winter without an icestorm. When Robert Frost gazed at bowed birch trees and tried to think that boys had bent them playing, he knew better: "Icestorms do that." They do that and a lot more, trimming disease and weakness out of the tree—the old tree's friend, as pneumonia used to be the old man's. Some of us provide life-support systems for our precious shrubs, boarding them over against the ice, for the icestorm takes the young or unlucky branch or birch as well as the rotten or feeble. One February morning we look out our windows over yards and fields littered with kindling, small twigs and great branches. We look out at a world turned into one diamond, ten thousand carats in the line of sight, twice as many facets. What a dazzle of spinning refracted light, spider webs of cold brilliance attacking our eyeballs! All winter we wear sunglasses to drive, more than we do in summer, and never so much as after an icestorm, with its painful glaze reflecting from maple and birch, granite boulder and stone wall, turning electric wires into bright silver filaments. The snow itself takes on a crust of ice, like the finish of a clay pot, that carries our weight and sends us swooping and sliding. It's worth your life to go for the mail. Until sand and salt redeem the highway, Route 4 is quiet. We cancel the appointment with the dentist, stay home, and marvel at the altered universe, knowing that midday sun will strip ice from tree and roof and restore our ordinary white winter world.
>
> —Donald Hall, *Seasons at Eagle Pond*

WHY USE DESCRIPTION?

Descriptions help readers create mental images of a subject or scene. To do this, the writer uses concrete, specific detail ("The floodwater turned the carpet into a slippery mess that smelled like dead fish and covered the electronic insides of the TV with a thin coat of black mud") rather than abstract, general impressions ("The flood soaked everything in the living room"). You can put descriptive detail to work for a variety of purposes, however.

You might choose to focus on a particular place or scene, using description to convey and support your thoughts and conclusions about it. Writing of this sort often appears in brief essays focusing on a limited scene: a beach in winter, a small corner of the Sonoran Desert, or a mall parking lot just before Christmas, for example. On the other hand, a description of a typical family apartment in Cairo might provide important conclusions and support for a study of family structure in Egypt, or descriptions of the Arctic landscape might contribute to an understanding of the habits of polar bears. When used for such expository purposes, descriptive writing goes beyond simply recording details to offering conclusions and explanations of the effects of a setting on those who live in it.

You might also use descriptive writing to create a portrait of a person. To do this, you combine descriptive detail with narration (see Chapter 11), usually in the form of brief but representative incidents. Your aim is to highlight the characteristics of your subject: details of appearance, speech, action, and feeling. In such a context, descriptive detail serves to support and convey your understanding of an individual's outlook and motivation, a sense of his or her personality, and your insight into the individual's influence on others.

Technical descriptions, common in scientific and professional writing, are another use for descriptive writing. In this form of writing, you provide a precise understanding of the elements of a subject and their relationship, and in so doing you convey necessary information or evidence to support your conclusions. Biologists, for example, might describe features of a frog that are marks of evolution or function; art historians might focus on color, line, shape, and brush stroke as a way of supporting a thesis about an artist or a particular painting.

CHOOSING A STRATEGY

Descriptive writing generally follows one of two strategies— *objective* description or *subjective* description—though some overlapping is also common. In objective description you aim at conveying the details of a subject thoroughly and accurately without suggesting your feelings or biases and without trying to evoke an emotional response from readers. Scientific papers, business reports, and academic writing often take this stance. In choosing details, writers of objective descriptions aim at precision and try to avoid emotional overtones. In arranging the details for presentation, writers either pay attention to the need to support a conclusion or to the function of the object or process being presented, as in the following example.

Cathode Ray Tube

The most familiar example is a television picture tube, and the simplest kind is the black and white. The inside of the tube is coated with a *phosphor*, a substance that glows when struck by electrons. At the rear of the tube (the neck) is an electron gun that shoots a beam of electrons toward the front. Electromagnetic coils or electrically charged metal plates direct this stream from side to side and top to bottom, forming a glow-picture of the "message" being received by the cathode ray tube. Color tubes are similar except that the face is coated with thousands of groups of dots. Each group, called a *pixel* (picture element), consists of three dots, one for each of the three primary colors—red, green, and blue.

—Herman Schneider and Leo Schneider, *The Harper Dictionary*
of Science in Everyday Language

In subjective description, however, you make your values and feelings clear and often encourage readers to respond emotionally. Often, instead of describing how something *is* objectively, you describe how it *seems* subjectively. To do this, you may make occasional use of direct statement, but you are likely to find it more effective to rely on a choice of vivid, concrete, or emotionally laden detail or on the connotations of words. *Connotations* are the feelings or associations that accompany a word, not its dictionary or literal meaning. Subjective descriptions express your conclusions about a subject or your attitudes toward it. Thus, in arranging details for presentation, you should pay attention to the dominant impression or interpretation you wish to convey as well as to the arrangement of details in the setting (right to left, top to bottom, for example).

In creating a subjective description, pay attention to the dominant impression you create, making sure it conveys and supports your overall purpose or interpretation. In the following passage, for example, the dominant impression clearly conveys the writer's insights into the effects of atmosphere—in this case, fog—on human perceptions, even though she does not directly state this conclusion.

It begins in late afternoon, a wall of gray blocking the entrance to the harbor, moving imperceptibly, closing in. The sun becomes a bright thing in the sky for a moment before a thick grayness takes over. Trails of vapor drift by. Roads taper off into mist. Pine trees, encircled by the fog, take on different shapes. Inside vacation houses, people make tea, read books, play cards with old decks. Outside, the air smells of soaked wharves. Down by the rocks the surf crashes, but it is a muffled sound, heard while asleep. Bay bushes hunch together, woolly and wet. Walking through fields of Queen Anne's lace, lupine, and goldenrod, their colors muted, is like moving through dreamland. A foghorn blows. Other people are out—a figure appears near the raspberry bushes, spectral, with a basket. A dog runs by, and from the leaves drops fall.

—Susan Minot, "Lost in the Light of Gray"

DEVELOPING DESCRIPTION

The first and most important job in descriptive writing is to select the details. The questions you ask about a subject can help you identify significant details and suggest ways of interpreting it.

For scenes or objects:

- What does it look like (colors, shapes, height, depth)?
- What does it sound like (loud, soft, rasping, soothing, musical, like a lawn mower)?
- What does it smell like (smoky, acrid, like gasoline, like soap, like a wood fire)?
- What does it feel like (smooth, sticky, like a cat's fur, like a spider's web, like grease)?
- What does it taste like (bitter, salty, like grass, like feathers)?

For emotions or ideas:

- What effect does it have on behavior (anger: red face, abrupt gestures)?
- What is it like (freedom: like taking a deep breath of air after leaving a smoky room)?

For people:

- What does the person look like (hair neatly combed, rumpled blouse, muddy boots)?
- What are some characteristic behaviors (rubs hands on skirt, picks ear)?
- What has the person done or said (cheated on a chemistry test, said cruel things to friends)?
- How do others respond to the person (turn to her for advice, call him a "slob")?

Successful subjective descriptions generally focus on a single *dominant impression,* which can act in place of a conclusion or thesis. To create a dominant impression, you select those details that will help create a mood or atmosphere or emphasize a feature or quality. But more than the materials themselves are involved in creating a dominant impression. The words you choose, and both their literal and suggestive meanings (denotations and connotations), convey an impression. So, too, do the arrangements of words in sentences, as in the use of short, hurried sentences to help convey a sense of urgency or excitement.

The actual arrangement of the material is perhaps less troublesome in description than in most other expository patterns. Nonetheless, you need to follow a sequence that is clear to your reader and that helps you achieve your purpose or support your thesis. A clear spatial organization, for example, will help readers understand a visually complex subject. You can move from left to right, top to bottom, or near to far. You can describe a person from head to toe, or vice versa, or begin with the most noticeable feature and work from there. Or you could start with an overall view of a scene and then move to a focal point.

A chronological arrangement enables you to look at a scene from several perspectives: early morning, midday, and night, for example, or in different weather conditions. Such a strategy allows you to make a point by contrasting the scenes, and it provides variety and interest. A thematic organization emphasizes the dominant impression or thesis through focus and repetition. You might emphasize by repeating clusters of key words (grim, grasping, hard, short-tempered) or images (pink ribbons, the scent of violets). You might also arrange segments of the description by increasing order of importance or in another manner that best supports a thesis.

You can also choose a point of view, either first person ("I looked . . .") or third person ("He sighed . . . ," "It moved . . ."). You might also choose a perspective, including the location of the observer and any limitation on the observer's ability to see and understand, perhaps observing a familiar family scene from a child's perspective to provide a new understanding of relationships.

Whatever techniques you choose, however, try to avoid excessive description, which creates confusion and boredom, or description without a clear purpose, which offers your readers no goal or reward for their effort.

Student Essay

In preparing the following essay, Carey Braun tried to combine technical descriptions of the effects of light with her subjective responses and perceptions. In linking the two, she makes some interesting observations about the way we humans are linked to the natural world.

Bright Light
by Carey Braun

The sun woke me by sneaking its way through the narrow cracks of the vertical blinds. I squinted at the bright sun, then kept my eyes closed and enjoyed its warmth on my face and shoulders. After a time, I slid across the bed to the window and peeked through the blinds to look out on a day that reminded me of *my* version of Andrew Lloyd Webber's song, "*Light* changes everything"—or at least the sun does.

What better place to see light, feel light, and become one with the sun, I thought, than at the beach? I rushed out of bed, got dressed, had a bite of breakfast, grabbed my bathing suit and suntan lotion, and headed for the beach.

As I stepped out of the car in the parking lot, I felt a sunwarmed breeze across my face. It blew my hair across my cheek and made me wonder what it would be like to be a bird, about to skim across the waves of wind with the sun on my back. I hurried down the walkway. On each side of the path, dilapidated summer cottages managed to look fresh and new in the early morning rays. Crossing the hot sand, I stepped gingerly on it, a recognition that even this early in the day we need to shape our actions to the sun's heat and power.

I sat on the blanket and rubbed the suntan lotion over my body. My skin shined, reflecting the sun's rays and making me seem for a moment like a second source of light. But soon I began to feel like a frying pan that would sizzle if a drop of water hit me. In the background I could hear the sound of many boom boxes blending together forming a lighthearted hymn that took away thoughts of everything else but this time and place.

Initial setting
Time: morning

*Thesis—
stated
somewhat
indirectly*

*Observer
moves from
place to
place—
observations
show the
effect of light
at different
times of day*

*Observer is
also
participant*

*Detailed,
specific
observations*

Time: Midday

People were splashing the water, sending luminous drops into the air and breaking the surface of the water into a million mirroring pieces. During brief breaks in the music and the sounds of splashing, I could hear the sound of birds singing.

The sun's heat relaxed me so that I fell asleep. When I woke, there was sweat covering my face and my arms and refracting the sun's rays. If I looked just right, I could see rainbow dots on the surface of my skin. I woke up slowly and decided to head for the cool, refreshing water in front of me. I could feel my body temperature dropping as it moved into the water. As I dove into a wave, chills went through my body like shock waves. I was ready to move back to the beach and the sun.

Appeals to a variety of senses

I couldn't taste the sun, but as I walked back to my blanket, I licked the salt off my lips, which had dried quickly in the heat. Salt, I decided, must be the taste of light, at least this morning. The salt on my skin made it feel like stretched leather, tight across my cheekbones and shoulders and stiffening at my joints. I walked across the glinting sand, through midday air heated to luminous, shimmering waves, to the outdoor shower.

More senses

As I let the water wash away the salt, I looked at the sky and realized that the sun was beginning to descend. The subtle change in light made me feel cooler even though the sand was just as hot as I returned to my blanket. As the light turned to afternoon, people began looking at each other, perhaps noticing the growing shadows and the loss of brilliance. Light now turned to haze, luminous and bright, but still haze. People began straggling up the sand, looking as if their energy, too, had begun to wane. The music left and the song that remained was the crash of waves, glinting here and there as the growing fog broke to let through a stray ray.

Transition to late afternoon

Change in mood and effects of light

I gathered my belongings and shook all the sand off. As I drove away, I took one last look in the mirror to mourn the passing of the sun's power and light; startled by the electrifying colors of reds, yellows, and oranges spreading from the horizon through the sky, I realized once again the power of light to change everything.

Restates thesis

SUZANNE BERNE

Writer Suzanne Berne earned a B.A. in English from Wesleyan University and an M.F.A. from the University of Iowa Writers' Workshop. Among her works are *Missing Lucile* (2010), a biography of the grandmother she never met, as well as the psychological novels *A Perfect Arrangement* (2001) and *The Ghost at the Table* (1997). She has taught at Harvard University and Wellesley College. She is currently an associate English professor at Boston College.

Ground Zero

Soon after the two towers of the World Trade Center collapsed under terrorist attack on September 11, 2001, hospital staff and police officers began referring to the site as "ground zero," meaning "a scene of great devastation." Berne's description of "Ground Zero" was originally published in the *New York Times* as "Where Nothing Says Everything" on April 21, 2002.

On a cold, damp March morning, I visited Manhattan's financial   1
district, a place I'd never been, to pay my respects at what used
to be the World Trade Center. Many other people had chosen to do
the same that day, despite the raw wind and spits of rain, and so the
first thing I noticed when I arrived on the corner of Vesey and
Church Streets was a crowd.

Standing on the sidewalk, pressed against aluminum police   2
barricades, wearing scarves that flapped into their faces and woolen
hats pulled over their ears, were people apparently from everywhere. Germans, Italians, Japanese. An elegant-looking Norwegian
family in matching shearling coats. People from Ohio and California
and Maine. Children, middle-aged couples, older people. Many of
them were clutching cameras and video recorders, and they were all
craning to see across the street, where there was nothing to see.

At least, nothing is what it first looked like, the space that is now   3
ground zero. But once your eyes adjust to what you are looking at,
"nothing" becomes something much more potent, which is absence.

But to the out-of-towner, ground zero looks at first simply like a   4
construction site. All the familiar details are there: the wooden scaf-
folding; the cranes, the bulldozers, and forklifts; the trailers and
construction workers in hard hats; even the dust. There is the pound
of jackhammers, the steady beep-beep-beep of trucks backing up,
the roar of heavy machinery.

So much busyness is reassuring, and it is possible to stand look-   5
ing at the cranes and trucks and feel that mild curiosity and hope-
fulness so often inspired by construction sites.

Then gradually your eyes do adjust, exactly as if you have   6
stepped from a dark theater into a bright afternoon, because what
becomes most striking about this scene is the light itself.

Ground zero is a great bowl of light, an emptiness that seems   7
weirdly spacious and grand, like a vast plaza amid the dense tangle
of streets in lower Manhattan. Light reflecting off the Hudson River
vaults into the site, soaking everything—especially on an overcast
morning—with a watery glow. This is the moment when absence
begins to assume a material form, when what is not there becomes
visible.

Suddenly you notice the periphery, the skyscraper shrouded in   8
black plastic, the boarded windows, the steel skeleton of the shattered Winter Garden. Suddenly there are the broken steps and
cracked masonry in front of Brooks Brothers. Suddenly there are the
firefighters, the waiting ambulance on the other side of the pit, the
police on every corner. Suddenly there is the enormous cross made
of two rusted girders.

And suddenly, very suddenly, there is the little cemetery attached   9
to St. Paul's Chapel, with tulips coming up, the chapel and grounds
miraculously undamaged except for a few plastic-sheathed grave-
stones. The iron fence is almost invisible beneath a welter of dried
pine wreaths, banners, ribbons, laminated poems and prayers and
photographs, swags of paper cranes, withered flowers, baseball
hats, rosary beads, teddy bears. And flags, flags everywhere, little
American flags fluttering in the breeze, flags on posters drawn by
Brownie troops, flags on T-shirts, flags on hats, flags streaming by,
tied to the handles of baby strollers.

It takes quite a while to see all of this; it takes even longer to   10
come up with something to say about it.

An elderly man standing next to me had been staring fixedly   11
across the street for some time. Finally he touched his son's elbow
and said: "I watched those towers being built. I saw this place when
they weren't there." Then he stopped, clearly struggling with, what
for him, was a double negative, recalling an absence before there
was an absence. His son, waiting patiently, took a few photographs.
"Let's get out of here," the man said at last.

Again and again I heard people say, "It's unbelievable." And   12
then they would turn to each other, dissatisfied. They wanted to say
something more expressive, more meaningful. But it *is* unbelievable,

to stare at so much devastation, and know it for devastation, and yet recognize that it does not look like the devastation one has imagined.

Like me, perhaps, the people around me had in mind images   13 from television and newspaper pictures: the collapsing buildings, the running office workers, the black plume of smoke against a bright blue sky. Like me, they were probably trying to superimpose those terrible images onto the industrious emptiness right in front of them. The difficulty of this kind of mental revision is measured, I believe, by the brisk trade in World Trade Center photograph booklets at tables set up on street corners.

Determined to understand better what I was looking at, I decided   14 to get a ticket for the viewing platform beside St. Paul's. This proved no easy task, as no one seemed to be able to direct me to South Street Seaport, where the tickets are distributed. Various police officers whom I asked for directions waved me vaguely toward the East River, differing degrees of boredom and resignation on their faces. Or perhaps it was a kind of incredulousness. Somewhere around the American Stock Exchange, I asked a security guard for help and he frowned at me, saying, "You want tickets to the disaster?"

Finally I found myself in line at a cheerfully painted kiosk, watch-   15 ing a young juggler try to entertain the crowd. He kept dropping the four red balls he was attempting to juggle, and having to chase after them. It was noon; the next available viewing was at 4 P.M.

Back I walked, up Fulton Street, the smell of fish in the air, to wan-   16 der again around St. Paul's. A deli on Vesey Street advertised a view of the World Trade Center from its second-floor dining area. I went in and ordered a pastrami sandwich, uncomfortably aware that many people before me had come to that same deli for pastrami sand-wiches who would never come there again. But I was here to see what I could, so I carried my sandwich upstairs and sat down be-side one of the big plate-glass windows.

And there, at last, I got my ticket to the disaster.   17

I could see not just into the pit now, but also its access ramp,   18 which trucks had been traveling up and down since I had arrived that morning. Gathered along the ramp were firefighters in their black helmets and black coats. Slowly they lined up, and it became clear that this was an honor guard, and that someone's remains were being carried up the ramp toward the open door of an ambulance.

Everyone in the dining room stopped eating. Several people   19
stood up, whether out of respect or to see better, I don't know. For a
moment, everything paused.

Then the day flowed back into itself. Soon I was outside once   20
more, joining the tide of people washing around the site. Later, as I
huddled with a little crowd on the viewing platform, watching people scrawl their names or write "God Bless America" on the plywood
walls, it occurred to me that a form of repopulation was taking effect,
with so many visitors to this place, thousands of visitors, all of us
coming to see the wide emptiness where so many were lost. And by
the act of our visiting—whether we are motivated by curiosity or
horror or reverence or grief, or by something confusing that combines them all—that space fills up again.

MEANINGS AND VALUES

1. What is the significance of the observation: "This is the moment
    when absence begins to assume a material form, when what is not
    there becomes visible" (Par. 7)?

2. What does the author mean when she refers to "my ticket to the
    disaster" (Par. 17). Why do you think she phrases it this way?

EXPOSITORY TECHNIQUES

1. Does the writer use *objective* description or *subjective* description in
    this essay? How so?

2. What sights, sounds, and other sensory details does Berne employ to
    describe the scene at Ground Zero? List examples.

3. What would you say is the dominant impression of the writer's
    descriptive essay? Explain your answer.

DICTION AND VOCABULARY

1. What is the tone of this essay (Guide: *Style/Tone*)? Explain your
    answer.

2. If you do not know the meaning of some of the following words,
    consult a dictionary: *potent* (Par. 3); *jackhammers* (4); *periphery* (8);
    welter (9).

READ TO WRITE

1. **Collaborating:** Discuss historic landmarks that your group members have visited. Examples might include the Statue of Liberty, Stonehenge, Graceland, a California mission, the pyramids of Egypt, or some other. Did the actual appearance of these landmarks match expectations? What was the dominant impression, and what details did they base that on? Choose one of the landmarks and, as a group, write a brief report.

2. **Considering Audience:** What is your emotional response to this reading selection? What details does Berne use that stir this response in you? Would you have the same response if you had never heard of Ground Zero?

3. **Developing an Essay:** Visit a public place in your vicinity, such as a park, theater, or library. Try to observe it as though you had never seen it before. Write a descriptive essay that conveys a dominant impression, using either a subjective or objective strategy or a combination of both.

(NOTE: Suggestions for topics requiring development by DESCRIPTION are on pp. 368–369 at the end of this chapter.)

GEORGE SIMPSON

GEORGE SIMPSON, born in Virginia in 1950, received his B.A. in journalism from the University of North Carolina at Chapel Hill. He went to work for *Newsweek* in 1972, and in 1978 he became public affairs director for that magazine. Before joining *Newsweek,* Simpson worked for two years as a writer and editor for the *Carolina Financial Times* in Chapel Hill, North Carolina, and as a reporter for the *News-Gazette* in Lexington, Virginia. He received the Best Feature Writing award from Sigma Delta Chi in 1972 for a five-part investigative series on the University of North Carolina football program. He has written stories for the *New York Times, Sport, Glamour,* the *Winston-Salem* (North Carolina) *Journal,* and *New York.*

The War Room at Bellevue

"The War Room at Bellevue" was first published in *New York* magazine. The author chose, for good reason, to stay strictly within a time sequence as he described the emergency ward. This essay is also noteworthy for its cumulative descriptive effect, which was accomplished almost entirely with objective details.

Bellevue. The name conjures up images of an indoor war zone: the wounded and bleeding lining the halls, screaming for help while harried doctors in blood-stained smocks rush from stretcher to stretcher, fighting a losing battle against exhaustion and the crushing number of injured. "What's worse," says a longtime Bellevue nurse, "is that we have this image of being a hospital only for . . ." she pauses, then lowers her voice, "for crazy people." 1

Though neither battlefield nor Bedlam is a valid image, there is something extraordinary about the monstrous complex that spreads for five blocks along First Avenue in Manhattan. It is said best by the head nurse in Adult Emergency Service: "If you have any chance for survival, you have it here." Survival—that is why they come. Why do injured cops drive by a half-dozen other hospitals to be treated at Bellevue? They've seen the Bellevue emergency team in action. 2

9:00 P.M. It is a Friday night in the Bellevue emergency room. The after-work crush is over (those who've suffered through the day, only to come for help after the five-o'clock whistle has blown) and it is nearly silent except for the mutter of voices at the admitting desk, where administrative personnel discuss who will go for coffee. 3

Across the spotless white-walled lobby, ten people sit quietly, passively, in pastel plastic chairs, waiting for word of relatives or to see doctors. In the past 24 hours, 300 people have come to the Bellevue Adult Emergency Service. Fewer than 10 percent were true emergencies. One man sleeps fitfully in the emergency ward while his heartbeat, respiration, and blood pressure are monitored by control consoles mounted over his bed. Each heartbeat trips a tiny bleep in the monitor, which attending nurses can hear across the ward. A half hour ago, doctors in the trauma room withdrew a six-inch stiletto blade from his back. When he is stabilized, the patient will be moved upstairs to the twelve-bed Surgical Intensive Care Unit.

9:05 P.M. An ambulance backs into the receiving bay, its red and yellow lights flashing in and out of the lobby. A split second later, the glass doors burst open as a nurse and an attendant roll a mobile stretcher into the lobby. When the nurse screams, "Emergency!" the lobby explodes with activity as the way is cleared to the trauma room. Doctors appear from nowhere and transfer the bloodied body of a black man to the treatment table. Within seconds his clothes are stripped away, revealing a tiny stab wound in his left side. Three doctors and three nurses rush around the victim, each performing a task necessary to begin treatment. Intravenous needles are inserted into his arms and groin. A doctor draws blood for the lab, in case surgery is necessary. A nurse begins inserting a catheter into the victim's penis and continues to feed in tubing until the catheter reaches the bladder. Urine flows through the tube into a plastic bag. Doctors are glad not to see blood in the urine. Another nurse records pulse and blood pressure.   4

The victim is in good shape. He shivers slightly, although the trauma room is exceedingly warm. His face is bloodied, but shows no major lacerations. A third nurse, her elbow propped on the treatment table, asks the man a series of questions, trying to quickly outline his medical history. He answers abruptly. He is drunk. His left side is swabbed with yellow disinfectant and a doctor injects a local anesthetic. After a few seconds another doctor inserts his finger into the wound. It sinks in all the way to the knuckle. He begins to rotate his finger like a child trying to get a marble out of a milk bottle. The patient screams bloody murder and tries to struggle free.   5

Meanwhile in the lobby, a security guard is ejecting a derelict who has begun to drink from a bottle hidden in his coat pocket. "He's a regular, was in here just two days ago," says a nurse. "We checked him pretty good then, so he's probably okay now. Can you believe those were clean clothes we gave him?" The old man, blackened by filth, leaves quietly.   6

9:15 P.M. A young Hispanic man interrupts, saying his pregnant   7
girl friend, sitting outside in his car, is bleeding heavily from her
vagina. She is rushed into an examination room, treated behind
closed doors, and rolled into the observation ward, where, much
later in the night, a gynecologist will treat her in a special room—the
same one used to examine rape victims. Nearby, behind curtains,
the neurologist examines an old white woman to determine if her
headaches are due to head injury. They are not.

9:45 P.M. The trauma room has been cleared and cleaned merci-   8
lessly. The examination rooms are three-quarters full—another
overdose, two asthmatics, a young woman with abdominal pains.
In the hallway, a derelict who has been sleeping it off urinates all
over the stretcher. He sleeps on while attendants change his clothes.
An ambulance—one of four that patrol Manhattan for Bellevue
from 42nd Street to Houston, river to river—delivers a middle-aged
white woman and two cops, the three of them soaking wet. The
woman has escaped from the psychiatric floor of a nearby hospital
and tried to drown herself in the East River. The cops fished her
out. She lies on a stretcher shivering beneath white blankets. Her
eyes stare at the ceiling. She speaks clearly when an administrative
worker begins routine questioning. The cops are given hospital
gowns and wait to receive tetanus shots and gamma globulin—a
hedge against infection from the befouled river water. They will
hang around the E.R. for another two hours, telling their story to as
many as six other policemen who show up to hear it. The woman is
rolled into an examination room, where a male nurse speaks gently:
"They tell me you fell into the river." "No," says the woman, "I
jumped. I have to commit suicide." "Why?" asks the nurse. "Because I'm insane and I can't help [it]. I have to die." The nurse gradually discovers the woman has a history of psychological problems.
She is given dry bedclothes and placed under guard in the hallway.
She lies on her side, staring at the wall.

The pace continues to increase. Several more overdose victims   9
arrive by ambulance. One, a young black woman, had done a strip-
tease on the street just before passing out. A second black woman is
semiconscious and spends the better part of her time at Bellevue al-
ternately cursing at and pleading with the doctors. Attendants find
a plastic bottle coated with methadone in the pocket of a Hispanic
O.D. The treatment is routinely the same, and sooner or later involves vomiting. Just after doctors begin to treat the O.D., he vomits
great quantities of wine and methadone in all directions. "Lovely
business, huh?" laments one of the doctors. A young nurse confides

that if there were other true emergencies, the overdose victims
would be given lower priority. "You can't help thinking they did it
to themselves," she says, "while the others are accident victims."

10:30 P.M. A policeman who twisted his knee struggling with an   10
"alleged perpetrator" is examined and released. By 10:30, the lobby is
jammed with friends and relatives of patients in various stages of treatment and recovery. The attendant who also functions as a translator for
Hispanic patients adds chairs to accommodate the overflow. The medical walk-in rate stays steady—between eight and ten patients waiting.
A pair of derelicts, each with battered eyes, appear at the admitting
desk. One has a dramatically swollen face laced with black stitches.

11:30 P.M. The husband of the attempted suicide arrives. He   11
thanks the police for saving his wife's life, then talks at length with
doctors about her condition. She continues to stare into the void and
does not react when her husband approaches her stretcher.

Meanwhile, patients arrive in the lobby at a steady pace. A   12
young G.I. on leave has lower-back pains; a Hispanic man com-
plains of pains in his side; occasionally parents hurry through the
adult E.R. carrying children to the pediatric E.R. A white woman of
about 50 marches into the lobby from the walk-in entrance. Dried
blood covers her right eyebrow and upper lip. She begins to perform. "I was assaulted on 28th and Lexington, I was," she says
grandly, "and I don't have to take it *anymore*. I was a bride 21 years
ago and, God, I was beautiful then." She has captured the attention
of all present. "I was there when the boys came home—on Memorial
Day—and I don't have to take this kind of treatment."

As midnight approaches, the nurses prepare for the shift   13
change. They must brief the incoming staff and make sure all reports are up-to-date. One young brunet says, "Christ, I'm gonna go
home and take a shower—I smell like vomit."

11:50 P.M. The triage nurse is questioning an old black man about 14
chest pains, and a Hispanic woman is having an asthma attack, when
an ambulance, its sirens screaming full tilt, roars into the receiving
bay. There is a split-second pause as everyone drops what he or she is
doing and looks up. Then all hell breaks loose. Doctors and nurses are
suddenly sprinting full-out toward the trauma room. The glass doors
burst open and the occupied stretcher is literally run past me. Cops
follow. It is as if a comet has whooshed by. In the trauma room it all
becomes clear. A half-dozen doctors and nurses surround the lifeless
form of a Hispanic man with a shotgun hole in his neck the size of
your fist. Blood pours from a second gaping wound in his chest. A res-
pirator is slammed over his face, making his chest rise and fall as if he

were breathing. "No pulse," reports one doctor. A nurse jumps on a stool and, leaning over the man, begins to pump his chest with her palms. "No blood pressure," screams another nurse. The ambulance driver appears shaken, "I never thought I'd get here in time," he stutters. More doctors from the trauma team upstairs arrive. Wrappings from syringes and gauze pads fly through the air. The victim's eyes are open yet devoid of life. His body takes on a yellow tinge. A male nurse winces at the gunshot wound. "This guy really pissed off somebody," he says. This is no ordinary shooting. It is an execution. IV's are jammed into the body in the groin and arms. One doctor has been plugging in an electrocardiograph and asks everyone to stop for a second so he can get a reading. "Forget it," shouts the doctor in charge. "No time." "Take it easy, Jimmy," someone yells at the head physician. It is apparent by now that the man is dead, but the doctors keep trying injections and finally they slit open the chest and reach inside almost up to their elbows. They feel the extent of the damage and suddenly it is all over. "I told 'em he was dead," says one nurse, withdrawing. "They didn't listen." The room is very still. The doctors are momentarily disgusted, then go on about their business. The room clears quickly. Finally there is only a male nurse and the still-warm body, now waxy-yellow, with huge ribs exposed on both sides of the chest and giant holes in both sides of the neck. The nurse speculates that this is yet another murder in a Hispanic political struggle that has brought many such victims to Bellevue. He marvels at the extent of the wounds and repeats, "This guy was really blown away."

Midnight. A hysterical woman is hustled through the lobby 15 into an examination room. It is the dead man's wife, and she is nearly delirious. "I know he's dead, I know he's dead," she screams over and over. Within moments the lobby is filled with anxious relatives of the victim, waiting for word on his condition. The police are everywhere asking questions, but most people say they saw nothing. One young woman says she heard six shots, two louder than the other four. At some point, word is passed that the man is, in fact, dead. Another woman breaks down in hysterics; everywhere young Hispanics are crying and comforting each other. Plainclothes detectives make a quick examination of the body, check on the time of pronouncement of death, and begin to ask questions, but the bereaved are too stunned to talk. The rest of the uninvolved people in the lobby stare dumbly, their injuries suddenly paling in light of a death.

12:30 A.M. A black man appears at the admissions desk and says 16 he drank poison by mistake. He is told to have a seat. The ambulance brings in a young white woman, her head wrapped in white gauze. She is wailing terribly. A girl friend stands over her, crying, and a boyfriend clutches the injured woman's hands, saying, "I'm here, don't worry, I'm here." The victim has fallen downstairs at a friend's house. Attendants park her stretcher against the wall to wait for an examination room to clear. There are eight examination rooms and only three doctors. Unless you are truly an emergency, you will wait. One doctor is stitching up the eyebrow of a drunk who's been punched out. The friends of the woman who fell down the stairs glance up at the doctors anxiously, wondering why their friend isn't being treated faster.

1:10 A.M. A car pulls into the bay and a young Hispanic asks if a 17
shooting victim has been brought here. The security guard blurts out, "He's dead." The young man is stunned. He peels his tires leaving the bay.

1:20 A.M. The young woman of the stairs is getting stitches in a 18
small gash over her left eye when the same ambulance driver who brought in the gunshot victim delivers a man who has been stabbed in the back on East 3rd Street. Once again the trauma room goes from 0 to 60 in five seconds. The patient is drunk, which helps him endure the pain of having the catheter inserted through his penis into his bladder. Still he yells, "That hurts like a bastard," then adds sheepishly, "Excuse me, ladies." But he is not prepared for what comes next. An X-ray reveals a collapsed right lung. After just a shot of local anesthetic, the doctor slices open his side and inserts a long plastic tube. Internal bleeding had kept the lung pressed down and prevented it from reinflating. The tube releases the pressure. The ambulance driver says the cops grabbed the guy who ran the eight-inch blade into the victim's back. "That's not the one," says the man. "They got the wrong guy." A nurse reports that there is not much of the victim's type blood available at the hospital. One of the doctors says that's okay, he won't need surgery. Meanwhile blood pours from the man's knife wound and the tube in his side. As the nurses work, they chat about personal matters, yet they respond immediately to orders from either doctor. "How ya doin'?" the doctor asks the patient. "Okay," he says. His blood spatters on the floor.

So it goes into the morning hours. A Valium overdose, a woman 19
who fainted, a man who went through the windshield of his car. More overdoses. More drunks with split eyebrows and chins. The doctors and nurses work without complaint. "This is nothing, about normal, I'd say," concludes the head nurse. "No big deal."

MEANINGS AND VALUES

1. What is the author's point of view? (See "Guide to Terms": *Point of View.*) How is this reflected by the tone? (Guide: *Style/Tone.*)

2. Does Simpson ever slip into sentimentality—a common failing when describing the scenes of death and tragedy? (Guide: *Sentimentality.*) If so, where? If not, how does he avoid it?

3. Cite at least six facts learned from reading this piece that are told, not in general terms but by specific, concrete details—for example, that a high degree of cleanliness is maintained at Bellevue, illustrated by "the spotless white-walled lobby" (Par. 3) and "the trauma room has been cleared and cleaned mercilessly" (Par. 8). What are the advantages of having facts presented in this way?

EXPOSITORY TECHNIQUES

1. Do you consider the writing to be primarily objective or impressionistic? What is the dominant impression, if any?

2. What is the value of using a timed sequence in such a description?

3. Does it seem to you that any of this description is excessive—that is, unnecessary to the task at hand? If so, how might the piece be revised?

4. List, in skeletal form, the facts learned about the subject from reading the two-paragraph introduction. How well does it perform the three basic purposes of an introduction? (Guide: *Introductions.*)

5. What is the significance of the rhetorical question in Paragraph 2? (Guide: *Rhetorical Questions.*) Why is it rhetorical?

6. Is the short closing effective? (Guide: *Closings.*) Why, or why not?

DICTION AND VOCABULARY

1. Cite the clichés in Paragraphs 4, 5, 8, and 14. (Guide: *Clichés.*) What justification, if any, can you offer for their use?

2. Cite the allusion in Paragraph 2, and explain its meaning and source. (Guide: *Figures of Speech.*)

3. Simpson uses some slang and other colloquialisms. Cite as many of these as you can. (Guide: *Colloquial Expressions.*) Is their use justified? Why, or why not?

READ TO WRITE

1. **Collaborating:** Working in a group, discuss a job or an activity (sport, organization) that to an outsider might seem hectic or hazardous. Consider describing it in an essay so that readers can come to understand it more clearly.

2. **Considering Audience:** Descriptive writing can create events for readers who have not experienced them. Much of the power of Simpson's writing comes from the sensational nature of the subjects he describes and his careful selection of detail. If you have witnessed or participated in some other kind of extreme experience, help your readers understand it by describing and explaining it with the same mix of detail and commentary that Simpson offers.

3. **Developing an Essay:** Consider arranging an expository essay of your own by using a time frame as Simpson does. Your purposes for using this device need not be the same, however, and you can use this strategy for expository patterns other than description.

(NOTE: Suggestions for topics requiring development by DESCRIPTION are on pp. 368–369 at the end of this chapter.)

DANIEL THOMAS COOK

Daniel Thomas Cook teaches at Rutgers University/Camden in the Department of Childhood Studies. His research focuses on children as consumers, and he has published widely on this topic. His books include *The Commodification of Childhood: The Children's Clothing Industry and the Rise of the Child Consumer* (2004), *Symbolic Childhood* (2002), and *The Lived Experiences of Public Consumption* (2008). He is also the founder of The Consumer Studies Research Network for the exchange of information about the ways in which commodification and market logic pervade our lives and interactions. His most recent book, co-authored with John Wall, is *Children and Armed Conflict* (2011).

Children of the Brand

Description can play an important role in expository writing even if it takes up only part of an essay. Daniel Thomas Cook uses the pattern to introduce his topic and to provide support for his generalizations in "Children of the Brand." In addition, his descriptions suggest similar experiences that readers can bring with them to the essay to help understand his conclusions and judge their value.

As I sat in the café of a Borders bookstore in Chicago huddled over my laptop and struggling to write about children and commercialism, I was interrupted by an annoying clamor of loud talk, screams and laughter. I looked over and to my horror discovered it was a group of . . . kids! How dare children disrupt my ruminations on childhood! 1

Accepting my fate, I behaved like a social researcher: I observed the scene. "Welcome to Borders Explorers," exclaimed their hostess in a voice intended for seven-year-olds. "We are excited to have you here. We have a lot of fun things planned for your stay with us." On each table stood a cardboard cutout of the "Border Explorer"—a goofy-looking cartoon character sporting winged goggles and an outfit that intimated a '50s version of a "futuristic" space suit. Clearly a boy (explorers are still male, apparently), the character displayed a gigantic "B" on his belt. 2

Daniel Thomas Cook, "Children of the Brand." This article is reprinted with permission from *In These Times* magazine, December 25, 2006, and is available at www.inthesetimes.com

As the students colored in an image of the Borders Explorer   3
character, the staff member explained the morning's plan. Each table would be given several topics, such as "seals" and "mountains,"
to be divided among the students, who would then go to the children's section and find books on the topic.

The children's section was clearly "kid-themed," with an en-   4
tranceway in colorful "kid letters," a soft stars-and-planets carpet,
floor-level displays and a nonlinear arrangement of bookshelves.
The iconography and organization of the section revealed the same
method of age ascendance that I had found in my historical research on the rise of the child consumer. The books and small toys
intended for the youngest children were situated in the back corner; the age ladder progressively moved up toward the entrance
area where items intended for the oldest children (9 and 10-year-
olds) were displayed. Such an arrangement is designed to avoid exposing the older children to undesirable "babyish" things—which
could "pollute" them by association—while giving the younger
children, who must pass through this area, a feeling of maturity,
perhaps even of desire.

Brands and Branding

Delightful and insidious at once, Borders endeavors to brand the ex-   5
perience of reading and exploring ideas. Paradoxically, Borders
strives, on the one hand, to stimulate the children's curiosity and, on
the other, to numb their critical faculties with characters, arts-and-
crafts activities and merchandise placement. They're encouraged to
explore everything about Borders—except of course the company's
brand strategy.

Branding resides, first and foremost, in the realm of design. The   6
quintessential marriage of art and commerce, branding, when it
works best, is inspired by aesthetic sensibility and intuition, and
guided by market research. Brands—their iconography, acoustics,
tastes, physical feelings and smells—coax us to react but not to analyze. Every moment is to be infused not just with "style" or "beauty,"
but with emotional bonding to a corporate entity. At least, this is the
dream of brand managers. Art, in its most general sense, serves as an
ideal vehicle for connecting human emotions to a material object because it strikes us at a pre-analytic level. We experience it and react to
it before we can reflect on it.

However, corporate ingenuity and the colonization of art and de-   7
sign for promotional effect is not the entire story. Children and adults,

after all, want things, buy things and identify with things. We are not completely helpless creatures, but active beings searching for meaning and significance.

Meaning-full Brands

The kids' market has proven lucrative (well into $100 billion an-   8
nually), in large part because both kids and parents derive personal well-being from the goods and images of contemporary
consumer capitalism. When asked why she put "Blue's Clues"
characters on her four-year-old's birthday cake, a 33-year-old
mother told me that a simple "Happy Birthday" was generic and
not special.

Brands—in their artful presence as icons, images and styles—   9
seek to accomplish the somewhat contradictory task of allowing
people to forge personal identities out of mass-produced, mass-
distributed, readily available goods and images. To grasp the
power of brand appeal, one need only think of those who tattoo
the Nike swoosh on their bodies, name their kids after global
brands like Puma or spend hours blogging about their favorite
products.

Retailers, designers, marketers and merchandisers have   10
known for the better part of a century something that social scientists are now just learning. To cultivate a consumer market at a
deep level, beyond simple functional need, consumers must be approached and addressed as having desires and aspirations that
transcend the specific product at hand. For many of us, as brand
managers have discovered, the "need" for belonging, for intimacy,
for respect, for individuality and for being seen as someone worthy in the eyes of others is what drives consumption and brand attachment. Some of the key "needs" of children, who by default are
relatively powerless economically (but quite powerful emotionally), include recognition, aspiration and a sense of ownership
over their world.

Kids aspire to be older than they are at whatever age because,   11
early in life, they recognize their position on the lower rungs of the
social ladder. Hence retailers, like Borders, design spaces that encode
both aspiration to older, more autonomous identities and distance
from younger, undesirable selves. Any savvy package designer
knows that a child's product, if it is to have any chance on the market, must appear to appeal to the age group just older than the intended end-user. Something intended for a six-year-old boy will

probably not do well if a six-year-old is pictured on it—better an eight-year-old.

Making such appeals directly to a child is, historically speaking, 12 new and revolutionary. The recognition and appeasement of the child's point of view in commercial contexts began in the '30s and marked a change not only in marketing and merchandising, but in parent-child relations as well. The child's view now must be acknowledged, addressed and satisfied in many arenas of social life. For a parent to do otherwise is to set themselves up as morally suspect.

The strongest institutional urge to "know" and speak to the 13 child's view comes from the world of marketing, branding and design. It is marketers, often more than parents, who are in tune with kids and their worlds. They visit children's bedrooms and query them about their decorating, clothing and music choices. They attend girls' sleepover parties and convene focus groups to observe "tweens" discussing the benefits of various products. In doing so, marketers venerate children's commercial choices as a democratic exercise. They insist that, in this way, they are "empowering" children.

These children certainly appeared to be "empowered" as they 14 actively delved into the books. But, I had to wonder, if it is the kind of power that will transcend its corporate inspired origins and help the kids navigate contemporary life, or if this "category management" will serve only to infuse brand attachment into the minds of those just learning about the world. It is almost criminal to discourage the next generation from reading and engaging with books. This day, however, was not about books or reading for the young Explorers. It was about engineering the Borders™ experience and cultivating consumers, ultimately re-empowering those who already have the power to produce experiences in addition to products.

MEANINGS AND VALUES

1. What setting does the writer describe in Paragraph 4? State in your own words the interpretation he offers of the setting.

2. What does the writer explain as the goal of branding?

3. According to the essay, what do brands provide for people?

4. In your own words, explain the "contradictory task" (Par. 9) that brands achieve.

Expository Techniques

1. a. What does the writer describe in Paragraph 1? How does this description contrast with the descriptions in the paragraphs that follow?

    b. Which description does the writer wish us to view positively and which negatively?

2. Paragraphs 1–4 provide descriptions the writer echoes elsewhere in the text. Where does he do so?

3. What examples does the writer provide in Paragraphs 8, 9, and 13? Does he provide an appropriate balance of generalization and examples in these paragraphs? (See "Guide to Terms": *Evaluation*.)

4. In general, does the essay provide enough balance between description and interpretation so that the overall aim can be called *expository*?

5. Where, if at all, does the writer argue for a particular point of view on branding and similar activities?

Diction and Vocabulary

1. What does the author mean when he says Borders is "Delightful and insidious at once . . ." (Par. 5)? In what way is this a paradox, as the writer suggests elsewhere in the paragraph? (Guide: *Paradox*.)

2. If you do not know the meaning of some of the following terms, look them up in a dictionary: *ruminations* (Par. 1); *iconography, ascendance* (4); *insidious* (5); *quintessential, acoustics* (6); *lucrative, generic* (8); *aspirations, transcend, default* (10); *appeasement* (12); *query* (13).

Read to Write

1. **Collaborating:** Working in a group, prepare a description of some other setting (such as a store, a camp, a bank, or a library) in which the arrangement of space, the objects, and the colors or sounds conveys messages about what is most important and what is less important.

2. **Considering Audience:** Has this writer done enough to take into account people who might not agree with his conclusions? What other perspectives can you imagine people having on the scenes he describes? Write out these perspectives or objections to his conclusions. Then write out what you think the author might say in response to them.

3. **Developing an Essay:** Go to a store that children are likely to visit. Take notes on the setting and on the behavior of the children you see at the store. Use these notes to create an essay that, like Cook's, draws conclusions from a description.

(NOTE: Suggestions for topics requiring development by DESCRIPTION are on pp. 368–369 at the end of this chapter.)

Issues and Ideas

Expressing Memories

- Donna Tartt, *A Garden Party*
- E. B. White, *Once More to the Lake*

DONNA TARTT

DONNA TARTT was born in 1963 in Greenwood, Mississippi. She attended the University of Mississippi and Bennington College. Her first novel, *The Secret History,* was published in 1992 and her second, *The Little Friend,* in 2003, winning the WH Smith Literary Award and making the list of finalists for the Orange Prize for Fiction. She has also published nonfiction essays and short stories.

A Garden Party

The power of childhood experiences over your values and perspectives as well as the briefness of life (and beauty) are some of the ideas explored through description in this essay, originally published in the *Guardian* (U.K.) newspaper and in *When We Were Young: An Anthology of Childhood.* Instead of describing a single scene in this essay, Tartt presents several detailed examples, each related to the central theme.

Not long ago, my little godson came to stay with me for the first time: his first summer vacation, and also his first trip to the countryside. Though still an infant, not yet able to speak, his eyes were round and ringing with astonishment all weekend long. Everything at my house was shocking and utterly new: velvet sofa cushions, purple flowers, elderly pug (bigger than he was, a frightening but friendly lion). In the photographs from that weekend (swimming pool; absurd yellow kiddie float) his face is alight with violent wonder—an expression very similar to the dazed, incredulous joy that I remember on the faces of some somber little hill-children in India at the watermelon sparklers I gave them. These were a racy treat of my American childhood—clear candies of a biting, gorgeous pink, deliciously sour, smooth and sparkling like jewels when you took them out of your mouth and held them up to the light after you'd sucked on them for a while. But though they are pretty enough to look at, their taste is the real stunner—an overpowering electric tang to make a grown-up's eyes water, but that children adore. As a child I craved these candies, was driven mad by them, saved my nickels and dimes for them—all the children on my school bus did—but there, in the high Himalayas, they were unheard of, pure magic: I might as well have been handing out rubies.

Of course, it's not at all remarkable that children are captivated by new things, because to children everything is new. But what is remarkable is how fleeting impressions of childhood delight can linger and change and vanish and reappear unexpectedly over the years, winking like fireflies throughout the arduous and complicated darks of a lifetime. It has been remarked that a poet's most powerful, passionate metaphors—the ones that recur again and again, the ones that carry the deepest personal meaning—are fixed irrevocably in the mind before the age of 12. So, too, I think, for the rest of us. Someday, long after I am dead, my little godson may be an old man of 80 or 90 sitting in a deck chair in Miami Beach, inexplicably transfixed with a wordless pang of joy at a striped beach ball, at dazzling turquoise pool water—just as someday (I hope) a particular impossible shade of watermelon pink, glimpsed in passing, may perhaps strike an old lady in a Himalayan hill village as the very sweetness of youth.

Quite often there's a pattern to these haphazard and apparently random flashes of childhood memory—a pattern that doesn't emerge or make itself known until later in life. One particularly vivid memory that has stayed with me throughout my life, and will be with me until I die, is of the first time I saw a hummingbird. The incident was inconsequential enough; I was about four years old, and had accompanied my beloved great-grandmother (then in her late 70s) to a garden party given for a distant relative: a young bride-to-be. It was springtime; the azaleas were in spectacular bloom; the astonishing little ruby-throated creature flew right in front of me—down at my eye level, practically in front of my face—and hovered there for some moments before it buzzed forward, then backward, then flew away across the green lawn for ever.

That was all. It can have lasted no more than 10 seconds, yet this tiny incident has left a much more intense and lasting impression on me than many of the great landmark events of my childhood. For many years, I wondered exactly why I remembered this

2

3

4

specific incident so vividly and not some thing else, something more powerful. Why the hummingbird? What was it trying to tell me? Why had this memory, and not some other, struck me so forcefully in the first place; why does it come back to me so persistently, in memory and in dream?

Only now—at mid-life, in my 40th year—am I starting to realise what the hummingbird means, and why, at unexpected moments, it returns to me still. It is a premonition of heaven, and of death. My great-grandmother (who was leaning beside me, holding my hand, as the hummingbird paused in mid-air before me) did not have long to live. Nor did the bride herself—lovely laughing Ginger, who died young, of cancer. I couldn't have understood it then, and scarcely understand it now, but my entire subsequent impressions of death, and beauty, and mutability, and the brevity of life itself are somehow crystallised perfectly in those few moments, when the tiny iridescent hummingbird darted before my face, hovered briefly, then flew away. All I know of the sublime is somehow encapsulated and encoded in that instant: flowers everywhere, white-gloved ladies in pastel dresses. Then beautiful Ginger, in an apple-green dress, kneeling to say hello.

5

MEANINGS AND VALUES

1. Where in the essay does the writer announce the central theme (thesis)? (See "Guide to Terms": *Thesis.*) State the central theme in your own words.

2. Why should this essay be regarded as expository in purpose rather than simply a vivid re-creation of experiences? (Guide: *Purpose.*)

3. If you have read E. B. White's essay, "Once More to the Lake" (beginning on p. 359), compare Tartt's views on death, beauty, and life's briefness with White's.

EXPOSITORY TECHNIQUES

1. What "fleeting impressions of childhood delight" does the writer present as examples in this essay?

2. Where does the writer locate the statement of the essay's central theme (thesis) in relationship to the two main examples? Why do you think she chose this location?

3. Can the watermelon candy and the hummingbird be considered symbols? (Guide: *Symbol.*) If so, what does each symbolize?

DICTION AND VOCABULARY

1. Identify the words and phrases the writer uses in Paragraph 1 to help readers imagine the taste and appearance of the watermelon candy. How effective are her choices in conveying the candy's qualities? (Guide: *Diction.*)

2. What words does the writer use in Paragraph 5 to emphasize the briefness and fragility of life and beauty? (Guide: *Diction.*)

3. If you do not know the meaning of some of the following words, look them up in the dictionary: *pug, incredulous, somber* (Par. 1); *captivated, arduous, irrevocably, inexplicably, transfixed* (2); *haphazard, inconsequential* (3); *premonition, subsequent, mutability, brevity, iridescent, sublime, encapsulated* (5).

READ TO WRITE

1. **Collaborating:** Working in a group, use the following questions and make up others like them in order to examine the relationship among places, childhood experiences, and values, and develop a list of possible topics for writing. Do many people today have a chance to return to the homes or neighborhoods in which they grew up, which helped shape their values and personalities? Are experiences with food, weather, natural settings, animals, or social events likely to be central to people's values? How are the childhood memories of people who grew up in settings unlike those described by Tartt likely to differ? Are their values likely to differ also?

2. **Considering Audience:** Consider how readers who grew up in settings very different from those described by Tartt likely to respond to her essay. Write an essay describing the likely reactions of such readers, focusing especially on passages they might not fully appreciate or to which they might respond negatively.

3. **Developing an Essay:** Prepare an essay describing one or more experiences you had as a child, paying particular attention to the physical and sensory details. Follow Tartt's lead and deal with questions of change, loss, growth, continuity, death, and beauty, offering your insights, of course, and not Tartt's.

(NOTE: Suggestions for topics requiring development by DESCRIPTION are on pp. 368–369 at the end of this chapter.)

E. B. WHITE

E. B. WHITE, distinguished essayist, was born in Mount Vernon, New York, in 1899 and died in 1985 in North Brooklin, Maine. A graduate of Cornell University, White worked as a reporter and advertising copywriter, and in 1926 he joined the staff of the *New Yorker* magazine. After 1937 he did most of his writing at his farm in Maine, for many years contributing a regular column, "One Man's Meat," to *Harper's* magazine and freelance editorials for the "Notes and Comments" column of the *New Yorker.* White also wrote children's books, two volumes of verse, and, with James Thurber, *Is Sex Necessary?* (1929). With his wife, Katherine White, he compiled *A Subtreasury of American Humor* (1941). Collections of his own essays include *One Man's Meat* (1942), *The Second Tree from the Corner* (1953), *The Points of My Compass* (1962), and *Essays of E. B. White* (1977). In 1959 he revised and enlarged William Strunk's *The Elements of Style,* a textbook still widely used in college classrooms. White received many honors and writing awards for his crisp, highly individual style and his sturdy independence of thought.

Once More to the Lake

In this essay White relies primarily on description to convey his sense of the passage of time and the power of memory. The vivid scenes and the clear yet expressive prose in this essay are characteristic of his writing.

August 1941

One summer, along about 1904, my father rented a camp on a   1
lake in Maine and took us all there for the month of August. We all got ringworm from some kittens and had to rub Pond's Extract on our arms and legs night and morning, and my father rolled over in a canoe with all his clothes on; but outside of that the vacation was a success and from then on none of us ever thought there was any place in the world like that lake in Maine. We returned summer after summer—always on August 1 for one month. I have since become a salt-water man, but sometimes in summer there are days when the restlessness of the tides and the fearful cold of the sea water and the incessant wind that blows across the afternoon and into the evening make me wish for the placidity of a lake in the woods. A few weeks ago this feeling got so strong I bought myself a couple of bass hooks and a spinner and returned to the lake where we used to go, for a week's fishing and to revisit old haunts.

I took along my son, who had never had any fresh water up his   2
nose and who had seen lily pads only from train windows. On the
journey over to the lake I began to wonder what it would be like.
I wondered how time would have marred this unique, this holy
spot—the coves and streams, the hills that the sun set behind, the
camps and the paths behind the camps. I was sure that the tarred
road would have found it out, and I wondered in what other ways
it would be desolated. It is strange how much you can remember
about places like that once you allow your mind to return into the
grooves that lead back. You remember one thing, and that suddenly
reminds you of another thing. I guess I remembered clearest of all
the early mornings, when the lake was cool and motionless, remembered how the bedroom smelled of the lumber it was made of and of
the wet woods whose scent entered through the screen. The parti-
tions in the camp were thin and did not extend clear to the top of the
rooms, and as I was always the first up I would dress softly so as not
to wake the others, and sneak out into the sweet outdoors and start
out in the canoe, keeping close along the shore in the long shadows
of the pines. I remembered being very careful never to rub my pad-
dle against the gunwale for fear of disturbing the stillness of the
cathedral.

The lake had never been what you would call a wild lake. There   3
were cottages sprinkled around the shores, and it was in farming
country although the shores of the lake were quite heavily wooded.
Some of the cottages were owned by nearby farmers, and you would
live at the shore and eat your meals at the farmhouse. That's what
our family did. But although it wasn't wild, it was a fairly large and
undisturbed lake and there were places in it that, to a child at least,
seemed infinitely remote and primeval.

I was right about the tar: it led to within half a mile of the shore.   4
But when I got back there, with my boy, and we settled into a camp
near a farmhouse and into the kind of summertime I had known, I
could tell that it was going to be pretty much the same as it had been
before—I knew it, lying in bed the first morning, smelling the bedroom and hearing the boy sneak quietly out and go off along the
shore in a boat. I began to sustain the illusion that he was I, and
therefore, by simple transposition, that I was my father. This sensation persisted, kept cropping up all the time we were there. It was
not an entirely new feeling, but in this setting it grew much stronger.
I seemed to be living a dual existence. I would be in the middle of
some simple act, I would be picking up a bait box or laying down a
table fork, or I would be saying something, and suddenly it would

be not I but my father who was saying the words or making the gesture. It gave me a creepy sensation.

We went fishing the first morning. I felt the same damp moss covering the worms in the bait can, and saw the dragonfly alight on the tip of my rod as it hovered a few inches from the surface of the water. It was the arrival of this fly that convinced me beyond any doubt that everything was as it always had been, that the years were a mirage and that there had been no years. The small waves were the same, chucking the rowboat under the chin as we fished at anchor, and the boat was the same boat, the same color green and the ribs broken in the same places, and under the floorboards the same fresh-water leavings and débris—the dead helgramite, the wisps of moss, the rusty discarded fishhook, the dried blood from yesterday's catch. We stared silently at the tips of our rods, at the dragonflies that came and went. I lowered the tip of mine into the water, tentatively, pensively dislodging the fly, which darted two feet away, poised, darted two feet back, and came to rest again a little farther up the rod. There had been no years between the ducking of this dragonfly and the other one—the one that was part of memory. I looked at the boy, who was silently watching his fly, and it was my hands that held his rod, my eyes watching. I felt dizzy and didn't know which rod I was at the end of.

We caught two bass, hauling them in briskly as though they were mackerel, pulling them over the side of the boat in a businesslike manner without any landing net, and stunning them with a blow on the back of the head. When we got back for a swim before lunch, the lake was exactly where we had left it, the same number of inches from the dock, and there was only the merest suggestion of a breeze. This seemed an utterly enchanted sea, this lake you could leave to its own devices for a few hours and come-back to, and find that it had not stirred, this constant and trustworthy body of water. In the shallows, the dark, water-soaked sticks and twigs, smooth and old, were undulating in clusters on the bottom against the clean ribbed sand, and the track of the mussel was plain. A school of minnows swam by, each minnow with its small individual shadow, doubling the attendance, so clear and sharp in the sunlight. Some of the other campers were in swimming, along the shore, one of them with a cake of soap, and the water felt thin and clear and unsubstantial. Over the years there had been this person with the cake of soap, this cultist, and here he was. There had been no years.

Up to the farmhouse to dinner through the teeming, dusty field, the road under our sneakers was only a two-track road. The middle

5

6

7

track was missing, the one with the marks of the hooves and the splotches of dried, flaky manure. There had always been three tracks to choose from in choosing which track to walk in; now the choice was narrowed down to two. For a moment I missed terribly the middle alternative. But the way led past the tennis court, and something about the way it lay there in the sun reassured me; the tape had loosened along the backline, the alleys were green with plantains and other weeds, and the net (installed in June and removed in September) sagged in the dry noon, and the whole place steamed with midday heat and hunger and emptiness. There was a choice of pie for dessert, and one was blueberry and one was apple, and the waitresses were the same country girls, there having been no passage of time, only the illusion of it as in a dropped curtain—the waitresses were still fifteen; their hair had been washed, that was the only difference—they had been to the movies and seen the pretty girls with the clean hair.

Summertime, oh, summertime, pattern of life indelible, the fade-proof lake, the woods unshatterable, the pasture with the sweetfern and the juniper forever and ever, summer without end; this was the background, and the life along the shore was the design, their tiny docks with the flagpole and the American flag floating against the white clouds in the blue sky, the little paths over the roots of the trees leading from camp to camp and the paths leading back to the outhouses and the can of lime for sprinkling, and at the souvenir counters at the store the miniature birch-bark canoes and the postcards that showed things looking a little better than they looked. This was the American family at play, escaping the city heat, wondering whether the newcomers in the camp at the head of the cove were "common" or "nice," wondering whether it was true that the people who drove up for Sunday dinner at the farmhouse were turned away because there wasn't enough chicken.   8

It seemed to me, as I kept remembering all this, that those times   9
and those summers had been infinitely precious and worth saving. There had been jollity and peace and goodness. The arriving (at the beginning of August) had been so big a business in itself, at the railway station the farm wagon drawn up, the first smell of the pine-laden air, the first glimpse of the smiling farmer, and the great importance of the trunks and your father's enormous authority in such matters, and the feel of the wagon under you for the long ten-mile haul, and at the top of the last long hill catching the first view of the lake after eleven months of not seeing this cherished body of water. The shouts and cries of the other campers when they saw

you, and the trunks to be unpacked, to give up their rich burden. (Arriving was less exciting nowadays, when you sneaked up in your car and parked it under a tree near the camp and took out the bags and in five minutes it was all over, no fuss, no loud wonderful fuss about trunks.)

Peace and goodness and jollity. The only thing that was wrong   10 now, really, was the sound of the place, an unfamiliar nervous sound of the outboard motors. This was the note that jarred, the one thing that would sometimes break the illusion and set the years moving. In those other summertimes all motors were inboard; and when they were at a little distance, the noise they made was a sedative, an ingredient of summer sleep. They were one-cylinder and two-cylinder engines, and some were make-and-break and some were jump-spark, but they all made a sleepy sound across the lake. The one-lungers throbbed and fluttered, and the twin-cylinder ones purred and purred, and that was a quiet sound, too. But now the campers all had outboards. In the daytime, in the hot mornings, these motors made a petulant, irritable sound; at night, in the still evening when the afterglow lit the water, they whined about one's ears like mosquitoes. My boy loved our rented outboard, and his great desire was to achieve single-handed mastery over it, and authority, and he soon learned the trick of choking it a little (but not too much), and the adjustment of the needle valve. Watching him I would remember the things you could do with the old one-cylinder engine with the heavy flywheel, how you could have it eating out of your hand if you got really close to it spiritually. Motorboats in those days didn't have clutches, and you would make a landing by shutting off the motor at the proper time and coasting in with a dead rudder. But there was a way of reversing them, if you learned the trick, by cutting the switch and putting it on again exactly on the final dying revolution of the flywheel, so that it would kick back against compression and begin reversing. Approaching a dock in a strong following breeze, it was difficult to slow up sufficiently by the ordinary coasting method, and if a boy felt he had complete mastery over his motor, he was tempted to keep it running beyond its time and then reverse it a few feet from the dock. It took a cool nerve, because if you threw the switch a twentieth of a second too soon you would catch the flywheel when it still had speed enough to go up past center, and the boat would leap ahead, charging bull-fashion at the dock.

We had a good week at the camp. The bass were biting well and   11 the sun shone endlessly, day after day. We would be tired at night and lie down in the accumulated heat of the little bedrooms after the long hot day and the breeze would stir almost imperceptibly out-side and the smell of the swamp drift in through the rusty screens. Sleep would come easily and in the morning the red squirrel would be on the roof, tapping out his gay routine. I kept remembering every-thing, lying in bed in the mornings—the small steamboat that had a long rounded stern like the lip of a Ubangi, and how quietly she ran on the moonlight sails, when the older boys played their mandolins and the girls sang and we ate doughnuts dipped in sugar, and how sweet the music was on the water in the shining night, and what it had felt like to think about girls then. After breakfast we would go up to the store and the things were in the same place—the minnows in a bottle, the plugs and spinners disarranged and pawed over by the youngsters from the boys' camp, the Fig Newtons and the Bee-man's gum. Outside, the road was tarred and cars stood in front of the store. Inside, all was just as it had always been, except there was more Coca-Cola and not so much Moxie and root beer and birch beer and sarsaparilla. We would walk out with the bottle of pop apiece and sometimes the pop would backfire up our noses and hurt. We explored the streams, quietly, where the turtles slid off the sunny logs and dug their way into the soft bottom; and we lay on the town wharf and fed worms to the tame bass. Everywhere we went I had trouble making out which was I, the one walking at my side, the one walking in my pants.

One afternoon while we were there at that lake a thunderstorm   12
came up. It was like the revival of an old melodrama that I had seen long ago with childish awe. The second-act climax of the drama of the electrical disturbance over a lake in America had not changed in any important respect. This was the big scene, still the big scene. The whole thing was so familiar, the first feeling of oppression and heat and a general air around camp of not wanting to go very far away. In mid-afternoon (it was all the same) a curious darkening of the sky, and a lull in everything that had made life tick; and then the way the boats suddenly swung the other way at their moorings with the com-ing of a breeze out of the new quarter, and the premonitory rumble. Then the kettle drum, then the snare, then the bass drum and cym-bals, then crackling light against the dark, and the gods grinning and licking their chops in the hills. Afterward the calm, the rain steadily rustling in the calm lake, the return of light and hope and spirits, and the campers running out in joy and relief to go swimming in the rain, their bright cries perpetuating the deathless joke about how they were getting simply drenched, and the children screaming with delight at

the new sensation of bathing in the rain, and the joke about getting drenched linking the generations in a strong indestructible chain. And the comedian who waded in carrying an umbrella.

When the others went swimming, my son said he was going in, too. He pulled his dripping trunks from the line where they had hung all through the shower and wrung them out. Languidly, and with no thought of going in, I watched him, his hard little body, skinny and bare, saw him wince slightly as he pulled up around his vitals the small, soggy, icy garment. As he buckled the swollen belt, suddenly my groin felt the chill of death.   13

MEANINGS AND VALUES

1. In what ways have the lake and its surroundings remained the same since White's boyhood? In what ways have they changed? Be specific.

2. Can the lake be considered a personal symbol for White? (See "Guide to Terms": *Symbol.*) If so, what does it symbolize?

3. At one point in the essay, White says, "I seemed to be living a dual existence" (Par. 4). What is the meaning of this statement? How does this "dual existence" affect his point of view in the essay? (Guide: *Point of View.*) Is the dual existence emphasized more in the first half of the essay or the second half? Why?

4. Where in the essay does White link differences between the lake now and in his youth with a difference between his son's outlooks and his own? Is this distance between father and son caused by changes in the world around them or merely the passage of time? Explain.

5. After spending a day on the lake, White remarks, "There had been no years" (Par. 6). What other direct or indirect comments does he make about time and change? Be specific.

6. What is the tone of the essay? (Guide: *Style/Tone.*) Does the tone change or remain the same throughout the essay?

7. What is meant by the closing phrase of the essay, "suddenly my groin felt the chill of death" (Par. 13)? Is this an appropriate way to end the essay? Why, or why not?

EXPOSITORY TECHNIQUES

1. In the first part of the essay, White focuses on the unchanged aspects of the lake; in the second part, he begins acknowledging the passage of time. Where does this shift in attitude take place? What strategies, including transitional devices, does White use to signal to the reader the shift in attitude? Be specific.

2.   How does White use the discussion of outboard motors and inboard motors (Par. 10) to summarize the differences between life at the lake in his youth and at the time of his return with his son?

3.   Many of the descriptive passages in this essay convey a dominant impression, usually an emotion or mood. Discuss how the author's choice of details and the author's comments suggest that the impressions are more a reflection of the observer's perspective than an objective description of the lake. (Guide: *Syntax; Diction.*)

4.   In many places the author combines description and comparison. Select a passage from the essay and discuss in detail how he combines the patterns. In what ways is the combination of description and comparison appropriate to the theme and the point of view of the essay?

DICTION AND VOCABULARY

1.   How much do the connotations of the words used in Paragraph 8 contribute to the dominant impression the author is trying to create? (Guide: *Connotation/Denotation.*) In Paragraph 10? What do these connotations suggest about the relation of person to place? Of observer to subject of observation?

2.   Is the diction in this passage sentimental: "Summertime, oh, summertime, pattern of life indelible, the fade-proof lake, the woods unshatterable, the pasture with the sweetfern and the juniper forever and ever, summer without end. . . ." (Par. 8)? (Guide: *Sentimentality.*) If so, why would the author choose to use this style in the passage? Does the passage contain an allusion? If so, what is alluded to and why? (Guide: *Figures of Speech.*)

3.   In what sense can a tennis court steam "with midday heat and hunger and emptiness" (Par. 7)?

4.   What kind of paradox is presented in this passage: "the waitresses were the same country girls, there having been no passage of time, only the illusion of it as in a dropped curtain—the waitresses were still fifteen; their hair had been washed, that was the only difference—they had been to the movies and seen the pretty girls with the clean hair" (Par. 7)? (Guide: *Paradox.*)

5.   Study the author's uses of the following words, consulting the dictionary as needed: *incessant, placidity* (Par. 1); *gunwale* (2); *primeval* (3); *transposition* (4); *helgramite, pensively* (5); *petulant* (10); *premonitory* (12); *languidly* (13).

READ TO WRITE

1.   **Collaborating:** Working with a group, make a list of your memorable vacations and holidays, then choose three and develop for each a tentative thesis statement that sums up the meaning of the event.

2. **Considering Audience:** In his descriptions, White creates symbols to convey his ideas about the passing of time. How else might readers respond to the incidents White describes? To what extent might responses be shaped by differing religious, social, economic, or cultural backgrounds? Prepare a short essay considering the possible range of reactions.

3. **Developing an Essay:** Drawing on the strategies White employs in "Once More to the Lake," choose some place you remember from your childhood and have seen recently, and write a description of it comparing its present appearance with your memories of it. As you write, take into account the relationships of place and person, permanence and change, and the effect of experience on perception.

(NOTE: Suggestions for topics requiring development by DESCRIPTION follow.)

Writing Suggestions for Chapter 10

DESCRIPTION

1. Primarily by way of impressionistic description that focuses on a single dominant impression, show and explain the mood or atmosphere of one of the following:

   a. A country fair

   b. A ball game

   c. A rodeo

   d. A wedding

   e. A funeral

   f. A busy store

   g. A ghost town

   h. A cave

   i. A beach in summer (or winter)

   j. An antique shop

   k. A party

   l. A family dinner

   m. A traffic jam

   n. A medical or dental waiting room

   o. An airport (or a bus depot)

   p. An automobile race (or a horse race)

   q. A home during one of its rush hours

   r. The last night of holiday shopping

   s. A natural scene at a certain time of day

   t. The campus at examination time

   u. A certain person at a time of great emotion—for example, joy, anger, or grief

2. Using objective description as your basic pattern, explain the functional qualities or the significance of one of the following:

   a. A house for sale

   b. A public building

   c. A dairy barn

   d. An ideal workshop (or hobby room)

e. An ideal garage

f. A fast-food restaurant

g. The layout of a town (or airport)

h. The layout of a farm

i. A certain type of boat

j. A sports complex

SETTINGS

Some settings give us insights into human behavior. Choose a kind of behavior from the list below and create a description of a setting and any activity within it that offers insights into the behavior.

1. How children develop values
2. How family conflicts develop
3. How we learn compassion
4. How we develop ways to reduce conflict
5. How we learn to recognize beauty
6. How we develop an appreciation for hard work
7. How we come to recognize personality in animals
8. How people come to understand the effects of their anger
9. How films, paintings, or music affect people in different ways
10. How sporting events draw varied reactions from people

COLLABORATIVE EXERCISES

1. Have each member of your team brainstorm a list of words that describe the mood or atmosphere he or she feels when attending any one of the events listed in 1a–c. From your individual lists, look for similar experiences and moods. Collaboratively write an essay based on one of those events and the team similarities.

2. Have each member of the group describe a designated building on campus. Compare and contrast your descriptions.

3. Consider an ideal gymnasium or dormitory. Have each student in the group research this building by talking to other students on campus. Share your results and write a collaborative essay incorporating each member's research.

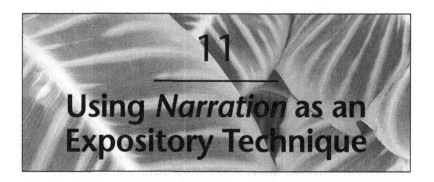

11

Using *Narration* as an Expository Technique

When is narration a pattern of exposition rather than a story told for its own purposes? The answer: when it serves to explain a subject, present conclusions, or support an interpretation or a thesis. For example, a writer who wishes to explain the role of risk-taking individuals (rather than corporations) in developing new ideas and products might tell the story of an entrepreneur who perfected the frozen French fry in the early 1950s only to discover that there was little demand for his product. The story would emphasize his perseverance in struggling to develop a market for the product—a perseverance that paid off for all concerned a decade later when the rapidly growing fast-food industry discovered the usefulness of frozen fries for ready-in-a-minute menus.

Whether you use narration as the pattern for an entire essay or for support and explanation within an essay, your readers will expect you to do certain things. They will expect your narrative to help them understand *what happened*, including the *who, where, what*, and *to whom* of events. They will expect the narrative to *recreate* events, showing (through concrete detail or the actual words of participants) rather than merely telling what happened (through summary). Finally, your readers will expect your narrative to help them understand the *significance* of the events. They will look for the point you are making, for what you have to say about the events, or for the way the events support your thesis.

In a book explaining the extraordinary character and physical courage of early Antarctic explorers, the writer Edwin Mickleburgh offers the following narrative to support his thesis about the explorer Ernest Shackleton's abilities as a leader and about the courage of his crew.

> For anyone who has looked up from the sullen South Georgia shore [an island near Antarctica] towards the soaring, razor-edged peaks and the terrible chaos of glaciers topped by swirling clouds and scoured by mighty winds, the knowledge of the crossing made by these three men adds a wider dimension to an already awe-inspiring sight. How they did it, God only knows, but they crossed the island in thirty-six hours. They were fortunate that the weather held, although many times great banks of fog rolled in from the open sea, creeping toward them over the snow and threatening to obscure their way. Confronted by precipices of ice and walls of rock they had often to retrace their steps, adding many miles to the journey. They walked almost without rest. At one point they sat down in an icy gully, the wind blowing the drift around them, and so tired were they that Worseley and Crean fell asleep immediately. Shackleton, barely able to keep himself awake, realized that to fall asleep under such conditions would prove fatal. After five minutes he woke the other two, saying that they had slept for half an hour.

Introduces narrative and its relation to writer's main point

Narrative

> —Edwin Mickleburgh,
> *Beyond the Frozen Sea: Visions of Antarctica*

WHY USE NARRATION?

Perhaps the most familiar form of expository narrative is the personal narrative, based on personal experience or observation, that offers insights into events or conclusions about relationships and the importance of certain kinds of experience. These include memoirs focusing on the author's personal and intellectual development, on an unusual and significant childhood event, or on other experiences. They include autobiographies of media stars, politicians, and other well-known people, especially those that shed light on the fields in which they have worked or on the important events they have witnessed. And they include personal narratives embedded in other kinds of works in order to give the works a sense of authenticity.

Another use of narrative is to present a profile on an unfamiliar or unusual activity or the people involved in it. Typically, such a narrative begins by presenting an interesting person in action (a day in the life of a computer game creator, for example) or by focusing on an activity (workers changing light bulbs on the spire of the Empire State Building; divers searching in deep water for wreckage from an airplane crash). As a way of creating drama and interest, such narratives frequently reveal surprising tensions or contradictions, such as the quiet home life and personal kindness of an offshore boat racer also known for his fearlessness, abrasiveness, spectacular crashes, and narrow escapes from death.

A narrative can also provide a framework for commentary and analysis, with passages of narrative interspersed with discussions of the significance and implications of the events. Or narratives can add convincing detail or emotional force to explanations built around some other expository pattern, such as comparison (Chapter 5), cause-and-effect (Chapter 8), or definition (Chapter 9).

CHOOSING A STRATEGY

A narrative is a chronological account of events. You do not always have to present the events in chronological order or give them all equal emphasis. When you are creating an event for expository purposes, begin your planning process with questions like these:

- What events are most important to my purpose for writing?
- What ideas and emotions surrounding the events are worth sharing with my readers?
- What point do I want to make with this narrative?

Your answers to questions like these should help you limit the time frame of your narrative and focus on the most important events of the story. Many writers are gripped by a compulsion to get all the details of a story down—important and unimportant. Radical surgery often helps. Instead of covering a whole week or day, consider focusing on the single most important incident—the four or five minutes when all the forces came together—and summarizing the rest.

Remember that you can arrange the events to suit your purpose(s). In basic form, a narrative sets the scene; introduces characters; presents, in chronological order, episodes that introduce a conflict or prepare for the central event; then, finally, explores in detail the most important incident in which the conflict is resolved or the writer's outlook is made clear. Yet the chronological approach can make it hard to emphasize the most important element. You may instead want to start in the middle of things, perhaps at the climactic episode, and fill in prior events through flashbacks. Or you might stop in the middle of events to provide important background information or comment on the characters and their actions.

And you need to choose whether to provide an explicit thesis statement to organize your narrative and direct commentary on the events, or to let the events speak for themselves, assuming that their relationship to your main point will be sufficiently clear to readers.

DEVELOPING A NARRATIVE

As you draft and revise a narrative, pay attention to the following concerns that can contribute to the success (or failure) of your efforts.

- **Selection of Details.** You will probably have many more details you might include in a narrative than you need. Keep in mind that too many details can overwhelm readers, making them lose sight about the point the narrative is making or the explanation it is offering. Focused, unified writing makes use only of those details that are most relevant to the writer's purpose and desired effect. Whenever possible, try to include concrete, specific details that make the narrative vivid and believable and that will be likely to hold your readers' interest.
- **Time Order.** You can employ straight chronology, relating events as they happened, or the flashback method, leaving the sequence temporarily in order to go back and relate some now-significant happening of a time prior to the main action. If you use flashback, do so deliberately, not merely because you neglected to mention the episode earlier.
- **Transitions.** Watch out for overly simple and repetitive transitions between events in the narrative: "And then we. . . . And then she. . . . And then we . . ." As you revise, make a conscious effort to create variety in transitions: "next," "following," "subsequently," "as a consequence," "reacting to," "later," "meanwhile," "at the same time," "concurrently," and the like.
- **Point of View.** Decide whether you want to tell the story from the point of view of a participant, such as yourself or a character, or from the overall perspective of a spectator. The vividness and immediacy possible from a participant's point of view can make the narrative more dramatic, but the spectator's point of view can allow for an easier transition from narrative to commentary and may be especially useful in expository writing. Whichever point of view you choose, keep it consistent throughout the narrative.
- **Dialogue.** Remember that quoting the words of participants can help make narrative more convincing and dialogue, which can reveal conflicting perspectives among the participants, can also be a springboard to your commentary on the meaning of the events.

Student Essay

One important use of narrative in expository writing is to explore values and the ways they change. In the following essay, Hrishikesh Unni uses flashback and a dream sequence to explain a set of personal values—love of ivory and of ivory carvings—that may be unfamiliar to many of his readers. He then returns to the main narrative of his encounter with a herd of elephants in Zambia and uses it to explain his change in attitude toward ivory collecting.

Elephants, Ivory, and an Indelible Experience
by Hrishikesh Unni

The roar of the engine increased to a crescendo as the driver revved the engine of the open van. This sound broke the monotonous atmosphere of the dry and deserted African grassland of the Luangwa Valley in Zambia and made me shift in my rear seat. I had been sitting there for at least three hours since noon and had not seen any game, apart from the impala and zebra that intermittently spotted the grasslands. These creatures are a common sight in all national parks in Zambia, including the Luangwa. The drought had taken its toll. What was once a land filled with green vegetation was turned into a brown and heavily scorched area by the menacing October sun that was callously beating down on my back. I clutched my Canon camera even more firmly and could feel the heat radiating from the surface of its black case.

"You sure are unlucky, aren't you, Hrishi? No elephants yet!" said Musa, the guide, who was the only other person in the spacious van besides Banda.

Banda was a local driver who could only speak the local language, Nyanga. I merely nodded to this statement, admitting my disappointment. I had come all the way from Ndola (another town in Zambia) to see the well-known elephants of the Luangwa National Park. I had given up hope because it was the third and final day of my visit, and I had not seen any so far. What irritated me was the fact that I had lost a long-awaited opportunity to see these beasts. To overcome my disappointment, I looked at the metallic body of the van that

Opening incident—starts in the middle of events

Unusual, exotic—gets readers' attention

Appeals to senses

Uses quotation

Fills in background of events

was painted white. It blazed in the sun and blinded my
eyes. It reminded me of something I had once loved
and treasured: ivory.

Uses key word
to set off
flashbacks

I had an affinity for ivory. I loved its color, texture, and
appearance. My positive feelings for this substance had
begun after I received my first ivory carving for my ninth
birthday from a Zambian friend. It was a superb carving
of a baby elephant, and I instantly liked it. I would gaze
at it, admiring its dominant white color and its smooth
texture. Also, its different shades of light brown never
seemed to bore me. Since receiving that gift, I had
bought every ivory item I could get my hands on and
had a magnificent collection that I kept in my room.

Introduces his
values

Flashbacks—
source of
values

My eyes could no longer take the glare and in an attempt to reduce the strain, I allowed my eyelids to drop
over them. I realized how tired I was when I closed my
eyes. Every muscle in my body seemed to be screaming
in desperation, ordering my brain to sleep. I felt sleep
gradually overtake me like an ivy conquering an old dilapidated castle. Soon I was fast asleep and dreaming of
the time. . . .

Back to main
narrative

Dream event

I entered my room and switched on my titanium-
white tube light. I stared in awe as the light fell on my
ivory collection, enhancing its already immaculate
white coating. The furniture in my room consisted of a
bed, a table, a chair, and a couple of shelves that were
attached to the wall. It was decorated with my extrava-
gant ivory collection. I stood at the doorway and began surveying the room, casting my eyes on each and
every piece of ivory. I admired and absorbed every detail of the carvings and was aware of the hours of work
involved in creating a single delicate carving from a
long curved elephant tusk. The dexterity and skill the
African craftsmen possessed amazed me, and I never
got tired of looking at my collection. I saw a variety of
things: old traditional men, dogs, a range of birds,
daggers, kudu, impala, elephants, rhino, leopards,
cheetahs—all in ivory. My eyes finally came to rest on
the carving I admired the most—an elephant bull,

which I had named Tusker Bull. It was the largest piece I had. Its place on the highest shelf and its majestic posture gave it an authority over the other animals in my collection. Its ominous, evil eyes and its cocked ears portrayed tyranny. I had a sudden urge to look into its lifeless eye. I daringly did this and saw a look I had never seen before. It was one of anger and rage. This look sent a chill down my spine as I wondered if my imagination was mocking me. The look in its eye seemed to be saying. . . .

Explains values; love of ivory helps readers understand appeal of art that may be unfamiliar to them

"Wake up, Hrishi, elephants!" shouted the guide.

I awoke with a jump, expecting to see my room, but the heat waves of the national park that enveloped me made me aware that I was a long way away from there. The painful process of adjusting to the amber sunlight took quite a while. The sky was an orange-yellow, and the ground seemed to have darkened to a beige color. It was nearly dusk, and I realized I had been sleeping for at least two hours. Musa repeated the word "elephant," the word I longed to hear. I knew he had spotted a couple of them.

Brief transition paragraph

Back to main narrative

"Where?" I asked anxiously.

He pointed in between two brown-colored thickets and said, "By that dry waterhole."

He was right, and I could see the posterior of two African elephants. I could not see the entire waterhole because the dry trees and scrub that had adapted to drought conditions partially obliterated our view. I was filled with excitement as images of elephants and my ivory collection flashed in my mind. I quickly set my camera to "operate" as the driver steered the van toward the elephants. We took an unorthodox and meandering path toward the elephants. As the van cut through the dry scrub, I could hear the twigs being crushed by its enormous tires and the dry grass, grazing and caressing the sides of the van. We finally reached the brown-colored thicket, and the driver deftly steered around it enabling us to see the entire expanse of the waterhole that merely had shallow puddles of water.

What we saw shocked us. There were not two elephants; there were two thousand of them! From where
we were before, we could only get a glimpse of this
enormous herd.

"What a sight! Ten years in this business, and I have
not seen this many at once!" exclaimed Musa.

"Hitut, hitut!" said Banda, in awe.

Everywhere I looked, I only saw elephants. They completely superimposed the entire landscape, which now
looked like a dark gray Persian carpet. The faint sunlight
that reflected off the elephants transformed the color of
their bodies to a stone-gray. It was an absolutely fantastic
and awesome sight! I began surveying them in the manner I surveyed my ivory collection in my dream, slowly
and meticulously, but this time I wasn't looking at elephant ivory carvings but at real elephants. My eyes
swept across the herd, and I was amazed at the unique
behavior of each individual elephant I saw. There were
numerous bulls with gigantic tusks. Their white tusks
contrasted with their black bodies and made me think
of ivory. From our position the tusks looked like curved
toothpicks. The females were nurturing and tending to
their playful calves. The elephants were of different
sizes, but all the bulls were above eleven feet. Their
postures conveyed a strong sense of magnanimity as
they marched slowly in unison, every step serving a purpose. I admired the ease with which they moved, taking
all the time in the world. They deliberately swung their
trunks from side to side, like pendulums, and their tails
moved naturally to their rhythmic walk. The mild deep
grunts of the bulls were amplified by the wind that blew
toward us. This natural sound enabled them to coax the
members of the herd that were extremely slow. The
pitch of this sound was lower than the sound the baby
elephants made, which was like notes played on a trum-
pet that was not in tune. The calves pranced around
playfully and used their trunks to mock and tease each
other, not aware of their vulnerability to predators. A
huge bull raised its head and arched its trunk in a form

*Experience of
seeing
elephants
more
dramatic and
moving than
their
representa-
tions in ivory*

*Concrete
details appeal
to senses
throughout
narrative*

of imperious salute. He was definitely the largest and seemed to be leading the herd, ready to admonish the herd of any potential danger. I wanted a photo of this elephant.

"Let's get closer, I want a photo of that bull," I said, pointing to the conspicuous animal.

Dialogue

"I think we'll be asking for trouble if we get any closer. This herd is definitely overprotective because there are so many young," replied Musa.

"Oh, come on, this is the only opportunity we've had of seeing so many elephants. I mean, this is a rare sight, and we haven't seen any all day. I want that bull. We must get closer," I persisted.

Musa and Banda conversed in the local language about my idea. I could tell Banda was not pleased, but finally he reluctantly nodded his head in apparent consent.

"Okay, but Banda says only a couple of meters," he said firmly.

I gave them both a "thumbs up" sign showing my appreciation. Banda furtively drove the van toward the herd that had not noticed us yet, and he stopped near it. As a precaution he left the engine on and did not remove his foot from the accelerator, establishing a ready position to take off if something went terribly wrong. From the expressions on Banda's and Musa's faces, I could tell that they were not pleased. I was told that the elephants were used to the sound of the van, and if you maintained a safe distance, you would be fine even if they were aware of you. I knew the elephants had seen us because some turned their heads in our direction.

Now we were a dangerous fifteen meters from the herd, and I was now in a position to take a photo of the largest elephant that was closer to us than the rest of the herd. I set the flash on my camera and peered at the bull through the eyepiece. It was out of focus, and I had the lateral view of the elephant. I quickly brought it into focus and waited, hoping it would turn toward me. I had to wait for approximately forty seconds until the moment I longed for arrived, but it was a moment I have never forgotten to this day. The bull turned its head towards me, and I stared into its eye the way I stared into the eye of the elephant carving in my dream. I saw the same look of rage and anger in its eye. The menacing look seemed to be accusing me of an unforgivable crime I seemed to have committed. I avoided its eyes and pressed the button on my camera. This was a big mistake because the flash disturbed the elephant, and it let out an ear-shattering sound that I had never heard before. This sound seemed to be the warning alarm because it caused the whole herd to simultaneously bellow in this fashion. It sounded like a loud never-ending echo, which punished our ears. The ground reverberated beneath us as they moved impetuously and tried to form a cordon around their young. There were so many of them, causing them to nearly trample on each other. Some began running away from us, while others advanced toward us, their ears flapping rapidly and fervently in a form of defense. What had once been a calm and benign atmosphere turned into a calamitous one at the push of a camera button.

Link to dream sequence— effect on his values

I was speechless and could hear Musa shouting, "Tieni, tieni fast!" to the driver. Instinctively, Banda slammed the foot on the accelerator causing the engine to roar strongly, but this sound was barely audible due to the louder angry grunts of the elephants. He then turned the van away from the herd in an attempt to reach safety.

"Abuil abuil ei tiuti hamba isa tieni tieni fast!" shouted Musa frantically to Banda as he ducked below a seat. I did not know what this had meant, but I soon found out. The massive bull, which I had tried to photograph, began charging at us from the rear, flapping its ears vigorously and grunting vehemently. Its tusks were raised, like a tank with two white-colored barrels, ready for battle. I had a clear view of its tusks and they made me think of ivory—yet not as a smooth and attractive substance, as I once did, but as something dangerous to be in

Dramatic climax of narrative

possession of. Now the thought of ivory did not amaze me but frightened me. I have never seen ivory the same way since that day. At that moment, the image of Tusker Bull, my biggest piece in the ivory collection, flashed into my mind. It seemed as if it had come alive and was after me. I was surprised at the pace the bull was running because I didn't expect such a large animal to run at such a fast speed. I honestly thought I was going to die and was terrified because it was merely ten feet away from the van and was gaining on us. I held on to the side of the van and shut my eyes, not looking behind me. Yet, I could see the elephant in my mind, charging angrily at us. Banda was doing his best to escape from this animal, but his efforts seemed to be futile.

Reference to dream sequence and to underlying discussion of values

It seemed hours had passed when suddenly Musa yelled in relief, "It's stopped! It's stopped!" pointing at the elephant that had become stationary.

It gave an indignant salute that meant to say, "Don't ever come near my herd again. We are much more powerful than you."

Warning symbolic of writer's changed perspectives

"Hiny in hyi it fl, ungo," replied Banda in a tone of relief.

"Are you all right?" Musa asked me.

Since I was in a state of shock, I did not say a word and merely nodded.

"We'll be at the lodge soon so don't worry. It's over, and everything will be all right," said Musa.

I responded to him with a slight smile and then closed my eyes, while thinking of my close brush with death. The roar of the engine increased to a crescendo as the driver revved the engine of the open van and followed the dusty route to Mfuwe Lodge of the Luangwa National Park of Zambia.

The ten-minute encounter with the elephants and the charging bull changed my perspective of elephants and gave me second thoughts about collecting ivory. This frightening experience made me aware of how protective an elephant community is and of the similarities in its character to that of a human society. It was during this time that I realized the natural power these animals

Discussion of changed values— summarizes main ideas of essay

possess and that a human is only able to overpower them with the use of guns and other weapons. My respect for these animals and nature in general has increased. I felt that the elephants were trying to make me aware of the cruelty of people and how they have killed elephants to get ivory. Just the fact that I collected ivory betrayed my insensitivity toward these creatures. I burned my collection when I got home, and now I am no longer interested in collecting ivory. Now I don't value my collection in terms of money but in terms of the amount of life that was wasted in obtaining every piece that was present in my collection. I was taught a lesson by the victims that I feel is the best way to be punished. I will never collect ivory again, and I am planning to become part of the organization that plans to ban ivory and abolish poaching. Yes, the actual substance of ivory I will continue to admire, but differently, because I now think that ivory looks best on an elephant and not as carvings placed on a shelf in my room.

GEOFFREY CANADA

GEOFFREY CANADA is the president/CEO of the Harlem Children's Zone in New York City. He is the author of *Fist Stick Knife Gun: A Personal History of Violence in America* (1995) and *Reaching Up for Manhood: Transforming the Lives of Boys in America* (1998).

Pain

"Pain," an excerpt from the book *Reaching Up for Manhood,* draws on the writer's training and experience as a psychologist. He uses the narrative to explain the power of memory in our lives, especially memory of painful experiences. His particular focus is on boys and on the ways they are taught to repress the wounds caused by painful experiences. Nonetheless, it should be easy for readers to apply his insights to the experiences of girls.

Boys are taught to suffer their wounds in silence. To pretend that   1
it doesn't hurt, outside or inside. So many of them carry the scars of childhood into adulthood, never having come to grips with the pain, the anger, the fear. And that pain can change boys and bring doubts into their lives, though more often than not they have no idea where those doubts come from. Pain can make you afraid to love or cause you to doubt the safety of the ground you walk on. I know from my own experience that some pain changes us forever.

It all started because there was no grass. Actually, there was   2
grass, you just couldn't walk on it.

In the late fifties and early sixties, the projects were places peo-   3
ple moved to get away from tenement buildings like mine. We couldn't move into the projects because my mother was a single parent. Today most projects are crammed full of single parents, but when I was a child your application for the projects was automatically rejected if that was your situation. The projects were places for people on the way up. They had elevators, they were well maintained, and they had grass surrounding them. Grass like we had never seen before. The kind of grass that was like walking on carpet. Grass that yelled out to little girls and boys to run and tumble and do cartwheels and roll around on it. There was just one problem, it was off limits to people. All the projects had signs that said "Keep Off the Grass." And there were men keeping their eyes open for children who dared even think of crossing the single-link chain that

enclosed it. The projects didn't literally have the only grass we could find in the Bronx. Crotona Park, Pelham Bay Park, and Van Cortland Park were available to us. But the grass in those parks was a sparse covering for dirt, rocks, and twigs. You would never think about rolling around in that grass, because if you did you'd likely be rolling in dog excrement or over a hard rock.

There was one other place where we found grass in our neighborhood. Real grass. Lawn-like grass. It was in the side yard of a small church that was on the corner of Union Avenue and Home Street. The church was small and only open on Sundays. The yard and its precious grass were enclosed by a four-foot-high fence. We were not allowed in the yard by the pastor of the church.   4

Occasionally we would sneak in to retrieve a small pink Spaulding ball that had gone off course during a game of stickball or punch ball, but if we were seen climbing the fence there would be a scene, with screams, yells, and threats to tell our parents. So although we often looked at that soft grass with longing, the churchyard was off limits.   5

It would have stayed off limits if it had not been for football. Football came into my life one fall when I was nine years old, and I played it every fall for the rest of my childhood and adolescence. But football in the inner city looked very different than football played other places. The sewer manhole covers were the end zones. Anywhere in the street was legal playing territory, but not the sidewalk. There could be no tackling on pavement, so the game was called two-hand touch. If you touched an opponent with both hands, play had to stop. The quarterback called colorful plays: "Okay now. David, you go right in front of the blue Chevy. I'm gonna fake it to you. Geoff, see the black Ford on the right? No, don't look, stupid—they're gonna know our play. You go there, stop, then cross over toward William's stoop. I'll look for you short. Richard, go to the first sewer and turn around and stop. I'll pump it to you, go long, Geoff, you hike on three. Ready! Break!"   6

All we needed was grass. All our eyes were drawn to the churchyard. A decision had to be made. Rory was the first to bring it up. "We should sneak into the churchyard and play tackle."   7

We all walked over to Home Street and, out of sight of front windows, climbed over the fence and walked onto the grass. A thick carpet of grass that felt like falling on a mattress. We were in heaven.   8

Football in the churchyard was everything we had imagined. We could finally block and tackle and not worry about   9 falling on the hard concrete or asphalt streets. We didn't have to worry about cars coming down the block the way we did when we played two-hand touch. And because we were able to tackle, we could have running plays. We loved it. We played for hours on end.

There was one problem with our football field, which was about thirty yards long and fifteen yards wide: at the far end there was a built-in barbecue pit, right in the middle of the end zone. If we were running with the football, or going out for a pass, we had to avoid the barbecue pit with its metal rods along the top, set into its concrete sides. We knew that no matter what you were doing when in that area of the yard, you had to keep one eye on the barbecue pit. To run into its concrete sides—or, even worse, the metal bars—would be very painful and dangerous.

I was fast and crafty. I loved to play split end on the offense. I could fake out the other kids and get free to catch the ball. I had one problem, though—I hadn't mastered catching a football thrown over my head. To do this you have to lean your head back and watch as the football descends into your hands. Keep your eye on the ball, that's the trick to catching one over the shoulder. We all wanted to go deep for "the bomb"—a ball thrown as far as possible, where a receiver's job is to run full speed and catch it with outstretched hands. It took me forever to learn to concentrate on the football, with my head back as far as it would go, while running full speed. But finally I mastered it. I was now a truly dangerous receiver. If you played too far away from me I could catch the ball short, and if you came too close I could run right by the slower boys and catch the bomb.

The move I did on Ned was picture perfect. I ran ten yards, turned around, and faced Walter. He pumped the ball to me. I felt Ned take a step forward, going for the fake as I turned and ran right by him. Walter launched the bomb. As the football left his hand I stopped looking over my shoulder at him and started my sprint to the end zone. After running ten yards I tilted my head back and looked up at the bright blue fall sky. Nothing. I looked forward again and ran harder, then looked up again. There it was, the brown leather football falling in a perfect arc toward the earth, toward where I would be in three seconds, toward the winning touchdown.

And then pain. The bar of the barbecue pit caught me in midstride in the middle of my shin. I went down in a flurry of ashes, legs and arms flying every which way. The pain was all-enveloping. I grabbed my leg above and below where it had hit; I couldn't bear

10

11

12

13

to touch the place where it had slammed into the bar. The pain was too much. I lay flat on the ground, trying to cry out. I could only make a humming sound deep in the back of my throat. My friends gathered around and I tried to act like a big boy, the way I had been taught. I tried not to cry. Then the pain consumed me and I couldn't see any of my friends anymore. I howled and then cried and then howled some more. The boys saw the blood seeping through my dungarees and my brother John said, "Let me see. Be still. Let me see." He rolled my pants leg up to my knee to look at the damage. All the other boys who had been playing or watching were in a circle around me. They all grimaced and turned away. I knew it was bad then, and I howled louder.

Catching the metal bar in full stride with my shin had crushed a 14 quarter-sized hole in my leg. The skin was missing and even to this day I can feel the indentation in my shinbone where the bar gouged out a small piece of bone. I was off my feet for a few days and it took about two weeks for my shin to heal completely. Still, I was at the age where sports and friends meant everything to me. I couldn't wait to play football in the churchyard again, but I was a much more cautious receiver than before.

Several years later, when I finished the ninth grade at a junior 15 high school in the South Bronx and was preparing to go to high school, I knew that my life had reached a critical juncture. My high school prospects were grim. I didn't pass the test to get into the Bronx High School of Science (I was more interested in girls than prep work), so my choices were either Morris High School or Clinton High School. Both of these were poor academically and suffered from a high incidence of violence. I asked my mother if I could stay with my grandparents in the house they had just built in Wyandanch, a quiet, mostly African-American town on Long Island. She agreed and they agreed, so I went there for my three years of high school.

That first year I went out for the junior varsity football team at 16 Wyandanch High and played football as a receiver. I was a good receiver. The years of faking out kids on the narrow streets of the Bronx made me so deceptive that I couldn't be covered in the wide-open area of a real football field. But I had one problem—I couldn't catch the bomb. My coach would scream at me after the ball had slipped through my fingers or bounced off my hands. "Geoff! What's the matter with you? Concentrate, goddamn it! Concentrate!" I couldn't. No matter how I tried to focus on the ball coming down out of the sky, at the last minute I would have to look down.

To make sure the ground wasn't playing tricks on me. No hidden booby traps. What happened in the churchyard would flash into my mind and even though I knew I was in a wide-open field, I'd have to glance down at the ground. I never made it as a receiver in high school. I finished my career as quarterback. Better to be looking at your opponent, knowing he wanted to tackle you, sometimes even getting hit without seeing it coming, but at least being aware of that possibility. Never again falling into the trap of thinking you were safe, running free, only you and the sky and a brown leather ball dropping from it.

Boys are conditioned not to let on that it hurts, never to say, 17 "I'm still scared." I've written here only about physical trauma, but every day in my work I deal with boys undergoing almost unthinkable mental trauma from violence or drug abuse in the home, or carrying emotional scars from physical abuse or unloving parents. I have come to see that in teaching boys to deny their own pain we inadvertently teach them to deny the pain of others. I believe this is one of the reasons so many men become physically abusive to those they supposedly love. Pain suffered early in life often becomes the wellspring from which rage and anger flow, emotions that can come flooding over the banks of restraint and reason, often drowning those unlucky enough to get caught in their way. We have done our boys an injustice by not helping them to acknowledge their pain. We must remember to tell them "I know it hurts. Come let me hold you. I'll hold you until it stops. And if you find out that the hurt comes back, I'll hold you again. I'll hold you until you're healed."

Boys are taught by coaches to play with pain. They are told by 18 parents that they shouldn't cry. They watch their heroes on the big screen getting punched and kicked and shot, and while these heroes might groan and yell, they never cry. And even some of us who should know better don't go out of our way to make sure our boys know about our pain and tears, and how we have healed ourselves. By sharing this we can give boys models for their own healing and recovery.

Even after I was grown I believed that ignoring pain was part 19 of learning to be a man, that I could get over hurt by simply willing it away. I had forgotten that when I was young I couldn't run in an open field without looking down, that with no one to talk to me about healing, I spent too many years unable to trust the ground beneath my feet.

MEANINGS AND VALUES

1. What is the main expository point (thesis) of the essay, and where does the writer state it? (See "Guide to Terms": *Unity*.)

2. What desires or aspirations did grass represent for the writer as a young man?

3. a. What, according to the writer, are the consequences of painful experiences (physical or emotional) suffered in youth?

    b. Why might the writer have chosen to focus on the consequences of pain for boys? How might the essay's conclusions be applied to or adapted for understanding the experiences of girls?

EXPOSITORY TECHNIQUES

1. Which paragraphs in the essay are devoted primarily to retelling events? Which focus on analyzing the events and generalizing about behavior?

2. Why do you think the writer waited until the end of the essay to offer an extended discussion of the psychological consequences of painful events? Where else in the essay might he have undertaken such an explanation?

3. Discuss the strategies the writer employs to create transitions between the paragraphs in the following pairs: 1 and 2, 5 and 6, 6 and 7, 12 and 13, and 17 and 18.

DICTION AND VOCABULARY

1. Discuss the use of the repetition of the word *pain* and its synonyms in Paragraph 17 to provide emphasis for the writer's main ideas. (Guide: *Emphasis*.)

2. For what purposes does the writer employ repetition and parallel structures in Paragraph 3? (Guide: *Parallel Structure*.)

3. Look up in a dictionary any of the following words with which you are unfamiliar: *excrement* (Par. 3); *grimaced* (13); *trauma, wellspring* (17).

READ TO WRITE

1. **Collaborating:** Working in a group, list and describe briefly the earliest recollections that each group member has of a painful event, either physical or emotional. From the list, choose several that your group finds particularly intriguing and plan a narrative essay around each one.

2. **Considering Audience:** How might girls' (and women's) experiences of pain differ from the experience described in Canada's essay? Write a brief essay exploring the similarities and differences between boys' and girls' experiences of pain.

3. **Developing an Essay:** Think of some central event from your youth that continues to affect your behavior today, positively or negatively. Write a narrative similar to Canada's, emphasizing that distinguishing part of your experience and commenting on the way such experiences are likely to affect many other people. To expand your perspective on the events, include your point of view, then and now, and describe the reactions of others to the events.

(NOTE: Suggestions for topics requiring development by NARRATION are on pp. 412–413 at the end of this chapter.)

LANGSTON HUGHES

LANGSTON HUGHES (1902–1967) was a poet, novelist, playwright, and columnist of African American, European American, and Native American descent. Born in Joplin, Missouri, he was elected class poet while in elementary school in Lincoln, Illinois. His first book of poetry, *The Weary Blues,* was published in 1926 and contains one of his best known poems, "The Negro Speaks of Rivers." Hughes is a major poet of the Harlem Renaissance, a movement of 1920s and 1930s when African Americans migrating to urban areas in the North achieved a new literary and intellectual expression involving a shared black cultural identity.

Salvation

When the young Langston Hughes was still in school, his father and mother separated, and his mother entrusted him to the care of her own mother in Lawrence, Kansas, while she traveled looking for work. Hughes writes of his maternal grandmother, "Something about my grandmother's stories (without her ever having said so) taught me the uselessness of crying about anything." His own story of a childhood experience's impact on his future is found in Hughes's 1940 autobiography *The Big Sea.*

I was saved from sin when I was going on thirteen. But not really saved. It happened like this. There was a big revival at my Auntie Reed's church. Every night for weeks there had been much preaching, singing, praying, and shouting, and some very hardened sinners had been brought to Christ, and the membership of the church had grown by leaps and bounds. Then just before the revival ended, they held a special meeting for children, "to bring the young lambs to the fold." My aunt spoke of it for days ahead. That night I was escorted to the front row and placed on the mourners' bench with all the other young sinners, who had not yet been brought to Jesus.

My aunt told me that when you were saved you saw a light, and something happened to you inside! And Jesus came into your life! And God was with you from then on! She said you could see and hear and feel Jesus in your soul. I believed her. I had heard a great many old people say the same thing and it seemed to me they ought to know. So I sat there calmly in the hot, crowded church, waiting for Jesus to come to me.

The preacher preached a wonderful rhythmical sermon, all   3
moans and shouts and lonely cries and dire pictures of hell, and
then he sang a song about the ninety and nine safe in the fold,
but one little lamb was left out in the cold. Then he said: "Won't
you come? Won't you come to Jesus? Young lambs, won't you
come?" And he held out his arms to all us young sinners there
on the mourners' bench. And the little girls cried. And some of
them jumped up and went to Jesus right away. But most of us
just sat there.

A great many older people came and knelt around us and   4
prayed, old women with jet black faces and braided hair, old men
with work-gnarled hands. And the church sang a song about the
lower lights are burning, some poor sinners to be saved. And the
whole building rocked with prayer and song.

Still I kept waiting to *see* Jesus.   5

Finally all the young people had gone to the altar and were   6
saved, but one boy and me. He was a rounder's son named Westley.
Westley and I were surrounded by sisters and deacons praying. It
was very hot in the church, and getting late now. Finally Westley
said to me in a whisper: "God damn! I'm tired o' sitting here. Let's
get up and be saved." So he got up and was saved.

Then I was left all alone on the mourners' bench. My aunt came   7
and knelt at my knees and cried, while prayers and songs swirled
all around me in the little church. The whole congregation prayed
for me alone, in a mighty wail of moans and voices. And I kept waiting serenely for Jesus, waiting, waiting—but he didn't come.
I wanted to see him, but nothing happened to me. Nothing! I wanted
something to happen to me, but nothing happened.

I heard the songs and the minister saying: "Why don't you   8
come? My dear child, why don't you come to Jesus? Jesus is waiting
for you. He wants you. Why don't you come? Sister Reed, what is
this child's name?"

"Langston," my aunt sobbed.   9

"Langston, why don't you come? Why don't you come and be   10
saved? Oh, Lamb of God! Why don't you come?"

Now it was really getting late. I began to be ashamed of myself,   11
holding everything up so long. I began to wonder what God thought
about Westley, who certainly hadn't seen Jesus either, but who was
now sitting proudly on the platform, swinging his knickerbockered
legs and grinning down at me, surrounded by deacons and old
women on their knees praying. God had not struck Westley dead for

taking his name in vain or for lying in the temple. So I decided that maybe to save further trouble, I'd better lie, too, and say that Jesus had come, and get up and be saved.

So I got up.   12

Suddenly the whole room broke into a sea of shouting, as they   13
saw me rise. Waves of rejoicing swept the place. Women leaped in the air. My aunt threw her arms around me. The minister took me by the hand and led me to the platform.

When things quieted down, in a hushed silence, punctuated by   14
a few ecstatic "Amens," all the new young lambs were blessed in the name of God. Then joyous singing filled the room.

That night, for the last time in my life but one—for I was a big   15
boy twelve years old—I cried. I cried, in bed alone, and couldn't stop. I buried my head under the quilts, but my aunt heard me. She woke up and told my uncle I was crying because the Holy Ghost had come into my life, and because I had seen Jesus. But I was really crying because I couldn't bear to tell her that I had lied, that I had deceived everybody in the church, and I hadn't seen Jesus, and that now I didn't believe there was a Jesus any more, since he didn't come to help me.

MEANINGS AND VALUES

1. Describe the actions of the congregation during the revival meeting that put pressure on the writer to be saved.

2. What does the writer say he was crying about after the revival meeting? Why doesn't he tell his aunt the real reasons why he is upset?

EXPOSITORY TECHNIQUES

1. Scan the reading selection for transition words between events in the narrative. List those transition words.

2. Paragraph 4 is short, but it contains many specific details. Restate those details and explain how they help focus the narrative.

3. Does the author use dialogue in this narrative? Quote an example. Does the dialogue in general make the narrative more convincing? Does it reveal conflicting perspectives among the churchgoers?

DICTION AND VOCABULARY

1. What is the author's point in using exclamation marks in the first three sentences of Paragraph 2? Does the technique work as he intended it? Explain your answer.

2. If you do not know the meaning of some of the following words, consult a dictionary: *revival* (Par. 1); *dire* (3); *rounder, deacon* (6); *ecstatic* (14).

READ TO WRITE

1. **Collaborating:** In a group of writers, brainstorm memories of incidents that did not turn out as you expected them to. Take turns interviewing each other about the events, then choose one of the incidents and collaborate in writing a brief summary of it in the form of a newspaper article. Use transition words to indicate time order.

2. **Considering Audience:** Suppose Hughes's autobiographical narrative in this reading selection were delivered as a letter to his aunt. How do you think she would respond? Write a letter to Hughes, taking on the role of his aunt. You can choose to assume that Hughes is still a boy, or that he is now an adult as you write. Tell him how you feel about his confession.

3. **Developing an Essay:** Write a journal entry about a time when you felt pressured by friends, family, or society to lie or pretend about something. Drawing from the journal entry and using the Hughes essay as a model, write your own first-person narrative about this situation. In your description, use specific details that are vivid, convincing, and focused on conveying how this incident made you feel at the time. Remember to communicate the reasons why you think it is important to tell readers this story.

(NOTE: Suggestions for topics requiring development by NARRATION are on pp. 412–413 at the end of this chapter.)

SANDRA CISNEROS

> Mexican American author SANDRA CISNEROS is best known for her
> coming-of-age novel, *The House on Mango Street* (1984), about a
> Latina girl growing up in a poor Chicago neighborhood. She
> earned a B.A. from Loyola University Chicago in 1976 and an
> M.F.A. from the University of Iowa Writers' Workshop in 1978. Her
> experimental writing style interweaves Spanish and English. Other
> works by Cisneros include *Woman Hollering Creek and Other Stories*
> (1991), *Caramelo* (2002), and *Vintage Cisneros* (2004).

Only Daughter

With one foot in Mexican culture and the other in Anglo-American
culture, Sandra Cisneros grew up as the only sister among six
brothers, an experience she drew upon in her later writing. "Only
Daughter" first appeared in the November 1990 issue of *Glamour*
magazine.

Once, several years ago, when I was just starting out my writing   1
career, I was asked to write my own contributor's note for an
anthology I was part of. I wrote: "I am the only daughter in a family
of six sons. *That* explains everything."

Well, I've thought about that ever since, and yes, it explains   2
a lot to me, but for the reader's sake I should have written: "I am the
only daughter in a *Mexican* family of six sons." Or even: "I am the only
daughter of a Mexican father and a Mexican-American mother." Or:
"I am the only daughter of a working-class family of nine." All of these
had everything to do with who I am today.

I was/am the only daughter and *only* a daughter. Being an only   3
daughter in a family of six sons forced me by circumstance to spend
a lot of time by myself because my brothers felt it beneath them to
play with a *girl* in public. But that aloneness, that loneliness, was
good for a would-be writer—it allowed me time to think and think,
to imagine, to read and prepare myself.

Being only a daughter for my father meant my destiny would   4
lead me to become someone's wife. That's what he believed. But
when I was in the fifth grade and shared my plans for college with
him, I was sure he understood. I remember my father saying, *"Que
bueno, mi'ja,* that's good." That meant a lot to me, especially since
my brothers thought the idea hilarious. What I didn't realize was
that my father thought college was good for girls—good for finding
a husband. After four years in college and two more in graduate

school, and still no husband, my father shakes his head even now and says I wasted all that education.

In retrospect, I'm lucky my father believed daughters were   5
meant for husbands. It meant it didn't matter if I majored in something silly like English. After all, I'd find a nice professional eventually, right? This allowed me the liberty to putter about embroidering my little poems and stories without my father interrupting with so much as a "What's that you're writing?"

But the truth is, I wanted him to interrupt. I wanted my father   6
to understand what it was I was scribbling, to introduce me as "My only daughter, the writer." Not as "This is only my daughter. She teaches." *Es maestra*—teacher. Not even *profesora*.

In a sense, everything I have ever written has been for him, to   7
win his approval even though I know my father can't read English words, even though my father's only reading includes the brown-ink *Esto* sports magazines from Mexico City and the bloody *¡Alarma!* magazines that feature yet another sighting of *La Virgen de Guadalupe* on a tortilla or a wife's revenge on her philandering husband by bashing his skull in with a *molcajete* (a kitchen mortar made of volcanic rock). Or the *fotonovelas,* the little picture paperbacks with tragedy and trauma erupting from the characters' mouths in bubbles.

My father represents, then, the public majority. A public who is   8
uninterested in reading, and yet one whom I am writing about and for, and privately trying to woo.

When we were growing up in Chicago, we moved a lot because   9
of my father. He suffered bouts of nostalgia. Then we'd have to let go of our flat, store the furniture with mother's relatives, load the station wagon with baggage and bologna sandwiches, and head south. To Mexico City.

We came back, of course. To yet another Chicago flat, another   10
Chicago neighborhood, another Catholic school. Each time, my father would seek out the parish priest in order to get a tuition break, and complain or boast: "I have seven sons."

He meant *siete hijos,* seven children, but he translated it as   11
"sons." "I have seven sons." To anyone who would listen. The Sears Roebuck employee who sold us the washing machine. The short-order cook where my father ate his ham-and-eggs breakfasts. "I have seven sons." As if he deserved a medal from the state.

My papa. He didn't mean anything by that mistranslation, I'm   12
sure. But somehow I could feel myself being erased. I'd tug my father's sleeve and whisper: "Not seven sons. Six! and *one daughter.*"

When my oldest brother graduated from medical school, he ful-   13
filled my father's dream that we study hard and use this—our heads,

instead of this — our hands. Even now my father's hands are thick and yellow, stubbed by a history of hammer and nails and twine and coils and springs. "Use this," my father said, tapping his head, "and not this," showing us those hands. He always looked tired when he said it.

Wasn't college an investment? And hadn't I spent all those 14 years in college? And if I didn't marry, what was it all for? Why would anyone go to college and then choose to be poor? Especially someone who had always been poor.

Last year, after ten years of writing professionally, the financial 15 rewards started to trickle in. My second National Endowment for the Arts Fellowship. A guest professorship at the University of California, Berkeley. My book, which sold to a major New York publishing house.

At Christmas, I flew home to Chicago. The house was throb- 16 bing, same as always; hot *tamales* and sweet *tamales* hissing in my mother's pressure cooker, and everybody—my mother, six brothers, wives, babies, aunts, cousins—talking too loud and at the same time, like in a Fellini film, because that's just how we are.

I went upstairs to my father's room. One of my stories had just 17 been translated into Spanish and published in an anthology of Chicano writing, and I wanted to show it to him. Ever since he recovered from a stroke two years ago, my father likes to spend his leisure hours horizontally. And that's how I found him, watching a Pedro Infante movie on Galavisión and eating rice pudding.

There was a glass filmed with milk on the bedside table. There 18 were several vials of pills and balled Kleenex. And on the floor, one black sock and a plastic urinal that I didn't want to look at but looked at anyway. Pedro Infante was about to burst into song, and my father was laughing.

I'm not sure if it was because my story was translated into 19 Spanish, or because it was published in Mexico, or perhaps because the story dealt with Tepeyac, the *colonia* my father was raised in and the house he grew up in, but at any rate, my father punched the mute button on his remote control and read my story.

I sat on the bed next to my father and waited. He read it very 20 slowly. As if he were reading each line over and over. He laughed at all the right places and read lines he liked out loud. He pointed and asked questions: "Is this So-and-so?" "Yes," I said. He kept reading.

When he was finally finished, after what seemed like hours, my 21 father looked up and asked: "Where can we get more copies of this for the relatives?"

Of all the wonderful things that happened to me last year, that 22 was the most wonderful.

MEANINGS AND VALUES

1. Explain the significance to the writer of her father's comment, "I have seven sons" (Pars. 10–12).

2. Why do you suppose the author writes to win her father's approval?

3. Explain the significance to the writer of:"'Use this,' my father said, tapping his head, 'and not this,' showing us those hands. He always looked tired when he said it" (Par. 13).

4. What is the significance of the last paragraph of the essay?

EXPOSITORY TECHNIQUES

1. Cisneros divides her narrative essay into two parts: background details to introduce a scene, followed by a detailed scene or story with a point. Locate where in the essay the detailed scene begins. Explain its point.

2. Explain how the narrative technique of dialogue adds to your enjoyment and understanding of this essay.

DICTION AND VOCABULARY

1. Cisneros uses many Spanish phrases throughout the essay, some translated and some not. Explain how this adds or detracts from your reading experience.

2. If you do not know the meaning of some of the following words, consult a dictionary: *destiny* (Par. 4); *retrospect, putter about* (5); *nostalgia* (9); *anthology, Chicano* (17).

READ TO WRITE

1. **Collaborating:** In your writer's group, tell stories about times that members have tried to please their parents. Choose one of the stories and write it together as a brief scene with dialogue that makes a point.

2. **Considering Audience:** Is this essay equally powerful in reaching people who are children of immigrant parents and those whose parents were born in this country? Why or why not?

3. **Developing an Essay:** Write a journal entry about a situation or event that was the source of an ambition of yours, for example, wanting to become an attorney or an artist. Distill this situation into a single telling incident with a beginning, middle, and end. Using specific detail and dialogue, recount the incident in a narrative essay that explains how you first decided to dedicate yourself to that ambition.

(NOTE: Suggestions for topics requiring development by NARRATION are on pp. 412–413 at the end of this chapter.)

Issues and Ideas

Dramatizing Ethical Dilemmas

- Martin Gansberg, *Thirty-Eight Who Saw Murder Didn't Call the Police*
- George Orwell, *Shooting an Elephant*

MARTIN GANSBERG

MARTIN GANSBERG was born in Brooklyn, New York, in 1920 and re-ceived a Bachelor of Social Sciences degree from St. John's Univer-sity. He has been an editor and reporter for the *New York Times,* including a three-year period as editor of its international edition in Paris. He also served on the faculty of Fairleigh Dickinson University. Gansberg has written for many magazines, including *Diplomat, Catholic Digest, Facts,* and *U.S. Lady.*

Thirty-Eight Who Saw Murder Didn't Call the Police

"Thirty-Eight Who Saw Murder . . ." was written for the *New York Times* in 1964, and for obvious reasons it has been anthologized frequently since then. Cast in a deceptively simple news style, it still provides material for serious thought, as well as a means of studying the use and technique of narration.

For more than half an hour 38 respectable, law-abiding citizens in Queens watched a killer stalk and stab a woman in three sepa-rate attacks in Kew Gardens.

Twice their chatter and the sudden glow of their bedroom lights interrupted him and frightened him off. Each time he returned, sought her out, and stabbed her again. Not one person telephoned the police during the assault; one witness called after the woman was dead.

1

2

That was two weeks ago today.   3

Still shocked is Assistant Chief Inspector Frederick M. Lussen, in   4
charge of the borough's detectives and a veteran of 25 years of homicide investigations. He can give a matter-of-fact recitation on many
murders. But the Kew Gardens slaying baffles him—not because it is
a murder, but because the "good people" failed to call the police.

"As we have reconstructed the crime," he said, "the assailant   5
had three chances to kill this woman during a 35-minute period. He
returned twice to complete the job. If we had been called when he
first attacked, the woman might not be dead now."

This is what the police say happened beginning at 3:20 A.M in   6
the staid, middle-class, tree-lined Austin Street area:

Twenty-eight-year-old Catherine Genovese, who was called   7
Kitty by almost everyone in the neighborhood, was returning home
from her job as manager of a bar in Hollis. She parked her red Fiat in
a lot adjacent to the Kew Gardens Long Island Rail Road Station,
facing Mowbray Place. Like many residents of the neighborhood,
she had parked there day after day since her arrival from Connecticut a year ago, although the railroad frowns on the practice.

She turned off the lights of her car, locked the door, and started   8
to walk the 100 feet to the entrance of her apartment at 82–70 Austin
Street, which is in a Tudor building, with stores in the first floor and
apartments on the second.

The entrance to the apartment is in the rear of the building be-   9
cause the front is rented to retail stores. At night the quiet neighborhood is shrouded in the slumbering darkness that marks most
residential areas.

Miss Genovese noticed a man at the far end of the lot, near a seven-   10
story apartment house at 82–40 Austin Street. She halted. Then, ner-
vously, she headed up Austin Street toward Lefferts Boulevard, where
there is a call box to the 102nd Police Precinct in nearby Richmond Hill.

She got as far as a street light in front of a bookstore before the man   11
grabbed her. She screamed. Lights went on in the 10-story apartment
house at 82–67 Austin Street, which faces the bookstore. Windows slid
open and voices punctuated the early-morning stillness.

Miss Genovese screamed: "Oh, my God, he stabbed me! Please   12
help me! Please help me!"

From one of the upper windows in the apartment house, a man   13
called down: "Let that girl alone!"

The assailant looked up at him, shrugged and walked down   14
Austin Street toward a white sedan parked a short distance away.
Miss Genovese struggled to her feet.

Lights went out. The killer returned to Miss Genovese, now try-   15
ing to make her way around the side of the building by the parking
lot to get to her apartment. The assailant stabbed her again.

"I'm dying!" she shrieked, "I'm dying!"   16

Windows were opened again, and lights went on in many   17
apartments. The assailant got into his car and drove away. Miss
Genovese staggered to her feet. A city bus, Q-10, the Lefferts Boulevard line to Kennedy International Airport, passed. It was 3:35 A.M.

The assailant returned. By then, Miss Genovese had crawled to   18
the back of the building, where the freshly painted brown doors
to the apartment house held out hope for safety. The killer tried the
first door; she wasn't there. At the second door, 82–62 Austin Street,
he saw her slumped on the floor at the foot of the stairs. He stabbed
her a third time—fatally.

It was 3:50 by the time the police received their first call, from a   19
man who was a neighbor of Miss Genovese. In two minutes they were
at the scene. The neighbor, a 70-year-old woman, and another woman
were the only persons on the street. Nobody else came forward.

The man explained that he had called the police after much de-   20
liberation. He had phoned a friend in Nassau County for advice and
then he had crossed the roof of the building to the apartment of the
elderly woman to get her to make the call.

"I didn't want to get involved," he sheepishly told the police.   21

Six days later, the police arrested Winston Moseley, a 29-year-   22
old business-machine operator, and charged him with homicide.
Moseley had no previous record. He is married, has two children
and owns a home at 133–19 Sutter Avenue, South Ozone Park,
Queens. On Wednesday, a court committed him to Kings County
Hospital for psychiatric observation.

When questioned by the police, Moseley also said that he had   23
slain Mrs. Annie May Johnson, 24, of 146–12 133rd Avenue, Jamaica,
on Feb. 29 and Barbara Kralik, 15, of 174–17 140th Avenue, Spring-
field Gardens, last July. In the Kralik case, the police are holding
Alvin L. Mitchell, who is said to have confessed to that slaying.

The police stressed how simple it would have been to have got-   24
ten in touch with them. "A phone call," said one of the detectives,
"would have done it." The police may be reached by dialing "O" for
operator or SPring 7–3100.

Today witnesses from the neighborhood, which is made up of   25
one-family homes in the $35,000 to $60,000 range with the exception
of the two apartment houses near the railroad station, find it difficult to explain why they didn't call the police.

A housewife, knowingly if quite casually, said, "We thought it was a lover's quarrel." A husband and wife both said, "Frankly, we were afraid." They seemed aware of the fact that events might have been different. A distraught woman, wiping her hands on her apron, said, "I didn't want my husband to get involved." 26

One couple, now willing to talk about that night, said they heard the first screams. The husband looked thoughtfully at the bookstore where the killer first grabbed Miss Genovese. 27

"We went to the window to see what was happening," he said, "but the light from our bedroom made it difficult to see the street." The wife, still apprehensive, added: "I put out the light and we were able to see better." 28

Asked why they hadn't called the police, she shrugged and replied: "I don't know." 29

A man peeked out from the slight opening in the doorway to his apartment and rattled off an account of the killer's second attack. Why hadn't he called the police at the time? "I was tired," he said without emotion. "I went back to bed." 30

It was 4:25 A.M. when the ambulance arrived to take the body of Miss Genovese. It drove off. "Then," a solemn police detective said, "the people came out." 31

MEANINGS AND VALUES

1. What is Gansberg's central (expository) theme? How might he have developed this theme without using narration at all? Specify what patterns of exposition he could have used instead. Would any of them have been as effective as narration *for the purpose?* Why, or why not?

2. Why has this narrative account of old news (the murder made its only headlines in 1964) retained its significance to this day? Are you able to see in this event a paradigm of any larger condition or situation? If so, explain, using examples as needed to illustrate your ideas.

EXPOSITORY TECHNIQUES

1. What standard introductory technique is exemplified in the first paragraph? (See "Guide to Terms": *Introductions.*) How effective do you consider it? If you see anything ironic in the fact stated there, explain the irony. (Guide: *Irony.*)

2. Where does the main narration begin? What, then, is the function of the preceding paragraphs?

3. Study several of the paragraph transitions within the narration itself to determine Gansberg's method of advancing the time sequence (to avoid overuse of "and then"). What is the technique? Is another needed? Why, or why not?

4. What possible reasons do you see for the predominant use of short paragraphs in this piece? Does this selection lose any effectiveness because of the short paragraphs?

5. Undoubtedly, the author selected with care the few quotations from witnesses that he uses. What principle or principles do you think applied to his selection?

6. Explain why you think the quotation from the "solemn police detective" was, or was not, deliberately and carefully chosen to conclude the piece. (Guide: *Closings.*)

7. Briefly identify the point of view of the writing. (Guide: *Point of View.*) Is it consistent throughout? Show the relation, as you see it, between this point of view and the author's apparent attitude toward his subject matter.

DICTION AND VOCABULARY

1. Why do you think the author used no difficult words in this narration? Do you find the writing at all belittling to college people because of this fact? Why, or why not?

READ TO WRITE

1. **Collaborating:** Gansberg's narration is written as a news account except that it clearly editorializes about the apathetic attitude of citizens. Working in a group, identify the places in the essay that Gansberg injects his bias. With your group, rewrite those sections where Gansberg expresses his perspective, taking the opposite point of view—supporting people who do not get involved in a situation like the one presented in the essay.

2. **Considering Audience:** The general plot of this story is as believable for audiences of the twenty-first century as it was for audiences of the 1960s—perhaps even more so because levels of violence in society have increased in the intervening decades. However, how might the behaviors of the people involved have been different if the incident had occurred today? Write out your answer and a brief explanation of it.

3. **Developing an Essay:** Though he certainly has his own view of the events he reports, Gansberg allows readers to question the motivations of the observers and to make their own judgments about the lack of involvement. Prepare an account of some incident you witnessed and use a similar approach. Call attention to the various

motivations expressed by the participants, to any inconsistencies in their behavior, and to any other elements you wish readers to analyze and question. The event itself need not be of more than local significance (an account of a meeting or a sports event can offer interesting insights, for example), but your exposition should offer readers insights worth considering.

(NOTE: Suggestions for topics requiring development by NARRATION are on pp. 412–413 at the end of this chapter.)

GEORGE ORWELL

The name GEORGE ORWELL, pen name of Eric Arthur Blair (1903–1950), is synonymous with social justice and opposition to totalitarianism. The English author and journalist is best known for two classic works: *Animal Farm* (1945), an allegorical novella condemning Stalin-era communism, and *Nineteen Eighty-Four* (1949), a science fiction novel about a suppressive dystopia. Orwell was born in India, educated in England, and served as a foreign news correspondent covering the Spanish Civil War (1936–1939) while participating in direct combat.

Shooting an Elephant

In 1922, before India's independence from British rule, Orwell joined the Indian Imperial Police and was posted in Burma (now Myanmar). His youthful experiences among a people hostile to colonial rule inspired this essay, originally published in 1936 in the periodical *New Writing*.

In Moulmein, in Lower Burma, I was hated by large numbers of people—the only time in my life that I have been important enough for this to happen to me. I was sub-divisional police officer of the town, and in an aimless, petty kind of way anti-European feeling was very bitter. No one had the guts to raise a riot, but if a European woman went through the bazaars alone somebody would probably spit betel juice over her dress. As a police officer I was an obvious target and was baited whenever it seemed safe to do so. When a nimble Burman tripped me up on the football field and the referee (another Burman) looked the other way, the crowd yelled with hideous laughter. This happened more than once. In the end the sneering yellow faces of young men that met me everywhere, the insults hooted after me when I was at a safe distance, got badly on my nerves. The young Buddhist priests were the worst of all. There were several thousands of them in the town and none of them seemed to have anything to do except stand on street corners and jeer at Europeans.

All this was perplexing and upsetting. For at that time I had already made up my mind that imperialism was an evil thing and the sooner I chucked up my job and got out of it the better. Theoretically—and secretly, of course—I was all for the Burmese and all against their oppressors, the British. As for the job I was doing, I hated it more bitterly than I can perhaps make clear. In a job like that you see the dirty work of Empire at close quarters. The wretched prisoners huddling in the stinking cages of the lockups, the grey, cowed faces of the long-term convicts, the scarred buttocks of the men who had been flogged with bamboos—all these oppressed me with an intolerable sense of guilt. But I could get nothing into perspective. I was young and ill-educated and I had had to think out my problems in the utter silence that is imposed on every Englishman in the East. I did not even know that the British Empire is dying, still less did I know that it is a great deal better than the younger empires that are going to supplant it. All I knew was that I was stuck between my hatred of the empire I served and my rage against the evil-spirited little beasts who tried to make my job impossible. With one part of my mind I thought of the British Raj as an unbreakable tyranny, as something clamped down, in *saecula saeculorum*, upon the will of prostrate peoples; with another part I thought that the greatest joy in the world would be to drive a bayonet into a Buddhist priest's guts. Feelings like these are the normal by-products of imperialism; ask any Anglo-Indian official, if you can catch him off duty.

One day something happened which in a roundabout way was enlightening. It was a tiny incident in itself, but it gave me a better glimpse than I had had before of the real nature of imperialism—the real motives for which despotic governments act. Early one morning the sub-inspector at a police station the other end of the town rang me up on the phone and said that an elephant was ravaging the bazaar. Would I please come and do something about it? I did not know what I could do, but I wanted to see what was happening and I got on to a pony and started out. I took my rifle, an old .44 Winchester and much too small to kill an elephant, but I thought the noise might be useful *in terrorem*. Various Burmans stopped me on the way and told me about the elephant's doings. It was not, of course, a wild elephant, but a tame one which had gone "must." It had been chained up, as tame elephants always are when their attack of "must" is due, but on the previous night it had broken its chain and escaped. Its mahout, the only person who could manage it when it was in that state, had set out in pursuit, but had taken the wrong direction and was now twelve hours' journey away, and in the morning the elephant had suddenly reappeared in the town. The Burmese population had no weapons and were quite helpless against it. It had already destroyed somebody's bamboo hut, killed a cow, and raided some fruit-stalls and devoured the stock; also it had met the municipal rubbish van and, when the driver jumped out and took to his heels, had turned the van over and inflicted violences upon it.

3

The Burmese sub-inspector and some Indian constables were   4
waiting for me in the quarter where the elephant had been seen. It
was a very poor quarter, a labyrinth of squalid bamboo huts,
thatched with palm-leaf, winding all over a steep hillside. I remember
that it was a cloudy, stuffy morning at the beginning of the rains.
We began questioning people as to where the elephant had gone,
and, as usual, failed to get any definite information. That is invariably
the case in the East; a story always sounds clear enough at a
distance, but the nearer you get to the scene of events the vaguer it
becomes. Some of the people said that the elephant had gone in one
direction, some said that he had gone in another, some professed not
even to have heard of an elephant. I had almost made up my mind
that the whole story was a pack of lies, when we heard yells a little
distance away. There was a loud, scandalized cry of "Go away, child!
Go away this instant!" and an old woman with a switch in her hand
came round the corner of a hut, violently shooing away a crowd of
naked children. Some more women followed, clicking their tongues
and exclaiming; evidently there was something that the children
ought not to have seen. I rounded the hut and saw a man's dead
body sprawling in the mud. He was an Indian, a black Dravidian
coolie, almost naked, and he could not have been dead many
minutes. The people said that the elephant had come suddenly
upon him round the corner of the hut, caught him with its trunk,
put its foot on his back, and ground him into the earth. This was the
rainy season and the ground was soft, and his face had scored a
trench a foot deep and a couple of yards long. He was lying on his
belly with arms crucified and head sharply twisted to one side. His
face was coated with mud, the eyes wide open, the teeth bared and
grinning with an expression of unendurable agony. (Never tell me, by
the way, that the dead look peaceful. Most of the corpses I have seen
looked devilish.) The friction of the great beast's foot had stripped the
skin from his back as neatly as one skins a rabbit. As soon as I saw the
dead man I sent an orderly to a friend's house nearby to borrow an
elephant rifle. I had already sent back the pony, not wanting it to go
mad with fright and throw me if it smelled the elephant.

The orderly came back in a few minutes with a rifle and five cartridges,   5
and meanwhile some Burmans had arrived and told us that
the elephant was in the paddy fields below, only a few hundred yards
away. As I started forward practically the whole population of
the quarter flocked out of the houses and followed me. They had seen
the rifle and were all shouting excitedly that I was going to shoot the
elephant. They had not shown much interest in the elephant when he

was merely ravaging their homes, but it was different now that he was going to be shot. It was a bit of fun to them, as it would be to an English crowd; besides they wanted the meat. It made me vaguely uneasy. I had no intention of shooting the elephant—I had merely sent for the rifle to defend myself if necessary—and it is always unnerving to have a crowd following you. I marched down the hill, looking and feeling a fool, with the rifle over my shoulder and an ever-growing army of people jostling at my heels. At the bottom, when you got away from the huts, there was a metalled road and beyond that a miry waste of paddy fields a thousand yards across, not yet ploughed but soggy from the first rains and dotted with coarse grass. The elephant was standing eight yards from the road, his left side towards us. He took not the slightest notice of the crowd's approach. He was tearing up bunches of grass, beating them against his knees to clean them and stuffing them into his mouth.

I had halted on the road. As soon as I saw the elephant I knew 6
with perfect certainty that I ought not to shoot him. It is a serious matter to shoot a working elephant—it is comparable to destroying a huge and costly piece of machinery—and obviously one ought not to do it if it can possibly be avoided. And at that distance, peacefully eating, the elephant looked no more dangerous than a cow. I thought then and I think now that his attack of "must" was already passing off; in which case he would merely wander harmlessly about until the mahout came back and caught him. Moreover, I did not in the least want to shoot him. I decided that I would watch him for a little while to make sure that he did not turn savage again, and then go home.

But at that moment I glanced round at the crowd that had fol- 7
lowed me. It was an immense crowd, two thousand at the least and growing every minute. It blocked the road for a long distance on either side. I looked at the sea of yellow faces above the garish clothes—faces all happy and excited over this bit of fun, all certain that the elephant was going to be shot. They were watching me as they would watch a conjurer about to perform a trick. They did not like me, but with the magical rifle in my hands I was momentarily worth watching. And suddenly I realized that I should have to shoot the elephant after all. The people expected it of me and I had got to do it; I could feel their two thousand wills pressing me forward, irresistibly. And it was at this moment, as I stood there with the rifle in my hands, that I first grasped the hollowness, the futility of the white man's dominion in the East. Here was I, the white man with his gun, standing in front of the unarmed native crowd—seemingly the leading actor of the piece; but in reality I was only an absurd puppet pushed to and fro

by the will of those yellow faces behind. I perceived in this moment that when the white man turns tyrant it is his own freedom that he destroys. He becomes a sort of hollow, posing dummy, the conventionalized figure of a sahib. For it is the condition of his rule that he shall spend his life in trying to impress the "natives," and so in every crisis he has got to do what the "natives" expect of him. He wears a mask, and his face grows to fit it. I had got to shoot the elephant. I had committed myself to doing it when I sent for the rifle. A sahib has got to act like a sahib; he has got to appear resolute, to know his own mind and do definite things. To come all that way, rifle in hand, with two thousand people marching at my heels, and then to trail feebly away, having done nothing—no, that was impossible. The crowd would laugh at me. And my whole life, every white man's life in the East, was one long struggle not to be laughed at.

But I did not want to shoot the elephant. I watched him beating his bunch of grass against his knees, with the preoccupied grandmotherly air that elephants have. It seemed to me that it would be murder to shoot him. At that age I was not squeamish about killing animals, but I had never shot an elephant and never wanted to. (Somehow it always seems worse to kill a *large* animal.) Besides, there was the beast's owner to be considered. Alive, the elephant was worth at least a hundred pounds; dead, he would only be worth the value of his tusks, five pounds, possibly. But I had got to act quickly. I turned to some experienced-looking Burmans who had been there when we arrived, and asked them how the elephant had been behaving. They all said the same thing: he took no notice of you if you left him alone, but he might charge if you went too close to him. 8

It was perfectly clear to me what I ought to do. I ought to walk up to within, say, twenty-five yards of the elephant and test his behavior. If he charged I could shoot, if he took no notice of me it would be safe to leave him until the mahout came back. But also I knew that I was going to do no such thing. I was a poor shot with a rifle and the ground was soft mud into which one would sink at every step. If the elephant charged and I missed him, I should have about as much chance as a toad under a steamroller. But even then I was not thinking particularly of my own skin, only of the watchful yellow faces behind. For at that moment, with the crowd watching me, I was not afraid in the ordinary sense, as I would have been if I had been alone. A white man mustn't be frightened in front of "natives"; and so, in general, he isn't frightened. The sole thought in my mind was that if anything went wrong those two thousand Burmans would see me pursued, caught, trampled on, and reduced to a 9 grinning corpse like that Indian up the hill. And if that happened it was quite probable that some of them would laugh. That would never do. There was only one alternative. I shoved the cartridges into the magazine and lay down on the road to get a better aim.

The crowd grew very still, and a deep, low, happy sigh, as of 10 people who see the theatre curtain go up at last, breathed from innumerable throats. They were going to have their bit of fun after all. The rifle was a beautiful German thing with cross-hair sights. I did not then know that in shooting an elephant one would shoot to cut an imaginary bar running from ear-hole to ear-hole. I ought, therefore, as the elephant was sideways on, to have aimed straight at his ear-hole; actually I aimed several inches in front of this, thinking the brain would be further forward.

When I pulled the trigger I did not hear the bang or feel the 11 kick—one never does when a shot goes home—but I heard the devilish roar of glee that went up from the crowd. In that instant, in too short a time, one would have thought, even for the bullet to get there, a mysterious, terrible change had come over the elephant. He neither stirred nor fell, but every line on his body had altered. He looked suddenly stricken, shrunken, immensely old, as though the frightful impact of the bullet had paralyzed him without knocking him down. At last, after what seemed a long time—it might have been five seconds, I dare say—he sagged flabbily to his knees. His mouth slobbered. An enormous senility seemed to have settled upon him. One could have imagined him thousands of years old. I fired again into the same spot. At the second shot he did not collapse but climbed with desperate slowness to his feet and stood weakly upright, with legs sagging and head drooping. I fired a third time. That was the shot that did for him. You could see the agony of it jolt his whole body and knock the last remnant of strength from his legs. But in falling he seemed for a moment to rise, for as his hind legs collapsed beneath him he seemed to tower upwards like a huge rock toppling, his trunk reaching skywards like a tree. He trumpeted, for the first and only time. And then down he came, his belly towards me, with a crash that seemed to shake the ground even where I lay.

I got up. The Burmans were already racing past me across the 12 mud. It was obvious that the elephant would never rise again, but he was not dead. He was breathing very rhythmically with long rattling gasps, his great mound of a side painfully rising and falling. His mouth was wide open—I could see far down into the caverns of pale pink throat. I waited a long time for him to die, but his breathing did not weaken. Finally I fired my two remaining shots into the spot where I thought his heart must be. The thick blood welled out of him like red velvet, but still he did not die. His body did not even jerk when the shots hit him, the tortured breathing continued without a pause. He was dying, very slowly and in great agony, but in some world remote from me where not even a bullet could damage him further. I felt that I had got to put an end to that dreadful noise. It seemed dreadful to see the great beast lying there, powerless to move and yet powerless to die, and not even to be able to finish him. I sent back for my small rifle and poured shot after shot into his heart and down his throat. They seemed to make no impression. The tortured gasps continued as steadily as the ticking of a clock.

In the end I could not stand it any longer and went away.   13
I heard later that it took him half an hour to die. Burmans were bringing dahs and baskets even before I left, and I was told they had stripped his body almost to the bones by the afternoon.

Afterwards, of course, there were endless discussions about the   14
shooting of the elephant. The owner was furious, but he was only an Indian and could do nothing. Besides, legally I had done the right thing, for a mad elephant has to be killed, like a mad dog, if its owner fails to control it. Among the Europeans opinion was divided. The older men said I was right, the younger men said it was a damn shame to shoot an elephant for killing a coolie, because an elephant was worth more than any damn Coringhee coolie. And afterwards I was very glad that the coolie had been killed; it put me legally in the right and it gave me a sufficient pretext for shooting the elephant. I often wondered whether any of the others grasped that I had done it solely to avoid looking a fool.

Meanings and Values

1.   What reasons does the author offer for his statement: "In Moulmein, in Lower Burma, I was hated by large numbers of people" (Par. 1)?

2.   In the writer's opinion, was it necessary to shoot the elephant? What would the consequences of shooting it be? Of not shooting it?

3.   In Paragraph 3, Orwell says that the incident he narrates gave him a better understanding of "imperialism—the real motives for which despotic governments act." What does he mean, and how does this tie in with the last sentence of the essay?

EXPOSITORY TECHNIQUES

1. The author begins his narration of the incident of shooting the elephant with the transition "One day" (Par. 3). Scan the essay and underline other transitions between events in the narration of this incident.

2. The essay uses very little dialogue. Is this a problem, in your opinion?

3. At what point in the essay does Orwell go into the most detail? Why?

DICTION AND VOCABULARY

1. What is the author's tone in this essay (see "Guide to Terms": *Style/ Tone*)? Explain your answer.

2. Why do you suppose the writer uses Latin phrases such as *saecula saeculorum* ("from time immemorial") in Paragraph 2? In what contexts would one have normally encountered Latin phrases in the early twentieth century?

3. If you do not know the meaning of some of the following words, consult a dictionary: *jeer* (Par. 1), *tyranny, prostrate* (2), *despotic* (3), *labyrinth* (4), *ravaging* (5), *mahout* (6), *futility, conventionalized, resolute* (7), *squeamish* (8), *pretext* (14).

READ TO WRITE

1. **Collaborating:** In his essay, Orwell states that he acted as he did in order to avoid looking foolish. He implies that imperialist governments do the same. On the Internet, research the term *saving face* and discuss your findings with your writer's group. Share times that you or someone you know or have read about acted in order to save face.

2. **Considering Audience:** Take on the role of one of the Burmese spectators and rewrite the incident described by Orwell from his or her point of view.

3. **Developing an Essay:** Using Orwell's essay and the stories shared in question 1 as a jumping-off point, write a first-person narrative describing a time you acted a certain way in order to save face. Use specific details focused on the point you are making in your narrative.

(NOTE: Suggestions for topics requiring development by NARRATION follow.)

Writing Suggestions for Chapter 11

NARRATION

Set 1

Use narration as a primary or partial pattern (e.g., in developed examples or in comparison) for one of the following expository themes or another suggested by them. Avoid the isolated personal account that has little broader significance. Remember, too, that development of the essay should itself make your point, without excessive moralizing.

1. People can still succeed without a college education.
2. The world still has unexplored territories to discover.
3. When people succeed in communicating, they can learn to get along with each other.
4. Even with "careful" use of capital punishment, innocent people can be executed.
5. Sports don't always build character.
6. Physical danger can make us more aware of ourselves and our values.
7. Conditioning to the realities of the job is as important for police officers as it is in professional training.
8. It is possible for employees themselves to determine when they have reached their highest level of competence.
9. Wartime atrocities are not a new development.
10. "Date rape" and sexual harassment on the job are devastating and generally unexpected.
11. Both heredity and environment shape personality.
12. Physical and mental handicaps can be overcome in some ways, but they are still a burden.
13. Toxic wastes pose a problem for many communities.
14. Hunting is a worthwhile and challenging sport.
15. Lack of money places considerable stress on a family or a marriage.
16. Exercise can become an obsession.

17. People who grow up in affluent surroundings don't understand what it is like to worry about money, to be hungry, or to live in a dangerous neighborhood.
18. Some jobs are simply degrading, either because of the work or because of the fellow workers.

Set 2

Some events in our lives are so important that they suggest generalizations about larger issues. Develop an expository essay built around one of these events, and use the narration to make a larger point of significance to readers.

 a. A first kiss
 b. Staying away from home for several days for the first time
 c. Learning to swim (or some other challenging activity)
 d. Being rejected
 e. Rejecting someone
 f. Losing a parent
 g. A major operation
 h. A serious accident
 i. Being humiliated
 j. Winning

COLLABORATIVE EXERCISES

1. Consider item 6 from the list of writing suggestions. Have each member of a group relate a story of physical danger and self-awareness that affected the group member or a friend. Each group member can then combine the examples into a unified paper narrating the effects that physical dangers may have upon people. When the papers are completed, group members can compare them and discuss the different choices the writers made.

2. Item 9 from the list of writing suggestions addresses analyzing wartime atrocities. Have each member of your group choose some wartime atrocity (e.g., from the Gulf War, the Holocaust, or the like). Group members can then choose from these examples to create unified narratives.

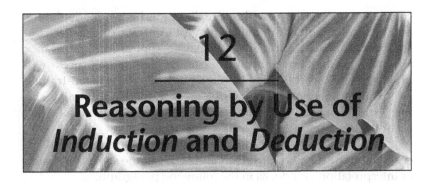

12

Reasoning by Use of Induction and Deduction

Sometimes you can best explain a subject by asking readers to follow the line of reasoning you use to *understand it:* either *inductive reasoning* or *deductive reasoning. Induction* is the process by which we accumulate evidence until, at some point, we can make the "inductive leap" and thus reach a useful *generalization.* The science laboratory employs this technique: hundreds of tests and experiments and analyses may be required before the scientist will generalize, for instance, that a disease is caused by a certain virus. It is also one of the primary techniques of the prosecuting attorney who presents pieces of inductive evidence, asking the jury to make the inductive leap and conclude that the accused did indeed kill the victim.

Whereas induction is the method of reaching a potentially useful generalization (for example, people attending meetings after lunch are invariably less attentive than those at morning meetings), *deduction* is the method of *using* such a generality, now accepted as a fact (for example, because we need an attentive audience, we had better schedule this meeting at 10:30 A.M. rather than 1:00 P.M.). Working from a generalization already formulated—by ourselves, by someone else, or by tradition—we may deduce that a specific thing or circumstance that fits into the generality will act the same. Hence, if we are convinced that orange-colored food tastes bad, we will be reluctant to try pumpkin pie.

A personnel manager may have discovered over the years that electrical engineering majors from Central College are invariably well trained in their field. His induction may have been based on the evidence of observations, records, and opinions of people at his company; and, perhaps without realizing it, he has made the usable generalization about the training of Central College electrical engineering majors. Later, when he has an application from Nancy Ortega, a graduate of Central College, his deductive process will probably work as follows: Central College turns out well-trained electrical engineering majors; Ortega was trained at Central; therefore, Ortega must be well trained. Here he has used a generalization for a specific case.

In written form, you can use inductive reasoning to help readers explore the details of a subject and arrive at the same conclusion or interpretation you do, as in the following paragraph.

> Roaming the site, I can't help noticing that when men start cooking, the hardware gets complicated. Custom-built cookers—massive contraptions of cast iron and stainless steel—may cost $15,000 or more; they incorporate the team's barbecue philosophy. "We burn straight hickory under a baffle," Jim Garts, coleader of the Hogaholics, points out as he gingerly opens a scorching firebox that vents smoke across a water tray beneath a 4-by-8-foot grill. It's built on a trailer the size of a mobile home. Other cookers have been fashioned from a marine diesel engine; from a '76 [Nissan], with grilling racks instead of front seats, a chimney above the dash, and coals under the hood; and as a 15-foot version of Elvis Presley's guitar (by the Graceland Love Me Tenderloins). It's awesome ironmongery.

Preliminary observation states topic

Inductive evidence/details

Inductive generalization

> —Daniel Cohen,
> "Cooking-Off for Fame and Fortune"

You can use deductive reasoning to help readers use a generalization as a way of understanding a complex situation or complicated evidence and details, as in this paragraph.

> It is an everyday fact of life that competitors producing similar products claim that their own goods or services are better than those of their rivals. Every product advertised—from pain relievers to fried chicken—is claimed to be better than its competitor's. If all these companies sued for libel, the courts would be so overloaded with cases that they would grind to a halt. For years courts dismissed criticisms of businesses, products, and performances as expressions of opinion. When a restaurant owner sued a guidebook

Background for generalization

Deductive generalizations

to New York restaurants for giving his establishment a
bad review, he won a $20,000 verdict in compensatory
damages and $5 in punitive damages. But this was
overturned by the court of appeals. The court held
that, with the exception of one item, the allegedly li-
belous statements were expressions of opinion, not
fact. Among these statements were that the "dumplings,
on our visit, resembled bad ravioli . . . chicken with chili
was rubbery and the rice . . . totally insipid. . . ."
Obviously, it would be impossible to prove the nature
of the food served at that particular meal. What is
tender to one palate may be rubbery to another. The
one misstatement of fact, that the Peking duck was
served in one dish instead of three, was in my opinion, a minor and insignificant part of the entire review.
Had the review of the restaurant been considered as a
whole . . . , this small misstatement of fact would have
been treated as *de minimis*. That is a well-established
doctrine requiring that minor matters not be considered by the courts. In this case, the court held that the
restaurant was a public figure and had failed to prove
actual malice.

Specific instance
to be explained
using the
generalizations

—Lois G. Forer,
*A Chilling Effect: The Mounting
Threat of Libel and Invasion of Privacy Actions
to the First Amendment*

WHY USE INDUCTION AND DEDUCTION?

One useful way to think of induction and deduction is as a way of
arriving at a generalization (induction) and of applying a generalization as an explanatory strategy (deduction). Once you start thinking of the patterns this way, you can develop questions to help you
decide when to employ them in your writing. You might ask, for
example, "Why should I lead readers through the process of arriving at a generalization when I could simply announce it at the beginning of an essay and then provide examples, comparisons, and
other kinds of evidence to explain the generalization and show how
reasonable it is?" One answer is that you employ induction whenever the process of arriving at a generalization is as important as
the conclusion itself. For example, in explaining a particular kind of
childhood behavior, you may also wish to model for readers a way
of drawing conclusions about such behavior.

Another occasion when induction is an appropriate pattern of explanation is when the evidence leading to your conclusion is quite complicated or your conclusion is unusual or surprising. In such cases, readers may be more likely to understand and agree with your conclusion if you lead them through the process of reasoning. Inductive reasoning is also appropriate when you want to create tension or drama by building toward your conclusion or when you want to arrive at it by considering and rejecting other explanations until you arrive at a satisfactory one.

Before employing deduction as an explanatory strategy, you might ask, "How will my readers benefit if I use deductive reasoning to guide my explanation?" The importance of deductive reasoning as an explanatory pattern lies in the careful logic (and hence reliability) it can lend to conclusions. Put in simplified form (which, in writing, it seldom is), the deductive process is also called a "syllogism"—with the beginning generality known as the "major premise" and the specific that fits into the generality known as the "minor premise." For example:

Major premise—Orange-colored food is not fit to eat.
Minor premise—Pumpkin pie is orange-colored.
Conclusion—Pumpkin pie is not fit to eat.

As this example makes clear, however, deductive reasoning can be only as reliable as the original generalizations that were used as deductive premises. If the generalizations themselves were based on flimsy or insufficient evidence, any future deduction using them is likely to be erroneous.

Working together, induction and deduction can be good strategies for exploring an unfamiliar or complicated topic. Inductive reasoning can suggest a generalization about the topic; deductive reasoning can use the generalization to explore and explain whatever details, applications, and consequences call for understanding.

CHOOSING A STRATEGY

The organization of writing employing induction, deduction, or both generally parallels the process of reasoning. The following example may make this clear. Suppose that after a careful process of reasoning, you concluded that your family's dog treats you and other family members as if they were part of her own dog pack. This would be a somewhat startling conclusion for many readers, so to help make your explanation convincing, you might wish to follow an inductive-deductive pattern.

> *Tentative Thesis* (to be presented in full at the end of the essay): My family's dog treats me, my parents, and my siblings as if we were all members of the same pack of dogs.
>
> *Inductive Explanation:* Dogs behave in ways that surprise humans.
>
>> 1. They often try to sleep with their owners or members of the family. Dogs in packs like to sleep together.
>> 2. Dogs often like to carry around bits of smelly clothing (ugh!) from their owners or family members. Dogs in packs recognize and relate to each other through scent.
>> 3. Dogs choose one family member as most important and others as less so. Dog packs are strictly hierarchical; a dog is content when he or she can recognize the "alpha" dog and his or her own place in the pack.
>> 4, 5, 6. . . .
>
> *Inductive Generalization:* Dogs relate to humans in ways similar to the ways they relate to other dogs in a pack.
>
> *Deductive Explanation:* Much of my dog's behavior can be explained by considering my family as her pack.
>
>> 1. Every time one of the family sits down, our female beagle comes over and falls asleep on one of our feet. She's "cuddling" with us and feeling comfortable when she is literally "in touch" with her pack.
>> 2. I have lots of single socks; the dog has the other ones, which she chews, then "lovingly" drapes over her head or muzzle when she falls asleep in her bed. My dog isn't trying to be a pest or to cause me trouble. She's "complimenting" me by letting me know that my scent is an important element in her life.
>> 3. My mother says that even though she feeds and walks the dog, our beagle still thinks my father and my brothers are the most important people in the house. Beagles aren't politically correct; the lead dog is still generally a male, even if the "dog" walks on two legs.
>> 4, 5, 6. . . .

One particularly effective and familiar pattern of induction in writing is the "process of elimination." If it can be shown, for instance, that "A" does not have the strength to swing the murder weapon, that "B" was in a drunken sleep at the time of the crime, and that "C" had recently become blind and could not have found her way to the boathouse, then we may be ready for the inductive leap—that the foul deed must have been committed by "X," the only other person on the island. This organization can help you explain to readers why a particular explanation or interpretation of a subject is the only reasonable one.

Details of the subject to be explained
Explanation 1
    Strengths and weaknesses
Explanation 2
    Strengths and weaknesses
Explanation 3
    Strengths and weaknesses
Explanation 4, 5. . . .
Deductive Generalization
    This explanation is the only one with significant strengths and few significant weaknesses. It is probably the most accurate one.

DEVELOPING INDUCTION AND DEDUCTION

To develop an explanation using induction and deduction, you need to pay attention to the logic of your reasoning. These two faults are common in induction: (1) the use of *flimsy* evidence—mere opinion, hearsay, or analogy, none of which can support a valid generalization—instead of verified facts or opinions of reliable authorities; and (2) the use of *too little* evidence, leading to a premature inductive leap. The amount of evidence needed in any situation depends, of course, on purpose and audience. The success of two Central College graduates might be enough to convince some careless personnel director that all Central College electrical engineering graduates would be good employees, but two laboratory tests would not convince medical researchers that they had learned anything worthwhile about a disease-causing virus.

Deductive reasoning can fall victim to questionable premises or any of a number of flaws in logic. Induction and deduction are highly logical processes, and any trace of weakness can seriously undermine an exposition that depends on their reasonableness. Although no induction or deduction ever reaches absolute, 100 percent certainty, we should try to get from these methods as high a degree of *probability* as possible.

Student Essay

In the following essay, Sheilagh Brady shows how an essay can use induction and deduction to organize a complicated explanation in a way readers will consider clear and easy to understand. She takes readers through the history of MADD, leading up to some of its key positions, then explores the positions in detail.

Mad About MADD

Sheilagh Brady

On May 3, 1980, Cari Lightner was walking through a suburban neighborhood on her way to a church carnival in Fair Oaks, California, when she was killed by a hit-and-run drunk driver. The driver was Clarence Busch, 46 years old with four prior arrests for drunk driving. Busch had just been released on bail for a hit-and-run drunk-driving charge a week before.

Background

Cari's mother, Candy Lightner, was 33 at the time, a divorced mother of two other children working as a real estate agent. She was told by two police officers investigating the accident that Busch would probably receive little jail time, if any, because "'That's the way the system works'" (Lightner and Hathaway 224).

Faced with these circumstances, many of us might have concluded that the only possible responses were despair and frustrated rage. Candy Lightner reached another conclusion. Mulling over the police officers' words during dinner the same night, Lightner conceived of the organization that eventually became MADD, Mothers Against Drunk Driving. She felt the need to do something to take away her pain. MADD became a way for her to use her anger and to come to terms with the death of her daughter. For the next five years, Lightner devoted her time and effort to the creation of MADD.

Events in the history of MADD and its efforts lead up to the inductive conclusion

Lightner moved to Dallas, Texas, the eventual headquarters of MADD, to begin working on organizing the new group. In March 1983, NBC aired a documentary, "Mothers Against Drunk Driving: The Candy Lightner Story." According to James B. Jacobs, MADD chapters doubled across the United States by 1985, and in the same year *Time* magazine reported that there were 320 chapters nationwide, and 600,000 volunteers and donors (Otto 41).

MADD's response to drunk driving has been to emphasize jail sentences and legislation. MADD members get angry when people feel "that a killer drunk driver deserves a lesser penalty than other homicidal offenders" (Jacobs). MADD has been successful in focusing public attention on the problems associated with drinking and driving and mobilizing legal changes to create stiffer penalties for drunk driving. MADD aims to have these stiffer penalties made mandatory and plea bargaining abolished (Voas and Lacey 126–27).

Not only has MADD focused public attention but it has also had considerable effect on local, state, and federal governments. In 1988, S. Ungerleider and S. A. Bloch did an evaluation of MADD that has been summarized as concluding that MADD was "more successful in state legislatures where a large number of laws were enacted in an effort to produce more severe sanctions for the drunk driving offense" (qtd. in Voas and Lacey 137).

Yet according to Dave Russel, a member of the Rhode Island Chapter of MADD, the past few years have been difficult. During the 1980s legislation was passed quickly because of the sudden public support through pressure groups concerned about drinking and driving. Since then, the progress of drunk-driving legislation has slowed considerably. Russel says that the number of deaths per year has steadily decreased since 1980 but that alcohol related accidents still take close to 19,000 lives each year. As a response to this situation, MADD chapters nationally have concluded that there is still a need for more drunk-driving legislation, even if legislators do not see it.

Having reached this conclusion, MADD chapters nationwide have decided to submit three different bills annually to their state legislatures. Some states have turned these bills into laws, but many have not. Just what are these MADD chapters proposing? Are the laws they want enacted reasonable or unreasonable?

Inductive generalization

One bill aims to reduce the BAC (blood alcohol content) level from .10 to .08 as the legal limit of intoxication. In 1988 in a report focusing on BAC levels, researchers Moskowitz and Robinson found that although theoretically impairment begins with the first drink, significant impairment occurs in most people at .05 BAC or lower. At the Surgeon General's Workshop, December 14–16, 1988, C. Everett Koop called for lowering the BAC limit in all states to .08, as did the National Highway Transportation Safety Administration in reports sent to the United States Congress. According to MADD's national office, lowering the BAC level to .08 will reduce drunk driving by making it more likely that drunk drivers will be caught, and also by acting to discourage driving under the influence. If research evidence and reliable authorities suggest reducing the BAC level from .10 to .08 will save lives, then most of us are likely to conclude that the legislative proposal seems reasonable.

First deductive explanation

Another bill is the ALR Bill or the Administrative License Revocation Bill. This law would eliminate the period between the arrest of a drunk driver and the hearing suspending the license. Right now, in many states, that period is supposed to be around 30 days but inevitably becomes much longer, a delay that allows the drunk driver to continue driving for that much longer legally under a valid license. The ALR would be a process that would allow the police officer to take the drunk driver's license if there is a refusal to take the breathalyzer test. In return, the driver would be given a temporary permit, good for ten to fifteen days, following an appearance at a hearing. If the driver does not appear for the hearing or cannot provide reasonable evidence for refusing the test, the license is suspended.

Second deductive explanation

In the case of a "no show," the driver must appear later
to answer to the charge against him or her, but what is
important is that the license will have already been
suspended.

The Administrative License Revocation was recom-
mended by the Presidential Commission on Drunk Driving, which developed the National Commission Against
Drunk Driving. According to several researchers,
"Administrative revocation has widespread support among
researchers, highway safety experts, and the public in
general because it has been shown to be an effective
administrative action that protects innocent drivers" in
an experiment conducted in California, Washington, and
Minnesota (Peck, Sadler, and Perrine). Most of us would
probably conclude that ALR is a reasonable procedure,
yet 17 states have not yet turned the ALR bill into a law.

Last, MADD chapters propose annually an Open
Container Law requiring that open containers of alcohol
not be allowed in the passenger compartments of ve-
hicles. According to MADD's national chapter, it is fundamental to separate drinking and driving because this
separation is essential to the public interest and to the
public's understanding of the crisis created by drunk
driving. MADD argues that banning open containers of
alcoholic beverages in a vehicle is one way to make sure
drivers do not start drinking while driving or become
even more intoxicated while driving. Moskowitz and
Robinson, in *Effects of Low Doses of Alcohol on Driving
Skills*, report that drinking while driving is dangerous because ingesting even a small amount of alcohol begins
the impairment process. For most of us, the Open Container Law probably also seems quite reasonable.

Even though the bills proposed by MADD chapters
are likely to seem reasonable to most people, many
states have not turned them into laws. At the same
time, the combination of alcohol and driving remains a
problem. Nineteen thousand deaths per year may be
lower than in previous years, but this is still too many
avoidable tragedies. One appropriate response is for

**Third
deductive
explanation**

each of us to become involved in working for a solution. If MADD's three proposals seem reasonable to you, if they are not yet law in your state, and if you want these policies in place to protect you, your family, and your friends, call your local MADD chapter and ask what you can do to help.

Works Cited

Jacobs, James B. *Drunk Driving: An American Dilemma.* Chicago: U of Chicago P, 1989. Print.

Lightner, Candy, and Nancy Hathaway. "The Other Side of Sorrow." *Ladies' Home Journal* Sept. 1990: 158–224. Print.

Moskowitz, H., and C. D. Robinson. *Effects of Low Doses of Alcohol on Driving Skills.* Washington: National Highway Traffic Safety Administration, 1988. Print.

Otto, Friedrich. "Seven Who Succeeded." *Time* 7 Jan. 1985: 40. Print.

Peck, Raymond C., D. D. Sadler, and M. W. Perrine. "The Comparative Effectiveness of Alcohol Rehabilitation and Licensing Control Actions for Drunk Driving Offenders: A Review of the Literature." *Alcohol, Drugs and Driving: Abstracts and Reviews* 1.1 (1985): 15–39. Print.

Russel, Dave. Personal interview. 19 Nov. 1993. MS.

Voas, Robert B., and John H. Lacey. "Drunk Driving Enforcement, Adjudication, and Sanctions in the United States." *Drinking and Driving: Advances in Research and Prevention.* Ed. Robert E. Mann and R. Jean Wilson. New York: Guilford, 1990. 130–45. Print.

NANCY FRIDAY

NANCY FRIDAY is the author of numerous books, including My Mother, My Self: The Daughter's Search for Identity (1977); Jealousy (1985); My Secret Garden: Women's Sexual Fantasies (1988); and Our Looks, Our Lives: Sex, Beauty, Power, and the Need to Be Seen (1999). Her most recent book is Beyond My Control: Forbidden Fantasies in an Uncensored Age (2009).

The Age of Beauty

In "The Age of Beauty," first published in the *New York Times Magazine*, Friday uses induction and deduction to explain a parallel process of personal discovery and change. Her effective use of the pattern illustrates its versatility.

I had stood, all eagerness and impatience, while my sister's old evening dress was pinned on me before that fateful dance at the yacht club. I didn't even know enough to look critically at the mirror and see that the strapless gown didn't suit me, especially after the dark brown velvet straps had been added to keep the dress up on my flat chest. I placed no value on looks. Having not had this rite of passage explained to me, I hadn't a clue that beauty was *the* prerequisite to adolescent stardom. Certainly, this new longing for boys had made me awkward in their presence; but I had noticed that they were awkward, too. Accustomed to being chosen first for any team of girls, I didn't question success that night, couldn't remember failure, so carefully had I buried nursery angers under trophies of recent accomplishments. I'm sure I was prepared to solve any hesitancy the boys might have in approaching us girls by taking the initiative myself. Assuming responsibility was who I was. In recent years my life had been a great adventure, in which there had been no comparisons made to my mother and sister. In my mind, they were boring in their tedious arguing over my sister's looks and her evenings with boys.

That night at the yacht club marked the end of childhood, the finish of that adventure story with me as heroine. In one momentous night I took it all in and made my concession speech to myself. I watched my friends, whose leader I had been for years, watched them happy in the arms of desirable boys, and I recognized what they had that I lacked; saw it so clearly that I can recreate the film

1

2

today, frame by frame: they had a look I lacked that went beyond beauty. It wasn't curls, breasts, prettiness, but a quality of acquiescence: the agreeable offer to be led instead of to lead. My own face was too eager, too open, too sure of itself. I needed a mask. I needed a new face that belied the intelligent leader inside and portrayed the little girl, no, the tiny, helpless baby who hadn't been held enough in the first years of life and had been waiting all these years for boys now to care for her.

I stood in my horrible dress, shoulder blades pressing into the wall, watching my dear friends dance by in the arms of handsome boys, with a frozen, ghastly smile on my face, denying I needed to be rescued. Why, even the girl who couldn't hit a ball danced by. Though they all whispered for me to hide in the ladies' room, I stood my ground. 3

Miserable as I was, I recognized the work ahead: the girl I had invented, so full of words waiting to be spoken and skills to be mastered, she had to be pushed down like an ugly jack-in-the-box. No boy was going to take a package like me. 4

A part of me was filled with rage at having to abandon what I thought to be a fine person. But I had no voice for rage. I belonged to a family of women who wept, and by not weeping I had made myself different from my mother and sister. But that night I became a woman; I wept and wept after someone's father drove me home while the rest of my group went off to a late party with boys. I showed my grief but not my rage. I did what most women still do: I swallowed anger, choked on it. I bowed my head, in part to be shorter, but also, like a cornered cow, to signal I had given up. 5

By morning I had buried and mourned my 11-year-old self, the leader, the actress, the tree climber, and had become an ardent beauty student. From now on I would ape my beautiful friends, smile the group smile, walk the group walk and, what with hanging my head and bending my knees, approximate as best I could the group look. 6

I have a photograph of myself taken in our yard on what looks like The First Day of Adolescence. I am sitting in a white wicker chair, hunched forward, staring at the ground, hands tightly clasped in my lap, swathed in the loser's agony of defeat. I remember the box camera aimed at me and that awful skirt and sweater, which had been my sister's—as had the awful dress at the yacht club, fine for a beauty but oh, so wrong for the tomboy I had been. 7

Twenty years later, I would go through countless hours of physical therapy to realign my spine, which has never recovered 8 from the bent-leg posture I mastered in learning the art of being less. Neither professional success, great friendships nor the love of men could recapture the self-confidence, the inner vision and, yes, the kindness of generosity I owned before I lost myself in the external mirrors of adolescence.

MEANINGS AND VALUES

1. In Paragraph 2, Friday says, "That night at the yacht club marked the end of childhood, the finish of that adventure story with me as the heroine." Explain the significance of that one evening. What did it symbolize for Friday? (See "Guide to Terms": *Symbol.*)

2. What does Friday mean when she says, "It wasn't curls, breast, prettiness, but a quality of acquiescence: the agreeable offer to be led instead of to lead" (Par. 2)? How is Friday defining the "role" of a successful woman from her adolescent perspective?

3. Why did Friday have to undergo physical therapy for her spine (Par. 8)? What is the significance of this reference as the conclusion of her essay?

EXPOSITORY TECHNIQUES

1. What inductive generalizations does the adolescent Friday make? Does the author still regard that generalization as valid? Why, or why not?

2. Throughout the essay, the author uses masculine imagery to describe her youthful self, for example "adventure story" (Par. 2), "the girl who couldn't hit a ball" (3), and "the loser's agony of defeat" (7). Why might she have used such masculine and athletic references?

3. What is the tone of Friday's essay? (Guide: *Tone.*) Is it successful in supporting the inductive pattern that she presents?

DICTION AND VOCABULARY

1. Look up any of the following words with which you may be unfamiliar: *tedious* (Par. 1); *acquiescence* (2); *ardent* (6); *swathed* (7).

READ TO WRITE

1. **Collaborating:** In a group, share stories from your adolescence that had a particular impact on the way that you defined yourself. Do group members share any similar experiences? Write a collaborative essay using one of those similar experiences as a basis for an inductive essay.

2. **Considering Audience:** Most women who read this essay would have some understanding of Friday's experiences. The image of the dress, the moving from "tomboy" to adolescent "girl," and the effort to "fit" are somewhat universal examples for young women. What images might be universal for men? Think of experiences that young boys have that mark their adolescence. Write an essay similar to Friday's looking at some adult male behaviors that may be outcomes of adolescent experiences. You may have to do some research in the form of interviews.

3. **Developing an Essay:** Think of something physical or emotional that is part of your adult character and that developed as a result of adolescent experiences. Write an essay incorporating an inductive generalization like Friday's to help your reader understand the impact of adolescence on your life.

(NOTE: Essays requiring development by means of INDUCTION and DEDUCTION are on p. 440 at the end of this chapter.)

Issues and Ideas

Digital Realities

* JC Herz, *Superhero Sushi*

JC HERZ

JC HERZ was a graduate student at Harvard University when she set out to explore the world of video games. Her reports on this virtual world have appeared in numerous magazines and in two books she authored, *Surfing on the Internet* (1995) and *Joystick Nation: How Videogames Ate Our Quarters, Won Our Hearts, and Rewired Our Minds* (1997). She was the *New York Times*'s first computer game critic and is currently producing a documentary on the history of videogames.

Superhero Sushi

For JC Herz, induction and deduction serve to explain the complicated mixture of American and Japanese characteristics and cultures that appear in the figures of video game heroes. The essay is a detailed and sometimes disturbing (though entertaining) exploration of the worlds of virtual reality and their complex relationships to everyday life. This essay first appeared in *Joystick Nation.*

After walloping her opponent, *Tekken 2*'s heroine, Michelle Chang, swivels within the videogame arena and turns to face the camera, the viewer, the players. And it's a disconcerting moment, because she looks at you intelligently, and there are so many polygons in her face that she almost seems real, and because she is such a confusing mix of signals. She's a slender girl who beats up rippling hypermasculine bruisers. She's computer generated, yet more true-to-life than most of the silicon-enhanced, digitally retouched dreamgirls staring vacantly out from real world magazine racks. She's got an Asian name but ambiguous features—a Western nose, almond-shaped eyes. If you saw her on the street, you'd peg her as Amerasian. 1

In a way, she is a perfect metaphor for videogames themselves. She's a hybrid, of mixed Asian and American heritage, a creature 2 made possible by the technological innovation of two hemispheres. Videogame characters are a bicontinental crossbreed of American and Japanese pop culture, with elements of Japanese comic books (manga) and animation as well as Western comics and science fiction.

On the Pacific side, videogames' family resemblance to manga   3
and Japanimation are undeniable. In some cases, the games themselves are playable translations of popular Japanese comic books and animated films. In the last decade, hundreds of manga titles have been made into videogames in Japan, crossing over into the United States as manga shifts from cult status to mass acceptance, mostly via MTV. *Dragonball* alone has spawned six arcade games, a dozen titles for the Super Famicon (the Japanese equivalent of the Super NES), and a *Dragonball* Game Boy cartridge.

The salient feature of manga heroes—and the game characters   4
based on them—is a preternatural cuteness and almost freakish baby-like quality, which takes the form of oversized heads, tiny noses, and saucerlike, impossibly liquid eyes. This way of drawing characters translated easily into early videogames, which didn't have the graphic resolution to represent characters with adult proportions. Small, cute characters had fewer pixels per inch and were easier to use, and so videogames borrowed, for reasons of expediency, what manga had developed as a matter of convention. Even a character like Mario the Plumber, who's supposed to be an adult, with facial hair no less, is rendered with the roly-poly proportions of a child, like a manga character. You would expect characters to take on mature dimensions as technology enables videogame manufacturers to animate large, complex, realistic forms. But instead, companies like Sega hew even closer to the babyland aesthetic. To paraphrase Gordon Gekko in *Wall Street*, cuteness is good. Cuteness works.

The reason cuteness works, as Scott McCloud notes in *Under-*   5
standing Comics,[1] is that abstraction fosters identification. It is only because an animated character is abstract and cartoony that we can project our own expressions onto him. We can't really map ourselves onto truly realistic characters—we see them as objects, separated from us by their details. To use an annoying but useful postmodern term, they read as the Other. The most realistically rendered characters in videogames are usually enemies. The good guys are rounded, simplified, and childlike, a puttylike visual glove into which our

[1]Scott McCloud, *Understanding Comics: The Invisible Art* (New York: HarperCollins, 1993).

own hands and faces fit. If anything, early videogames were especially powerful in this sense. The more photorealistic characters become, the less we relate to them. Seeing a cast of TV actors in a full-motion video makes you into more of a spectator or an editor than a part of the story, whereas the polygon people in *Tekken 2* are easy to slide into, and a character like Mario or Sonic is even easier to identify with. A primitive, completely minimal figure like Pac-Man takes this link between pixel and personality to the nth degree. Characters in *Mortal Kombat* have fingers and stubble. You watch them. Pac-Man has one black dot for an eye, and you *become* him.

Videogame companies are well aware of this, which is why their   6
figureheads are all round and minimal and cute, just like, well, jeepers, just like Mickey Mouse. Sega is even working on a version of *Virtua Fighter 2* called *Virtua Fighter Kizu* ("kizu" is Japlish for "kids") where all the adult martial arts characters are rendered with gigantic toddler heads. From a distance, it looks like ferocious dueling lollipops. If you count the height of their hair, the giant toddlers' heads are as tall as the rest of their bodies. The eyes are bigger than their flying fists.

Americans usually read these saucer eyes as Western, as a sign   7
of whiteness. After all, the reasoning goes, Western eyes are bigger and rounder than Asian eyes. This must be the way that they see us. And for some strange reason, they're drawing us all over their comic books. But actually, that's not the case, says Matt Thorn, a doctoral candidate at Columbia University who is writing his dissertation on teen-girl comic books in Japan. "Japanese readers don't think of the characters as white," he says. "Of course, they have these huge eyes. And so to us, the characters do look white, because Westerners expect that the Japanese will represent themselves the way that Westerners represent them. That is, we have these certain standardized ways of indicating to a viewer this character is Asian or this character is black or this character is anything but white, including the slanty eyes and the black hair. And of course, the Japanese don't draw themselves that way. Those characters aren't white, and the readers don't think of them as being white, despite those features. There's a concept in linguistics called the unmarked category. And in the West, which is white-dominated, white is the unmarked category. Everything else is marked and has to be indicated, but white is taken for granted. But in Japan, Japanese is the unmarked category, the one that's taken for granted. They've developed that style with the huge eyes—that's the way that they've developed for drawing people, which means Japanese people. And when they want to indicate that a character is not Japanese, they have different ways of doing it.

Like, for white people and black people they use exaggerated features. Like for white people, they'll have big noses or really big bodies or really sharply defined eyelashes."

So within a typical martial arts videogame, the racial continuum is deceptive. It's not a simple matter of ethnic blur. It's a matter of reading the signs in completely different ways. All the indeterminate characters that to Western eyes would read as white look Japanese to kids playing the games in Tokyo. Figuratively speaking, we read these faces left to right. The Japanese read them up and down. This isn't their way of drawing us. It's their way of drawing themselves. Meanwhile, both sets of videogame players look at the screen and think the characters look native. It's counterintuitive. But when you think about it, really, *no one* has eyes that big.

There are characters in videogames that are visibly Asian, the way Westerners would draw Asians. But these characters are never supposed to be from Japan. They are supposed to be from China or Korea or Mongolia or some other part of Asia. "The irony," says Thorn, "is that the techniques that Westerners use to draw Asians are the same techniques the Japanese use when they're drawing Asians other than themselves. So you'll have a manga in which there are Japanese characters, which to us read as white. And then you'll have a Chinese character, and the Chinese character is drawn in such a way as to indicate to players that this character is not Japanese but Chinese. And they'll use the same kinds of techniques that we use: the straight black hair, the slanty eyes, etc."

And Americans? Usually, when a videogame character hails from the United States, he's blond. He's broad. He's buff. And he's larger than life, or at least larger than the other videogame characters. He looks more like an American comic book character than a manga hero. And he's not nearly as unassuming and cute. In fact, the more videogames borrow from American comic books, the less cute they get. Whereas Japanese manga characters are generally childlike and unassuming, American cartoon heroes in the Marvel/DC vein are, if anything, hyperadult. "In America," writes comic book historian Fred Schodt, "almost every comic book hero is a 'superhero' with bulging biceps (or breasts, as the case may be), a face and physique that rigidly adhere to the classical traditions, invincibly accompanied by superpowers, and a cloying, moralistic personality."[2] Like the drawings in a Western

8

9

10

[2]Frederik Schodt, *Manga Manga: The World of Japanese Comics* (Tokyo: Kodansha, 1983), 77, 78.

superhero comic, American characters in Japanese fighting games have wildly distorted, hyperrealistic, hypersexual bodies. And in American software houses, where Superman takes native precedence over Speed Racer and Astro Boy, the videogames themselves are absolutely devoid of blinking sweetness, offering instead the beloved stateside menagerie of larger-than-life comic book mutants. Capcom's *Marvel Superheroes* arcade cabinet, which is seven feet tall and physically towers over its Japanese counterparts, pumps out sound effects at blockbuster volume and stars veiny, spandex-clad standbys like the Incredible Hulk, Spiderman, and Captain America. The arcade game is, essentially, a moving comic book that replaces Pow! Boom! Zap! bubbles with gut-rattling audio effects. In this way, a Marvel Comics videogame is a more intense comic book experience than the paper it's based on. Comic book characters have always been drawn swooping and swinging and flying through the air. Now they can do it in real time. Comic book videogames are comic books squared. And with this added dimension the blurry line between comic books and videogames finally dissolves.

This blur between media is epitomized by *Comix Zone*, a videogame for the Sega Saturn. The premise, whose only precedent is Swedish pop group A-Ha's *Take on Me* video, is that your character, Sketch, is trapped in a Marvelesque comic book universe and forced to battle through it, panel by panel, combating enemies drawn by Mortus, an evil comic book artist. Along the way, helper characters yell out from the corner of the screen ("Watch out, Sketch!") in comic book dialogue boxes. The object, ultimately, is to defeat the evil illustrator and rip yourself out of his two-dimensional paper universe. It's like an Escher drawing, where you break out of one trompe l'oeil tableau only to find yourself in another impossible illusion. Beyond the simulated comic book page is a simulated TV cartoon, when, really, there aren't any pages, or any television, for that matter. There are only the conventions of paper and television, twined around each other, to float the action of a videogame.

Of course, to kids playing *Comix Zone* or *Marvel Superheroes* or *Tekken 2*, the distinction between comic book and videogame or Asian and Western is completely irrelevant. The only categories they recognize are "fun" and "not fun." If you walk into an arcade, you don't see white kids choosing white characters and black kids choosing black characters. Kids routinely choose any and all of these options and don't think twice about it, because the only factor in their decision is a given character's repertoire of kick-ass fighting moves. Ironically, all considerations of race, sex, and nationality are shunted aside in the videogame arena, where the only goal is to clobber everyone indiscriminately.

But on a deeper level, the kids playing these games intui- 13 tively understand that they're operating in a disembodied environment where your virtual skin doesn't have to match your physical one, and that you can be an Okinawan karate expert, a female Thai kickboxer, a black street fighter from the Bronx, or a six-armed alien from outer space, all within the span of a single game. Members of the previous generation might have a problem with the idea of playing a Japanese schoolgirl in a combat game. At the very least, they would be aware of their decision to choose this character, and maybe even a little smug about being enlightened enough to do so. For kids of the eighties and nineties, shuffling videogame bodies and faces is like playing with a remote control. The game starts, cycles through a bunch of avatars, and you punch the fire button when you see one you like. It's channel surfing.

In this milieu, the classic distinctions between heroes and vil- 14 lains break down. In older videogames, and in all previous media, the good guys look one way and the bad guys look another. It may be as simple as black hats and white hats or as fraught as cowboys and Indians. In movies and TV shows, we know what the hero and the villain are supposed to look like, and those images are very loaded. Heroes talk like midwestern news anchors and own dogs. Bad guys speak with foreign accents and stroke cats. Heroines are slender and blond and adorably helpless. Bad girls have dark hair and red nails and hips and guns they're ready to use. And because of the way these people look, and the way they're lit, it's clear for whom you're supposed to root.

But in an arcade fighting game like *Virtua Fighter 2*, you can't do 15 that, because those categories don't exist at all. You can play any character, and it's every gladiator for himself. This type of videogame doesn't label opposing forces as evil or good, because that would imply a scripted outcome, that the designated "hero" is supposed to win, when really no one is supposed to win. Everyone is supposed to play. It's the skill of the competitors that determines who wins and who loses. In a videogame, unlike in novels or movies or other fictions like history, no one—not even the game designer—knows the outcome of a given contest. And so it's impossible to cast a moral hair light on one character versus another.[3] There are no heroes and villains in a round-robin martial arts game. There are only combatants, each with his or her own special weapons, attributes, and fighting style. In the post–Cold War world, this seems an evenhanded approach. Everyone's a hero. Everyone is also a monster.

Or, to paraphrase the Red Dog beer motto, you are your own   16
monster. Now that the videogame hero is freed from the cosmetic constraints of gallant poster boyhood, you can play a whole menagerie of creatures, from werewolves to ice creatures to dinosaurs. Superhuman strength and/or demonic powers seem to be the only prerequisites for inclusion in the videogame bestiary, which draws from martial arts movies, Arthurian legend, the Greek pantheon, science fiction, Norse mythology, and Jurassic Park. And that's just *Primal Rage*, one of the hotter fighting games of 1996.

Primal Rage is mythic stuff. It's a fight-to-the-death among an-   17
gry, violent demigods who are also dinosaurs. According to the epic back story, "Before there were humans, gods walked the earth. They embodied the essence of Hunger, Survival, Life, Death, Insanity, Decay, Good, and Evil. They fought countless battles up through the Mesozoic Wars." When these conflicts threatened to destroy the planet, a wiser, more mature deity in another dimension decided to launch a kind of mythological NATO peacekeeping mission to shut them up. "He was not powerful enough to kill the gods," the story goes, "so instead he banished one to a rocky tomb within the moon. This disrupted the fragile balance between the gods; pandemonium ensued, and a great explosion threw clouds of volcanic dust into the atmosphere. The dinosaurs died out, and the surviving gods went into suspended animation. Now, the impact of a huge meteor strikes the Earth. Its destructive force wipes out civilization, rearranges the continents, and frees the imprisoned gods. Get ready to rumble . . . ."

The game ensues, throwing you into a kind of fossil fantasy   18
Ragnarok scenario where you choose one of these reptilian gods to fight against all the others. Each of them has its own repertoire of decay-related weapons, most of which involve bodily functions. The God of Survival is a crafty velociraptor lacking in brute strength but incredibly agile and slippery.

---

[3]This becomes patently obvious when you play a game like *Tekken 2*, where even the more wholesome characters are monstrously broad-shouldered, earnest, square-jawed, and monumental in the style of socialist realism. This is when you realize that monstrosity is in the eye of the beholder. This is also when you realize that most of the superheroes we hold up for children to admire are freaks.

In addition to its personal eccentricities, each character also has 19
a coordinated epic backdrop. The fire-breathing Tyrannosaurus rex
dukes it out in the Inferno, an active volcanic island oozing lava.
The serpentine Goddess of Insanity fights on a Stonehengian knoll
under a full moon with petrified enemies planted like lawn sculp-
tures in the background. And, if you make it through all these
themed battlegrounds, the final scene of *Primal Rage* is set in a dino-
saur graveyard littered with the bones of fallen reptiles. Red cracks
split the ground, and a huge vortex swirls in the sky as you leap,
bite, and strike as best you can against a very scary-looking, dragon-
ish God of Death. It's a perfect frappé of paleontology and the su-
pernatural, prehistory and the apocalypse. Like the science fiction
universe, videogames are where technology melts into the occult.
This is a place where missile launchers and mojo are both legitimate
weapons. All the old monsters, harpies, dragons, and divinities are
excavated from their mythological sediment, sampled, looped, re-
mixed, cross-faded, and digitally recycled. Videogames do to dusty
legends what deejays do to vintage vinyl. They weave the old
grooves into something accessible to teenagers.

And increasingly, it doesn't matter where those teenagers are. 20
The same way a transcendent house mix leaps from a mixing board
in London to sound systems in Tokyo, Los Angeles, and Helsinki,
good videogames have a way of becoming popular everywhere. It's
all digital. And a certain echelon of global youth all have access
to the technology. So if it's fun, it quickly goes transnational. And in
the process, it ceases to connote nationality. A successful dance track
or videogame doesn't read Japanese or American, German, or British.
It's all just pop. And it's yours for fifty cents.

The finest digital architects on the planet have built these play- 21
grounds out of comic books, Hong Kong cinema, scroll paintings
and music videos, ancient monsters and digital technology. They
pour in their myths and suck out quarters.

And this is what it's about, finally, as the cultural streams of 22
East and West swirl into the Tastee-Freez of global entertainment.
Mythic figures resonate, all the more if they're engaged in some
kind of combat or action adventure, real or simulated, the most popular forms being basketball and video games. They resonate for the
same reasons mythic figures have always resonated. Only now,
the audience numbers in the millions, and the object is not to celebrate ancestors or teach lessons or curry favor with the spirits. It's
commerce. And the people transmitting their stories to the next generation aren't priests or poets or medicine women. They're

multinational corporations. And they are not trying to appease the gods. They are trying to appease the shareholders. It's not just video-games. It's everything, with the possible exception of the Internet. All the mythic pop stars in Hollywood, the NBA, and MTV are purchasable commodities. Videogames are just the logical extreme, because all the superheroes in them are computer generated for maximum resonance and marketing kick. Unlike sports stars or actors, they don't get addicted, arrested, or petulant. They perform. They may look and act superhuman. They may throw lightning or breathe fire. And when you're in the game, they may really inspire or scare you. But unlike the mythic monsters that preceded them, videogame demons are caged in their arcade cabinets, firmly under the control of their corporate wardens. Demigods used to make people docile. Now it's the other way around. It is Sega and Namco and Capcom and Williams Entertainment, finally, that have tamed the dragons.

MEANINGS AND VALUES

1. Explain the significance of the title of the essay. How does it connect to Herz's message?

2. Why does Herz open with a description of a female, Japanese video character? What is significant about this character as opposed to other characters that Herz might have chosen to use in an introduction?

3. What is the significance of Paragraph 4? Does technology control other images that we see? Can it define or create stereotypes? Please explain.

4. In the first section of this essay (Pars. 1–11), Herz explains the different images of heroes from different nations. But in Paragraph 12, she makes a clear shift into limiting the importance of gender, race, and nationality. What is the significance of this shift?

EXPOSITORY TECHNIQUES

1. Herz repeatedly uses comparison and contrast in this essay. Identify the different things that she compares. How successful is this technique for a reader who may have limited knowledge of video games?

2. What is the thesis of this essay? (See "Guide to Terms": *Thesis.*) What type of reasoning (inductive, deductive, or a combination of both) does Herz employ to clarify and support the thesis?

3. Herz uses the second person (*you*) at various points in the essay. How effective is this? Why might she have chosen that technique in the places that she did?

DICTION AND VOCABULARY

1. Identify slang and jargon in "Superhero Sushi." (Guide: *Slang*.) Is the use of such language excessive? Could a person unfamiliar with video games and the language associated with them understand the essay? Please explain.

2. To what age group(s) is this essay targeted? Explain how Herz's language helps to define the age of her intended audience.

READ TO WRITE

1. **Collaborating:** List as many video game characters as you can think of and identify their race, gender, nationality, or species (if appropriate). Working with a group, compare your lists. Write a plan for an essay analyzing the various trends in video game characters.

2. **Considering Audience:** This essay clearly will be more easily understood by readers who have played video games or at least observed others play them. Using Herz's thesis as the basis for an essay, write a similar piece for an audience that might be less familiar with such technology.

3. **Developing an Essay:** Choose two or three virtual characters with which you are familiar, then go to a local arcade and study the newest games. Write an essay similar to Herz's that uses these characters collectively as a basis for an inductive generalization about the latest trends in video game characters.

(NOTE: Suggestions for essays requiring development by INDUCTION and DEDUCTION follow.)

Writing Suggestions for Chapter 12

INDUCTION AND DEDUCTION

Choose one of the following unformed topics and shape your central theme from it. This could express the view you prefer or an opposing view. Develop your composition primarily by use of induction, alone or in combination with deduction. Unless otherwise directed by your instructor, be completely objective and limit yourself to exposition, rather than engaging in argumentation.

1. Little League baseball (or the activities of Boys & Girls Clubs of America, Boy Scouts, Girl Scouts, etc.) as a molder of character
2. Conformity as an expression of insecurity
3. Pop music as a mirror of contemporary values
4. The status symbol as a motivator to success
5. The liberal arts curriculum and its relevance to success in a career
6. Student opinion as the guide to better educational institutions
7. The role of public figures (including politicians, movie stars, and business people) in shaping attitudes and fashions
8. The values of education, beyond dollars and cents
9. Knowledge and its relation to wisdom
10. The right of individuals to select the laws they obey
11. Videogames as molders of morals
12. The "other" side of one ecological problem
13. The value of complete freedom from worry
14. Homosexuality as inborn or as voluntary behavior
15. Raising mentally challenged children at home
16. Fashionable clothing as an expression of power (or as a means of attaining status)

COLLABORATIVE EXERCISE

Using number 3, 5, or 10 from the Writing Suggestions list above, have each member of your group write an inductive generalization for the topic. Then as a group, create a plan for a unified essay that presents one of the inductive generalizations.

13

Using Patterns for *Argument*

Argument and exposition have many things in common. They both use the basic patterns of exposition; they share a concern for the audience; and they often deal with similar subjects, including social trends (changing social relationships, the growth of the animal rights movement), recent developments (the creation of new strains of plants through genetic manipulation, developments in health care), and issues of widespread concern (the quality of education, the effects of pollution). As a result, the study of argument is a logical companion to the study of exposition. Yet the two kinds of writing have very different purposes.

Expository writing shares information and ideas; it explores issues and explains problems. Argumentative writing has a different motivation. It asks readers to choose one side of an issue or take a particular action, whether it is to choose a career, vote for a candidate, or build a new highway. In exposition we select facts and ideas to give a clear, interesting, and thorough picture of a subject. In argument we select facts and ideas that provide strong support for our point of view and arrange this evidence in the most logical and persuasive order, taking care to provide appropriate background information and to acknowledge and refute opposing points of view.

The evidence we choose for an argument is determined to a great extent by the attitudes and needs of the people we are trying to persuade. For example, suppose you want to argue successfully for a new approach to secondary education in your community—an approach that enrolls students in "mini-schools" according to their interests. Your essay would need to provide enough examples, facts, and reasons to convince parents and community leaders that the approach would be best for *their* children, not just for children in general. You would need to show that the community could afford the approach and that the benefits would justify the added expense. To be effective, moreover, your essay would also need to answer possible objections to the proposal and demonstrate that it is preferable to other approaches a reasonable school board and community might consider.

Your argumentative writing needs to focus on your thesis: the opinion you wish readers to share, the action you want them to undertake, or the assertion you wish them to endorse. The twin poles of argumentative writing—your thesis and the needs and values of your readers—need to be linked by evidence and reasoning. Evidence and reasoning extend your thesis to readers, and they bring readers closer to it.

WHY USE ARGUMENT?

Argumentative writing responds to situations in which there are two or more conflicting points of view. An argument attempts to resolve or at least modify disagreements by encouraging people to agree upon an action or a point of view. You can recognize an argumentative thesis and an argumentative essay by the writer's evident awareness of opposing perspectives. When readers are likely to require good reasons before they will agree with your thesis or when they are likely to resist your point of view, your situation is one that calls for argumentative writing.

In addition, a simple argumentative essay can serve one of three purposes. Some essays ask readers to agree with a *value judgment* ("The present daycare system is inadequate and inefficient"). Others propose a *specific action* ("Money from the student activity fee at this college should be used to establish and staff a fitness program available to all students"). And still others advance an *opinion* quite different from that held by most people ("The supposed 'revolution' of Web shopping is no more than the logical next step in catalog retailing").

In situations calling for more complex arguments, however, you should feel free to combine these purposes as long as the relationship among them is made clear to the reader. In a complex argument, for instance, you might *first* show that the city government is inefficient and corrupt and *then* argue that it is better to change the city charter to eliminate the opportunities for the abuse of power than it is to try to vote a new party into office or to support a reform faction within the existing political machine.

Some people draw a distinction between situations calling for *logical argument* (usually called, simply, *argument*) and *persuasive argument* (usually termed *persuasion*). Whereas logical argument appeals to reason, persuasive argument appeals to the emotions. The aim of both, however, is to convince, and they are nearly always blended into whatever mixture seems most likely to do the convincing. After all, reason and emotion are both important human elements. The two often work together, with reason helping to change minds and emotion helping to prompt action.

CHOOSING A STRATEGY

Argument begins with an issue, moves to a thesis (or assertion) addressing the issue, and concludes with evidence and reasoning to convince readers and deal with opposing perspectives. This is an admittedly oversimplified view of the components of an argument (and the process of composing), yet it serves to point out that choosing strategies for an argumentative essay calls for a number of different activities.

First, you need to *identify an issue* that you can effectively address through argument. Without an issue—a difference in point of view—you have nothing to argue about. Some issues will take a clear shape before you begin writing: matters of social justice, environmental regulation, civil and criminal law, education, community relationships, and the like are filled with familiar and significant matters of disagreement and difference. In preparing to address such an issue, you need to make sure that you understand them well enough to present them in clearly defined form to readers and to provide appropriate background. You should be ready to stress the significance of an issue and the need to make a judgment or take an action.

Some familiar issues have been argued so often that readers are not likely to be receptive to further argument; others are matters of taste that are beyond argument. For instance, no amount of reasoning is likely to convince people who dislike action movies to begin enjoying them. And some issues involve matters of deeply held religious or ethical beliefs that are difficult, if not impossible, to address through logical argument.

Many issues will take a clear shape only when you think and write about them, however. Perhaps you have been irritated for some time by the concert arrangements at a local civic center, and you believe other people share your irritation. Your irritation is not itself an issue, but it can point to one. If you propose changing the arrangements, and you realize that your proposals are not the only ones that ought to be considered, then you have begun to shape an issue. As you write, you need to be ready to explain the issue to your readers, perhaps drawing on their own irritation with the arrangements to stress the importance of considering changes. Of course, when an issue takes shape in your writing, the opposing points of view are probably not well developed, if at all. For instance, you may not be aware of any alternate concert arrangements that other people have proposed, but you can probably think of some plausible alternatives to your own. In exploring them for readers, however, you identify the opposing points of view that create the issue.

Next, you need to *articulate your stance.* At the heart of an argumentative essay is the opinion you want readers to share or the action you are proposing they undertake. Being able to state this *thesis* (or *proposition*) concisely and clearly to yourself is essential to developing your strategy for an argumentative essay. Conveying your thesis in convincing form is, after all, the main purpose of the essay. Expressing your stance concisely and clearly in a *thesis statement* is perhaps the best way to alert readers to the point of your argument.

Some writers like to arrive at a sharply focused thesis statement early in the process of composing and use it to guide the selection and arrangement of evidence, for example,

> The inconvenience and discontent that accompanies concerts at the Civic Center can be greatly reduced by moving the box office further away from the main entrance doors, doubling the number of rest rooms, improving the lighting, and removing the temporary seating that partially obstructs the central aisles.

Other writers settle on a tentative ("working") thesis, which they revise as an essay takes shape. In either case, checking frequently to see that factual evidence and supporting ideas or arguments are clearly linked to the thesis is a good way for writers to make sure their finished essays are coherent, unified arguments.

Finally, you need to develop evidence and reasoning that supports your thesis and arrange it in ways that readers will consider clear and convincing. Variety in evidence gives writers a chance to present an argument fully and persuasively. Examples, facts and figures, statements from authorities, personal experience, or the experience of other people—all these can be valuable sources of support.

The basic patterns of exposition, too, can be supporting strategies. For example, to persuade people to take driving lessons at an automobile racing school, you might tell the story of someone whose life was saved through the evasive maneuver she learned in her first day at such a school. Or you might follow this narrative example with a classification of the most common kinds of accidents, comparing them, in turn, with the parallel kinds of safety lessons the schools provide.

The expository patterns can also be easily adapted to argumentative purposes. Writers frequently turn to example, comparison and contrast, cause and effect, definition, and induction or deduction to organize arguments. A series of *examples* can be an effective way of showing that a government social policy does not work and in fact hurts the people it is supposed to serve. *Comparison and contrast* can guide choices among competing products, among ways of disposing of toxic waste, or among ways of revising student loan policies. *Cause and effect* can organize an argument over who is to blame for a problem or over the possible consequences of a new program. *Definition* is helpful when a controversy hinges on the interpretation of a key term or when the meaning of an important word is itself the subject of disagreement. *Induction* and *deduction* are useful in argument because they provide the kind of careful, logical reasoning necessary to convince many readers, especially those who may at first have little sympathy for the writer's opinion.

An argument need not be restricted to a single pattern. The choice of a pattern or a combination of patterns depends on the subject, the specific purpose, and the kinds of evidence needed to convince the audience to which the essay is directed. Some arguments about complicated, significant issues use so many patterns that they can be called *complex arguments.*

In arranging your evidence and reasoning, you should also consider the potential impact on readers. Three common and effective arrangements from which you can choose are ascending order, refutation-proof, and pro-con. In an *ascending order* arrangement, the strongest, most complex, or most emotionally moving evidence comes last, where it can build on the rest of the evidence in the essay and is likely to have the greatest impact on readers, as in the following example.

Introduction: The issue—some people are trying to have genetically altered farm products banned while others are arguing for an increase in the number of such products.

Tentative thesis: Despite a few drawbacks, genetically altered farm products are a great benefit to us all.

Support 1: The regulations governing genetic alteration and extensive testing means the products are generally quite safe; problems have been minor and worries have not been warranted by experience.

Support 2: Genetic alteration can create crops that are more resistant to disease and that are easier to cook and digest.

Support 3: Genetic alteration can make farms more productive and in so doing lower food costs, make more food available, and help fight undernourishment throughout the world [strongest, most moving support; even if there are some problems, these benefits may outweigh them].

Conclusion: Sums up, restates, and reinforces the thesis and the evidence.

In a *refutation-proof* arrangement, the writer acknowledges opposing points of view early in the essay and then goes on to show why the author's outlook is superior.

Tentative thesis: Genetically altered farm products benefit farmers and consumers.

Opposing points of view: Genetically engineered products are often less tasty and less nutritious; they can have unintended health consequences for farmers and consumers.

Refutation: The products can be engineered to be both tasty and nutritious—the choice is up to the producers and consumers; all natural products can have unintended consequences, and we forget this when dealing with "scientific products"; more extensive testing can help us deal with any unfortunate consequences.

Support 1: Genetically altered products can be more disease and pest-resistant, reducing the dangers of exposure to pesticides and other chemicals.

Support 2: Genetically altered products provide greater variety for consumers and choices for farmers looking for products appropriate for their soil and climate.

Support 3, 4, 5. . . .

Conclusion

A *pro-con* arrangement allows the writer to present an opposing point of view and then refute it, continuing until all opposition has been dealt with and all positive arguments voiced. This strategy is particularly useful when there is a strong opposition to the writer's thesis.

> Tentative thesis: The benefits of genetically altered farm products far outweigh the liabilities.
> Con 1: The engineered products may end up replacing "natural" ones.
> Pro 1: Some "natural" products may be less common, but the success of organic and other specialty products indicates that there will be a demand for both "new" and "natural" foods.
> Con 2: Genetically altered products are often designed for the needs of large corporate farms and will contribute to the demise of smaller, family farms.
> Pro 2: The shift to larger farms and agribusinesses has been occurring for many reasons other than genetic engineering of crops; the new crops will have only a small effect, if any.
> Con 3, 4, 5. . . .
> Pro 3, 4, 5. . . .
> Conclusion

DEVELOPING ARGUMENTS

In developing an argument, you need to pay attention to your choice of evidence and to make sure your reasoning is clear and logical. It is never possible to arrive at absolute proof—argument, after all, assumes that there are at least two sides to the matter under discussion—yet a carefully constructed case will convince many readers.

One way to construct arguments is to follow the pattern of *data-warrant-claim reasoning* as outlined by the philosopher Stephen Toulmin. *Data* correspond to your evidence and *claim* to your thesis or assertion. *Warrant* refers to the mental process by which a reader connects the data to the claim. To argue effectively, you need to show your readers how the warrant connects the data to your claim, as in the following sequence.

> Data: Children's books are relatively expensive, generally costing between ten and thirty dollars.
> Warrant: Buying children a variety of books can be very expensive.

Warrant: Children learn to love books by reading; playing with books on a regular basis is something that helps them become good readers.

Warrant: Children get easily bored with a book, so they need a variety of books to keep them occupied—though the book that bores them today will interest them tomorrow and the day after.

Claim: The high cost of children's books keeps many children from learning to love books and becoming better readers.

At the same time, a flaw in logic can undermine an otherwise reasonable argument and destroy a reader's confidence in its conclusions. The introduction to Chapter 12, "Reasoning by Use of *Induction* and *Deduction*," discusses some important errors to avoid in reasoning or in choosing evidence. Here are some others:

Post hoc ergo propter hoc ("After this therefore because of this")— Just because one thing happened *after* another does not mean that the first event caused the second. In arguing without detailed supporting evidence that a recent drop in the crime rate is the result of a newly instituted anticrime policy, a writer might be committing this error, because there are other equally plausible explanations: a drop in the unemployment rate, for example, or a reduction in the number of people in the 15–25 age bracket, the segment of the population that is responsible for a high proportion of all crimes.

Begging the question—A writer "begs the question" when he or she assumes the truth of something that is still to be proven. An argument that begins this way, "The recent, unjustified rise in utility rates should be reversed by the state legislature," assumes that the rise is "unjustified," though this important point needs to be proven.

Ignoring the question—A writer may "ignore the question" by shifting attention away from the issue at hand to some loosely related or even irrelevant matter: for example, "Senator Jones's plan for encouraging new industries cannot be any good because in the past he has opposed tax cuts for corporations" (this approach shifts attention away from the merits of Senator Jones's proposal). A related problem is the *ad hominem* (toward the person) argument, which substitutes personal attack for a discussion of the issue in question.

Student Essay

In recent years, many new foods have been developed, including some that are substitutes for "natural foods." The development of these products has gone hand-in-hand with growing controversies over their safety, with most people willing to at least listen to the criticisms on the grounds that food safety is one of the most important public health issues all of us face. In the face of such controversy, Julie Richardson sets out to defend an "artificial" food, olestra, in her essay, "The Fight on Fat Controversy."

The Fight on Fat Controversy

by Julie Richardson

Today, Americans are realizing the importance of a healthy lifestyle, which includes exercising and following a balanced diet. Reducing fat in the diet decreases the risk of health problems such as heart disease and obesity and is a vital step in achieving an improved lifestyle. Food manufacturers are responding to the consumer's needs by adding more reduced-fat foods to product lines. A trip down the grocery aisle is evidence of the increased "better-for-you" products, tempting the consumer with less salt, less sugar, and sugarless, lower fat, and nonfat items.

Background

Importance of topic for readers

After nine years of research, the U.S. Food & Drug Administration (FDA) approved a fat-free cooking oil known as olestra to be used in frying savory snacks. Olestra has been hailed as a breakthrough solution for millions of Americans who are looking to reduce fat and calories from the foods they want to eat without sacrificing the quality of taste. Excitement, curiosity, and confusion have followed the new lineup of products made with olestra. This new discovery is slowly yet dramatically changing food processing, and consumers need to educate themselves on the facts surrounding this innovative alternative to fat.

Information about specific issue/ disagreement

"Confusion" suggests potential disagreements

Olestra, marketed by Procter & Gamble as Olean, is made from vegetable oil and sugar, then used in place of regular cooking oils or fats. This revolutionary fat substitute does not break down like other fats; instead, it passes through the stomach and intestines without being digested or absorbed by the body. As a result, olestra provides all the taste of vegetable oil but none of the calories or harmful saturated fats of regular vegetable oils. The results are snacks that taste great with no fat and half of the calories.

Heralded as a waistline-whittling savior by millions of consumers, olestra has been condemned by others as a nutritional saboteur with distressing gastrointestinal side effects. The Center for Science in the Public Interest (CSPI) believes there are serious health risks when products made with olestra are consumed. This nonprofit health group believes the FDA should ban olestra or, at the very least, require a prominent warning label on the front of packages stating that olestra can cause severe side effects. Currently there is only a small warning on the back of packaging, warning consumers that they could experience soft stools when consuming olestra.

Challengers of olestra also advocate that the body is robbed of vitamins or carotenoids (found in fresh fruits and vegetables) that have already been digested. Michael Jacobson, executive director of CSPI, reveals that carotenoids protect against chronic diseases. Jacobson also states that long-term use of olestra in snack foods is likely to cause thousands of cases of cancer and heart disease each year. Opponents of olestra believe additional research should be completed to ensure the protection of consumers' health.

Proponents of olestra, including Procter & Gamble and the FDA, are quick to point out the fallacy of olestra "robbing" the body of vitamins and carotenoids that have already been digested, as Jacobson implies. Olestra can only interact with vitamins or carotenoids that are in the digestive system at the exact same time as the olestra; and even then, the level of interaction has

Concise statement of issue

Arguments against the product

More arguments against

Arguments and evidence for the product— refuting opponents of olestra

not been outside the acceptable range. Results from the
FDA Advisory Committee review in June 1998 determined there is no direct evidence that carotenoids are
responsible for lower risk of disease, which disproves
Jacobson's theory that carotenoids protect against
chronic diseases. These results also show the absurdity
of Jacobson's claim that long-term use of olestra causes
cancer.

Frito-Lay has been allowed to fortify their WOW!
Chips with extra vitamins to insure there is no net loss
or reduction in vitamin levels due to normal absorp-
tion. However, the FDA is preventing Frito-Lay from
adding extra carotenoids to their WOW! Chips because the jury in the scientific community is still out as
to whether or not carotenoids are actually good or
bad. In a study conducted in Sweden, a compelling
argument raises the possibility of carotenoids actually
causing cancer.

> Admits to
> some validity
> in worries
> about the
> product

Michael Jacobson's research is anecdotal and unsci-
entific. Most of his research is obtained through ques-
tionnaires completed on the CSPI Web site, not in a
laboratory by scientists. In contrast, P&G has spent
25 years and $200 million researching olestra, in one of
the most comprehensive reviews of any food additive in
history. The FDA received 150,000 pages of data from
studies of 8,000 adults and children. Results from a
follow-up study were reviewed in June 1998 by a FDA
panel of leading health, medical, and nutrition experts
who overwhelmingly reaffirmed the safety of Olean.
The committee also discussed the possibility of remov-
ing or rewording the warning label on Frito-Lay's WOW!
Chips.

> Direct
> refutation of
> major
> objections
> supported by
> statistics and
> authoritative
> testimony

Another issue of concern with olestra rivals is the
labeling of "fat-free" on snacks made with olestra.
Opponents feel the packaging is misleading to consumers
since olestra is an indigestible fat. I do understand the dispute over labeling, even though olestra technically is a fat
substitute and does not have the same effect as regular
fat in the body.

> Agrees with
> objections to
> packaging of
> product

Side effects from olestra in some people have given way for public scrutiny. Olestra's larger and tighter molecules pass through the body undigested. Since the olestra is mixed in with other food products in the digestive system, it may physically soften the stool, similar to adding oil or water to bread dough. The symptoms experienced may depend on consumption, other eaten foods, and the individual body reaction.

Another objection

Followed by two paragraphs of refutation

Prior to olestra's approval, it was determined that digestive symptoms were common among the general population. As recorded in the FDA's report on olestra in 1996, 40 percent of adults noted that they experienced some digestive effect within the past month. Also, a study published in the *Journal of the American Medical Association* (January 1998) said that potato chips made with Olean are no more likely to cause digestive changes than potato chips made with regular vegetable oil.

Common digestive symptoms are caused by a range of other foods, such as beans, some milk products, and fruit, especially in those who eat too much. Usually when people determine that certain foods do not agree with them, they avoid them. To ban olestra since it may cause diarrhea in some instances is like banning milk because it causes illness for those that are lactose intolerant.

Opponents of olestra, namely the CSPI group, have fought loud and hard at attacking the new fat substitute by relying on the media to circulate their allegations. They have become the nation's most familiar nutrition watchdog group; however, some people may view CSPI's intentions as being more interested in publicity rather than protecting the public's interest. Let's face it, the media loves drama brought on by interest groups representing "victims," and CSPI is good at digging out victims from their Web site. According to a *Reader's Digest* article titled, "Attack of the Food Police," Jacobson has not only thrashed olestra, but has also attempted bans on movie theater popcorn and Chinese food.

Questions motivation of opponents

CSPI has also petitioned the Federal Trade Commission to stop deceptive multimillion-dollar advertising campaigns for Olean and products made with it. As a result, Michael Jacobson persuaded *The New England Journal of Medicine* to pull Olean advertisements on the basis that *NEJM* was biased and had received funds from manufacturer, Procter & Gamble, for its support.

The truth of the matter is that *NEJM* elected to discontinue the Olean ad because it did not want to compromise its position while receiving advertising money from P&G. It is common for prestigious magazines to make decisions such as this to protect their interests; however, it was even more critical with Olean. The backlash and rhetoric the magazine would receive from Jacobson if it were to publish a positive report on olestra while still accepting ad funds from P&G would be damaging to its credibility. This is a good example of the effectiveness of Jacobson's scare tactics and persuasiveness.

Refutes the reasoning of criticisms of the product

Since Olean's approval, tens of millions of people have eaten over half-a-billion servings of new snacks made with this ingredient. These consumers have avoided more than 10 million pounds of fat and 40 billion calories, fat and calories they would have eaten in full-fat snacks. That's particularly noteworthy, considering the country's struggle with obesity and concern for cardiovascular diseases.

Pro-evidence of safety (facts)

Proctor & Gamble is continuing to study olestra, including possible nutrient depletion, and will report its findings to the FDA. The company has signed agreements with 12 other firms interested in making olestra snacks. P&G has tested olestra in several other foods, such as ice cream and mayonnaise, and states it will submit another application to the FDA for olestra's use within a year.

Evidence of trustworthiness of the manufacturer

I believe the protests made by opponents of olestra to be exaggerated, unfounded, and sensationalized. The Center for Science in the Public Interest is leading the crusade against olestra in its typical melodramatic fashion by twisting and eliminating the true facts.

Argumentative proposition implied throughout— now stated directly

Consumers owe it to themselves to be aware of the organizations supporting olestra, such as The Food & Drug Administration, The American Medical Association, The American Dietetics Association, The American Academy of Pediatrics, and The National Consumer League.

The evidence from years of research has proven that olestra can be worked into a healthy diet, just like any other food. Olestra has confirmed its safety and effectiveness to the medical and scientific community as well as gained momentum in the consumer's "fight on fat" battle. Olestra alone is not the answer to trim the fat off America's belly; however, it is a safe and effective way to enjoy favorite foods without sacrificing the taste. Olestra has opened the doors; now it's up to the American people to open their eyes to the truth. As Abraham Lincoln said "Truth is generally the best vindication against slander," and the truth of olestra's safety will prevail over Michael Jacobson and the CSPI group.

Summarizes evidence for and ends with a quotation summing up the writer's opinion of critics

Issues and Ideas
Persuading an Audience

CHRISTOPHER B. DALY

> CHRISTOPHER B. DALY grew up in Medford, Massachusetts. He now lives with his family in Newton, Massachusetts, and is a freelance writer and contributor to magazines.

How the Lawyers Stole Winter

> In this essay, which appeared first in *Atlantic Monthly*, Daly uses comparison to make the case that in our attempts to prevent dangerous accidents, we (and, in particular, the lawyers among us) have not only stolen some enjoyment from our lives but also lessened responsibility for our own actions. He suggests that the result may be more danger, not less.

When I was a boy, my friends and I would come home from school each day, change our clothes (because we were not allowed to wear "play clothes" to school), and go outside until dinnertime. In the early 1960s in Medford, a city on the outskirts of Boston, that was pretty much what everybody did. Sometimes there might be flute lessons, or an organized Little League game, but usually not. Usually we kids went out and played.

In winter, on our way home from the Gleason School, we would go past Brooks Pond to check the ice. By throwing heavy stones onto it, hammering it with downed branches, and, finally, jumping on it, we could figure out if the ice was ready for skating. If it was, we would hurry home to grab our skates, our sticks, and whatever other gear we had, and then return to play hockey for the rest of the day. When the streetlights came on, we knew it was time to jam our cold, stiff feet back into our green rubber snow boots and get home for dinner.

I had these memories in mind recently when I moved, with my   3
wife and two young boys, into a house near a lake even closer to Boston, in the city of Newton. As soon as Crystal Lake froze over, I grabbed my skates and headed out. I was not the first one there, though: the lawyers had beaten me to the lake. They had warned the town recreation department to put it off limits. So I found a sign that said DANGER. THIN ICE. NO SKATING.

Knowing a thing or two about words myself, I put my own   4
gloss on the sign. I took it to mean *When the ice is thin, there is danger and there should be no skating.* Fair enough, I thought, but I knew that the obverse was also true: *When the ice is thick, it is safe and there should be skating.* Finding the ice plenty thick, I laced up my skates and glided out onto the miraculous glassy surface of the frozen lake. My wife, a native of Manhattan, would not let me take our two boys with me. But for as long as I could, I enjoyed the free, open-air de-light of skating as it should be. After a few days others joined me, and we became an outlaw band of skaters.

What we were doing was once the heart of winter in New   5
England—and a lot of other places, too. It was clean, free exercise that needed no StairMasters, no health clubs, no appointments, and hardly any gear. Sadly, it is in danger of passing away. Nowadays it seems that every city and town and almost all property holders are so worried about liability and lawsuits that they simply throw up a sign or a fence and declare that henceforth there shall be no skating, and that's the end of it.

As a result, kids today live in a world of leagues, rinks, rules,   6
uniforms, adults, and rides—rides here, rides there, rides every-where. It is not clear that they are better off; in some ways they are clearly *not* better off.

When I was a boy skating on Brooks Pond, there were no   7
grown-ups around. Once or twice a year, on a weekend day or a holiday, some parents might come by with a thermos of hot cocoa. Maybe they would build a fire (which we were forbidden to do), and we would gather round.

But for the most part the pond was the domain of children. In   8
the absence of adults, we made and enforced our own rules. We had

hardly any gear—just some borrowed hockey gloves, some hand-me-down skates, maybe an elbow pad or two—so we played a clean form of hockey, with no high-sticking, no punching, and almost no checking. A single fight could ruin the whole afternoon. Indeed, as I remember it, thirty years later, it was the purest form of hockey I ever saw—until I got to see the Russian national team play the game.

But before we could play, we had to check the ice. We became   9
serious junior meteorologists, true connoisseurs of cold. We learned that the best weather for pond skating is plain, clear cold, with starry nights and no snow. (Snow not only mucks up the skating surface but also insulates the ice from the colder air above.) And we learned that moving water, even the gently flowing Mystic River, is a lot less likely to freeze than standing water. So we skated only on the pond. We learned all the weird whooping and cracking sounds that ice makes as it expands and contracts, and thus when to leave the ice.

Do kids learn these things today? I don't know. How would   10
they? We don't let them. Instead we post signs. Ruled by lawyers, cities and towns everywhere try to eliminate their legal liability. But try as they might, they cannot eliminate the underlying risk. Liability is a social construct; risk is a natural fact. When it is cold enough, ponds freeze. No sign or fence or ordinance can change that.

In fact, by focusing on liability and not teaching our kids how   11
to take risks, we are making their world more dangerous. When we were children, we had to learn to evaluate risks and handle them on our own. We had to learn, quite literally, to test the waters. As a result, we grew up to be savvier about ice and ponds than any kid could be who has skated only under adult supervision on a rink.

When I was a boy, despite the risks we took on the ice no one I   12
knew ever drowned. The only people I heard about who drowned were graduate students at Harvard or MIT who came from the tropics and were living through their first winters. Not knowing (after all, how could they?) about ice on moving water, they would innocently venture out onto the half-frozen Charles River, fall through, and die. They were literally out of their element.

Are we raising a generation of children who will be out of their   13
element? And if so, what can we do about it? We cannot just roll back the calendar. I cannot tell my six-year-old to head down to the lake by himself to play all afternoon—if for no other reason than that he would not find twenty or thirty other kids there, full of the collective wisdom about cold and ice that they had inherited, along

with hockey equipment, from their older brothers and sisters. Somewhere along the line that link got broken.

The whole setting of childhood has changed. We cannot change   14
it again overnight. I cannot send my children out by themselves yet, but at least some of the time I can go out there with them. Maybe that is a start.

As for us, last winter was a very unusual one. We had ferocious   15
cold (near-zero temperatures on many nights) and tremendous snows (about a hundred inches in all). Eventually a strange thing happened. The town gave in—sort of. Sometime in January the recreation department "opened" a section of the lake, and even dispatched a snowplow truck to clear a good-sized patch of ice. The boys and I skated during the rest of winter. Ever vigilant, the town officials kept the THIN ICE signs up, even though their own truck could safely drive on the frozen surface. And they brought in "lifeguards" and all sorts of rules about the hours during which we could skate and where we had to stay.

But at least we were able to skate in the open air, on real ice.   16
And it was still free.

MEANINGS AND VALUES

1.   Summarize in your own words the issue the author is addressing in this essay. In what ways is this issue representative of similar issues in other settings and climates? Explain. Does this "representativeness" make the argument significant and interesting for people who are not worried about thin ice and have no interest in skating? Why, or why not? (See "Guide to Terms": *Evaluation*.)

2.   Daly presents his examples of growing up in the early 1960s as illustrations of a good way to teach children responsibility and to allow them to have healthy fun. Does he succeed in doing so? If so, what details in the examples or statements of interpretation are most convincing? If not, what keeps the examples from being successful?

3.   What opposing points of view, if any, does Daly acknowledge? Would the essay be more (or less) effective if he spent more time dealing with possible objections to his argument? Make a list of possible objections to his argument and evidence that could be used to support them.

4.   Does the writer offer possible answers to the problem he identifies? If so, what are they? Does the essay make a clear case that lawyers are to blame for the problem? If not, does this weaken the essay? Why, or why not?

ARGUMENTATIVE TECHNIQUES

1. Why does the writer wait until Paragraph 6 to offer an argumentative proposition (thesis)? What role(s) do the opening paragraphs play? Do they explain an issue or problem? Do they provide evidence that can be used to support the thesis? Be specific in your answer, and point to specific evidence to support your conclusions. (Guide: *Introductions.*)

2. Which sentence or sentences state the argumentative proposition (thesis)? (Guide: *Thesis.*) Restate it in your own words. Are all parts of the essay clearly related to this thesis? If not, what are the functions of any parts not clearly related to the thesis? (Guide: *Unity.*) How is the comparison-contrast pattern related to the thesis? Explain. Would another arrangement of ideas and evidence be likely to provide more convincing development and support for the thesis? What arrangement, and why?

3. In what ways does the concluding sentence "echo" the beginning of the essay? Which paragraphs should be considered the conclusion of the essay? What functions do they perform? (Guide: *Closings.*)

DICTION AND VOCABULARY

1. The effectiveness of this essay depends to a considerable extent on the writer's ability to make the account of his childhood experiences seem like a realistic ideal and not merely a sentimental, nostalgic excursion. How does the diction in Paragraphs 1–2 and 7–9 aid him in staying away from too much sentimentality while at the same time making the experience seem attractive and worth reclaiming? If you think the examples are overly sentimental, explain why. (Guide: *Sentimentality.*)

2. What words with positive connotations does Daly associate with skating and playing hockey (see Pars. 4 and 8)? (Guide: *Connotation/ Denotation.*) How do the connotations of these words help support his thesis?

3. If you do not know the meaning of some of the following words, look them up in a dictionary: *gloss, obverse* (Par. 4); *high-sticking, checking* (8); *meteorologists, connoisseurs* (9); *liability, construct* (10); *vigilant* (15).

READ TO WRITE

1. **Collaborating:** Working in a group, make a list of other valuable childhood activities that have been curtailed, limited, or threatened by legal concerns. Should we ignore these concerns, find a way to accommodate them, or come up with different and less dangerous activities? Consider making an issue from this general subject area the focus of an argumentative essay.

2. **Considering Audience:** Using Daly's essay as a model, argue that in an attempt to deal with a problem, threat, or danger, we have taken steps that create more problems and dangers by taking away the need to be responsible for our actions. In developing the essay, acknowledge that many readers have legitimate fears, and avoid being too critical of such readers.

3. **Developing an Essay:** Begin an argumentative essay of your own with examples of how things should be, then develop your argument by contrasting how they are with how they ought to be.

(NOTE: Suggestions for topics requiring development by ARGUMENT are on p. 528 at the end of this chapter.)

STEPHANIE MILLS

STEPHANIE MILLS is an activist and writer. She has written and edited a number of books on environmental and social issues, including *In Praise of Nature* (ed.) (1991); *In Service of the Wild: Restoring and Reinhabiting Damaged Land* (1995); *Turning Away from Technology: A New Vision for the 21st Century* (ed.) (1997); *Epicurean Simplicity* (2002); and *On Gandhi's Path* (2010).

Could You Live with Less?

The examples in this essay, first published in *Glamour* magazine, are drawn from Mills's experience and, she suggests, are arguments intended primarily to justify her frugal, natural lifestyle. It should be clear to most readers, however, that she intends them to encourage readers to take seriously the choices she has made and perhaps even make similar choices themselves. What helps make this essay more than a statement of personal belief is the time Mills spends dealing with potential objections to her reasoning. In appearing to deal with objections, she is actually arguing in favor of her outlook—and addressing these arguments to readers, hoping to persuade them to agree with her.

Compared to the lifestyle of the average person on Earth, my days are lush with comfort and convenience: I have a warm home, enough to eat, my own car. But compared to most of my urban American contemporaries, I live a monastically simple life. 1

Since 1984 I've made my home outside a small city in lower Michigan, where the winters are snowy but not severely cold. My snug 720-square-foot house is solar- and wood-heated. No thermostat, just a cast-iron stove. There's electric lighting, indoor plumbing, a tankless water heater, a secondhand refrigerator and range—but no microwave oven, no dishwasher, no blow-dryer, no cordless phone. My gas-sipping compact station wagon has 140,000 miles on it and spreading patches of rust. I've never owned a television set. My home entertainment center consists of a thousand books, a CD-less stereo system, a picture window and two cats. 2

Part of the reason I live the way I do is that as a freelance writer, my income is unpredictable and at best fairly unspectacular. Thus it behooves me to keep in mind the difference between wants and 3 needs. Like all human beings, I have some needs that are absolute: about 2,500 calories a day, a half a gallon of water to drink, a sanitary means of disposing of my bodily wastes, water to bathe in, something muscular to do for part of the day and a warm, dry place to sleep. To stay sane I need contact with people and with nature, meaningful work and the opportunity to love and be loved.

I don't need, nor do I want, to complicate my life with gadgets.   4
I want to keep technology at the periphery rather than at the center of my life, to treat it like meat in Chinese cuisine—as a condiment rather than as a staple food. Technology should abet my life, not dominate or redefine it. A really good tool—like a sharp kitchen knife, a wheelbarrow or a baby carrier, all of which have been with us in some form for thousands of years—makes a useful difference but doesn't displace human intelligence, character or contact the way higher technologies sometimes do. Working people need the tools of their trade, and as a writer, I do have a fax, but I've resisted the pressure to buy a personal computer. A manual typewriter has worked well for me so far. Noticing that the most computer-savvy people I know are always pining for more megabytes and better software, I've decided not to climb on the purchasing treadmill of planned obsolescence.

Doing with less is easier when I remember that emotional needs   5
often get expressed as material wants, but can never, finally, be satisfied that way. If I feel disconnected from others, a cellular phone won't cure that. If I feel like I'm getting a little dowdy, hours on a tanning bed can't eradicate self-doubt.

Why live in a snowy region when I don't use central heat?   6
I moved here for love several years ago, and while that love was brief, my affection for this place has grown and grown. I like the roots I've put down; living like Goldilocks, moving from chair to chair, seems like not much of a life to me.

Being willfully backward about technology suits my taste—I like   7
living this way. Wood heat feels good, better than the other kinds. (Central heating would make my home feel like it was just anywhere.) Fetching firewood gets me outdoors and breathing (sometimes gasping) fresh air in the wintertime when it's easy to go stale. It's hard, achy work to split and stack the eight or 12 cords of stove wood I burn annually. I've been known to seek help to get it done. But the more of it I do myself, the more I can brag to my city friends.

My strongest motivation for living the way I do is my knowl-   8
edge, deep and abiding, that technology comes at a serious cost to the planet and most of its people. Burning fossil fuels has changed

the Earth's climate. Plastics and pesticides have left endocrine-disrupting chemicals everywhere—in us and in wildlife, affecting reproductive systems. According to Northwest Environment Watch in Seattle, the "clean" computer industry typically generates 139 pounds of waste, 49 of them toxic, in the manufacture of each 55-pound computer.

I refuse to live as if that weren't so. In this, I'm not unique.   9
There are many thousands of Americans living simply, questioning technology, fighting to preserve what remains of nature. We're bucking the tide, acting consciously and succeeding only a little. Yet living this way helps me feel decent within myself—and that, I find, is one luxury worth having.

MEANINGS AND VALUES

1. To what extent does the title of this essay act as a statement of the argumentative thesis (admittedly an *indirect* statement)? Is the thesis stated anywhere else in the essay? If not, does it need to be? (See "Guide to Terms": *Unity*.)

2. Summarize in your own words the issue the author is addressing in this essay. What evidence is there in the essay that the writer's purpose is to take a stand on the issue rather than simply to make a statement of personal belief? (Guide: *Purpose*.)

3. What opposing points of view does Mills acknowledge? Identify each and tell how effective you think she is at rebutting it. (Guide: *Evaluation*.) Do you think other readers are likely to agree with your estimate of Mills's success or failure? Why? What kinds of readers would be likely to disagree with you, if any?

ARGUMENTATIVE TECHNIQUES

1. Why does the writer not announce her argumentative proposition (thesis) clearly in the opening paragraphs of the essay? What role(s) do the opening paragraphs play? Do they explain an issue or problem? Do they provide evidence that can be used to support the thesis? Be specific in your answer, and point to specific evidence to support your conclusions. (Guide: *Introductions*.)

2. Examine the opening sentences of Paragraphs 3–8. How are they related to the argumentative thesis? Which parts of the essay, if any, do not support or explain the thesis? Could the essay be revised in any way to make it more unified? (Guide: *Thesis; Unity*.)

3. In what ways does the concluding paragraph sentence "echo" or refer to the beginning of the essay? What appeal to readers to agree with her does Mills offer in the conclusion? (Guide: *Closings*.)

DICTION AND VOCABULARY

1. The effectiveness of this essay depends to a considerable extent on the writer's ability to make her way of living seem like a realistic ideal and not merely an impractical, foolish, or sentimental exercise. How do the diction and the details in Paragraphs 3–4 and 7–8 emphasize the realistic and practical side of her way of living and help her stay away from too much sentimentality or nostalgia in portraying a lifestyle many will see as pointing back to the "good old times"? If you think the examples are overly sentimental, explain why. (Guide: *Sentimentality*.)

2. What words with positive connotations does Mills associate with her lifestyle (see Pars. 3, 4, 6, 7, and 8)? (Guide: *Connotation/Denotation*.) How do the connotations of these words help support her thesis?

READ TO WRITE

1. **Collaborating:** Working in a group, list other ways of living that most people might not endorse immediately. Decide with your group which patterns of development might be used for an essay defending one of these ways of living.

2. **Considering Audience:** Envision yourself as a modern suburban or urban dweller reading Mills's essay (this will not be much of a stretch for many people). Write a letter to the editor of the magazine in which it appeared (*Glamour*), responding to the issue from your perspective.

3. **Developing an Essay:** Mills clearly lets her readers know how she feels without excessive moralizing. Choose a controversial issue and write an essay similar to Mills's in which you share your belief without judging harshly or openly criticizing those in opposition.

(NOTE: Suggestions for essays requiring development by ARGUMENT are on p. 528 at the end of this chapter).

ANNA QUINDLEN

ANNA QUINDLEN has been a reporter and columnist for the *New York Times* and a columnist for *Newsweek*. She has written many novels: *Object Lessons* (1991), *One True Thing* (1994), *Black and Blue* (1998), *Blessings* (2002), *Rise and Shine* (2006), and *Every Last One* (2010). Her books of nonfiction essays include *Living Out Loud* (1988), *Thinking Out Loud* (1993), *How Reading Changed My Life* (1998), *Loud and Clear* (2004), *Imagined London* (2004), *Being Perfect* (2005), and *Good Dog. Stay.* (2007).

The Drug That Pretends It Isn't

In this essay, Quindlen employs a particularly useful (and flexible) argument strategy: choose a definition about which most people agree, and then show that a controversial subject or issue fits within the definition. Quindlen begins by pointing out that most people see illegal drug use as a big problem, and then argues that we need to view alcohol as a drug and its misuse as a significant problem. She builds on this framework, too, paying attention to arguments and evidence likely to be most persuasive to her readers.

Spring break in Jamaica, and the patios of the waterfront bars are   1
so packed that it seems the crowds of students must go tumbling into the aquamarine sea, still clutching their glasses. Even at the airport one drunken young man with a peeling nose argues with a flight attendant about whether he can bring his Red Stripe, kept cold in an insulated sleeve, aboard the plane heading home.

The giggle about Jamaica for American visitors has always been   2
the availability of ganja; half the T-shirts in the souvenir shops have slogans about smoking grass. But the students thronging the streets of Montego Bay seem more comfortable with their habitual drug of choice: alcohol.

Whoops! Sorry! Not supposed to call alcohol a drug. Some of   3
the people who lead antidrug organizations don't like it because they fear it dilutes the message about the "real" drugs, heroin, cocaine, and marijuana. Parents are offended by it: as they try to figure out which vodka bottle came from their party and which from their teenager's, they sigh and say, "Well, at least it's not drugs." And naturally the lobbyists for the industry hate it. They're power guys, these guys: The wine guy is George W.'s brother-in-law, the beer

guy meets regularly with House majority whip Tom DeLay. When you lump a cocktail in with a joint, it makes them crazy.

And it's true: Booze and beer are not the same as illegal drugs. 4 They're worse. A policy research group called Drug Strategies has produced a report that calls alcohol "America's most pervasive drug problem" and then goes on to document the claim. Alcohol-related deaths outnumber deaths related to drugs four to one. Alcohol is a factor in more than half of all domestic violence and sexual assault cases. Between accidents, health problems, crime, and lost productivity, researchers estimate alcohol abuse costs the economy $167 billion a year. In 1995 four out of every ten people on probation said they were drinking when they committed a violent crime, while only one in ten admitted using illicit drugs. Close your eyes and substitute the word blah-blah for alcohol in any of those sentences, and you'd have to conclude that an all-out war on blah-blah would result.

Yet when members of Congress tried to pass legislation that 5 would make alcohol part of the purview of the nation's drug czar, the measure failed. Mothers Against Drunk Driving faces opposition to both its education programs and its public service ads from principals and parents who think illicit drugs should be given greater priority. The argument is this: Heroin, cocaine, and marijuana are harmful and against the law, but alcohol is used in moderation with no ill effects by many people.

Here's the counterargument: There are an enormous number of 6 people who cannot and will never be able to drink in moderation. And what they leave in their wake is often more difficult to quantify than DWIs or date rapes. In his memoir *A Drinking Life*, Pete Hamill describes simply and eloquently the binges, the blackouts, the routine: "If I wrote a good column for the newspaper, I'd go to the bar and celebrate; if I wrote a poor column, I would drink away my regret. Then I'd go home, another dinner missed, another chance to play with the children gone, and in the morning, hung over, thick-tongued, and thick-fingered, I'd attempt through my disgust to make amends." Hamill and I used to drink, when we were younger, at a dark place down a short flight of stairs in the Village called the Lion's Head. There were book jackets covering the walls that I used to look at covertly with envy. But then I got older, and when I passed the Head I sometimes thought of how many books had never been written at all because of the drinking.

Everyone has a friend/an uncle/a coworker/a spouse/a neigh- 7 bor who drinks too much. A recent poll of seven thousand adults found that 82 percent said they'd even be willing to pay more for a drink if the money was used to combat alcohol abuse. New Mexico and Montana already use excise taxes on alcohol to pay for treatment programs. It's probably just coincidence that, as Drug Strategies reports, the average excise tax on beer is nineteen cents a gallon, while in Missouri and Wisconsin, homes to Anheuser-Busch and Miller, respectively, the tax is only six cents.

A wholesale uprising in Washington against Philip Morris, which 8 owns Miller Brewing and was the largest donor of soft money to the Republicans in 1998, or against Seagram's, which did the same for the Democrats in 1996, doesn't seem likely. Homeschooling is in order, a harder sell than even to elected officials, since many parents prefer lessons that do not require self-examination. Talking about underage drinking and peer pressure lets them off the hook by suggesting that it's all about sixteen-year-olds with six-packs. But the peer group is everywhere, from the frogs that croak "Bud" on commercials to those tiresome folks who behave as if wine were as important as books (it's not) to parents who drink to excess and teach an indelible life lesson.

Prohibition was cooked up to try to ameliorate the damage that 9 drinking does to daily life. It didn't work. But there is always self-prohibition. It's not easy, since all the world's a speakeasy. "Not even wine?" Hamill recalls he was asked at dinner parties after he stopped. Of course, children should not drink, and people who sell them alcohol should be prosecuted. Of course, people should not drink and drive, and those who do should be punished. But twenty-one is not a magic number, and the living room is not necessarily a safe place. There is a larger story that needs to be told, loud and clear, in homes and schools and on commercials given as much prominence and paid for in the same way as those that talk about the dangers of smack or crack: that alcohol is a mind-altering, mood-altering drug, and that lots of people should never start to drink at all. "I have no talent for it," Hamill told friends. Just like that.

MEANINGS AND VALUES

1. Summarize the reasons why, as this essay claims, people resist viewing alcohol as a drug.

2. Summarize the arguments and evidence the essay offers in favor of viewing alcohol as a drug.

3. Where in this essay does the writer offer readers a definition of illegal drugs, and in what ways does she provide this definition? Will the definition be precise enough so that most readers will be able to follow the argument? Why, or why not? (See "Guide to Terms": *Evaluation*.)

ARGUMENTATIVE TECHNIQUES

1. Identify the thesis statement in this essay. Tell why you find it either clear, focused, and appropriately limited in scope or unclear, vague, and too broad (or too narrow). (Guide: *Thesis.*)

2. What strategy does the writer employ to introduce opposing points of view? What strategies does she employ to introduce her refutation of the opposing points of view?

3. Identify the elements of this essay that are consistent with a refutation proof organization (see p. 446). Does the essay, in general, follow a refutation-proof pattern? Why, or why not?

4. Can this essay be said to combine strategies of definition and refutation-proof? If so, why? If not, why not?

DICTION AND VOCABULARY

1. Discuss how the author's choice of words in Paragraphs 3 and 8 is a strategy for criticizing people and groups unwilling to take strong measures against alcohol use and abuse. (Guide: *Diction.*)

2. Analyze the use of the words "blah-blah" in Paragraph 4 as a strategy consistent with the author's use of definition for purposes of argument.

3. What words or phrases in Paragraph 7 are used ironically? (Guide: *Irony.*)

4. If you do not know the meaning of some of the following words, look them up in a dictionary: *aquamarine* (Par. 1); *lobbyists* (3); *purview* (5); *eloquently, amends, covertly* (6); *excise* (7).

READ TO WRITE

1. **Collaborating:** Working in a group, focus on drinking or some other activity some people may regard as "recreational" and others as "dangerous." List as many reasons as you can for each judgment. Summarize these *pro* and *con* perspectives in a brief informative essay.

2. **Considering Audience:** The range of responses to Quindlen's essay is likely to be broad, depending on a reader's experiences, values, and background. Identify four kinds of people likely to have differing responses, and summarize briefly the likely responses from each kind of reader as well as reasons for the responses.

3. **Developing an Essay:** Using Quindlen's essay as a model, develop an argumentative essay of your own about how a particular activity generally regarded in either a positive or negative light should be redefined as the opposite.

(NOTE: Suggestions for topics requiring development by ARGUMENT are on p. 528 at the end of this chapter.)

ANDREW O'HEHIR

Andrew O'Hehir has written both film and book reviews for *Salon.com* and *Sight and Sound*. He is primarily interested in "indie" films. O'Hehir currently lives in Brooklyn, New York, with his wife and children.

The Myth of Media Violence

This serious argument, published online at *Salon.com*, has nonetheless an often informal tone. It addresses an issue about which people have strong opinions which often run contrary to facts and research, as this writer points out. One of the writer's main tactics in this essay is to look at the reasoning commonly used about media violence (both induction and deduction) and point out its many faults.

Kids these days. They're all wasting their spare hours, or so we're   1
told, with immoral trash like *Grand Theft Auto*, the now-notorious series of slickly decorated and powerfully addictive video games. As Senator Hillary Clinton explained at a forum hosted by the Kaiser Family Foundation, "They're playing a game that encourages them to have sex with prostitutes and then murder them."

Fans of "GTA" claim this is a typical nongamer's misinterpreta-   2
tion—it might be possible to kill hookers in the game, but it won't necessarily help you win—but let's let that go. There's no doubt that GTA allows you, for example, to play the role of an ex-con trying to take over a vice-addled city by gunning down drug lords, cops, low-flying aircraft and pretty much everything and everybody else. These games revel in their pseudo-noir amorality, and they're basically designed to be loathed by parents, school principals and tweedy psychologists.

Clinton's attack on the latest manifestation of the Media   3
Demon—you know, the evil force within video games, action movies, rap songs, comic books, dime novels, Judas Priest records played backward and, I don't know, Javanese puppet theater and cave hieroglyphics—is a depressingly familiar ploy in American politics.

Andrew O'Hehir, "The Myth of Media Violence," *Salon.com*, March 17, 2005. This article first appeared in Salon.com, at http://www.Salon.com. An online version remains in the Salon archives. Reprinted with permission.

When you can't make any progress against genuine social problems, or, like Senator Clinton, you seem religiously committed to triangulating every issue and halving the distance between yourself and Jerry Falwell, you go after the people who sell fantasy to teenagers.

What might be most interesting about this latest vapidity, in fact, is what Clinton didn't say. Five years ago, in the wake of the Columbine massacre, we were told that there was no serious debate about whether media violence contributed to teenage crime in the real world. A clear link had been established, the case was closed, and the only question was what we were going to do about it. By contrast, Clinton's comments were surprisingly mild and almost entirely subjective. She called violent and debauched entertainment a "silent epidemic," essentially arguing that it has effects, but we don't quite know what they are.

Over the long haul, Clinton said, violent media might teach kids "that it's okay to dis people because they're women or they're a different color or they're from a different place." Perhaps more to the point, she added: "Parents worry their children will not grow up with the same values they did because of the overwhelming presence of the media." That was it—no claims that we were breeding a nation of perverts and murderers, and no mention of all the supposed science indicating a link between simulated mayhem and the real thing. Playing GTA and watching Internet porn might lead your kids to "dis" somebody, or to grow up with different values from yours (or anyway to make you concerned that they might). Katy, bar the door!

As dopey as Clinton's remarks are, I don't mean to ridicule parents and educators for their legitimate concerns. Of course, I'm not certain that violent movies and games (or, for that matter, dumb-ass sitcoms and vapid reality shows) are harmless. My own kids are still too young for this question to matter much, but of course, I hold onto the naive hope that they'll spend their formative years hiking the Appalachians and reading about the Byzantine Empire, rather than vegetating in media sludge. But it's long past time to face the fact that, while it's legitimate not to like violent media, or to believe it's psychologically deadening in various ways, the case that it directly leads to real-life violence has pretty much collapsed.

Hillary Clinton's equivocation may be something of a compulsive family trait, but it also reflects how muddy this issue has become since the summer of 2000, when the American Medical Association, the American Psychiatric Association, the American Academy of Child and Adolescent Psychiatry, and several other

professional busybody organizations issued a joint statement proclaiming that "well over 1,000 studies" had shown a direct connection between media violence and "juvenile aggression." In 2002,
Harvard psychologist Steven Pinker wrote that it had become an
article of faith "among conservative politicians and liberal health
professionals alike . . . that violence in the media is a major cause of
American violent crime."

Actually, there never was any such consensus in the academic   8
fields of psychology, criminology, or media studies. And there
weren't well over a thousand studies of media violence either—that
was one of the many myths and legends that sprung up around this
question. In the years since then, the mavericks have been increasingly heard from. Even in the theatrical United States Senate hearings convened a few days after the Columbine shootings in 1999,
MIT professor Henry Jenkins observed that the idea that violent entertainment had consistent and predictable effects on viewers was
"inadequate and simplistic," adding almost poetically that most
young people don't absorb entertainment passively, but rather
move "nomadically across the media landscape, cobbling together
a personal mythology of symbols and stories taken from many different places."

Jenkins was a lonely voice at the time, but more recently the   9
edifice of mainstream certainty has begun to crumble. Psychologists
like Pinker, Jonathan Freedman, Jonathan Kellerman, and Melanie
Moore have counterattacked against their own establishment, arguing that media-violence research to date has been flawed and incon-
clusive at best, and a grant-funding scam at worst. Some have gone
further, suggesting that violent entertainment provides a valuable
fantasy outlet for the inevitable rage of childhood and adolescence,
and probably helps more children than it hurts. . . .

We've also heard from criminologists, lawyers, and literary   10
scholars as the tide of counterarguments has swelled. The latest of
these last is Harold Schechter, a professor at Queens College in New
York whose book, *Savage Pastimes*, provides an eye-opening survey
of gruesome entertainment throughout the history of Western civilization. Schechter's main point concerns what scholars call the "peri-
odicity" of campaigns like Senator Clinton's latest screed. Every
time a technological shift occurs (such as from books to movies,
radio to TV, movies to video games), he argues, it produces a new
medium for gruesome entertainment aimed at adolescent audiences, and produces a renewed outrage among the self-appointed
guardians of civilization.

One remarkable example not cited by Schecter: In 1948, there   11
was an enormous uproar in Canada over a meaningless killing committed by two boys, ages 13 and 11. Pretending to be highwaymen, they hid near a road with a stolen rifle and shot at a passing car, killing a passenger. When it was revealed that they were avid readers of crime comic books, the anticomics movement swelled. This story bears an uncanny similarity to a recent case, examined in *Salon*, in which two boys, ages 15 and 13, stole their father's rifle, hid near a highway, and shot at a passing car, killing a passenger. The youths defended themselves on the grounds that playing *Grand Theft Auto* made them do it.

The Jeremiahs who condemn violent entertainment, whether   12
crime comics or *Grand Theft Auto*, also invariably lament the passage of a golden age, generally contemporaneous with their own childhoods, when entertainment was healthful and wholesome, suitable for infants and grannies alike. I don't mean to impugn Granny, who may have a healthy appetite for phony bloodshed, but these moral guardians' sunny views of the past either reflect fuzzy memories or whopping hypocrisy.

Schechter offers an amusing catalog of the outrageous blood-   13
shed and mayhem found in popular entertainment since time immemorial, from the classics (as he observes, the onstage blinding of Gloucester in "King Lear"—"out, vile jelly"—is one of the most traumatic acts of violence in any medium) to the pornographic sadism of Grand-Guignol theater, the lurid sensationalism of turn-of-the-century "penny papers," and the ugly misogyny of Mickey Spillane's best-selling pulp novels. Undoubtedly Hillary Clinton would prefer that today's kids read books instead of playing GTA, and Schechter might suggest *Seth Jones: or, The Captives of the Frontier*, a wilderness adventure that was one of the best-selling kids' books of the nineteenth century. In one scene, the hero comes upon the corpse of a man who has been tied to a tree by Indians and burned to death: "Every vestige of the flesh was burned off to the knees, and the bones, white and glistening, dangled to the crisp and blackened members above! The hands, tied behind, had passed through the fire unscathed, but every other part of the body was literally roasted!" Seth is greatly relieved, however, to discover that the victim was not a white man. As Schechter says, it's impossible to imagine anyone publishing this as kiddie lit today, both for its gore quotient and its casual racism.

In another dime novel of the period, a rattling Western adven-   14
ture called *Deadwood Dick on Deck*, Schechter reports that more

than 100 people are killed in the first two chapters, a figure that fans of *Resident Evil* and *Doom* can only view with awe and veneration. Then there's the gruesome "comic" yarn Schechter digs up from 1839, in which that authentic American hero, Davy Crockett, engages in a "scentiforous fight" with an individual referred to as "a pesky great bull nigger" (and also as "Blackey," "Mr. Nig" and "snow-ball"). Crockett ends the battle by gouging out one of his adversary's eyes, feeling "the bottom of the socket with end of my thum."

Schechter knows what you're thinking: At least those kids were   15 reading, and as reprehensible by our standards as those books may have been, there's really no comparison between the printed page and the "hyperkinetic visuals of movies and computer games." The only answer to this is maybe and maybe not; critics of pop culture always assume that new technologies have rendered kids incapable of telling the difference between reality and fantasy, and so far they've always been wrong. Schechter writes that for children who had never seen a movie or a video game, "the printed page was a PlayStation, and penny dreadfuls were state-of-the-art escapism, capable of eliciting a shudder or thrill every bit as intense as the kind induced by today's high-tech entertainment." The relativist position that each generation is equally affected by the media available to it is supported by ample historical evidence, from the way that the audiences at early film screenings rose in panic when on-screen trains bore down upon them to the wildly Dionysian effect of that hypersexual, morals-corroding music, swing.

If Senator Clinton might prefer an outdoor family activity in the   16 sunny American heartland, there's always the example of Owensboro, Kentucky, where on August 14, 1936, some 20,000 citizens of all ages crowded into the courthouse square. It was a "jolly holiday," according to newspaper reports. Hot dogs, popcorn, and soft drinks were sold, and there was a mixture of cheers and catcalls—but no general disorder, as the local paper angrily insisted—when sheriff's deputies brought a man named Rainey Bethea out to the scaffold, where he was hanged.

Schechter cites the infamous opening pages of Michel Fou-   17 cault's *Discipline and Punish*, which recount the horrible tortures inflicted in 1757 on Robert François Damiens, the attempted assassin of Louis XV. In 1305 in London, Scottish rebel William Wallace was hanged and revived, castrated and disemboweled while still alive, and finally decapitated and dismembered, with the pieces coated in boiling tar and strung up in various public places. (When

Mel Gibson played Wallace in *Braveheart*, we saw none of that.) Sometimes it's the little things that tell the story: During the Reign of Terror in revolutionary France, children were given 2-foot-tall toy guillotines they could use to behead birds and mice.

Schechter doesn't bring up the Bethea execution to paint white 18 Kentuckians of the Depression as depraved rubes; his point is that we actually have come a long way in seven decades. We're free to regard violent movies and video games as loathsome, but we also have to admit they reflect at least a partially successful sublimation of what William James called "our aboriginal capacity for murderous excitement." Few of us are eager for the return of public executions (except perhaps the programming executives at Fox) and no real cops or prostitutes were harmed during the creation of *Grand Theft Auto*. Although a few juveniles charged with murder, or their victims' families, have argued that video games were responsible for murder, kids who play video-game shooters aren't outside gunning down the neighbors, possibly because that would mean getting off their butts and leaving behind the overlit universe of their TV or computer screen.

As Schechter says, there are two linked assumptions that un- 19 derpin all the hysteria about purported media-influenced violence in the last 20 years, if not longer. Assumption No. 1 is that we live in an especially violent time in human history, surrounded by serial killers, hardened teenage "superpredators," genocidal atrocities, and all sorts of amoral mayhem. Assumption No. 2 is that our popular entertainment is far more violent than the entertainment of the past, and presents that violence in more graphic and bloodthirsty detail. For critics of media violence, from the Clintons to Dave Grossman to the leadership of the child-psychiatry establishment, these assumptions go essentially unchallenged, and the conclusion they draw is that there is a causal or perhaps circular relationship between these "facts": Media violence breeds real violence, which leads to ever more imaginative media violence, and so on.

A longtime crime buff who has written several books about no- 20 torious murderers, Schechter mounts an impressive case in *Savage Pastimes* that, if anything, our pop culture is less bloody-minded than that of the past. Anyone who looks back at the 1950s, when Schechter himself was a child, and remembers only *Leave It to Beaver* and Pat Boone needs to read his discourse on the hugely popular *Davy Crockett* miniseries of 1954, "whose level of carnage," he writes, "remains unsurpassed in the history of televised children's entertainment." This series, with its barrage of "shootings, stabbings, scalpings, stranglings," was broadcast on Wednesday nights at 7:30 PM, and presented as the acme of wholesome family fare.

In fact, as Schechter demonstrates, fifties TV was profoundly 21 rooted in guns and gunfire, to a degree that would provoke widespread outrage today. But there are factors he doesn't consider, or considers only in passing, that fuel people's perceptions that the past was less violent, both in real and symbolic terms. Those fifties TV shows were mostly westerns, of course, which meant that they presented themselves as instructive fables of American history in [their] most masculine, individualistic form. They were racially and politically uncomplicated; *Gunsmoke* and *Bonanza* developed a social conscience in the sixties, but the white screen cowboys of the fifties were heroes, and the whites, Indians, and Mexicans around them were clearly divided into good guys and bad.

In other words, while *Davy Crockett* and *Have Gun Will Travel* 22 and *The Rifleman* were loaded with violence, it was mostly reassuring violence, presented without splatter and without moral consequences. The graphic media violence of our age, whether in *Taxi Driver* or *Reservoir Dogs* or *CSI* or *Grand Theft Auto*, is deliberately unsettling, meant to fill viewers with dread and remind them that life is an uncertain, morally murky affair. This might put us closer to the murder-obsessed Victorian age than to the scrubbed fifties, and in examining both eras, it's important to remember that this message can be delivered badly or well, used for a cheap roller-coaster effect or a tremendous *King Lear* catharsis. (It's also worth pointing out that Jib Fowles disagrees with Schechter, arguing, "It does appear that television violence has been slowly growing in volume and intensity since 1950.")

But if Assumption No. 2 looks questionable, Assumption No. 1 23 is just flat-out false. As Fowles painstakingly details in *The Case for Television Violence*, violence has clearly been decreasing in the Western world for the last 500 years; as far as we can tell from uneven record keeping, the murder rate in medieval Europe was several times higher than it is today, even in relatively violent societies like the United States. While the twentieth century has seen some spikes in violent crime—correlating less to the arrival of television than to the proportion of young men in the population—the downward trend since about 1980 has reinforced the general tendency. As Rhodes puts it, "We live in one of the least violent eras in peacetime human history."

Again, there are some complicating ambiguities here, although 24 they don't make the absolute numbers look any different. If you're convinced that we live amid a psychotic crime wave, well, blame the media. Murder has become an increasingly rare crime, and most of it is pretty unglamorous—poor people, many of them black and brown, killing each other in petty disputes over love affairs or insultingly small amounts of money. But whenever something truly ghoulish happens—a serial killer hacks up some white girls or a mom drowns her kids in the tub—we're exposed to so many pseudo-news stories and movies of the week that it seems as if society is totally out of its gourd and such things are happening every day.

I don't think there's any question that the sense of dislocation   25
this produces, while unmeasurable by social science, can be profound. We know this as the "mean world" syndrome, and it's the reason why, for instance, my wife's 90-something grandparents not only don't go outside after dark but also refuse to answer the phone. (Apparently the depraved criminals roaming the suburban streets can teleport themselves through the phone lines.) Our obsession with violent crime may indeed be at an all-time high, even as crime itself keeps becoming rarer. Perhaps TV has made us so frightened that we've mostly stopped killing each other.

There's far more that one could and perhaps should say about   26
the essentially adolescent character of our civilization, fatally torn between the impulses of Eros and Thanatos. But the point I'm struggling toward is that while you can't prove that media violence *doesn't* lead to real violence—and only an idiot would assert that no one has ever been inspired to commit a crime by a book or movie or video game—our definitions of "media" and "violence" may need some rethinking. And as a general proposition, the simplistic consensus of a few years ago stands on exceedingly shaky ground. "This whole episode of studying television violence," as Fowles told Rhodes in 2000, "is going to be seen by history as a travesty. It's going to be used in classes as an example of how social science can just go totally awry."

Most likely it will be seen in the same way that we now see psy-   27
chologist Frederic Wertham's infamous fifties campaign against horror comics—as an understandable, if in retrospect laughable, response to the unknown. Wertham interviewed juvenile offenders and found that most of them read comic books; ergo, comics led to juvenile crime. There was widespread panic about juvenile delinquency in that decade (which actually saw record lows in crime of all kinds), and he had found an appropriately disreputable scapegoat. While Wertham focused his ire on the gore-drenched horror

comics, with their rotting zombies and sadistic scientists, he also wrote that Wonder Woman was a lesbian, Batman and Robin were a man-boy couple and Superman was a fascist. (So he got those right, at least.)

Attorney and author Marjorie Heins has pointed out that the con-   28
flict between pop culture and its critics is literally as old as Western civilization: Plato thought that unsavory art should be censored, while Aristotle argued that violent and upsetting drama had a cathartic effect and helped purge the undesirable emotions of spectators. Jib Fowles suggests that these periodic culture wars are mostly a way of displacing anxieties about class, race, and gender, as well as, most obviously, a proxy war between middle-aged adults and the succeeding generations whose culture they can't quite understand.

Perhaps the most sensible words on this subject that I've dis-   29
covered come from comics author Gerard Jones, in a 2000 *Mother Jones* article that became, in part, the basis for his book *Killing Monsters*. "I'm not going to argue that violent entertainment is harmless," he wrote. "I am going to argue that it's helped hundreds of people for every one it's hurt, and that it can help far more if we learn to use it well. I am going to argue that our fear of 'youth violence' isn't well-founded on reality, and that the fear can do more harm than the reality. We act as though our highest priority is to prevent our children from growing up into murderous thugs—but modern kids are far more likely to grow up too passive, too distrustful of themselves, too easily manipulated."

That expresses, I suspect, exactly what many parents of more or   30
less my generation feel about their kids and the media. To be fair, I also think it's a more honest, less red-state-coded version of what Hillary Clinton was trying to say. We know that the media stew most of us marinate in is tremendously powerful, but we don't understand its power, so we fear it. Furthermore, even if violent entertainment has always been with us, as Harold Schechter argues, it's *supposed* to scare us, because it calls up emotions and impulses we don't usually want to think about, because it summons demons from below our conscious minds and before our approved history. That's its job.

Ultimately, we can't protect our kids from being frightened or   31
unsettled by things they will inevitably encounter, whether while reading Dostoevsky or playing the latest zombie-splattering incarnation of *Resident Evil*. We can't stop them from forging their own culture out of fragments and shards they collect along the way, a culture specifically intended to confuse and alienate us. But I think

Jones is right: Most of us don't have to worry about breeding little homicidal maniacs. What's far more plausible, and more dangerous, is that we'll raise a pack of sedentary, cynical little button-pushing consumption monsters who never go outside. Now that's scary.

MEANINGS AND VALUES

1. How would you describe the tone of this essay? (See "Guide to Terms": *Tone.*) Does it vary anywhere in the essay? If so, where?

2. To what extent does the tone support or undermine the purpose and argumentative proposition of the essay? (Guide: *Purpose, Thesis.*)

3. What argumentative proposition does the writer advance in this essay? Where does he state it?

ARGUMENTATIVE TECHNIQUES

1. a. Which sections of this essay are taken up by summaries and refutations of points of view that differ from the writer's?

   b. Does the writer spend too much time on other points of view? Why, or why not? (Guide: *Evaluation.*)

2. Discuss the use of transitions at the beginnings of Paragraphs 28, 29, 30, 31, 35, and 36. (Guide: *Transitions.*) How do they advance the argument and guide the reader? Are they effective? (Guide: *Evaluation.*)

3. This essay uses a number of detailed examples. Make a list of them, and indicate which you think are particularly effective or ineffective and why.

DICTION AND VOCABULARY

1. Tell what the specific, concrete diction contributes to the effectiveness of the examples in Paragraphs 11, 19, and 23. (Guide: *Concrete/Abstract, Diction.*)

2. Does the offensiveness of some of the language in Paragraphs 11, 19, and 23 undermine the writer's purpose? Why, or why not? (Guide: *Purpose, Evaluation.*)

3. If you do not know the meaning of some of the following terms, look them up in a dictionary: *pseudo-noir* (Par. 2); *debauched* (4); *consensus, nomadically* (8); *Jeremiahs* (12); *Grand-Guignol* (13); *hyperkinetic* (15); *disembowled* (17); *simplistic* (26); *unsavory* (28).

READ TO WRITE

1. **Collaborating:** Most of us have experience with media violence. Working with a group, ask each person to write a paragraph about specific examples of media violence they have witnessed and the effects (or lack of them) that this violence had for them.

2. **Considering Audience:** Do different people with different personalities respond to media violence in varied ways? Prepare a questionnaire about media violence and ask your friends or classmates to respond to it, then summarize the results.

3. **Developing an Essay:** Follow O'Hehir's approach, and argue against many of the widely held opinions on an issue, criticizing them using tactics similar to O'Hehir's.

(NOTE: Suggestions for topics requiring development by use of ARGUMENT are on p. 528 at the end of this chapter.)

AL GORE

Environmental activist and author AL GORE won the Nobel Peace Prize in 2007 for his work on climate change. He was the subject of the 2007 documentary on that topic, *An Inconvenient Truth*. After graduating from Harvard, serving in the Army during the Vietnam War, and working as an investigative journalist, he won a seat in the U.S. House of Representatives and subsequently became a U.S. senator. Al Gore was the 45th vice president of the United States from 1993 to 2001 under President Bill Clinton. A Democrat, he won the popular vote in the 2000 presidential election but lost to Republican candidate George W. Bush in a disputed result. Gore has written several books, including *An Inconvenient Truth* (2006), *The Assault on Reason* (2007), and *Our Choice* (2009).

The Time to Act Is Now

Scientists have long warned that global warming has dire consequences. Gore's discussion of our role in halting global warming originally appeared in the online magazine *Salon* on November 4, 2005. The United States Environmental Protection Agency imposed the nation's first regulations on greenhouse gas emissions on January 2, 2011.

It is now clear that we face a deepening global climate crisis that 1 requires us to act boldly, quickly and wisely, "Global warming" is the name it was given a long time ago. But it should be understood for what it is: a planetary emergency that now threatens human civilization on multiple fronts. Stronger hurricanes and typhoons represent only one of many new dangers as we begin what someone has called "a nature hike through the Book of Revelation."

As I write, my heart is heavy due to the suffering the people of 2 the Gulf Coast have endured. In Florida, Alabama, Mississippi, Louisiana, and Texas, and particularly in New Orleans, thousands have experienced losses beyond measure as our nation and the world witnessed scenes many of us thought we would never see in this great country. But unless we act quickly, this suffering will be but a beginning.

The science is extremely clear: global warming may not affect 3 the frequency of hurricanes, but it makes the average hurricane stronger, magnifying its destructive power. In the years ahead, there will be more storms like Katrina, unless we change course. Indeed, we have had two more Category 5 storms since Katrina—including Wilma, which before landfall was the strongest hurricane ever measured in the Atlantic.

We know that hurricanes are heat engines that thrive on warm water. We know that heat-trapping gases from our industrial society are warming the oceans. We know that, in the past thirty years, the number of Category 4 and 5 hurricanes globally has almost doubled. It's time to connect the dots:

- Last year, the science textbooks had to be rewritten. They used to say, "It's impossible to have a hurricane in the South Atlantic." We had the first one last year, in Brazil. Japan also set an all-time record for typhoons last year: ten. The previous record was seven.
- This summer, more than two hundred cities in the United States broke all-time heat records. Reno, Nevada, set a new record with ten consecutive days above one hundred degrees, Tucson, Arizona, tied its all-time record of thirty-nine consecutive days above one hundred degrees. New Orleans—and the surrounding waters of the Gulf—also hit an all-time high.
- This summer, parts of India received record rainfall—thirty-seven inches fell in Mumbai in twenty-four hours, killing more than one thousand people.
- The new extremes of wind and rain are part of a larger pattern that also includes rapidly melting glaciers worldwide, increasing desertification, a global extinction crisis, the ravaging of ocean fisheries, and a growing range for disease "vectors" like mosquitoes, ticks, and many other carriers of viruses and bacteria harmful to people.

All of these are symptoms of a deeper crisis: the "Category 5" collision between our civilization—as we currently pursue it—and the earth's environment.

Sixty years ago, Winston Churchill wrote about another kind of gathering storm. When Neville Chamberlain tried to wish that threat away with appeasement, Churchill said, "This is only the beginning of the reckoning. This is only the first sip, the first foretaste, of a bitter cup which will be proffered to us year by year—unless by a supreme recovery of moral health and martial vigor, we rise again and take our stand for freedom."

For more than fifteen years, the international community has   7
conducted a massive program to assemble the most accurate scientific assessment on global warming. Two thousand scientists,
in a hundred countries, have produced the most elaborate, well-
organized scientific collaboration in the history of humankind and
have reached a consensus as strong as it ever gets in science. As Bill
McKibben points out, there is no longer any credible basis to doubt
that the earth's atmosphere is warming because of human activities.
There is no longer any credible basis to doubt that we face a string of
terrible catastrophes unless we prepare ourselves and deal with the
underlying causes of global warming.

Scientists around the world are sounding a clear and urgent   8
warning. Global warming is real, it is already under way, and the
consequences are totally unacceptable.

Why is this happening? Because the relationship between hu-   9
mankind and the earth has been utterly transformed. To begin with,
we have quadrupled the population of our planet in the past hundred years. And secondly, the power of the technologies now at our
disposal vastly magnifies the impact each individual can have on
the natural world. Multiply that by six and a half billion people, and
then stir into that toxic mixture a mind-set and an attitude that say
it's OK to ignore scientific evidence—that we don't have to take responsibility for the future consequences of present actions—and
you get this violent and destructive collision between our civilization and the earth.

There are those who say that we can't solve this problem—that   10
it's too big or too complicated or beyond the capacity of political
systems to grasp.

To those who say this problem is too difficult, I say that we have   11
accepted and met such challenges in the past. We declared our liberty, and then won it. We designed a country that respected and
safeguarded the freedom of individuals. We abolished slavery. We
gave women the right to vote. We took on Jim Crow and segregation. We cured fearsome diseases, landed on the moon, won two
wars simultaneously—in the Pacific and in Europe. We brought
down communism, we defeated apartheid. We have even solved a
global environmental crisis before: the hole in the stratospheric
ozone layer.

So there should be no doubt that we can solve this crisis too.   12
We must seize the opportunities presented by renewable energy, by
conservation and efficiency, by some of the harder but exceedingly
important challenges such as carbon capture and sequestration.

The technologies to solve the global-warming problem exist; if we have the determination and wisdom to use them.

But there is no time to wait. In the 1930s, Winston Churchill also wrote of those leaders who refused to acknowledge the clear and present danger: "They go on in strange paradox, decided only to be undecided, resolved to be irresolute, adamant for drift, solid for fluidity, all powerful to be impotent. The era of procrastination, of half-measures, of soothing and baffling expedients, of delays, is coming to a close. In its place, we are entering a period of consequences." 13

With Hurricane Katrina, the melting of the Arctic ice cap and careless ecological mayhem, we, too, are entering a period of consequences. This is a moral moment. This is not ultimately about any scientific debate or political dialogue. Ultimately it is about who we are as human beings. It is about our capacity to transcend our own limitations. 14

The men and women honored as warriors and heroes have risen to this new occasion. On the surface, they share little in common: scientists, ministers, students, politicians, activists, lawyers, celebrities, inventors, world leaders. But each of them recognized the threat that climate change poses to the planet—and responded by taking immediate action to stop it. Their stories should inspire and encourage us to see with our hearts, as well as our heads, the unprecedented response that is now called for. 15

As these heroes demonstrate, we have everything we need to face this urgent challenge. All it takes is political will. And in our democracy, political will is a renewable resource. 16

MEANINGS AND VALUES

1. Explain the concept of global warming as Gore presents it in this essay.

2. What possible solutions to the problem of global warming does the writer suggest?

3. What reasons, if any, does the writer offer for the refusal to recognize global warming as a crisis?

ARGUMENTATIVE TECHNIQUES

1. Is the writer's argument logical (appealing to reason), persuasive (appealing to the emotions), or both? Give examples to support your answer.

2. In his argument, the author often uses cause and effect as an organizational mode. Give examples from the essay.

3. In which paragraph of this essay does Gore state an opposing point of view to his argument? Do you think he should have stated it earlier? Why or why not?

4. To what international crisis in history does the author compare global warming? Is this effective, in your opinion? How so?

DICTION AND VOCABULARY

1. State the paragraph number in which the writer uses a rhetorical question (see "Guide to Terms": *Rhetorical Questions*). Is it effective? Why or why not?

2. If you do not know the meaning of some of the following words, consult a dictionary: *typhoons* (Par. 1); *ravaging* (4); *proffered* (6); *mindset* (9); *stratospheric, ozone* (11); *paradox* (13); *mayhem* (14).

READ TO WRITE

1. **Collaborating:** In a group of writers, discuss whether reading Al Gore's essay has a) added to your prior knowledge about global warming, and b) changed your mind about the issue in any way. Write a brief report together summarizing the views of your group.

2. **Considering Audience:** From the point of view of a reader who doubts that global warming is a serious threat, write a letter to Al Gore disputing his claims.

3. **Developing an Essay:** Research a current environmental problem. Taking a firm stand on the issue, argue for a convincing solution to this problem. Remember to take the opposing viewpoint into account by addressing its concerns.

(NOTE: Suggestions for essays requiring development by ARGUMENT are on p. 528 at the end of this chapter.)

MARK TWAIN

Author, humorist, abolitionist, and supporter of women's rights
Samuel Langhorne Clemens (1835–1910), better known by his
pen name of MARK TWAIN, was born in Florida, Missouri. When he
was four, the family moved to Hannibal, Missouri, a town on the
banks of the Mississippi River. His childhood experiences there, as
well as a stint as steamboat pilot, inspired his famous novels *The
Adventures of Tom Sawyer* (1876) and *Adventures of Huckleberry
Finn* (1884). Twain was a major influence on American literature.
Among his many works are *Life on the Mississippi* (1883), *A Connecticut Yankee in King Arthur's Court* (1889), and *The Tragedy of
Pudd'nhead Wilson* (1894).

The Damned Human Race

Written close to the end of his life, between 1905 and 1909, Mark
Twain's classic essay "The Damned Human Race" was published
after his death in *Letters from the Earth*, a collection of Twain's work
edited in 1939 by Bernard DeVoto and published in 1962.

I have been studying the traits and dispositions of the "lower ani-   1
mals" (so-called), and contrasting them with the traits and dispositions of man. I find the result humiliating to me. For it obliges me
to renounce my allegiance to the Darwinian theory of the Ascent of
Man from the Lower Animals; since it now seems plain to me that
the theory ought to be vacated in favor of a new and truer one, this
new and truer one to be named the *Descent* of Man from the Higher
Animals.

In proceeding toward this unpleasant conclusion I have not   2
guessed or speculated or conjectured, but have used what is commonly called the scientific method. That is to say, I have subjected
every postulate that presented itself to the crucial test of actual experiment, and have adopted it or rejected it according to the result.
Thus I verified and established each step of my course in its turn
before advancing to the next. These experiments were made in the
London Zoological Gardens, and covered many months of painstak-
ing and fatiguing work.

Before particularizing any of the experiments, I wish to state   3
one or two things which seem to more properly belong in this place
than further along. This in the interest of clearness. The massed

experiments established to my satisfaction certain generalizations, to wit:

1. That the human race is of one distinct species. It exhibits slight variations—in color, stature, mental caliber, and so on—due to climate, environment, and so forth; but it is a species by itself, and not to be confounded with any other.
2. That the quadrupeds are a distinct family, also. This family exhibits variations—in color, size, food preferences and so on; but it is a family by itself.
3. That the other families—the birds, the fishes, the insects, the reptiles, etc.—are more or less distinct, also. They are in the procession. They are links in the chain which stretches down from the higher animals to man at the bottom.

Some of my experiments were quite curious. In the course of my reading I had come across a case where, many years ago, some hunters on our Great Plains organized a buffalo hunt for the entertainment of an English earl—that, and to provide some fresh meat for his larder. They had charming sport. They killed seventy-two of those great animals; and ate part of one of them and left the seventy-one to rot. In order to determine the difference between an anaconda and an earl—if any—I caused seven young calves to be turned into the anaconda's cage. The grateful reptile immediately crushed one of them and swallowed it, then lay back satisfied. It showed no further interest in the calves, and no disposition to harm them. I tried this experiment with other anacondas; always with the same result. The fact stood proven that the difference between an earl and an anaconda is that the earl is cruel and the anaconda isn't; and that the earl wantonly destroys what he has no use for, but the anaconda doesn't. This seemed to suggest that the anaconda was not descended from the earl. It also seemed to suggest that the earl was descended from the anaconda, and had lost a good deal in the transition. 4

I was aware that many men who have accumulated more millions of money than they can ever use have shown a rabid hunger for more, and have not scrupled to cheat the ignorant and the helpless out of their poor servings in order to partially appease that appetite. I furnished a hundred different kinds of wild and tame animals the opportunity to accumulate vast stores of food, but none of them would do it. The squirrels and bees and certain birds made accumulations, but stopped when they had gathered a winter's supply, and could not be persuaded to add to it either honestly or by 5 chicanery. In order to bolster up a tottering reputation the ant pretended to store up supplies, but I was not deceived. I know the ant. These experiments convinced me that there is this difference between man and the higher animals: he is avaricious and miserly, they are not.

In the course of my experiments I convinced myself that among the animals man is the only one that harbors insults and injuries, broods over them, waits till a chance offers, then takes revenge. The passion of revenge is unknown to the higher animals. 6

Roosters keep harems, but it is by consent of their concubines; therefore no wrong is done. Men keep harems, but it is by brute force, privileged by atrocious laws which the other sex were allowed no hand in making. In this matter man occupies a far lower place than the rooster. 7

Cats are loose in their morals, but not consciously so. Man, in his descent from the cat, has brought the cat's looseness with him but has left the unconsciousness behind—the saving grace which excuses the cat. The cat is innocent, man is not. 8

Indecency, vulgarity, obscenity—these are strictly confined to man; he invented them. Among the higher animals there is no trace of them. They hide nothing; they are not ashamed. Man, with his soiled mind, covers himself. He will not even enter a drawing room with his breast and back naked, so alive are he and his mates to indecent suggestion. Man is "The Animal that Laughs." But so does the monkey, as Mr. Darwin pointed out; and so does the Australian bird that is called the laughing jackass. No—Man is the Animal that Blushes. He is the only one that does it—or has occasion to. 9

At the head of this article we see how "three monks were burnt to death" a few days ago, and a prior "put to death with atrocious cruelty." Do we inquire into the details? No; or we should find out that the prior was subjected to unprintable mutilations. Man—when he is a North American Indian—gouges out his prisoner's eyes; when he is King John, with a nephew to render untroublesome, he uses a red-hot iron; when he is a religious zealot dealing with heretics in the Middle Ages, he skins his captive alive and scatters salt on his back; in the first Richard's time he shuts up a multitude of Jew families in a tower and sets fire to it; in Columbus's time he captures a family of Spanish Jews and—but *that* is not printable; in our day in England a man is fined ten shillings for beating his mother nearly to death with a chair, and another man is fined forty shillings for having four pheasant eggs in his possession without being able to satisfactorily explain how he got them. Of all the animals, man is the 10 only one that is cruel. He is the only one that inflicts pain for the pleasure of doing it. It is a trait that is not known to the higher animals. The cat plays with the frightened mouse; but she has this excuse, that she does not know that the mouse is suffering. The cat is moderate—unhumanly moderate: she only scares the mouse, she does not hurt it; she doesn't dig out its eyes, or tear off its skin, or drive splinters under its nails—man-fashion; when she is done playing with it she makes a sudden meal of it and puts it out of its trouble. Man is the Cruel Animal. He is alone in that distinction.

The higher animals engage in individual fights, but never in organized masses. Man is the only animal that deals in that atrocity of atrocities, War. He is the only one that gathers his brethren about him and goes forth in cold blood and with calm pulse to exterminate his kind. He is the only animal that for sordid wages will march out, as the Hessians did in our Revolution, and as the boyish Prince Napoleon did in the Zulu war, and help to slaughter strangers of his own species who have done him no harm and with whom he has no quarrel. 11

Man is the only animal that robs his helpless fellow of his country—takes possession of it and drives him out of it or destroys him. Man has done this in all the ages. There is not an acre of ground on the globe that is in possession of its rightful owner, or that has not been taken away from owner after owner, cycle after cycle, by force and bloodshed. 12

Man is the only Slave. And he is the only animal who enslaves. He has always been a slave in one form or another, and has always held other slaves in bondage under him in one way or another. In our day he is always some man's slave for wages, and does that man's work; and this slave has other slaves under him for minor wages, and they do *his* work. The higher animals are the only ones who exclusively do their own work and provide their own living. 13

Man is the only Patriot. He sets himself apart in his own country, under his own flag, and sneers at the other nations, and keeps multitudinous uniformed assassins on hand at heavy expense to grab slices of other people's countries, and keep *them* from grabbing slices of *his*. And in the intervals between campaigns he washes the blood off his hands and works for "the universal brotherhood of man"—with his mouth. 14

Man is the Religious Animal. He is the only Religious Animal. He is the only animal that has the True Religion—several of them. He is the only animal that loves his neighbor as himself, and cuts his throat if his theology isn't straight. He has made a graveyard of the 15 globe in trying his honest best to smooth his brother's path to happiness and heaven. He was at it in the time of the Caesars, he was at it in Mahomet's time, he was at it in the time of the Inquisition, he was at it in France a couple of centuries, he was at it in England in Mary's day, he has been at it ever since he first saw the light, he is at it today in Crete—as per the telegrams quoted above—he will be at it somewhere else tomorrow. The higher animals have no religion. And we are told that they are going to be left out, in the Hereafter. I wonder why? It seems questionable taste.

Man is the Reasoning Animal. Such is the claim. I think it is 16 open to dispute. Indeed, my experiments have proven to me that he is the Unreasoning Animal. Note his history, as sketched above. It seems plain to me that whatever he is he is *not* a reasoning animal. His record is the fantastic record of a maniac, I consider that the strongest count against his intelligence is the fact that with that record back of him he blandly sets himself up as the head animal of the lot: whereas by his own standards he is the bottom one.

In truth, man is incurably foolish. Simple things which the 17 other animals easily learn, he is incapable of learning. Among my experiments was this. In an hour I taught a cat and a dog to be friends. I put them in a cage. In another hour I taught them to be friends with a rabbit. In the course of two days I was able to add a fox, a goose, a squirrel and some doves. Finally a monkey. They lived together in peace; even affectionately.

Next, in another cage I confined an Irish Catholic from Tipper-18 ary, and as soon as he seemed tame I added a Scotch Presbyterian from Aberdeen. Next a Turk from Constantinople; a Greek Christian from Crete; an Armenian; a Methodist from the wilds of Arkansas; a Buddhist from China; a Brahman from Benares. Finally, a Salvation Army Colonel from Wapping. Then I stayed away two whole days. When I came back to note results, the cage of Higher Animals was all right, but in the other, there was but a chaos of gory odds and ends of turbans and fezzes and plaids and bones and flesh—not a specimen left alive. These Reasoning Animals had disagreed on a theological detail and carried the matter to a Higher Court.

One is obliged to concede that in true loftiness of character, 19 Man cannot claim to approach even the meanest of the Higher Animals. It is plain that he is constitutionally incapable of approaching that altitude; that he is constitutionally afflicted with a Defect which must make such approach forever impossible, for it is manifest that this defect is permanent in him, indestructible, ineradicable.

I find this Defect to be *the Moral Sense*. He is the only animal   20
that has it. It is the secret of his degradation. It is the quality *which
enables him to do wrong*. It has no other office. It is incapable of performing any other function. It could never have been intended to
perform any other. Without it, man could do no wrong. He would
rise at once to the level of the Higher Animals.

Since the Moral Sense has but the one office, the one capacity—   21
to enable man to do wrong—it is plainly without value to him. It is
as valueless to him as is disease. In fact, it manifestly *is* a disease.
Rabies is bad, but it is not so bad as this disease. Rabies enables a
man to do a thing which he could not do when in a healthy state:
kill his neighbor with a poisonous bite. No one is the better man for
having rabies. The Moral Sense enables a man to do wrong. It enables him to do wrong in a thousand ways. Rabies is an innocent
disease, compared to the Moral Sense. No one, then, can be the better man for having the Moral Sense. What, now, do we find the Primal Curse to have been? Plainly what it was in the beginning: the
infliction upon man of the Moral Sense; the ability to distinguish
good from evil; and with it, necessarily, the ability to *do* evil; for
there can be no evil act without the presence of consciousness of it in
the doer of it.

And so I find that we have descended and degenerated, from   22
some far ancestor—some microscopic atom wandering at its pleasure between the mighty horizons of a drop of water perchance—
insect by insect, animal by animal, reptile by reptile, down the long
highway of smirchless innocence, till we have reached the bottom
stage of development—namable as the Human Being. Below
us—nothing.

MEANINGS AND VALUES

1. Explain, in your own words, what the author's story about the anaconda says about humankind.

2. Greed and a desire for revenge are two of the human character traits
   that the writer discusses. Name two others from the reading.

3. According to the author, "Of all the animals, man is the only one that
   is cruel" (Par. 10). What support does he give for this statement? Is it
   convincing? How so?

4. After stating that humans are the only animals who blush (Par. 9),
   the writer adds "He is the only one that does it—or has occasion to."
   Explain the significance of this comment.

5.   Surprisingly, the author claims that having a moral sense is a defect. What reasons does he offer to support this unusual claim? Do you think that the author means us to take this claim literally? Explain your answer.

ARGUMENTATIVE TECHNIQUES

1.   The author tells us he used the scientific method to arrive at his conclusions. Is this essay an example of the scientific method or of inductive reasoning? Explain why or why not.

2.   Does Twain use appeals to the emotions (persuasive argument) in this essay? If so, how?

DICTION AND VOCABULARY

1.   Irony consists of saying one thing on the surface but meaning the opposite (see "Guide to Terms": *Irony*). In the second half of Twain's essay, he classifies human qualities commonly considered to be virtues, such as reason, patriotism, piety, and morality, as faults. Is he being ironic, in your opinion, or does he truly believe these qualities to be defects? Explain your answer.

2.   If you do not know the meaning of some of the following words, consult a dictionary: *postulate* (Par. 2); *quadrupeds* (3); *anaconda* (4); *scrupled, avaricious* (5); *sordid* (11); *loftiness* (19); *degenerated, smirchless* (22).

READ TO WRITE

1.   **Collaborating:** In a group of writers, divide into two teams. One side will argue the position that humans are basically good, and one side will take the stance that humans are basically evil. Debate the issue. Together, write a brief summary of your debate.

2.   **Considering Audience:** As Twain's audience, how do you react to his pessimism about human nature? Do you appreciate his use of humor? Were you shocked by any of the examples he used? Explain your answers.

3.   **Developing an Essay:** Refute Twain's observation in Paragraph 21 that having a moral sense is bad because it allows people to tell the difference between good and evil, and therefore allows people to consciously choose to do evil. Take the stand that having a moral sense is good because it allows people to consciously choose to do *good*. Provide examples that support your claim, use both logical reasoning and emotional persuasion, and end your essay with a call to action.

(NOTE: Suggestions for essays requiring development by ARGUMENT are on p. 528 at the end of this chapter.)

ELIZABETH SVOBODA

ELIZABETH SVOBODA was born in the suburbs of Western New York. She graduated from Yale University in 2003 and now writes for various publications on a number of eclectic topics, which she approaches from a unique and often unorthodox perspective. She currently lives in San Jose, California, with her husband.

I Am Not a Puzzle, I Am a Person

In this essay, first published online at *Salon.com*, the writer reports on a controversy over the appropriate definition and treatment of autism. Though the aim at first seems expository, it is in fact argumentative. The writer structures the essay as an argument and advances a particular perspective on autism through the people whose experiences and ideas she describes—without taking an explicit position herself. Clearly, however, she agrees with those parents who take a moderate approach in favor of "neurodiversity."

Long before her son Michelangelo's first birthday, Dana Commandatore began to suspect he was different. The other babies she knew babbled animatedly to everyone in sight. Michelangelo, though, never took much interest in children his age, and by the time he was 18 months old, he still wasn't speaking. Determined to find out what was wrong, Commandatore took her son to the pediatrician. "They sent us for a hearing test. The technicians were trying to put the headphones on and Michelangelo wouldn't let them do it," she recalls. "One tech said to the other, 'It seems more like autism than a hearing problem.' I turned around and said, 'What?'"

When Michelangelo's autism diagnosis was confirmed soon after, the verdict was more of a relief than anything else—it seemed to suggest a clear course of action. "We knew who he was," Commandatore says. "Now we knew what to do." In the process of scouring the Internet, she stumbled across Web sites run by autistic adults who advocated a school of thought they called "neurodiversity." Autism was not a "disease," their reasoning went, but a "neurological variation" that ought to be as respected as a difference like skin color or sexual orientation. The Centers for Disease Control and

1

2

Elizabeth Svoboda, "I Am Not a Puzzle, I Am a Person," *Salon.com*, April 27, 2009. This article first appeared in Salon.com, at http://www.Salon.com. An online version remains in the Salon archives. Reprinted with permission.

Prevention estimates that the prevalence of autism spectrum disorders in the U.S. is about 1 in every 150 8-year-olds.

The advocates' core message—that autistic people should be cel- 3
ebrated for their uniqueness, not aggressively "normalized"— struck
a chord with Commandatore. She began learning more about the
movement and went to hear Ari Ne'eman, president of the Autistic
Self Advocacy Network, give a lecture. "I am not a person at all who
joins groups. I'm not religious," Commandatore says. "But when
I found Ari's Web site and saw him speak, he put into words what
I had been thinking."

Like the deaf culture movement before it, the so-called autistic 4
culture movement continues to gain traction, boasting thousands of
adherents among parents, patients and healthcare professionals.
And the rhetoric is often as strident as anything out of the deaf-
pride movement. Some autistic people even use the pejorative term
"curebie" to refer to people who hope for a cure for the condition.
Organizations like Autism Network International view efforts to
cure autism as similar to misguided efforts to cure homosexuality
and left-handedness.

As its associated swag—buttons and T-shirts proclaiming "I am 5
not a puzzle, I am a person"—suggests, the movement aims to redefine autism as something to be valued and protected, not obliterated. Proponents insist that forcing autistic people to behave like
"neurotypicals," a term that borders on insulting, squelches the very
qualities that make them unique. "The real ends for autistic people
should be quality of life, full access in society, the kinds of things we
support and are working for," Ne'eman says. "Parents have been
told that the way to approach these things is to support research for
a cure, but our belief is that that's not the most effective paradigm."

In other words, Jenny McCarthy can go jump off a cliff. While 6
the Hollywood comedian's claims that childhood shots cause autism may be well-intentioned, Ne'eman says, her message has a per-
nicious and probably untrue implication: If we stopped giving kids
"toxic" vaccines, autism wouldn't exist. Not only does this message
distract from pragmatic efforts to get autistic kids the social support
they need, it implies that autistic children are inherently less valuable than their normal counterparts. "The cure paradigm sends a
message that there is somehow a normal person under the autistic
person, and that's a significant denial of who we are."

But it's not just anti-vaccine diatribes that raise autistic culture 7
crusaders' ire. Their primary target is something much broader and
more insidious: the general therapeutic approach to autism in the

medical community. Many autistic rights advocates have spoken out against applied behavioral analysis (ABA), the most common type of autism therapy, developed by UCLA psychologist Ivar Lovaas in the 1960s and '70s, with the goal of helping autistic children achieve "normal intellectual and educational" functioning. The therapy, which uses repetition and rewards to reinforce new skills, is geared toward extinguishing autistic behaviors such as "stimming" (making repetitive body movements) and failing to make eye contact. One sign of the treatment's success, Lovaas suggested, might be for school personnel to perceive an autistic child as "indistinguishable" from his or her normal peers.

Approaches like this miss the point entirely, says Kathleen Seidel, the webmaster of Neurodiversity.com and the mother of a child on the autism spectrum. Instead of trying to coerce autistic kids to behave like "neurotypicals," therapists should focus on helping them deal more effectively with the non-autistic world. "A person's nervous system is not fundamentally going to change—an autistic person is going to remain autistic throughout his or her lifetime," Seidel says. "And it can be very problematic and a source of stress for an autistic child to have to suppress certain mannerisms."   8

Equally problematic, says Dora Raymaker, a Portland, Ore., artist with autism, is the tendency for medical professionals to impose "normal" behaviors on autistic people—even when those behaviors do not necessarily improve their ability to function. Rather than undergoing continual and grueling speech therapy, Raymaker has fought to express herself via text chat, the communication medium with which she feels most at home. "If we'd done this interview on the telephone you would have been lucky to get much more than disjointed, stuttering, completely non sequitur responses from me," she told me in an instant-message conversation. "But because you allowed me to do this interview through text-only media where I can slow down, really understand you, and bypass my difficulties with spoken language, I'm able to give you intelligent, on topic answers."   9

The key assumption that underlies much autistic culture discourse is that any autism-related limitations can be worked around and dealt with in a way that does not compromise the autistic individual's core "personhood." When such workarounds are found, Raymaker asserts, the concept of a "cure" becomes irrelevant. "Do I need a pill to make me suddenly able to have phone conversations, or do I need you to be able to find a middle ground that bypasses my disabilities?"   10

Some parents and therapists counter that this kind of active op- 11
position to suppressing autistic symptoms is a niche crusade—one
mounted by a small, visible group of high-functioning autistics who
don't represent the autistic population at large. If a child stages
screaming outbursts in the classroom or has trouble stringing together a complete sentence, New Brunswick lawyer Harold Doherty
argues, does it really make sense to treat that child's condition as "a
different neurological way of being," instead of a disease that imposes severe limitations?

"Some of these advocates oppose a cure and they appear in 12
court proceedings. In all these cases, they're talking about other
people's children," says Doherty, whose son Conor is autistic. "Who
gives them the authority to represent autistics? What does Ari
Ne'eman know about Conor? He has no real investment in my son's
life. There's a denial in this movement of the challenges of more autistic individuals. It's not a feel-good story to talk about kids who
are smashing their heads into things."

The question of whether autism should be considered a medi- 13
cal condition or a variation in neural wiring isn't just one of seman-
tics. If autistic-rights advocates win their court battles, many
treatment programs could stop receiving government money. In
2004, for instance, autistic-rights crusader Michelle Dawson convinced the Canadian Supreme Court to overturn an appeal that
would have provided state funding for ABA therapy. If similar legal
efforts succeed in the U.S., says Massachusetts psychologist Teresa
Bolick, autistic children could be hampered in acquiring the skills
they need to interact with the world.

"One of the main dangers of saying, 'This is not a developmen- 14
tal disorder,' is that federal and state governments don't usually
fund intervention for differences," Bolick says. "Parents say, 'But
what if his natural personality is to be a hermit? What if my son just
wants to be like Thoreau?' I say, 'You know what, if he wants to be
Thoreau, that's terrific.' But we need to give people the skills so they
can choose whether to be like Thoreau or like a more social
person."

Bolick adds that the justification many autistic culture advo- 15
cates give for slamming ABA—that the therapy is condescending and
attempts to turn autistic children into people they're not—is strained
and largely outmoded. "If we look at contemporary ABA, we see tremendous attention to the individual and tremendous appreciation
for personality," she says. "Old-fashioned behavior modification has
the reputation of using aversives and denying individual freedoms,

but that's not the way good treatments are anymore. For the most part, reinforcement is driven by what the kid wants to do. One kid loves it when his teaching assistant draws for him, so he'll do anything if she'll draw."

Ne'eman disputes the accuracy of this portrayal, citing cases in 16 which autistic children were abused and restrained in the name of "therapy." "There are very significant problems with the way in which intervention is approached," he says. "The founders of ABA quite unabashedly practiced the use of aversives, including electric shock, and this is something that continues to this day."

In some cases, inappropriate therapeutic interventions may be 17 a catalyst for antisocial behavior, says Ann Bauer, a Salon essayist who recently wrote about her autistic son Andrew's violent outbursts. "I believe deeply that one contributor to Andrew's recent behavior is a system that treats him inappropriately," Bauer says. "We had an overworked and apathetic state caseworker who consistently placed my son in homes developed for people with IQs of 70 or below because she couldn't see the difference between this and high-functioning autism. I'm not sure I wouldn't have gone insane myself if housed in such a place." Still, she does not solely blame the system for Andrew's furious rampages. "This is not to say that I don't hold my son responsible for his behaviors. He behaves cognitively and socially in a way that is completely out of sync with the rest of our world. I guess what I'm saying is, it's complicated. Is there something wrong with him or something wrong with society or both?"

In theory, neurodiversity advocates fall squarely into the some- 18 thing-wrong-with-society camp. The problem isn't that they or their children are defective, their thinking goes, but that society simply isn't capable yet of giving them the accommodations they need. In practice, though, many pro-neurodiversity families take a more nuanced stance on therapy and treatment than heated message-board debates might suggest. Safeguarding a child's dignity and teaching him to navigate a neurotypical world, they reason, don't have to be mutually exclusive. "Michelangelo has had a form of ABA three times a week," Commandatore says, "but it is so loose and we control and guide it. We just say, 'Look, we don't stop any stimming behavior.' But that doesn't mean you let him do whatever he wants. If he's stimming and hurting something, you have to stop that. You have to realize what is important and what isn't."

Arriving at such realizations is easier said than done. While the 19 autistic culture movement may come off as dogmatic at times,

Commandatore says the question of how to raise autistic kids in the spirit of neurodiversity has no clear-cut answer. Her child-rearing strategies don't radiate from a single ideological core—they're more cobbled-together, day-by-day solutions to various issues that crop up. Instead of trying to train her son out of his personality quirks, such as strong reactions to loud and sudden noises, she says, "We've given him headphones that he can use in public, these big 1970s speaker headphones. If he starts to panic, he asks for his headphones and we give them to him." She and her husband have also taught Michelangelo how to do deep-breathing exercises whenever he finds himself in a stressful situation, as he did this winter when his first-grade class began preparations for a holiday singing performance. "He was nervous. He said, 'Mama, I don't want to sing.'"

Rather than making her son practice the songs over and over until they became rote, as some therapists might recommend, Commandatore decided to give him a choice. "I said, 'Look, if you don't want to try this, you don't have to. I just want you to go up there and stand with your friends, and remember that Mama and Papa love you and we will be here for you.'" Though Michelangelo was skeptical, he agreed to give it a shot. When it came time for his moment in the limelight, he closed his eyes and took a deep breath. A smile slowly spread across his face as he burst into song.

20

MEANINGS AND VALUES

1. Which paragraphs outline the issue addressed in this essay? State it in your own words.

2. a. With which person in the essay does the writer seem to agree most fully? Please support your answer with specific evidence from the text.

   b. State in your own words the thesis or argumentative proposition endorsed by the person you identified in answering *a*, above. (See "Guide to Terms": *Thesis*.)

3. State any objections to the argumentative proposition that the writer presents in this essay.

ARGUMENTATIVE TECHNIQUES

1. a. What perspective on the issue does the writer present in Paragraphs 1–5?

   b. Why do you think the writer chose to begin this way?

2. Paragraphs 6–12 look at other approaches to autism and argue why they are wrong or inappropriate. Which paragraphs provide summaries? Which provide arguments against? Which provide both?

3. In what ways does the title of the essay attract readers' attention? In what ways does it summarize the argumentative proposition?

DICTION AND VOCABULARY

1. Describe how the writer uses diction to make Dana Commandatore and her stand on the issue seem sensible and sympathetic.

READ TO WRITE

1. **Collaborating:** Working in a group, create a list of the qualities you think most people associate with autism (or alcoholism, schizophrenia, or some other named condition). Then make a note of how the lists of people in the group might differ based on their experience or knowledge.

2. **Considering Audience:** Sometimes readers need to learn a good deal more about an issue before they can form an opinion or agree with an argumentative proposition. Choose two important issues, and write out in brief form what you think most readers will need to learn about each before they can form an opinion or agree with an argumentative proposition.

3. **Developing an Essay:** Using Svoboda's approach, report on an issue in such a way that the people whose ideas, words, and experiences you report help convince readers to share their perspective.

(NOTE: Suggestions for topics requiring development by ARGUMENT are on p. 528 at the end of this chapter.)

MARGARET ATWOOD

MARGARET ATWOOD was born in Ottawa, Ontario, in 1939. After attending college in Canada, she went to graduate school at Harvard University. She has had a distinguished career as a novelist, poet, and essayist, and is generally considered to be one of the central figures in contemporary Canadian literature and culture. Atwood's international reputation as a writer rests on her novels, including *The Edible Woman* (1960), *Surfacing* (1972), *Life Before Man* (1979), *Bodily Harm* (1982), *The Handmaid's Tale* (1986), *Cat's Eye* (1989), *The Robber Bride* (1993), *Alias Grace* (1996), *The Blind Assassin* (2000), *Oryx and Crake* (2003), *The Penelopiad* (2005), and *The Year of the Flood* (2009), and her short story collections, including *Bluebeard's Egg and Other Stories* (1986) and *Good Bones* (1992), although she has written poetry, television plays, and children's books as well. Her essays were collected in the volume *Second Words* (1982) and have continued to appear in newspapers and magazines such as *Ms., Harper's, Globe and Mail, The Nation, Maclean's, Washington Post, Harvard Educational Review, The Humanist, The New Republic,* and *Architectural Digest.* As an essayist, Atwood frequently writes about issues in contemporary culture and society, including the nature of Canadian culture and relationships between Canada and the United States.

Pornography

In the following essay, Atwood addresses the question of pornography with a directness and originality that are characteristic of her work. This essay originally appeared in *Chatelaine Magazine,* a mass-circulation women's magazine. As you read the selection, consider how well it addresses both the concerns of its original audience and the concerns about pornography a somewhat wider audience might have. Note also how she makes use of definition and a number of other expository patterns.

When I was in Finland a few years ago for an international writers' conference, I had occasion to say a few paragraphs in public on the subject of pornography. The context was a discussion of political repression, and I was suggesting the possibility of a link between the two. The immediate result was that a male journalist took several large bites out of me. Prudery and pornography are two halves of the same coin, said he, and I was clearly a prude. What could you expect from an Anglo-Canadian? Afterward, a couple of pleasant Scandinavian men asked me what I had been so worked

1

up about. All "pornography" means, they said, is graphic depictions of whores, and what was the harm in that?

Not until then did it strike me that the male journalist and I had   2
two entirely different things in mind. By "pornography," he meant
naked bodies and sex. I, on the other hand, had recently been doing
the research for my novel *Bodily Harm*, and was still in a state of
shock from some of the material I had seen, including the Ontario
Board of Film Censors' "outtakes." By "pornography," I meant
women getting their nipples snipped off with garden shears, having
meat hooks stuck into their vaginas, being disemboweled; little girls
being raped; men (yes, there are some men) being smashed to a pulp
and forcibly sodomized. The cutting edge of pornography, as far as I
could see, was no longer simple old copulation, hanging from the
chandelier or otherwise: it was death, messy, explicit and highly sadistic. I explained this to the nice Scandinavian men. "Oh, but that's
just the United States," they said. "Everyone knows they're sick." In
their country, they said, violent "pornography" of that kind was not
permitted on television or in movies; indeed, excessive violence of
any kind was not permitted. They had drawn a clear line between
erotica, which earlier studies had shown did not incite men to more
aggressive and brutal behavior toward women, and violence, which
later studies indicated did.

Some time after that I was in Saskatchewan, where, because of   3
the scenes in *Bodily Harm*, I found myself on an open-line radio
show answering questions about "pornography." Almost no one
who phoned in was in favor of it, but again they weren't talking
about the same stuff I was, because they hadn't seen it. Some of
them were all set to stamp out bathing suits and negligees, and, if
possible, any depictions of the female body whatsoever. God, it was
implied, did not approve of female bodies, and sex of any kind, including that practiced by bumblebees, should be shoved back into
the dark, where it belonged. I had more than a suspicion that *Lady
Chatterley's Lover*, Margaret Laurence's *The Diviners*, and indeed
most books by most serious modern authors would have ended up
as confetti if left in the hands of these callers.

For me, these two experiences illustrate the two poles of the   4
emotionally heated debate that is now thundering around this issue.
They also underline the desirability and even the necessity of defining the terms. "Pornography" is now one of those catchalls, like
"Marxism" and "feminism," that have become so broad they can
mean almost anything, ranging from certain verses in the Bible, ads
for skin lotion and sex tests for children to the contents of *Penthouse*,

Naughty '90s postcards and films with titles containing the word
Nazi that show vicious scenes of torture and killing. It's easy to say
that sensible people can tell the difference. Unfortunately, opinions
on what constitutes a sensible person vary.

But even sensible people tend to lose their cool when they start   5
talking about this subject. They soon stop talking and start yelling,
and the name-calling begins. Those in favor of censorship (which
may include groups not noticeably in agreement on other issues,
such as some feminists and religious fundamentalists) accuse the
others of exploiting women through the use of degrading images,
contributing to the corruption of children, and adding to the general
climate of violence and threat in which both women and children
live in this society; or, though they may not give much of a hoot
about actual women and children, they invoke moral standards and
God's supposed aversion to "filth," "smut" and deviated *perversion,*
which may mean ankles.

The camp in favor of total "freedom of expression" often comes   6
out howling as loud as the Romans would have if told they could no
longer have innocent fun watching the lions eat up Christians. It too
may include segments of the population who are not natural bedfel-
lows: those who proclaim their God-given right to freedom, including the freedom to tote guns, drive when drunk, drool over chicken
porn and get off on videotapes of women being raped and beaten,
may be waving the same anticensorship banner as responsible liber-
als who fear the return of Mrs. Grundy, or gay groups for whom
sexual emancipation involves the concept of "sexual theater." *Whatever turns you on* is a handy motto, as is *A man's home is his castle* (and
if it includes a dungeon with beautiful maidens strung up in chains
and bleeding from every pore, that's his business).

Meanwhile, theoreticians theorize and speculators speculate. Is   7
today's pornography yet another indication of the hatred of the
body, the deep mind-body split, which is supposed to pervade
Western Christian society? Is it a backlash against the women's
movement by men who are threatened by uppity female behavior in
real life, so like to fantasize about women done up like outsize par-
cels, being turned into hamburger, kneeling at their feet in slave-like
adoration or sucking off guns? Is it a sign of collective impotence, of
a generation of men who can't relate to real women at all but have to
make do with bits of celluloid and paper? Is the current flood just a
result of smart marketing and aggressive promotion by the money
men in what has now become a multibillion-dollar industry? If they
were selling movies about men getting their testicles stuck full of

knitting needles by women with swastikas on their sleeves, would they do as well, or is this penchant somehow peculiarly male? If so, why? Is pornography a power trip rather than a sex one? Some say that those ropes, chains, muzzles and other restraining devices are an argument for the immense power female sexuality still wields in the male imagination: you don't put these things on dogs unless you're afraid of them. Others, more literary, wonder about the shift from the 19th-century Magic Woman or Femme Fatale image to the lollipop-licker, airhead or turkey-carcass treatment of women in porn today. The proporners don't care much about theory; they merely demand product. The antiporners don't care about it in the final analysis either; there's dirt on the street, and they want it cleaned up, now.

It seems to me that this conversation, with its *You're-a-prude/ You're-a-pervert* dialectic, will never get anywhere as long as we continue to think of this material as just "entertainment." Possibly we're deluded by the packaging, the format: magazine, book, movie, theatrical presentation. We're used to thinking of these things as part of the "entertainment industry," and we're used to thinking of ourselves as free adult people who ought to be able to see any kind of "entertainment" we want to. That was what the First Choice pay-TV debate was all about. After all, it's only entertainment, right? Entertainment means fun, and only a killjoy would be antifun. What's the harm?   8

This is obviously the central question: *What's the harm?* If there isn't any real harm to any real people, then the antiporners can tsk-tsk and/or throw up as much as they like, but they can't rightfully expect more legal controls or sanctions. However, the no-harm position is far from being proven.   9

(For instance, there's a clear-cut case for banning—as the federal government has proposed—movies, photos and videos that depict children engaging in sex with adults: real children are used to make the movies, and hardly anybody thinks this is ethical. The possibilities for coercion are too great.)   10

To shift the viewpoint, I'd like to suggest three other models for looking at "pornography"—and here I mean the violent kind.   11

Those who find the idea of regulating pornographic materials repugnant because they think it's Fascist or Communist or otherwise not in accordance with the principles of an open democratic society should consider that Canada has made it illegal to disseminate material that may lead to hatred toward any group because of race or religion. I suggest that if pornography of the violent kind   12 depicted these acts being done predominantly to Chinese, to blacks, to Catholics, it would be off the market immediately, under the present laws. Why is hate literature illegal? Because whoever made the law thought that such material might incite real people to do real awful things to other real people. The human brain is to a certain extent a computer: garbage in, garbage out. We only hear about the extreme cases (like that of American multimurderer Ted Bundy) in which pornography has contributed to the death and/or mutilation of women and/or men. Although pornography is not the only factor involved in the creation of such deviance, it certainly has upped the ante by suggesting both a variety of techniques and the social acceptability of such actions. Nobody knows yet what effect this stuff is having on the less psychotic.

Studies have shown that a large part of the market for all kinds 13 of porn, soft and hard, is drawn from the 16-to-21-year-old population of young men. Boys used to learn about sex on the street, or (in Italy, according to Fellini movies) from friendly whores, or, in more genteel surroundings, from girls, their parents, or, once upon a time, in school, more or less. Now porn has been added, and sex education in the schools is rapidly being phased out. The buck has been passed, and boys are being taught that all women secretly like to be raped and that real men get high on scooping out women's digestive tracts.

Boys learn their concept of masculinity from other men: is this 14 what most men want them to be learning? If word gets around that rapists are "normal" and even admirable men, will boys feel that in order to be normal, admirable and masculine they will have to be rapists? Human beings are enormously flexible, and how they turn out depends a lot on how they're educated, by the society in which they're immersed as well as by their teachers. In a society that advertises and glorifies rape or even implicitly condones it, more women get raped. It becomes socially acceptable. And at a time when men and the traditional male role have taken a lot of flak and men are confused and casting around for an acceptable way of being male (and, in some cases, not getting much comfort from women on that score), this must be at times a pleasing thought.

It would be naïve to think of violent pornography as just harm- 15 less entertainment. It's also an educational tool and a powerful propaganda device. What happens when boy educated on porn meets girl brought up on Harlequin romances? The clash of expectations can be heard around the block. She wants him to get down on his knees with a ring, he wants her to get down on all fours with a ring in her nose. Can this marriage be saved?

Pornography has certain things in common with such addictive   16
substances as alcohol and drugs: for some, though by no means for
all, it induces chemical changes in the body, which the user finds
exciting and pleasurable. It also appears to attract a "hard core" of
habitual users and a penumbra of those who use it occasionally but
aren't dependent on it in any way. There are also significant numbers of men who aren't much interested in it, not because they're
undersexed but because real life is satisfying their needs, which may
not require as many appliances as those of users.

For the "hard core," pornography may function as alcohol does   17
for the alcoholic: tolerance develops, and a little is no longer enough.
This may account for the short viewing time and fast turnover in porn
theaters. Mary Brown, chairwoman of the Ontario Board of Film Censors, estimates that for every one mainstream movie requesting
entrance to Ontario, there is one porno flick. Not only the quantity consumed but the quality of explicitness must escalate, which may
account for the growing violence: once the big deal was breasts, then it
was genitals, then copulation, then that was no longer enough and the
hard users had to have more. The ultimate kick is death, and after that,
as the Marquis de Sade so boringly demonstrated, multiple death.

The existence of alcoholism has not led us to ban social drink-   18
ing. On the other hand, we do have laws about drinking and driving, excessive drunkenness and other abuses of alcohol that may
result in injury or death to others.

This leads us back to the key question: what's the harm? Nobody   19
knows, but this society should find out fast, before the saturation
point is reached. The Scandinavian studies that showed a connection
between depictions of sexual violence and increased impulse toward
it on the part of male viewers would be a starting point, but many
more questions remain to be raised as well as answered. What, for
instance, is the crucial difference between men who are users and
men who are not? Does using affect a man's relationship with actual
women, and, if so, adversely? Is there a clear line between erotica and
violent pornography, or are they on an escalating continuum? Is this a
"men versus women" issue, with all men secretly siding with the proporners and all women secretly siding against? (I think not; there *are*
lots of men who don't think that running their true love through the
Cuisinart is the best way they can think of to spend a Saturday night,
and they're just as nauseated by films of someone else doing it as
women are.) Is pornography merely an expression of the sexual confusion of this age or an active contributor to it?

Nobody wants to go back to the age of official repression, when   20
even piano legs were referred to as "limbs" and had to wear panta-
loons to be decent. Neither do we want to end up in George
Orwell's *1984*, in which pornography is turned out by the State to
keep the proles in a state of torpor, sex itself is considered dirty and
the approved practice it only for reproduction. But Rome under the
emperors isn't such a good model either.

If all men and women respected each other, if sex were consid-   21
ered joyful and life-enhancing instead of a wallow in germ-filled
glop, if everyone were in love all the time, if, in other words, many
people's lives were more satisfactory for them than they appear to
be now, pornography might just go away on its own. But since this
is obviously not happening, we as a society are going to have to
make some informed and responsible decisions about how to deal
with it.

MEANINGS AND VALUES

1. What is the writer's term for the specific type of pornography she is objecting to?

2. Atwood re-categorizes violent pornography in order to change the reader's preconception of it as entertainment, stating in Paragraph 11 that she will suggest three other models for considering it. Name two of three categories she develops.

EXPOSITORY TECHNIQUES

1. Atwood begins her persuasive argument with an extended narrative anecdote set at an international writers' conference in Finland. Is this strategy effective? Why or why not?

2. In Paragraph 9, Atwood poses a rhetorical question, "Where's the harm?" that echoes an earlier question in Paragraph 1: "...what was the harm in that?" In Paragraph 19, she writes, "This leads us back to the key question: what's the harm?" What is Atwood's purpose in repeating this question, and, in your opinion, is it effective?

3. The writer makes occasional use of sardonic humor. Point to one instance of this in the essay. Is she undermining the seriousness of her message in so doing? Explain your answer.

DICTION AND VOCABULARY

1. In paragraph 7, the writer coins two new words to represent the opposite poles of the debate about violent pornography. What are they? Are they effective? Why or why not?

2. The writer shifts between formal diction (using words such as "penumbra" and "continuum") and slang ("flick," "glop"). Why do you think she does this?

3. Atwood seems to be trying to strike a calm and reasonable tone in the midst of what she describes as an "emotionally heated debate." Does she succeed, and what do you make of her success or failure?

READ TO WRITE

1. **Collaborating:** In a group of writers, discuss whether you, like Atwood, believe that there could be a link between political oppression and the use of violent pornography. Alternatively, discuss whether you believe that violence against women in current video games should be censored and your reasons pro or con.

2. **Considering Audience:** Atwood wrote this article for a Canadian women's magazine readership. At the end of her article is a call to action: "...We as a society are going to have to make some informed and responsible decisions about how to deal with it." Responding as a reader (male or female) of the magazine article, how would you answer Atwood's call to action? Write as though you were composing a letter to the editor of *Chatelaine* magazine.

3. **Developing an Essay:** Develop an persuasive essay taking a stand on whether or not to ban or censor a particular media product, such as a video game, a film, an Internet site, a magazine, or some other. Include a clear call to action, and use both definition and classification as expository techniques in your essay.

(NOTE: Suggestions for essays requiring development by ARGUMENT are on p. 528 at the end of this chapter.)

SARAH MIN

Writer SARAH MIN worked at *Glamour* magazine at the time she published this essay in the late 1990s.

Language Lessons

Issues of bilingualism and bilingual education along with proposals for "English Only" in government and schools have drawn much interest over the past decade. Sarah Min takes a somewhat different, and personal, approach to bilingualism, arguing for its importance through her own story.

Even though I could understand only snippets of their conversation, I comprehended enough to know that the manicurists at the nail salon were talking about me.   1

What a shame! Another Korean who cannot speak the language, the woman filing my fingernails said to her colleague, both of them shaking their heads in disapproval. Her remark hit me, and I stumbled for the right words to defend myself.   2

The fact is, I traded my own Korean voice to give my parents their English ones: My mom and dad came to this country 27 years ago with an English vocabulary dominated by brand names like Tropicana and Samsonite. But they were determined to master the language of their new home. When I was in grade school, my dad read my English textbooks and asked me to give him the same lessons I had learned that day. On long car trips, my parents spent the confined hours in our Impala station wagon practicing their pronunciation aloud. My brother and I, captive tutors, led them in oral exercises, repeating the difficult distinction between *ear* and *year, war* and *wore.*   3

As my parents' fluency increased, their use of Korean dwindled. Though they spoke to each other in their native tongue, with my brother and me they used only one language: English. They didn't want us to speak Korean, they said, because they didn't want even a trace of an accent to infect our American-style speech.   4

Still, I absorbed bits and pieces of Korean, important phrases   5
like "Oh-mo-mo" and "Whey-goo-deh?"—the equivalent of "Oh
no!" and "What's your problem?"—subtleties that can't be precisely
translated but are understood as readily as "oy vey" or "cool." In
private, I'd practice the sound effects—the gasps and clucks that are
a part of the Korean language.

In public, though, I was reluctant to speak. My words sounded   6
clunky, choppy, unlike the rhythmic cadences of my mother's voice.
Once when I attempted conversation with a Korean-speaking
woman in my neighborhood, my efforts were clearly unimpressive:
She snickered at my accent and answered me in English. By the time
I was in college, I had stopped trying to speak Korean, a decision
only I noticed. No one expected me to speak the language anyway.

Yet I always felt that a part of me had been silenced. As I got   7
older and moved to a city where I met more Koreans, I began to feel
as the women in the nail salon did: That those of us who didn't
speak Korean had something to be ashamed of, that we were distancing ourselves from our cultural heritage. Language, after all, involves much more than the ability to communicate. It conveys a
desire to understand and participate in a culture, to make it one's
own. Could I ever fully understand and appreciate my heritage if I
couldn't speak the language of my ancestors?

So I registered for a course in Korean at an adult education   8
school. I expected my classmates to be Americans who were going
abroad, but I discovered most of the students had come for the same
reason that I had: to find their Korean voices.

To my surprise, I picked up the language quickly. Even though   9
my vocabulary was limited and my grammar was rough, I realized I
knew quite a bit, as if the Korean words had been lurking somewhere in a quiet corner of my brain. The teacher taught phrases that
sounded familiar and came to me effortlessly; I practiced the new
tongue placements and inflections to hide my American accent. The
first time I called my parents and said, in flawless Korean, "Hello,
we haven't spoken in such a long time," I was 24 years old, but they
reacted as proudly as if I were a toddler who had just uttered her
first words. And when I walked into a Korean restaurant and casually greeted the waiter, who responded in Korean that I could sit
anywhere I liked, I knew he took me for the genuine article.

Now whenever I visit my parents, I ask them to speak Korean   10
with me at least some of the time. Although I'm still struggling, still
studying so I can become more fluent, I know enough now that my
parents can tell me stories, jokes and proverbs that would otherwise

have gotten garbled in the static of translation. Eagerly, I listen, laugh and nod in full understanding.

Being able to speak Korean has some surprising bonuses: In   11
American restaurants, my dad and I figure the tip right in front of the waiter. And among Koreans, knowing the language forges an almost instant camaraderie.

That day at the nail salon, when I finally worked up the cour-   12
age to respond to the manicurist, I spoke slowly, but confidently: *I understand you and yes, it is shameful that I can only speak a little.*

The young woman polishing my fingernails paused. She looked   13
up at me and smiled, as if she were seeing me for the first time. And, for the first time, I too was seeing a new part of myself: a proud Korean American who could finally hear her own voice.

Meanings and Values

1. Min devotes much of Paragraphs 3 and 4 in her essay to a discussion of her parents' efforts to learn English and to encourage their children to speak English. Explain why her parents may have felt they needed to do this. As a young girl, how does Min react to her parents' effort?

2. What feelings inspired Min to take adult education courses in Korean (Par. 8)? Is she justified in her concerns about heritage? How important are these cultural issues in the contemporary America?

Argumentative Techniques

1. The anecdote in Min's introduction (Pars. 1 and 2) is readdressed in her conclusion. What element of surprise does she incorporate into this story? Does she convince her reader of the importance of her conversation with the manicurists?

2. Much of Min's argument is in the form of narrative. How effective is this technique? Why do you think she chose a first-person narrative for this topic?

Diction and Vocabulary

1. Are there any words in this essay with which you are unfamiliar? Why might Min have used a basic vocabulary for this piece? Who might her target audience include?

2. Min writes this as an autobiographical narrative. Point to specific uses of transitions, dialogue, and other techniques that help the narrative have a storylike quality.

READ TO WRITE

1. **Collaborating:** Working in a group, list the native languages of your ancestors. How many of you still speak that language? Discuss with your teammates the reasons why you feel that your family no longer speaks in the native tongue, or if your family still does, why the members have chosen to continue. Compare your reasons and look for underlying cultural connections regarding the maintenance of native tongues. Keeping in mind your group discussions, write an individual paper in a style similar to Min's discussing your use or lack of use of your family's native tongue. If your ancestry is of English-speaking people, write about a friend or someone you know who has had this issue arise in his or her family.

2. **Considering Audience:** Min says, "And among Koreans, knowing the language forges an almost instant camaraderie" (Par. 11). Would non-Korean readers identify with this statement? Does her point apply to others besides Koreans? Write a short analysis explaining your response.

3. **Developing an Essay:** Min's essay clearly encourages the maintaining of a native tongue, but not at the sacrifice of learning English when living in the United States. This is one facet of a debate on language. Research the question of whether or not the United States should have a unified language and the impact of maintaining a native tongue in some capacity. Consider the unifying qualities of language both inside and outside of the cultural boundaries. Write an argumentative essay employing multiple patterns of development in which you address the issue of either the adoption of a national language, the use of native languages in the household, or the acceptance of bilingualism or multilingualism in society.

(NOTE: Suggestions for essays requiring development by ARGUMENT are on p. 528 at the end of this chapter.)

MARTIN LUTHER KING JR.

MARTIN LUTHER KING JR. (1929–1968), was a Baptist minister, the president of the Southern Christian Leadership Conference, and a respected leader in the nationwide movement for equal rights for blacks. He was born in Atlanta, Georgia, and earned degrees from Morehouse College (A.B., 1948), Crozer Theological Seminary (B.D., 1951), Boston University (Ph.D., 1955), and Chicago Theological Seminary (D.D., 1957). He held honorary degrees from numerous other colleges and universities and was awarded the Nobel Peace Prize in 1964. Some of his books are *Stride Toward Freedom* (1958), *Strength to Love* (1963), and *Why We Can't Wait* (1964). King was assassinated April 4, 1968, in Memphis, Tennessee.

Letter from Birmingham Jail[1]

This letter, written to King's colleagues in the ministry, is a reasoned explanation for his actions during the civil rights protests in Birmingham. It is a good example of both persuasion and logical argument. Here the two are completely compatible, balancing each other in rather intricate but convincing and effective patterns.

My Dear Fellow Clergymen: 1

While confined here in the Birmingham city jail, I came across 2 your recent statement calling my present activities "unwise and untimely." Seldom do I pause to answer criticism of my work and ideas. If I sought to answer all the criticisms that cross my desk, my secretaries would have little time for anything other than such correspondence in the course of the day, and I would have no time for constructive work. But since I feel that you are men of genuine good will and that your criticisms are sincerely set forth, I want

---

[1]This response to a published statement by eight fellow clergymen from Alabama (Bishop C. C. J. Carpenter, Bishop Joseph A. Durick, Rabbi Hilton L. Grafman, Bishop Paul Hardin, Bishop Holan B. Harmon, the Reverend George M. Murray, the Reverend Edward V. Ramage, and the Reverend Earl Stallings) was composed under somewhat constricting circumstances. Begun on the margins of the newspaper in which the statement appeared while I was in jail, the letter was continued on scraps of writing paper supplied by a friendly Negro trusty, and concluded on a pad my attorneys were eventually permitted to leave me. Although the text remains in substance unaltered, I have indulged in the author's prerogative of polishing it for publication.— *King's note.*

to try to answer your statement in what I hope will be patient and reasonable terms.

I think I should indicate why I am here in Birmingham, since you have been influenced by the view which argues against "outsiders coming in." I have the honor of serving as president of the Southern Christian Leadership Conference, an organization operating in every southern state, with headquarters in Atlanta, Georgia. We have some eighty-five affiliated organizations across the South, and one of them is the Alabama Christian Movement for Human Rights. Frequently we share staff, educational, and financial resources with our affiliates. Several months ago the affiliate here in Birmingham asked us to be on call to engage in a nonviolent direct-action program if such were deemed necessary. We readily consented, and when the hour came, we lived up to our promise. So I, along with several members of my staff, am here because I was invited here. I am here because I have organizational ties here.

But more basically, I am in Birmingham because injustice is here. Just as the prophets of the eighth century b.c. left their villages and carried their "thus saith the Lord" far beyond the boundaries of their home towns, and just as the Apostle Paul left his village of Tarsus and carried the gospel of Jesus Christ to the far corners of the Greco-Roman world, so am I compelled to carry the gospel of freedom beyond my own home town. Like Paul, I must constantly respond to the Macedonian call for aid.

Moreover, I am cognizant of the interrelatedness of all communities and states. I cannot sit idly by in Atlanta and not be concerned about what happens in Birmingham. Injustice anywhere is a threat to justice everywhere. We are caught in an inescapable network of mutuality, tied in a single garment of destiny. Whatever affects one directly, affects all indirectly. Never again can we afford to live with the narrow, provincial "outside agitator" idea. Anyone who lives inside the United States can never be considered an outsider within its bounds.

You deplore the demonstrations taking place in Birmingham. But your statement, I am sorry to say, fails to express a similar concern for the conditions that brought about the demonstrations. I am sure that none of you would want to rest content with the superficial kind of social analysis that deals merely with effects and does not grapple with underlying causes. It is unfortunate that demonstrations are taking place in Birmingham, but it is even more unfortunate that the city's white power structure left the Negro community with no alternative.

In any nonviolent campaign there are four basic steps: collection of the facts to determine whether injustices exist; negotiation;

self-purification; and direct action. We have gone through all these steps in Birmingham. There can be no gainsaying the fact that racial injustice engulfs this community. Birmingham is probably the most thoroughly segregated city in the United States. Its ugly record of brutality is widely known. Negroes have experienced grossly unjust treatment in the courts. There have been more unsolved bombings of Negro homes and churches in Birmingham than in any other city in the nation. These are the hard, brutal facts of the case. On the basis of these conditions, Negro leaders sought to negotiate with the city fathers. But the latter consistently refused to engage in good-faith negotiation.

Then, last September, came the opportunity to talk with leaders of Birmingham's economic community. In the course of the negotiations, certain promises were made by the merchants—for example, to remove the stores' humiliating racial signs. On the basis of these promises, the Reverend Fred Shuttlesworth and the leaders of the Alabama Christian Movement for Human Rights agreed to a moratorium on all demonstrations. As the weeks and months went by, we realized that we were the victims of a broken promise. A few signs, briefly removed, returned; the others remained.   8

As in so many past experiences, our hopes had been blasted, and the shadow of deep disappointment settled upon us. We had no alternative except to prepare for direct action, whereby we would present our very bodies as a means of laying our case before the conscience of the local and the national community. Mindful of the difficulties involved, we decided to undertake a process of self-purification. We began a series of workshops on nonviolence, and we repeatedly asked ourselves: "Are you able to accept blows without retaliating?" "Are you able to endure the ordeal of jail?" We decided to schedule our direct-action program for the Easter season, realizing that except for Christmas, this is the main shopping period of the year. Knowing that a strong economic-withdrawal program would be the by-product of direct action, we felt that this would be the best time to bring pressure to bear on the merchants for the needed change.   9

Then it occurred to us that Birmingham's mayoral election was coming up in March, and we speedily decided to postpone action until after election day. When we discovered that the Commissioner of Public Safety, Eugene "Bull" Connor, had piled up enough votes to be in the run-off, we decided again to postpone action until the day after the run-off so that the demonstrations could not be used to cloud the issues. Like many others, we waited to see Mr. Connor defeated, and to this end we endured postponement after postponement. Having   10 aided in this community need, we felt that our direct-action program could be delayed no longer.

You may well ask, "Why direct action? Why sit-ins, marches, and so forth? Isn't negotiation a better path?" You are quite right in calling for negotiation. Indeed, this is the very purpose of direct action. Nonviolent direct action seeks to create such a crisis and foster such a tension that a community which has constantly refused to negotiate is forced to confront the issue. It seeks so to dramatize the issue that it can no longer be ignored. My citing the creation of tension as part of the work of the nonviolent-resister may sound rather shocking. But I must confess that I am not afraid of the word "tension." I have earnestly opposed violent tension, but there is a type of constructive, nonviolent tension which is necessary for growth. Just as Socrates felt that it was necessary to create a tension in the mind so that individuals could rise from the bondage of myths and half-truths to the unfettered realm of creative analysis and objective appraisal, so must we see the need for nonviolent gadflies to create the kind of tension in society that will help men rise from the dark depths of prejudice and racism to the majestic heights of understanding and brotherhood. 11

The purpose of our direct-action program is to create a situation so crisis-packed that it will inevitably open the door to negotiation. I therefore concur with you in your call for negotiation. Too long has our beloved Southland been bogged down in a tragic effort to live in monologue rather than dialogue. 12

One of the basic points in your statement is that the action that I and my associates have taken in Birmingham is untimely. Some have asked: "Why didn't you give the new city administration time to act?" The only answer that I can give to this query is that the new Birmingham administration must be prodded about as much as the outgoing one, before it will act. We are sadly mistaken if we feel that the election of Albert Boutwell as mayor will bring the millennium to Birmingham. While Mr. Boutwell is a much more gentle person than Mr. Connor, they are both segregationists, dedicated to maintenance of the status quo. I have hoped that Mr. Boutwell will be reasonable enough to see the futility of massive resistance to desegregation. But he will not see this without pressure from devotees of civil rights. My friends, I must say to you that we have not made a single gain in civil rights without determined legal and nonviolent pressure. Lamentably, it is an historical fact that privileged groups seldom give up their privileges voluntarily. Individuals may see the moral light and voluntarily give up their unjust posture; but, 13 as Reinhold Niebuhr has reminded us, groups tend to be more immoral than individuals.

We know through painful experience that freedom is never voluntarily given by the oppressor; it must be demanded by the oppressed. Frankly, I have yet to engage in a direct-action campaign that was "well timed" in the view of those who have not suffered unduly from the disease of segregation. For years now I have heard the word "Wait!" It rings in the ear of every Negro with piercing familiarity. This "Wait" has almost always meant "Never." We must come to see, with one of our distinguished jurists, that "justice too long delayed is justice denied."

We have waited for more than 340 years for our constitutional and God-given rights. The nations of Asia and Africa are moving with jetlike speed toward gaining political independence, but we still creep at horse-and-buggy pace toward gaining a cup of coffee at a lunch counter. Perhaps it is easy for those who have never felt the stinging darts of segregation to say, "Wait." But when you have seen vicious mobs lynch your mothers and fathers at will and drown your sisters and brothers at whim; when you have seen hate-filled policemen curse, kick, and even kill your black brothers and sisters; when you see the vast majority of your twenty million Negro brothers smothering in an airtight cage of poverty in the midst of an affluent society; when you suddenly find your tongue twisted and your speech stammering as you seek to explain to your six-year-old daughter why she can't go to the public amusement park that has just been advertised on television, and see tears welling up in her eyes when she is told that Funtown is closed to colored children, and see ominous clouds of inferiority beginning to form in her little mental sky, and see her beginning to distort her personality by developing an unconscious bitterness toward white people; when you have to concoct an answer for a five-year-old son who is asking, "Daddy, why do white people treat colored people so mean?"; when you take a cross-country drive and find it necessary to sleep night after night in the uncomfortable corners of your automobile because no motel will accept you; when you are humiliated day in and day out by nagging signs reading "white" and "colored"; when your first name becomes "nigger," your middle name becomes "boy" (however old you are) and your last name becomes "John," and your wife and mother are never given the respected title "Mrs."; when you are harried by day and haunted by night by the fact that you are a Negro, living constantly at tiptoe stance, never quite knowing what to expect next, and are plagued with inner fears and outer resentments; when you

14

15

are forever fighting a degenerating sense of "nobodiness"—then you will understand why we find it difficult to wait. There comes a time when the cup of endurance runs over, and men are no longer willing to be plunged into the abyss of despair. I hope, sirs, you can understand our legitimate and unavoidable impatience.

You express a great deal of anxiety over our willingness to break laws. This is certainly a legitimate concern. Since we so diligently urge people to obey the Supreme Court's decision of 1954 outlawing segregation in the public schools, at first glance it may seem rather paradoxical for us consciously to break laws. One may well ask: "How can you advocate breaking some laws and obeying others?" The answer lies in the fact that there are two types of laws: just and unjust. I would be the first to advocate obeying just laws. One has not only a legal but a moral responsibility to obey just laws. Conversely, one has a moral responsibility to disobey unjust laws. I would agree with St. Augustine that "an unjust law is no law at all."

Now, what is the difference between the two? How does one determine whether a law is just or unjust? A just law is a man-made code that squares with the moral law or the law of God. An unjust law is a code that is out of harmony with the moral law. To put it in the terms of St. Thomas Aquinas: An unjust law is a human law that is not rooted in eternal law and natural law. Any law that uplifts human personality is just. Any law that degrades human personality is unjust. All segregation statutes are unjust because segregation distorts the soul and damages the personality. It gives the segregator a false sense of superiority and the segregated a false sense of inferiority. Segregation, to use the terminology of the Jewish philosopher Martin Buber, substitutes an "I-it" relationship for an "I-thou" relationship and ends up relegating persons to the status of things. Hence segregation is not only politically, economically, and sociologically unsound, it is morally wrong and sinful. Paul Tillich has said that sin is separation. Is not segregation an existential expression of man's tragic separation, his awful estrangement, his terrible sinfulness? Thus it is that I can urge men to obey the 1954 decision of the Supreme Court, for it is morally right; and I can urge them to disobey segregation ordinances, for they are morally wrong.

Let us consider a more concrete example of just and unjust laws. An unjust law is a code that a numerical or power majority group compels a minority group to obey but does not make binding on itself. This is *difference* made legal. By the same token, a just law is a code that a majority compels a minority to follow and that it is willing to follow itself. This is *sameness* made legal.

Let me give another explanation. A law is unjust if it is inflicted   19
on a minority that, as a result of being denied the right to vote, had
no part in enacting or devising the law. Who can say that the legislature of Alabama which set up that state's segregation laws was democratically elected? Throughout Alabama all sorts of devious
methods are used to prevent Negroes from becoming registered vot-
ers, and there are some counties in which, even though Negroes
constitute a majority of the population, not a single Negro is registered. Can any law enacted under such circumstances be considered
democratically structured?

Sometimes a law is just on its face and unjust in its application.   20
For instance, I have been arrested on a charge of parading without a
permit. Now, there is nothing wrong in having an ordinance which
requires a permit for a parade. But such an ordinance becomes
unjust when it is used to maintain segregation and to deny citizens
the First Amendment privilege of peaceful assembly and protest.

I hope you are able to see the distinction I am trying to point out.   21
In no sense do I advocate evading or defying the law, as would the
rabid segregationist. That would lead to anarchy. One who breaks an
unjust law must do so openly, lovingly, and with a willingness to
accept the penalty. I submit that an individual who breaks a law that
conscience tells him is unjust, and who willingly accepts the penalty of
imprisonment in order to arouse the conscience of the community
over its injustice, is in reality expressing the highest respect for the law.

Of course, there is nothing new about this kind of civil disobe-   22
dience. It was evidenced sublimely in the refusal of Shadrach,
Meshach, and Abednego to obey the laws of Nebuchadnezzar, on
the ground that a higher moral law was at stake. It was practiced
superbly by the early Christians, who were willing to face hungry
lions and the excruciating pain of chopping blocks rather than submit to certain unjust laws of the Roman Empire. To a degree, academic freedom is a reality today because Socrates practiced civil
disobedience. In our own nation, the Boston Tea Party represented a
massive act of civil disobedience.

We should never forget that everything Adolf Hitler did in Ger-   23
many was "legal" and everything the Hungarian freedom fighters
did in Hungary was "illegal." It was "illegal" to aid and comfort a
Jew in Hitler's Germany. Even so, I am sure that, had I lived in Germany at the time, I would have aided and comforted my Jewish
brothers. If today I lived in a Communist country where certain
principles dear to the Christian faith are suppressed, I would openly
advocate disobeying that country's anti-religious laws.

I must make two honest confessions to you, my Christian and   24
Jewish brothers. First, I must confess that over the past few years
I have been gravely disappointed with the white moderate. I have
almost reached the regrettable conclusion that the Negro's great
stumbling block in his stride toward freedom is not the White Citizen's Counciler or the Ku Klux Klanner, but the white moderate, who
is more devoted to "order" than to justice; who prefers a negative
peace which is the absence of tension to a positive peace which is the
presence of justice; who constantly says, "I agree with you in the goal
you seek, but I cannot agree with your methods of direct action";
who paternalistically believes he can set the timetable for another
man's freedom; who lives by a mythical concept of time and who
constantly advises the Negro to wait for a "more convenient season."
Shallow understanding from people of good will is more frustrating
than absolute misunderstanding from people of ill will. Lukewarm
acceptance is much more bewildering than outright rejection.

I had hoped that the white moderate would understand that law   25
and order exist for the purpose of establishing justice and that when
they fail in this purpose they become the dangerously structured dams
that block the flow of social progress. I had hoped that the white moderate would understand that the present tension in the South is a necessary phase of the transition from an obnoxious negative peace, in
which the Negro passively accepted his unjust plight, to a substantive
and positive peace, in which all men will respect the dignity and worth
of human personality. Actually, we who engage in nonviolent direct
action are not the creators of tension. We merely bring to the surface
the hidden tension that is already alive. We bring it out in the open,
where it can be seen and dealt with. Like a boil that can never be cured
so long as it is covered up but must be opened with all its ugliness to
the natural medicines of air and light, injustice must be exposed, with
all the tension its exposure creates, to the light of human conscience
and the air of national opinion, before it can be cured.

In your statement you assert that our actions, even though peace-   26
ful, must be condemned because they precipitate violence. But is this a
logical assertion? Isn't this like condemning a robbed man because his
possession of money precipitated the evil act of robbery? Isn't this like
condemning Socrates because his unswerving commitment to truth
and his philosophical inquiries precipitated the act by the misguided
populace in which they made him drink hemlock? Isn't this like condemning Jesus because his unique God-consciousness and never-
ceasing devotion to God's will precipitated the evil act of crucifixion?
We must come to see that, as the federal courts have consistently

affirmed, it is wrong to urge an individual to cease his efforts to gain his basic constitutional rights because the quest may precipitate violence. Society must protect the robbed and punish the robber.

I had also hoped that the white moderate would reject the myth   27 concerning time in relation to the struggle for freedom. I have just received a letter from a white brother in Texas. He writes: "All Christians know that the colored people will receive equal rights eventually, but it is possible that you are in too great a religious hurry. It has taken Christianity almost two thousand years to accomplish what it has. The teachings of Christ take time to come to earth." Such an attitude stems from a tragic misconception of time, from the strangely irrational notion that there is something in the very flow of time that will inevitably cure all ills. Actually, time itself is neutral; it can be used either destructively or constructively. More and more I feel that the people of ill will have used time much more effectively than have the people of good will. We will have to repent in this generation not merely for the hateful words and actions of the bad people, but for the appalling silence of the good people. Human progress never rolls in on wheels of inevitability; it comes through the tireless efforts of men willing to be co-workers with God, and without this hard work, time itself becomes an ally of the forces of social stagnation. We must use time creatively, in the knowledge that the time is always ripe to do right. Now is the time to make real the promise of democracy and transform our pending national elegy into a creative psalm of brotherhood. Now is the time to lift our national policy from the quicksand of racial injustice to the solid rock of human dignity.

You speak of our activity in Birmingham as extreme. At first I   28 was rather disappointed that fellow clergymen would see my non-violent efforts as those of an extremist. I began thinking about the fact that I stand in the middle of two opposing forces in the Negro community. One is a force of complacency, made up in part of Negroes who, as a result of long years of oppression, are so drained of self-respect and a sense of "somebodiness" that they have adjusted to segregation; and in part of a few middle-class Negroes who, because of a degree of academic and economic security and because in some ways they profit by segregation, have become insensitive to the problems of the masses. The other force is one of bitterness and hatred, and it comes perilously close to advocating violence. It is expressed in the various black nationalist groups that are springing up across the nation, the largest and best-known being Elijah Muhammad's Muslim movement. Nourished by the Negro's frustration

over the continued existence of racial discrimination, this movement is made up of people who have lost faith in America, who
have absolutely repudiated Christianity, and who have concluded
that the white man is an incorrigible "devil."

I have tried to stand between these two forces, saying that we   29
need emulate neither the "do-nothingism" of the complacent nor
the hatred and despair of the black nationalist. For there is the more
excellent way of love and nonviolent protest. I am grateful to God
that, through the influence of the Negro church, the way of nonviolence became an integral part of our struggle.

If this philosophy had not emerged, by now many streets of the   30
South would, I am convinced, be flowing with blood. And I am further convinced that if our white brothers dismiss as "rabble-rousers"
and "outside agitators" those of us who employ nonviolent direct
action, and if they refuse to support our nonviolent efforts, millions
of Negroes will, out of frustration and despair, seek solace and security in black-nationalist ideologies—a development that would inevitably lead to a frightening racial nightmare.

Oppressed people cannot remain oppressed forever. The yearn-   31
ing for freedom eventually manifests itself, and that is what has
happened to the American Negro. Something within has reminded
him of his birthright of freedom, and something without has reminded him that it can be gained. Consciously or unconsciously, he
has been caught up by the *Zeitgeist,* and with his black brothers of
Africa and his brown and yellow brothers of Asia, South America,
and the Caribbean, the United States Negro is moving with a sense
of great urgency toward the promised land of racial justice. If one
recognizes this vital urge that has engulfed the Negro community,
one should readily understand why public demonstrations are taking place. The Negro has many pent-up resentments and latent frus-
trations, and he must release them. So let him march; let him make
prayer pilgrimages to the city hall; let him go on freedom rides—
and try to understand why he must do so. If his repressed emotions
are not released in nonviolent ways, they will seek expression
through violence; this is not a threat but a fact of history. So I have
not said to my people, "Get rid of your discontent." Rather, I have
tried to say that this normal and healthy discontent can be chan-
neled into the creative outlet of nonviolent direct action. And now
this approach is being termed extremist.

But though I was initially disappointed at being categorized as   32
an extremist, as I continued to think about the matter I gradually
gained a measure of satisfaction from the label. Was not Jesus an

extremist for love: "Love your enemies, bless them that curse you, do good to them that hate you, and pray for them which despitefully use you, and persecute you." Was not Amos an extremist for justice: "Let justice roll down like waters and righteousness like an everflowing stream." Was not Paul an extremist for the Christian gospel: "I bear in my body the marks of the Lord Jesus." Was not Martin Luther an extremist: "Here I stand; I cannot do otherwise, so help me God." And John Bunyan: "I will stay in jail to the end of my days before I make a butchery of my conscience." And Abraham Lincoln: "This nation cannot survive half slave and half free." And Thomas Jefferson: "We hold these truths to be self-evident, that all men are created equal . . . ." So the question is not whether we will be extremists, but what kind of extremists we will be. Will we be extremists for hate or for love? Will we be extremists for the preservation of injustice or for the extension of justice? In that dramatic scene on Calvary's hill three men were crucified. We must never forget that all three were crucified for the same crime—the crime of extremism. Two were extremists for immorality, and thus fell below their environment. The other, Jesus Christ, was an extremist for love, truth, and goodness, and thereby rose above his environment. Perhaps the South, the nation, and the world are in dire need of creative extremists.

I had hoped that the white moderate would see this need. Perhaps I was too optimistic; perhaps I expected too much. I suppose I should have realized that few members of the oppressor race can understand the deep groans and passionate yearnings of the oppressed race, and still fewer have the vision to see that injustice must be rooted out by strong, persistent, and determined action. I am thankful, however, that some of our white brothers in the South have grasped the meaning of this social revolution and committed themselves to it. They are still all too few in quantity, but they are big in quality. Some—such as Ralph McGill, Lillian Smith, Harry Golden, James McBride Dabbs, Anne Braden, and Sarah Patton Boyle—have written about our struggle in eloquent and prophetic terms. Others have marched with us down nameless streets of the South. They have languished in filthy, roach-infested jails, suffering the abuse and brutality of policemen who view them as "dirty nigger-lovers." Unlike so many of their moderate brothers and sisters, they have recognized the urgency of the moment and sensed the need for powerful "action" antidotes to combat the disease of segregation.   33

Let me take note of my other major disappointment. I have been so greatly disappointed with the white church and its leadership. Of course, there are some notable exceptions. I am not unmindful of the   34 fact that each of you have taken some significant stands on this issue. I commend you, Reverend Stallings, for your Christian stand on this past Sunday, in welcoming Negroes to your worship service on a nonsegregated basis. I commend the Catholic leaders of this state for integrating Spring Hill College several years ago.

But despite these notable exceptions, I must honestly reiterate 35 that I have been disappointed with the church. I do not say this as one of those negative critics who can always find something wrong with the church. I say this as a minister of the gospel, who loves the church; who has nurtured in its bosom; who has been sustained by its spiritual blessings and who will remain true to it as long as the cord of life shall lengthen.

When I was suddenly catapulted into the leadership of the bus 36 protest in Montgomery, Alabama, a few years ago, I felt we would be supported by the white church. I felt that the white ministers, priests, and rabbis of the South would be among our strongest allies. Instead, some have been outright opponents, refusing to understand the freedom movement and misrepresenting its leaders; all too many others have been more cautious than courageous and have remained silent behind the anesthetizing security of stained glass windows.

In spite of my shattered dreams, I came to Birmingham with the 37 hope that the white religious leadership of this community would see the justice of our cause and, with deep moral concern, would serve as the channel through which our just grievances could reach the power structure. I had hoped that each of you would understand. But again I have been disappointed.

I have heard numerous southern religious leaders admonish 38 their worshipers to comply with a desegregation decision because it is the law, but I have longed to hear white ministers declare: "Follow this decree because integration is morally right and because the Negro is your brother." In the midst of blatant injustices inflicted upon the Negro, I have watched white churchmen stand on the sideline and mouth pious relevancies and sanctimonious trivialities. In the midst of a mighty struggle to rid our nation of racial and economic injustice I have heard many ministers say: "Those are social issues, with which the gospel has no real concern." And I have watched many churches commit themselves to a completely otherworldly religion which makes a strange, un-Biblical distinction between body and soul, between the sacred and the secular.

I have traveled the length and breadth of Alabama, Mississippi, 39 and all the other southern states. On sweltering summer days and crisp autumn mornings I have looked at the South's beautiful churches with their lofty spires pointing heavenward. I have beheld the impressive outlines of her massive religious-education buildings. Over and over I have found myself asking: "What kind of people worship here? Who is their God? Where were their voices when the lips of Governor Barnett dripped with words of interposition and nullification? Where were they when Governor Wallace gave a clarion call for defiance and hatred? Where were their voices of support when bruised and weary Negro men and women decided to rise from the dark dungeons of complacency to the bright hills of creative protest?"

Yes, these questions are still in my mind. In deep disappoint-   40
ment I have wept over the laxity of the church. But be assured that my tears have been tears of love. There can be no deep disappointment where there is not deep love. Yes, I love the church. How could I do otherwise? I am in the rather unique position of being the son, the grandson, and the great-grandson of preachers. Yes, I see the church as the body of Christ. But, oh! How we have blemished and scarred that body through social neglect and through fear of being nonconformists.

There was a time when the church was very powerful—in the   41
time when the early Christians rejoiced at being deemed worthy to suffer for what they believed. In those days the church was not merely a thermometer that recorded the ideas and principles of popular opinion; it was a thermostat that transformed the mores of society. Whenever the early Christians entered a town, the people in power became disturbed and immediately sought to convict the Christians for being "disturbers of the peace" and "outside agitators." But the Christians pressed on, in the conviction that they were "a colony of heaven," called to obey God rather than man. Small in number, they were big in commitment. They were too God-intoxicated to be "astronomically intimidated." By their effort and example they brought an end to such ancient evils as infanticide and gladiatorial contests.

Things are different now. So often the contemporary church is a   42
weak, ineffectual voice with an uncertain sound. So often it is an archdefender of the status quo. Far from being disturbed by the presence of the church, the power structure of the average community is consoled by the church's silent—and often even vocal—sanction of things as they are.

But the judgment of God is upon the church as never before. If   43
today's church does not recapture the sacrificial spirit of the early church, it will lose its authenticity, forfeit the loyalty of millions, and

be dismissed as an irrelevant social club with no meaning for the twentieth century. Every day I meet young people whose disappointment with the church has turned into outright disgust.

Perhaps I have once again been too optimistic. Is organized religion too inextricably bound to the status quo to save our nation and the world? Perhaps I must turn my faith to the inner spiritual church, the church within the church, as the true *ekklesia* and the hope of the world. But again I am thankful to God that some noble souls from the ranks of organized religion have broken loose from the paralyzing chains of conformity and joined us as active partners in the struggle for freedom. They have left their secure congregations and walked the streets of Albany, Georgia, with us. They have gone down the highways of the South on tortuous rides for freedom. Yes, they have gone to jail with us. Some have been dismissed from their churches, have lost the support of their bishops and fellow ministers. But they have acted in the faith that right defeated is stronger than evil triumphant. Their witness has been the spiritual salt that has preserved the true meaning of the gospel in these troubled times. They have carved a tunnel of hope through the dark mountain of disappointment. 44

I hope the church as a whole will meet the challenge of this decisive hour. But even if the church does not come to the aid of justice, I have no despair about the future. I have no fear about the outcome of our struggle in Birmingham, even if our motives are at present misunderstood. We will reach the goal of freedom in Birmingham and all over the nation, because the goal of America is freedom. Abused and scorned though we may be, our destiny is tied up with America's destiny. Before the pilgrims landed at Plymouth, we were here. Before the pen of Jefferson etched the majestic words of the Declaration of Independence across the pages of history, we were here. For more than two centuries, our forbears labored in this country without wages; they made cotton king; they built the homes of their masters while suffering gross injustice and shameful humiliation—and yet out of a bottomless vitality they continued to thrive and develop. If the inexpressible cruelties of slavery could not stop us, the opposition we now face will surely fail. We will win our freedom because the sacred heritage of our nation and the eternal will of God are embodied in our echoing demands. 45

Before closing I feel impelled to mention one other point in your statement that has troubled me profoundly. You warmly commended the Birmingham police force for keeping "order" and "preventing violence." I doubt that you would have so warmly commended the police force if you had seen its dogs sinking their teeth into unarmed, 46 nonviolent Negroes. I doubt that you would so quickly commend the policemen if you were to observe their ugly and inhumane treatment of Negroes here in the city jail; if you were to watch them push and curse old Negro women and young Negro girls; if you were to see them slap and kick old Negro men and young boys; if you were to observe them, as they did on two occasions, refuse to give us food because we wanted to sing our grace together. I cannot join you in your praise of the Birmingham police department.

It is true that the police have exercised a degree of discipline in handling the demonstrators. In this sense they have conducted themselves rather "nonviolently" in public. But for what purpose? To preserve the evil system of segregation. Over the past few years I have consistently preached that nonviolence demands that the means we use must be as pure as the ends we seek. I have tried to make clear that it is wrong to use immoral means to attain moral ends. But now I must affirm that it is just as wrong, or perhaps even more so, to use moral means to preserve immoral ends. Perhaps Mr. Connor and his policemen have been rather nonviolent in public, as was Chief Pritchett in Albany, Georgia, but they have used the moral means of nonviolence to maintain the immoral end of racial injustice. As T. S. Eliot has said, "The last temptation is the greatest treason: To do the right deed for the wrong reason." 47

I wish you had commended the Negro sit-inners and demonstrators of Birmingham for their sublime courage, their willingness to suffer, and their amazing discipline in the midst of great provocation. One day the South will recognize its real heroes. They will be the James Merediths, with the noble sense of purpose that enables them to face jeering and hostile mobs, and with the agonizing loneliness that characterizes the life of the pioneer. They will be old, oppressed, battered Negro women, symbolized in a seventy-two-year-old woman in Montgomery, Alabama, who rose up with a sense of dignity and with her people decided not to ride segregated buses, and who responded with ungrammatical profundity to one who inquired about her weariness: "My feets is tired, but my soul is at rest." They will be the young high school and college students, and young ministers of the gospel and a host of their elders, courageously and nonviolently sitting in at lunch counters and willingly going to jail for conscience's sake. One day the South will know that when these disinherited children of God sat down at lunch counters, they were in reality standing up for what is best in the American dream and for the most sacred values in our Judaeo-Christian heritage, thereby bringing our nation back to those great wells of democracy which 48 were dug deep by the founding fathers in their formulation of the Constitution and the Declaration of Independence.

Never before have I written so long a letter. I'm afraid it is much 49 too long to take your precious time. I can assure you that it would have been much shorter if I had been writing from a comfortable desk, but what else can one do when he is alone in a narrow jail cell, other than write long letters, think long thoughts, and pray long prayers?

If I have said anything in this letter that overstates the truth and 50 indicates an unreasonable impatience, I beg you to forgive me. If I have said anything that understates the truth and indicates my having a patience that allows me to settle for anything less than brotherhood, I beg God to forgive me.

I hope this letter finds you strong in the faith. I also hope that cir- 51 cumstances will soon make it possible for me to meet each of you, not as an integrationist or a civil-rights leader but as a fellow clergyman and a Christian brother. Let us all hope that the dark clouds of racial prejudice will soon pass away and the deep fog of misunderstanding will be lifted from our fear-drenched communities, and in some not too distant tomorrow the radiant stars of love and brotherhood will shine over our great nation with all their scintillating beauty.

Yours for the cause of Peace and Brotherhood, 52
MARTIN LUTHER KING JR. 53

MEANINGS AND VALUES

1. What does King say are the four basic steps in a nonviolent campaign?

2. In what ways does King say he is disappointed in the white moderate?

3. Name some examples King gives when he says "One day the South will recognize its real heroes."

EXPOSITORY TECHNIQUES

1. According to the introduction to this chapter, "An argument attempts to resolve or at least modify disagreements by encouraging people to agree upon an action or a point of view." Given that King wrote his letter to white clergymen to explain his actions in organizing a campaign against segregation, does his argument attempt to get the other ministers to agree on a) an action or b) a point of view?

2. King uses both logic and emotion in his letter. Give one example of each.

3. Point to one example of King's restating the objections of his audience. What is his purpose, in your opinion, of restating the objection?

DICTION AND VOCABULARY

1. In Paragraph 24, King uses a simile to strengthen the point that injustice must be exposed. What is the simile? Is it effective, in your opinion?

2. King often uses the device of the rhetorical question. Find and list two examples. What is the purpose of King's use of rhetorical questions?

READ TO WRITE

1. **Collaborating:** In a group of writers, discuss King's concept of just and unjust laws and why he believes it is morally acceptable to break an unjust law (Paragraphs 15 through 20). Write down the main points of your discussion of King's concept, then use the bullet points to develop a brief oral presentation, using examples contributed by your group from personal experience and current events. Be sure that your group's presentation takes a stand for or against King's claim that it is acceptable to break an unjust law.

2. **Considering Audience:** Taking into account what you can determine about King's audience of fellow clergyman based on what he says in his letter, research the incident he writes about. Next, taking the point of view of one of the clergyman King writes to, write an answer to King's letter. Be sure to answer his main points.

3. **Developing an Essay:** Develop a persuasive essay, using both logic and emotion, about one of the ideas raised in King's "Letter from Birmingham Jail." Some ideas might be: the concept of the "creative extremist" (paragraph 31); just and unjust laws (Paragraphs 15 through 20); the idea that "oppressed people cannot remain oppressed forever," (Paragraph 30); or some other. Develop a clear thesis statement and use contemporary examples from personal experience and/or current events.

(NOTE: Suggestions for essays requiring development by ARGUMENT follow.)

Writing Suggestions for Chapter 13

Choose one of the following topic areas, identify an issue (a conflict or problem) within it, and prepare an essay that tries to convince readers to share your opinion about the issue and to take any appropriate action. Use a variety of evidence in your essay, and choose any pattern of development you consider proper for the topic, for your thesis, and for the intended audience.

1. Gun control
2. The quality of education in American elementary and secondary schools
3. Treatment of critically ill newborn babies
4. Hunting
5. Stem-cell research
6. Censorship in public schools and libraries
7. College athletics
8. The problem of toxic waste or a similar environmental problem
9. Careers versus family responsibilities
10. The separation of church and state
11. Law on the drinking age or on drunk driving
12. Evolution versus creationism
13. Medical ethics
14. Government spending on social programs
15. The quality of television programming
16. The impact of divorce
17. The effects of television viewing on children
18. Professional sports
19. Violence in service of an ideal or belief
20. Scholarship and student loan policies
21. Low pay for public service and the helping professions
22. Cheating in college courses
23. Drug and alcohol abuse
24. Product safety and reliability
25. Government economic or social policy

COLLABORATIVE ACTIVITIES

As you prepare an essay on one of the given topics (1–25) or on some other topic, make a list of the evidence for your opinion. Share the list with one or more readers. Ask the reader to rank each piece of evidence for persuasiveness, using a scale of 1 (unpersuasive) to 5 (very persuasive).

14

Further Readings: Combining Patterns

JASON KELLY

JASON KELLY'S articles have appeared in a number of publications, including *The Atlanta Journal Constitution, The European, Forbes ASAP,* and the online magazine *PopPolitics.* He currently lives in Atlanta, Georgia.

The Great TV Debate

In "The Great TV Debate" (published by *PopPolitics* in 2001), Jason Kelly addresses a topic that is familiar to many parents: how much television is too much? Using persuasive logic, comparison, and cause-and-effect analysis, Kelly conveys a message about the importance of finding a middle ground while simultaneously expressing his own ambivalence about where the line should be drawn.

I worry about a lot of things related to my son. September 11   1
brought almost more than I could bear. Today, for instance, I'm
worried that he's pushing other kids at his day care center. Alas,
there are a few constant worries, including this one: Am I already
letting him turn his brain to mush?

When I got this assignment, I set out to try and understand the   2
latest salvos in the great TV debate. I'd planned to do a sensibly
journalistic, fully objective treatment of both sides. Then I realized
that, especially as a dad, that's nearly, if not totally, impossible.

My wife and I have operated under the notion that I'd ascribe 3
to most people—we allow our son, Owen, age 2, to watch some television, though we worry about him watching too much. We'll give
into the pressure a little too often, pushing in a Teletubbies or Elmo
video when we need a mental break, or need to actually get something done.

It's worth confessing here that I like TV, and maybe slightly 4
more than the average bear. I watch enough shows regularly to have
strong opinions about, and feelings for, fake people: Carrie on *Sex
and the City*, Jack on *Will and Grace*, Donna on *West Wing*. I do feel
like I know them. I, of course, hide behind my occupation as a
"writer," tricking myself (but not others, I'm afraid) into thinking
that watching these shows is really work, as if talking about them in
important terms—"Sorkin's gift for writing that crisp, banter-y dialogue makes these shows feel more like plays than movies"—will
make them important, will turn them into high art.

And so, actually, I feel slightly ashamed of my own viewing 5
habits. Why not include my son in my neuroses ("Paging Dr. Frasier
Crane")? These overlapping guilts lead to a creeping sense of hypocrisy, whereby I deprive my son of watching *Clifford: The Big Red
Dog* but, when he leaves the room, quickly switch over to *Today*, so I
can see Katie banter with Matt about listening to the *Shrek*
soundtrack in her minivan. At least Clifford's got a "big idea of the
day"—usually something like "respect" or "sharing"—on at the end
of every show. Katie and Matt just have Willard and his jelly jars
every few days.

In the great American spirit of rationalization, I've convinced 6
myself that my son—who goes to day care during the week—actually
watches less TV than a kid who stays at home full-time with a parent
or a nanny. I know that occasionally his teachers roll in the television
and slip in a video, but it's certainly not every day. Owen has always
been somewhat fickle about watching TV, and in this I see the tenden-
cies that stay with you through adulthood. Sometimes, the dude just
wants to chill out and watch the Teletubbies (or, in his lingo, simply
"Tubbies"). Other times, he's far too busy, and actually walks over
and turns it off in favor of reading a book, coloring or building Lego
towers.

I spent hours on the Web sifting through searches on "Kids and 7
TV," looking for guidance. While on the Cartoon Network site,
I came across a link for "TV Parental Guidelines." That's the site for
the classification system that puts the little box on the screen that
says "TV-MA (mature audiences only)," for example. The

guidelines, at least for me, have become more or less invisible; they're pretty broad and based on the quite-flawed Motion Picture Association of America guidelines, which say it's okay for 13-year-olds to both see and hear the F-bomb.

The Fox Kids TV site was suitably frightening to me, with its   8
animation and teasers—"It's the stinkiest Ripping Friends ever!!" The site for the PBS shows (for better or worse, the only shows we let Owen watch) was similarly predictable in its "We're really about education here" language. Drilling through the Teletubbies, I noted the repeated use of carefully chosen words like "safe," "friendly," and "stimulating."

After wading through the positive messages from the purvey-   9
ors themselves, I found the Washington, D.C.-based TV-Turnoff Network, which appears to have a reputable staff and advisory board. I gave them a call, and they mailed me a packet of materials supporting a TV-free lifestyle, including the requisite bumper stickers. The one that made me chuckle was designed to mimic the warnings on cigarette boxes: "Surgeon General's Warning: Television Promotes Illiteracy." They also feature some startling statistics, like the fact that the average 2- to 17-year-old viewer watches nearly 20 hours of TV per week. And that 73 percent of American parents would like to limit their kids' TV-watching.

Writing this story forced the topic to the front of my mind, and   10
as I chatted with friends and colleagues, even interview subjects for other stories, about various other topics, I often tried to sneak this one in. One friend told me that his kids watch about an hour of TV a month. It took me a full minute to stop saying "Wow." He and his wife both work and have had a full-time nanny since their now-7- and 9-year-old children were born. The nanny knows that no TV is the rule. "And the nanny's a TV junkie" in her off-hours, my friend tells me.

In an odd turn of events, two days later we go with another   11
family on a Sunday outing, loading three adults and three kids comfortably into their family minivan, one of the new, decked-out Honda Odysseys. The high-end versions of these veritable cruise ships on wheels have a VCR and video screen installed; the player sits in the middle console up front, and the screen flips down from the ceiling just behind the front seats. Our hour-plus trip was nearly silent. We could've ridden for days it seemed, despite the fact that we had three sub-6-year-olds in the car.

Somewhere in the middle of these two extremes is where I fall,   12
and, by the looks of it, so does a lot of America. Schools across the

country embrace the idea of using TV as a learning tool and are aided by groups like Cable in the Classroom and Channel One, which provide special programming. The latter is the much-ballyhooed 11-year-old network that broadcasts to roughly 12,000 American middle, junior, and high schools; the network claims those schools represent more than 8 million students and 400,000 educators. There is, however, a catch: Channel One also broadcasts commercials. So while the kids are learning more about, say, life in space, they're also being told to eat Mars bars.

More pointedly, many of the kids TV shows—led by the grand- 13 daddy of educational TV, *Sesame Street*—encourage kids to read. *Clifford the Big Red Dog*, we're told at the end of his PBS show, wants us to "be the best-read dog on the block." And in fact, Clifford was born as a book character himself, then migrated to PBS. *Teletubbies* and others took the reverse path. But they all stress the value of reading. My own son seems to have no problem reading and watching TV, often at the same time. It's a brand of multitasking I'm sure my wife and I have encouraged by example, as we talk on the phone, listen to the radio, cook dinner, and read a magazine, all in one fluid, continuous motion.

I'm starting to come to grips with the idea that this is just how it 14 is, that we live in an information and media-drenched society. We can't stop it, as the wise man said, we can only hope to contain it. Then, as I'm putting all my thoughts together, I come across one more thing that makes me throw my hands up.

Neil Postman's *Amusing Ourselves to Death* is a book I read in 15 college that paints a stark picture of what TV is doing to us and our children. He spends 163 pages undermining just about every idea set forth by the Cable in the Classrooms and PBS's of the world, namely that "educational television" is a contradiction in terms. While his data is old—the book was published in 1985—his arguments likely have more, not less, relevance.

And his voice, while somewhat histrionic, does echo in my ears: 16 "Like the alphabet or the printing press, television has by its power to control the time, attention, and cognitive habits of our youth gained the power to control their education."

And so I end much like I began—pretty damn confused, with 17 my finger poised uncertainly in front of the "play" button.

LESLIE MARMON SILKO

LESLIE MARMON SILKO was born in 1948 in Albuquerque, New Mexico. She was raised on the Laguna Pueblo Reservation and attended the University of New Mexico (B.A., 1969). Formerly on the English faculty of the University of Arizona, Silko now focuses full-time on her writing, for which she has received many awards, including a MacArthur Foundation grant. Much of Silko's writing draws on Native American traditions and myths and on the interactions of Native American cultures and perspectives with the contemporary world. Her novels include the much-praised *Ceremony* (1977), *Almanac of the Dead* (1991), and *Gardens in the Dunes* (1999). She has also published a volume of poetry, *Laguna Woman* (1974); a collection of short stories, *Storyteller* (1981); an autobiography, *Sacred Water* (1993); and a collection of essays, *Yellow Woman and a Beauty of the Spirit* (1996). Her 2010 memoir is *The Turquoise Ledge*.

Yellow Woman and a Beauty of the Spirit

"Yellow Woman and a Beauty of the Spirit" comes from the book with the same title. In this essay, Silko recalls her differences in appearance from other Laguna Pueblo children, the result of her mixed ancestry, and uses this memory as a springboard to an explanation of the traditional Pueblo disregard of physical appearance and emphasis instead on individual qualities of spirit as the basis of true beauty. She also discusses the Pueblo disregard of fixed gender, work, and family roles, but a correspondingly strong emphasis is on the quality of relationships among people, animals, and the land. As in much of her work, Silko's perspective lies at the center of the intersection between cultures.

From the time I was a small child, I was aware that I was different. I looked different from my playmates. My two sisters looked different too. We didn't look quite like the other Laguna Pueblo children, but we didn't look quite white either. In the 1880s, my great-grandfather had followed his older brother west from Ohio to the New Mexico Territory to survey the land for the U.S. government. The two Marmon brothers came to the Laguna Pueblo reservation because they had an Ohio cousin who already lived there.

The Ohio cousin was involved in sending Indian children thousands of miles away from their families to the War Department's big Indian boarding school in Carlisle, Pennsylvania. Both brothers married full-blood Laguna Pueblo women. My great-grandfather had first married my great-grandmother's older sister, but she died in childbirth and left two small children. My great-grandmother was fifteen or twenty years younger than my great-grandfather. She had attended Carlisle Indian School and spoke and wrote English beautifully.

I called her Grandma A'mooh because that's what I heard her   2 say whenever she saw me. *A'mooh* means "granddaughter" in the Laguna language. I remember this word because her love and her acceptance of me as a small child were so important. I had sensed immediately that something about my appearance was not acceptable to some people, white and Indian. But I did not see any signs of that strain or anxiety in the face of my beloved Grandma A'mooh.

Younger people, people my parents' age, seemed to look at the   3 world in a more modern way. The modern way included racism. My physical appearance seemed not to matter to the old-time people. They looked at the world very differently; a person's appearance and possessions did not matter nearly as much as a person's behavior. For them, a person's value lies in how that person interacts with other people, how that person behaves toward the animals and the earth. That is what matters most to the old-time people. The Pueblo people believed this long before the Puritans arrived with their notions of sin and damnation, and racism. The old-time beliefs persist today; thus I will refer to the old-time people in the present tense as well as the past. Many worlds may coexist here.

I spent a great deal of time with my great-grandmother. Her   4 house was next to our house, and I used to wake up at dawn, hours before my parents or younger sisters, and I'd go wait on the porch swing or on the back steps by her kitchen door. She got up at dawn, but she was more than eighty years old, so she needed a little while to get dressed and to get the fire going in the cookstove. I had been carefully instructed by my parents not to bother her and to behave, and to try to help her any way I could. I always loved the early mornings when the air was so cool with a hint of rain smell in the breeze. In the dry New Mexico air, the least hint of dampness smells sweet.

My great-grandmother's yard was planted with lilac bushes   5 and iris; there were four o'clocks, cosmos, morning glories, and hollyhocks, and old-fashioned rosebushes that I helped her water. If the garden hose got stuck on one of the big rocks that lined the path in the yard, I ran and pulled it free. That's what I came to do early every morning: to help Grandma water the plants before the heat of the day arrived.

Grandma A'mooh would tell about the old days, family stories about relatives who had been killed by Apache raiders who stole the sheep our relatives had been herding near Swahnee. Sometimes she read Bible stories that we kids liked because of the illustrations of Jonah in the mouth of a whale and Daniel surrounded by lions. Grandma A'mooh would send me home when she took her nap, but when the sun got low and the afternoon began to cool off, I would be back on the porch swing, waiting for her to come out to water the plants and to haul in firewood for the evening. When Grandma was eighty-five, she still chopped her own kindling. She used to let me carry in the coal bucket for her, but she would not allow me to use the ax. I carried armloads of kindling too, and I learned to be proud of my strength.

I was allowed to listen quietly when Aunt Susie or Aunt Alice came to visit Grandma. When I got old enough to cross the road alone, I went and visited them almost daily. They were vigorous women who valued books and writing. They were usually busy chopping wood or cooking but never hesitated to take time to answer my questions. Best of all they told me the *hummah-hah* stories, about an earlier time when animals and humans shared a common language. In the old days, the Pueblo people had educated their children in this manner; adults took time out to talk to and teach young people. Everyone was a teacher, and every activity had the potential to teach the child.

But as soon as I started kindergarten at the Bureau of Indian Affairs day school, I began to learn more about the differences between the Laguna Pueblo world and the outside world. It was at school that I learned just how different I looked from my classmates. Sometimes tourists driving past on Route 66 would stop by Laguna Day School at recess time to take photographs of us kids. One day, when I was in the first grade, we all crowded around the smiling white tourists, who peered at our faces. We all wanted to be in the picture because afterward the tourists sometimes gave us each a penny. Just as we were all posed and ready to have our picture taken, the tourist man looked at me. "Not you," he said and motioned for me to step away from my classmates. I felt so embarrassed that I wanted to disappear. My classmates were puzzled by the tourists' behavior, but I knew the tourists didn't want me in their snapshot because I looked different, because I was part white.

6

7

8

In the view of the old-time people, we are all sisters and broth-   9
ers because the Mother Creator made all of us—all colors and all
sizes. We are sisters and brothers, clanspeople of all the living beings around us. The plants, the birds, fish, clouds, water, even the
clay—they all are related to us. The old-time people believe that all
things, even rocks and water, have spirit and being. They understood that all things want only to continue being as they are; they
need only to be left as they are. Thus the old folks used to tell us
kids not to disturb the earth unnecessarily. All things as they were
created exist already in harmony with one another as long as we do
not disturb them.

As the old story tells us, Tse'itsi'nako, Thought Woman, the Spi-   10
der, thought of her three sisters, and as she thought of them, they
came into being. Together with Thought Woman, they thought of the
sun and the stars and the moon. The Mother Creators imagined
the earth and the oceans, the animals and the people, and the *ka'tsina*
spirits that reside in the mountains. The Mother Creators imagined
all the plants that flower and the trees that bear fruit. As Thought
Woman and her sisters thought of it, the whole universe came into
being. In this universe, there is no absolute good or absolute bad;
they are only balances and harmonies that ebb and flow. Some years
the desert receives abundant rain, other years there is too little rain,
and sometimes there is so much rain that floods cause destruction.
But rain itself is neither innocent nor guilty. The rain is simply itself.

My great-grandmother was dark and handsome. Her expres-   11
sion in photographs is one of confidence and strength. I do not
know if white people then or now would consider her beautiful. I
do not know if the old-time Laguna Pueblo people considered her
beautiful or if the old-time people even thought in those terms. To
the Pueblo way of thinking, the act of comparing one living being
with another was silly, because each being or thing is unique and
therefore incomparably valuable because it is the only one of its
kind. The old-time people thought it was crazy to attach such importance to a person's appearance. I understood very early that
there were two distinct ways of interpreting the world. There was
the white people's way and there was the Laguna way. In the Laguna way, it was bad manners to make comparisons that might hurt
another person's feelings.

In everyday Pueblo life, not much attention was paid to one's   12
physical appearance or clothing. Ceremonial clothing was quite
elaborate but was used only for the sacred dances. The traditional
Pueblo societies were communal and strictly egalitarian, which

means that no matter how well or how poorly one might have dressed, there was no social ladder to fall from. All food and other resources were strictly shared so that no one person or group had more than another. I mention social status because it seems to me that most of the definitions of beauty in contemporary Western culture are really codes for determining social status. People no longer hide their face-lifts and they discuss their liposuctions because the point of the procedures isn't just cosmetic, it is social. It says to the world, "I have enough spare cash that I can afford surgery for cosmetic purposes."

In the old-time Pueblo world, beauty was manifested in behavior and in one's relationships with other living beings. Beauty was as much a feeling of harmony as it was a visual, aural, or sensual effect. The whole person had to be beautiful, not just the face or the body; faces and bodies could not be separated from hearts and souls. Health was foremost in achieving this sense of well-being and harmony; in the old-time Pueblo world, a person who did not look healthy inspired feelings of worry and anxiety, not feelings of well-being. A healthy person, of course, is in harmony with the world around her; she is at peace with herself too. Thus an unhappy person or spiteful person would not be considered beautiful. 13

In the old days, strong, sturdy women were most admired. One of my most vivid preschool memories is of the crew of Laguna women, in their forties and fifties, who came to cover our house with adobe plaster. They handled the ladders with great ease, and while two women ground the adobe mud on stones and added straw, another woman loaded the hod with mud and passed it up to the two women on ladders, who were smoothing the plaster on the wall with their hands. Since women owned the houses, they did the plastering. At Laguna, men did the basket making and the weaving of fine textiles; men helped a great deal with the child care too. Because the Creator is female, there is no stigma on being female; gender is not used to control behavior. No job was a man's job or a woman's job; the most able person did the work. 14

My Grandma Lily had been a Ford Model A mechanic when she was a teenager. I remember when I was young, she was always fixing broken lamps and appliances. She was small and wiry, but she could lift her weight in rolled roofing or boxes of nails. When she was seventy-five, she was still repairing washing machines in my uncle's coin-operated laundry. 15

The old-time people paid no attention to birthdays. When a person was ready to do something, she did it. When she no longer 16 was able, she stopped. Thus the traditional Pueblo people did not worry about aging or about looking old because there were no social boundaries drawn by the passage of years. It was not remarkable for young men to marry women as old as their mothers. I never heard anyone talk about "women's work" until after I left Laguna for college. Work was there to be done by any able-bodied person who wanted to do it. At the same time, in the old-time Pueblo world, identity was acknowledged to be always in a flux; in the old stories, one minute Spider Woman is a little spider under a yucca plant, and the next instant she is a sprightly grandmother walking down the road.

When I was growing up, there was a young man from a nearby 17
village who wore nail polish and women's blouses and permed his hair. People paid little attention to his appearance; he was always part of a group of other young men from his village. No one ever made fun of him. Pueblo communities were and still are very interdependent, but they also have to be tolerant of individual eccentricities because survival of the group means everyone has to cooperate.

In the old Pueblo world, differences were celebrated as signs of 18
the Mother Creator's grace. Persons born with exceptional physical or sexual differences were highly respected and honored because their physical differences gave them special positions as mediators between this world and the spirit world. The great Navajo medicine man of the 1920s, the Crawler, had a hunchback and could not walk upright, but he was able to heal even the most difficult cases.

Before the arrival of Christian missionaries, a man could dress 19
as a woman and work with the women and even marry a man without any fanfare. Likewise, a woman was free to dress like a man, to hunt and go to war with the men, and to marry a woman. In the old Pueblo worldview, we are all a mixture of male and female, and this sexual identity is changing constantly. Sexual inhibition did not begin until the Christian missionaries arrived. For the old-time people, marriage was about teamwork and social relationships, not about sexual excitement. In the days before the Puritans came, marriage did not mean an end to sex with people other than your spouse. Women were just as likely as men to have a *si'ash*, or lover.

New life was so precious that pregnancy was always appropri- 20
ate, and pregnancy before marriage was celebrated as a good sign. Since the children belonged to the mother and her clan, and women owned and bequeathed the houses and farmland, the exact determination of paternity wasn't critical. Although fertility was prized, infertility was no problem because mothers with unplanned pregnancies

gave their babies to childless couples within the clan in open adoption arrangements. Children called their mother's sisters "mother" as well, and a child became attached to a number of parent figures.

In the sacred kiva ceremonies, men mask and dress as women   21
to pay homage and to be possessed by the female energies of the spirit beings. Because differences in physical appearance were so highly valued, surgery to change one's face and body to resemble a model's face and body would be unimaginable. To be different, to be unique was blessed and was best of all.

THE TRADITIONAL CLOTHING of Pueblo women emphasized a   22
woman's sturdiness. Buckskin leggings wrapped around the legs protected her from scratches and injuries while she worked. The more layers of buckskin, the better. All those layers gave her legs the appearance of strength, like sturdy tree trunks. To demonstrate sisterhood and brotherhood with the plants and animals, the old-time people make masks and costumes that transform the human figures of the dancers into the animal beings they portray. Dancers paint their exposed skin; their postures and motions are adapted from their observations. But the motions are stylized. The observer sees not an actual eagle or actual deer dancing, but witnesses a human being, a dancer, gradually changing into a woman/buffalo or a man/deer. Every impulse is to reaffirm the urgent relationships that human beings have with the plant and animal world.

In the high desert plateau country, all vegetation, even weeds   23
and thorns, becomes special, and all life is precious and beautiful because without the plants, the insects, and the animals, human beings living here cannot survive. Perhaps human beings long ago noticed the devastating impact human activity can have on the plants and animals; maybe this is why tribal cultures devised the stories about humans and animals intermarrying, and the clans that bind humans to animals and plants through a whole complex of duties.

We children were always warned not to harm frogs or toads, the   24
beloved children of the rain clouds, because terrible floods would occur. I remember in the summer the old folks used to stick big bolls of cotton on the outside of their screen doors as bait to keep the flies from going in the house when the door was opened. The old folks staunchly resisted the killing of flies because once, long, long ago, when human beings were in a great deal of trouble, a Green Bottle Fly carried the desperate messages of human beings to the Mother Creator in the Fourth World, below this one. Human beings had outraged the Mother Creator by neglecting the Mother Corn altar while they dabbled with sorcery and magic. The Mother Creator

disappeared, and with her disappeared the rain clouds, and the plants and the animals too. The people began to starve, and they had no way of reaching the Mother Creator down below. Green Bottle Fly took the message to the Mother Creator, and the people were saved. To show their gratitude, the old folks refused to kill any flies.

THE OLD STORIES demonstrate the interrelationships that the   25
Pueblo people have maintained with their plant and animal clanspeople. Kochininako, Yellow Woman, represents all women in the old stories. Her deeds span the spectrum of human behavior and are mostly heroic acts, though in at least one story, she chooses to join the secret Destroyer Clan, which worships destruction and death. Because Laguna Pueblo cosmology features a female Creator, the status of women is equal with the status of men, and women appear as often as men in the old stories as hero figures. Yellow Woman is my favorite because she dares to cross traditional boundaries of ordinary behavior during times of crisis in order to save the Pueblo; her power lies in her courage and in her uninhibited sexuality, which the old-time Pueblo stories celebrate again and again because fertility was so highly valued.

The old stories always say that Yellow Woman was beautiful,   26
but remember that the old-time people were not so much thinking about physical appearances. In each story, the beauty that Yellow Woman possesses is the beauty of her passion, her daring, and her sheer strength to act when catastrophe is imminent.

In one story, the people are suffering during a great drought and   27
accompanying famine. Each day, Kochininako has to walk farther and farther from the village to find fresh water for her husband and children. One day she travels far, far to the east, to the plains, and she finally locates a freshwater spring. But when she reaches the pool, the water is churning violently as if something large had just gotten out of the pool. Kochininako does not want to see what huge creature had been at the pool, but just as she fills her water jar and turns to hurry away, a strong, sexy man in buffalo skin leggings appears by the pool. Little drops of water glisten on his chest. She cannot help but look at him because he is so strong and so good to look at. Able to transform himself from human to buffalo in the wink of an eye, Buffalo Man gallops away with her on his back. Kochininako falls in love with Buffalo Man, and because of this liaison, the Buffalo People agree to give their bodies to the hunters to feed the starving Pueblo. Thus Kochininako's fearless sensuality results in the salvation of the people of her village, who are saved by the meat the Buffalo People "give" to them.

My father taught me and my sisters to shoot .22 rifles when we   28
were seven; I went hunting with my father when I was eight, and I
killed my first mule deer buck when I was thirteen. The Kochininako stories were always my favorite because Yellow Woman had
so many adventures. In one story, as she hunts rabbits to feed her
family, a giant monster pursues her, but she has the courage and
presence of mind to outwit it.

In another story, Kochininako has a fling with Whirlwind Man   29
and returns to her husband ten months later with twin baby boys.
The twin boys grow up to be great heroes of the people. Once again,
Kochininako's vibrant sexuality benefits her people.

The stories about Kochininako made me aware that sometimes   30
an individual must act despite disapproval, or concern for appearances or what others may say. From Yellow Woman's adventures, I
learned to be comfortable with my differences. I even imagined that
Yellow Woman had yellow skin, brown hair, and green eyes like
mine, although her name does not refer to her color, but rather to
the ritual color of the east.

There have been many other moments like the one with the   31
camera-toting tourist in the schoolyard. But the old-time people always say, remember the stories, the stories will help you be strong.
So all these years I have depended on Kochininako and the stories
of her adventures.

Kochininako is beautiful because she has the courage to act in   32
times of great peril, and her triumph is achieved by her sensuality,
not through violence and destruction. For these qualities of the
spirit, Yellow Woman and all women are beautiful.

GEORGE ORWELL

GEORGE ORWELL (1903–1950), whose real name was Eric Blair, was a British novelist and essayist well known for his satire. He was born in India and educated at Eton in England; he was wounded while fighting in the Spanish Civil War. Later he wrote the books *Animal Farm* (1945), a satire on Soviet history; and *1984* (1949), a vivid picture of life in a projected totalitarian society. He was, however, also sharply aware of injustices in democratic societies and was consistently socialistic in his views. Many of Orwell's essays are collected in *Critical Essays* (1946), *Shooting an Elephant and Other Essays* (1950), and *Such, Such Were the Joys* (1953).

A Hanging

"A Hanging" is typical of Orwell's essays in its setting—Burma—and in its subtle but biting commentary on colonialism, on capital punishment, and even on one aspect of human nature itself. Although he is ostensibly giving a straightforward account of an execution, the author masterfully uses descriptive details and dialogue to create atmosphere and sharply drawn characterizations. The essay gives concrete form to a social message that is often delivered much less effectively in abstract generalities.

It was in Burma, a sodden morning of the rains. A sickly light, like yellow tinfoil, was slanting over the high walls into the jail yard. We were waiting outside the condemned cells, a row of sheds fronted with double bars, like small animal cages. Each cell measured about ten feet by ten and was quite bare within except for a plank bed and a pot for drinking water. In some of them brown, silent men were squatting at the inner bars, with their blankets draped round them. These were the condemned men, due to be hanged within the next week or two.

One prisoner had been brought out of his cell. He was a Hindu, a puny wisp of a man, with a shaven head and vague liquid eyes. He had a thick, sprouting mustache, absurdly too big for his body, rather like the mustache of a comic man on the films. Six tall Indian warders were guarding him and getting him ready for the gallows. Two of them stood by with rifles and fixed bayonets, while the others handcuffed him, passed a chain through his handcuffs and fixed it to their belts, and lashed his arms tight to his sides. They crowded very close about him, with their hands always on him in a careful, caressing grip, as though all the while feeling him to make sure he was there. It was like men handling a fish which is still alive and may jump back into the water. But he stood quite unresisting, yielding his arms limply to the ropes, as though he hardly noticed what was happening.

Eight o'clock struck and a bugle call, desolately thin in the wet air, floated from the distant barracks. The superintendent of the jail, who was standing apart from the rest of us, moodily prodding the gravel with his stick, raised his head at the sound. He was an army doctor, with a grey toothbrush mustache and a gruff voice. "For God's sake, hurry up, Francis," he said irritably. "The man ought to have been dead by this time. Aren't you ready yet?"

Francis, the head jailer, a fat Dravidian in a white drill suit and gold spectacles, waved his black hand. "Yes sir, yes sir," he bubbled. "All iss satisfactorily prepared. The hangman iss waiting. We shall proceed."

"Well, quick march, then. The prisoners can't get their breakfast till this job's over."

We set out for the gallows. Two warders marched on either side of the prisoner, with their rifles at the slope; two others marched close against him, gripping him by arm and shoulder, as though at once pushing and supporting him. The rest of us, magistrates and the like, followed behind. Suddenly, when we had gone ten yards, the procession stopped short without any order or warning. A dreadful thing had happened—a dog, come goodness knows whence, had appeared in the yard. It came bounding among us with a loud volley of barks and leapt round us wagging its whole body, wild with glee at finding so many human beings together. It was a large woolly dog, half Airedale, half pariah. For a moment it pranced around us, and then, before anyone could stop it, it had made a dash for the prisoner, and jumping up tried to lick his face. Everybody stood aghast, too taken aback even to grab the dog.

"Who let that bloody brute in here?" said the superintendent angrily. "Catch it, someone!"

A warder detached from the escort, charged clumsily after the dog, but it danced and gambolled just out of his reach, taking everything as part of the game. A young Eurasian jailer picked up a handful of gravel and tried to stone the dog away, but it dodged the stones and came after us again. Its yaps echoed from the jail walls. The prisoner, in the grasp of the two warders, looked on incuriously, as though this was another formality of the hanging. It was several minutes before someone managed to catch the dog. Then we put my handkerchief through its collar and moved off once more, with the dog still straining and whimpering.

It was about forty yards to the gallows. I watched the bare   9
brown back of the prisoner marching in front of me. He walked
clumsily with his bound arms, but quite steadily, with that bobbing
gait of the Indian who never straightens his knees. At each step his
muscles slid neatly into place, the lock of hair on his scalp danced
up and down, his feet printed themselves on the wet gravel. And
once, in spite of the men who gripped him by each shoulder, he
stepped lightly aside to avoid a puddle on the path.

It is curious; but till that moment I had never realized what it   10
means to destroy a healthy, conscious man. When I saw the prisoner
step aside to avoid the puddle, I saw the mystery, the unspeakable
wrongness, of cutting a life short when it is in full tide. This man
was not dying, he was alive just as we are alive. All the organs of his
body were working—bowels digesting food, skin renewing itself,
nails growing, tissues forming—all toiling away in solemn foolery.
His nails would still be growing when he stood on the drop, when
he was falling through the air with a tenth-of-a-second to live. His
eyes saw the yellow gravel and the grey walls, and his brain still remembered, foresaw, reasoned—even about puddles. He and we
were a party of men walking together, seeing, hearing, feeling, understanding the same world; and in two minutes, with a sudden
snap, one of us would be gone—one mind less, one world less.

The gallows stood in a small yard, separate from the main   11
grounds of the prison, and overgrown with tall prickly weeds. It
was a brick erection like three sides of a shed, with planking on top,
and above that two beams and a crossbar with the rope dangling.
The hangman, a greyhaired convict in the white uniform of the
prison, was waiting beside his machine. He greeted us with a servile
crouch as we entered. At a word from Francis the two warders, gripping the prisoner more closely than ever, half led, half pushed him
to the gallows and helped him clumsily up the ladder. Then the
hangman climbed up and fixed the rope round the prisoner's neck.

We stood waiting, five yards away. The warders had formed in   12
a rough circle round the gallows. And then, when the noose was
fixed, the prisoner began crying out to his god. It was a high, reiter-
ated cry of "Ram! Ram! Ram! Ram!" not urgent and fearful like a
prayer or cry for help, but steady, rhythmical, almost like the tolling
of a bell. The dog answered the sound with a whine. The hangman,
still standing on the gallows, produced a small cotton bag like a
flour bag and drew it down over the prisoner's face. But the sound,
muffled by the cloth, still persisted, over and over again: "Ram!
Ram! Ram! Ram! Ram!"

The hangman climbed down and stood ready, holding the   13
lever. Minutes seemed to pass. The steady, muffled crying from the
prisoner went on and on, "Ram! Ram! Ram!" never faltering for an
instant. The superintendent, his head on his chest, was slowly pok-
ing the ground with his stick; perhaps he was counting the cries,
allowing the prisoner a fixed number—fifty, perhaps, or a hundred.
Everyone had changed colour. The Indians had gone grey like bad
coffee, and one or two of the bayonets were wavering. We looked at
the lashed, hooded man on the drop, and listened to his cries—each
cry another second of life; the same thought was in all our minds;
oh, kill him quickly, get it over, stop that abominable noise!

Suddenly the superintendent made up his mind. Throwing up   14
his head he made a swift motion with his stick. "Chalo!" he shouted
almost fiercely.

There was a clanking noise, and then dead silence. The prisoner   15
had vanished, and the rope was twisting on itself. I let go of the dog,
and it galloped immediately to the back of the gallows; but when it
got there it stopped short, barked, and then retreated into a corner
of the yard, where it stood among the weeds, looking timorously
out at us. We went round the gallows to inspect the prisoner's body.
He was dangling with his toes pointed straight downwards, very
slowly revolving, as dead as a stone.

The superintendent reached out with his stick and poked the   16
bare brown body; it oscillated slightly. "*He's* all right," said the superintendent. He backed out from under the gallows, and blew out
a deep breath. The moody look had gone out of his face quite suddenly. He glanced at his wrist-watch. "Eight minutes past eight.
Well, that's all for this morning, thank God."

The warders unfixed bayonets and marched away. The dog, so-   17
bered and conscious of having misbehaved itself, slipped after them.
We walked out of the gallows yard, past the condemned cells with
their waiting prisoners, into the big central yard of the prison. The
convicts, under the command of warders armed with lathis, were
already receiving their breakfast. They squatted in long rows, each
man holding a tin pannikin, while two warders with buckets
marched around ladling out rice; it seemed quite a homely, jolly
scene, after the hanging. An enormous relief had come upon us now
that the job was done. One felt an impulse to sing, to break into a
run, to snigger. All at once everyone began chattering gaily.

The Eurasian boy walking beside me nodded towards the way   18
we had come, with a knowing smile. "Do you know, sir, our friend (he
meant the dead man) when he heard his appeal had been dismissed,

he pissed on the floor of his cell. From fright. Kindly take one of my cigarettes, sir. Do you not admire my new silver case, sir? From the boxwallah, two rupees eight annas. Classy European style."

Several people laughed—at what, nobody seemed certain.   19

Francis was walking by the superintendent, talking garrulously: 20
"Well, sir, all has passed off with the utmost satisfactoriness. It was all finished—flick! Like that. It iss not always so—oah, no! I have known cases where the doctor was obliged to go beneath the gallows and pull the prissoner's legs to ensure decease. Most disagreeable!"

"Wriggling about, eh? That's bad," said the superintendent.   21

"Ach, sir, it iss worse when they become refractory! One man,   22
I recall, clung to the bars of hiss cage when we went to take him out. You will scarcely credit, sir, that it took six warders to dislodge him, three pulling at each leg. We reasoned with him, 'My dear fellow,' we said, 'think of all the pain and trouble you are causing to us!' But no, he would not listen! Ach, he wass very troublesome!"

I found that I was laughing quite loudly. Everyone was laugh-   23
ing. Even the superintendent grinned in a tolerant way. "You'd better all come out and have a drink," he said quite genially. "I've got a bottle of whisky in the car. We could do with it."

We went through the big double gates of the prison into the   24
road. "Pulling at his legs!" exclaimed a Burmese magistrate suddenly, and burst into a loud chuckling. We all began laughing again. At that moment Francis' anecdote seemed extraordinarily funny. We all had a drink together, native and European alike, quite amicably. The dead man was a hundred yards away.

JEAN E. KILBOURNE

JEAN E. KILBOURNE is a feminist author, speaker, and filmmaker whose award-winning films *Still Killing Us Softly* and *Calling the Shots* explore the relationships between media and advertising images and our values and behaviors. She lectures regularly on alcohol and cigarette advertising, images of women in advertising, and related issues of media literacy. She is a graduate of Wellesley College and holds a doctorate in education from Boston University. She is the co-author with Diane E. Levin of *So Sexy So Soon* (2008).

Beauty . . . and the Beast of Advertising

In this essay, first published in *Media & Values* in 1989, Kilbourne analyzes the ways media images shape perceptions and values, particularly those of women. This essay blends a number of patterns, including definition, process analysis, and cause-and-effect analysis.

"You're a Halston woman from the very beginning," the adver-   1
tisement proclaims. The model stares provocatively at the viewer, her long blonde hair waving around her face, her bare chest partially covered by two curved bottles that give the illusion of breasts and a cleavage.

The average American is accustomed to blue-eyed blondes   2
seductively touting a variety of products. In this case, however, the blonde is about five years old.

Advertising is an over $100 billion a year industry and affects all   3
of us throughout our lives. We are each exposed to over 2,000 ads a day, constituting perhaps the most powerful educational force in society. The average adult will spend one and one-half years of his/her life watching television commercials. But the ads sell a great deal more than products. They sell values, images and concepts of success and worth, love and sexuality, popularity and normalcy. They tell us who we are and who we should be. Sometimes they sell addictions.

Advertising's foundation and economic lifeblood is the mass   4
media, and the primary purpose of the mass media is to deliver an audience to advertisers, just as the primary purpose of television programs is to deliver an audience for commercials.

Adolescents are particularly vulnerable, however, because they   5
are new and inexperienced consumers and are the prime targets of many advertisements. They are in the process of learning their values and roles and developing their self-concepts. Most teenagers are

sensitive to peer pressure and find it difficult to resist or even question the dominant cultural messages perpetuated and reinforced by the media. Mass communication has made possible a kind of nationally distributed peer pressure that erodes private and individual values and standards.

But what does society, and especially teenagers, learn from the   6
advertising messages that proliferate in the mass media? On the most obvious level they learn the stereotypes. Advertising creates a mythical, WASP-oriented world in which no one is ever ugly, overweight, poor, struggling or disabled either physically or mentally (unless you count the housewives who talk to little men in toilet bowls, animated germs in drains or muscle-bound giants clad in white clothing). And it is a world in which people talk only about products.

Housewives or Sex Objects

The aspect of advertising most in need of analysis and change is the   7
portrayal of women. Scientific studies and the most casual viewing yield the same conclusion: Women are shown almost exclusively as housewives or sex objects.

The housewife, pathologically obsessed by cleanliness and   8
lemon-fresh scents, debates cleaning products with herself and worries about her husband's "ring around the collar."

The sex object is a mannequin, a shell. Conventional beauty is   9
her only attribute. She has no lines or wrinkles (which would indicate she had the bad taste and poor judgment to grow older), no scars or blemishes—indeed, she has no pores. She is thin, generally tall and long-legged, and, above all, she is young. All "beautiful" women in advertisements (including minority women), regardless of product or audience, conform to this norm. Women are constantly exhorted to emulate this ideal, to feel ashamed and guilty if they fail, and to feel that their desirability and lovability are contingent upon physical perfection.

Creating Artificiality

The image is artificial and can only be achieved artificially (even the   10
"natural look" requires much preparation and expense). Beauty is something that comes from without; more than one million dollars is spent every hour on cosmetics. Desperate to conform to an ideal and impossible standard, many women go to great lengths to manipulate and change their faces and bodies. A woman is conditioned to view

her face as a mask and her body as an object, as *things* separate from and more important than her real self, constantly in need of alteration, improvement, and disguise. She is made to feel dissatisfied with and ashamed of herself, whether she tries to achieve "the look" or not. Objectified constantly by others, she learns to objectify herself. (It is interesting to note that one in five college-age women have an eating disorder.)

"When *Glamour* magazine surveyed its readers in 1984, 75 per- 11
cent felt too heavy and only 15 percent felt just right. Nearly half of those who were actually underweight reported feeling too fat and wanting to diet. Among a sample of college women, 40 percent felt overweight when only 12 percent actually were too heavy," according to Rita Freedman in her book *Beauty Bound*.

There is evidence that this preoccupation with weight begins at 12
ever-earlier ages for women. According to a recent article in *New Age Journal*, "Even grade-school girls are succumbing to sticklike standards of beauty enforced by a relentless parade of wasp-waisted fashion models, movie stars, and pop idols." A study by a University of California professor showed that nearly 80 percent of fourth-grade girls in the Bay Area are watching their weight.

A recent *Wall Street Journal* survey of students in four Chicago- 13
area schools found that more than half the fourth-grade girls were dieting and three-quarters felt they were overweight. One student said, "We don't expect boys to be that handsome. We take them as they are." Another added, "But boys expect girls to be perfect and beautiful. And skinny."

Dr. Steven Levenkron, author of *The Best Little Girl in the World*, 14
the story of an anorexic, says his blood pressure soars every time he opens a magazine and finds an ad for women's fashions. "If I had my way," he said, "every one of them would have to carry a line saying, 'Caution: This model may be hazardous to your health.'"

Women are also dismembered in commercials, their bodies sep- 15
arated into parts in need of change or improvement. If a woman has "acceptable" breasts, then she must also be sure that her legs are worth watching, her hips slim, her feet sexy, and that her buttocks look nude under her clothes ("like I'm not wearin' nothin'"). This image is difficult and costly to achieve and impossible to maintain (unless you buy the product)—no one is flawless and everyone ages. Growing older is the great taboo. Women are encouraged to remain little girls ("because innocence is sexier than you think"), to be passive and dependent, never too mature. The contradictory message— "sensual, but not too far from innocence"—places women in a

double bind; somehow we are supposed to be both sexy and virginal, experienced and naïve, seductive and chaste. The disparagement of maturity is, of course, insulting and frustrating to adult women, and the implication that little girls are seductive is dangerous to real children.

Influencing Sexual Attitudes

Young people also learn a great deal about sexual attitudes from the media and from advertising in particular. Advertising's approach to sex is pornographic; it reduces people to objects and de-emphasizes human contact and individuality. This reduction of sexuality to a dirty joke and of people to objects is the real obscenity of the culture. Although the sexual sell, overt and subliminal, is at a fevered pitch in most commercials, there is at the same time a notable absence of sex as an important and profound human activity.   16

There have been some changes in the images of women. Indeed, a "new woman" has emerged in commercials in recent years. She is generally presented as superwoman, who manages to do all the work at home and on the job (with the help of a product, of course, not of her husband or children or friends), or as the liberated woman, who owes her independence and self-esteem to the products she uses. These new images do not represent any real progress but rather create a myth of progress, an illusion that reduces complex sociopolitical problems to mundane personal ones.   17

Advertising images do not cause these problems, but they contribute to them by creating a climate in which the marketing of women's bodies—the sexual sell and dismemberment, distorted body image ideal and children as sex objects—is seen as acceptable.   18

This is the real tragedy, that many women internalize these stereotypes and learn their "limitations," thus establishing a self-fulfilling prophecy. If one accepts these mythical and degrading images, to some extent one actualizes them. By remaining unaware of the profound seriousness of the ubiquitous influence, the redundant message and the subliminal impact of advertisements, we ignore one of the most powerful "educational" forces in the culture—one that greatly affects our self-images, our ability to relate to each other, and effectively destroys any awareness and action that might help to change that climate.   19

A Guide to Terms

Abstract (See *Concrete/Abstract.*)

Allusion (See *Figures of Speech.*)

Analogy (See Chapter 6.)

Argument is writing that uses factual evidence and supporting ideas to convince readers to share the author's opinion on an issue or to take some action the writer considers appropriate or necessary. Like exposition, argument conveys information; however, it does so not to explain but to induce readers to favor one side in a conflict or to choose a particular course of action.

Some arguments appeal primarily to reason, others primarily to emotion. Most, however, mix reason and emotion in whatever way is appropriate for the issue and the audience. (See Chapter 13.)

Support for an argument can take a number of forms:

1. *Examples*—Real-life examples or hypothetical examples (used sparingly) can be convincing evidence if they are typical and if the author provides enough of them to illustrate all the major points in the argument or combines them with other kinds of evidence. (See Daly, Mills, Svoboda, and Min.) Some examples are *specific*, referring to particular people or events. (See Daly.) Others are *general*, referring to kinds of events or people, usually corresponding in some way to the reader's experiences. (See O'Hehir.)

2. *Facts and figures*—Detailed information about a subject, particularly if presented in statistical form, can help convince readers by showing that the author's perspective on an issue is consistent with what is known about the subject. (See O'Hehir and Quindlen.) But facts whose accuracy is questionable or statistics that are confusing can undermine an argument.

3. *Authority*—Supporting an argument with the ideas or the actual words of someone who is recognized as an expert can be an effective strategy as long as the author can show that the expert is a reliable witness and can combine the expert's opinion with other kinds of evidence that point in the same direction.

4. *Personal experience*—Examples drawn from personal experience or the experience of friends can be more detailed and vivid (and hence more convincing) than other kinds of evidence, but a writer should use this kind of evidence sparingly because readers may sometimes suspect that it represents no more than one person's way of looking at events. When combined with other kinds of evidence, however, examples drawn from personal experience can be an effective technique for persuasion. (See Daly, Svoboda.)

In addition, all the basic expository patterns can be used to support an argument. (See Chapter 13.)

Cause (See Chapter 8.)

Central Theme (See *Unity.*)

Classification (See Chapter 4.)

Clichés are tired expressions, perhaps once fresh and colorful, that have been overused until they have lost most of their effectiveness and become trite or hackneyed. The term is also applied, less commonly, to trite ideas or attitudes.

We may need to use clichés in conversation, of course, when the quick and economical phrase is an important and useful tool of expression— and when no one expects us to be constantly original. We are fortunate, in a way, to have a large accumulation of clichés from which to draw. To describe someone, without straining our originality very much, we can always declare that he is *as innocent as a lamb, as thin as a rail,* or *as fat as a pig;* that she is *as dumb as an ox, as sly as a fox,* or *as wise as an owl;* that he is *financially embarrassed* or *has a fly in the ointment* or that *her ship has come in;* or that, *last but not least, in this day and age,* the *Grim Reaper* has taken him to *his eternal reward.* There is indeed *a large stockpile* from which we can draw for ordinary conversation. But the trite expression, written down on paper, is a permanent reminder that the writer is either lazy or not aware of the dullness of stereotypes—or, even more damaging, it is a clue that the ideas themselves may be threadbare and therefore can be adequately expressed in threadbare language.

Occasionally, of course, a writer can use obvious clichés deliberately (see Frazier). But usually to be fully effective, writing must be fresh and should seem to have been written specifically for the occasion. Clichés, however fresh and appropriate at one time, have lost these qualities.

Closings are almost as much of a problem as introductions, and they are equally important. The function of a closing is simply "to close," of course, but this implies somehow tying the entire writing into a neat package, giving the final sense of unity to the whole endeavor, and thus leaving the reader with a sense of satisfaction instead of an uneasy feeling that there ought to be another page.

There is no standard length for closings. A short composition may be effectively completed with one sentence—or even without any real closing at all, if the last point discussed is a strong or climactic one. A longer piece of writing, however, may end more slowly, perhaps through several paragraphs.

A few types of weak endings are so common that warnings are in order here. Careful writers will avoid these faults: (1) giving the effect of suddenly tiring and quitting; (2) ending on a minor detail or an apparent afterthought; (3) bringing up a new point in the closing; (4) using any new qualifying remark in the closing (if writers want their opinions to seem less dogmatic or generalized, they should go back to do their qualifying where the damage was done), and (5) ending with an apology of any kind (authors who are not interested enough to become at least minor experts in their subject should not be wasting the reader's time).

Of the several acceptable ways of giving the sense of finality to a paper, the easiest is the *summary*, but it is also the least desirable for most short papers. Readers who have read and understood something only a page or two before probably do not need to have it reviewed for them. Such a review is apt to seem merely repetitious. Longer writings, of course, such as research or term papers, may require thorough summaries.

Several other closing techniques are available to writers. The following ones, which do not represent all the possibilities, are useful in many situations, and they can frequently be employed in combination:

1. *Using word signals*—for example, *finally, at last, thus, and so,* and *in conclusion,* as well as more original devices suggested by the subject itself. (See Simpson.)

2. *Changing the tempo*—usually a matter of sentence length or pace. This is a very subtle indication of finality, and it is difficult to achieve. (For examples of modified use, see Simpson, Fadiman, and Walker.)

3. *Restating the central idea of the writing*—sometimes a "statement" so fully developed that it practically becomes a summary itself. (See Catton and Carter.)

4. *Using climax*—a natural culmination of preceding points or, in some cases, the last major point itself. This is suitable, however, only if the materials have been so arranged that the last point is outstanding. (See Catton and Walker.)

5. *Making suggestions,* perhaps mentioning a possible solution to the problem being discussed—a useful technique for exposition as well as for argument, and a natural signal of the end.

6. *Showing the topic's significance,* its effects, or the universality of its meaning—a commonly used technique that, if carefully handled, is an excellent indication of closing. (See Quindlen and Klinkenborg.)

7. *Echoing the introduction*—a technique that has the virtue of improving the effect of unity by bringing the development around full circle, so to speak. The echo may be a reference to a problem posed or a significant expression, quotation, analogy, or symbol used in the introduction or elsewhere early in the composition. (See Min and Berendt.)

8. *Using some rhetorical device*—a sort of catchall category, but a good supply source that includes several very effective techniques: pertinent quotations, anecdotes and brief dialogues, metaphors, allusions, ironic comments, and various kinds of witty or memorable remarks. All, however, run the risk of seeming forced and hence amateurish; but properly handled, they make for an effective closing. (See White, Simpson, and King.)

Coherence is a quality of good writing that results from the presentation of all parts in logical and clear relations.

Coherence and unity are usually studied together and, indeed, are almost inseparable. But whereas unity refers to the relation of parts to the central theme (see *Unity*), coherence refers to their relations with each other. In a coherent piece of writing, each sentence, each paragraph, and each major division seem to grow out of those preceding them.

Several transitional devices (see *Transition*) help to make these relations clear, but far more fundamental to coherence is the sound organization of materials. From the first moment of visualizing the subject materials in pattern, the writer's goal must be clear and logical development. If it is, coherence is almost ensured.

Colloquial Expressions are characteristic of conversation and informal writing, and they are normally perfectly appropriate in those contexts. However, most writing done for college, business, or professional purposes is considered "formal" writing; for such usage, colloquialisms are too informal, too *folksy* (itself a word most dictionaries would label "colloq.").

Some of the expressions appropriate only for informal usage are *kid* (for child), *boss* (for employer), *flunk, buddy, snooze, gym, a lot of, phone, skin flicks,* and *porn*. In addition, contractions such as *can't* and *I'd* are usually regarded as colloquialisms and are never permissible in, for instance, a research or term paper.

Slang is defined as a low level of colloquialism, but it is sometimes placed "below" colloquialism in respectability; even standard dictionaries differ as to just what the distinction is. (Some of the examples in the preceding paragraph, if included in dictionaries at all, are identified both ways.) At any rate, slang generally comprises words either coined or given novel meanings in an attempt at colorful or humorous expression. Slang often becomes limp with overuse, however, losing whatever vigor it first had. In time, slang expressions either disappear completely or graduate to more acceptable colloquial status and thence, possibly, into standard usage. (This is one way in which our language is constantly changing.) But until their "graduations," slang and colloquialisms have an appropriate place in formal writing only if used sparingly and for special effect. Because dictionaries frequently differ in matters of usage, the student should be sure to use a standard edition approved by the instructor. (For further examples, see Frazier and Simpson, Pars. 8, 16, and 17.)

Comparison (See Chapter 5.)

Conclusions (See *Closings.*)

Concrete and **Abstract** words are both indispensable to the language, but a good rule in most writing is to use the concrete whenever possible. This policy also applies, of course, to sentences that express only abstract ideas, which concrete examples can often make clearer and more effective. Many expository and argumentative paragraphs are constructed with an abstract topic sentence and its concrete support. (See *Unity.*)

A concrete word names something that exists as an entity in itself, something that can be perceived by the human senses. We can see, touch, hear, and smell a horse—hence *horse* is a concrete word. But a horse's *strength* is not. We have no reason to doubt that strength exists, but it does not have an independent existence: something else must *be* strong or there is no strength. Hence *strength* is an abstract word.

Purely abstract reading is difficult for average readers; with no concrete images provided, they are constantly forced to make their own. Concrete writing helps readers to visualize and is therefore easier and faster to read. (See *Specific/General* for further discussion.)

Connotation and **Denotation** both refer to the meanings of words. Denotation is the direct, literal meaning of a word as it would be found in a dictionary, whereas connotation refers to the response a word *really* arouses in the reader or listener. (See Fadiman, Par. 14; Daly.)

There are two types of connotation: personal and general. Personal connotations vary widely, depending on the experiences and moods that an individual associates with the word. (This corresponds with personal symbolism; see *Symbol.*) *Waterfall* is not apt to have the same meaning for the happy young honeymooners at Yosemite as it has for the grieving mother whose child has just drowned in a waterfall. General connotations are those shared by many people. *Fireside,* far beyond its obvious dictionary definition, generally connotes warmth, security, and good companionship. *Mother,* which denotatively means simply "female parent," means much more connotatively.

A word or phrase considered less distasteful or offensive than a more direct expression is called a *euphemism,* and this is also a matter of connotation. The various expressions used instead of the more direct "four-letter words" referring to daily bathroom events are examples of euphemisms. *Remains* is often used instead of *corpse,* and a few newspapers still report people *passing away* and being *laid to rest* rather than *dying* and being *buried*.

But a serious respect for the importance of connotations goes far beyond euphemistic practices. Young writers can hardly expect to know all the different meanings of words for all their potential readers, but they can at least be aware that words do *have* different meanings. Of course, this is most important in persuasive writing—in political speeches, in advertising copywriting, and in any endeavor where some sort of public image is being created. When President Franklin Roosevelt began his series of informal radio talks, he called them "fireside chats," thus putting connotation to work. An advertising copywriter trying to evoke the feeling of love and tenderness associated with motherhood is not seriously tempted to use *female parent* instead of *mother*.

In exposition, where the primary purpose is to explain, the writer ordinarily tries to avoid words that may have emotional overtones, unless these can somehow be used to increase understanding. In argument, however, a writer may on occasion wish to appeal to the emotions.

Contrast (See Chapter 5.)

Deduction (See Chapter 12.)

Denotation (See *Connotation/Denotation*.)

Description (See Chapter 10.)

Diction refers simply to "choice of words," but, not so simply, it involves many problems of usage, some of which are explained under several other headings in this guide, for example, *Clichés, Colloquial Expressions, Connotation/Denotation,* and *Concrete/Abstract*—anything, in fact, that pertains primarily to word choices. But the characteristics of good diction may be more generally classified as follows:

  1. *Accuracy*—the choice of words that mean exactly what the author intends

  2. *Economy*—the choice of the simplest and fewest words that will convey the exact meaning intended

  3. *Emphasis*—the choice of fresh, strong words, avoiding clichés and unnecessarily vague or general terms

  4. *Appropriateness*—the choice of words that suit the subject matter, the prospective reader-audience, and the purpose of the writing

  (For contrasts of diction see Frazier, Walker, King, Murphy, Svoboda, and Carter.)

Division (See Chapter 4.)

Effect (See Chapter 8.)

Emphasis is almost certain to fall *somewhere,* and the author should be the one to decide where. A major point, not some minor detail, should be emphasized.

Following are the most common ways of achieving emphasis. Most of them apply to the sentence, the paragraph, or the overall writing—all of which can be seriously weakened by emphasis in the wrong places.

1. By *position*—The most emphatic position is usually at the end, the second most emphatic at the beginning. (There are a few exceptions, including news stories and certain kinds of scientific reports.) The middle, therefore, should be used for materials that do not deserve special emphasis. (See Catton, Par. 16; Fadiman for a final statement of considerable emotional effect.)

A sentence in which the main point is held until the last is called a *periodic sentence*, for example, "After a long night of suspense and horror, the cavalry arrived." In a *loose sentence*, the main point is disposed of earlier and followed by dependencies, for example, "The cavalry arrived after a long night of suspense and horror."

2. By *proportion*—Ordinarily, but not necessarily, important elements are given the most attention and thus automatically achieve a certain emphasis.

3. By *repetition*—Words and ideas may sometimes be given emphasis by reuse, usually in a different manner. If not cautiously handled, however, this method can seem merely repetitious, not emphatic. (See Atwood, who repeats words to give them varied meanings and highlight their importance.)

4. By *flat statement*—Although an obvious way to achieve emphasis is simply to *tell* the reader what is most important, it is often least effective, at least when used as the only method. Readers have a way of ignoring such pointers as "most important" and "especially true." (See Catton, Par. 16.)

5. By *mechanical devices*—Emphasis can be achieved by using italics (underlining), capital letters, or exclamation points. But too often these devices are used, however unintentionally, to cover deficiencies of content or style. Their use can quickly be overdone and their impact lost.

6. By *distinctiveness of style*—The author can emphasize subtly with fresh and concrete words or figures of speech, crisp or unusual structures, and careful control of paragraph or sentence lengths. These methods are used in many essays in this book: see Twain, who changes style radically for the second half of "Two Ways of Seeing a River"; Catton; Frazier, who parodies many different styles; and Fadiman.) *Verbal irony* (see *Irony*), including *sarcasm* (see Frazier and Atwood) and the rather specialized form known as *understatement*, is another valuable means of achieving distinctiveness of style and increasing emphasis.

Essay refers to a brief prose composition on a single topic, usually, but not always, communicating the author's personal ideas and impressions. Beyond this, because of the wide and loose application of the term, no satisfactory definition has been universally accepted.

Classifications of essay types have also been widely varied and sometimes not very meaningful. One basic and useful distinction, however, is between *formal* and *informal* essays, although many defy classification even in such broad categories as these. It is best to regard the two types as opposite ends of a continuum, along which most essays may be placed.

The formal essay usually develops an important theme through a logical progression of ideas, with full attention to unity and coherence, and in a serious tone. Although the style is seldom completely impersonal, it is literary rather than colloquial. (For examples of essays that are somewhere near the "formal" end of the continuum, see Fadiman, Cook, Klinkenborg, Catton, and Kilbourne.)

The informal, or personal, essay is less elaborately organized and more chatty in style. First-person pronouns, contractions, and other colloquial or even slang expressions are often freely used. Informal essays are less serious in apparent purpose than formal essays. Although most do contain a worthwhile message or observation of some kind, an important purpose of many is to entertain. (See Ventura and Tartt.)

The more personal and intimate informal essays may be classifiable as *familiar* essays, although, again, there is no well-established boundary. Familiar essays pertain to the author's own experience, ideas, or prejudices, frequently in a light and humorous style. (See White and Murphy.)

Evaluation of a literary piece, as for any other creative endeavor, is meaningful only when based on the answers to three questions: (1) What was the author's purpose? (2) How successfully was it fulfilled? and (3) How worthwhile was it?

An architect could hardly be blamed for designing a poor gymnasium if the commission had been to design a library. Similarly, an author who is trying to explain for us why women are paid less than men cannot be faulted for failing to make the reader laugh. An author whose purpose is simply to amuse (a worthy goal) should not be condemned for teaching little about trichobothria. (Nothing prevents the author from trying to explain pornography through the use of humor, or trying to amuse by comparing two Civil War generals, but in these situations the purpose has changed—and grown almost unbearably harder to achieve.)

An architect who was commissioned to design a gymnasium, and who, in fact, designed one, however, could be justifiably criticized on whether the building is successful and attractive *as a gymnasium*. If an author is examining matters of cognition and personality, the reader has a right to expect sound reasoning and clear expository prose; and varied, detailed support ought to be expected in an essay that looks at the physical basis of human behavior.

Many things are written and published that succeed very well in carrying out the author's intent—but simply are not worthwhile. Although this is certainly justifiable grounds for unfavorable criticism, readers should first make full allowance for their own limitations and perhaps their narrow range of interests, and they should evaluate the work as nearly as possible from the standpoint of the average reader for whom the writing was intended.

Figures of Speech are short, vivid comparisons, either stated or implied, but they are not literal comparisons (e.g., "Your car is like my car," which is presumably a plain statement of fact). Figures of speech are more imaginative. They imply analogy but, unlike analogy, are used less to inform than to make quick and forceful impressions. All figurative language is a comparison of unlikes, but the unlikes do have some interesting point of likeness, perhaps one never noticed before.

A *metaphor* merely suggests the comparison and is worded as if the two unlikes are the same thing—for example, "the language of the river" and "was turned to blood" (Twain, "Two Ways of Seeing a River," Par. 1) and "a great chapter in American life" (Catton, Par. 1). (For another example in this book, see King.)

A *simile* (which is sometimes classified as a special kind of metaphor) expresses a similarity directly, usually with the word *like* or *as*.

A *personification*, which is actually a special type of either metaphor or simile, is usually classified as a "figure" in its own right. In personification, inanimate things are treated as if they had the qualities or powers of a person. Some people would also label as personification any characterization of inanimate objects as animals or of animals as humans.

An *allusion* is literally any casual reference, any alluding, to something, but rhetorically it is limited to a figurative reference to a famous or literary person, event, or quotation, and it should be distinguished from the casual reference that has a literal function in the subject matter. Hence casual mention of Judas Iscariot's betrayal of Jesus is merely a reference, but calling a modern traitor a "Judas" is an allusion. A rooster might be referred to as "the Hitler of the barnyard," or a lover as a "Romeo." Many allusions refer to mythological or biblical persons or places. (See Simpson, Par. 2, for a discussion of some commonly employed allusions.)

Irony and paradox (both discussed under their own headings) and analogy (see Chapter 6) are also frequently classed as figures of speech, and there are several other less common types that are really subclassifications of those already discussed.

General (See *Specific/General.*)

Illustration (See Chapter 3.)

Impressionistic Description (See Chapter 10.)

Induction (See Chapter 12.)

Introductions give readers their first impressions, which often turn out to be the lasting ones. In fact, unless an introduction succeeds in somehow attracting a reader's interest, he or she probably will read no further. The importance of the introduction is one reason that writing it is nearly always difficult.

When the writer remains at a loss for how to begin, it may be a good idea to forget about the introduction for a while and go ahead with the main body of the writing. Later the writer may find that a suitable introduction has suggested itself or even that the way the piece begins is actually introduction enough.

Introductions may vary in length from one sentence in a short composition to several paragraphs or even several pages in longer and more complex expositions and arguments, such as research papers and reports of various kinds.

Good introductions in expository writing have at least three and sometimes four functions.

1. *To identify the subject and set its limitations,* thus building a solid foundation for unity. This function usually includes some indication of the central theme, letting the reader know what point is to be made about the subject. Unlike the other forms of prose, which can often benefit by some degree of mystery, exposition has the primary purpose of explaining, so the reader has a right to know from the beginning just *what* is being explained.

2. *To interest the readers,* and thus ensure their attention. To be sure of doing this, writers must analyze their prospective readers and the readers' interest in their subject. The account of a new X-ray technique would need an entirely different kind of introduction if written for doctors than if written for the campus newspaper.

3. *To set the tone* of the rest of the writing. (See *Style/Tone.*) Tone varies greatly in writing, just as the tone of a person's voice varies with the person's mood. One function of the introduction is to let the reader know the author's attitude since it may have a subtle but important bearing on the communication.

4. *Frequently,* but not always, *to indicate the plan of organization.* Although seldom important in short, relatively simple compositions and essay examinations, this function of introductions can be especially valuable in more complex papers.

These are the necessary functions of an introduction. For best results, keep these guidelines in mind: (1) Avoid referring to the title or even assuming that the reader has seen it. Make the introduction do all the introducing. (2) Avoid crude and uninteresting beginnings, such as "This paper is about . . . ." (3) Avoid going too abruptly into the main body—a smooth transition is at least as important here as anywhere else. (4) Avoid overdoing the introduction, either in length or in extremes of style.

Fortunately, there are many good ways to introduce expository writing (and argumentative writing), and several of the most useful are illustrated by the selections in this book. Many writings, of course, combine two or more of the following techniques for interesting introductions.

1. *Stating the central theme,* which is sometimes fully enough explained in the introduction to become almost a preview summary of the exposition or argument to come.

2. *Showing the significance of the subject,* or stressing its importance. (See Catton, Klinkenborg, and Simpson.)

3. *Giving the background of the subject,* usually in brief form, in order to bring the reader up-to-date as early as possible for a better understanding of the matter at hand.

4. *"Focusing down" to one aspect of the subject,* a technique similar to that used in some movies, showing first a broad scope (of subject area, such as a landscape) and then progressively narrowing views until the focus is on one specific thing (perhaps the name "O'Grady O'Connor" on a mailbox by a gate). (See also Rooney.)

5. *Using a pertinent rhetorical device* that will attract interest as it leads into the main exposition—for example, an anecdote, analogy, allusion, quotation, or paradox. (See Simpson.)

6. *Using a short but vivid comparison or contrast* to emphasize the central idea.

7. *Posing a challenging question,* the answering of which the reader will assume to be the purpose of the writing.

8. *Referring to the writer's experience with the subject,* perhaps even giving a detailed account of that experience. Some writings are simply continuations of experience so introduced, perhaps with the expository purpose of making the telling entirely evident only at the end or slowly unfolding it as the account progresses. (See White, Cook, and Daly.)

9. *Presenting a startling statistic or other fact* that will indicate the nature of the subject to be discussed.

10. *Making an unusual statement* that can intrigue as well as introduce. (See Frazier and Gansberg.)

11. *Making a commonplace remark* that can draw interest because of its very commonness in sound or meaning.

Irony, in its verbal form sometimes classed as a figure of speech, consists of saying one thing on the surface but meaning exactly (or nearly) the opposite—for example, "this beautiful neighborhood of ours" may mean that it is a dump. (For other illustrations, see Frazier and Walker.)

Verbal irony has a wide range of tones, from the gentle, gay, or affectionate to the sharpness of outright *sarcasm,* which is always intended to cut. It may consist of only a word or phrase, it may be a simple *understatement,* or it may be sustained as one of the major components of satire.

Irony can be an effective tool of exposition if its tone is consistent with the overall tone and if the writer is sure that the audience is bright enough to recognize it. In speech, a person usually indicates by voice or eye expression that he or she is not to be taken literally; in writing, the words on the page have to speak for themselves.

In addition to verbal irony, there is also an *irony of situation*, in which there is a sharp contradiction between what is logically expected to happen and what does happen—for example, a man sets a trap for an obnoxious neighbor and then gets caught in it himself. Or the ironic situation may simply be some discrepancy that an outsider can see while those involved cannot.

Logical Argument (See Chapter 13.)

Loose Sentence (See *Emphasis.*)

Metaphor (See *Figures of Speech.*)

Narration (See Chapter 11.)

Objective writing and **Subjective** writing are distinguishable by the extent to which they reflect the author's personal attitudes or emotions. The difference is usually one of degree, as few writing endeavors can be completely objective or subjective.

Objective writing, seldom used in its pure form except in business or scientific reports, is impersonal and concerned almost entirely with straight narration, with logical analysis, or with the description of external appearances. (For somewhat objective writing, see Simpson; and Staples, Par. 1.)

Subjective writing (in description called "impressionistic"—see Chapter 10) is more personalized, more expressive of the beliefs, ideals, or impressions of the author. Whereas in objective writing the emphasis is on the object being written about, in subjective writing the emphasis is on the way the author sees and interprets the object. (For some of the many examples in this book, see Tartt; Svoboda; and Staples, after Par. 1.)

Paradox is a statement or remark that, although seeming to be contradictory or absurd, actually contains some truth. Many paradoxical statements are also ironic.

Paragraph Unity (See *Unity.*)

Parallel Structure refers in principle to the same kind of "parallelism" that is studied in grammar: the principle that coordinate elements should have coordinate presentation, as in a pair or a series of verbs, prepositional phrases, or gerunds. It is often as much a matter of "balance" as it is of parallelism.

But the principle of parallel structure, far from being just a negative "don't mix" set of rules, is also a positive rhetorical device. Many writers use it as an effective means of stressing variety of profusion in a group of nouns or modifiers, or of emphasizing parallel ideas in sentence parts, in two or more sentences, or even in two or more paragraphs. At times it can also be useful stylistically to give a subtle poetic quality to the prose.

Periodic Sentence (See *Emphasis.*)

Persona refers to a character created as the speaker in an essay or the narrator of a story. The attitudes and character of a persona often differ from those of the author, and their persona may be created as a way of submitting certain values or perspectives to examination and criticism.

Personification (See *Figures of Speech.*)

Point of View in *argument* means the author's opinion on an issue or the thesis being advanced in an essay. In *exposition*, however, point of view is simply the position of the author in relation to the subject matter. Rhetorical point of view in exposition has little in common with the grammatical sort, and it differs somewhat from point of view in fiction.

A ranch in a mountain valley is seen differently by the ranch hand working at the corral, by the gardener deciding where to plant the petunias, by the artist or poet viewing the ranch from the mountainside, and by the geographer in a plane above, map-sketching the valley in relation to the entire range. It is the same ranch, but the positions and attitudes of the viewers are different.

So it is with expository prose. The position and attitude of the author are the important lens through which the reader sees the subject. Consistency is important, because if the lens is changed without sufficient cause and explanation, the reader will become disconcerted, if not annoyed.

Obviously, since the point of view is partially a matter of attitude, the tone and often the style of writing are closely linked to it. (See *Style/Tone.*)

The expository selections in this book provide examples of numerous points of view. Twain's are those of an authority in his own fields of experience and Cook's is that of both a participant and a researcher. In each of these (and the list could be extended to include all the selections in the book), the subject would seem vastly different if seen from some other point of view.

Process Analysis (See Chapter 7.)

Purpose that is clearly understood by the author before beginning to write is essential to both unity and coherence. A worthwhile practice, certainly in the training stages, is to write down the controlling purpose before even beginning to outline. Some instructors require both a statement of purpose and a statement of central theme, or thesis. (See *Unity; Thesis.*)

The most basic element of a statement of purpose is the commitment to "explain" or, in some assignments, to "convince" (argument). But the statement of purpose, whether written down or only decided upon, goes further.

Qualification is the tempering of broad statements to make them more valid and acceptable, the authors themselves admitting the probability of exceptions. This qualifying can be done inconspicuously, to whatever degree needed, by the use of *possibly, nearly always, most often, usually, frequently, sometimes,* or *occasionally.* Instead of saying, "Chemistry is the most valuable field of study," it would probably be more accurate and defensible to say that it is for *some* people or that it *can* be the most valuable.

Refutation of opposing arguments is an important element in most argumentative essays, especially when the opposition is strong enough or reasonable enough to provide a real alternative to the author's opinion. A refutation consists of a brief summary of the opposing point of view along with a discussion of its inadequacies, a discussion that often helps support the author's own thesis.

Here are three commonly used strategies for refutation:

1. *Pointing out weaknesses in evidence*—If an opposing argument is based on inaccurate, incomplete, or misleading evidence, or if the argument does not take into account some new evidence that contradicts it, then the refutation should point out these weaknesses.

2. *Pointing out errors in logic*—If an opposing argument is loosely reasoned or contains major flaws in logic, then the refutation should point these problems out to the reader.

3. *Questioning the relevance of an argument*—If an opposing argument does not directly address the issue under consideration, then the refutation should point out that even though the argument may well be correct, it is not worth considering because it is not relevant.

Refutations should always be moderate in tone and accurate in representing opposing arguments; otherwise, readers may feel that the writer has treated the opposition unfairly and as a result judge the author's own argument more harshly.

Rhetorical Questions are posed with no expectation of receiving an answer; they are merely structural devices for launching or furthering a discussion or for achieving emphasis.

Sarcasm (See *Irony.*)

Satire, sometimes called "extended irony," is a literary form that brings wit and humor to the serious task of pointing out frailties or evils of human institutions. It has thrived in Western literature since the time of the ancient Greeks, and English literature of the eighteenth century was particularly noteworthy for the extent and quality of its satire. Broadly, two types are recognized: *Horatian satire,* which is gentle and smiling, and which aims to correct by invoking laughter and sympathy; and *Ju-venalian satire*, which is sharper and points with anger, contempt, and/or moral indignation to corruption and evil.

Sentimentality, also called *sentimentalism,* is an exaggerated show of emotion, whether intentional or caused by lack of restraint. An author can sentimentalize almost any situation, but the trap is most dangerous when writing of timeworn emotional symbols or scenes—for example, a broken heart, mother love, a lonely death, or the conversion of a sinner. However sincere the author may be, if readers are not fully oriented to the worth and uniqueness of the situation described, they may be either resentful or amused at any attempt to play on their emotions. Sentimentality is, of course, one of the chief characteristics of melodrama. (For examples of writing that, less adeptly handled, could easily have slipped into sentimentality, see Catton, Staples, Simpson, and Gansberg.)

Simile (See *Figures of Speech.*)

Slang (See *Colloquial Expressions.*)

Specific and **General** terms, and the distinctions between the two, are similar to concrete and abstract terms (as discussed under their own heading), and for our purpose there is no real need to keep the two sets of categories separated. Whether *corporation* is thought of as "abstract" and *Ajax Motor Company* as "concrete," or whether they are assigned to "general" and "specific" categories, the principle is the same: in most writing, *Ajax Motor Company* is better.

But "specific" and "general" are relative terms. For instance, the word *apple* is more specific than *fruit* but less so than *Winesap*. And *fruit,* as general as it certainly is in one respect, is still more specific than *food.* Such relationships are shown more clearly in a series, progressing from general to specific: *food, fruit, apple, Winesap;* or *vehicle, automobile, Ford, Mustang.* Modifiers and verbs can also have degrees of specificity: *bright, red, scarlet;* or *moved, sped, careened.* It is not difficult to see the advantages to the reader—and, of course, to the writer who needs to communicate an idea clearly—in "the scarlet Mustang careened through the pass" instead of "the bright-colored vehicle moved through the pass."

Obviously, however, there are times when the general or the abstract term or statement is essential—for example, "A balanced diet includes some fruit" or "There was no vehicle in sight." But the use of specific language whenever possible is one of the best ways to improve diction and thus clarity and forcefulness in writing.

(Another important way of strengthening general, abstract writing is, of course, to use examples or other illustrations. See Chapter 3.)

Style and **Tone** are so closely linked and so often even elements of each other that it is best to consider them together.

But there is a difference. Think of two young men, each with his girlfriend on separate moonlit dates, whispering in nearly identical tender and loving tones of voice. One young man says, "Your eyes, dearest, reflect a thousand sparkling candles of heaven," and the other says, "Them eyes of yours—in this light—they sure do turn me on." Their *tones* were the same; their *styles* were considerably different.

The same distinction exists in writing. But, naturally, with more complex subjects than the effect of moonlight on a lover's eyes, there are more complications in separating the two qualities, even for the purpose of study.

The tone is determined by the *attitude* of writers toward their subject and toward their audience. Writers, too, may be tender and loving, but they may be indignant, solemn, playful, enthusiastic, belligerent, contemptuous—the list could be as long as a list of the many "tones of voice." (In fact, wide ranges of tone may be illustrated by essays in this book. Compare, for example, those of the two parts of Twain and Staples.)

Style, on the other hand, expresses the author's individuality through choices of words (see *Diction*), sentence patterns (see *Syntax*), and selection and arrangement of details and basic materials. (All these elements of style are illustrated in the contrasting statements of the moonstruck lads.) These matters of style are partially prescribed, of course, by the adopted tone, but they are still bound to reflect the writer's personality, mood, education, and general background.

(Some of the more distinctive styles—partially affected by and affecting tone—represented by selections in this book are those of Frazier, Fadiman, Tartt, White, Silko, Murphy, Staples, and Walker.)

Subjective Writing (See *Objective/Subjective*.)

Symbol refers to anything that although real itself also suggests something broader or more significant—not just in greater numbers, however. A person would not symbolize a group or even humankind itself, although a person might be typical or representative in one or more abstract qualities. On the most elementary level, even words are symbols—for example, *bear* brings to mind the furry beast itself. But more important is that things, persons, or even acts may also be symbolic if they invoke abstract concepts, values, or qualities apart from themselves or their own kind. Such symbols, in everyday life as well as in literature and the other arts, are generally classifiable according to three types, which, although terminology differs, we may label *natural, personal,* and *conventional.*

In a natural symbol, the symbolic meaning is inherent in the thing itself. The sunrise naturally suggests new beginnings to most people, an island is almost synonymous with isolation, and a cannon automatically suggests war; hence these are natural symbols. It does not matter that some things, by their nature, can suggest more than one concept.

Although a valley may symbolize security to one person and captivity to another, both meanings, contradictory as they might seem, are inherent, and in both respects the valley is a natural symbol.

The personal symbol, depending as it does on private experience or perception, is meaningless to others unless they are told about it or allowed to see its significance in context (as in literature). Although the color green may symbolize the outdoor life to the farm boy trapped in the gray city (in this respect perhaps a natural symbol), it can also symbolize romance to the young woman proposed to while wearing her green blouse, or dismal poverty to the woman who grew up in a weathered green shanty; neither of these meanings is suggested by something *inherent* in the color green, so they are personal symbols. Anything at all could take on private symbolic meaning, even the odor of marigolds or the sound of a lawnmower. The sunrise itself could mean utter despair, instead of fresh opportunities, to the man who has long despised his daily job and cannot find another.

Conventional symbols usually started as personal symbols, but continued usage in life or art permits them to be generally recognized for their broader meanings, which depend on custom rather than any inherent quality—for example, the olive branch for peace, the flag for love of country, the cross for Christianity, and the raised fist for revolutionary power.

Symbols are used less in expository and argumentative writing than in fiction and poetry, but a few authors represented in this book have either referred to the subtle symbolism of others or made use of it in developing their own ideas.

Syntax is a very broad term—too broad, perhaps, to be very useful—referring to the arrangement of words in a sentence. Good syntax implies the use not only of correct grammar but also of effective patterns. These patterns depend on sentences with good unity, coherence, and emphasis; on the use of subordination and parallel construction as appropriate; on economy; and on a consistent and interesting point of view. A pleasing variety of sentence patterns is also important in achieving effective syntax.

Theme (See *Unity.*)

Thesis In an argumentative essay, the central theme is often referred to as the thesis, and to make sure that readers recognize it, the thesis is often summed up briefly in a *thesis statement*. In a very important sense, the thesis is the center of an argument because the whole essay is designed to make the reader agree with it and, hence, with the author's opinion. (See *Unity.*)

Tone (See *Style/Tone.*)

Transition is the relating of one topic to the next, and smooth transition is an important aid to the coherence of a sentence, a paragraph, or an entire piece of writing. (See *Coherence.*)

The most effective coherence, of course, comes about naturally with sound development of ideas, one growing logically into the next—and that depends on sound organization. But sometimes beneficial even in this situation, particularly in going from one paragraph to the next, is the use of appropriate transitional devices.

Readers are apt to be sensitive creatures, easy to lose. (And, of course, the writers are the real losers since they are the ones who presumably have something they want to communicate.) If the readers get into a new paragraph and the territory seems familiar, chances are that they will continue. But if there are no identifying landmarks, they will often begin to feel uneasy and will either start worrying about their slow comprehension or take a dislike to the author and the subject matter. Either way, a communication block arises, and very likely the author will soon have fewer readers.

A good policy, then, unless the progression of ideas is exceptionally smooth and obvious, is to provide some kind of familiar identification early in the new paragraph to keep the reader feeling at ease with the different ideas. The effect is subtle but important. These familiar landmarks or transitional devices are sometimes applied deliberately but more often come naturally, especially when the prospective reader is kept constantly in mind at the time of writing.

An equally important reason for using some kinds of transitional devices, however, is a logical one: while functioning as bridges between ideas, they also assist the basic organization by pointing out the *relationship* of the ideas—and thus contributing still further to readability.

Transitional devices useful for bridging paragraph changes (and, some of them, to improve transitional flow within paragraphs) may be roughly classified as follows:

1. *Providing an "echo"* from the preceding paragraph. This may be the repetition of a key phrase or word, a pronoun referring back to such a word, or a casual reference to an idea. Such an echo cannot be superimposed on new ideas, but must, by careful planning, be made an organic part of them.

2. *Devising a whole sentence or paragraph* to bridge other important paragraphs or major divisions.

3. *Using parallel structure* in an important sentence of one paragraph and the first sentence of the next. This is a subtle means of making the reader feel at ease in the new surroundings, but it is seldom used because it is much more limited in its potential than the other methods of transition.

4. *Using standard transitional expressions*, most of which have the additional advantage of indicating relationship of ideas. Only a few of those available are classified below, but nearly all the selections in this book amply illustrate such transitional expressions:

Time—soon, immediately, afterward, later, meanwhile, after a while
Place—nearby, here, beyond, opposite
Result—as a result, therefore, thus, consequently, hence

Comparison—likewise, similarly, in such a manner

Contrast—however, nevertheless, still, but, yet, on the other hand, after all, otherwise

Addition—also, too, and, and then, furthermore, moreover, finally, first, second, third

Miscellaneous—for example, for instance, in fact, indeed, on the whole, in other words

Trite (See *Clichés.*)

Unity in writing is the same as unity in anything else—in a picture, a musical arrangement, or a campus organization—and that is a *one*-ness in which all parts contribute to an overall effect.

Many elements of good writing contribute in varying degrees to the effect of unity. Some of these are properly designed introductions and closings; consistency in point of view, tone, and style; sometimes the recurring use of analogy or thread of symbolism; and occasionally the natural time boundaries of an experience or event, as in the selections of Simpson, Gansberg, and Orwell.

But in most expository and argumentative writing the only dependable unifying force is the *central theme*, which every sentence and every word must somehow help to support. (The central theme is also called the *central idea* or the *thesis* when pertaining to the entire writing, and it is almost always called the *thesis* in argument. In an expository or argumentative paragraph it is the same as the *topic sentence*, which may be implied or, if stated, may be located anywhere in the paragraph but is usually placed first.) As soon as anything appears that is not related to the central idea, there are *two* units instead of one. Hence unity is basic to all other virtues of good writing, even to coherence and emphasis, the other two organic essentials. (See *Coherence; Emphasis.*)

An example of unity may be found in a single river system (for a practical use of analogy), with all its tributaries, big or little, meandering or straight, flowing into the main stream and making it bigger—or at least flowing into another tributary that finds its way to the main stream. This is *one* river system, an example of unity. Now picture another stream nearby that does not empty into the river but goes off in some other direction. There are now two systems, not one, and there is no longer unity.

It is the same way with writing. The central theme is the main river, flowing along from the first capital letter to the last period. Every drop of information or evidence must find its way into this theme-river, or it is not a part of the system. It matters not even slightly if the water is good, the idea-stream perhaps deeper and finer than any of the others: if it is not a tributary, it has no business pretending to be relevant to *this* theme of writing.

And that is why most students are required to state their central idea or thesis, usually in solid sentence form, before even starting to organize their ideas. If the writer can use only tributaries, it is very important to know from the start just what the river is.

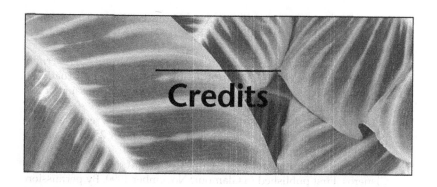

Credits

PHOTO CREDIT

To My Valentine: 1900s Greeting Card, UK. Source: The Advertising Archive.

TEXT CREDITS

Al Gore, 'The Time to Act Is Now" originally published in Salon. Copyright © 2005 by Al Gore, reprinted with permission of The Wylie Agency LLC.

Wil Haygood, "Underground Dads," from *The New York Times Magazine*, January 30, 1997. Copyright © 1997 by The New York Times. Reprinted by permission of the author.

Ernest Hemingway, "Camping Out" by Ernest Hemingway, 1920.

JC Herz, "Superhero Sushi," from *Joystick Nation: How Videogames Ate Our Quarters, Won Our Hearts, and Rewired Our Minds*. Reprinted by permission of International Creative Management, Inc. Copyright © 1997 by J. C. Herz.

Langston Hughes, "Salvation" from *The Big Sea* by Langston Hughes. Copyright © 1940 by Langston Hughes. Reprinted with permission of Farrar, Straus and Giroux, LLC.

Michael Jernigan, "Living the Dream" from *The New York Times*, October 11, 2009 © 2009 The New York Times. All rights reserved. Used by permission and protected by the Copyright Laws of the United States. The printing, copying, redistribution, or retransmission of this Content without express written permission is prohibited.

Mary Karr, "Dysfunctional Nation," *The New York Times*, May 12, 1996. Reprinted by permission of International Creative Management, Inc. Copyright © 1996 by Mary Karr for *The New York Times*.

Jason Kelly, "The Great TV Debate," *PopPolitics.com*, December 2001. Reprinted by permission of the author.

Jean Kilbourne, "Beauty . . . and the Beast of Advertising." Copyright © 1989 by Jean Kilbourne. Reprinted by permission of the author.

Martin Luther King Jr., "Letter from Birmingham Jail." Reprinted by arrangement with The Heirs to the Estate of Martin Luther King Jr., c/o Writers House as agent for the proprietor, New York, NY. Copyright 1963 Dr. Martin Luther King Jr; copyright renewed 1991 Coretta Scott King.

Verlyn Klinkenborg, "Our Vanishing Night," *National Geographic*, November 2008. Reprinted by permission of National Geographic Society.

Lori L'Heureux, "Stars." Reprinted by permission.

Sarah Lake, "Welcome to the Gym!" Reprinted by permission.

Jonah Lehrer, excerpt from "The Uses of Reason" from *How We Decide* by Jonah Lehrer. Copyright © 2009 by Jonah Lehrer. Reprinted by permission of Houghton Mifflin Harcourt Publishing Company. All rights reserved.

Jhumpa Lahiri, "My Two Lives" from *The New York Times*, March 6, 2006 © 2006 The New York Times. All rights reserved. Used by permission and protected by the Copyright Laws of the United States. The printing, copying, redistribution, or retransmission of this Content without express written permission is prohibited.

Index